Toyota Avensis
Owners Workshop Manual

John S. Mead

Models covered

(4264 - 320)

Toyota Avensis Hatchback, Saloon and Estate models with petrol engines, including special/limited editions

1.6 litre (1587 and 1598 cc), 1.8 litre (1762 and 1794 cc) and 2.0 litre (1998 cc)

Does not cover diesel engines, or Avensis Verso models
Does not cover new Avensis range introduced January 2003

© Haynes Publishing 2006

A book in the **Haynes Service and Repair Manual Series**

All rights reserved. No part of this book may be reproduced or transmitted in any form or by any means, electronic or mechanical, including photocopying, recording or by any information storage or retrieval system, without permission in writing from the copyright holder.

ISBN-10: **1 84425 264 7**
ISBN-13: **978 1 84425 264 0**

British Library Cataloguing in Publication Data
A catalogue record for this book is available from the British Library.

ABCDE
FGHIJ
KLMNO
PQRST

Printed in the USA

Haynes Publishing
Sparkford, Yeovil, Somerset BA22 7JJ, England

Haynes North America, Inc
861 Lawrence Drive, Newbury Park, California 91320, USA

Editions Haynes
4, Rue de l'Abreuvoir
92415 COURBEVOIE CEDEX, France

Haynes Publishing Nordiska AB
Box 1504, 751 45 UPPSALA, Sverige

Contents

LIVING WITH YOUR TOYOTA AVENSIS

Roadside repairs

Weekly checks

Lubricants and fluids

Tyre pressures

MAINTENANCE

Routine maintenance and servicing

Illegal Copying

It is the policy of Haynes Publishing to actively protect its Copyrights and Trade Marks. Legal action will be taken against anyone who unlawfully copies the cover or contents of this Manual. This includes all forms of unauthorised copying including digital, mechanical, and electronic in any form. Authorisation from Haynes Publishing will only be provided expressly and in writing. Illegal copying will also be reported to the appropriate statutory authorities.

Contents

Advanced driving

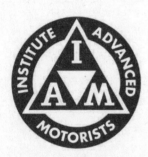

Many people see the words 'advanced driving' and believe that it won't interest them or that it is a style of driving beyond their own abilities. Nothing could be further from the truth. Advanced driving is straightforward safe, sensible driving - the sort of driving we should all do every time we get behind the wheel.

An average of 10 people are killed every day on UK roads and 870 more are injured, some seriously. Lives are ruined daily, usually because somebody did something stupid. Something like 95% of all accidents are due to human error, mostly driver failure. Sometimes we make genuine mistakes - everyone does. Sometimes we have lapses of concentration. Sometimes we deliberately take risks.

For many people, the process of 'learning to drive' doesn't go much further than learning how to pass the driving test because of a common belief that good drivers are made by 'experience'.

Learning to drive by 'experience' teaches three driving skills:

- ☐ Quick reactions. (Whoops, that was close!)
- ☐ Good handling skills. (Horn, swerve, brake, horn).
- ☐ Reliance on vehicle technology. (Great stuff this ABS, stop in no distance even in the wet...)

Drivers whose skills are 'experience based' generally have a lot of near misses and the odd accident. The results can be seen every day in our courts and our hospital casualty departments.

Advanced drivers have learnt to control the risks by controlling the position and speed of their vehicle. They avoid accidents and near misses, even if the drivers around them make mistakes.

The key skills of advanced driving are **concentration,** effective all-round **observation, anticipation** and **planning.** When **good vehicle handling** is added to these skills, all driving situations can be approached and negotiated in a safe, methodical way, leaving nothing to chance.

Concentration means applying your mind to safe driving, completely excluding anything that's not relevant. Driving is usually the most dangerous activity that most of us undertake in our daily routines. It deserves our full attention.

Observation means not just looking, but seeing and seeking out the information found in the driving environment.

Anticipation means asking yourself what is happening, what you can reasonably expect to happen and what could happen unexpectedly. (One of the commonest words used in compiling accident reports is 'suddenly'.)

Planning is the link between seeing something and taking the appropriate action. For many drivers, planning is the missing link.

If you want to become a safer and more skilful driver and you want to enjoy your driving more, contact the Institute of Advanced Motorists at www.iam.org.uk, phone 0208 996 9600, or write to IAM House, 510 Chiswick High Road, London W4 5RG for an information pack.

Working on your car can be dangerous. This page shows just some of the potential risks and hazards, with the aim of creating a safety-conscious attitude.

General hazards

Scalding

• Don't remove the radiator or expansion tank cap while the engine is hot.
• Engine oil, automatic transmission fluid or power steering fluid may also be dangerously hot if the engine has recently been running.

Burning

• Beware of burns from the exhaust system and from any part of the engine. Brake discs and drums can also be extremely hot immediately after use.

Crushing

• When working under or near a raised vehicle, always supplement the jack with axle stands, or use drive-on ramps. *Never venture under a car which is only supported by a jack.*
• Take care if loosening or tightening high-torque nuts when the vehicle is on stands. Initial loosening and final tightening should be done with the wheels on the ground.

Fire

• Fuel is highly flammable; fuel vapour is explosive.
• Don't let fuel spill onto a hot engine.
• Do not smoke or allow naked lights (including pilot lights) anywhere near a vehicle being worked on. Also beware of creating sparks (electrically or by use of tools).
• Fuel vapour is heavier than air, so don't work on the fuel system with the vehicle over an inspection pit.
• Another cause of fire is an electrical overload or short-circuit. Take care when repairing or modifying the vehicle wiring.
• Keep a fire extinguisher handy, of a type suitable for use on fuel and electrical fires.

Electric shock

• Ignition HT voltage can be dangerous, especially to people with heart problems or a pacemaker. Don't work on or near the ignition system with the engine running or the ignition switched on.

• Mains voltage is also dangerous. Make sure that any mains-operated equipment is correctly earthed. Mains power points should be protected by a residual current device (RCD) circuit breaker.

Fume or gas intoxication

• Exhaust fumes are poisonous; they often contain carbon monoxide, which is rapidly fatal if inhaled. Never run the engine in a confined space such as a garage with the doors shut.
• Fuel vapour is also poisonous, as are the vapours from some cleaning solvents and paint thinners.

Poisonous or irritant substances

• Avoid skin contact with battery acid and with any fuel, fluid or lubricant, especially antifreeze, brake hydraulic fluid and Diesel fuel. Don't syphon them by mouth. If such a substance is swallowed or gets into the eyes, seek medical advice.
• Prolonged contact with used engine oil can cause skin cancer. Wear gloves or use a barrier cream if necessary. Change out of oil-soaked clothes and do not keep oily rags in your pocket.
• Air conditioning refrigerant forms a poisonous gas if exposed to a naked flame (including a cigarette). It can also cause skin burns on contact.

Asbestos

• Asbestos dust can cause cancer if inhaled or swallowed. Asbestos may be found in gaskets and in brake and clutch linings. When dealing with such components it is safest to assume that they contain asbestos.

Special hazards

Hydrofluoric acid

• This extremely corrosive acid is formed when certain types of synthetic rubber, found in some O-rings, oil seals, fuel hoses etc, are exposed to temperatures above 400ºC. The rubber changes into a charred or sticky substance containing the acid. *Once formed, the acid remains dangerous for years. If it gets onto the skin, it may be necessary to amputate the limb concerned.*
• When dealing with a vehicle which has suffered a fire, or with components salvaged from such a vehicle, wear protective gloves and discard them after use.

The battery

• Batteries contain sulphuric acid, which attacks clothing, eyes and skin. Take care when topping-up or carrying the battery.
• The hydrogen gas given off by the battery is highly explosive. Never cause a spark or allow a naked light nearby. Be careful when connecting and disconnecting battery chargers or jump leads.

Air bags

• Air bags can cause injury if they go off accidentally. Take care when removing the steering wheel and/or facia. Special storage instructions may apply.

Diesel injection equipment

• Diesel injection pumps supply fuel at very high pressure. Take care when working on the fuel injectors and fuel pipes.

⚠ *Warning: Never expose the hands, face or any other part of the body to injector spray; the fuel can penetrate the skin with potentially fatal results.*

Remember...

DO

• Do use eye protection when using power tools, and when working under the vehicle.

• Do wear gloves or use barrier cream to protect your hands when necessary.

• Do get someone to check periodically that all is well when working alone on the vehicle.

• Do keep loose clothing and long hair well out of the way of moving mechanical parts.

• Do remove rings, wristwatch etc, before working on the vehicle – especially the electrical system.

• Do ensure that any lifting or jacking equipment has a safe working load rating adequate for the job.

DON'T

• Don't attempt to lift a heavy component which may be beyond your capability – get assistance.

• Don't rush to finish a job, or take unverified short cuts.

• Don't use ill-fitting tools which may slip and cause injury.

• Don't leave tools or parts lying around where someone can trip over them. Mop up oil and fuel spills at once.

• Don't allow children or pets to play in or near a vehicle being worked on.

1.8 litre Avensis Hatchback

Introduced in January 1998 as a replacement for the Carina-E, the Avensis was available as a 4-door Saloon, 5-door Hatchback and a 5-door Estate. In August 2000, the range underwent a facelift, with cosmetic revisions to the front bumper, headlights, bonnet and front grille. To coincide with the facelift, a new range of petrol engines, with variable valve timing, was introduced, replacing the existing units.

The petrol engines are all fuel injected, in-line, four-cylinder units of 1.6, 1.8 or 2.0 litre displacement with double overhead camshafts and 16 valves. All engines are normally aspirated, with the later VVT-i engines (August 2000 on), incorporating a hydraulically-controlled mechanism on the inlet camshaft which varies the valve timing. This facility improves the driveability, efficiency and emissions of the engines. All engines feature a comprehensive engine management system with extensive emission control equipment. Although two diesel engines were available, neither are covered in this manual.

All models are available with a 5-speed manual transmission, with a 4-speed automatic transmission optionally available on 1.8 and 2.0 litre engines.

Braking is by discs at the front, and by drums or discs at the rear. ABS and hydraulically operated power-assisted steering is standard on all models.

The front suspension is of the fully-independent MacPherson strut type, incorporating telescopic shock absorbers, coil springs and an anti-roll bar. The rear suspension is an independent dual-link strut arrangement with integral shock telescopic absorbers, coil springs and an anti-roll bar.

A wide range of standard and optional equipment is available within the range to suit virtually all tastes. Both a driver's and passenger's airbag are fitted as standard, together with side airbags, incorporated into the front seats. Additional curtain airbags and front seat belt pretensioners, are also available as either standard or optional equipment.

Provided that regular servicing is carried out in accordance with the manufacturer's recommendations, the Toyota Avensis will provide the enviable reliability for which this marque is famous. The engine compartment is relatively spacious, and most of the items requiring frequent attention are easily accessible.

Your Toyota Avensis Manual

The aim of this manual is to help you get the best value from your vehicle. It can do so in several ways. It can help you decide what work must be done (even should you choose to get it done by a garage), provide information on routine maintenance and servicing, and give a logical course of action and diagnosis when random faults occur. However, it is hoped that you will use the manual by tackling the work yourself. On simpler jobs it may even be quicker than booking the vehicle into a garage and going there twice, to leave and collect it. Perhaps most important, a lot of money can be saved by avoiding the costs a garage must charge to cover its labour and overheads.

The manual has drawings and descriptions to show the function of the various components so that their layout can be understood. Tasks are described and photographed in a clear step-by-step sequence.

References to the 'left-hand' and 'right-hand' sides of the vehicle are always in the sense of when viewed by a person sat in the driver's seat, facing forwards.

Acknowledgements

Thanks are due to Draper Tools Limited, who provided some of the workshop tools, and to all those people at Sparkford who helped in the production of this Manual.

We take great pride in the accuracy of information given in this manual, but vehicle manufacturers make alterations and design changes during the production run of a particular vehicle of which they do not inform us. No liability can be accepted by the authors or publishers for loss, damage or injury caused by errors in, or omissions from, the information given.

Avensis GS Estate

The following pages are intended to help in dealing with common roadside emergencies and breakdowns. You will find more detailed fault finding information at the back of the manual, and repair information in the main chapters.

If your car won't start and the starter motor doesn't turn

- ☐ If it's a model with automatic transmission, make sure the selector is in P or N.
- ☐ Open the bonnet and make sure that the battery terminals are clean and tight.
- ☐ Switch on the headlights and try to start the engine. If the headlights go very dim when you're trying to start, the battery is probably flat. Get out of trouble by jump starting (see next page) using a friend's car.

If your car won't start even though the starter motor turns as normal

- ☐ Is there fuel in the tank?
- ☐ Is there moisture on electrical components under the bonnet? Switch off the ignition, then wipe off any obvious dampness with a dry cloth (on later models, remove the plastic engine cover for access to the ignition components). Spray a water-repellent aerosol product (WD-40 or equivalent) on ignition and fuel system electrical connectors like those shown in the photos).

A Check the security and condition of the battery connections.

B Check the security of the ignition coil(s) electrical connectors.

C Check the security of the airflow meter wiring connector.

Check that electrical connections are secure (with the ignition switched off) and spray them with a water-dispersant spray like WD-40 if you suspect a problem due to damp

D Check that all fuses are still in good condition and none have blown.

E Check the security of the HT leads (pre-August 2000 engines).

Jump starting

When jump-starting a car using a booster battery, observe the following precautions:

✔ Before connecting the booster battery, make sure that the ignition is switched off.

✔ Ensure that all electrical equipment (lights, heater, wipers, etc) is switched off.

✔ Take note of any special precautions printed on the battery case.

✔ Make sure that the booster battery is the same voltage as the discharged one in the vehicle.

✔ If the battery is being jump-started from the battery in another vehicle, the two vehicles MUST NOT TOUCH each other.

✔ Make sure that the transmission is in neutral (or PARK, in the case of automatic transmission).

 HAYNES HiNT *Jump starting will get you out of trouble, but you must correct whatever made the battery go flat in the first place. There are three possibilities:*

1 The battery has been drained by repeated attempts to start, or by leaving the lights on.

2 The charging system is not working properly (alternator drivebelt slack or broken, alternator wiring fault or alternator itself faulty).

3 The battery itself is at fault (electrolyte low, or battery worn out).

1 Connect one end of the red jump lead to the positive (+) terminal of the flat battery

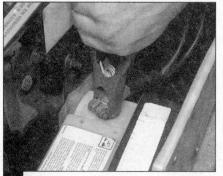

2 Connect the other end of the red lead to the positive (+) terminal of the booster battery.

3 Connect one end of the black jump lead to the negative (-) terminal of the booster battery

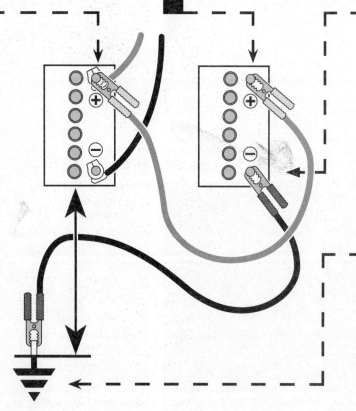

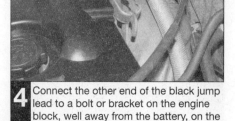

4 Connect the other end of the black jump lead to a bolt or bracket on the engine block, well away from the battery, on the vehicle to be started.

5 Make sure that the jump leads will not come into contact with the cooling fan, drivebelts or other moving parts of the engine.

6 Start the engine using the booster battery and run it at idle speed. Switch on the lights, rear window demister and heater blower motor, then disconnect the jump leads in the reverse order of connection. Turn off the lights etc.

Wheel changing

⚠️ *Warning: Do not change a wheel in a situation where you risk being hit by other traffic. On busy roads, try to stop in a lay-by or a gateway. Be wary of passing traffic while changing the wheel – it is easy to become distracted by the job in hand.*

Preparation

☐ When a puncture occurs, stop as soon as it is safe to do so.
☐ Park on firm level ground, if possible, and well out of the way of other traffic.
☐ Use hazard warning lights if necessary.

☐ If you have one, use a warning triangle to alert other drivers of your presence.
☐ Apply the handbrake and engage first or reverse gear (or Park on models with automatic transmission).

☐ Chock the wheel diagonally opposite the one being removed – a couple of large stones will do for this.
☐ If the ground is soft, use a flat piece of wood to spread the load under the jack.

Changing the wheel

1 From inside the luggage compartment, fold back the carpet and remove the cover panel.

2 Release the jack from its location and remove it from the luggage compartment.

3 Lift the carpet then unscrew the spare wheel retainer from the centre of the wheel. Lift out the spare wheel together with the tool kit bag.

4 Prise off the wheel trim (where fitted), using the bevelled end of the wheelbrace, then slacken each wheel nut by a half turn.

5 Engage the jack head with the reinforced jacking point located near the end of the sill (don't jack the vehicle at any other point of the sill). Turn the handle clockwise until the wheel is raised clear of the ground.

6 Unscrew the wheel nuts and remove the wheel.

Finally . . .

☐ Remove the wheel chocks.
☐ Stow the jack and tools in the spare wheel.
☐ Check the tyre pressure on the wheel just fitted. If it is low, or if you don't have a pressure gauge with you, drive slowly to the nearest garage and inflate the tyre to the correct pressure.
☐ Have the damaged tyre or wheel repaired as soon as possible.

Note: *Some models may be supplied with a special lightweight 'space-saver' spare wheel, the tyre being narrower than standard, and marked TEMPORARY USE ONLY. The space-saver spare wheel is intended only for temporary use, and must be replaced with a standard wheel as soon as possible. Drive with particular care with this wheel fitted, especially through corners and when braking – Toyota recommend a maximum speed of 50 mph when the special spare wheel is in use.*

7 Fit the spare wheel, then fit and screw on the nuts. Lightly tighten the nuts with the wheelbrace, then lower the vehicle to the ground.

8 Securely tighten the wheel nuts in the sequence shown, then refit the wheel trim. The wheel nuts should be slackened and retightened to the correct torque (103 Nm) at the earliest possible opportunity.

Identifying leaks

Puddles on the garage floor or drive, or obvious wetness under the bonnet or underneath the car, suggest a leak that needs investigating. It can sometimes be difficult to decide where the leak is coming from, especially if the engine bay is very dirty already. Leaking oil or fluid can also be blown rearwards by the passage of air under the car, giving a false impression of where the problem lies.

 Warning: Most automotive oils and fluids are poisonous. Wash them off skin, and change out of contaminated clothing, without delay.

 The smell of a fluid leaking from the car may provide a clue to what's leaking. Some fluids are distinctively coloured. It may help to clean the car carefully and to park it over some clean paper overnight as an aid to locating the source of the leak.
Remember that some leaks may only occur while the engine is running.

Sump oil

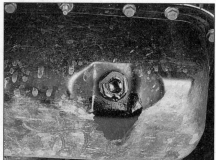

Engine oil may leak from the drain plug...

Oil from filter

...or from the base of the oil filter.

Gearbox oil

Gearbox oil can leak from the seals at the inboard ends of the driveshafts.

Antifreeze

Leaking antifreeze often leaves a crystalline deposit like this.

Brake fluid

A leak occurring at a wheel is almost certainly brake fluid.

Power steering fluid

Power steering fluid may leak from the pipe connectors on the steering rack.

Towing

When all else fails, you may find yourself having to get a tow home – or of course you may be helping somebody else. Long-distance recovery should only be done by a garage or breakdown service. For shorter distances, DIY towing using another car is easy enough, but observe the following points:

☐ Use a proper tow-rope – they are not expensive. The vehicle being towed must display an ON TOW sign in its rear window.

☐ Always turn the ignition key to the 'On' position when the vehicle is being towed, so that the steering lock is released, and the direction indicator and brake lights work.

☐ Only attach the tow-rope to the towing eyes provided.

☐ Before being towed, release the handbrake and select neutral on the transmission. On models with automatic transmission, do not exceed 30 mph (50 kph) and do not tow for more than 30 miles (50 km). If in doubt, do not tow, or transmission damage may result.

☐ Note that greater-than-usual pedal pressure will be required to operate the brakes, since the vacuum servo unit is only operational with the engine running.

☐ Greater-than-usual steering effort will also be required if the engine is not running.

☐ The driver of the car being towed must keep the tow-rope taut at all times to avoid snatching.

☐ Make sure that both drivers know the route before setting off.

☐ Only drive at moderate speeds and keep the distance towed to a minimum. Drive smoothly and allow plenty of time for slowing down at junctions.

Introduction

There are some very simple checks which need only take a few minutes to carry out, but which could save you a lot of inconvenience and expense.

These *Weekly checks* require no great skill or special tools, and the small amount of time they take to perform could prove to be very well spent, for example:

☐ Keeping an eye on tyre condition and pressures, will not only help to stop them wearing out prematurely, but could also save your life.

☐ Many breakdowns are caused by electrical problems. Battery-related faults are particularly common, and a quick check on a regular basis will often prevent the majority of these.

☐ If your car develops a brake fluid leak, the first time you might know about it is when your brakes don't work properly. Checking the level regularly will give advance warning of this kind of problem.

☐ If the oil or coolant levels run low, the cost of repairing any engine damage will be far greater than fixing the leak, for example.

Underbonnet check points

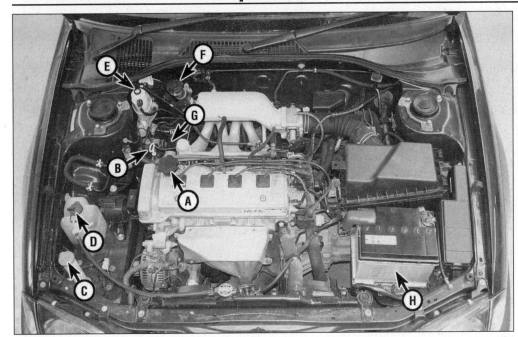

◄ 1.8 litre engine (pre-August 2000) (others similar)

A Engine oil filler cap
B Engine oil level dipstick
C Washer fluid reservoir
D Coolant expansion tank
E Brake fluid reservoir
F Clutch fluid reservoir
G Power steering fluid reservoir
H Battery

◄ 1.8 litre engine (post-August 2000) (others similar)

A Engine oil filler cap
B Engine oil level dipstick
C Washer fluid reservoir
D Coolant expansion tank
E Brake fluid reservoir
F Clutch fluid reservoir
G Power steering fluid reservoir
H Battery

Engine oil level

Before you start
✔ Make sure that the car is on level ground.
✔ Check the oil level before the car is driven, or at least 5 minutes after the engine has been switched off.

 HAYNES HiNT *If the oil is checked immediately after driving the vehicle, some of the oil will remain in the upper engine components, resulting in an inaccurate reading on the dipstick.*

The correct oil
Modern engines place great demands on their oil. It is very Important that the correct oil for your car is used (see *Lubricants and fluids*).

Car care
● If you have to add oil frequently, you should check whether you have any oil leaks. Place some clean paper under the car overnight, and check for stains in the morning. If there are no leaks, then the engine may be burning oil.
● Always maintain the level between the upper and lower dipstick marks (see photos 2 and 3). If the level is too low, severe engine damage may occur. Oil seal failure may result if the engine is overfilled by adding too much oil.

1 The dipstick top is brightly coloured for easy identification (see *Underbonnet check points* for exact location). Withdraw the dipstick. Using a clean rag or paper towel, wipe all the oil from the dipstick. Insert the clean dipstick into the tube as far as it will go, then withdraw it again.

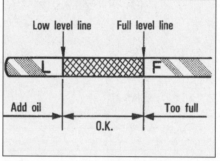

3 . . . or in the hatched area indicating MAX and MIN between the upper (F) mark and lower (L) mark. Approximately 1.0 litre of oil will raise the level from the lower mark to the upper mark.

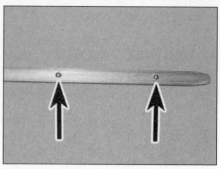

2 Note the oil level on the end of the dipstick, which should be between the maximum and minimum marks . . .

4 Oil is added through the filler cap. Unscrew the cap and top up the level; a funnel may help to reduce spillage. Add the oil slowly, checking the level on the dipstick often. Don't overfill (see *Car Care*).

Coolant level

 Warning: Do not attempt to remove the expansion tank pressure cap when the engine is hot, as there is a very great risk of scalding. Do not leave open containers of coolant about, as it is poisonous.

Car Care
● With a sealed-type cooling system, adding coolant should not be necessary on a regular basis. If frequent topping-up is required, it is likely there is a leak. Check the radiator, all hoses and joint faces for signs of staining or wetness, and rectify as necessary.

● It is important that antifreeze is used in the cooling system all year round, not just during the winter months. Don't top up with water alone, as the antifreeze will become diluted.

1 The coolant level varies with the temperature of the engine. When the engine is cold, the coolant level should be between the FULL and LOW marks on the expansion tank.

2 If topping-up is necessary, wait until the engine is cold then remove the expansion tank cap. The expansion tank is not pressurised since the pressure cap is located in the top of the radiator, however the system should be topped-up with the engine cold.

3 Add a mixture of water and antifreeze to the expansion tank until the coolant level is up to the FULL level mark, then refit the cap.

Clutch fluid level

Warning:
● *Brake fluid can harm your eyes and damage painted surfaces, so use extreme caution when handling and pouring it.*
● *Do not use fluid that has been standing open for some time, as it absorbs moisture from the air.*
● *Do not mix different types of fluid; mixing can cause damage to the system*

● *Make sure that your car is on level ground.*
● *The fluid level in the reservoir will drop slightly but the fluid level must never be allowed to drop below the MIN mark.*

Safety first!

● If the reservoir requires repeated topping-up this is an indication of a fluid leak somewhere in the system, which should be investigated immediately.

1 The MAX and MIN marks are indicated on the clutch fluid reservoir filler neck. The fluid level must be kept between these two marks.

2 If topping-up is necessary, first wipe clean the area around the filler cap to prevent dirt entering the hydraulic system.

3 Carefully prise off the cap using your fingers, and inspect the fluid and filler neck. If the fluid is dirty the hydraulic system should be drained and refilled (see Chapter 6).

4 Carefully add fluid, taking care not to spill it onto the surrounding components. Use only the specified fluid. After topping-up to the correct level, securely refit the cap and wipe off any spilt fluid. Note the special rubber float in the filler neck.

Brake fluid level

Warning: Brake fluid can harm your eyes and damage painted surfaces, so use extreme caution when handling and pouring it. Do not use fluid which has been standing open for some time, as it absorbs moisture from the air, which can cause a dangerous loss of braking effectiveness.

● *Make sure that your car is on level ground.*
● *The fluid level in the reservoir will drop slightly but the fluid level must never be allowed to drop below the MIN mark.*

Safety first!

● If the reservoir requires repeated topping-up, this is an indication of a fluid leak somewhere in the system, which should be investigated immediately.
● If a leak is suspected, the car should not be driven until the braking system has been checked. Never take any risks where brakes are concerned.

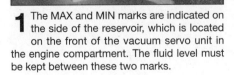

1 The MAX and MIN marks are indicated on the side of the reservoir, which is located on the front of the vacuum servo unit in the engine compartment. The fluid level must be kept between these two marks.

2 If topping-up is necessary, first wipe the area around the filler cap with a clean rag before removing the cap.

3 Carefully add fluid, avoiding spilling it on surrounding paintwork. Use only the specified hydraulic fluid; mixing different types of fluid can cause damage to the system and/or a loss of braking effectiveness. After filling to the correct level, refit the cap securely and wipe off any spilt fluid.

Tyre condition and pressure

It is very important that tyres are in good condition, and at the correct pressure - having a tyre failure at any speed is highly dangerous. Tyre wear is influenced by driving style - harsh braking and acceleration, or fast cornering, will all produce more rapid tyre wear. As a general rule, the front tyres wear out faster than the rears. Interchanging the tyres from front to rear ("rotating" the tyres) may result in more even wear. However, if this is completely effective, you may have the expense of replacing all four tyres at once!

Remove any nails or stones embedded in the tread before they penetrate the tyre to cause deflation. If removal of a nail does reveal that the tyre has been punctured, refit the nail so that its point of penetration is marked. Then immediately change the wheel, and have the tyre repaired by a tyre dealer.

Regularly check the tyres for damage in the form of cuts or bulges, especially in the sidewalls. Periodically remove the wheels, and clean any dirt or mud from the inside and outside surfaces. Examine the wheel rims for signs of rusting, corrosion or other damage. Light alloy wheels are easily damaged by "kerbing" whilst parking; steel wheels may also become dented or buckled. A new wheel is very often the only way to overcome severe damage.

New tyres should be balanced when they are fitted, but it may become necessary to re-balance them as they wear, or if the balance weights fitted to the wheel rim should fall off. Unbalanced tyres will wear more quickly, as will the steering and suspension components. Wheel imbalance is normally signified by vibration, particularly at a certain speed (typically around 50 mph). If this vibration is felt only through the steering, then it is likely that just the front wheels need balancing. If, however, the vibration is felt through the whole car, the rear wheels could be out of balance. Wheel balancing should be carried out by a tyre dealer or garage.

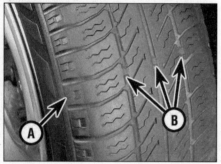

1 *Tread Depth - visual check*
The original tyres have tread wear safety bands (B), which will appear when the tread depth reaches approximately 1.6 mm. The band positions are indicated by a triangular mark on the tyre sidewall (A).

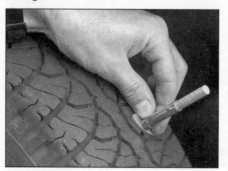

2 *Tread Depth - manual check*
Alternatively, tread wear can be monitored with a simple, inexpensive device known as a tread depth indicator gauge.

3 *Tyre Pressure Check*
Check the tyre pressures regularly with the tyres cold. Do not adjust the tyre pressures immediately after the vehicle has been used, or an inaccurate setting will result.

Tyre tread wear patterns

Shoulder Wear

Underinflation (wear on both sides)
Under-inflation will cause overheating of the tyre, because the tyre will flex too much, and the tread will not sit correctly on the road surface. This will cause a loss of grip and excessive wear, not to mention the danger of sudden tyre failure due to heat build-up.
Check and adjust pressures
Incorrect wheel camber (wear on one side)
Repair or renew suspension parts
Hard cornering
Reduce speed!

Centre Wear

Overinflation
Over-inflation will cause rapid wear of the centre part of the tyre tread, coupled with reduced grip, harsher ride, and the danger of shock damage occurring in the tyre casing.
Check and adjust pressures

If you sometimes have to inflate your car's tyres to the higher pressures specified for maximum load or sustained high speed, don't forget to reduce the pressures to normal afterwards.

Uneven Wear

Front tyres may wear unevenly as a result of wheel misalignment. Most tyre dealers and garages can check and adjust the wheel alignment (or "tracking") for a modest charge.
Incorrect camber or castor
Repair or renew suspension parts
Malfunctioning suspension
Repair or renew suspension parts
Unbalanced wheel
Balance tyres
Incorrect toe setting
Adjust front wheel alignment
Note: *The feathered edge of the tread which typifies toe wear is best checked by feel.*

Power steering fluid level

Before you start
✔ Make sure that the car is on level ground.

✔ Set the steering wheel straight ahead.

✔ The engine should be turned off.

Safety first!
● The need for frequent topping-up indicates a leak, which should be investigated immediately.
● If a leak is suspected, the car should not be driven until the braking system has been checked. Never take any risks where brakes are concerned.

 HAYNES HINT *For the check to be accurate, the steering must not be turned once the engine has been stopped.*

1 On later 1.6 and 1.8 litre models, and all 2.0 litre models, the reservoir is mounted on the right-hand side of the engine compartment. The MAX and MIN level marks are on the side of the translucent reservoir. With the engine cold, the fluid level should be within the COLD range on the reservoir; if it is hot the level should be within the HOT range.

2 On 1.6 and 1.8 litre models pre-August 2000, the power steering fluid reservoir is integral with the power steering pump, located at the right-hand rear of the engine. The reservoir filler cap incorporates a dipstick with HOT and COLD range level markings. Wipe clean the area around the reservoir filler neck, before unscrewing the filler cap/dipstick from the reservoir.

3 With the engine stopped check the level through the side of the reservoir, or dip the fluid with the reservoir cap/dipstick by screwing it fully back into place. Add fluid if necessary to bring the level within the HOT or COLD range according to engine temperature. Use the specified type of fluid and do not overfill the reservoir. When the level is correct, screw on the cap securely

Washer fluid level

● Screenwash additives not only keep the windscreen clean during bad weather, they also prevent the washer system freezing in cold weather – which is when you are likely to need it most. Don't top-up using plain water, as the screenwash will become diluted, and will freeze in cold weather.

 Warning: On no account use engine coolant antifreeze in the screen washer system – this may damage the paintwork.

1 The washer fluid reservoir is located at the front right-hand side of the engine compartment. To check the fluid level, open the cap, place your thumb over the vent hole in the centre of the cap, and withdraw the cap and tube. The fluid level can then be seen in the transparent tube.

2 If topping-up is necessary, add water and a screenwash additive in the quantities recommended on the bottle.

Wiper blades

Note: *Fitting details for wiper blades vary according to model, and according to whether genuine Toyota wiper blades have been fitted. Use the procedures and illustrations shown as a guide for your car.*

1 Check the condition of the wiper blades; if they are cracked or show any signs of deterioration, or if the glass swept area is smeared, renew them. Wiper blades should be renewed annually.

2 To remove a windscreen wiper blade, pull the arm fully away from the screen until it locks. Swivel the blade through 90°, then depress the locking clip at the base of the mounting block.

3 Move the blade down the arm to disengage the mounting block, then slide the blade from the arm. Don't forget to check the tailgate wiper blade as well (where applicable).

Battery

Caution: Before carrying out any work on the vehicle battery, read the precautions given in 'Safety first!' at the start of this manual.

✔ Make sure that the battery tray is in good condition, and that the clamp is tight. Corrosion on the tray, retaining clamp and the battery itself can be removed with a solution of water and baking soda. Thoroughly rinse all cleaned areas with water. Any metal parts damaged by corrosion should be covered with a zinc-based primer, then painted.

✔ Periodically (approximately every three months), check the charge condition of the battery as described in Chapter 5A.

✔ If the battery is flat, and you need to jump start your vehicle, see *Roadside Repairs*.

1 The battery is located on the left-hand side of the engine compartment. Check the tightness of the battery cable clamps to ensure good electrical connections. You should not be able to move them. Also check each cable for cracks and frayed conductors.

2 If corrosion (white, fluffy deposits) is evident, remove the cables from the battery terminals.

HAYNES HiNT

Battery corrosion can be kept to a minimum by applying a layer of petroleum jelly to the clamps and terminals after they are reconnected.

3 Clean them with a small wire brush, then refit them. Automotive stores sell a useful tool for cleaning the battery post . . .

4 . . . as well as the battery cable clamps.

Electrical systems

✔ Check all external lights and the horn. Refer to the appropriate Sections of Chapter 12 for details if any of the circuits are found to be inoperative.

✔ Visually check all accessible wiring connectors, harnesses and retaining clips for security, and for signs of chafing or damage.

HAYNES HiNT *If you need to check your brake lights and indicators unaided, back up to a wall or garage door and operate the lights. The reflected light should show if they are working properly.*

1 If a single indicator light, brake light or headlight has failed, it is likely that a bulb has blown and will need to be renewed. Refer to Chapter 12 for details. If both brake lights have failed, it is possible that the brake/stop-light switch operated by the brake pedal has failed. Refer to Chapter 9 for details.

2 If more than one indicator light or tail light has failed it is likely that either a fuse has blown or that there is a fault in the circuit (see Chapter 12). The main fuses are located behind the pull-out stowage box in the facia on the driver's side . . .

3 . . . and in the fuse/relay box in the engine compartment.

4 To renew a blown fuse, remove it, where applicable using the plastic tool provided. Fit a new fuse of the same rating, available from vehicle accessory shops. It is important that you find the reason that the fuse blew (see *Electrical fault finding* in Chapter 12).

Lubricants and fluids

Engine . . . . Multigrade engine oil, viscosity SAE 5W/30 or 10W/30 to API SJ or better

Cooling system . . . . Toyota long-life coolant or ethylene glycol-based antifreeze and soft water

Clutch system . . . . Hydraulic fluid to SAE J1703F or DOT 4

Manual gearbox . . . . Hypoid gear oil, viscosity SAE 75W/90 to API GL-3

Automatic transmission:

All except 2.0 litre models post-August 2000 . . . . Dexron type II, or type III, automatic transmission fluid (ATF)

2.0 litre models post-August 2000 . . . . Toyota type T-IV automatic transmission fluid

Braking system . . . . Hydraulic fluid to SAE J1703F or DOT 4

Power steering . . . . Dexron type II or type III automatic transmission fluid (ATF)

Tyre pressures

Note: *The following pressures apply only to original-equipment tyres at speeds of up to 100 mph and may vary if any other make or type of tyre is fitted; check with the tyre manufacturer or supplier for correct pressures if necessary. For pressures at higher speeds, consult the vehicle's handbook or your Toyota dealer.*

All models	Front	Rear
185/65 R14 86H tyres	2.2 bar (32 psi)	2.2 bar (32 psi)
195/60 R15 88H tyres	2.2 bar (32 psi)	2.2 bar (32 psi)
Space-saver spare tyre	4.2 bar (61 psi)	4.2 bar (61 psi)

Chapter 1
Routine maintenance and servicing

Contents

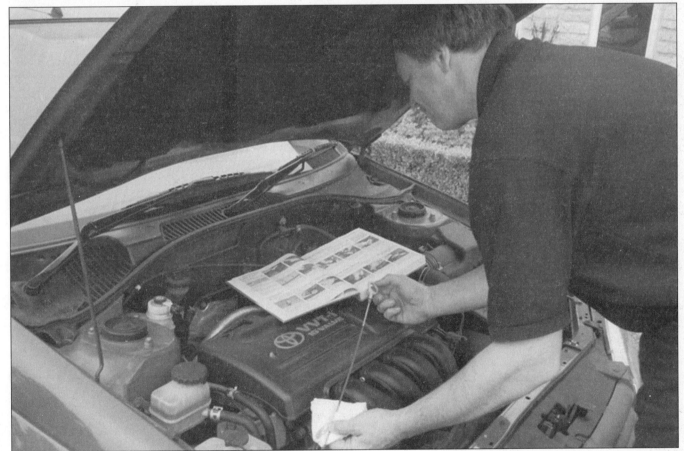

Degrees of difficulty

Easy, suitable for novice with little experience | **Fairly easy,** suitable for beginner with some experience | **Fairly difficult,** suitable for competent DIY mechanic | **Difficult,** suitable for experienced DIY mechanic | **Very difficult,** suitable for expert DIY or professional

Lubricants and fluids

Refer to *Weekly checks*

Capacities

Engine oil (including filter)

Pre-August 2000 models:
1.6 litre engines	3.0 litres
1.8 litre engines	3.7 litres
2.0 litre engines	3.9 litres

Post-August 2000 models:
1.6 and 1.8 litre engines.................................	3.7 litres
2.0 litre engines	4.2 litres

Cooling system (approximate)

Pre-August 2000 models:
1.6 and 1.8 litre engines.................................	6.2 litres
2.0 litre engines	7.6 litres

Post-August 2000 models:
1.6 and 1.8 litre engines.................................	5.6 litres

2.0 litre engines:
Manual transmission models	5.7 litres
Automatic transmission models	6.2 litres

Manual transmission

1.6 and 1.8 litre engines.................................	1.9 litres
2.0 litre engines	2.2 litres

Automatic transmission

Refilling after draining (approximate):

Pre-August 2000 models:
1.8 litre engines..	3.1 litres
2.0 litre engines..	3.3 litres

Post-August 2000 models:
1.8 litre engines..	3.1 litres
2.0 litre engines..	4.0 litres

Fuel tank

All models..	60 litres

Cooling system

Antifreeze mixture:
50% antifreeze	Protection down to –37°C

Note: *Refer to antifreeze manufacturer for latest recommendations. Toyota antifreeze is normally supplied premixed.*

Auxiliary drivebelt – pre-August 2000 models

Deflection (tension check):

1.6 and 1.8 litre engines:
Alternator/coolant pump drivebelt	11.5 to 13.5 mm
Air conditioning compressor drivebelt	8.5 to 9.5 mm
Power steering pump drivebelt...........................	6.0 to 8.0 mm

2.0 litre engines:
Alternator drivebelt.....................................	13.0 to 19.0 mm
Alternator/air conditioning compressor drivebelt..............	9.0 to 11.0 mm
Power steering pump drivebelt...........................	10.0 to 13.0 mm

Ignition system

Spark plugs:

Pre-August 2000 models:

1.6 and 1.8 litre engines	Denso SK20R – P13
Electrode gap (new)	1.3 mm
Electrode gap (used)	1.4 mm
2.0 litre engines	Denso PK20TR11
Electrode gap (new)	1.1 mm
Electrode gap (used)	1.3 mm

Post-August 2000 models:

1.6 and 1.8 litre engines	Denso K16R – U11
Electrode gap	1.1 mm
2.0 litre engines	Denso SK20R11
Electrode gap	1.1 mm
Spark plug HT lead resistances	25 k ohms per HT lead maximum

Brakes

Brake pad lining minimum thickness	2.0 mm
Brake shoe friction material minimum thickness	1.0 mm
Handbrake lever travel	4 to 7 clicks of ratchet
Front brake disc minimum thickness	23.0 mm
Rear brake disc minimum thickness	9.0 mm

Torque wrench settings

	Nm	lbf ft
Pre-August 2000 models:		
Alternator mounting bolts:		
Alternator-to-mounting bracket bolts	54	40
Alternator to adjustment link	19	14
Cylinder block drain plug:		
1.6 and 1.8 litre engines	34	25
2.0 litre engines	25	18
Manual transmission oil filler/level and drain plugs:		
1.6 and 1.8 litre engines	39	29
2.0 litre engines	49	36
Roadwheel nuts	103	76
Spark plugs:		
1.6 and 1.8 litre engines	23	17
2.0 litre engines	18	13
Sump drain plug:		
1.6 and 1.8 litre engines	34	25
2.0 litre engines	37	27
Post-August 2000 models:		
Cylinder block drain plug	8	6
Ignition coil mounting bolts	10	7
Manual transmission oil filler/level and drain plugs:		
1.6 and 1.8 litre engines	39	29
2.0 litre engines	49	36
Roadwheel nuts	103	76
Spark plugs:		
1.6 and 1.8 litre engines	25	18
2.0 litre engines	19	14
Sump drain plug:		
1.6 and 1.8 litre engines	37	27
2.0 litre engines	25	18

The maintenance intervals in this manual are provided with the assumption that you, not the dealer, will be carrying out the work. These are the minimum maintenance intervals recommended by us for vehicles driven daily. If you wish to keep your vehicle in peak condition at all times, you may wish to perform some of these procedures more often. We encourage frequent maintenance, because it enhances the efficiency, performance and resale value of your vehicle. If you drive in dusty areas, tow a trailer, idle or drive at low speeds for extended periods, or drive for short distances (less than four miles), shorter intervals are also recommended.

When the vehicle is new, it should be serviced by a factory-authorised dealer service department, in order to preserve the factory warranty.

Every 250 miles or weekly
☐ Refer to *Weekly checks*

Every 5000 miles or 6 months – whichever comes first
☐ Renew the engine oil and filter (Section 3)

Note: *Toyota recommends that the engine oil and filter are changed every 10 000 miles or 12 months. However, oil and filter changes are good for the engine, and we recommend that the oil and filter are renewed more frequently, especially if the car is used mainly for short journeys.*

Every 10 000 miles or 12 months – whichever comes first
☐ Check the condition of the auxiliary drivebelt(s), and renew if necessary (Section 4)
☐ Clean the air filter element (Section 5)
☐ Check the battery (Section 6)
☐ Check the automatic transmission fluid level (Section 7)
☐ Check the condition of the brake pads and discs (Section 8)
☐ Check the tightness of the roadwheel nuts (Section 9)
☐ Lubricate all hinges and locks (Section 10)
☐ Check the condition, operation and security of all seat belts (Section 11)
☐ Carry out a road test (Section 12)

Every 20 000 miles or 2 years – whichever comes first
☐ Renew the pollen filter (Section 13)
☐ Check the engine coolant strength (Section 14)
☐ Check and adjust the brake pedal (Section 15)
☐ Check and adjust the handbrake (Section 16)
☐ Check all underbonnet components and hoses for fluid leaks (Section 17)
☐ Check the manual transmission oil level (Section 18)
☐ Check the exhaust system (Section 19)
☐ Check the evaporative emission control system (Section 20)
☐ Check the steering and suspension components for condition and security (Section 21)
☐ Check the condition of the driveshaft rubber gaiters and CV joints (Section 22)
☐ Check the rear brake shoes and drums – models with rear drum brakes (Section 23)
☐ Renew the brake fluid (Section 24)
☐ Check the body for corrosion (Section 25)
☐ Renew the battery in the alarm/locking remote handset (Section 26)

Every 40 000 miles or 3 years – whichever comes first
☐ Renew the air filter element (Section 5)
☐ Renew the engine coolant (Section 27)

Every 40 000 miles or 4 years – whichever comes first
☐ Renew the spark plugs – except engines fitted with platinum-tipped spark plugs (Section 28)
☐ Renew the fuel filter (Section 29)
☐ Renew the transmission oil/fluid (Section 30)

Every 60 000 miles or 6 years – whichever comes first
☐ Renew the spark plugs – engines fitted with platinum-tipped spark plugs only (Section 28)
☐ Renew the timing belt – pre-August 2000 models (Section 31)
☐ Check and adjust the valve clearances (Section 32)

Underbonnet view of a pre-August 2000 1.8 litre model (manual transmission)

1 Engine oil filler cap
2 Engine oil dipstick
3 Engine oil filter
4 Radiator pressure cap
5 Exhaust gas lean mixture sensor
6 Alternator
7 Windscreen/tailgate washer fluid reservoir
8 Coolant expansion tank
9 Brake master cylinder fluid reservoir
10 Clutch master cylinder fluid reservoir
11 Power steering pump
12 Ignition coil
13 Air cleaner housing
14 Fuse/relay box
15 Battery

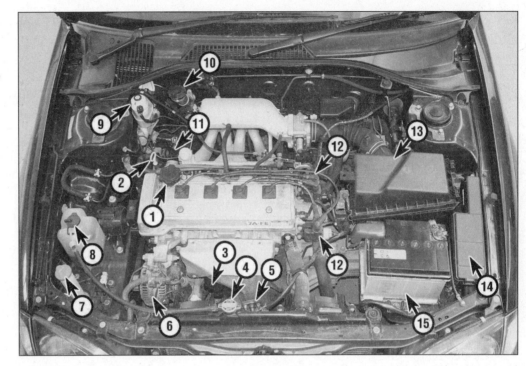

Underbonnet view of a pre-August 2000 2.0 litre model (automatic transmission)

1 Engine oil filler cap
2 Alternator
3 Engine oil filter
4 Engine oil dipstick
5 Radiator pressure cap
6 Windscreen/tailgate washer fluid reservoir
7 Coolant expansion tank
8 Power steering fluid reservoir
9 Brake master cylinder fluid reservoir
10 EGR valve and modulator
11 Air cleaner housing
12 Fuse/relay box
13 Battery
14 Automatic transmission fluid dipstick

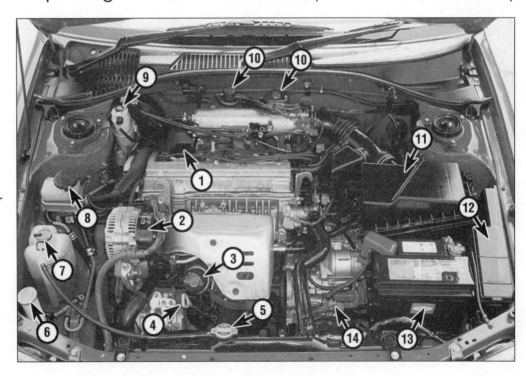

Underbonnet view of a post-August 2000 1.8 litre model (manual transmission)

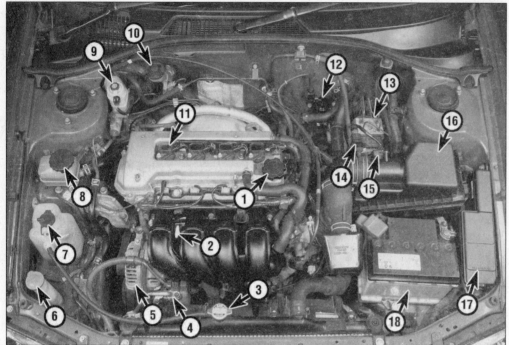

1 Engine oil filler cap
2 Engine oil dipstick
3 Radiator pressure cap
4 Air conditioning compressor
5 Alternator
6 Windscreen/tailgate washer fluid reservoir
7 Coolant expansion tank
8 Power steering fluid reservoir
9 Brake master cylinder fluid reservoir
10 Clutch master cylinder fluid reservoir
11 Ignition coils
12 Fuel filter
13 ABS hydraulic unit
14 Evaporative emission system solenoid valve
15 Airflow meter
16 Air cleaner housing
17 Fuse/relay box
18 Battery

Underbonnet view of a post-August 2000 2.0 litre model (manual transmission)

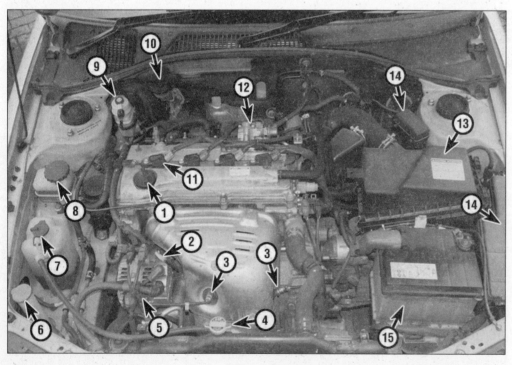

1 Engine oil filler cap
2 Engine oil dipstick
3 Exhaust gas oxygen sensor
4 Radiator pressure cap
5 Alternator
6 Windscreen/tailgate washer fluid reservoir
7 Coolant expansion tank
8 Power steering fluid reservoir
9 Brake master cylinder fluid reservoir
10 Clutch master cylinder fluid reservoir
11 Ignition coils
12 High-pressure fuel pump
13 Air cleaner housing
14 Fuse/relay box
15 Battery

Front underbody view of a post-August 2000 1.8 litre model

1 Sump drain plug
2 Oil filter
3 Radiator drain tap
4 Longitudinal crossmember
5 Manual transmission
6 Front brake caliper
7 Suspension arm control link
8 Driveshaft inner CV joint
9 Steering track rod
10 Front suspension lower arm
11 Front subframe
12 Exhaust front downpipe

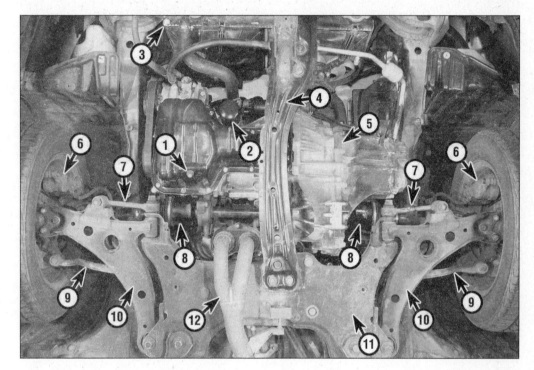

Rear underbody view of a post-August 2000 1.8 litre model

1 Spare wheel well
2 Fuel tank filler hose
3 Rear suspension lower arm
4 Rear suspension strut/ shock absorber
5 Rear subframe
6 Handbrake cable
7 Rear suspension radius rod
8 Exhaust tailpipe and silencer
9 Exhaust heat shield
10 Fuel tank

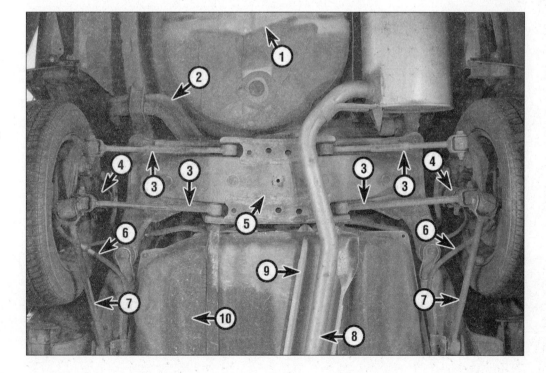

1 Introduction

1 This Chapter is designed to help the home mechanic maintain his/her vehicle for safety, economy, long life and peak performance.

2 The Chapter contains a master maintenance schedule, and Sections dealing specifically with each task in the schedule. Visual checks, adjustments, component renewal and other helpful items are included. Refer to the accompanying illustrations of the engine compartment and the underside of the vehicle for the locations of the various components.

3 Servicing your vehicle in accordance with the mileage/time maintenance schedule and the following Sections will provide a planned maintenance programme, which should result in a long and reliable service life. This is a comprehensive plan, so maintaining some items but not others at the specified service intervals will not produce the same results.

4 As you service your vehicle, you will discover that many of the procedures can – and should – be grouped together, because of the particular procedure being performed, or because of the proximity of two otherwise-unrelated components to one another. For example, if the vehicle is raised for any reason, the exhaust can be inspected at the same time as the suspension and steering components.

5 The first step in this maintenance programme is to prepare yourself before the actual work begins. Read through all the Sections relevant to the work to be carried out, then make a list and gather all the parts and tools required. If a problem is encountered, seek advice from a parts specialist, or a dealer service department.

2 Regular maintenance

1 If, from the time the vehicle is new, the routine maintenance schedule is followed closely, and frequent checks are made of fluid levels and high-wear items, as suggested throughout this manual, the engine will be kept in relatively good running condition, and the need for additional work will be minimised.

2 It is possible that there will be times when the engine is running poorly due to the lack of regular maintenance. This is even more likely if a used vehicle, which has not received regular and frequent maintenance checks, is purchased. In such cases, additional work may need to be carried out, outside of the regular maintenance intervals.

3 If engine wear is suspected, a compression test (refer to Chapter 2A or 2B) will provide valuable information regarding the overall performance of the main internal components. Such a test can be used as a basis to decide on the extent of the work to be carried out. If, for example, a compression test indicates serious internal engine wear, conventional maintenance as described in this Chapter will not greatly improve the performance of the engine, and may prove a waste of time and money, unless extensive overhaul work is carried out first.

4 The following operations are those most often required to improve the performance of a generally poor-running engine:

Primary operations

a) Clean, inspect and test the battery ('Weekly checks', Section 6 and Chapter 5A).
b) Check all the engine-related fluids ('Weekly checks').
c) Check the condition and tension of the auxiliary drivebelts (Section 4).
d) Renew the spark plugs (Section 28).
e) Check the condition of the air filter, and renew if necessary (Section 5).
f) Check the fuel filter (Section 29).
g) Check the condition of all hoses, and check for fluid leaks (Section 17).

5 If the above operations do not prove fully effective, carry out the following secondary operations:

Secondary operations

All items listed under Primary operations, plus the following:

a) Check the charging system (Chapter 5A).
b) Check the ignition system (Chapter 5B).
c) Check the fuel system (Chapter 4A).
d) Check the emissions control systems (Chapter 4B).

Every 5000 miles or 6 months

3 Engine oil and filter renewal

1 Frequent oil and filter changes are the most important preventative maintenance procedures which can be undertaken by the DIY owner. As engine oil ages, it becomes diluted and contaminated, which leads to premature engine wear.

2 Before starting this procedure, gather together all the necessary tools and materials. Also make sure that you have plenty of clean rags and newspapers handy, to mop-up any spills. Ideally, the engine oil should be warm, as it will drain better, and more built-up sludge will be removed with it. Take care, however, not to touch the exhaust or any other hot parts of the engine when working under the vehicle. To avoid any possibility of scalding, and to protect yourself from possible skin irritants and other harmful contaminants in used engine oils, it is advisable to wear gloves when carrying out this work. Access to the underside of the vehicle will be greatly improved if it can be raised on a lift, driven onto ramps, or jacked up and supported on axle stands (see Jacking and vehicle support). Whichever method is chosen, make sure that the vehicle remains level or, if it is at an angle, that the drain plug is at the lowest point.

3 Remove the oil filler cap from the engine camshaft cover (turn it anti-clockwise and withdraw it) (see illustration).

4 Using a spanner, or preferably a suitable socket and bar, slacken the drain plug about half a turn (see illustration). Position the draining container under the drain plug, then remove the plug completely (see Haynes Hint). Recover the sealing ring from the drain plug.

3.3 Remove the oil filler cap from the camshaft cover

3.4 Slacken the engine oil drain plug (arrowed)

HAYNES HiNT *Keep the drain plug pressed into the sump while unscrewing it by hand the last couple of turns. As the plug releases, move it away sharply so the stream of oil issuing from the sump runs into the container, not up your sleeve.*

5 Allow some time for the oil to drain, noting that it may be necessary to reposition the container as the oil flow slows to a trickle.

6 After all the oil has drained, wipe the drain plug and the sealing washer with a clean rag. Examine the condition of the sealing washer – renew it if it shows signs of scoring or other damage which may prevent an oil-tight seal. Clean the area around the drain plug opening, and refit the plug complete with the washer. Tighten the plug securely – preferably to the specified torque, using a torque wrench.

7 Move the container under the oil filter which is located at the front right-hand side of the cylinder block **(see illustrations)**.

8 Use an oil filter removal tool (if required) to slacken the filter initially, then unscrew it by hand the rest of the way **(see illustration)**. Empty the oil from the old filter into the container.

9 Use a clean rag to remove all oil, dirt and sludge from the filter sealing area on the engine. Check the old filter to make sure that the rubber sealing ring has not stuck to the engine. If it has, carefully remove it.

10 Apply a light coating of clean engine oil to the sealing ring on the new filter, then screw the filter into position on the engine **(see illustration)**. Lightly tighten the filter until its sealing ring contacts the block, then tighten it through a further two-thirds of a turn.

11 Remove the old oil and all tools from under the vehicle then, if applicable, lower the vehicle to the ground.

12 Fill the engine through the filler in the camshaft cover, using the correct grade and type of oil (refer to *Weekly checks* for details of topping-up). Pour in half the specified quantity of oil first, then wait a few minutes for the oil to drain into the sump. Continue to add oil, a small quantity at a time, until the level is up to the lower mark on the dipstick. Adding

3.7a Oil filter (arrowed) – pre-August 2000 engines

3.7b Oil filter (arrowed) – post-August 2000 engines

3.8 Using a chain strap to remove the oil filter

3.10 Apply a light coating of clean engine oil to the sealing ring on the new filter

approximately a further 1.0 litre will bring the level up to the upper mark on the dipstick.

13 Start the engine and run it for a few minutes, while checking for leaks around the oil filter seal and the sump drain plug. Note that there may be a delay of a few seconds before the low oil pressure warning light goes out when the engine is first started, as the oil circulates through the new oil filter and the engine oil galleries before the pressure builds-up. Do not run the engine above idle speed while the warning light is on.

14 Stop the engine, and wait a few minutes for the oil to settle in the sump once more. With the new oil circulated and the filter now completely full, recheck the level on the dipstick, and add more oil as necessary.

15 Dispose of the used engine oil and filter safely, with reference to *General repair procedures* at the rear of this manual. Do not discard the old filter with domestic household waste. The facility for waste oil disposal provided by many local council refuse tips generally has a filter receptacle alongside.

Every 10 000 miles or 12 months

4 Auxiliary drivebelt(s) check and renewal

1 On 1.6 and 1.8 litre engines pre-August 2000, two or three drivebelts are fitted. The main drivebelt drives the coolant pump and alternator from the crankshaft pulley, and a secondary drivebelt drives the power steering pump from the coolant pump pulley. Where air conditioning is fitted, the compressor is driven by a separate drivebelt from the crankshaft pulley.

2 On 2.0 litre engines pre-August 2000, two drivebelts are fitted. The main drivebelt drives the alternator from the crankshaft pulley. On models with air conditioning the main drivebelt is longer and drives the air conditioning compressor in addition to the alternator. The power steering pump is driven by a separate drivebelt from the crankshaft pulley.

3 On all post-August 2000 engines, a single drivebelt is used to drive the alternator, power steering pump and, where fitted, the air conditioning compressor, from the crankshaft pulley. The belt is adjusted automatically, by means of a spring-loaded tensioner mechanism.

Checking

4 Apply the handbrake, slacken the front right-hand roadwheel bolts, then jack up the front of the car and support it on axle stands (see *Jacking and vehicle support*). Remove the right-hand front roadwheel.

5 Remove the plastic wheel arch liner under the right-hand front wing with reference to Chapter 11.

6 Using a socket and extension bar fitted to the crankshaft pulley bolt, rotate the crankshaft so that the entire length of each drivebelt can be examined. Examine the drivebelts for

cracks, splitting, fraying or damage. Check also for signs of glazing (shiny patches) and for separation of the belt plies. Renew the belt if worn or damaged.

 Turning the engine will be much easier if the spark plugs are removed first (Section 28).

7 If the condition of the belt is satisfactory, check the drivebelt tension (pre-August 2000 engines) as described below under the relevant sub-heading.

Alternator – pre-August 2000
Removal

8 If not already done, proceed as described in paragraphs 4 and 5.

9 Disconnect the battery negative terminal

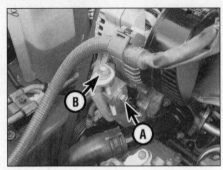

4.10 Alternator lower adjusting lockbolt (A) and adjuster bolt (B) – 2.0 litre engines pre-August 2000

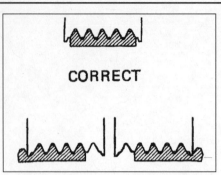

4.12 When refitting a drivebelt, ensure it is centred – it must not overlap either edge of the pulleys

4.15 Checking the tension of the alternator drivebelt – 1.6 and 1.8 litre engines pre-August 2000

(refer to *Disconnecting the battery* in the Reference Chapter).

10 Slacken the alternator upper pivot bolt, then slacken the alternator lower adjusting lockbolt **(see illustration)**.

11 Back off the adjuster bolt (on the lower link bracket) to relieve the tension in the drivebelt, then slip the drivebelt from the pulleys.

Refitting

12 Fit the belt around the pulleys, ensuring that the belt is of the correct type if it is being renewed and is correctly engaged with the ribs on the pulley **(see illustration)**. Take up the slack in the belt by tightening the adjuster bolt. Tension the drivebelt as described in the following paragraphs.

Tensioning

13 If not already done, proceed as described in paragraphs 4 and 5.

14 Correct tensioning of the drivebelt will ensure that it has a long life. Beware, however, of overtightening, as this can cause wear in the alternator or coolant pump bearings.

15 On 1.6 and 1.8 litre engines, the belt tension is checked at the mid-point between the alternator and coolant pump pulleys on the upper belt run. Apply finger or thumb pressure by pressing down on the drivebelt, and check that it deflects by the amount given in the Specifications **(see illustration)**.

16 On 2.0 litre engines without air conditioning, the belt tension is checked at the mid-point between the crankshaft and alternator pulleys. On engines with air

conditioning, the belt tension is checked at the mid-point between the alternator and air conditioning compressor pulleys. Apply finger or thumb pressure by pressing down on the drivebelt, and check that it deflects by the amount given in the Specifications.

17 On all engines, to adjust the belt tension, with the alternator upper pivot bolt and lower adjusting lockbolt loose, turn the adjuster bolt until the correct tension is achieved. Rotate the crankshaft a couple of times, recheck the tension, then securely tighten both the alternator mounting pivot and adjusting lockbolts.

18 Refit the wheel arch liner and roadwheel, then reconnect the battery, and lower the vehicle to the ground.

Air conditioning compressor – 1.6 and 1.8 litre pre-August 2000

Removal

19 If not already done, proceed as described in paragraphs 4 and 5.

20 Remove the alternator drivebelt as described earlier in this Section.

21 Loosen the idler pulley bolt then back off the adjuster bolt (on the idler pulley bracket) to relieve the tension in the drivebelt, and slip the drivebelt from the pulleys **(see illustration)**.

Refitting

22 Fit the belt around the pulleys, ensuring that the belt is of the correct type if it is being renewed, and is correctly engaged with the ribs on the pulley **(see illustration 4.12)**.

Take up the slack in the belt by tightening the adjuster bolt. Tension the drivebelt as described in the following paragraphs.

Tensioning

23 If not already done, proceed as described in paragraphs 4 and 5.

24 Correct tensioning of the drivebelt will ensure that it has a long life. Beware, however, of overtightening, as this can cause wear in the compressor bearings.

25 The belt tension is checked at the mid-point between the compressor and crankshaft pulleys on the lower belt run. Apply finger or thumb pressure by pressing on the drivebelt, and check that it deflects by the amount given in the Specifications.

26 To adjust, with the idler pulley bolt loose, turn the adjuster bolt until the correct tension is achieved. Rotate the crankshaft a couple of times, recheck the tension, then securely tighten the idler pulley bolt.

27 Refit and tension the alternator drivebelt as described earlier in this Section.

28 On completion, refit the wheel arch liner and roadwheel, then reconnect the battery, and lower the vehicle to the ground.

Power steering pump – pre-August 2000

Removal

29 If not already done, proceed as described in paragraphs 4 and 5.

30 Remove the alternator drivebelt as described earlier in this Section.

31 Loosen the power steering pump pivot and adjuster lockbolts, then swivel the pump towards the engine and slip the drivebelt from the pulleys **(see illustration)**.

Refitting

32 Fit the belt around the pulleys, ensuring that the belt is of the correct type if it is being renewed, and is correctly engaged with the ribs on the pulley **(see illustration 4.12)**. Take up the slack in the belt by swivelling the pump away from the engine. Tension the drivebelt as described in the following paragraphs.

Tensioning

33 If not already done, proceed as described in paragraphs 4 and 5.

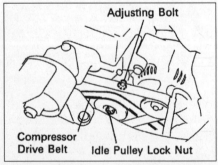

4.21 Air conditioning compressor drivebelt idler pulley details – 1.6 and 1.8 litre engines pre-August 2000

4.31 Power steering pump adjuster lockbolt (arrowed) – 1.6 and 1.8 litre engines pre-August 2000

34 Correct tensioning of the drivebelt will ensure that it has a long life. Beware, however, of overtightening, as this can cause wear in the power steering pump bearings.

35 The belt tension is checked at the mid-point between the pulleys on the upper belt run. Apply finger or thumb pressure by pressing on the drivebelt, and check that it deflects by the amount given in the Specifications.

36 To adjust, with the pump pivot bolt loose, swivel the pump away from the engine until the correct tension is achieved then tighten the adjuster lockbolt. Rotate the crankshaft a couple of times, then recheck the tension.

37 Refit and tension the alternator drivebelt as described earlier in this Section.

38 On completion, refit the wheel arch liner and roadwheel, then reconnect the battery, and lower the vehicle to the ground.

Auxiliary – post-August 2000

Removal

39 If not already done, proceed as described in paragraphs 4 and 5.

40 Disconnect the battery negative terminal (refer to *Disconnecting the battery* in the Reference Chapter).

41 Using a spanner or deep socket on the hexagonal section, rotate the tensioner clockwise to relieve the tension on the belt **(see illustration)**.

42 Lift the belt from the pulleys **(see illustration)**.

4.41 Use a spanner on the hexagonal section (arrowed) of the auxiliary drivebelt tensioner – post-August 2000 engines

Refitting

43 Fit the new belt to the pulleys then, holding the tensioner clockwise, fit the belt around the tensioner pulley, and gently release the tensioner.

5	Air filter element check and clean

Pre-August 2000 engines

1 Withdraw the inlet air temperature sensor from the grommet on the air cleaner lid **(see illustration)**.

2 Slacken the retaining clip and detach the air inlet duct from the air cleaner lid **(see illustration)**.

4.42 Rotate the tensioner clockwise and slip the belt off the pulleys – post-August 2000 engines

3 Release the two retaining clips securing the air cleaner lid to the base. Lift up the right-hand side of the lid, slide it sideways and release it from the two lugs on the air cleaner base **(see illustrations)**.

Post-August 2000 engines

4 Withdraw the evaporative emission system solenoid valve from its location at the rear of the air cleaner lid, or air inlet duct **(see illustrations)**.

5 Disconnect the wiring connector from the airflow meter on the side of the air cleaner lid **(see illustration)**.

6 On 2.0 litre engines, disconnect the engine breather hose from the air inlet duct, and withdraw the inlet air temperature sensor from the grommet on the air cleaner lid **(see illustrations)**.

5.1 Withdraw the inlet air temperature sensor from the air cleaner lid . . .

5.2 . . . then slacken the clip and detach the air inlet duct – pre-August 2000 engines

5.3a Release the two retaining clips . . .

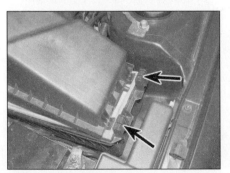

5.3b . . . then lift up the air cleaner lid and release it from the two lugs on the base (arrowed) – pre-August 2000 engines

5.4a On 1.6 and 1.8 litre engines, withdraw the emission system solenoid valve from the air cleaner lid . . .

5.4b . . . or, on 2.0 litre engines, from the air inlet duct (arrowed) – post-August 2000 engines

5.5 Disconnect the wiring connector from the airflow meter on the air cleaner lid – post-August 2000 engines

5.6a On 2.0 litre engines, disconnect the breather hose (arrowed) from the air inlet duct . . .

5.6b . . . and withdraw the inlet air temperature sensor (arrowed) from the air cleaner lid – post-August 2000 engines

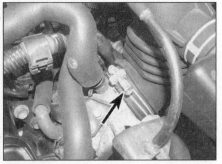

5.7 Slacken the clip (arrowed) securing the air inlet duct to the throttle housing – post-August 2000 engines

5.8a Release the two retaining clips securing the air cleaner lid to the base . . .

5.8b . . . then lift up the lid, detach the air inlet duct and withdraw the lid and duct assembly – post-August 2000 engines

7 Slacken the retaining clip securing the air inlet duct to the throttle housing **(see illustration)**.

8 Release the two retaining clips securing the air cleaner lid to the base. Lift up the right-hand side of the lid, while at the same time detaching the air inlet duct from the throttle housing. Slide the lid sideways to release it from the two lugs on the air cleaner base, then lift the lid and duct assembly off the air cleaner base **(see illustrations)**.

All engines

9 Lift the filter element from the air cleaner base, noting which way round it is fitted **(see illustration)**.

10 Check that the element is not damaged, oily or excessively dirty.

11 To clean the element, blow from its

underside using compressed air then blow off its upper surfaces.

12 Wipe clean the inside of the air cleaner body, then refit the element using a reversal of the removal procedure.

---

6 Battery and electrolyte level check

1 The battery is located on the left-hand side of the engine compartment.

2 On batteries with removable cell covers, the electrolyte level in the battery should be checked (and if necessary topped-up) at the interval given at the beginning of this Chapter; the check should be made more often if the car is operated in high ambient temperature

conditions. Maintenance-free batteries (usually identifiable by a label on the battery top) do not require topping-up and the cell covers are not removable.

3 On some batteries, the case is translucent and incorporates minimum (or lower) and maximum (or upper) level marks; with the vehicle parked on level ground, the electrolyte level in each cell must be maintained between these marks **(see illustration)**. On batteries without a translucent case and level marks, the electrolyte level must be maintained just above the top of the cell plates.

4 If topping-up is necessary, proceed as described in the following paragraph.

5 Remove the cell covers from the top of the battery then carefully add distilled or de-ionized water to raise the electrolyte level in each cell but do not overfill. With the electrolyte level replenished, refit the cell covers.

6 The exterior of the battery should be inspected periodically for damage such as a cracked case or cover.

7 Check the tightness of the battery cable terminal clamps to ensure good electrical connections, and check the entire length of each cable for cracks and frayed conductors.

8 If corrosion (visible as white, fluffy deposits) is evident, remove the cable terminal clamps from the battery terminals, clean them with a small wire brush then refit them. Corrosion can be kept to a minimum by applying a layer of petroleum jelly to the clamps and terminals after they are reconnected.

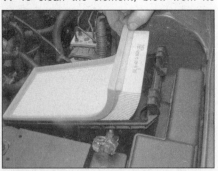

5.9 Lift the filter element from the air cleaner base, noting which way round it is fitted

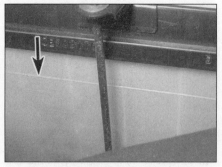

6.3 The electrolyte level can be viewed though the battery casing

7.4 Withdraw the automatic transmission fluid dipstick from its tube

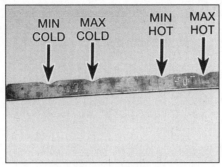

7.6a Transmission fluid level markings on the early type dipstick . . .

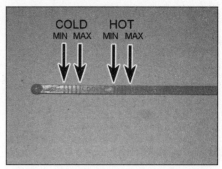

7.6b . . . and on the later type dipstick

9 Make sure that the battery tray is in good condition and the retaining clamp is tight.

10 Corrosion or deposits on the tray, retaining clamp and the battery itself can be removed with a solution of water and baking soda. Thoroughly rinse all cleaned areas with cold water.

11 Any metal parts of the vehicle damaged by such corrosion should be covered with a zinc-based primer then painted.

12 Further information on the battery, charging and jump starting can be found in Chapter 5A and in the preliminary sections of this Manual.

7 Automatic transmission fluid level check

1 The level of the automatic transmission fluid should be carefully maintained. Low fluid level can lead to slipping or loss of drive, while overfilling can cause foaming, loss of fluid and transmission damage.

2 The transmission fluid level should only be checked when the transmission is hot (at its normal operating temperature). If the vehicle has just been driven over 10 miles (15 miles in a cold climate), and the fluid temperature is 71 to 80°C, the transmission is hot.

Caution: If the vehicle has just been driven for a long time at high speed or in city traffic in hot weather, or if it has been pulling a trailer, an accurate fluid level reading cannot be obtained. In these circumstances, allow the fluid to cool down for about 30 minutes.

3 Park the vehicle on level ground, apply the handbrake, and start the engine. While the engine is idling, depress the brake pedal and move the selector lever through all the gear positions, beginning and ending in P.

4 With the engine still idling, remove the dipstick from its tube **(see illustration)**. Note the condition and colour of the fluid on the dipstick.

5 Wipe the fluid from the dipstick with a clean rag, and re-insert it into the filler tube until the cap seats.

6 Pull the dipstick out again, and note the fluid level. On early transmissions, the level should be between the two notches on the

dipstick, either side of the word HOT. On later transmissions, the level should be between the upper and lower lines on the dipstick, below the word HOT **(see illustrations)**.

7 Note that there are also markings on the dipstick to be used if the fluid is cold. On early transmissions, there are two notches on the dipstick either side of the word COOL. On later transmissions, there are upper and lower lines on the dipstick just below the word COOL. If the car has not been driven for about five hours, and the fluid is at or below room temperature, the fluid should be between the two notches, or the two lines in the COOL sector of the dipstick. Checking the level with the fluid cold should only be used for reference and the level must be checked again when the fluid is hot.

8 If the fluid level is near or below the appropriate lower notch or line, stop the engine, and add the specified automatic transmission fluid through the dipstick tube, using a clean funnel if necessary. It is important not to introduce dirt into the transmission when topping-up.

9 Add the fluid a little at a time, and keep checking the level as previously described until it is correct.

10 The need for regular topping-up of the transmission fluid indicates a leak, which should be found and rectified without delay.

11 The condition of the fluid should also be checked along with the level. If the fluid on the dipstick is black or a dark reddish-brown colour, or if it has a burned smell, the fluid should be changed (see Chapter 7B). If you

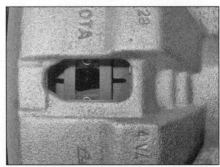

8.5 Check the brake pad friction material thickness by looking through the inspection window in the caliper

are in doubt about the condition of the fluid, purchase some new fluid, and compare the two for colour and smell.

8 Brake pad and disc check

Note: *For detailed photographs of the brake system, refer to Chapter 9.*

1 The work described in this Section should be carried out at the specified intervals, or whenever a defect is suspected in the braking system. Any of the following symptoms could indicate a potential brake system defect:

a) *The vehicle pulls to one side when the brake pedal is depressed.*

b) *The brakes make scraping or dragging noises when applied.*

c) *Brake pedal travel is excessive.*

d) *The brake fluid requires repeated topping-up.*

2 A thorough inspection should be made to confirm the thickness of the linings, as follows.

3 Jack up the front or rear of the vehicle, as applicable, and support it on axle stands (see *Jacking and vehicle support*). Where rear brake pads are fitted, also jack up the rear of the vehicle and support on axle stands.

4 For better access to the brake calipers, remove the wheels.

5 Look through the inspection window in the caliper, and check that the thickness of the friction lining material on each of the pads is not less than the recommended minimum thickness given in the Specifications **(see illustration)**. **Note:** *Bear in mind that the lining material is normally bonded to a metal backing plate.*

6 If it is difficult to determine the exact thickness of the pad linings, or if you are at all concerned about the condition of the pads, then remove them from the calipers for further inspection (refer to Chapter 9).

7 Check the remaining brake caliper(s) in the same way.

8 If any one of the brake pads has worn down to, or below, the specified limit, *all four* pads at that end of the car must be renewed as a set (ie, all the front pads or all the rear pads).

9 Measure the thickness of the discs with

a micrometer, if available, to make sure that they still have service life remaining. If any disc is thinner than the specified minimum thickness, renew it (refer to Chapter 9). In any case, check the general condition of the discs. Look for excessive scoring and discolouration caused by overheating. If these conditions exist, remove the relevant disc and have it resurfaced or renewed (refer to Chapter 9).

10 Before refitting the wheels, check all brake lines and hoses (refer to Chapter 9). In particular, check the flexible hoses in the vicinity of the calipers, where they are subjected to most movement. Bend them between the fingers (but do not actually bend them double, or the casing may be damaged) and check that this does not reveal previously-hidden cracks, cuts or splits.

9 Roadwheel nut tightness check
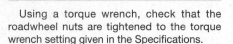

Using a torque wrench, check that the roadwheel nuts are tightened to the torque wrench setting given in the Specifications.

10 Hinge and lock check and lubrication

1 All hinges and locks (doors, bonnet, tailgate, boot, and fuel filler flap) should be examined for correct operation and any defects rectified.
2 Lubricate the moving parts of the hinges and locks with a little engine oil, and apply a little multi-purpose grease to the contact surfaces of the locks and strikers.

11 Seat belt check
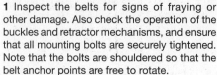

1 Inspect the belts for signs of fraying or other damage. Also check the operation of the buckles and retractor mechanisms, and ensure that all mounting bolts are securely tightened. Note that the bolts are shouldered so that the belt anchor points are free to rotate.
2 If there is any sign of damage, or any doubt about the condition of a belt, it must be renewed. If the vehicle has been involved in a collision, any belts in use at the time should be renewed as a matter of course, and all other belts should be checked carefully.
3 Use only warm water and non-detergent soap when cleaning the belt webbing. Never use chemicals that could attack the belt fabric and reduce its effectiveness. Keep the belts fully extended until they have dried – do not apply heat to accelerate drying.

12 Road test

Instruments and electrical equipment

1 Check the operation of all instruments and electrical equipment.
2 Make sure that all instruments read correctly, and switch on all electrical equipment in turn, to check that it functions properly.

Steering and suspension

3 Check for any abnormalities in the steering, suspension, handling or road feel.
4 Drive the vehicle, and check that there are no unusual vibrations or noises.
5 Check that the steering feels positive, with no excessive sloppiness, or roughness,

and check for any suspension noises when cornering and driving over bumps.

Drivetrain

6 Check the performance of the engine, clutch (if applicable), transmission and driveshafts.
7 Listen for any unusual noises from the engine, clutch and transmission.
8 Make sure that the engine runs smoothly when idling, and that there is no hesitation when accelerating.
9 Check that, where applicable, the clutch action is smooth and progressive, that the drive is taken up smoothly, and that the pedal travel is not excessive. Also listen for any noises when the clutch pedal is depressed.
10 On manual transmission models, check that all gears can be engaged smoothly without noise, and that the gear lever action is smooth and not abnormally vague or notchy.
11 On automatic transmission models, make sure that all gearchanges occur smoothly, without snatching, and without an increase in engine speed between changes. Check that all the gear positions can be selected with the vehicle at rest. If any problems are found, they should be referred to a Toyota dealer.
12 Listen for a metallic clicking sound from the front of the vehicle, as the vehicle is driven slowly in a circle with the steering on full-lock. Carry out this check in both directions. If a clicking noise is heard, this indicates wear in a driveshaft joint, in which case the joint should be renewed.

Braking system

13 Make sure that the vehicle does not pull to one side when braking, and that the wheels do not lock when braking hard.
14 Check that there is no vibration through the steering when braking.
15 Check that the handbrake operates correctly without excessive movement of the lever, and that it holds the vehicle stationary on a slope.

Every 20 000 miles or 2 years

13 Pollen filter renewal

1 Working under the facia on the driver's side, pull back the carpet for access to the front of the heater/air conditioning unit.
2 Depress the retaining tabs and lift off the pollen filter cover (see illustration).
3 Slide the lower pollen filter out from the heater/air conditioning unit. Reach up and pull down the upper filter, and slide the upper filter out in the same way (see illustrations).
4 Check the condition of the filters, and renew them if dirty.
5 Fit the new upper filter, noting that according to filter type, it may be necessary to break off

the detachable plastic centre section of the filter frame, to allow it to locate correctly (see illustration).

13.2 Depress the retaining tabs and lift off the pollen filter cover

6 Fit the new lower filter, followed by the filter cover, then fold back the carpet.

13.3a Slide out the lower pollen filter . . .

13.3b ... pull down the upper pollen filter ...

13.3c ... and slide the upper filter out in the same way

13.5 If necessary, break off the detachable plastic centre section of the filter frame, to allow it to locate correctly

14 Engine coolant strength check

Warning: Wait until the engine is cold before starting this procedure.

1 The coolant antifreeze strength can be checked using a proprietary tester obtained from a car accessory shop. One type of tester acts similar to a battery hydrometer and has five small plastic balls within a clear tube – the coolant strength is determined by the number of balls floating in the coolant.

2 To use the tester, lift the cap from the coolant expansion tank and draw out some of the coolant. Hold the tester vertical and check the number of balls floating. After making the test disperse the coolant into the expansion tank and refit the cap.

3 If the strength of the coolant is low, drain the coolant and refill with the correct strength as described in Section 27.

4 Check the coolant level with reference to *Weekly checks*.

15 Brake pedal check and adjustment

Refer to the procedures in Chapter 9.

16 Handbrake check and adjustment

In service, the handbrake should be fully applied within 4 to 7 clicks of the handbrake lever ratchet. On drum brake models, the handbrake lever travel will normally be kept within these limits by the self-adjusting mechanism on the rear brake shoes. Periodic manual adjustment may be necessary, however, to compensate for cable stretch, and this is carried out by means of the cable adjuster on the side of the handbrake lever. On disc brake models, the handbrake shoes, located inside the rear brake disc/drum assemblies, must first be adjusted manually to compensate for lining wear, and then the

handbrake cable can be adjusted by means of the adjuster on the handbrake lever, to provide the specified lever travel (ratchet clicks). Refer to Chapter 9 for the full adjustment procedure according to type.

17 Hose and fluid leak check

Cooling system

Warning: Refer to the safety information given in 'Safety first!' and Chapter 3 before disturbing any of the cooling system components.

1 Carefully check the radiator and heater coolant hoses along their entire length. Renew any hose which is cracked, swollen or which shows signs of deterioration. Cracks will show up better if the hose is squeezed. Pay close attention to the clips that secure the hoses to the cooling system components. Hose clips that have been over-tightened can pinch and puncture hoses, resulting in cooling system leaks.

2 Inspect all the cooling system components (hoses, joint faces, etc) for leaks. Where any problems of this nature are found on system components, renew the component or gasket with reference to Chapter 3.

3 A leak from the cooling system will usually show up as white or rust-coloured deposits, on the area surrounding the leak (**see Haynes Hint**).

Fuel

Warning: Refer to the safety information given in 'Safety first!' and Chapter 4A before disturbing any of the fuel system components.

4 From within the engine compartment, check the security of all fuel pipe attachments and unions, and inspect the fuel pipes for kinks, chafing and deterioration.

5 To identify fuel leaks between the fuel tank and the engine bay, the vehicle should be raised and securely supported on axle stands (see *Jacking and vehicle support*). Inspect the fuel tank and filler neck for punctures, cracks and other damage. The connection between the filler neck and tank is especially critical. Sometimes a rubber filler neck or connecting

hose will leak due to loose retaining clamps or deteriorated rubber.

6 Carefully check all rubber hoses and metal fuel lines leading away from the fuel tank. Check for loose connections, deteriorated hoses, kinked lines, and other damage. Pay particular attention to the vent pipes and hoses, which often loop up around the filler neck and can become blocked or kinked, making tank filling difficult. Follow the fuel supply and return lines to the front of the vehicle, carefully inspecting them all the way for signs of damage or corrosion. Renew damaged sections as necessary.

Engine oil

7 Inspect the area around the cylinder head cover, cylinder head, oil filter and sump joint faces. Bear in mind that, over a period of time, some very slight seepage from these areas is to be expected – what you are really looking for is any indication of a serious leak caused by gasket failure. Engine oil seeping from the base of the timing belt cover or the transmission bellhousing may be an indication of crankshaft or input shaft oil seal failure. Should a leak be found, renew the failed gasket or oil seal by referring to the appropriate Chapters in this manual.

Air conditioning refrigerant

Warning: Refer to the safety information given in 'Safety first!' and Chapter 3, regarding the dangers of disturbing any of the air conditioning system components.

A leak in the cooling system will usually show up as white- or rust-coloured deposits on the area adjoining the leak.

8 The air conditioning system is filled with a liquid refrigerant, which is retained under high pressure. If the air conditioning system is opened and depressurised without the aid of specialised equipment, the refrigerant will immediately turn into gas and escape into the atmosphere. If the liquid comes into contact with your skin, it can cause severe frostbite. In addition, the refrigerant contains substances which are environmentally damaging; for this reason, it should not be allowed to escape into the atmosphere.

9 Any suspected air conditioning system leaks should be immediately referred to a Toyota dealer or air conditioning specialist. Leakage will be shown up as a steady drop in the level of refrigerant in the system.

10 Note that water may drip from the condenser drain pipe, underneath the car, immediately after the air conditioning system has been in use. This is normal, and should not be cause for concern.

Brake (and clutch) fluid

 Warning: Refer to the safety information given in 'Safety first!' and Chapter 9, regarding the dangers of handling brake fluid.

11 With reference to Chapter 9, examine the area surrounding the brake pipe unions at the master cylinder for signs of leakage. Check the area around the base of fluid reservoir, for signs of leakage caused by seal failure. Also examine the brake pipe unions at the ABS hydraulic unit.

12 If fluid loss is evident, but the leak cannot be pinpointed in the engine bay, the brake calipers and underbody brake lines and should be carefully checked with the vehicle raised and supported on axle stands. Leakage of fluid from the braking system is serious fault that must be rectified immediately.

13 Refer to Chapter 6 and check for leakage around the hydraulic fluid line connections to the clutch master cylinder at the bulkhead, and to the clutch slave cylinder, bolted to the side of the transmission bellhousing.

14 Brake/clutch hydraulic fluid is a toxic substance with a watery consistency. New fluid is almost colourless, but it becomes darker with age and use.

18.2 Manual transmission oil filler/level plug (arrowed)

Unidentified fluid leaks

15 If there are signs that a fluid of some description is leaking from the vehicle, but you cannot identify the type of fluid or its exact origin, park the vehicle overnight and slide a large piece of card underneath it. Providing that the card is positioned in roughly in the right location, even the smallest leak will show up on the card. Not only will this help you to pinpoint the exact location of the leak, it should be easier to identify the fluid from its colour. Bear in mind, though, that the leak may only be occurring when the engine is running!

Vacuum hoses

16 Although the braking system is hydraulically-operated, the brake servo unit amplifies the effort you apply at the brake pedal, by making use of the vacuum created in the inlet manifold. Vacuum is ported to the servo by means of a large-bore hose. Any leaks that develop in this hose will reduce the effectiveness of the braking system.

17 In addition, many of the underbonnet components, particularly the emission control components, are driven by vacuum supplied from the inlet manifold via narrow-bore hoses. A leak in a vacuum hose means that air is being drawn into the hose (rather than escaping from it) and this makes leakage very difficult to detect. One method is to use an old length of vacuum hose as a kind of stethoscope – hold one end close to (but not in) your ear and use the other end to probe the area around the suspected leak. When the end of the hose is directly over a vacuum leak, a hissing sound will be heard clearly through the hose. Care must be taken to avoid contacting hot or moving components, as the engine must be running when testing in this manner. Renew any vacuum hoses that are found to be defective.

18 Manual transmission oil level check

1 Park the car on a level surface. The oil level must be checked before the car is driven, or at least 5 minutes after the engine has been switched off. If the oil is checked immediately after driving the car, some of the oil will remain distributed around the transmission components, resulting in an inaccurate level reading. To improve access, position the car over an inspection pit, or raise the car off the ground and position it on axle stands, making sure the vehicle remains level to the ground.

2 Wipe clean the area around the filler/ level plug, which is on the front face of the transmission. Unscrew the plug and clean it **(see illustration)**.

3 Check the oil level with your finger, or by inserting a home-made dipstick made from a short length of wire bent to shape. The oil level should be no more than 5.0 mm below the lower edge of the filler/level hole.

A certain amount of oil may have gathered behind the filler/level plug and will often trickle out when it is removed; this does **not** necessarily indicate that the level is correct. To ensure that a true level is established, wait until the initial trickle has stopped, then add oil as necessary until a trickle of new oil can be seen emerging. The level will be correct when the flow ceases; use only good-quality oil of the specified type.

4 On completion refit the filler/level plug and tighten to the specified torque.

19 Exhaust system check

1 With the engine cold (at least an hour after the vehicle has been driven), check the complete exhaust system from the engine to the end of the tailpipe. The exhaust system is most easily checked with the vehicle raised on a hoist, or suitably supported on axle stands, so that the exhaust components are readily visible and accessible.

2 Check the exhaust pipes and connections for evidence of leaks, severe corrosion and damage. Make sure that all brackets and mountings are in good condition, and that all relevant nuts and bolts are tight. Leakage at any of the joints or in other parts of the system will usually show up as a black sooty stain in the vicinity of the leak.

3 Rattles and other noises can often be traced to the exhaust system, especially the brackets and mountings. Move the pipes and silencers from side to side on the rubber mountings. If the components are able to come into contact with the body or suspension parts, secure the system with new mountings.

20 Evaporative emission control system check

Refer to Chapter 4B and check that all wiring and hoses are correctly connected to the evaporative loss system components.

21 Steering, suspension and roadwheel check

Front suspension and steering

1 Chock the rear wheels then jack up the front of the car and support it on axle stands (see *Jacking and vehicle support*).

2 Visually inspect the balljoint dust covers and the steering gear gaiters for splits, chafing or deterioration. Any wear of these components will cause loss of lubricant, together with dirt and water entry, resulting in rapid deterioration of the balljoints or steering gear.

3 Check the power-assisted steering fluid hoses for chafing or deterioration, and the pipe and hose unions for fluid leaks. Also check for signs of fluid leakage under pressure from the steering gear rubber gaiters, which would indicate failed fluid seals within the steering gear.

4 Grasp the roadwheel at the 12 o'clock and 6 o'clock positions, and try to rock it **(see illustration)**. Very slight free play may be felt, but if the movement is appreciable, further investigation is necessary to determine the source. Continue rocking the wheel while an assistant depresses the footbrake. If the movement is now eliminated or significantly reduced, it is likely that the hub bearings are at fault. If the free play is still evident with the footbrake depressed, then there is wear in the suspension joints or mountings.

5 Now grasp the wheel at the 9 o'clock and 3 o'clock positions, and try to rock it as before. Any movement felt now may again be caused by wear in the hub bearings or the steering track rod balljoints. If the outer track rod end balljoint is worn, the visual movement will be obvious. If the inner joint is suspect, it can be felt by placing a hand over the rack-and-pinion rubber gaiter, and gripping the track rod. If the wheel is now rocked, movement will be felt at the inner joint if wear has taken place.

6 Using a large screwdriver or flat bar, check for wear in the suspension mounting bushes by levering between the relevant suspension component and its attachment point. Some movement is to be expected, as the mountings are made of rubber, but excessive wear should be obvious. Also check the condition of any visible rubber bushes, looking for splits, cracks or contamination of the rubber.

7 With the vehicle standing on its wheels, have an assistant turn the steering wheel back-and-forth, about an eighth of a turn each way. There should be very little, if any, lost movement between the steering wheel and roadwheels. If this is not the case, closely observe the joints and mountings previously described, but in addition check the steering column universal joints for wear, and also check the rack-and-pinion steering gear itself.

Rear suspension

8 Chock the front wheels then jack up the rear of the car and support it on axle stands (see *Jacking and vehicle support*). Remove the rear roadwheels.

9 Check the rear hub bearings for wear, using the method described for the front hub bearings (paragraph 4).

10 Using a large screwdriver or flat bar, check for wear in the suspension mounting bushes by levering between the relevant suspension component and its attachment point. Some movement is to be expected, as the mountings are made of rubber, but excessive wear should be obvious. Check the condition of the shock absorbers and their bushes/mountings.

Roadwheel check and balancing

11 Periodically remove the roadwheels, and clean any dirt or mud from the inside and outside surfaces. Examine the wheel rims for signs of rusting, corrosion or other damage. Light alloy wheels are easily damaged by kerbing whilst parking, and steel wheels may become dented or buckled. Renewal of the wheel is very often the only course of remedial action possible.

12 The balance of each wheel and tyre assembly should be maintained, not only to avoid excessive tyre wear, but also to avoid wear in the steering and suspension components. Wheel imbalance is normally signified by vibration through the vehicle's bodyshell, although in many cases it is particularly noticeable through the steering wheel. Conversely, it should be noted that wear or damage in suspension or steering components may cause excessive tyre wear. Out-of-round or out-of-true tyres, damaged wheels and wheel bearing wear/ maladjustment also fall into this category. Balancing will not usually cure vibration caused by such wear.

13 Wheel balancing may be carried out with the wheel either on or off the vehicle. If balanced on the vehicle, ensure that the wheel-to-hub relationship is marked in some way prior to subsequent wheel removal, so that it may be refitted in its original position.

22 Driveshaft rubber gaiter and constant velocity (CV) joint check

1 With the vehicle raised and securely supported on stands (see *Jacking and vehicle support*), turn the steering onto full lock, then slowly rotate the roadwheel. Inspect the condition of the outer constant velocity (CV) joint gaiters, squeezing the gaiters to open out the folds **(see illustration)**. Check for signs of cracking, splits or deterioration of the gaiter, which may allow the grease to escape, and lead to water and grit entry into the joint. Also check the security and condition of the retaining clips. Repeat these checks on the inner CV joints. If any damage or deterioration is found, the gaiters should be renewed (see Chapter 8).

2 At the same time, check the general condition of the CV joints themselves by first holding the driveshaft and attempting to rotate the wheel. Repeat this check by holding the inner joint and attempting to rotate the driveshaft. Any appreciable movement indicates wear in the joints, wear in the driveshaft splines, or a loose driveshaft retaining nut.

23 Rear brake shoe check

Note: *For detailed photographs of the brake system, refer to Chapter 9.*

21.4 Check for wear in the hub bearings by grasping the wheel and trying to rock it

1 The work described in this Section should be carried out at the specified intervals, or whenever a defect is suspected in the braking system. Any of the following symptoms could indicate a potential brake system defect:

a) The vehicle pulls to one side when the brake pedal is depressed.
b) The brakes make scraping or dragging noises when applied.
c) Brake pedal travel is excessive.
d) The brake fluid requires repeated topping-up.

2 Chock the front wheels then jack up the rear of the car and support it on axle stands (see *Jacking and vehicle support*). For better access, remove the rear roadwheels.

3 To check the brake shoe lining thickness without removing the brake drums, prise the inspection hole plugs from the backplates, and use an electric torch and mirror to inspect the linings of the leading brake shoes. Check that the thickness of the lining material on the brake shoes is not less than the recommendation given in the Specifications.

4 If it is difficult to determine the exact thickness of the brake shoe linings, or if you are at all concerned about the condition of the shoes, then remove the rear drums for a more comprehensive inspection (refer to Chapter 9).

5 With the drum removed, check the shoe return and hold-down springs for correct installation, and check the wheel cylinders for leakage of brake fluid. Check the friction surface of the brake drums for scoring and discoloration. If excessive, the drum should be resurfaced or renewed.

22.1 Checking the driveshaft gaiters for damage

6 Before refitting the wheels, check all brake lines and hoses (refer to Chapter 9). On completion, fully apply the handbrake and check that the rear wheels are locked. The handbrake also requires periodic adjustment, and if its travel seems excessive, refer to Section 16.

24 Brake fluid renewal

The procedure is similar to that for the bleeding of the hydraulic system as described in Chapter 9, except that the brake fluid reservoir should be emptied by syphoning, and allowance should be made for the old fluid to be removed from the circuit when bleeding a section of the circuit.

25 Body corrosion check

1 Jack up the front and rear of the vehicle and support on axle stands (see *Jacking and vehicle support*).
2 Working from the front to the rear of the vehicle, check the condition of the entire vehicle structure for signs of corrosion, especially near the load-bearing areas. These include chassis box sections, side sills, crossmembers, pillars, and all suspension, steering, braking system and seat belt mountings and anchorages.
3 Check that the anti-corrosion sealing materials on the underbody are intact. Where necessary re-apply the material.
4 In the engine compartment, examine the front suspension upper mountings and inner wing panels, also the lower areas of the front valance for signs of corrosion.
5 Inside the vehicle, lift the carpets where possible and check the floor and inner surfaces of the sills for signs of corrosion.
6 Check the drain holes in the doors for blockages and clear by probing with wire.
7 Where body corrosion is evident, consult a Toyota dealer to have it repaired.

26 Remote control battery renewal

The alarm remote control battery should be renewed at the specified intervals to ensure correct operation of the alarm system. Obtain a new battery from a Toyota dealer and fit it in accordance with the instructions supplied.

Every 40 000 miles or 3 years

27 Coolant renewal

⚠️ *Warning: Wait until the engine is cold before starting this procedure. Do not allow antifreeze to come in contact with your skin, or with the painted surfaces of the vehicle. Rinse off spills immediately with plenty of water. Never leave antifreeze lying around in an open container, or in a puddle in the driveway or on the garage floor. Children and pets are attracted by its sweet smell, but antifreeze can be fatal if ingested.*

Draining

1 If the engine is cold, unscrew and remove the pressure cap from the radiator. If it is not possible to wait until the engine is cold, place a cloth over the pressure cap and slowly unscrew it. Wait until all pressure has escaped, then remove the cap.
2 On all models a radiator drain tap is provided on the lower left-hand or right-hand side of the radiator and a cylinder block

27.2 Radiator drain tap (arrowed)

drain tap is provided in the following location according to model **(see illustration)**. To gain access to the drain taps, remove the engine compartment undershield on the left-hand or eight-hand side, as applicable, with reference to Chapter 11.

Pre-August 2000 models
1.6 and 1.8 litre engines:
   Front right-hand side of cylinder block.
2.0 litre engines:
   Rear left-hand side of cylinder block.

Post-August 2000 models
1.6 and 1.8 litre engines:
   Rear right-hand side of cylinder block.
2.0 litre engines:
   In the oil cooler return hose adjacent to the engine oil filter.
3 Position suitable containers beneath the drain taps, then open the taps and allow the coolant to drain. With all the coolant drained, close the drain taps; if the system needs to be flushed after draining refer to the following sub-Section. Refit the engine compartment undershield(s) on completion.
4 When draining the cooling system, do not forget about the coolant in the expansion tank. The heater hoses and matrix also contain engine coolant, although no recommendations are made to attend to this as the relatively small amount of coolant will circulate back into the main volume of coolant in the engine during heater usage.

Cooling system flushing

5 If coolant renewal has been neglected, or if the antifreeze mixture has become diluted then, in time, the cooling system may gradually lose efficiency, as the coolant passages become restricted due to rust, scale deposits, and other sediment. The cooling system efficiency can be restored by flushing the system clean.
6 The radiator should be flushed independently of the engine, to avoid unnecessary contamination.

Radiator flushing

7 To flush the radiator disconnect the top and bottom hoses from the radiator.
8 Insert a garden hose into the radiator top inlet. Direct a flow of clean water through the radiator, and continue flushing until clean water emerges from the radiator bottom outlet.
9 If after a reasonable period, the water still does not run clear, the radiator can be flushed with a good proprietary cooling system cleaning agent. It is important that the manufacturer's instructions are followed carefully. If the contamination is particularly bad, remove the radiator then insert the hose in the radiator bottom outlet, and reverse-flush the radiator.

Engine flushing

10 To flush the engine, remove the thermostat (see Chapter 3).
11 With the bottom hose disconnected from the radiator, insert a garden hose into the coolant housing. Direct a clean flow of water through the engine, and continue flushing until clean water emerges from the radiator bottom hose.
12 When flushing is complete, refit the thermostat and reconnect the hoses (see Chapter 3).

Cooling system filling

13 Before attempting to fill the cooling system, reconnect all hoses, close all drain taps, and make sure that all clips are in good condition and tight. Note that an antifreeze mixture must be used all year round, to prevent corrosion of the engine components (see following sub-Section).
14 Slowly add new coolant (50/50 mix of antifreeze and coolant) to the radiator until the level reaches the bottom of the filler neck.

Note that Toyota genuine antifreeze is normally supplied premixed. While filling, compress the radiator hoses frequently to purge airlocks from the system.

15 Fill the expansion tank with coolant to the MAX level mark.

16 With the radiator cap still removed, start the engine and allow it to idle until heat can be felt through the radiator top hose. Accelerate the engine briefly several times, then switch off the ignition and allow the engine to cool (preferably for an hour).

17 Top-up the level in the radiator to the filler neck and refit the radiator cap. Top-up the level in the expansion tank to the MAX mark.

18 Start the engine and run it at 3000 rpm for half a minute. Stop the engine then remove the radiator cap and top-up the level if necessary. Refit the cap.

19 Check for leaks, particularly around disturbed components.

Antifreeze mixture

20 The antifreeze should always be renewed at the specified intervals. This is necessary not only to maintain the antifreeze properties, but also to prevent corrosion which would otherwise occur as the corrosion inhibitors become progressively less effective.

21 Always use an ethylene-glycol based antifreeze which is suitable for use in mixed-metal cooling systems.

22 Before adding antifreeze, the cooling system should be completely drained, preferably flushed, and all hoses checked for condition and security.

23 After filling with antifreeze, a label should be attached to the expansion tank, stating the type and concentration of antifreeze used, and the date installed. Any subsequent topping-up should be made with the same type and concentration of antifreeze.

24 Do not use engine antifreeze in the washer system, as it will cause damage to the vehicle paintwork. A screenwash additive should be added to the washer system in the quantities stated on the bottle.

Every 40 000 miles or 4 years

28 Spark plug renewal

Note: *On pre-August 2000 engines fitted with platinum-tipped spark plugs, the renewal interval is every 60 000 miles/6 years.*

1 The correct functioning of the spark plugs is vital for the correct running and efficiency of the engine. It is essential that the plugs fitted are appropriate for the engine (a suitable type is specified at the beginning of this Chapter). If this type is used and the engine is in good condition, the spark plugs should not need attention between scheduled renewal intervals. Spark plug cleaning is rarely necessary, and should not be attempted unless specialised equipment is available, as damage can easily be caused to the firing ends.

Pre-August 2000 engines

2 If the marks on the original-equipment spark plug (HT) leads cannot be seen, mark the leads 1 to 4, to correspond to the cylinder the lead serves (No 1 cylinder is at the timing belt end of the engine). Pull the leads from the plugs by gripping the end fitting, not the lead, otherwise the lead connection may be fractured. Note that as the spark plugs are deeply recessed, the HT lead end fittings are extended.

3 It is advisable to remove the dirt from the spark plug recesses using a clean brush, vacuum cleaner or compressed air before removing the plugs, to prevent dirt dropping into the cylinders.

⚠ *Warning: Wear eye protection when using compressed air.*

4 Unscrew the plugs using a spark plug spanner, suitable box spanner or a deep socket and extension bar. Keep the socket aligned with the spark plug – if it is forcibly moved to one side, the ceramic insulator may be broken off, however since the spark plugs are deeply recessed this is not likely to be a problem until the plugs are being withdrawn. As each plug is removed, examine it as follows.

5 Examination of the spark plugs will give a good indication of the condition of the engine. If the insulator nose of the spark plug is clean and white, with no deposits, this is indicative of a weak mixture or too hot a plug (a hot plug transfers heat away from the electrode slowly, a cold plug transfers heat away quickly).

6 If the tip and insulator nose are covered with hard black-looking deposits, then this is indicative that the mixture is too rich. Should the plug be black and oily, then it is likely that the engine is fairly worn, as well as the mixture being too rich.

7 If the insulator nose is covered with light tan to greyish-brown deposits, then the mixture is correct and it is likely that the engine is in good condition.

8 The spark plug electrode gap is of considerable importance as, if it is too large or too small, the size of the spark and its efficiency will be seriously impaired. If new spark plugs are being fitted, the gap should be set to the value given in the Specifications for new spark plugs. If the original spark plugs have not reached the recommended mileage/time renewal interval, they may be re-used providing the electrode gap does not exceed the value given in the Specifications for used spark plugs. Toyota specify that the electrode gap on a used platinum-tipped spark plug *must not* be adjusted.

9 To set the gap on new spark plugs, measure it with a feeler blade or wire gauge, and then bend the outer plug electrode until the correct gap is achieved **(see illustrations)**. The centre electrode should never be bent, as this may crack the insulator and cause plug failure, if nothing worse. If using feeler blades, the gap is correct when the appropriate-size blade is a firm sliding fit.

10 Special spark plug electrode gap adjusting tools are available from most motor accessory shops, or from some spark plug manufacturers.

11 Before fitting the spark plugs, check that the threaded connector sleeves are tight, and that the plug exterior surfaces and threads are clean **(see Haynes Hint overleaf)**.

12 Remove the rubber hose (if used), and tighten the plug to the specified torque using the spark plug socket and a torque wrench. Refit the remaining spark plugs in the same manner.

13 Connect the HT leads in their correct order, making sure they are pushed fully home on the spark plugs.

Post-August 2000 engines

14 Remove the plastic cover from the top of the engine. On 1.6 and 1.8 litre engines, the cover is secured by two nuts at the front and two plastic fasteners at the rear. On 2.0 litre engines, the cover is secured by four nuts.

15 Ensure the ignition is switched off, then disconnect the wiring connectors from the ignition coils **(see illustration)**.

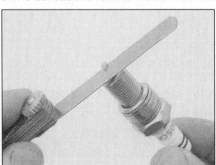

28.9a Measuring the spark plug gap with a feeler blade

28.9b Measuring the spark plug gap with a wire gauge

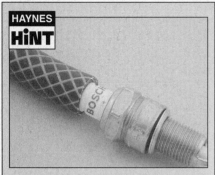

It is very often difficult to insert spark plugs into their holes without cross-threading them. To avoid this possibility, fit a short length of 5/16 inch internal diameter rubber hose over the end of the spark plug. The flexible hose acts as a universal joint to help align the plug with the plug hole. Should the plug begin to cross-thread, the hose will slip on the spark plug, preventing thread damage to the cylinder head.

16 On 1.6 and 1.8 litre engines, undo the two bolts securing the plastic wiring harness protector to the camshaft cover and move the harness to one side **(see illustration)**.
17 Undo the bolts and pull the ignition coils from the top of the spark plugs **(see illustration)**.
18 Unscrew the plugs using a spark plug spanner, suitable box spanner or a deep socket and extension bar. Keep the socket aligned with the spark plug – if it is forcibly moved to one side, the ceramic insulator may be broken off, however since the spark plugs are deeply recessed this is not likely to be a problem until the plugs are being withdrawn. As each plug is removed, examine it as follows.
19 Examination of the spark plugs will give a good indication of the condition of the engine. If the insulator nose of the spark plug is clean and white, with no deposits, this is indicative of a weak mixture or too hot a plug (a hot plug transfers heat away from the electrode slowly, a cold plug transfers heat away quickly).
20 If the tip and insulator nose are covered with hard black-looking deposits, then this is

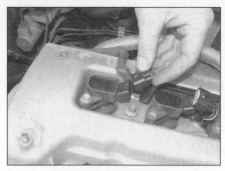

28.15 disconnect the wiring connectors from the ignition coils . . .

indicative that the mixture is too rich. Should the plug be black and oily, then it is likely that the engine is fairly worn, as well as the mixture being too rich.
21 If the insulator nose is covered with light tan to greyish-brown deposits, then the mixture is correct and it is likely that the engine is in good condition.
22 The spark plug electrode gap is of considerable importance as, if it is too large or too small, the size of the spark and its efficiency will be seriously impaired. The gap should be set to the value given in the Specifications.
23 To set the gap, measure it with a feeler blade or wire gauge, and then bend the outer plug electrode until the correct gap is achieved **(see illustrations 28.9a and 28.9b)**. The centre electrode should never be bent, as this may crack the insulator and cause plug failure, if nothing worse. If using feeler blades, the gap is correct when the appropriate-size blade is a firm sliding fit.
24 Special spark plug electrode gap adjusting tools are available from most motor accessory shops, or from some spark plug manufacturers.
25 Before fitting the spark plugs, check that the threaded connector sleeves are tight, and that the plug exterior surfaces and threads are clean **(see Haynes Hint)**.
26 Remove the rubber hose (if used), and tighten the plug to the specified torque using the spark plug socket and a torque wrench. Refit the remaining spark plugs in the same manner.

27 Refit the ignition coils to the top of the spark plugs and secure with the retaining bolts, tightened to the specified torque.
28 On 1.6 and 1.8 litre engines, refit the plastic wiring harness protector to the camshaft cover and tighten the retaining bolts securely.
29 On completion, refit the plastic cover to the top of the engine.

29 Fuel filter renewal

⚠️ *Warning: Before carrying out the following operation, refer to the precautions given in 'Safety first!' at the beginning of this manual, and follow them implicitly. Petrol is a highly-dangerous and volatile liquid, and the precautions necessary when handling it cannot be overstressed.*

1 The fuel filter is located in the engine compartment, mounted on the left-hand side of the engine compartment bulkhead.
2 Open the bonnet, then refer to Chapter 4A and depressurise the fuel system.
3 Position a suitable container beneath the filter to catch spilt fuel.
4 Undo the fuel inlet pipe union nut at the base of the filter, while counterholding the union on the filter with a second spanner.
5 On early models, the fuel outlet hose is attached to the top of the filter by means of a banjo union. Undo the banjo union bolt and recover the copper washer located each side of the union **(see illustration)**. Note that new washers will be required for refitting. Tape or plug the disconnected union end to minimise fuel loss.
6 On later models, the fuel outlet hose is secured to the filter by means of a quick-release fitting. Remove the plastic locking collar, then squeeze the tabs on each side of the fitting to release it **(see illustrations)**. Tape or plug the disconnected hose end to minimise fuel loss.
7 Unscrew the two retaining bolts (or nuts) and remove the fuel filter from the vehicle.
8 Fit the new filter using a reversal of the removal procedure. On early models, position

28.16 . . . on 1.6 and 1.8 litre engines, undo the two bolts and move the plastic wiring harness protector to one side . . .

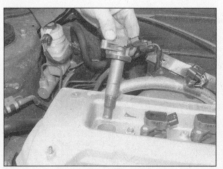

28.17 . . . then undo the bolts and pull the ignition coils off the spark plugs – post-August 2000 engines

29.5 On early models, undo the fuel filter outlet hose banjo union bolt (arrowed)

a new copper washer on each side of the banjo union and tighten the union bolt securely.

9 Start the engine and check the filter pipe and hose connections for leaks. On completion, stop the engine.

30 Transmission oil/fluid renewal

Refer to the procedures described in Chapter 7A (manual transmission) or 7B (automatic transmission).

29.6a On later models, remove the plastic locking collar . . .

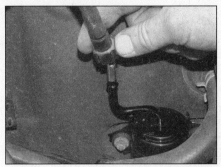

29.6b . . . then squeeze the tabs on each side of the fuel filter outlet hose fitting to release it

Every 60 000 miles or 6 years

31 Timing belt renewal

Refer to the procedures contained in Chapter 2A.

32 Valve clearance check and adjustment

Refer to the procedures contained in Chapter 2A or 2B as applicable.

Chapter 2 Part A:
Pre-August 2000 engine in-car repair procedures

Contents

Degrees of difficulty

Easy, suitable for novice with little experience		**Fairly easy,** suitable for beginner with some experience	✦	**Fairly difficult,** suitable for competent DIY mechanic	✦	**Difficult,** suitable for experienced DIY mechanic	✦	**Very difficult,** suitable for expert DIY or professional	

Specifications

General

Engine type.	Four-cylinder, in-line, double-overhead camshafts, 16 valve
Engine code*:	
1.6 litre engines	4A-FE
1.8 litre engines	7A-FE
2.0 litre engines	3S-FE
Capacity:	
1.6 litre engines	1587 cc
1.8 litre engines	1762 cc
2.0 litre engines	1998 cc
Bore:	
1.6 litre engines	81.0 mm
1.8 litre engines	81.0 mm
2.0 litre engines	86.0 mm
Stroke:	
1.6 litre engines	77.0 mm
1.8 litre engines	85.5 mm
2.0 litre engines	86.0 mm
Direction of crankshaft rotation	Clockwise (viewed from right-hand side of vehicle)
Cylinder compression pressures:	
Standard:	
1.6 and 1.8 litre engines	13.5 bar
2.0 litre engines.	13.0 bar
Minimum:	
1.6 and 1.8 litre engines	10.0 bar
2.0 litre engines.	9.5 bar
Maximum difference between cylinders.	1.0 bar
Firing order	1–3–4–2
No 1 cylinder location.	Timing belt (right-hand) end of the engine
Direction of crankshaft rotation	Clockwise (seen from right-hand side of car)

* Note: *See' Vehicle identification' in the Reference Chapter for details of engine code location.*

Camshaft and followers

Drive:

1.6 and 1.8 litre engines	Toothed belt to exhaust camshaft sprocket, anti-backlash gears from exhaust to inlet camshaft
2.0 litre engines	Toothed belt to inlet camshaft sprocket, anti-backlash gears from inlet to exhaust camshaft

	Standard	Maximum
Camshaft endfloat:		
1.6 and 1.8 litre engines:		
Inlet camshaft	0.030 to 0.085 mm	0.11 mm
Exhaust camshaft	0.035 to 0.090 mm	0.11 mm
2.0 litre engines:		
Inlet camshaft	0.045 to 0.100 mm	0.12 mm
Exhaust camshaft	0.030 to 0.085 mm	0.10 mm
Gear backlash:		
Standard	0.02 to 0.20 mm	
Maximum	0.30 mm	
Distance between free ends of inlet camshaft sub-gear spring:		
1.6 and 1.8 litre engines	17.0 to 17.6 mm	
2.0 litre engines	22.5 to 22.9 mm	

Timing belt

Tensioner spring free length:

1.6 litre engines	36.9 mm
1.8 litre engines	31.76 mm
2.0 litre engines	46.0 mm

Valve clearances (engine cold)

	Inlet	Exhaust
1.6 and 1.8 litre engines	0.15 to 0.25 mm	0.25 to 0.35 mm
2.0 litre engines	0.19 to 0.29 mm	0.28 to 0.38 mm

Lubrication system

Oil pump type:

1.6 and 1.8 litre engines	Bi-rotor driven from front of crankshaft
2.0 litre engines	Trochoidal rotor, driven by timing belt

System pressure – at normal operating temperature:

At idle speed	0.3 bar (minimum)
At 3000 rpm	5.0 bar

Oil pump clearances:	Standard	Maximum
1.6 and 1.8 litre engines:		
Outer rotor-to-pump body clearance	0.080 to 0.180 mm	0.200 mm
Rotor side clearance (endfloat):		
1.6 litre engines	0.025 to 0.075 mm	0.100 mm
1.8 litre engines	0.025 to 0.085 mm	0.100 mm
Inner rotor-to-outer rotor tip clearance:		
1.6 litre engines	0.060 to 0.180 mm	0.350 mm
1.8 litre engines	0.025 to 0.085 mm	0.350 mm
2.0 litre engines:		
Outer rotor-to-pump body clearance	0.100 to 0.160 mm	0.200 mm
Inner rotor-to-outer rotor tip clearance	0.040 to 0.160 mm	0.200 mm

Torque wrench settings

	Nm	lbf ft
1.6 and 1.8 litre engines		
Alternator adjusting bar to cylinder block	39	29
Alternator bracket bolts	26	19
Camshaft bearing cap bolts	13	10
Camshaft cover	6	4
Camshaft sprocket bolt	59	44
Connecting rod big-end cap nuts/bolts:*		
Stage 1:		
1.6 litre engines	29	21
1.8 litre engines	25	18
Stage 2	Angle-tighten a further 90°	
Coolant inlet elbow (small) to cylinder head	15	11
Coolant inlet elbow to cylinder head	20	15
Coolant outlet elbow to cylinder head	15	11
Crankshaft left-hand oil seal housing bolts	9	7
Crankshaft pulley bolt	118	87

Torque wrench settings (continued)

	Nm	lbf ft

1.6 and 1.8 litre engines (continued)

Cylinder head bolts:
Stage 1	29	21
Stage 2	Angle-tighten a further 90°	
Stage 3	Angle-tighten a further 90°	
Driveplate-to-crankshaft bolts (automatic transmission)	64	47
Engine lifting eye fasteners	27	20
Engine-to-transmission lower attachment bolts	43	32
Engine-to-transmission reinforcing plate bolts	43	32
Engine-to-transmission upper attachment bolts	64	47
Engine/transmission longitudinal crossmember bolts	73	54

Engine/transmission mountings:
Front mounting bracket through-bolt	87	64
Front mounting to crossmember	72	53
Left-hand mounting bracket through-bolt	87	64
Left-hand mounting bracket-to-transmission	52	38
Rear mounting bracket through-bolt	87	64
Rear mounting bracket to subframe	72	53
Rear mounting bracket to transmission	64	47
Right-hand mounting bracket to cylinder block	51	38
Right-hand mounting bracket-to-cylinder head (nut)	28	21
Flywheel-to-crankshaft bolts (manual transmission)	78	58
Main bearing cap bolts	60	44
Oil cooler pipe union bolt	34	25
Oil dipstick tube	9	7
Oil filter housing/oil pressure regulator valve housing stud	54	40
Oil pick-up tube/strainer nuts and bolts	9	7
Oil pressure relief valve plug on oil filter housing	37	27
Oil pump cover screws	10	7
Oil pump housing-to-cylinder block bolts	21	15
Rear engine plate to cylinder block	6	4
Roadwheel nuts	103	76

Sump nuts and bolts:
1.6 litre engines	5	4

1.8 litre engines:
Main sump to cylinder block	16	12
Main sump to oil pump	8	6
Main sump to oil seal housing	8	6
Secondary sump to main sump	5	4
Timing belt tensioner pulley bolt	37	27
Towing eye-to-longitudinal crossmember	39	29

2.0 litre engines

Alternator bracket to cylinder head	42	31
Camshaft bearing cap bolts	19	14
Camshaft cover	44	32
Camshaft sprocket bolt	54	40

Connecting rod big-end cap nuts:*
Stage 1	25	18
Stage 2	Angle-tighten a further 90°	
Crankshaft left-hand oil seal housing bolts	13	10
Crankshaft pulley bolt	108	80

Cylinder head bolts:
Stage 1	49	36
Stage 2	Angle-tighten a further 90°	
Driveplate-to-crankshaft bolts (automatic transmission)	83	61
Engine lifting eye	25	18
Engine-to-transmission lower attachment bolts	43	32

Engine-to-transmission reinforcing plate bolts/nuts:
M8 bolts	21	15
M10 bolts	44	32
Nuts	44	32
Engine-to-transmission upper attachment bolts	64	47
Engine/transmission longitudinal crossmember bolts	73	54

Torque wrench settings (continued)

	Nm	lbf ft
2.0 litre engines (continued)		
Engine/transmission mountings:		
Front mounting bracket through-bolt	87	64
Front mounting to crossmember	72	53
Left-hand mounting bracket through-bolt	87	64
Left-hand mounting bracket to transmission	52	38
Rear mounting bracket through-bolt	87	64
Rear mounting bracket to subframe.	72	53
Rear mounting bracket to transmission	64	47
Right-hand mounting bracket to cylinder block	51	38
Flywheel-to-crankshaft bolts (manual transmission)	88	65
Main bearing cap bolts.	59	44
Oil cooler retaining nut	9	7
Oil filter mounting stud	78	58
Oil pick-up pipe	6	4
Oil pump cover to housing	9	7
Oil pump housing-to-cylinder block bolts	9	7
Oil pump sprocket	24	18
Rear engine plate to cylinder block	9	7
Roadwheel nuts	103	76
Sump nuts and bolts	5	4
Timing belt idler pulley to cylinder block	42	31
Timing belt tensioner pulley bolt	42	31
Sump nuts and bolts	5	4

* New bolts/nuts must be used

1 General information

How to use this Chapter

Chapter 2 is divided into three Parts; A, B and C. Repair operations that can be carried out with the engine in the vehicle are described in Parts A and B. Part C covers the removal of the engine/transmission as a unit, and describes the engine dismantling and overhaul procedures.

In Parts A and B, the assumption is made that the engine is installed in the vehicle, with all ancillaries connected. If the engine has been removed for overhaul, the preliminary dismantling information which precedes each operation may be ignored.

Engine description

The engine is of in-line 4-cylinder design and is mounted transversely. A cast iron cylinder block and cast aluminium cylinder head are fitted.

1.6 and 1.8 litre engines have twin overhead camshafts, with two inlet valves and two exhaust valves per cylinder. Valve clearance adjustment is by means of shims located directly between the bucket-type followers and the camshaft lobes. The exhaust camshaft is driven from the crankshaft sprocket by the toothed timing belt, while the inlet camshaft is driven from the exhaust camshaft via a pair of gears; each camshaft is supported by five bearings. The pistons are attached to their connecting rods by semi-floating gudgeon pins. The cast iron crankshaft runs in five main bearings; endfloat is controlled by semi-

circular thrustwashers at the central main bearing. There are minor differences between the two engines; on 1.8 litre engines the sump is in two sections instead of one, and the connecting rod caps are secured with bolts instead of nuts.

2.0 litre engines are similar to the 1.6 and 1.8 litre engines described previously, however the timing belt drives the inlet camshaft, and the exhaust camshaft is driven by gears from the inlet camshaft. The cylinder block is of a different casting and the oil pump is located in its own housing bolted to the front of the cylinder block and driven by the timing belt. The coolant pump is bolted to the cylinder block and is also driven by the timing belt.

Operations with engine in car

The following work can be carried out with the engine in the car:
- a) *Valve clearance adjustment.*
- b) *Removal and refitting of the timing belt, sprockets and tensioner.*
- c) *Renewal of the camshaft oil seal(s).*
- d) *Removal and refitting of the camshafts and followers.*
- e) *Removal and refitting of the cylinder head.*
- f) *Removal and refitting of the sump.*
- g) *Removal and refitting of the oil pump.*
- h) *Removal and refitting of the flywheel/ driveplate.*
- i) *Renewal of the crankshaft oil seals.*
- j) *Renewal of the engine mountings.*

Note: *It is possible to remove the pistons and connecting rods (after removing the cylinder head and sump) without removing the engine, although this is not recommended. Work of this nature is more easily and thoroughly completed with the engine on the bench, as described in Chapter 2C.*

2 Compression test

1 When engine performance is down, or if misfiring occurs which cannot be attributed to the ignition or fuel systems, a compression test can provide diagnostic clues as to the engine's condition. If the test is performed regularly, it can give warning of trouble before any other symptoms become apparent.

2 The engine must be fully warmed-up to normal operating temperature, the battery must be fully-charged, and all the spark plugs must be removed (see Chapter 1). The aid of an assistant will also be required.

3 Disable the ignition system by disconnecting the wiring multiplug connectors at the ignition coils (see Chapter 5B).

4 Fit a compression tester to the No 1 cylinder spark plug hole – the type of tester which screws into the plug thread is to be preferred.

5 Have the assistant hold the throttle wide open, and crank the engine on the starter motor; after one or two revolutions, the compression pressure should build-up to a maximum figure, and then stabilise. Record the highest reading obtained.

6 Repeat the test on the remaining cylinders, recording the pressure in each.

7 All cylinders should produce very similar pressures; any difference greater than that specified indicates the existence of a fault. Note that the compression should build-up quickly in a healthy engine; low compression on the first stroke, followed by gradually increasing pressure on successive strokes, indicates worn piston rings. A low compression reading on the first stroke, which does not

build-up during successive strokes, indicates leaking valves or a blown head gasket (a cracked head could also be the cause).

8 If the pressure in any cylinder is reduced to the specified minimum or less, carry out the following test to isolate the cause. Introduce 5 ml of clean oil into that cylinder through its spark plug hole and repeat the test.

9 If the addition of oil temporarily improves the compression pressure, this indicates that bore or piston wear is responsible for the pressure loss. No improvement suggests that leaking or burnt valves, or a blown head gasket, may be to blame.

10 A low reading from two adjacent cylinders is almost certainly due to the head gasket having blown between them. Renew the head gasket if this is the case.

11 If one cylinder is about 20 percent lower than the others and the engine has a slightly rough idle, a worn camshaft lobe could be the cause.

12 On completion of the test, refit the spark plugs, then reconnect the ignition coil wiring.

3 Top dead centre (TDC) for No 1 piston – locating

1 Disconnect the battery negative terminal (refer to *Disconnecting the battery* in the Reference Chapter).

2 On 1.6 and 1.8 litre engines, remove the camshaft cover as described in Section 4. On 2.0 litre engines, unbolt and remove the upper timing belt cover, and recover the gasket.

3 The timing marks are marked on the lower timing belt cover at intervals of 5°, and the crankshaft pulley rim incorporates a notch for alignment with the timing marks. The 0° mark indicates TDC (top dead centre), and when the notch is aligned with this mark, the pistons in cylinders 1 and 4 are at TDC **(see illustration)**.

4 Using a spanner (or socket and extension bar) applied to the crankshaft pulley bolt, rotate the crankshaft clockwise until the notch on the crankshaft pulley rim is aligned with the 0° mark on the timing belt cover. Note that it will be necessary to remove the undershield from beneath the engine for access to the crankshaft pulley. Remove all four spark plugs; this will make the engine easier to turn; refer to Chapter 1 for details.

5 With the crankshaft in this position, Nos 1 and 4 pistons are now at TDC, with one of them on the compression stroke. Verify that No 1 piston is on the compression stroke by observing the camshaft sprocket; the hole in the sprocket should be aligned with the timing mark cut-out on the camshaft right-hand bearing cap. If this is not the case, rotate the crankshaft one full turn (360°) clockwise until the sprocket hole is aligned with the bearing cap cut-out. Use a drill or dowel rod through the hole in the sprocket and check that it aligns with the cut-out in the cap **(see illustration)**.

3.3 Timing marks on the crankshaft pulley and lower timing belt cover

6 Once No 1 cylinder piston has been positioned at TDC on the compression stroke, TDC for any of the other pistons can then be located by rotating the crankshaft clockwise 180° at a time and following the firing order (see Specifications).

4 Camshaft cover – removal and refitting

1.6 and 1.8 litre engines

Removal

1 Disconnect the battery negative terminal (refer to *Disconnecting the battery* in the Reference Chapter).

2 Disconnect the crankcase ventilation hoses from the camshaft cover **(see illustration)**.

4.2 Disconnecting the crankcase ventilation hoses from the camshaft cover – 1.6 and 1.8 litre engines

4.4b ... lift off the cover ...

3.5 Check the camshaft is at TDC by inserting a dowel rod through the hole into the bearing cap cut-out

3 Disconnect the HT leads from their locating clips and from their spark plugs, and release any other relevant wiring/cable clips.

4 Unscrew the domed retaining nuts and washers, then remove the cover and gasket **(see illustrations)**.

Refitting

5 Examine the condition of the cover gasket and spark plug tube seals, and renew if necessary. The tube seals may be prised or drifted out and the new ones fitted using a suitably-sized socket or section of tube **(see illustrations)**.

6 Refitting is a reversal of the removal procedure, but apply a little sealant to the cylinder head as shown **(see illustrations)** and ensure that the gasket seats correctly in the cover before the cover is fitted; as the cover is being fitted, ensure that the spark plug tube seals seat correctly.

4.4a Remove the domed retaining nuts and washers ...

4.4c ... and remove the gasket – 1.6 and 1.8 litre engines

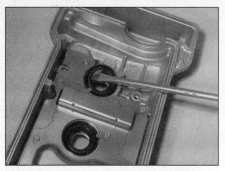

4.5a Prise out the spark plug tube seals . . .

4.5b . . . and fit new ones – 1.6 and 1.8 litre engines

4.6a Apply sealant on each side of the right-hand exhaust camshaft mounting caps . . .

4.6b . . . and also over the semi-circular cover on the right-hand end of the inlet camshaft – 1.6 and 1.8 litre engines

2.0 litre engines

Removal

7 Disconnect the battery negative terminal (refer to *Disconnecting the battery* in the Reference Chapter).

4.10a Remove the special nuts . . .

4.10b . . . and seals . . .

4.10c . . . and remove the camshaft cover – 2.0 litre engines

4.12a Applying sealant to the cylinder head before refitting the camshaft cover – 2.0 litre engines

the cover and gasket. Note that the cover is retained with special nuts screwed onto the spark plug tubes together with seals **(see illustrations)**. Keep the seals in order so they can be refitted in their original positions.

Refitting

11 Examine the condition of the cover gasket and spark plug tube seals, and renew if necessary.
12 Refitting is a reversal of removal, but apply a little sealant where the camshaft bearing caps meet the cylinder head and over the semi-circular plugs at each end of the exhaust camshaft, and ensure that the gasket seats correctly in the cover. As the cover is being fitted, ensure that the spark plug tube seals seat correctly, in their original locations, and with their tabs pointing towards the timing belt end of the engine. Tighten the retaining nuts to the specified torque **(see illustrations)**.

5 Valve clearance check and adjustment

1 The valve clearances must be checked and adjusted with the engine cold.
2 Remove the camshaft cover as described in Section 4.
3 Set No 1 piston at TDC on compression as described in Section 3.
4 Using feeler blades, check and record the clearances of the following valves; the feeler blade should be a firm sliding fit between the shim on the follower and the camshaft lobe **(see illustration)**.

Inlet camshaft	No 1 inlet valves
Inlet camshaft	No 2 inlet valves
Exhaust camshaft	No 1 exhaust valves
Exhaust camshaft	No 3 exhaust valves

5 Using a socket on the crankshaft pulley, turn the engine 360° clockwise and align the notch in the pulley with the 0° mark on the timing belt cover. This will set No 4 piston at TDC on compression.
6 Using feeler blades, check and record the clearances of the following valves; the feeler blade should be a firm sliding fit between the shim on the follower and the camshaft lobe.

8 Unclip the HT leads from their guides, then disconnect the leads from the spark plugs noting their locations.
9 Disconnect the PCV hoses from the centre and left-hand end of the camshaft cover.
10 Unscrew the retaining nuts, then remove

4.12b Tightening the special nuts on 2.0 litre engines

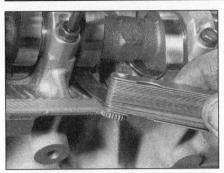

5.4 Checking the valve clearances with a feeler blade

Inlet camshaft	No 3 inlet valves
Inlet camshaft	No 4 inlet valves
Exhaust camshaft	No 2 exhaust valves
Exhaust camshaft	No 4 exhaust valves

7 Compare the recorded clearances with the clearances given in the Specifications, and note the valves which require adjustment.

8 If adjustment is required on the inlet valves of 1.6 and 1.8 litre engines, it will be necessary to remove the inlet camshaft as described in Section 9 in order to remove the existing shims and fit new ones. For the exhaust valves of these engines, and for all valves on 2.0 litre engines, the shims can be exchanged without removing the camshafts, provided that a special Toyota tool (or suitable alternative) is obtained to depress and hold the camshaft followers down. Using a socket on the crankshaft pulley, turn the engine over until the camshaft lobe over the shim to be removed, is pointing upward. With the camshaft follower held depressed, the shim is removed using a suitable screwdriver and a magnetic probe (possibly a magnetised screwdriver). It should be possible to use a suitable alternative tool to depress and hold the camshaft followers down, however, if the tool is not available the camshafts can be removed by following the procedure described in Section 9 and the shim removed using a small screwdriver **(see illustration)**. Adjustment should be made on each valve separately to ensure the shims are fitted in the correct locations.

9 Measure the thickness of the removed shim using a micrometer **(see illustration)**, then calculate the thickness of the required shim using the following formula where the

5.8 Using a small screwdriver to remove a shim from the top of the follower

variables are T (the thickness of the removed shim), A (the valve clearance measured), V (the required valve clearance as given in the Specifications) and N (the thickness of the new shim required):

$$N = T + (A - V)$$

Shims are available in a variety of sizes, and the shim selected (from your Toyota dealer) should be as close as possible to the calculated value.

10 Install the new shim on the follower, with its thickness marking facing downwards.

11 Repeat the process for all the remaining shims that require renewal, then refit the camshafts (if removed) with reference to Section 9.

12 On completion refit the camshaft cover as described in Section 4.

---

6 Timing belt –
removal, inspection
and refitting

1.6 and 1.8 litre engines

Removal

1 Disconnect the battery negative terminal (refer to *Disconnecting the battery* in the Reference Chapter).

2 Remove the camshaft cover (see Section 4).

3 Loosen the bolts securing the drive pulley to the coolant pump one or two turns – the bolts are easier to loosen before removing the drivebelt **(see illustration)**. **Note:** *The pulley must be moved to one side later in order to remove the middle timing belt cover.*

5.9 Measuring a shim with a micrometer

4 Firmly apply the handbrake, then jack up the front of the car and support it securely on axle stands (see *Jacking and vehicle support*). Remove the right-hand roadwheel, then unbolt and remove the undershield from under the right-hand side of the engine compartment.

5 Remove the auxiliary drivebelt(s) (alternator, power steering and air conditioning, as applicable), as described in Chapter 1.

6 Unscrew the bolts securing the pulley to the coolant pump and move the pulley as far to the rear as possible **(see illustration)**. Note that there is insufficient room to remove the pulley completely due to the body inner panel, however the pulley must be moved to one side to remove the middle timing belt cover.

7 Remove the spark plugs (see Chapter 1).

8 Set the engine at TDC for No 1 cylinder as described in Section 3.

9 The crankshaft must now be held stationary while the crankshaft pulley bolt is loosened. Toyota technicians use a special tool bolted to the crankshaft pulley to hold the crankshaft, and a similar tool can be fabricated out of flat metal bar. Alternatively, on manual transmission models, have an assistant engage top gear and depress the brake pedal. On automatic transmission models, remove the starter motor (Chapter 5A) and use a wide-bladed screwdriver engaged with the starter ring gear to hold the crankshaft stationary.

10 Unscrew the crankshaft pulley bolt and slide the pulley off of the end of the crankshaft. If it is tight, use a suitable puller to remove it **(see illustrations)**.

11 Unbolt and remove the upper, middle and lower timing belt covers **(see illustrations)**.

6.3 Loosening the coolant pump pulley bolts before removing the auxiliary drivebelts – 1.6 and 1.8 litre engines

6.6 Coolant pump pulley moved fully to the rear in order to remove the middle timing belt cover – 1.6 and 1.8 litre engines

6.10a Removing the crankshaft pulley bolt – 1.6 and 1.8 litre engines

6.10b Sliding the pulley off the end of the crankshaft – 1.6 and 1.8 litre engines

12 Slide the outer timing belt guide from the crankshaft, noting which way round it is fitted **(see illustration)**.

13 If the timing belt is to be re-used, mark it with an arrow to indicate its direction of rotation. Also mark it in relation to the crankshaft and camshaft sprockets as an aid to refitting.

14 Loosen the bolt securing the timing belt tensioner to the cylinder block. Using a screwdriver and protective card, lever the tensioner rearwards to release the tension from the belt, then tighten the bolt to retain the tensioner in this position.

15 Slide the timing belt from the camshaft and crankshaft sprockets **(see illustration)**. To enable the timing belt to be fully removed, the weight of the engine must be taken off the right-hand engine/transmission mounting and the mounting separated (see Section 16). Support the engine under the sump using a jack and block of wood before disconnecting the mounting.

16 Do not alter the position of the camshaft or crankshaft sprockets with the timing belt removed.

Inspection

17 With the timing belt removed, check it thoroughly for damage and deterioration. In particular check for cracking at the base of the teeth.

18 In addition to the regular renewal called for as part of the service schedule (Chapter 1), the timing belt should be renewed, regardless of age or mileage, if it appears to be defective

6.11a Removing the middle timing belt cover . . .

in any manner or if it has been in contact with water, oil or steam.

19 Check that the tensioner pulley turns smoothly without any signs of roughness. Also check that the free length of the pulley spring is as given in the Specifications – if it has stretched, renew it **(see illustration)**.

Refitting

20 Before refitting the timing belt, check that the small hole in the camshaft sprocket is in the 12 o'clock position and is centrally aligned with the timing mark cut-out on the camshaft right-hand bearing cap; also check that the TDC marks on the crankshaft sprocket and the oil pump housing are aligned.

21 Locate the timing belt on the crankshaft and camshaft sprockets, making sure that the sprockets remain at their TDC positions and the belt is taut between the front extremities of the camshaft and crankshaft sprockets. If the original belt is being refitted, ensure that the arrow marked on the belt during removal faces the correct way and that the belt-to-sprocket marks are correctly aligned. Refit the right-hand engine/transmission mounting and tighten the bolts to the specified torque.

22 Slacken the tensioner bolt and allow the tensioner to return under spring pressure so that the pulley bears on the timing belt. Do not tighten the bolt at this stage.

23 Temporarily install the crankshaft pulley bolt.

24 Use a spanner or socket on the crankshaft pulley bolt to turn the crankshaft clockwise (viewed from the vehicle's right-hand side)

6.11b . . . and lower timing belt cover – 1.6 and 1.8 litre engines

through two full turns, then check that the camshaft and crankshaft sprocket timing marks remain aligned. If the marks are not correctly aligned, reposition the timing belt on the sprockets as previously described, then rotate the crankshaft through two further turns and recheck.

25 Tighten the tensioner pulley bolt to the specified torque, then use a spring balance to check that there is 5 to 6 mm of belt deflection midway between the front run of the belt when a load of 2 kg is applied. If adjustment is required, move the tensioner pulley slightly.

26 Remove the temporarily-installed crankshaft pulley bolt.

27 Refit the timing belt guide to the crankshaft, ensuring that its concave side is outermost, then refit the timing belt covers and tighten the bolts.

28 Slide the crankshaft pulley onto the end of the crankshaft, then tighten the bolt to the specified torque while holding the crankshaft stationary as described for the removal procedure.

29 Locate the pulley on the coolant pump drive flange, and tighten the retaining bolts.

30 If removed, refit the starter motor (See Chapter 5A).

31 Refit and tension the auxiliary drivebelt(s) as described in Chapter 1.

32 Refit the undershield and right-hand road-wheel and lower the vehicle to the ground.

33 Refit the camshaft cover (see Section 4).

34 Refit the spark plugs (see Chapter 1).

35 On completion, reconnect the battery negative terminal.

6.12 Slide the outer timing belt guide from the crankshaft key – 1.6 and 1.8 litre engines

6.15 Removing the timing belt from the camshaft sprocket – 1.6 and 1.8 litre engines

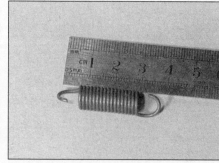

6.19 Checking the free length of the timing belt tensioner spring – 1.6 and 1.8 litre engines

2.0 litre engines

Removal

36 Disconnect the battery negative terminal (refer to *Disconnecting the battery* in the Reference Chapter).

37 Firmly apply the handbrake, then jack up the front of the car and support it securely on axle stands (see *Jacking and vehicle support*). Remove the right-hand roadwheel, then unbolt and remove the undershield from under the right-hand side of the engine compartment.

38 Remove the auxiliary drivebelt(s) (alternator, power steering and air conditioning, as applicable), as described in Chapter 1.

39 Remove the right-hand engine/transmission mounting as described in Section 16.

40 Remove the alternator as described in Chapter 5A.

41 Remove the spark plugs (see Chapter 1).

42 Set the engine at TDC for No 1 cylinder (see Section 3).

43 The crankshaft must now be held stationary while the crankshaft pulley bolt is loosened. Toyota technicians use a special tool bolted to the crankshaft pulley to hold the crankshaft, and a similar tool can be fabricated out of flat metal bar. Alternatively, on manual transmission models, have an assistant engage top gear and depress the brake pedal. On automatic transmission models, remove the starter motor (Chapter 5A) and use a wide-bladed screwdriver engaged with the starter ring gear to hold the crankshaft stationary.

44 Unscrew the crankshaft pulley bolt and slide the pulley off of the end of the crankshaft. If it is tight, use a suitable puller to remove it.

45 Unbolt and remove the upper and lower timing belt covers and, where fitted, recover the gaskets.

46 Slide the outer timing belt guide from the crankshaft.

47 If the timing belt is to be re-used, mark it with an arrow to indicate its direction of rotation. Also mark it in relation to the crankshaft and camshaft pulleys as an aid to refitting.

48 Loosen the bolt securing the timing belt tensioner to the cylinder block. Using a screwdriver and protective card, lever the tensioner rearwards to release the tension from the belt, then tighten the bolt to retain the tensioner in this position.

49 Slide the timing belt from the camshaft, crankshaft, oil pump and coolant pump sprockets and remove it from the engine.

50 Do not alter the position of the camshaft or crankshaft sprockets with the timing belt removed.

Inspection

51 With the timing belt removed, check it thoroughly for damage and deterioration. In particular check for cracking at the base of the teeth.

52 In addition to the regular renewal called for as part of the service schedule (Chapter 1), the timing belt should be renewed, regardless of age or mileage, if it appears to be defective in any manner or if it has been in contact with water, oil or steam.

53 Check that the tensioner and idler pulleys turn smoothly without any signs of roughness. Also check that the free length of the tensioner pulley spring is as given in the Specifications – if it has stretched, renew it.

Refitting

54 Before refitting the timing belt, check that the small hole in the camshaft sprocket is in the 12 o'clock position and is centrally aligned with the timing mark cut-out on the camshaft right-hand bearing cap. Also check that the TDC notch on the crankshaft sprocket flange is aligned with the TDC mark on the oil pump housing. As a further check, temporarily place the lower timing belt cover and the crankshaft pulley in position and check that the notch in the pulley is aligned with the 0° mark on the cover. Remove the pulley and cover after the check.

55 Fit the timing belt on the sprockets and idlers, ensuring that the sprocket positions do not alter and that the belt is taut on the front run between the camshaft, coolant pump and crankshaft sprockets. If the original belt is being refitted, ensure that the arrow marked on the belt during removal faces the correct way and that the belt-to-sprocket marks are correctly aligned.

56 Slacken the tensioner bolt and allow the tensioner to return under spring pressure so that the pulley bears on the timing belt. Do not tighten the bolt at this stage. Carry out the following procedure to set the tensioner.

  a) *Refit the outer timing belt guide concave side facing outwards, then refit the lower timing belt cover together with a new gasket (where applicable) and tighten the bolts.*

  b) *Refit the crankshaft pulley, and tighten the bolt to the specified torque.*

  c) *Turn the crankshaft clockwise nearly two complete revolutions, then turn it slowly to bring the TDC marks into alignment. Do not turn the crankshaft anti-clockwise. If the TDC marks do not align at this stage, remove the timing belt and carry out the refitting procedure again.*

  d) *Turn the crankshaft clockwise one complete turn then continue turning until the timing mark is aligned with the 45° BTDC mark on the lower timing belt cover.*

  e) *Tighten the tensioner bolt to the specified torque.*

57 Refit the upper timing belt cover together with a new gasket (where applicable), and tighten the retaining bolts.

58 Refit the right-hand engine/transmission mounting, and securely tighten the bolts.

59 Refit the spark plugs (see Chapter 1).

60 Refit the alternator, and if removed, the starter motor (see Chapter 5A).

61 Refit and tension the auxiliary drivebelt(s) as described in Chapter 1.

62 Refit the undershield and right-hand roadwheel, then lower the vehicle to the ground.

63 On completion, reconnect the battery negative terminal.

7 Timing belt sprocket(s) and pulleys – removal, inspection and refitting

Removal

1 Remove the timing belt as described in Section 6. Where only a camshaft sprocket is being removed, it is not necessary to remove the crankshaft pulley or the lower timing belt cover. Also it is not necessary to remove the right-hand engine mounting if the original timing belt is to be refitted.

2 On 2.0 litre engines, remove the camshaft cover as described in Section 4.

Camshaft sprocket

3 Use a spanner on the flats provided to hold the camshaft stationary, then unscrew the bolt and remove the sprocket from the end of the camshaft (**see illustrations**).

Crankshaft sprocket

4 Slide the crankshaft sprocket from the key on the end of the crankshaft using two levers if necessary (**see illustration**). To prevent damage to the oil pump housing, position card or pieces of wood beneath the levers.

5 If necessary, remove the key from the groove in the crankshaft and place in a container for safe-keeping.

7.3a Remove the retaining bolt . . .

7.3b . . . and the camshaft sprocket

7.4 Removing the crankshaft sprocket

7.8 Removing the tensioner pulley

7.16 TDC marks on the crankshaft sprocket and oil pump housing

7.21a Locate the tensioner pulley on the oil pump housing . . .

7.21b . . . and insert the bolt

Oil pump sprocket (2.0 litre engines)

6 A suitable tool will be required to hold the sprocket stationary as the retaining nut is slackened. In the absence of the Toyota special tool, a suitable alternative can be made from two lengths of steel strip bolted together to form a forked end. Drill a hole at the end of each fork, insert a suitable bolt and secure with a nut. The bolts can then be engaged with the holes in the sprocket to prevent rotation.

7 With the sprocket held stationary with the tool, undo the retaining nut and withdraw the sprocket from the oil pump shaft.

Tensioner pulley

8 Loosen the mounting bolt to release the spring tension, then unhook the spring, unscrew the mounting bolt and remove the tensioner from the oil pump housing or cylinder head, as applicable (see illustration).

Idler pulley (2.0 litre engines)

9 Unscrew the bolt and remove the idler pulley from the oil pump housing.

Inspection

10 Inspect the teeth of the sprockets for signs of nicks and damage. The teeth are not prone to wear, and should normally last the life of the engine.

11 Spin the tensioner and idler pulleys by hand, and check for any roughness or tightness. Do not attempt to clean them with solvent, as this may enter the bearings. If wear is evident, renew the tensioner and/or idler pulley as necessary.

Refitting

Camshaft sprocket

12 Locate the camshaft sprocket on the end of the camshaft, making sure that the location pin engages with the groove in the sprocket.

13 Insert the bolt and tighten to the specified torque while holding the camshaft stationary with a spanner on the flats provided.

14 Refit the timing belt with reference to Section 6. On 2.0 litre engines refit the camshaft cover.

Crankshaft sprocket

15 If removed, locate the key in the groove in the crankshaft making sure that its top edge is parallel with the crankshaft.

16 Slide the crankshaft sprocket on the crankshaft, flanged side first. If the sprocket becomes tight on the key, remove it and check that the key is pressed fully into the groove.

8.2 Drilling holes in the camshaft oil seal prior to removal – 1.6 and 1.8 litre engines

Check that the TDC mark is aligned correctly (see illustration).

17 Refit the timing belt with reference to Section 6. On 2.0 litre engines refit the camshaft cover.

Oil pump sprocket (2.0 litre engines)

18 Locate the sprocket on the oil pump shaft and refit the retaining nut. Hold the sprocket stationary using the method employed for removal, and tighten the nut to the specified torque.

19 Refit the timing belt (see Section 6).

20 Refit the camshaft cover.

Tensioner pulley

21 Hook the spring onto the pulley and oil pump housing, then refit the pulley and insert the bolt (see illustrations).

22 Lever the pulley against the spring and retain in this position by tightening the bolt.

23 Refit the timing belt (see Section 6).

24 On 2.0 litre engines, refit the camshaft cover.

Idler pulley (2.0 litre engines)

25 Apply locking fluid to the threads of the mounting bolt.

26 Locate the idler pulley on the oil pump housing then insert the mounting bolt and tighten to the specified torque.

27 Refit the timing belt (see Section 6).

28 Refit the camshaft cover.

---

8 Camshaft oil seal(s) – renewal

1.6 and 1.8 litre engines

1 Remove the camshaft sprocket as described in Section 7.

2 Punch or drill two small holes opposite each other in the seal, but take care not to damage the surface of the camshaft. Screw a self-tapping screw into each hole and pull on the screws with pliers to extract the seal (see illustration).

3 Wipe clean the seal location and check the contact surface on the camshaft for excessive wear. If a deep groove is evident, it will be necessary to renew the camshaft.

4 Lubricate the lips of the new seal with a little

multi-purpose grease and ease the seal over the end of the camshaft. Using a socket as a drift which bears only on the seal's hard outer edge, drive the seal squarely into position until it seats on its locating shoulder, then wipe off any surplus grease **(see illustrations)**.
5 Refit the camshaft sprocket with reference to Section 7.

2.0 litre engines

6 Remove the camshaft sprocket and tensioner pulley as described in Section 7.
7 Unbolt and remove the inner timing belt cover from the end of the cylinder head.
8 Punch or drill two small holes opposite each other in the seal. Screw a self-tapping screw into each hole and pull on the screws with pliers to extract the seal.
9 Wipe clean the seal location and check the contact surface on the camshaft for excessive wear. If a deep groove is evident, it will be necessary to renew the camshaft.
10 Lubricate the lips of the new seal with a little multi-purpose grease and ease the seal over the end of the camshaft. Using a socket as a drift which bears only on the seal's hard outer edge, drive the seal squarely into position until it seats on its locating shoulder, then wipe off any surplus grease.
11 Refit the inner timing belt cover and tighten the bolts.
12 Refit the camshaft sprocket and tensioner pulley with reference to Section 7.

9 Camshafts and followers
– removal, inspection and refitting

Removal

1 Remove the camshaft sprocket as described in Section 7.
2 Before removing the camshafts, use a dial gauge to measure the endfloat of each camshaft. This must be within specification; if it exceeds its maximum permissible limit, the camshaft(s) and/or cylinder head must be renewed.

1.6 and 1.8 litre engines

3 Using an open-ended spanner or adjustable spanner on the camshaft hexagonal section,

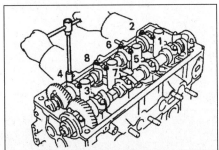

9.6a Inlet camshaft bearing cap bolt slackening sequence – 1.6 and 1.8 litre engines

8.4a Ease the new oil seal over the end of the camshaft . . .

set the inlet camshaft drive gear service bolt hole to the 12 o'clock position; the lobes of numbers one and three cylinders should now be pushing evenly on their followers **(see illustration)**.
4 Progressively slacken the inlet camshaft right-hand bearing cap retaining bolts, a little at a time, then remove the bearing cap **(see illustration)**.
5 To release the pressure of the sub-gear spring, secure the inlet camshaft sub-gear to its main gear using a 6 mm bolt (16 to 20 mm long) inserted through the service bolt hole.
6 Progressively slacken the inlet camshaft bearing cap bolts, a little at a time, in sequence, until all valve spring pressure has been relieved **(see illustration)**. Remove the bearing caps, noting their correct fitted positions, then lift out the camshaft. The caps are marked with an I, and an arrow points to the timing belt end of the engine **(see illustrations)**. Do not

9.3 Using an adjustable spanner on the hexagonal section on the inlet camshaft – 1.6 and 1.8 litre engines

9.6b Inlet camshaft caps are marked I and numbered, with an arrow towards the timing belt end of the engine – 1.6 and 1.8 litre engines

8.4b . . . and drive it into position with a socket – 1.6 and 1.8 litre engines

attempt to prise out the camshaft or it will be damaged; if the camshaft cannot be lifted out, retighten No 3 bearing cap then loosen each of its bolts alternately whilst pulling upwards the camshaft gear.
Caution: Make sure that the bolts are loosened progressively otherwise the force on the cylinder head thrust faces may damage the cylinder head and/or camshaft.
7 Rotate the exhaust camshaft so that the sprocket locating pin is at approximately the 7 o'clock position; the lobes of numbers one and three cylinders should be pushing evenly on their followers.
8 Progressively slacken the exhaust camshaft right-hand bearing cap retaining bolts, a little at a time, then remove the bearing cap. If it is tight, do not prise it out but leave it in position with the bolts removed.
9 Progressively slacken the exhaust

9.4 Removing the right-hand bearing cap from the inlet camshaft – 1.6 and 1.8 litre engines

9.6c Removing the inlet camshaft – 1.6 and 1.8 litre engines

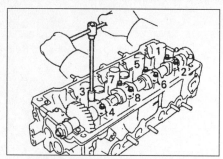

9.9a Exhaust camshaft bearing cap bolt slackening sequence – 1.6 and 1.8 litre engines

9.9b Exhaust camshaft caps are marked E and numbered, with an arrow towards the timing belt end of the engine – 1.6 and 1.8 litre engines

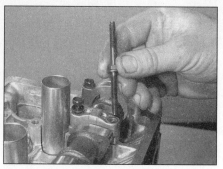

9.9c Remove the bolts . . .

9.9d . . . the bearing caps . . .

9.9e . . . and the exhaust camshaft – 1.6 and 1.8 litre engines

camshaft bearing cap bolts, a little at a time, in sequence, until all valve spring pressure has been relieved (see illustration). Remove the bearing caps, noting their correct fitted positions, then lift out the camshaft (see illustrations). Do not attempt to prise it out

or it will be damaged; if the camshaft cannot be lifted out, retighten No 3 bearing cap then loosen each of its bolts alternately whilst pulling upwards the camshaft gear.
Caution: Make sure that the bolts are loosened progressively otherwise the

force on the cylinder head thrust faces may damage the cylinder head and/or camshaft.
10 If necessary, lift out the shims and camshaft followers, keeping all components in order for refitting to their original locations (see illustration).
11 The inlet camshaft sub-gear can be removed as follows. Mount the camshaft by its hexagonal section in a soft-jawed vice and screw in two further bolts to act as leverage points. Using a screwdriver between these bolts, apply pressure in a clockwise direction to hold the sub-gear against the torsional spring pressure, then remove the bolt inserted to secure the sub-gear to the main gear, and carefully allow the sub-gear to rotate anti-clockwise until all spring pressure is released. Remove the sub-gear securing circlip then remove the wave washer, sub-gear and spring (see illustrations).

9.10 Removing the camshaft followers – 1.6 and 1.8 litre engines

9.11a Use two bolts to hold the inlet camshaft sub-gear tensioned while the retaining bolts is removed – 1.6 and 1.8 litre engines

9.11b Remove the circlip . . .

9.11c . . . the wave washer . . .

9.11d . . . the sub-gear . . .

9.11e . . . and the spring – 1.6 and 1.8 litre engines

9.12 Inlet and exhaust camshafts showing the drive gears – 2.0 litre engines

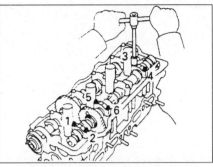

9.15 Exhaust camshaft bearing cap bolt slackening sequence – 2.0 litre engines

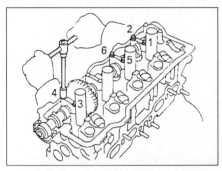

9.19 Inlet camshaft bearing cap bolt slackening sequence – 2.0 litre engines

2.0 litre engines

12 Using an open-ended spanner on its hexagonal section, set the inlet camshaft sprocket locating pin between 10° and 45° before TDC (camshaft angle); the lobes of numbers two and four cylinders should now be pushing evenly on their followers **(see illustration)**.

13 To release the pressure of the sub-gear spring, secure the exhaust camshaft sub-gear to its main gear using a 6 mm bolt (16 to 20 mm long).

14 Unbolt and remove the inner timing belt cover from the end of the cylinder head. Progressively slacken the exhaust camshaft left-hand bearing cap bolts, a little at a time, then remove the cap.

15 Working in several stages, in sequence, progressively slacken the exhaust camshaft bearing cap bolts but leaving the bolts of No 3 cap engaged several threads **(see illustration)**. Remove the Nos 1, 2 and 4 bearing caps, having noted their markings and their correct fitted positions.

16 Unscrew the bolts of the No 3 cap, then remove the cap and lift out the exhaust camshaft keeping it level so that it does not bind on the cylinder head.

Caution: Make sure that the bolts are loosened progressively otherwise the force on the cylinder head thrust faces may damage the cylinder head and/or camshaft.

17 Using an open-ended spanner on the camshaft hexagonal section, set the inlet camshaft sprocket locating pin between 80° and 115° before TDC (camshaft angle); the lobes of numbers one and three cylinders should now be pushing evenly on their followers.

18 Progressively unscrew the bolts of the right-hand bearing cap, then remove the cap and oil seal.

19 Working in several stages in sequence **(see illustration)**, progressively slacken the camshaft bearing cap bolts but leaving the bolts of No 2 cap engaged several threads.

Caution: Make sure that the bolts are loosened progressively otherwise the force on the cylinder head thrust faces may damage the cylinder head and/or camshaft.

20 Remove the Nos 1, 3 and 4 bearing caps, having noted their markings and their correct fitted positions.

21 Unscrew the bolts of the No 2 cap, then remove the cap and lift out the inlet camshaft keeping it level so that it does not bind on the cylinder head.

22 Lift out the shims and camshaft followers, keeping all components in order for refitting to their original locations.

23 The exhaust camshaft sub-gear can be removed as follows. Mount the camshaft by its hexagonal section in a soft-jawed vice and screw in two further bolts to act as leverage points. Using a screwdriver between these bolts, apply pressure in a clockwise direction to hold the sub-gear against the torsional spring pressure, then remove the first bolt (inserted to secure the sub-gear to the main gear) and carefully allow the sub-gear to rotate anti-clockwise until all spring pressure is released. Remove the sub-gear securing circlip then remove the washer, sub-gear and spring.

Inspection

24 Visually examine the cam followers, shims, cam lobes and bearing journals for scuffing, score marks, pitting and evidence of overheating (blue, discoloured areas). Look for flaking away of the hardened surface layer of each cam lobe.

25 If in any doubt as to the condition of the camshafts and associated components, have them examined and measured by an engine reconditioning specialist.

26 If the camshaft sub-gear has been removed, install the camshafts and check

the gear backlash using a dial gauge. If the backlash is outside specification, the camshafts must be renewed. Remove the camshafts (as described above) upon completion of the check.

27 Using calipers, check that the distance between the ends of the sub-gear torsional spring is as specified (with the spring in a 'free state'); renew the spring if not.

28 Before reassembling the inlet camshaft gear, check that there are no signs of chipping or cracking on any of the teeth (check also the exhaust camshaft gear); the camshaft must be renewed if any such fault is evident.

Refitting

1.6 and 1.8 litre engines

29 If it was dismantled, reassemble the inlet camshaft sub-gear, reversing the method of dismantling; remove the two bolts used as leverage points once the single bolt is in place securing the sub-gear to the main gear.

30 Install the camshaft followers and shims to their original bores, having lightly oiled the bores; check that the followers can be rotated smoothly in the bores by hand.

31 Lightly oil the exhaust camshaft journals and cam lobes, then place the exhaust camshaft on the cylinder head so that the sprocket locating pin is positioned as described in paragraph 8; the cam lobes of number one and number three cylinders should push evenly on their followers.

32 Apply sealant to the camshaft right-hand bearing cap location on the cylinder head **(see illustration)**, then refit the camshaft bearing

9.32a Apply sealant to the front edges of the exhaust camshaft right-hand bearing cap . . .

9.32b . . . then refit the cap on the cylinder head – 1.6 and 1.8 litre engines

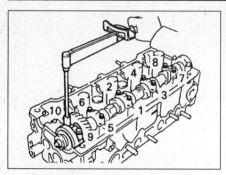

9.32c Bearing cap bolt tightening sequence for the exhaust camshaft – 1.6 and 1.8 litre engines

9.32d Tightening the exhaust camshaft bearing cap bolts to the specified torque – 1.6 and 1.8 litre engines

9.35a Lowering the inlet camshaft into the cylinder head – 1.6 and 1.8 litre engines

9.35b Installation marks on the gears of the inlet and exhaust camshafts – 1.6 and 1.8 litre engines

9.36a Refitting the inlet camshaft bearing caps – 1.6 and 1.8 litre engines

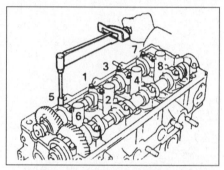

9.36b Bearing cap bolt tightening sequence for the inlet camshaft – 1.6 and 1.8 litre engines

caps in their original fitted positions. Lightly oil the heads and threads of the bolts then insert and tighten them evenly and progressively to their specified torque setting in sequence **(see illustrations)**.

33 Install a new camshaft oil seal as described in Section 8.

34 Lightly oil the inlet camshaft journals and cam lobes. Also lightly oil the camshaft bearing cap bolt threads and heads.

35 Set the exhaust camshaft locating pin to the 9 o'clock position just above the upper surface of the cylinder head, then engage the inlet camshaft gear with that of the exhaust camshaft so that their installation marks are aligned. Once the camshaft gears are correctly engaged, roll the inlet gear down the exhaust gear until the inlet camshaft is seated in the cylinder head **(see illustrations)**.

36 Refit the inlet camshaft bearing caps

(with the exception of the right-hand cap), and their bolts, in their original fitted positions **(see illustration)**. Evenly and progressively, in sequence, tighten the bolts to their specified torque setting **(see illustration)**.

37 Unscrew the bolt securing the sub-gear to the main gear **(see illustration)**.

38 Refit the inlet camshaft right-hand bearing cap so that its arrow points toward the timing belt end of the engine, and tighten its retaining bolts (lightly oiled) alternately to their specified torque; if difficulty is experienced fitting the bearing cap, push the camshaft towards the cylinder head left-hand end.

39 Using an open-ended spanner, rotate the exhaust camshaft clockwise so that its locating pin is in the 12 o'clock position. Check that the TDC marks on the outer face of the camshaft gears align and that the installation marks are both in the 12 o'clock position.

40 If all is well, refit the camshaft sprocket as described in Section 6. Note that the valve clearances should be checked (see Section 5) before the camshaft cover is refitted.

2.0 litre engines

41 If it was dismantled, reassemble the exhaust camshaft sub-gear, reversing the method of dismantling; remove the two bolts used as leverage points once the single bolt is in place securing the sub-gear to the main gear.

42 Install the camshaft followers and shims to their original bores, having lightly oiled the bores; check that the followers can be rotated smoothly in the bores by hand.

43 Lightly oil the inlet camshaft journals and cam lobes, then place the inlet camshaft on the cylinder head so that the camshaft sprocket locating pin is positioned as described in paragraph 17; the cam lobes of number one and number three cylinders should push evenly on their followers.

44 Apply a bead of sealant to the camshaft right-hand bearing cap, then refit the camshaft bearing caps in their original fitted positions. Lightly oil the heads and threads of the bolts then insert and tighten them evenly and progressively to their specified torque setting in sequence **(see illustration)**.

45 Install a new camshaft oil seal as described in Section 8.

46 Lightly oil the exhaust camshaft journals and cam lobes. Also lightly oil the camshaft bearing cap bolt threads and heads.

47 Set the inlet camshaft locating pin to

9.37 Unscrewing the bolts securing the sub-gear to the main gear on the inlet camshaft – 1.6 and 1.8 litre engines

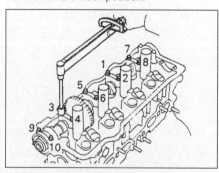

9.44 Inlet camshaft bearing cap bolt tightening sequence – 2.0 litre engines

the position described in paragraph 12, then engage the exhaust camshaft gear with that of the inlet camshaft so that their timing marks are aligned. Once the camshaft gears are correctly engaged, roll the exhaust gear down the inlet gear until the exhaust camshaft is seated in the cylinder head. Note that there are two sets of marks on the camshaft gears; assembly reference marks and timing marks. Ensure that the timing marks, **not** the assembly reference marks are aligned when engaging the gears **(see illustration)**.

48 Refit the exhaust camshaft bearing caps and their bolts in their original positions. Evenly and progressively, in sequence, tighten the bolts to their specified torque setting **(see illustration)**.

49 Unscrew the bolt securing the sub-gear to the main gear.

50 Refit the inner timing belt cover and secure with the bolts.

51 Refit the camshaft sprocket as described in Section 6. Note that the valve clearances should be checked (see Section 5) before the camshaft cover is refitted.

10 Cylinder head – removal and refitting

HAYNES HINT *To aid refitting, note the locations of all relevant brackets and the routing of hoses and cables before removal.*

Removal

1 Disconnect the battery negative terminal (refer to *Disconnecting the battery* in the Reference Chapter).

2 Drain the cooling system (see Chapter 1).

3 On 1.6 and 1.8 litre engines, loosen the bolts securing the pulley to the coolant pump drive flange.

4 Remove the auxiliary drivebelt(s) (see Chapter 1).

5 Remove the alternator as described in Chapter 5A.

6 Remove the exhaust manifold (Chapter 4A).

7 Disconnect the HT leads from the spark plugs and release them from the support on the left-hand end of the cylinder head.

8 Remove both ignition coils as described in Chapter 5B.

9 Disconnect the wiring, bottom hose and heater hoses from the coolant inlet housing on the left-hand end of the cylinder head. Also disconnect the top hose from the outlet on the left-hand end of the cylinder head **(see illustrations)**. On 2.0 litre engines disconnect the earth wiring, knock sensor wiring and EGR valve wiring.

10 Disconnect the wiring connector from the camshaft sensor.

11 On 2.0 litre engines remove the EGR valve

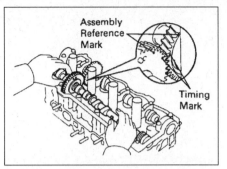

9.47 Assembly reference marks and timing marks on the camshaft gears – 2.0 litre engines

and vacuum modulator with reference to Chapter 4B.

12 Loosen the clips and remove the air duct from between the throttle housing and the air cleaner **(see illustration)**.

13 Disconnect the wiring and hoses, and accelerator cable, from the throttle housing.

14 Unbolt and remove the inlet manifold support bracket from the rear of the engine. Note that it is not necessary to completely remove the lower mounting bolt, but it must be loosened to enable the inlet manifold to be withdrawn from the studs on the cylinder head.

15 Unscrew the bolt and remove the lifting eye from the left-hand end of the cylinder head.

16 Identify the location of the wiring harness to the cylinder head and inlet manifold, then disconnect it and position to one side.

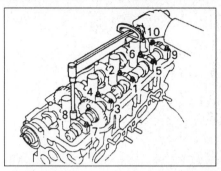

9.48 Exhaust camshaft bearing cap bolt tightening sequence – 2.0 litre engines

17 Disconnect the two PCV hoses from the camshaft cover.

18 Disconnect the vacuum hose from the right-hand end of the inlet manifold.

19 Unscrew the union bolt then disconnect the fuel inlet hose from the left-hand end of the fuel rail. Recover the copper washers.

20 Disconnect the wiring from the fuel injectors.

21 Unscrew the mounting bolts and remove the fuel rail and injectors as described in Chapter 4A. Recover the spacers from the inlet manifold.

22 Unscrew the nuts and bolts and withdraw the inlet manifold from the studs on the cylinder head. Recover the gasket.

23 At the rear of the engine, unscrew the nuts securing the coolant pump inlet to the cylinder head. Disconnect the hose from the coolant pump and remove the inlet and gasket.

10.9a Removing the bottom hose . . .

10.9b . . . and top hose

10.9c Disconnecting the wiring from the temperature sensor

10.12 Removing the air duct from the throttle housing

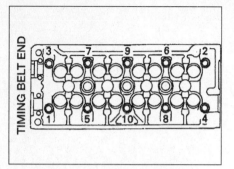

10.34a Cylinder head bolt slackening sequence – 1.6 litre engines

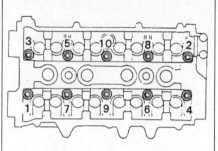

10.34b Cylinder head bolt slackening sequence – 1.8 and 2.0 litre engines

24 Remove the spark plugs as described in Chapter 1.

25 Remove the camshaft cover as described in Section 4 of this Chapter.

26 Unbolt and remove the upper (2.0 litre engines) or upper and middle (1.6 and 1.8 litre engines) timing belt covers.

27 Position the engine at TDC as described in Section 3 of this Chapter.

28 Mark the timing belt and camshaft sprocket in relation to each other as an aid to refitting.

29 Loosen the timing belt tensioner pulley retaining bolt, move the tensioner to the rear as far as possible and retighten the retaining bolt. For access to the tensioner pulley bolt on 1.6 and 1.8 litre engines, prise out the rubber grommet from the lower timing belt cover and slacken the bolt using a socket inserted through the hole in the cover.

30 Ease the timing belt from the camshaft sprocket, making sure that it remains engaged with the crankshaft sprocket. Tie the belt to one side but **do not** bend it excessively.

31 If necessary, unbolt the alternator mounting bracket from the front of the cylinder head.

32 Remove the inlet and exhaust camshafts as described in Section 9.

33 Prise the semi-circular plug from the camshaft cut-out at the right-hand end of the cylinder head.

34 Working in sequence, progressively slacken the cylinder head bolts by half a turn at a time, until all bolts can be unscrewed by hand **(see illustrations)**. A splined socket will be required for this procedure.

35 Lift out the cylinder head bolts and recover the washers.

36 Rock the cylinder head to release the gasket, then lift it from the two locating dowels on the cylinder block and position it on the bench. Remove the gasket from the top of the block **(see illustrations)**. If they are a loose fit in the block, remove the locating dowels and store them with the head for safe-keeping.

37 If the cylinder head is to be dismantled for overhaul, refer to Part C of this Chapter.

Preparation for refitting

38 Check the condition of the cylinder head bolts, and particularly their threads, whenever they are removed. Wash the bolts and wipe dry, then check each for any sign of visible wear or damage, renewing any bolt if necessary. Although Toyota do not actually specify that the bolts be renewed when disturbed, it is recommended that they are.

39 The mating faces of the cylinder head and cylinder block/crankcase must be perfectly clean before refitting the head. Use a hard plastic or wood scraper to remove all traces of gasket and carbon; also clean the piston crowns. Take particular care, as the surfaces are damaged easily. Also, make sure that the carbon is not allowed to enter the oil and water passages – this is particularly important for the lubrication system, as carbon could block the oil supply to any of the engine's components. Using adhesive tape and paper, seal the water, oil and bolt holes in the cylinder block/crankcase. To prevent carbon entering the gap between the pistons and bores, smear a little grease in the gap. After cleaning each

piston, use a small brush to remove all traces of grease and carbon from the gap, then wipe away the remainder with a clean rag. Clean all the pistons in the same way.

40 Check the mating surfaces of the cylinder block/crankcase and the cylinder head for nicks, deep scratches and other damage. If slight, they may be removed carefully with a file, but if excessive, machining may be the only alternative to renewal.

41 If warpage of the cylinder head gasket surface is suspected, use a straight-edge to check it for distortion. Refer to Part C of this Chapter if necessary.

Refitting

42 Wipe clean the mating surfaces of the cylinder head and cylinder block/crankcase. Check that the two locating dowels are in position at each end of the cylinder block/crankcase surface. Check that the crankshaft is still at the TDC position.

43 Fit a new gasket to the cylinder block/crankcase surface, aligning it with the locating dowels.

44 Carefully refit the cylinder head to the block and align it with the locating dowels.

45 Locate the washers on the cylinder head bolts, then lightly oil the threads of the bolts and the surfaces under the heads.

46 Enter each bolt into the holes (do not drop them in) and screw in, by hand until finger-tight. Note that on 1.6 and 1.8 litre engines, the longer bolts are located beneath the exhaust camshaft position **(see illustration)**.

47 Working progressively and in sequence, tighten the cylinder head bolts to their Stage 1 torque setting, using a torque wrench and socket **(see illustrations)**.

48 Go around again in the specified sequence and angle-tighten the head bolts through the specified Stage 2 angle. It is recommended that an angle-measuring gauge is used during this stage, to ensure accuracy **(see illustration)**. If an angle-measuring gauge is not available, mark the side of each bolt with a dab of paint before angle-tightening them. If each bolt is marked on the side facing the timing belt end of the engine, it will be easy to determine when they have been tightened through the 90° Stage 2 angle (all the paint marks will be facing the inlet manifold side of the engine).

10.36a Lift the cylinder head from the block . . .

10.36b . . . and remove the gasket

10.46 1.6 and 1.8 litre engines have the longer head bolts beneath the exhaust camshaft – 1.6 litre engine

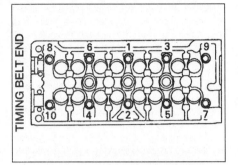

10.47a Cylinder head bolt tightening sequence – 1.6 and 2.0 litre engines

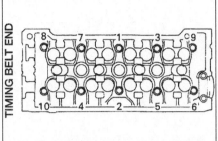

10.47b Cylinder head bolt tightening sequence – 1.8 litre engines

10.47c Tightening the cylinder head bolts to the Stage 1 torque setting

10.48 Angle-tightening the cylinder head bolts to the Stage 2 angle

10.50a Apply sealant to the semi-circular plug . . .

10.50b . . . and put it in the cut-out at the right-hand end of the cylinder head with the protrusion on the outside

49 On 1.6 and 1.8 litre engines only, and again working in the specified sequence, angle-tighten the bolts to the Stage 3 angle. Where used, the paint marks should now be facing the flywheel end of the engine.

50 Apply suitable sealant (consult a Toyota dealer) to the semi-circular plug and insert it in the cut-out at the right-hand end of the cylinder head **(see illustrations)**.

51 Refit the inlet and exhaust camshafts as described in Section 8.

52 On 2.0 litre engines, refit the inner timing belt cover.

53 Where removed, refit the alternator mounting bracket to the front of the cylinder head and tighten the bolts to the specified torque.

54 Locate the timing belt on the camshaft sprocket making sure that the previously-made marks are correctly aligned. Check that the TDC mark on the crankshaft pulley is still aligned.

55 Tension the timing belt with reference to the applicable paragraphs of Section 5 (according to engine type) then, on 1.6 and 1.8 litre engines, refit the rubber grommet to the lower timing belt cover.

56 Check that the TDC timing marks are correctly aligned with reference to Section 5.

57 Refit the upper, or upper and middle, timing belt covers, as applicable.

58 Refit the camshaft cover (see Section 4).

59 Refit the spark plugs (see Chapter 1).

60 Refit the coolant pump inlet together with a new gasket and tighten the nuts.

61 Reconnect the hose to the inlet.

62 Refit the inlet manifold together with a new gasket (refer to Chapter 4A if necessary).

63 Refit the fuel rail and injectors with reference to Chapter 4A.

64 Reconnect the injector wiring.

65 Refit the fuel inlet union to the left-hand end of the fuel rail together with new copper washers, and tighten the bolt.

66 Reconnect the PCV hoses to the camshaft cover.

67 Reconnect the wiring harness to the inlet manifold and cylinder head.

68 Refit the lifting eye to the cylinder head.

69 Refit the support bracket to the inlet manifold and tighten the bolts.

70 Reconnect the wiring and hoses, and accelerator cable, to the throttle housing.

71 Refit the air duct between the throttle housing and air cleaner.

72 On 2.0 litre engines reconnect the earth wiring, knock sensor wiring and the EGR valve wiring.

73 Reconnect the wiring and hoses to the coolant inlet housing.

74 Reconnect the camshaft sensor wiring connector.

75 On 2.0 litre engines refit the EGR valve and vacuum modulator (see Chapter 4B).

76 Refit the ignition coils with reference to Chapter 4A, then reconnect the HT leads to the spark plugs and support.

77 Refit the exhaust manifold with reference to Chapter 4A.

78 Refit the alternator with reference to Chapter 5A.

79 Refit the coolant pump pulley (1.6 and 1.8 litre engines) then refit and tension the auxiliary drivebelt(s) (see Chapter 1).

80 Refill the cooling system (see Chapter 1).

81 Reconnect the battery negative terminal.

82 Start the engine, warm it up to normal operating temperature, and check for oil and coolant leaks.

11 Sump – removal and refitting

Removal

1 Disconnect the battery negative terminal (refer to *Disconnecting the battery* in the Reference Chapter).

2 Firmly apply the handbrake, then jack up the front of the car and support it securely on axle stands (see *Jacking and vehicle support*).

3 Unbolt and remove the undershields from beneath the engine, then drain the engine oil as described in Chapter 1.

4 Connect a hoist and lifting tackle to the engine lifting bracket at the left-hand end of the cylinder head, and raise the hoist to just take the weight of the engine.

5 Remove the engine/transmission longitudinal crossmember as follows **(see illustration)**.

a) *Unscrew the two securing bolts, and remove the towing eye from the crossmember.*

b) *Prise out the cover plugs, and unscrew the two bolts securing the front engine/transmission mounting to the crossmember.*

c) *Where applicable, unscrew the securing bolt and release the air conditioning pipe clamp from the crossmember.*

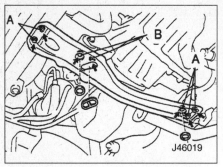

11.5 Longitudinal crossmember retaining bolts (A) and front engine/transmission mounting bracket bolts (B)

d) Prise out the rear cover plug and unscrew the five securing bolts, two at the front and three at the rear, and remove the crossmember.

6 Remove the exhaust system front downpipe as described in Chapter 4A. Where applicable, unscrew the securing bolts and remove the engine-to-transmission reinforcing plate. Recover any spacers if fitted, noting their locations.

7 Where an oil cooler is fitted, unscrew the union bolt and recover the copper washers. Seal the end of the hose with tape to prevent entry of dust and dirt.

8 Where fitted, disconnect the wiring connector at the oil level sensor.

9 Unscrew and remove all the sump (secondary sump on 1.8 litre engines) retaining bolts and nuts **(see illustration)**.

10 Break the joint by striking the sump with

11.9 Sump nuts and bolts

the palm of your hand, then lower the sump and withdraw it from underneath the vehicle. If necessary use a suitable tool (such as a scraper blade) to free the sump from the sealant.

11 On 1.8 litre engines, if necessary, the main sump may be unbolted from the cylinder block after removing the baffle plate and the pick-up tube and strainer with reference to Section 12.

Refitting

12 Clean all traces of sealant from the mating surfaces of the cylinder block/crankcase/main sump, oil pump, left-hand oil seal housing and sump, then use a clean rag to wipe out the sump and the engine's interior.

13 Ensure that the sump and cylinder block/crankcase mating surfaces are clean and dry. Apply a continuous bead of suitable sealant (consult a Toyota dealer) to the mating

surfaces of the sump, making sure that the bead goes around the inner edges of the bolt holes. On 1.8 litre engines, refit the main sump and oil pick-up tube first and tighten the bolts to the specified torque.

14 Offer up the sump and refit its retaining nuts and bolts. Tighten them evenly and progressively to the specified torque.

15 Where fitted, refit the oil cooler union together with new copper washers and tighten the union bolt.

16 Where fitted, reconnect the wiring connector at the oil level sensor.

17 Refit the engine-to-transmission reinforcing plate, together with the spacers where fitted.

18 Refit the exhaust system front downpipe section as described in Chapter 4A.

19 Refit the engine/transmission longitudinal crossmember, together with the engine mountings and tighten the bolts to the specified torque. Remove the engine support hoist and lifting tackle.

20 Refit the undershields and securely tighten the retaining screws.

21 Reconnect the battery negative terminal and lower the vehicle to the ground.

22 Fill the engine with oil as described in Chapter 1.

12 Oil pump and pick-up tube – removal, inspection and refitting

Removal

1 Remove the timing belt, tensioner, crankshaft sprocket and, where applicable, the oil pump sprocket and idler pulleys as described in Sections 6 and 7. Remove the Woodruff key from the crankshaft and store it with the pulley for safe-keeping **(see illustration)**.

2 Remove the crankshaft position sensor as described in Chapter 4A. On 1.6 and 1.8 litre engines, unbolt and remove the oil dipstick pipe.

3 Remove the sump as described in Section 11, however, on 1.8 litre engines only remove the secondary sump at this stage.

4 On 1.8 litre engines unbolt the baffle plate from the main sump.

5 Undo the bolts/nuts securing the oil pick-up tube/strainer, then remove it with its gasket **(see illustrations)**. On 2.0 litre engines remove the sump baffle plate at the same time.

6 On 1.8 litre engines unbolt and remove the main sump.

7 Withdraw the engine oil dipstick, then on 1.6 and 1.8 litre engines, unbolt and withdraw the guide tube and recover the rubber grommet from the oil pump housing.

8 Unscrew the pump retaining bolts, noting their correct fitted positions, then remove the pump and recover the gasket or rubber seal; if necessary carefully tap the pump with a soft-faced mallet to release it **(see illustrations)**.

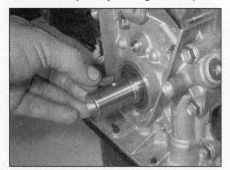

12.1 Remove the Woodruff key from the front of the crankshaft

12.5a Remove the oil pick-up tube/strainer assembly . . .

12.5b . . . and recover the gasket on the oil pump housing

12.8a Unscrew the retaining bolts . . .

12.8b . . . remove the oil pump . . .

12.8c . . . and recover the gasket

12.9a Remove the cover from the oil pump housing . . .

Inspection

9 Remove the screws securing the body cover to the pump housing then lift off the cover. Withdraw the drive and driven rotors **(see illustrations)**. On 2.0 litre engines recover the O-ring.

10 Dismantle the relief valve assembly after removing the spring retaining circlip; take care not to allow the spring to fly out and cause injury or damage, and note the order and orientation of the components as they are removed **(see illustrations)**.

11 Measure the oil pump clearances with a feeler blade. If the outer rotor-to-body clearance or side clearance is incorrect, the rotors and/or pump body must be renewed; if the rotor tip clearance is incorrect only the rotors need be renewed. If severe wear is evident, the oil pump assembly must be renewed complete **(see illustrations)**.

12 Check the relief valve components for

12.9b . . . and remove the drive rotor . . .

12.9c . . . and driven rotor

wear and damage. Coat the valve piston with clean engine oil then check that it falls slowly into its bore under its own weight; if this is not the case, renew the complete valve assembly.

13 Renew the crankshaft right-hand oil seal as described in Section 14.

14 Reassemble the oil pump by lubricating the rotors then inserting them in the pump body, with their marks facing the pump body cover, then locate the body cover and tighten the screws to the specified torque.

15 The relief valve is reassembled by

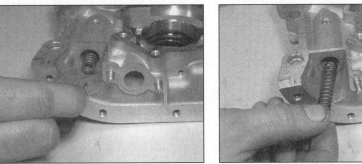

12.10a Removing the relief valve cap . . .

12.10b . . . spring . . .

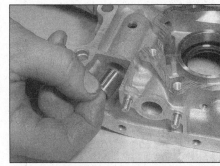

12.10c . . . and plunger

12.11a Using feeler blades to check the outer rotor-to-body clearance . . .

12.11b . . . the rotor tip clearance . . .

12.11c . . . and the side clearance

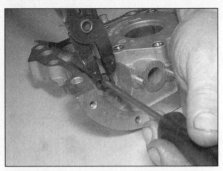

12.15 When refitting the circlip to the oil pump housing, depress the spring cap with a screwdriver

reversing the order of dismantling, ensuring that the valve piston is fitted the correct way around and that the circlip is securely located in its groove. When inserting the circlip use a screwdriver to depress the spring cap **(see illustration)**.

Refitting

16 Clean the sump and ensure that the oil pick-up pipe/strainer is clear.

17 Thoroughly clean the pump's sump mating face and ensure that the engine block-to-pump mating faces are clean.

18 Lightly oil the crankshaft oil pump drive and oil seal contact surfaces.

19 Position a new pump gasket on the cylinder block, or locate a new rubber seal in the pump body groove, according to engine, then refit the pump. On 1.6 and 1.8 litre engines, ensure that the drive rotor engages

with the crankshaft drive. Refit the pump bolts and tighten them to their specified torque.

20 On 1.6 and 1.8 litre engines, fit a new O-ring to the base of the engine oil dipstick guide tube, lubricating it with oil, then install the guide tube and tighten the bolt; refit the dipstick.

21 Refit the Woodruff key to the crankshaft, then refit the sprockets, pulleys and timing belt components as described in Sections 7 and 6.

22 On 1.8 litre engines refit the main sump with reference to Section 11.

23 Using a new gasket, refit the oil pick-up pipe/strainer and tighten its nuts and bolts to their specified torque. On 2.0 litre engines refit the sump baffle plate at the same time.

24 On 1.8 litre engines refit the baffle plate to the main sump.

25 Refit the sump as described in Section 11.

---

13 Oil cooler and pressure regulating valve – general information

1.6 and 1.8 litre engines

Oil cooler

1 The oil cooler is mounted between the radiator and the radiator grille **(see illustration)**.

2 The oil cooler hose connections are secured by clips. If the unions on the sump and oil filter housing are to be removed, new washers (behind the union and behind its bolt) will be

required on refitting; tighten the union bolts to the specified torque.

Oil pressure regulating valve

3 The valve is located in the combined oil filter housing/oil pressure regulator valve housing on the forward-facing side of the cylinder block.

4 To remove the valve, unscrew and remove the hexagon-headed plug on its base (with the washer) then withdraw the spring and valve piston noting their orientation; catch oil spillage in a container **(see illustrations)**. Refitting is a reversal of the removal procedure, but fit a new washer and tighten the hexagon-headed plug to its specified torque.

5 To remove the combined oil filter housing/oil pressure regulator valve housing, remove the oil filter (Chapter 1), then disconnect the union and remove the washers; catch oil spillage in a suitable container. Remove the filter mounting stud with its washer; remove the combined housing and its O-ring **(see illustrations)**. The valve assembly can now be removed (paragraph 4), if required.

6 Test the pressure regulator by coating the valve piston with clean engine oil and checking that it slides into its housing bore under its own weight; if not, renew the complete assembly.

7 Refitting is a reversal of the removal procedure, bearing in mind the following points:

a) Use a new O-ring and sealing washers and tighten all fastenings to the specified torque.

b) Fit a new oil filter with reference to Chapter 1, then top-up the engine oil as described in 'Weekly checks'.

13.1 Engine oil cooler location (arrowed) – 1.6 and 1.8 litre engines

13.4a Remove the plug . . .

13.4b . . . spring . . .

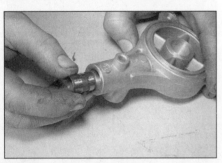

13.4c . . . and valve piston from the oil pressure regulating valve – 1.6 and 1.8 litre engines

13.5a Remove the stud securing the oil filter/oil pressure regulator valve housing to the cylinder block – 1.6 and 1.8 litre engines

13.5b The O-ring in located in the housing groove – 1.6 and 1.8 litre engines

14.1a Levering out the right-hand crankshaft seal from the oil pump housing

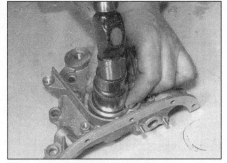

14.1b Using a hammer and socket to drive in the new oil seal

14.5 Removing the oil seal from the left-hand oil seal housing

2.0 litre engines

Oil cooler

8 The oil cooler is located at the base of the oil filter on the forward facing side of the cylinder block.

9 Firmly apply the handbrake, then jack up the front of the car and support it securely on axle stands (see *Jacking and vehicle support*).

10 Drain the cooling system as described in Chapter 1. Alternatively, clamp the oil cooler coolant hoses directly above the cooler, and be prepared for some coolant loss as the hoses are disconnected.

11 Release the hose clips, and disconnect the coolant hoses from the oil cooler.

12 Remove the oil filter (Chapter 1), then remove the filter mounting stud with its washer.

13 Undo the oil cooler retaining nut, then withdraw the oil cooler and recover the sealing O-ring.

14 Refitting is a reversal of the removal procedure, bearing in mind the following points:
  a) *Use a new O-ring and and tighten all fastenings to the specified torque.*
  b) *Fit a new oil filter with reference to Chapter 1, then top-up the engine oil as described in 'Weekly checks'.*
  c) *Refill or top-up the cooling system as described in Chapter 1 or 'Weekly checks'.*

14 Crankshaft oil seals
– renewal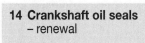

Right-hand seal

1 To renew the seal with the oil pump removed from the vehicle, carefully prise out the old seal using a flat-bladed screwdriver **(see illustration)**. Clean the seal housing and polish off any burrs or raised edges which may have caused the seal to fail in the first place. Apply multi-purpose grease to the new seal, then drive it squarely into position using a suitably-sized tubular drift, such as a socket, which bears only on the hard outer edge of the seal; the outer face of the seal should be flush with the pump face **(see illustration)**.

15.3 Using paint marks to mark the relationship of the flywheel/driveplate to its crankshaft flange

2 To renew the seal with the oil pump in place on the vehicle, first remove the timing belt (Section 6), then remove the crankshaft sprocket (Section 7).

3 Punch or drill two small holes opposite each other in the seal. Screw a self-tapping screw into each hole and pull on the screws with pliers to extract the seal. Clean the seal housing and polish off any burrs or raised edges which may have caused the seal to fail in the first place. Lubricate the lips of the new seal with clean engine oil and apply a smear of grease to the outer edge of the seal. Ease the seal over the end of the crankshaft and drive it squarely into position as described above.

4 Wipe off any excess grease then refit the crankshaft sprocket and install the timing belt as described earlier.

15.4b Removing the flywheel bolts

15.4a Home-made tool for locking the flywheel when loosening the retaining bolts

Left-hand seal

5 To renew the seal with its housing removed from the vehicle, work as described in paragraph 1 above **(see illustration)**.

6 To renew the seal with its housing in place in the vehicle, first remove the flywheel/driveplate (Section 15); the seal can then be renewed as described in paragraph 3.

7 Wipe off any excess grease, then refit the flywheel/driveplate.

15 Flywheel/driveplate
– removal, inspection and refitting

Removal

1 Remove the transmission as described in Chapter 7A or 7B according to type.

2 On manual transmission models, remove the clutch assembly as described in Chapter 6.

3 Mark the relationship of the flywheel/driveplate to its crankshaft flange **(see illustration)**.

4 Prevent the flywheel from turning by locking the ring gear teeth with a large flat-bladed screwdriver or by bolting a home-made tool to one of the transmission mounting bolt holes in the cylinder block **(see illustration)**. Progressively slacken the flywheel/driveplate retaining bolts, then remove the bolts and lift off the flywheel/driveplate **(see illustration)**.

Inspection

5 Examine the flywheel for scoring on its clutch driven plate face; if evident it may be possible for a competent engineering works to machine the surface, but renewal is the preferable option. Check the flywheel/driveplate carefully for signs of distortion, or any hairline cracks around the bolt holes or cracks radiating outwards from the centre; renewal will be required if evident.

6 If the ring gear is worn or damaged it may be possible to renew it separately, but this job should be entrusted to a Toyota dealer or engineering works.

Refitting

7 Clean the flywheel/driveplate and crankshaft flange faces, and remove all traces of thread locking compound from the retaining bolts.

 If a suitable tap is not available, cut two slots down the threads of one of the old bolts with a hacksaw, and use the bolt to remove the locking compound from the threads.

8 Locate the flywheel/driveplate on its crankshaft flange, aligning the marks made on removal. Apply a little threadlocking compound to the threads of the retaining bolts, then fit the bolts and progressively tighten them to the specified torque setting.

9 Remove the ring gear locking tool.

10 On manual transmission models refit the clutch as described in Chapter 6.

16.7a Unscrew the bolts securing the right-hand mounting to the inner wing panel . . .

16.7c . . . then withdraw the right-hand engine mounting – 1.6 and 1.8 litre engines

15.4c Removing the flywheel

11 Refit the transmission as described in Chapter 7A or 7B.

16 Engine/transmission mountings – inspection and renewal

Inspection

1 If improved access is required, firmly apply the handbrake, then jack up the front of the car and support it securely on axle stands (see *Jacking and vehicle support*).

2 Check the mounting rubber to see if it is cracked, hardened or separated from the metal at any point; renew the mounting if any such damage or deterioration is evident.

3 Check that all mounting fasteners are securely tightened; use a torque wrench to check if possible.

4 Using a large screwdriver or a crowbar,

16.7b . . . the upper bolt, and the two lower nuts from the studs . . .

16.8 Left-hand engine/transmission mounting through-bolt and nut (arrowed)

check for wear in the mounting by carefully levering against it to check for free play; where this is not possible, enlist the aid of an assistant to move the engine/transmission unit back-and-forth, or from side-to-side while you watch the mounting. While some free play is to be expected even from new components, excessive wear should be obvious. If excessive free play is found, check first that the fasteners are correctly secured, then renew any worn components as described below.

Renewal

5 The engine/transmission mountings can be unbolted and removed once the weight of the engine/transmission unit is taken off them using either a suitable hoist, an engine support bar or a jack with an interposed block of wood. Lifting eyes are provided on the engine.

6 The mountings are located in the following positions:

a) *Right-hand mounting, at the timing belt (right-hand) end of the engine.*

b) *Left-hand mounting, at the left-hand end of the transmission to the rear of the battery tray.*

c) *A front mounting between the cylinder block and the longitudinal crossmember.*

d) *A rear mounting between the rear of the transmission and the subframe.*

7 To remove the right-hand mounting, undo the bolts securing the mounting to the inner wing panel. Undo the nuts and bolts (one or two of each, depending on engine type) securing the mounting bracket to the bracket on the engine. The mounting assembly can now be withdrawn from the engine compartment **(see illustrations)**. Undo the through-bolt to separate the mounting bracket from the mounting rubber.

8 Access to the left-hand mounting is gained by removing the air cleaner assembly (see Chapter 4A), followed by the battery and tray (see Chapter 5A). It will be necessary to move the engine wiring loom to one side, and to release the air conditioning pipes from their support clips (where applicable) in order to reach all of the bolts. After removal of the through-bolt, unscrew the mounting bracket bolts and withdraw the mounting assembly

16.9 Front engine/transmission mounting through-bolt and nut (arrowed)

from the transmission and inner wing panel **(see illustration)**.

9 It is necessary to raise and support the front of the vehicle in order to remove the front and rear engine mountings. After removal of the through-bolts the brackets may be unbolted from the longitudinal crossmember or subframe **(see illustration)**. Plastic blanking plates are fitted to the longitudinal crossmember to protect the heads of the bracket bolts.

10 There are a number of different versions of the mountings used according to engine size and transmission type so, when ordering new parts, ensure that full vehicle details are provided to enable the correct component(s) to be obtained. If possible, take the old component(s) along to your Toyota dealer for positive identification.

Chapter 2 Part B:
Post-August 2000 engine in-car repair procedures

Contents

Degrees of difficulty

Easy, suitable for novice with little experience	Fairly easy, suitable for beginner with some experience	Fairly difficult, suitable for competent DIY mechanic	Difficult, suitable for experienced DIY mechanic	Very difficult, suitable for expert DIY or professional

Specifications

General

Engine type	Four-cylinder, in-line, double-overhead camshafts, 16 valve, VVT-i (Variable Valve Timing intelligent)

Engine code*:
- 1.6 litre engines 3ZZ-FE
- 1.8 litre engines 1ZZ-FE
- 2.0 litre engines 1AZ-FSE

Capacity:
- 1.6 litre engines . . . . 1598 cc
- 1.8 litre engines . . . . 1794 cc
- 2.0 litre engines . . . . 1998 cc

Bore:
- 1.6 litre engines . . . . 79.0 mm
- 1.8 litre engines . . . . 79.0 mm
- 2.0 litre engines . . . . 86.0 mm

Stroke:
- 1.6 litre engines . . . . 81.5 mm
- 1.8 litre engines . . . . 91.5 mm
- 2.0 litre engines . . . . 86.0 mm

Cylinder compression pressures:
Standard:
- 1.6 and 1.8 litre engines . . . . 15.0 bar
- 2.0 litre engines . . . . 14.6 bar
- Minimum . . . . 10.0 bar
- Maximum difference between cylinders . . . . 1.0 bar

Firing order 1–3–4–2
No 1 cylinder location . . . . Timing chain (right-hand) end of engine
Direction of crankshaft rotation . . . . Clockwise (seen from right-hand side of car)

*Note: See 'Vehicle identification' in the Reference Chapter for details of engine code location.

Valve clearances (engine cold)

	Inlet	Exhaust
1.6 and 1.8 litre engines	0.15 to 0.25 mm	0.25 to 0.35 mm
2.0 litre engines	0.19 to 0.29 mm	0.30 to 0.40 mm

Cylinder head bolt length

	Standard	Maximum
1.6 and 1.8 litre engines	156.0 to 159.0 mm	159.5 mm
2.0 litre engines	161.3 to 162.7 mm	164.2 mm

Timing chain and sprockets

Timing chain wear length limit (maximum)	122.6 mm per 16 links
Camshaft sprocket diameter – with chain (minimum)	97.3 mm
Crankshaft sprocket diameter – with chain (minimum)	51.6 mm
Timing chain tensioner slipper wear limit (maximum)	1.0 mm
Timing chain vibration damper wear limit (maximum)	1.0 mm

Camshafts

	Standard	Maximum
Camshaft endfloat:		
1.6 and 1.8 litre engines	0.040 to 0.095 mm	0.11 mm
2.0 litre engines:		
Inlet camshaft	0.040 to 0.095 mm	0.11 mm
Exhaust camshaft	0.080 to 0.135 mm	0.15 mm

Lubrication system

Oil pump type:	
1.6 and 1.8 litre engines	Bi-rotor, driven directly from front of crankshaft
2.0 litre engines	Bi-rotor, chain driven from front of crankshaft
System pressure – at normal operating temperature:	
1.6 and 1.8 litre engines:	
At idle speed	0.3 bar (minimum)
At 3000 rpm	2.9 to 5.4 bar
2.0 litre engines:	
At idle speed	0.3 bar (minimum)
At 3000 rpm	2.5 to 5.4 bar

Oil pump clearances:	Standard	Maximum
1.6 and 1.8 litre engines:		
Outer rotor-to-pump body clearance	0.260 to 0.325 mm	0.325 mm
Rotor side clearance (endfloat)	0.025 to 0.071 mm	0.071 mm
Inner rotor-to-outer rotor tip clearance	0.040 to 0.160 mm	0.160 mm
2.0 litre engines:		
Outer rotor-to-pump body clearance	0.100 to 0.170 mm	0.325 mm
Rotor side clearance (endfloat)	0.030 to 0.085 mm	0.160 mm
Inner rotor-to-outer rotor tip clearance	0.080 to 0.160 mm	0.350 mm

Oil pump drive chain and sprockets (2.0 litre engines):	
Maximum chain wear length	52.4 mm per 8 links
Sprocket minimum diameter – with chain	48.2 mm
Maximum chain tensioner plate wear	0.5 mm

Torque wrench settings

1.6 and 1.8 litre engines	Nm	lbf ft
Auxiliary drivebelt tensioner:		
Mounting bolt	69	51
Mounting nut	29	21
Big-end bearing cap bolts*:		
Stage 1	20	15
Stage 2	Angle-tighten a further 90°	
Camshaft bearing cap bolts:		
No 1 cap	23	17
All other caps	13	10
Camshaft cover nuts/bolts:		
Bolts with washers	9	7
Nuts/bolts without washers	11	8
Camshaft sprocket bolts	54	40
Coolant pump	10	7
Crankshaft pulley bolt	138	102
Cylinder head bolts:		
Stage 1	49	36
Stage 2	Angle-tighten a further 90°	
Driveplate bolts (automatic transmission)	88	65
Engine/transmission mountings:		
Front mounting bracket through-bolt	87	64
Front mounting to crossmember	72	53
Left-hand mounting bracket through-bolt	87	64
Left-hand mounting bracket to transmission	52	38
Rear mounting bracket through-bolt	87	64
Rear mounting bracket to subframe	72	53
Rear mounting bracket to transmission	64	47
Right-hand mounting bracket to cylinder head	47	35

Torque wrench settings (continued)

	Nm	lbf ft

1.6 and 1.8 litre engines (continued)

	Nm	lbf ft
Engine-to-transmission lower attachment bolts	23	17
Engine-to-transmission upper attachment bolts	64	47
Engine/transmission longitudinal crossmember bolts	73	54
Flywheel bolts (manual transmission):		
Stage 1	49	36
Stage 2	Angle-tighten a further 90°	
Main bearing ladder bolts:		
12-point head bolts*:		
Stage 1	22	16
Stage 2	44	32
Stage 3	Angle-tighten a further 45°	
Stage 4	Angle-tighten a further 45°	
Hexagon head bolts	19	14
Oil filter union to main bearing ladder	30	22
Oil pick-up tube nuts/bolt	9	7
Oil pressure relief valve	37	27
Oil pump cover plate	10	7
Oil pump mounting bolts	9	7
Sump bolts/nuts.	9	7
Timing chain cover:		
10 mm head bolts/nut	13	10
12 mm head bolts.	19	14
Timing chain tensioner housing nuts	10	7
Timing chain tensioner nuts	9	7
Timing chain tensioner slipper bolt	19	14
Timing chain vibration damper bolts	9	7
VVT-i oil control valve bolt	9	7

2.0 litre engines

	Nm	lbf ft
Auxiliary drivebelt tensioner mounting nut/bolt	60	44
Auxiliary drivebelt tensioner stud bolt	9	7
Big-end bearing cap bolts*:		
Stage 1	25	18
Stage 2	Angle-tighten a further 90°	
Camshaft bearing cap bolts:		
No 1 caps.	30	22
All other caps	9	7
Camshaft cover nuts/bolts (see text Section 4):		
Bolts A	11	8
Bolts B	21	15
Bolts C	14	10
Nuts	11	8
Camshaft sprocket bolts	54	40
Crankshaft pulley bolt	170	125
Cylinder head bolts:		
Stage 1	79	58
Stage 2	Angle-tighten a further 90°	
Driveplate bolts (automatic transmission)	83	61
Engine-to-transmission lower attachment bolts	23	17
Engine-to-transmission reinforcing plate bolts:		
M8 bolts	21	15
M10 bolts	44	32
Nuts	44	32
Engine-to-transmission upper attachment bolts	64	47
Engine/transmission longitudinal crossmember bolts	73	54
Engine/transmission mountings:		
Front mounting bracket through-bolt.	87	64
Front mounting to crossmember	72	53
Left-hand mounting bracket through-bolt	87	64
Left-hand mounting bracket to transmission	52	38
Rear mounting bracket through-bolt	87	64
Rear mounting bracket to subframe.	72	53
Rear mounting bracket to transmission	64	47
Flywheel bolts (manual transmission).	130	96
Lower crankcase to cylinder block.	33	24

Torque wrench settings (continued)

	Nm	lbf ft
2.0 litre engines (continued)		
Main bearing cap bolts*:		
Stage 1	20	15
Stage 2	40	30
Stage 3	Angle-tighten a further 90°	
Oil cooler retaining nut	9	7
Oil filter mounting stud	79	58
Oil pressure relief valve	49	36
Oil pump chain tensioner	12	9
Oil pump cover plate	9	7
Oil pump mounting bolts	19	14
Oil pump sprocket nut	30	22
Sump bolts/nuts	9	7
Timing chain cover:		
10 mm head bolts/nut	9	7
12 mm head bolts	21	15
14 mm head bolts	43	32
Timing chain guide bolt	9	7
Timing chain tensioner housing nuts	10	7
Timing chain tensioner nuts	9	7
Timing chain tensioner slipper bolt	19	14
Timing chain vibration damper bolts	9	7
VVT-i oil control valve bolt	9	7

New bolts must be used

1 General information

How to use this Chapter

Chapter 2 is divided into three Parts; A, B and C. Repair operations that can be carried out with the engine in the vehicle are described in Parts A and B. Part C covers the removal of the engine/transmission as a unit, and describes the engine dismantling and overhaul procedures.

In Parts A and B, the assumption is made that the engine is installed in the vehicle, with all ancillaries connected. If the engine has been removed for overhaul, the preliminary dismantling information which precedes each operation may be ignored.

Engine description

The engines are twin overhead camshaft, water-cooled, four cylinder in-line units with Toyota's VVT-i variable valve timing system. The 1.6 and 1.8 litre engines are virtually identical, whereas the 2.0 litre is similar in most respects but with significant differences in the cylinder block area. All the engines are mounted transversely at the front of the car, together with the transmission to form a combined power unit.

The crankshaft is supported by five shell-type main bearings retained by traditional bearing caps on 2.0 litre engines, whilst the 1.6 and 1.8 litre engines are fitted with a cast main bearing 'ladder' fitted between the cylinder block and the oil sump. The connecting rod big-end bearings are also split shell-type and are attached to the pistons by fully-floating gudgeon pins. Each piston is fitted with two compression rings and one oil control ring.

Drive for the overhead camshafts is provided by a spring-tensioned timing chain. The valves are operated by 'solid' followers which are directly operated by the cam lobes; no adjustment shims are fitted, so the valve clearances are determined by the thickness of the followers themselves. This reduces the weight of the valve components and gives a virtually maintenance-free valve setup. The valves are each closed by a single valve spring and operate in guides integral in the aluminium alloy cylinder head.

The variable valve timing system allows the inlet camshaft timing to be varied under the control of the engine management system, to boost both low-speed torque and top-end power, as well as reducing exhaust emissions. The cylindrical VVT-i controller is fitted directly to the end of the inlet camshaft, and is supplied with two pressurised oil feeds through passages in the camshaft itself. An oil control valve, operated by the engine management system, is fitted to the cylinder head, and this is used to supply the pressurised oil to the controller through the two oil feeds. The controller contains four vane chambers – depending on which of the two oil feeds is enabled by the control valve, the oil pressure will turn the inlet camshaft clockwise (advance) or anti-clockwise (retard) to adjust the valve timing as required. If pressure is removed from both feeds, this induces a timing 'hold' condition. Thus the inlet valve timing is infinitely variable within a given range.

A rotor-type oil pump is used on all engines. On 1.6 and 1.8 litre engines, the pump is fitted directly over the end of, and driven directly by, the crankshaft. On 2.0 litre engines the pump is driven by the crankshaft via a separate chain.

Operations with engine in car

The following work can be carried out with the engine in the car:

a) Valve clearance adjustment.
b) Removal and refitting of the timing chain, sprockets and tensioner.
c) Removal and refitting of the camshafts and followers.
d) Removal and refitting of the cylinder head.
e) Removal and refitting of the sump.
f) Removal and refitting of the oil pump.
g) Removal and refitting of the flywheel/driveplate.
h) Renewal of the crankshaft oil seals.
i) Renewal of the engine mountings.

Note: *It is possible to remove the pistons and connecting rods (after removing the cylinder head and sump) without removing the engine, although this is not recommended. Work of this nature is more easily and thoroughly completed with the engine on the bench, as described in Chapter 2C.*

2 Compression test

1 When engine performance is down, or if misfiring occurs which cannot be attributed to the ignition or fuel systems, a compression test can provide diagnostic clues as to the engine's condition. If the test is performed regularly, it can give warning of trouble before any other symptoms become apparent.

2 The engine must be fully warmed-up to normal operating temperature and the battery must be fully-charged. The aid of an assistant will also be required.

3.3 Align the crankshaft pulley notch (arrowed) with the 0 (zero) on the timing cover

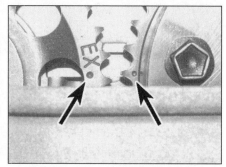

3.5a On 1.6 and 1.8 litre engines, the marks on the camshaft sprockets (arrowed) should be aligned with the top edge of the cylinder head

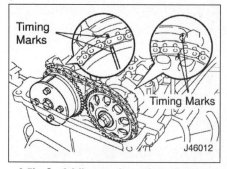

3.5b On 2.0 litre engines, the reference marks on the camshaft sprockets should be aligned with the corresponding marks on the adjacent bearing caps

3 Remove the ignition coils as described in Chapter 5B, then remove the spark plugs as described in Chapter 1.

4 Fit a compression tester to the No 1 cylinder spark plug hole – the type of tester which screws into the plug thread is to be preferred.

5 Have the assistant hold the throttle wide open, and crank the engine on the starter motor; after one or two revolutions, the compression pressure should build-up to a maximum figure, and then stabilise. Record the highest reading obtained.

6 Repeat the test on the remaining cylinders, recording the pressure in each.

7 All cylinders should produce very similar pressures; any difference greater than that specified indicates the existence of a fault. Note that the compression should build-up quickly in a healthy engine; low compression on the first stroke, followed by gradually increasing pressure on successive strokes, indicates worn piston rings. A low compression reading on the first stroke, which does not build-up during successive strokes, indicates leaking valves or a blown head gasket (a cracked head could also be the cause).

8 If the pressure in any cylinder is reduced to the specified minimum or less, carry out the following test to isolate the cause. Introduce 5 ml of clean oil into that cylinder through its spark plug hole and repeat the test.

9 If the addition of oil temporarily improves the compression pressure, this indicates that bore or piston wear is responsible for the pressure loss. No improvement suggests that leaking or burnt valves, or a blown head gasket, may be to blame.

10 A low reading from two adjacent cylinders is almost certainly due to the head gasket having blown between them. Renew the head gasket if this is the case.

11 If one cylinder is about 20 percent lower than the others and the engine has a slightly rough idle, a worn camshaft lobe could be the cause.

12 On completion of the test, refit the spark plugs (Chapter 1), and the ignition coils (Chapter 5B).

3 Top dead centre (TDC) for No 1 piston – locating

1 Disconnect the battery negative terminal (refer to *Disconnecting the battery* in the Reference Chapter).

2 Remove the camshaft cover as described in Section 4.

3 The timing marks are marked on the timing chain cover at intervals of 5°, and the crankshaft pulley rim incorporates a notch for alignment with the timing marks. The 0° mark indicates TDC (top dead centre), and when the notch is aligned with this mark, the pistons in cylinders 1 and 4 are at TDC **(see illustration)**.

4 Using a spanner (or socket and extension bar) applied to the crankshaft pulley bolt, rotate the crankshaft clockwise until the notch on the crankshaft pulley rim is aligned with the 0° mark on the timing chain cover. Note that it will be necessary to remove the undershield from beneath the engine for access to the crankshaft pulley. Remove all four spark plugs; this will make the engine easier to turn; refer to Chapter 1 for details.

5 Look at the camshaft lobes for No 1 cylinder. Both the inlet and exhaust camshaft lobes should be pointing away from the camshaft followers. If they are not, use the socket/spanner to rotate the crankshaft one complete revolution (360°) – now the lobes should be pointing away from the followers.

Additionally, on 1.6 and 1.8 litre engines, the reference marks on the inlet and exhaust camshaft sprockets should be aligned with the top of the cylinder head. On 2.0 litre engines, the reference marks on the inlet and exhaust camshaft sprockets should be aligned with the corresponding marks on the adjacent camshaft bearing caps **(see illustrations)**.

6 After the number one piston has been positioned at TDC on the compression stroke, TDC for any of the remaining pistons can be located by turning the crankshaft 180° and following the firing order.

4 Camshaft cover – removal and refitting

1.6 and 1.8 litre engines

Removal

1 Undo the two nuts, prise out the two plastic fasteners, and remove the plastic cover over the engine **(see illustrations)**.

2 Disconnect the two crankcase ventilation hoses from the camshaft cover.

3 Remove the ignition coils as described in Chapter 5B.

4 Working progressively around the camshaft cover, undo the six small bolts, the single stud bolt and the two nuts from the periphery, and the two longer bolts, with their seals, from the centre of the cover. Note the location of the

4.1a Undo the nuts then prise out the plastic fasteners . . .

4.1b . . . and lift off the plastic engine cover

4.5 Move the wiring harness clear, and lift off the camshaft cover and gasket

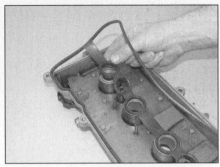

4.6 Ensure the camshaft cover gasket is pressed fully into the cover grooves

4.12 Undo the bolt (arrowed) and move the wiring harness clear of the camshaft cover – 2.0 litre engines

4.14 Undo the retaining bolt and move the vacuum solenoid valve clear of the camshaft cover – 2.0 litre engines

wiring harness support bracket which is also retained by one of the nuts.

5 Move the wiring harness clear, and lift the camshaft cover and gasket off the cylinder head **(see illustration)**. If the cover is stuck to the cylinder head, try to slip a flexible putty knife between the camshaft cover and cylinder head to break the seal.

Caution: Don't lever at the camshaft cover-to-cylinder head joint or damage to the sealing surfaces may occur, leading to oil leaks after the cover is refitted.

Refitting

6 Ensure that the mating surfaces of the camshaft cover and cylinder head are clean and dry prior to refitting the cover. The rubber sealing gasket can be re-used unless it has seen high mileage and the rubber has hardened or cracked. If so, pull out the rubber seal and thoroughly clean the contact surface in the camshaft cover. Install a new rubber seal, pressing it evenly into the groove around the underside of the cover **(see illustration)**.

7 Apply sealant (Toyota No 08826-00080 or equivalent) to the area where the timing chain cover abuts the cylinder head.

8 Refit the camshaft cover and tighten the nuts/bolts evenly and progressively to the specified torque.

9 Refit the ignition coils as described in Chapter 5B.

10 Reconnect the two crankshaft ventilation hoses to the camshaft cover, then start the engine and check for oil leaks. On completion, refit the plastic engine cover.

2.0 litre engines

Removal

11 Undo the four nuts and remove the plastic cover over the engine.

12 Undo the bolt securing the wiring harness support bracket to the right-hand end of the camshaft cover and move the harness clear of the cover **(see illustration)**.

13 Remove the high-pressure fuel pump as described in Chapter 4A.

14 Undo the bolt securing the vacuum solenoid valve to the inlet manifold **(see illustration)**. Position the solenoid valve clear of the camshaft cover.

15 Disconnect the crankshaft ventilation hoses from the camshaft cover.

16 Remove the ignition coils as described in Chapter 5B.

17 Working progressively around the camshaft

5.4 Checking the valve clearances with a feeler blade

cover, undo the nine bolts and two nuts securing the cover to the cylinder head, noting the location of the wiring harness support brackets, then lift off the cover and gasket. If the cover is stuck to the cylinder head, try to slip a flexible putty knife between the camshaft cover and cylinder head to break the seal.

Caution: Don't lever at the camshaft cover-to-cylinder head joint or damage to the sealing surfaces may occur, leading to oil leaks after the cover is refitted.

Refitting

18 Ensure that the mating surfaces of the camshaft cover and cylinder head are clean and dry prior to refitting the cover. The rubber sealing gasket can be re-used unless it has seen high mileage and the rubber has hardened or cracked. If so, pull out the rubber seal and thoroughly clean the contact surface in the camshaft cover. Install a new rubber seal, pressing it evenly into the groove around the underside of the cover **(see illustration 4.6)**.

19 Apply sealant (Toyota No 08826-00080 or equivalent) to the area where the timing chain cover abuts the cylinder head.

20 Refit the camshaft cover and tighten the nuts/bolts evenly and progressively to the specified torque. Bolt identification for torque wrench setting purposes is as follows:

Bolts A: 10 mm head bolts around the periphery of the cover.
Bolts B: 12 mm head bolts, either side of the high-pressure fuel pump mounting.
Bolts C: 10 mm head bolts in the centre of the cover.

21 Refit the ignition coils as described in Chapter 5B.

22 Reconnect the two crankshaft ventilation hoses.

23 Refit the vacuum solenoid valve to the inlet manifold and securely tighten the retaining bolt.

24 Refit the high-pressure fuel pump as described in Chapter 4A.

25 Secure the wiring harness support bracket to the cylinder head cover.

26 Start the engine and check for oil leaks. On completion, refit the plastic engine cover.

5 Valve clearance check and adjustment

1 The valve clearances must be checked and adjusted with the engine cold.

2 Remove the camshaft cover as described in Section 4.

3 Set No 1 piston at TDC on compression as described in Section 3.

4 Using feeler gauges, measure the clearance between the camshaft lobes and the cam followers of the inlet valves for cylinders 1 and 2, and the exhaust valves for cylinders 1 and 3. No 1 cylinder is at the timing chain end of the engine. Record the measurements obtained **(see illustration)**.

5 Turn the crankshaft one complete revolution (360°).

6 Using feeler gauges, measure the clearance between the camshaft lobes and the cam followers of the inlet valves for cylinders 3 and 4, and the exhaust valves for cylinders 2 and 4. Record the measurements obtained.

7 Compare the measurements obtained with those given in the Specifications. If any clearance is outside the specified range, remove the camshafts as described in Section 8.

8 With the camshafts removed, use a magnet to lift the relevant cam follower(s) from their location, then measure and record the thickness of the follower using a micrometer **(see illustration)**.

9 Determine the required thickness of the new follower using the following formula:

A = Measured valve clearance.
N = Thickness of new follower.
T = Thickness of the used follower.

1.6 and 1.8 litre engines
Inlet valves: $N = T + (A - 0.20 \text{ mm})$.
Exhaust valves: $N = T + (A - 0.30 \text{ mm})$.

2.0 litre engines
Inlet valves: $N = T + (A - 0.24 \text{ mm})$.
Exhaust valves: $N = T + (A - 0.35 \text{ mm})$.

10 Select a follower with a thickness as close as possible to the valve clearance calculated. Followers, which are available in 35 sizes in increments of 0.020 mm, range in size from 5.060 mm to 5.740 mm.

11 With all the followers in their correct locations, refit the camshafts as described in Section 8. Before refitting the camshaft cover, recheck the valve clearances as previously described, and, if necessary, remove the camshafts again and change followers as necessary.

---

6 Timing chain and sprockets
– removal, inspection
and refitting

Note: The photographs in this Section depict the timing chain and sprocket arrangement on 1.6 and 1.8 litre engines, with the inlet camshaft on the right and the exhaust camshaft on the left (when viewed from the timing chain end of the engine). On 2.0 litre engines, the camshaft positions are reversed and the inlet camshaft is on the left.

Removal

1 Disconnect the battery negative terminal (refer to Disconnecting the battery in the Reference Chapter).

2 Firmly apply the handbrake, then jack up the front of the car and support it securely on axle stands (see Jacking and vehicle support). Remove the right-hand roadwheel, then unbolt and remove the undershield from under the right-hand side of the engine compartment.

3 On 1.6 and 1.8 litre engines, drain the cooling system as described in Chapter 1.

5.8 Measure and record the thickness of the cam followers using a micrometer

4 Remove the auxiliary drivebelt as described in Chapter 1.

5 Remove the alternator as described in Chapter 5A.

6 Refer to Chapter 10 and unbolt the power steering pump. There is no need to disconnect the fluid pipes from the pump, suspend it from a suitable place on the bulkhead using cable ties/wire.

7 Remove the camshaft cover as described in Section 4.

8 Set No 1 piston at TDC on compression as described in Section 3.

9 The crankshaft must now be held stationary while the crankshaft pulley bolt is loosened. Toyota technicians use a special tool bolted to the crankshaft pulley to hold the crankshaft, and a similar tool can be fabricated out of flat metal bar. Alternatively, on manual transmission models, have an assistant

6.11 Undo the nut and bolt (arrowed) and remove the auxiliary belt tensioner assembly

6.15 Undo the two nuts and remove the chain tensioner assembly from the rear of the engine

engage top gear and depress the brake pedal. On automatic transmission models, remove the starter motor (Chapter 5A) and use a wide-bladed screwdriver engaged with the starter ring gear to hold the crankshaft stationary.

10 Unscrew the crankshaft pulley bolt and slide the pulley off of the end of the crankshaft. If it is tight, use a suitable puller to remove it

11 Undo the bolt/nut and remove the auxiliary drivebelt tensioner assembly **(see illustration)**.

12 On 2.0 litre engines, remove the sump as described in Section 10.

13 The engine must now be supported to enable the right-hand engine/transmission mounting to be removed. On 1.6 and 1.8 litre engines, the engine can be supported from above using either a suitable hoist or an engine support bar, or from below under the sump, using a jack with interposed block of wood. On 2.0 litre engines, it will be necessary to support the engine from above using a hoist or support bar.

14 With the engine securely supported, remove the right-hand engine/transmission mounting as described in Section 15. Additionally, on 1.6 and 1.8 litre engines, undo the three bolts and remove the engine mounting bracket from the timing cover **(see illustration)**.

15 Undo the two nuts and remove the chain tensioner assembly **(see illustration)**. On 2.0 litre engines, recover the gasket.

16 On 1.6 and 1.8 litre engines, undo the 6 bolts and remove the coolant pump **(see illustration)**.

6.14 Undo the bolts (arrowed) and remove the engine mounting bracket from the timing cover – 1.6 and 1.8 litre engines

6.16 Undo the 6 bolts (arrowed) and remove the coolant pump – 1.6 and 1.8 litre engines

6.19 Carefully prise the timing cover free, then remove the cover from the cylinder block and head

6.20 Withdraw the crankshaft angle sensor plate from the crankshaft

6.21 Undo the pivot bolt and remove the chain tensioner slipper

Discard the coolant pump O-ring seal, a new one must be fitted.

17 Undo the bolt and remove the crankshaft position sensor from the timing cover, then undo the bolt securing the wiring harness bracket clip and move the sensor to one side.

18 Undo the bolts/nuts securing the timing cover to the engine, then use a Torx socket to remove the auxiliary drivebelt tensioner mounting stud and the additional timing cover mounting stud. Note the locations of the various size bolts to aid refitting.

19 Use a flat-bladed screwdriver to carefully prise the timing cover free, then remove the cover from the cylinder block and head **(see illustration)**. Take great care not to damage the sealing surfaces.

20 Note which way round it's fitted, then withdraw the crankshaft angle sensor plate from the crankshaft **(see illustration)**.

21 Undo the pivot bolt at the base of the

chain tensioner slipper and remove the slipper **(see illustration)**.

22 On 2.0 litre engines, undo the retaining bolt and remove the timing chain guide located below the crankshaft sprocket.

23 Slide the sprocket (with the chain still fitted) from the crankshaft **(see illustration)**. If it's tight, use two flat-bladed screwdrivers to ease the sprocket free, then lift the chain from the camshaft sprockets.

24 Undo the bolts and remove the timing chain vibration damper **(see illustration)**.

25 Undo the centre bolt and remove the inlet camshaft sprocket. Use a spanner on the hexagonal section of the camshaft to prevent it from rotating **(see illustration)**. Repeat this procedure on the exhaust camshaft sprocket. **Note:** *The inlet sprocket with the VVT-i mechanism will be locked in the 'retarded' position.*

Inspection

26 Pull the timing chain taut by hand, and measure the length of 16 pins **(see illustration)**. Repeat this procedure at 3 or more sections of the chain. If any of the measurements obtained exceed the dimension given in the Specifications, the chain must be renewed.

27 Wrap the chain around the crankshaft sprocket and use a pair of vernier calipers to measure the diameter of the assembly **(see illustration)**. If the measurement obtained is less than that given in the Specifications, renew the chain and *all* the sprockets. Repeat this procedure on both camshaft sprockets.

28 Check the condition of the timing chain vibration damper and tensioner slipper. There should be no sign of cracking or damage. As the chain runs along the damper/slipper it will create two grooves along the damper/slipper length. The maximum depth of these grooves is 1.0 mm. If their depth exceeds this, renew the damper/slipper.

29 Using a small screwdriver, depress the top of the locking pawl on the tensioner assembly to disengage the pawl from the plunger, and check that the plunger moves smoothly in and out of the housing **(see illustration)**. Release the pawl and check that the plunger cannot be pushed into the housing with your finger.

Refitting

30 Align the locating hole on the VVT-i unit/sprocket with the locating pin on the inlet camshaft, then hold the camshaft in position with a spanner on the hexagonal section, and

6.23 Slide the sprocket and chain from the crankshaft

6.24 Undo the bolts and remove the chain vibration damper

6.25 With a spanner on the hexagonal section of the camshaft, slacken the sprocket retaining bolt

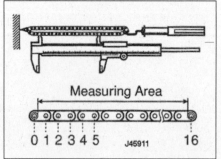

Measuring Area

0 1 2 3 4 5   16   J45911

6.26 Pull the chain taut, and measure the length over 16 pins as shown

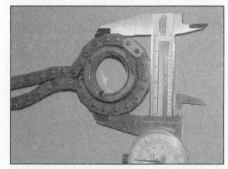

6.27 Wrap the chain around the sprocket and measure the diameter

attempt to rotate the sprocket anti-clockwise whilst gently pushing it against the camshaft. This is to ensure it's locked in the 'retarded' position. If the VVT-i unit is already in the 'retarded' position (as it should be) the sprocket will not move. If it's not, the sprocket will rotate anti-clockwise slightly until the locating pin on the end of the camshaft aligns with a further locating slot inside the VVT-i assembly **(see illustration)**. Fit the sprocket retaining bolt and tighten it to the specified torque, using a spanner on the hexagonal section of the camshaft to prevent it from rotating.

31 Align the locating hole in the exhaust sprocket with the locating pin on the exhaust camshaft, then fit the bolt and tighten it to the specified torque, using a spanner on the camshaft hexagonal section to prevent it from rotating. Note that the sprocket must be fitted with timing mark facing outwards **(see illustrations)**.

32 On 1.6 and 1.8 litre engines, check that the reference marks on the inlet and exhaust camshaft sprockets are aligned with the top of the cylinder head **(see illustration 3.5a)**. On 2.0 litre engines, the reference marks on the inlet and exhaust camshaft sprockets should be aligned with the corresponding marks on the adjacent camshaft bearing caps **(see illustration 3.5b)**. If necessary, using a spanner on the hexagonal section, rotate the camshaft(s) slightly to bring them into alignment.

33 Check that the locating key in the end of the crankshaft is in the 12 o'clock position (upright). If necessary, temporarily insert the

6.29 Press in the top of the locking pawl and check the plunger moves freely

crankshaft pulley bolt and turn the crankshaft slightly to this position **(see illustration)**.

34 Refit the timing chain vibration damper and tighten the bolts to the specified torque.

35 There are three yellow-coloured links on the timing chain (or two yellow coloured links and one orange or blue link on 2.0 litre engines) – two close together that correspond with the camshaft sprockets, and one which corresponds with the crankshaft sprocket. Engage the crankshaft sprocket with the timing chain, aligning the mark on the sprocket with the coloured link, then slide the sprocket over the end of the crankshaft, ensuring the locating key in the crankshaft aligns with the corresponding slot in the sprocket **(see illustration)**. If necessary, using a tubular spacer (or deep socket) and a hammer, tap the sprocket fully into position.

36 Engage the timing chain with the camshaft sprockets, ensuring the yellow-coloured links

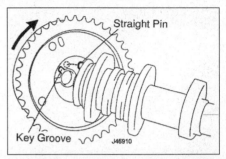
6.30 Align the pin on the camshaft with the locating hole in the VVT-i unit, and attempt to rotate the unit anti-clockwise. If the unit is not locked in the 'retarded' position, it will rotate slightly until the pin aligns with the key groove

align with the marks on the sprockets **(see illustration)**.

37 On 2.0 litre engines, refit the timing chain guide below the crankshaft sprocket and securely tighten the retaining bolt.

38 Place the chain tensioner slipper in position and refit the pivot bolt. Check that the slipper locates against the stopper projection on the cylinder head or cylinder block, then tighten the pivot bolt to the specified torque **(see illustrations)**.

39 Refit the crankshaft angle sensor plate with the F mark facing outwards **(see illustration)**.

40 Thoroughly clean the timing chain cover and engine block/cylinder gasket surfaces, removing all traces of the old sealant. Take the opportunity to renew the crankshaft oil seal in the timing chain cover as described in Section 12.

6.31a Fit the exhaust camshaft sprocket with the timing marks facing outwards ...

6.31b ... then tighten the bolt whilst holding the camshaft with a spanner at its hexagonal section

6.33 Set the crankshaft key in the 12 o'clock position (the key aligns with the mark on the oil pump body – arrowed)

6.35 Align the coloured link of the timing chain with the mark on the crankshaft sprocket (arrowed)

6.36 Align the marks on the sprockets (arrowed) with the yellow links on the timing chain

6.38a Place the chain tensioner slipper in position and refit the pivot bolt

6.38b Check that the slipper locates against the stopper projection (arrowed)

6.39 Fit the crankshaft angle sensor plate with the F mark (arrowed) facing outwards

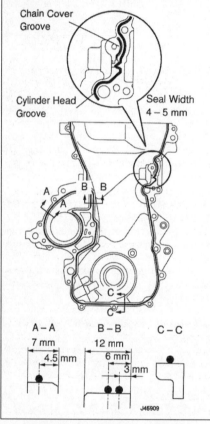

6.41a Timing chain cover sealant application details – 1.6 and 1.8 litre engines

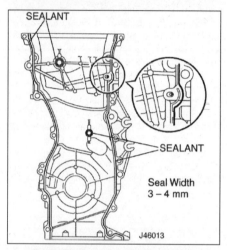

6.41b Timing chain cover sealant application details – 2.0 litre engines

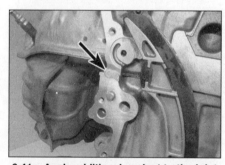

6.41c Apply additional sealant to the joint between the cylinder head and cylinder block (arrowed)

41 Apply a thin bead of sealant (Toyota No 08826-00080 or equivalent) to the timing cover gasket surfaces as shown, and also to the joint between the cylinder head and cylinder block. Fit the timing chain cover, and progressively and evenly tighten the bolts/nuts to the specified torques **(see illustrations)**. Note that the cover must be fitted within three minutes of the sealant being applied, otherwise the sealant must be completely removed and reapplied.

42 On 1.6 and 1.8 litre engines, fit a new O-ring seal to the coolant pump, then refit the pump and the engine mounting bracket. Tighten the bolts to the specified torque.

43 Refit the auxiliary drivebelt tensioner mounting stud to the timing cover, then refit the auxiliary drivebelt tensioner assembly. Tighten the retaining nut and bolt to the specified torque.

44 Refit the crankshaft pulley and tighten the retaining bolt to the specified torque. Prevent the crankshaft from rotating using the same method employed during removal.

45 On 2.0 litre engines, locate a new gasket over the timing chain tensioner mounting studs, with the projection on the gasket towards the flywheel/driveplate end of the engine.

46 Press in the top of the locking pawl to disengage it from the chain tensioner plunger, then use a finger to press the plunger fully into the tensioner housing. Retain the plunger in place with the hook on the side of the housing **(see illustrations)**.

47 Check the condition of the tensioner housing O-ring seal (1.6 and 1.8 litre engines) and renew if necessary. Fit the housing to the timing chain cover, taking care not to disturb the plunger hook. If the hook is disturbed and the plunger released, remove the housing and reset the plunger as previously described. Tighten the housing retaining bolts to the specified torque.

48 Rotate the crankshaft anti-clockwise a few degrees to release the hook retaining the tensioner plunger, then rotate it clockwise and check that the tensioner slipper is pushed against the chain by the plunger. If it isn't, use your finger or a screwdriver to push the slipper against the tensioner plunger and release the hook **(see illustration)**.

6.46a Disengage the locking pawl and press in the plunger . . .

6.46b . . . then retain it with the hook

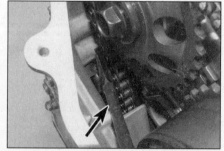

6.48 If necessary, use a screwdriver (arrowed) to push the chain against the slipper to release the tensioner plunger

49 Turn the crankshaft clockwise until the notch in the crankshaft pulley is aligned with the 0 (TDC) mark on the timing cover, and check that the marks on the camshaft sprockets align with the top of the cylinder head **(see illustrations 3.5a and 3.5b)**.

50 Refit the right-hand engine mounting as described in Section 15.

51 Refit the crankshaft position sensor and wiring harness clip to the timing cover, tightening the retaining bolts securely.

52 Refit the camshaft cover as described in Section 4.

53 On 2.0 litre engines, refit the sump as described in Section 10.

54 Refit the power steering pump and alternator as described in Chapters 10 and 5A respectively.

55 With reference to Chapter 1, refit the auxiliary drivebelt, refill the cooling system (1.6 and 1.8 litre engines), then top-up/refill the engine oil.

56 Refit the undershield and right-hand roadwheel, then lower the car to the ground. Reconnect the battery, then start the engine and check for oil/coolant leaks.

7.3 Undo the bolt and withdrawn the oil control valve from the cylinder head

7.6a Undo the oil control valve filter plug . . .

---

7 VVT-i (Variable Valve Timing) components – removal and refitting

Camshaft VVT-i unit

1 The VVT-i unit is integral with the inlet camshaft sprocket. Removal and refitting procedures are contained in Section 6 – no dismantling is recommended.

Oil control valve

2 Unplug the wiring connector from the oil control valve. The valve is located at the timing chain end of the cylinder head, on the inlet camshaft side.

3 Undo the bolt and withdraw the valve from the cylinder head **(see illustration)**. Be prepared for oil spillage.

4 Check the condition of the O-ring seal on the valve and renew if necessary.

5 Insert the valve into the cylinder head and tighten the retaining bolt to the specified torque. Reconnect the wiring plug.

Oil control valve filter

6 The filter is located at the timing chain end of the cylinder head, on the inlet camshaft side. Undo the plug and pull the filter from the plug **(see illustrations)**.

7 Clean the filter and ensure it's free from debris and damage.

8 Insert the filter into the cylinder head.

9 Check the condition of the plug sealing washer and renew if necessary. Refit the plug and tighten it securely.

8 Camshafts and followers – removal, inspection and refitting

Removal

1 Remove the timing chain as described in Section 6. There is no need to remove the camshaft sprockets unless you are renewing the camshafts.

2 Rotate the crankshaft 90° anti-clockwise to eliminate any possibility of accidental valve-to-piston contact during the camshaft removal procedure.

3 Working from the ends of the camshafts towards the centre, gradually and evenly slacken and remove the retaining bolts from camshaft bearing caps, then lift off the caps **(see illustration)**. On 2.0 litre engines, collect the upper bearing shell from the inlet camshaft No 1 bearing cap.

Caution: As the centre bearing cap bolts are being slackened, make sure the camshafts move up evenly. If one end or the other

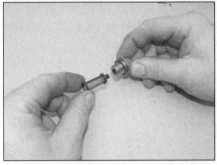

7.6b . . . then pull the filter from the plug

stops moving and the camshaft jams, start over by refitting the bearing caps. DO NOT try to lever or force the camshafts out.

4 Lift the camshaft straight up and out of the cylinder head **(see illustration)**. On 2.0 litre engines, collect the lower bearing shell from the inlet camshaft No 1 bearing in the cylinder head. Suitably mark the back of the shell to identify its fitted direction.

5 Clean the oil off the camshaft followers, mark them with a felt-tip marker and remove them. Store the camshaft followers and bearing caps in a suitably-marked compartmented box or similar so they can be reinstalled in their original locations **(see illustrations)**.

Inspection

6 Visually examine the cam followers, shims, cam lobes and bearing journals for scuffing, score marks, pitting and evidence of overheating (blue, discoloured areas). Look for

8.3 Lift off the camshaft bearing caps . . .

8.4 . . . then lift the camshaft straight up and out of the cylinder head

8.5a Lift out the camshaft followers . . .

8.5b . . . and store them in a suitably-marked compartmented box

flaking away of the hardened surface layer of each cam lobe. On 2.0 litre engines, similarly inspect the condition of the inlet camshaft bearing shells.

7 If in any doubt as to the condition of the camshafts and associated components, have them examined and measured by an engine reconditioning specialist, and obtain new components as necessary.

Refitting

8 Lubricate the exhaust camshaft followers with clean engine oil, then install them in their original locations. Repeat this procedure for the inlet camshaft followers.

9 On 2.0 litre engines, place the inlet camshaft lower bearing shell in position in the cylinder head, and place the upper bearing shell in No 1 bearing cap, ensuring that the tab on the shell engages with the notch in the cap.

10 Lubricate the inlet and exhaust camshaft lobes and bearing journals with clean engine oil.

11 On 1.6 and 1.8 litre engines, position both camshafts with the lobes for No 1 cylinder pointing upwards, away from the followers, and lay them in place in the cylinder head **(see illustration)**.

12 On 2.0 litre engines, position the inlet camshaft with the lobes for No 2 cylinder pointing upwards, away from the followers, and position the exhaust camshaft with the lobes for No 3 cylinder pointing upwards, away from the followers. Lay the camshafts in place in the cylinder head.

13 Refit the camshaft bearing caps to their original positions, with the arrow on each cap

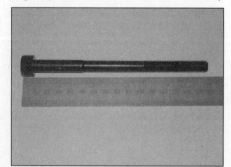

9.11 Measure the overall length of the cylinder head bolts

8.11 Position the No 1 cylinder camshaft lobes away from the followers – 1.6 and 1.8 litre engines

facing the timing chain end of the engine. Note that the exhaust bearing caps are marked E and the inlet caps are marked I, as well as being numbered 2 to 5 from the timing chain end **(see illustration)**. On 1.6 and 1.8 litre engines, No 1 bearing cap is the 'double' cap fitted adjacent to the timing chain. On 2.0 litre engines No 1 inlet bearing cap contains the bearing shell and No 1 exhaust bearing cap is plain.

14 Apply a little clean engine oil to the threads and underside of the heads, then install the retaining bolts and tighten them gradually and evenly to the specified torque, working from the centre of the camshafts outwards.

15 Align the camshaft sprocket timing marks **(see illustrations 3.5a and 3.5b)**, then rotate the crankshaft 90° clockwise, back to the TDC position (with the crankshaft key upright in the 12 o'clock position).

16 Refit the timing chain as described in Section 6.

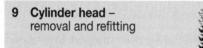

9 Cylinder head – removal and refitting

Note: *The engine must be completely cool before beginning this procedure.*

Removal

1 Disconnect the battery negative terminal (refer to *Disconnecting the battery* in the Reference Chapter).

2 Refer to Chapter 1 and drain the cooling system, then drain the engine oil and remove the oil filter.

3 Remove the throttle housing, fuel injectors, fuel rail, inlet and exhaust manifolds (see Chapter 4A).

4 Remove the timing chain and sprockets as described in Section 6.

5 Undo the bolt and withdraw the VVT-i oil control valve from the cylinder head **(see illustration 7.3)**.

6 Remove the camshafts and followers as described in Section 8.

7 Label and remove any remaining items, such as coolant fittings, tubes, cables, hoses or wires.

8 Using a 10 mm bi-hexagon bit, and working

8.13 The camshaft bearing caps are marked (arrowed) with E for exhaust, and I for inlet, numbered 1 to 5 (No 1 nearest the timing chain), and marked with an arrow which must point towards the timing chain

in the **reverse** of the sequence shown, progressively slacken the cylinder head bolts by half a turn at a time, until all bolts can be unscrewed by hand **(see illustrations 9.20a and 9.20b)**. Recover the washers.

9 Lift the cylinder head off the block. If it's stuck, very carefully pry up at the transmission end, beyond the gasket surface.

10 Remove all the external components from the cylinder head to allow for thorough cleaning and inspection. Refer to Chapter 2C, for cylinder head overhaul procedures.

Preparation for refitting

11 Check the condition of the cylinder head bolts, and particularly their threads, whenever they are removed. Wash the bolts and wipe dry, then check each for any sign of visible wear or damage, renewing any bolt if necessary. Measure the overall length of the bolts. If any of the bolts lengths exceeds the dimension given in the Specifications (indicating excessive stretching), renew all the cylinder head bolts **(see illustration)**.

12 The mating faces of the cylinder head and cylinder block/crankcase must be perfectly clean before refitting the head. Use a hard plastic or wood scraper to remove all traces of gasket and carbon; also clean the piston crowns. Take particular care, as the surfaces are damaged easily. Also, make sure that the carbon is not allowed to enter the oil and water passages – this is particularly important for the lubrication system, as carbon could block the oil supply to any of the engine's components. Using adhesive tape and paper, seal the water, oil and bolt holes in the cylinder block/crankcase. To prevent carbon entering the gap between the pistons and bores, smear a little grease in the gap. After cleaning each piston, use a small brush to remove all traces of grease and carbon from the gap, then wipe away the remainder with a clean rag. Clean all the pistons in the same way.

13 Check the mating surfaces of the cylinder block/crankcase and the cylinder head for nicks, deep scratches and other damage. If slight, they may be removed carefully with a file, but if excessive, machining may be the only alternative to renewal.

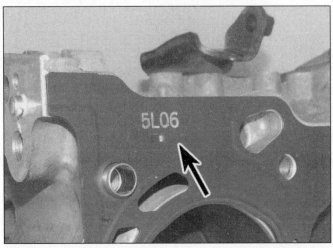

9.16 The 'Lot number' (arrowed) on the cylinder head gasket must face upwards

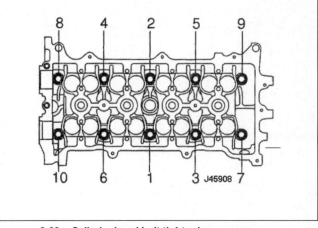

9.20a Cylinder head bolt tightening sequence – 1.6 and 1.8 litre engines

14 If warpage of the cylinder head gasket surface is suspected, use a straight-edge to check it for distortion. Refer to Part C of this Chapter if necessary.

Refitting

15 Refit any components that were removed from the cylinder head.

16 Position the new gasket over the locating dowels in the cylinder block. The 'Lot number' on the gasket must be facing upwards **(see illustration)**.

17 Carefully refit the cylinder head to the block and align it with the locating dowels.

18 Locate the washers on the cylinder head bolts, then lightly oil the threads of the bolts and the surfaces under the heads.

19 Enter each bolt into the holes (do not drop them in) and screw in, by hand until finger-tight.

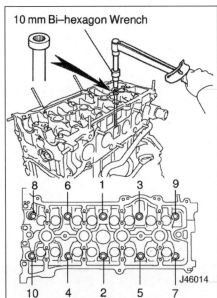

9.20b Cylinder head bolt tightening sequence – 2.0 litre engines

20 Working progressively and in sequence, tighten the cylinder head bolts to their Stage 1 torque setting, using a torque wrench and socket **(see illustrations)**.

21 Go around again in the specified sequence and angle-tighten the head bolts through the specified Stage 2 angle. It is recommended that an angle-measuring gauge is used during this stage, to ensure accuracy. If an angle-measuring gauge is not available, mark the side of each bolt with a dab of paint before angle-tightening them. If each bolt is marked on the side facing the timing chain end of the engine, it will be easy to determine when they have been tightened through the 90° Stage 2 angle.

22 The remainder of refitting is a reversal of removal, noting the following points:

a) *Refill the cooling system, then fit a new oil filter and refill the engine with oil (see Chapter 1).*

b) *Run the engine and check for leaks.*

c) *Road test the vehicle.*

10 Sump – removal and refitting

Removal

1 Disconnect the battery negative terminal (refer to *Disconnecting the battery* in the Reference Chapter).

2 Firmly apply the handbrake, then jack up the front of the car and support it securely on axle stands (see *Jacking and vehicle support*).

3 Unbolt and remove the undershields from beneath the engine, then drain the engine oil as described in Chapter 1.

4 On 2.0 litre engines, remove the exhaust system front downpipe as described in Chapter 4A.

5 Depending on transmission type, where applicable, unscrew the securing bolts and remove the engine-to-transmission reinforcing plate. Recover any spacers if fitted, noting their locations. Alternatively, pull down the plastic

cover slotted into the left-hand end of the cylinder block to access the left-hand sump bolts.

6 Undo and remove the retaining bolts/nuts and detach the sump from the cylinder block/crankcase. To do this, pry it free very carefully with a putty knife. Take care not to damage the mating surfaces of the sump and block/crankcase or oil leaks could develop.

7 On 1.6 and 1.8 litre engines, unbolt the pick-up tube/oil strainer assembly and remove it for cleaning. Discard the pick-up pipe gasket, a new one must be fitted.

Refitting

8 Use a scraper to remove all traces of old gasket material and sealant from the cylinder block/crankcase and sump. Take great care not to damage the mating surfaces.

9 Make sure the threaded bolt holes in the block/crankcase are clean.

10 On 1.6 and 1.8 litre engines, inspect the oil pump pick-up tube/oil strainer assembly for cracks and a blocked strainer. If the assembly was removed, clean it thoroughly and refit it, using a new gasket. Tighten the nuts/bolts to the specified torque.

11 Apply a 4 mm (approximately) wide bead of Toyota sealant No 08826-00080, or equivalent, to the sump flange, ensuring that the bead goes around the inside of the bolt holes **(see illustration)**. **Note:** *Refitting must*

10.11 Apply a bead of sealant to the sump flange, ensuring that the bead goes around the inside of the bolt holes

11.2 Oil pump retaining bolts (arrowed) – 1.6 and 1.8 litre engines

11.3a Undo the oil pressure relief valve plug . . .

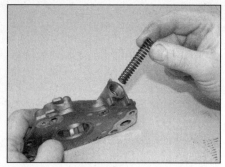

11.3b . . . and remove the relief valve spring . . .

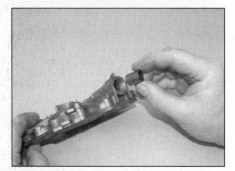

11.3c . . . and piston – 1.6 and 1.8 litre engines

11.4 Undo the screws and remove the oil pump cover – 1.6 and 1.8 litre engines

be completed within 3 minutes once the sealer has been applied.

12 Carefully position the sump on the cylinder block/crankcase and refit the bolts/nuts. Working from the centre outwards, tighten the bolts/nuts to the specified torque in three or four stages.

13 The remainder of refitting is the reverse of removal.

11 Oil pump – removal, inspection and refitting

1.6 and 1.8 litre engines

Removal

1 Remove the timing chain as described in Section 6.

2 Undo the five bolts and remove the oil pump

from the cylinder block (see illustration). Recover the oil pump gasket.

Inspection

3 Undo the plug and remove the oil pressure relief valve spring and piston (see illustrations).

4 Undo the retaining screws and remove the pump cover (see illustration).

5 Using a suitable marker pen, mark the outside face of the inner and outer rotors for correct reassembly. The rotors are stamped with assembly marks which should (theoretically) be visible with the pump cover removed. It is not uncommon, however for one or other of the rotors to be assembled with the assembly marks facing the pump body (ie, inwards). On reassembly, it is essential that the rotors are refitted in their original positions.

6 With the rotors correctly identified for reassembly, lift them out of the pump body.

7 Clean all components with solvent and inspect them for wear and damage. Use compressed air to blow through the oilways in the pump body.

8 Check the oil pressure relief valve piston sliding surface and valve spring. If either the spring or the piston is damaged, they must be renewed as a set. The piston must free to slide up and down the bore in the pump body without binding at any point.

9 Check the outer rotor-to-pump body clearance, rotor side clearance, and inner rotor-to-outer rotor tip clearance with a feeler gauge and compare the results with the clearances listed in the Specifications (see illustrations). If any clearance is excessive, renew the complete oil pump.

Refitting

10 Lubricate the pump rotors with clean engine oil, and place them in the pump body with the marks made on removal, or the rotor assembly marks, facing the pump cover.

11 Refit the pump cover and tighten the retaining screws to the specified torque.

12 Refit the oil pressure relief piston and spring, then tighten the plug to the specified torque.

13 Position a new gasket on the cylinder block, then refit the oil pump. Ensure the flats on the drive rotor align with the flats machined on the crankshaft, and tighten the bolts to the specified torque.

14 Refit the timing chain as described in Section 6.

11.9a Using a feeler gauge, measure the outer rotor-to-pump body clearance – 1.6 and 1.8 litre engines

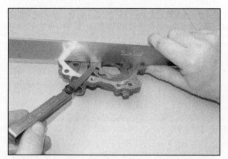

11.9b Using a straight-edge and feeler gauges, measure the rotor side clearance – 1.6 and 1.8 litre engines

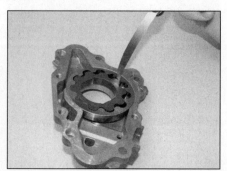

11.9c Measure the rotor tip clearance with a feeler gauge – 1.6 and 1.8 litre engines

2.0 litre engines

Removal

15 Remove the timing chain as described in Section 6.

16 Temporarily refit and tighten the crankshaft pulley bolt, then turn the crankshaft 90° anti-clockwise so that the crankshaft key is in the horizontal position. Remove the crankshaft pulley bolt.

17 Undo the retaining bolt and remove the oil pump drive chain tensioner plate and spring.

18 Undo and remove the oil pump sprocket retaining nut. To prevent rotation of the sprocket while the nut is slackened, insert a screwdriver through the hole in the sprocket and engage it with the oil pump body.

19 Slide the sprockets off the crankshaft and oil pump shaft and remove the drive chain.

20 Undo the three bolts and remove the oil pump from the cylinder block. Recover the oil pump gasket.

Inspection

21 Undo the plug and remove the oil pressure relief valve spring and piston.

22 Undo the seven bolts and remove the oil pump cover.

23 Using a suitable marker pen, mark the outside face of the inner and outer rotors for correct reassembly. The rotors are stamped with assembly marks which should (theoretically) be visible with the pump cover removed. It is not uncommon, however for the outer rotor to be assembled with the assembly marks facing the pump body (ie, inwards). On reassembly, it is essential that the rotors are refitted in their original positions.

24 With the rotors correctly identified for reassembly, lift them out of the pump body.

25 Clean all components with solvent and inspect them for wear and damage. Use compressed air to blow through the oilways in the pump body.

26 Check the oil pressure relief valve piston sliding surface and valve spring. If either the spring or the piston is damaged, they must be renewed as a set. The piston must free to slide up and down the bore in the pump body without binding at any point.

27 Check the outer rotor-to-pump body clearance, rotor side clearance, and inner rotor-to-outer rotor tip clearance with a feeler gauge and compare the results with the clearances listed in the Specifications. If any clearance is excessive, renew the complete oil pump.

28 Pull the oil pump drive chain taut by hand, and measure the length of 8 pins using vernier calipers. Repeat this procedure at 3 or more sections of the chain. If any of the measurements obtained exceed the dimension given in the Specifications, the chain must be renewed.

29 Wrap the chain around the oil pump sprocket and use vernier calipers to measure the diameter of the assembly. If the measurement obtained is less than that given in the Specifications, renew the chain and both sprockets.

30 Check the condition of the chain tensioner plate. There should be no sign of cracking or damage. As the chain runs along the tensioner plate it will create two grooves in the plate. The maximum depth of these grooves is 0.5 mm. If their depth exceeds this, renew the tensioner plate.

Refitting

31 Lubricate the pump rotors with clean engine oil, and place them in the pump body with the marks made on removal, or the rotor assembly marks, adjacent and facing the pump cover.

32 Refit the pump cover and tighten the retaining bolts to the specified torque.

33 Refit the oil pressure relief valve piston and spring, then tighten the plug to the specified torque.

34 Position a new gasket on the cylinder block, then refit the oil pump. Tighten the bolts to the specified torque.

35 Check that the crankshaft key is still in the horizontal position toward the inlet manifold side of the engine.

36 Turn the oil pump shaft so that the machined flat on the shaft is facing upward.

37 Engage the sprockets with the drive chain so that the reference mark on each sprocket is aligned with the coloured link on the chain.

38 Slide the sprockets and drive chain over the crankshaft and oil pump shaft. Engage the crankshaft sprocket with the crankshaft key, and the oil pump sprocket with the flat on the pump shaft.

39 Refit the oil pump sprocket retaining nut and tighten the nut to the specified torque.

40 Refit the chain tensioner plate, spring and retaining bolt, ensuring that the spring end locates behind the web on the crankcase and applies tension to the plate. Tighten the retaining bolt to the specified torque.

41 Temporarily refit the crankshaft pulley bolt and turn the crankshaft clockwise to bring the key in the end of the crankshaft back to the 12 o'clock position (upright). Remove the pulley bolt.

42 Refit the timing chain as described in Section 6.

12 Crankshaft oil seals
 – renewal

Right-hand seal

1 If the timing chain cover has been removed (part of the timing chain removal procedure), the seal can simply be driven from the cover using a hammer and punch **(see illustration)**. The new seal can then be fitted into place (spring towards the engine internals) using a block of wood and a hammer. The seal should be fitted with its outside edge flush with the timing cover.

12.1 Using a hammer and punch to remove the oil seal from the timing chain cover

2 If the timing cover is still in place, remove the auxiliary drivebelt as described in Chapter 1.

3 Remove the crankshaft pulley. To prevent the crankshaft from rotating whilst the crankshaft pulley central bolt is slackened, Toyota technicians use a special tool bolted to the crankshaft pulley to hold the crankshaft, and a similar tool can be fabricated out of flat metal bar. Alternatively, on manual transmission models, have an assistant engage top gear and depress the brake pedal. On automatic transmission models, remove the starter motor (Chapter 5A) and use a wide-bladed screwdriver engaged with the starter ring gear to hold the crankshaft stationary.

4 Punch or drill two small holes opposite each other in the seal. Screw a self-tapping screw into each hole and pull on the screws with pliers to extract the seal. Clean the seal housing and polish off any burrs or raised edges which may have caused the seal to fail in the first place. Lubricate the lips of the new seal with clean engine oil, then ease the seal over the end of the crankshaft and drive it squarely into position as described above.

5 Refit the crankshaft pulley and tighten the retaining bolt to the specified torque. Prevent the crankshaft from rotating using the same method employed during removal.

6 Refit the auxiliary drivebelt as described in Chapter 1.

Left-hand seal

7 Remove the flywheel/driveplate (Section 14); the seal can then be renewed as described in paragraph 4 **(see illustration)**.

8 On completion, refit the flywheel/driveplate.

12.7 Fit the crankshaft left-hand oil seal so the outer edge is flush with the housing

14.4 Home-made tool for locking the flywheel when loosening the retaining bolts

13 Oil cooler (2.0 litre engines) – removal and refitting

Removal

1 The oil cooler located above the oil filter at the base of the cylinder block.
2 Firmly apply the handbrake, then jack up the front of the car and support it securely on axle stands (see *Jacking and vehicle support*).
3 Drain the cooling system as described in Chapter 1. Alternatively, clamp the oil cooler coolant hoses directly above the cooler and be prepared for some coolant loss as the hoses are disconnected.
4 Release the hose clips, and disconnect the coolant hoses from the oil cooler.
5 Remove the oil filter (Chapter 1), then remove the filter mounting stud with its washer.
6 Undo the oil cooler retaining nut, then withdraw the oil cooler and recover the sealing O-ring.

Refitting

7 Refitting is a reversal of the removal procedure, bearing in mind the following points:
a) Use a new O-ring and and tighten all fastenings to the specified torque.
b) Fit a new oil filter with reference to Chapter 1, then top-up the engine oil as described in 'Weekly checks'.

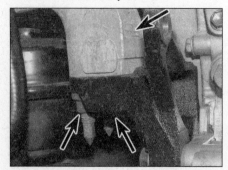

15.7a Right-hand engine mounting bracket-to-engine bracket retaining nuts/bolts (arrowed) – 1.6 and 1.8 litre engines

c) Refill or top-up the cooling system as described in Chapter 1 or 'Weekly checks'.

14 Flywheel/driveplate – removal, inspection and refitting

Removal

1 Remove the transmission as described in Chapter 7A or 7B according to type.
2 On manual transmission models, remove the clutch assembly as described in Chapter 6.
3 Mark the relationship of the flywheel/driveplate to its crankshaft flange.
4 Prevent the flywheel from turning by locking the ring gear teeth with a large flat-bladed screwdriver or by bolting a home-made tool to one of the transmission mounting bolt holes in the cylinder block **(see illustration)**. Progressively slacken the flywheel/driveplate retaining bolts, then remove the bolts and lift off the flywheel/driveplate.

Inspection

5 Examine the flywheel for scoring on its clutch driven plate face; if evident it may be possible for a competent engineering works to machine the surface, but renewal is the preferable option. Check the flywheel/driveplate carefully for signs of distortion, or any hairline cracks around the bolt holes or cracks radiating outwards from the centre; renewal will be required if evident.
6 If the ring gear is worn or damaged it may be possible to renew it separately, but this job should be entrusted to a Toyota dealer or engineering works.

Refitting

7 Clean the flywheel/driveplate and crankshaft flange faces, and remove all traces of thread locking compound from the retaining bolts.

> **HAYNES HINT** *If a suitable tap is not available, cut two slots down the threads of one of the old bolts with a hacksaw, and use the bolt to remove the locking compound from the threads.*

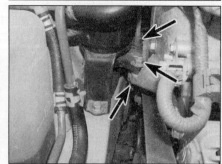

15.7b Right-hand engine mounting bracket-to-timing chain cover retaining nuts/bolts (arrowed) – 2.0 litre engines

8 Locate the flywheel/driveplate on its crankshaft flange, aligning the marks made on removal. Apply a little threadlocking compound to the threads of the retaining bolts, then fit the bolts and progressively tighten them to the specified torque setting.
9 Remove the ring gear locking tool.
10 On manual transmission models refit the clutch as described in Chapter 6.
11 Refit the transmission as described in Chapter 7A or 7B.

15 Engine/transmission mountings – inspection and renewal

Inspection

1 If improved access is required, firmly apply the handbrake, then jack up the front of the car and support it securely on axle stands (see *Jacking and vehicle support*).
2 Check the mounting rubber to see if it is cracked, hardened or separated from the metal at any point; renew the mounting if any such damage or deterioration is evident.
3 Check that all mounting fasteners are securely tightened; use a torque wrench to check if possible.
4 Using a large screwdriver or a crowbar, check for wear in the mounting by carefully levering against it to check for free play; where this is not possible, enlist the aid of an assistant to move the engine/transmission unit back-and-forth, or from side-to-side while you watch the mounting. While some free play is to be expected even from new components, excessive wear should be obvious. If excessive free play is found, check first that the fasteners are correctly secured, then renew any worn components as described below.

Renewal

5 The engine/transmission mountings can be unbolted and removed once the weight of the engine/transmission unit is taken off them using either a suitable hoist, an engine support bar or a jack with an interposed block of wood. Lifting eyes are provided on the engine.
6 The mountings are located in the following positions:
a) Right-hand mounting, at the timing chain (right-hand) end of the engine.
b) Left-hand mounting, at the left-hand end of the transmission to the rear of the battery tray.
c) A front mounting between the cylinder block and the longitudinal crossmember.
d) A rear mounting between the rear of the transmission and the subframe.
7 To remove the right-hand mounting, undo the bolts securing the mounting to the inner wing panel. Undo the three nuts/bolts securing the mounting bracket to the bracket on the engine, or to the timing chain cover **(see illustrations)**. The mounting assembly

can now be withdrawn from the engine compartment.

8 Access to the left-hand mounting is gained by removing the air cleaner assembly (see Chapter 4A), followed by the battery and tray (see Chapter 5A). It will be necessary to move the engine wiring loom to one side, and to release the air conditioning pipes from their support clips (where applicable) in order to reach all of the bolts. After removal of the through-bolt, unscrew the mounting bracket bolts and withdraw the mounting assembly from the transmission and inner wing panel **(see illustration)**.

9 It is necessary to raise and support the front of the vehicle in order to remove the front and rear engine mountings. After removal of the through-bolts the brackets may be unbolted from the longitudinal crossmember or subframe **(see illustration)**. Plastic blanking plates

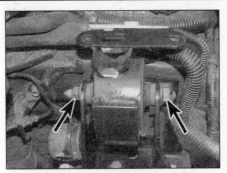

15.8 Left-hand engine/transmission mounting through-bolt and nut (arrowed)

15.9 Front engine/transmission mounting through-bolt and nut (arrowed)

are fitted to the longitudinal crossmember to protect the heads of the bracket bolts.

10 There are a number of different versions of the mountings used according to engine size and transmission type so, when ordering

new parts, ensure that full vehicle details are provided to enable the correct component(s) to be obtained. If possible, take the old component(s) along to your Toyota dealer for positive identification.

Notes

Chapter 2 Part C:
Engine removal and overhaul procedures

Contents

Degrees of difficulty

Easy, suitable for novice with little experience	Fairly easy, suitable for beginner with some experience	Fairly difficult, suitable for competent DIY mechanic	Difficult, suitable for experienced DIY mechanic	Very difficult, suitable for expert DIY or professional

Specifications

Cylinder head

Maximum gasket face warpage:
  Inlet and exhaust manifold faces:
    1.6 and 1.8 litre engines . . . . 0.10 mm
    2.0 litre engines engines . . . . 0.08 mm
  Cylinder head gasket face . . . . 0.05 mm
Valve seat angle . . . . 45°
Valve seat width . . . . 1.0 to 1.4 mm

Cylinder block

Maximum gasket face warpage. . . . . 0.05 mm
Cylinder bore diameter (nominal):
  Pre-August 2000 models:
    1.6 and 1.8 litre engines . . . . 81.00 to 81.03 mm
    2.0 litre engines. . . . . 86.00 to 86.03 mm
  Post-August 2000 models:
    1.6 and 1.8 litre engines . . . . 79.00 to 79.013 mm
    2.0 litre engines. . . . . 86.00 to 86.013 mm

Pistons and piston rings

Piston diameter:
Pre-August 2000 models:
    1.6 and 1.8 litre engines .... 80.905 to 80.935 mm
    2.0 litre engines .... 85.837 to 85.867 mm
Post-August 2000 models:
    1.6 and 1.8 litre engines .... 78.955 to 78.965 mm
    2.0 litre engines .... 85.925 to 85.935 mm

Piston ring end gap:	Standard	Maximum
Pre-August 2000 models:		
1.6 and 1.8 litre engines:		
Top compression ring	0.25 to 0.41 mm	1.11 mm
Second compression ring	0.24 to 0.40 mm	1.10 mm
Oil control ring	0.15 to 0.40 mm	1.10 mm
2.0 litre engines:		
Top compression ring	0.27 to 0.47 mm	1.07 mm
Second compression ring	0.45 to 0.65 mm	1.25 mm
Oil control ring	0.10 to 0.45 mm	1.05 mm
Post-August 2000 models:		
1.6 and 1.8 litre engines:		
Top compression ring	0.25 to 0.35 mm	1.05 mm
Second compression ring	0.35 to 0.50 mm	1.20 mm
Oil control ring	0.15 to 0.40 mm	1.05 mm
2.0 litre engines:		
Top compression ring	0.27 to 0.37 mm	0.90 mm
Second compression ring	0.37 to 0.47 mm	1.00 mm
Oil control ring	0.10 to 0.40 mm	0.80 mm

Crankshaft

Crankshaft endfloat:
Pre-August 2000 models:
    Standard .... 0.02 to 0.22 mm
    Maximum .... 0.30 mm
    Thrustwasher thickness .... 2.440 to 2.490 mm
Post-August 2000 models:
    1.6 and 1.8 litre engines:
        Standard .... 0.04 to 0.24 mm
        Maximum .... 0.30 mm
        Thrustwasher thickness .... 1.93 to 1.98 mm
    2.0 litre engines:
        Standard .... 0.04 to 0.24 mm
        Maximum .... 0.30 mm
        Thrustwasher thickness .... 2.430 to 2.480 mm

Valves and related components

Valve stem diameter:
Pre-August 2000 models:
    Inlet .... 5.970 to 5.985 mm
    Exhaust .... 5.965 to 5.980 mm
Post-August 2000 models:
    Inlet .... 5.470 to 5.485 mm
    Exhaust .... 5.465 to 5.480 mm
Valve spring free length:
Pre-August 2000 models:
    1.6 and 1.8 litre engines .... 42.4 mm
    2.0 litre engines .... 40.95 to 42.80 mm
Post-August 2000 models:
    1.6 and 1.8 litre engines .... 43.4 mm
    2.0 litre engines .... 45.7 mm

Torque wrench settings

Pre-August 2000 models

Refer to Chapter 2A specifications.

Post-August 2000 models

Refer to Chapter 2B specifications.

1 General information

Included in this Part of Chapter 2 are details of removing the engine/transmission from the car and general overhaul procedures for the cylinder head, cylinder block/crankcase and all other engine internal components.

The information given ranges from advice concerning preparation for an overhaul and the purchase of new parts, to detailed step-by-step procedures covering removal, inspection, renovation and refitting of engine internal components.

After Section 5, all instructions are based on the assumption that the engine has been removed from the car. For information concerning in-car engine repair, as well as the removal and refitting of those external components necessary for full overhaul, refer to Parts A or B of this Chapter, and to Section 5. Ignore any preliminary dismantling operations described in Parts A, or B that are no longer relevant once the engine has been removed from the car.

Apart from torque wrench settings, which are given at the beginning of Parts A and B, all specifications relating to engine overhaul are at the beginning of this Part of Chapter 2.

2 Engine overhaul – general information

It is not always easy to determine when, or if, an engine should be completely overhauled, as a number of factors must be considered.

High mileage is not necessarily an indication that an overhaul is needed, while low mileage does not preclude the need for an overhaul. Frequency of servicing is probably the most important consideration. An engine which has had regular and frequent oil and filter changes, as well as other required maintenance, should give many thousands of miles of reliable service. Conversely, a neglected engine may require an overhaul very early in its life.

Excessive oil consumption is an indication that piston rings, valve seals and/or valve guides are in need of attention. Make sure that oil leaks are not responsible before deciding that the rings and/or guides are worn. Perform a compression test, as described in Part A or Part B of this Chapter, to determine the likely cause of the problem.

Check the oil pressure with a gauge fitted in place of the oil pressure switch, and compare it with that specified. If it is extremely low, the main and big-end bearings, and/or the oil pump, are probably worn out.

Loss of power, rough running, knocking or metallic engine noises, excessive valve gear noise, and high fuel consumption may also point to the need for an overhaul, especially if they are all present at the same time. If a complete service does not remedy the situation, major mechanical work is the only solution.

A full engine overhaul involves restoring all internal parts to the specification of a new engine. During a complete overhaul, the pistons and the piston rings are renewed, and the cylinder bores are reconditioned. New main and big-end bearings are generally fitted; if necessary, the crankshaft may be reground, to compensate for wear in the journals. The valves are also serviced as well, since they are usually in less-than-perfect condition at this point. Always pay careful attention to the condition of the oil pump when overhauling the engine, and renew it if there is any doubt as to its serviceability. The end result should be an as-new engine that will give many trouble-free miles.

Critical cooling system components such as the hoses, thermostat and coolant pump should be renewed when an engine is overhauled. The radiator should also be checked carefully, to ensure that it is not clogged or leaking.

Before beginning the engine overhaul, read through the entire procedure to familiarise yourself with the scope and requirements of the job. Check on the availability of parts and make sure that any necessary special tools and equipment are obtained in advance. Most work can be done with typical hand tools, although a number of precision measuring tools are required for inspecting parts to determine if they must be renewed.

The services provided by an engineering machine shop or engine reconditioning specialist will almost certainly be required, particularly if major repairs such as crankshaft regrinding or cylinder reboring are necessary. Apart from carrying out machining operations, these establishments will normally handle the inspection of parts, offer advice concerning reconditioning or renewal and supply new components such as pistons, piston rings and bearing shells. It is recommended that the establishment used is a member of the Federation of Engine Re-Manufacturers, or a similar society.

Always wait until the engine has been completely dismantled, and until all components (especially the cylinder block/crankcase and the crankshaft) have been inspected, before deciding what service and repair operations must be performed by an engineering works. The condition of these components will be the major factor to consider when determining whether to overhaul the original engine, or to buy a reconditioned unit. Do not, therefore, purchase parts or have overhaul work done on other components until they have been thoroughly inspected. As a general rule, time is the primary cost of an overhaul, so it does not pay to fit worn or sub-standard parts.

As a final note, to ensure maximum life and minimum trouble from a reconditioned engine, everything must be assembled with care, in a spotlessly-clean environment.

3 Engine removal – methods and precautions

If you have decided that the engine must be removed for overhaul or major repair work, several preliminary steps should be taken.

Locating a suitable place to work is extremely important. Adequate work space, along with storage space for the car, will be needed. If a workshop or garage is not available, at the very least, a flat, level, clean work surface is required.

Cleaning the engine compartment and engine/transmission before beginning the removal procedure will help keep tools clean and organised.

An engine hoist will also be necessary. Make sure the equipment is rated in excess of the combined weight of the engine and transmission. Safety is of primary importance, considering the potential hazards involved in removing the engine/transmission from the car.

The help of an assistant is essential. Apart from the safety aspects involved, there are many instances when one person cannot simultaneously perform all of the operations required during engine/transmission removal.

Plan the operation ahead of time. Before starting work, arrange for the hire of or obtain all of the tools and equipment you will need. Some of the equipment necessary to perform engine/transmission removal and installation safely (in addition to an engine hoist) is as follows: a heavy duty trolley jack, complete sets of spanners and sockets as described in the rear of this manual, wooden blocks, and plenty of rags and cleaning solvent for mopping-up spilled oil, coolant and fuel. If the hoist must be hired, make sure that you arrange for it in advance, and perform all of the operations possible without it beforehand. This will save you money and time.

Plan for the car to be out of use for quite a while. An engineering machine shop or engine reconditioning specialist will be required to perform some of the work which cannot be accomplished without special equipment. These places often have a busy schedule, so it would be a good idea to consult them before removing the engine, in order to accurately estimate the amount of time required to rebuild or repair components that may need work.

During the engine/transmission removal procedure, it is advisable to make notes of the locations of all brackets, cable ties, earthing points, etc, as well as how the wiring harnesses, hoses and electrical connections are attached and routed around the engine and engine compartment. An effective way of doing this is to take a series of photographs of the various components before they are disconnected or removed; the resulting photographs will prove invaluable when the engine/transmission is refitted.

Always be extremely careful when removing and refitting the engine/transmission. Serious injury can result from careless actions. Plan ahead and take your time, and a job of this nature, although major, can be accomplished successfully.

The engine and transmission assembly is removed upwards from the engine compartment.

4 Engine and transmission – removal, separation and refitting

Note: *The engine can be removed from the car only as a complete unit with the transmission; the two are then separated for overhaul.*

Note: *Such is the complexity of the power unit arrangement on these vehicles, and the variations that may be encountered according to model and optional equipment fitted, that the following should be regarded as a guide to the work involved, rather than a step-by-step procedure. Where differences are encountered, or additional component disconnection or removal is necessary, make notes of the work involved as an aid to refitting.*

Removal

1 Firmly apply the handbrake, then jack up the front of the car and support it securely on axle stands (see *Jacking and vehicle support*). Remove both front roadwheels, then unbolt and remove the undershields from under the engine compartment.

2 Remove the bonnet as described in Chapter 11.

3 Depressurise the fuel system as described in Chapter 4A.

4 Remove the air cleaner assembly and inlet ducts as described in Chapter 4A.

5 Remove the battery and tray as described in Chapter 5A.

6 Drain the cooling system (see Chapter 1), saving the coolant if it is fit for re-use.

7 Drain the transmission oil/fluid with reference to Chapter 7A or 7B (as applicable). Refit and tighten the drain and filler plugs.

8 If the engine is to be dismantled, working as described in Chapter 1, drain the oil and if required remove the oil filter. Clean and refit the drain plug, tightening it to the specified torque (Chapter 1).

9 Remove the auxiliary drivebelt(s) as described in Chapter 1.

10 On models with air conditioning, refer to Chapter 3 and unbolt the air conditioning compressor from the engine, leaving the refrigerant pipes connected. Tie the compressor to one side.

11 Unbolt the power steering pump and, if clearance allows, tie the pump aside without disconnecting the hoses. Alternatively, remove the pump completely as described in Chapter 10.

12 The wiring loom must now be disconnected from the engine and transmission, and positioned to one side on the left-hand side of the engine compartment. It is not possible to disconnect the loom and leave the wiring on the engine. To ensure correct refitting, work methodically and make notes. Start at the alternator position on the front of the engine and work around to the rear, disconnecting all wiring that would impede engine/transmission removal. Clearly label all disconnected wiring and take photos or sketch the locations of connections and attachments.

13 Detach the accelerator cable from the throttle housing with reference to Chapter 4A, and position the cable to one side. On automatic transmission models also disconnect the kickdown cable.

14 Where applicable, position a suitable container beneath the front of the engine, then slacken the clips, or unscrew the union bolts securing the oil cooler hoses to the oil filter housing and sump. Recover the washers.

15 Unscrew the nuts securing the exhaust front downpipe to the exhaust manifold, then lower the downpipe and recover the sealing ring.

16 Remove the radiator as described in Chapter 3, then disconnect and remove the top and bottom hoses from the engine.

17 Note the location of the heater hoses on the left-hand side of the cylinder head, then loosen the clips and disconnect them.

18 Disconnect the vacuum hoses from the inlet manifold and throttle housing, noting their fitted locations.

19 Unscrew the union bolt and detach the fuel supply hose from the end of the fuel rail. Where applicable, also disconnect the fuel return hose. Position both hoses to one side and cover their ends to prevent entry of dust and dirt.

20 On manual transmission models, refer to Chapter 6 and unbolt the clutch slave cylinder from the front of the transmission and release it from the support brackets. Position it to one side. Also disconnect the gearchange selector cables with reference to Chapter 7A.

21 On automatic transmission models, disconnect the selector cable and starter inhibitor switch wiring from the transmission with reference to Chapter 7B. Also disconnect the transmission fluid cooler hoses.

22 Remove both driveshafts as described in Chapter 8.

23 Manoeuvre the engine hoist into position, and attach it to the engine using suitable lifting brackets on the cylinder head. To maintain the balance of the assembly, attach the hoist to the left-hand rear and right-hand front of the cylinder head. Raise the hoist until it is supporting the weight of the engine/transmission assembly.

24 Refer to Chapter 2A or 2B as applicable, and detach the front and rear, and left-hand and right-hand engine mountings, so as to enable the engine/transmission to be lifted upwards.

25 Make a final check that everything has been disconnected. Ensure that components such as the gearchange cables and driveshafts are secured so that they cannot be damaged on removal.

26 Lift the engine/transmission assembly from the engine compartment, making sure that nothing is trapped or damaged. Enlist the help of an assistant during this procedure, as it will be necessary to tilt the assembly slightly to clear the body panels.

Separation

27 With the engine/transmission assembly removed, support the assembly on suitable blocks of wood, on a workbench or, failing that, on a clean area of the workshop floor.

28 On automatic transmission models, where fitted, unscrew the securing bolts and remove the engine-to-transmission reinforcing plate, or remove the cover at the base of the bellhousing for access to the torque converter-to-driveplate bolts. Turn the crankshaft as necessary for access, and unscrew the six bolts.

29 Unscrew the retaining bolts, and remove the starter motor from the transmission (refer to Chapter 5A if necessary).

30 Ensure that both engine and transmission are adequately supported, then slacken and remove the bolts securing the transmission to the engine. Note the correct fitted positions of each bolt (and, where fitted, the relevant brackets) as they are removed, to use as a reference on refitting.

31 With the help of an assistant, withdraw the transmission from the engine. On manual transmission models, ensure that the weight of the transmission is not allowed to hang on the input shaft while it is engaged with the clutch disc. On automatic transmission models ensure that the torque converter remains fully engaged with the transmission.

32 If they are loose, remove the locating dowels from the engine or transmission, and keep them in a safe place.

Refitting

33 If the engine and transmission have been separated, perform the operations described below in paragraphs 34 to 39. If not, proceed as described from paragraph 40 onwards.

34 On manual transmission models, apply a smear of high-melting-point grease to the splines of the transmission input shaft. Do not apply too much, otherwise there is a possibility of the grease contaminating the clutch friction disc. Also ensure that the clutch release bearing is correctly engaged with the fork.

35 On automatic transmission models make sure that the torque converter is fully engaged with the transmission (see Chapter 7B).

36 Ensure that the locating dowels are correctly positioned in the engine or transmission. Carefully offer the transmission to the engine, until the locating dowels are engaged. On manual transmission models, ensure that the weight of the transmission is not allowed to hang on the input shaft.

37 Refit the transmission housing-to-engine bolts, ensuring that all the necessary brackets are correctly positioned, and tighten them to the specified torque setting.

38 Refit the starter motor and tighten the retaining bolts.

39 On automatic transmission models align the holes in the driveplate and torque converter then insert the bolts and tighten them to the specified torque (Chapter 7B). Refit the cover and tighten the bolts.

40 Reconnect the hoist and lifting tackle to the engine lifting brackets. With the aid of an assistant, lift the assembly into the engine compartment, making sure that it clears the surrounding components.

41 Refit the right-hand and left-hand engine mountings with reference to Chapter 2A or 2B.

42 Refit the front and rear engine mountings with reference to Chapter 2A or 2B. Remove the engine hoist.

43 The remainder of the refitting procedure is a direct reversal of the removal sequence, with reference to the relevant Chapters and noting the following points:

a) Ensure that the wiring harness is correctly routed and all connectors are correctly and securely reconnected.

b) Refill the transmission oil/fluid with reference to Chapter 7A or 7B (as applicable).

c) Refit and, where necessary adjust, the auxiliary drivebelts as described in Chapter 1.

d) On automatic transmission models adjust the kickdown cable and selector cable with reference to Chapter 7B, and top-up the fluid with reference to Chapter 1.

e) Refill the engine with oil as described in Chapter 1.

f) Refill the cooling system as described in Chapter 1.

g) On completion, start the engine and check for leaks.

5 Engine overhaul – dismantling sequence

1 It is much easier to dismantle and work on the engine if it is mounted on a portable engine stand. These stands can often be hired from a tool hire shop. Before the engine is mounted on a stand, the flywheel/driveplate should be removed, so that the stand bolts can be tightened into the end of the cylinder block/crankcase.

2 If a stand is not available, it is possible to dismantle the engine with it blocked up on a sturdy workbench, or on the floor. Be extra careful not to tip or drop the engine when working without a stand.

3 If you are going to obtain a reconditioned engine, all the external components must be removed first, to be transferred to the new engine (just as they will if you are doing a complete engine overhaul yourself). These components include the following:

a) Alternator, power steering pump and/or air conditioning compressor mounting brackets (as applicable).

b) Ignition coils, HT leads (where applicable) and spark plugs (Chapters 1 and 5B).

c) Coolant pump and thermostat/coolant outlet housing(s) (Chapter 3).

d) The fuel injection system components (Chapter 4A).

e) All electrical switches and sensors, and the engine wiring harness.

f) Inlet and exhaust manifolds (Chapter 4A).

g) Engine mountings (Part A or Part B of this Chapter).

h) Flywheel/driveplate (Part A or Part B of this Chapter).

Note: When removing the external components from the engine, pay close attention to details that may be helpful or important during refitting. Note the fitted position of gaskets, seals, spacers, pins, washers, bolts, and other small items.

4 If you are obtaining a short engine (which consists of the engine cylinder block/crankcase, crankshaft, pistons and connecting rods all assembled), then the cylinder head, sump, oil pump, and timing belt/chain components will have to be removed also.

5 If you are planning a complete overhaul, the engine can be dismantled, and the internal components removed, in the order given.

a) Timing belt covers, timing belt, sprockets, tensioner and idler pulleys (see Part A of this Chapter).

b) Timing chain cover, chain, sprockets and associated components (see Part B of this Chapter).

c) Inlet and exhaust manifolds (Chapter 4A).

d) Cylinder head (see Part A or B of this Chapter).

e) Sump (see Part A or B of this Chapter).

f) Piston/connecting rod assemblies (Section 9).

g) Flywheel/driveplate (see Part A or B of this Chapter).

h) Oil pump (see Part A or B of this Chapter).

i) Crankshaft (Section 10).

6 Before beginning the dismantling and overhaul procedures, make sure that you have all of the correct tools necessary. Refer to Tools and working facilities at the end of this manual for further information.

6 Cylinder head – dismantling

Note: New and reconditioned cylinder heads can be obtained from the manufacturer and engine overhaul specialists. Be aware that some specialist tools are required for the dismantling and inspection procedures, and new components may not be readily available. It may therefore be more practical and economical for the home mechanic to purchase a reconditioned head, rather than dismantle, inspect and recondition the original head.

1 Remove the cylinder head as described in Part A or B of this Chapter. This procedure includes removal of the camshafts, followers, and the inlet and exhaust manifolds. As applicable, unbolt and remove the coolant outlet and thermostat housing, the alternator upper mounting bracket, and any additional brackets, sensors or related components **(see illustrations)**.

2 Using a valve spring compressor, compress each valve spring in turn until the split collets can be removed. Release the compressor, and lift off the spring retainer, spring and spring seat. Withdraw the valve through the combustion chamber **(see illustrations)**.

3 If, when the valve spring compressor is screwed down, the spring retainer refuses to free and expose the split collets, gently tap

6.1a Removing the coolant outlet . . .

6.1b . . . the thermostat housing . . .

6.1c . . . and the alternator upper mounting bracket from the cylinder head

6.2a Using a compressor tool to compress the valve springs

6.2b Remove the spring retainer . . .

6.2c . . . spring . . .

6.2d . . . and spring seat . . .

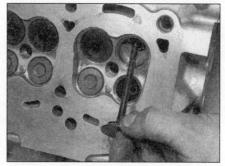

6.2e . . . then remove the valve from the combustion chamber

6.4 Using pliers or special removal tool, extract the valve stem seal from the top of the guide

the top of the tool, directly over the retainer, with a light hammer. This will free the retainer.

4 Using a pair of pliers or special removal tool, carefully extract the valve stem seal from the top of the guide **(see illustration)**.

5 It is essential that each valve is stored together with its collets, retainer, spring, and spring seat. The valves should also be kept in their correct sequence, unless they are so badly worn that they are to be renewed. If they are going to be kept and used again, place each valve assembly in a labelled polythene bag or similar small container. Note that the valves of No 1 cylinder are nearest to the timing belt/chain end of the engine.

7 Cylinder head and valves – cleaning and inspection

1 Thorough cleaning of the cylinder head and valve components, followed by a detailed inspection, will enable you to decide how much valve service work must be carried out during the engine overhaul. **Note:** *If the engine has been severely overheated, it is best to assume that the cylinder head is warped – check carefully for signs of this.*

Cleaning

2 Scrape away all traces of old gasket material from the cylinder head.

3 Scrape away the carbon from the combustion chambers and ports, then wash the cylinder head thoroughly with paraffin or a suitable solvent.

4 Scrape off any heavy carbon deposits that may have formed on the valves, then use a power-operated wire brush to remove deposits from the valve heads and stems.

Inspection

Note: *Be sure to perform all the following inspection procedures before concluding that the services of an engine overhaul specialist are required. Make a list of all items that require attention.*

Cylinder head

5 Inspect the head very carefully for cracks, evidence of coolant leakage, and other damage. If cracks are found, a new cylinder head should be obtained.

6 Use a straight-edge and feeler blade to check that the cylinder head surface is not distorted **(see illustration)**. If it is, it may be possible to have it machined by an engine overhaul specialist.

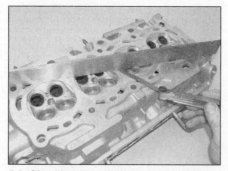

7.6 Checking the cylinder head surface for distortion

7 Examine the valve seats in each of the combustion chambers. If they are severely pitted, cracked, or burned, they will need to be renewed or recut by an engine overhaul specialist. If they are only slightly pitted, this can be removed by grinding-in the valve heads and seats with fine valve-grinding compound, as described below.

8 Check the valve guides for wear by inserting the relevant valve, and checking for side-to-side movement of the valve. A very small amount of movement is acceptable, however, if excessive, seek the advice of an engine overhaul specialist.

9 If in any further doubt as to the condition of the cylinder head, have it inspected by an engine overhaul specialist.

Valves

10 Examine the head of each valve for pitting, burning, cracks, and general wear. Check the valve stem for scoring and wear ridges. Rotate the valve, and check for any obvious indication that it is bent. Look for pits and excessive wear on the tip of each valve stem. Renew any valve that shows any signs of wear or damage.

11 If the valves are in satisfactory condition, they should be ground (lapped) into their respective seats, to ensure a smooth, gas-tight seal. If the seat is only lightly pitted, or if it has been recut, fine grinding compound only should be used to produce the required finish. Coarse valve-grinding compound should not be used, unless a seat is badly burned or deeply pitted. If this is the case, the cylinder head and valves should be inspected by an

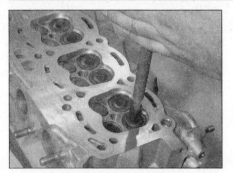

7.13 Grinding-in the valves

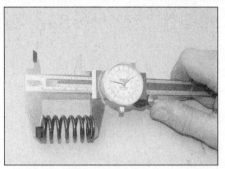

7.16 Measuring the free length of the valve springs

7.17 Checking the valve springs for squareness

expert, to decide whether seat recutting, or even the renewal of the valve or seat insert is required.

12 Valve grinding is carried out as follows. Place the cylinder head upside-down on a bench.

13 Smear a trace of the appropriate grade of valve-grinding compound on the seat face, and press a suction grinding tool onto the valve head. With a semi-rotary action, grind the valve head to its seat, lifting the valve occasionally to redistribute the grinding compound **(see illustration)**. A light spring placed under the valve head will greatly ease this operation.

14 If coarse grinding compound is being used, work only until a dull, matt even surface is produced on both the valve seat and the valve, then wipe off the used compound, and repeat the process with fine compound. When a smooth unbroken ring of light grey matt finish is produced on both the valve and seat, the grinding operation is complete. Do not grind-in the valves any further than absolutely necessary.

15 When all the valves have been ground-in, carefully wash off *all* traces of grinding compound using paraffin or a suitable solvent, before reassembling the cylinder head.

Valve components

16 Examine the valve springs for signs of damage and discoloration. The Toyota procedure for checking the condition of valve springs involves measuring the force necessary

to compress each spring to a specified height. This is not possible without the use of the Toyota special test equipment, and therefore spring checking must be entrusted to a Toyota dealer. A rough idea of the condition of the spring can be gained by measuring the spring free length, and comparing it to the length given in this Chapter's Specifications **(see illustration)**.

17 Stand each spring on a flat surface, and position a square alongside the edge of the spring **(see illustration)**. Measure the gap between the upper and lower edges of the spring and the square.

18 If any of the springs are damaged, distorted or have lost their tension, obtain a complete new set of springs. It is normal to renew the valve springs as a matter of course if a major overhaul is being carried out.

19 Renew the valve stem oil seals regardless of their apparent condition. They are normally supplied in the engine gasket set.

8 Cylinder head – reassembly

1 Working on the first valve, dip the new valve stem seal in clean engine oil and ease it over the valve stem onto the guide. Use a suitable socket or metal tube to press the seal firmly onto the guide. Note that although the seals are theoretically colour-coded for

identification purposes, in practice, the colour of the seals does not always agree with the Toyota documentation. On pre-August 2000 engines, the inlet seals should be brown or grey, and the exhaust seals should be black. On post-August 2000 engines, it is possible to discern an identification mark on the top of the seal face (you will probably need a magnifying glass to see this). With careful observation it will be seen that the exhaust valve stem seals are marked EX, and the inlet seals are marked IN **(see illustration)**. **Note:** *the inlet and exhaust valves require different seals – DO NOT mix them up.*

2 Lubricate the stems of the valves, and insert the valves into their original locations in the cylinder head. If new valves are being fitted, insert them into the locations to which they have been ground **(see illustration)**.

3 Refit the spring seat, then locate the valve spring on top of its seat and refit the spring retainer.

4 Compress the valve spring with the valve spring compressor tool, and locate the split collets in the recess in the valve stem. Release the compressor, then repeat this procedure on the remaining valves **(see Haynes hint)**.

5 With all the valves installed, place the cylinder head on blocks on the bench and, using a hammer and interposed block of wood, tap the end of each valve stem to settle the components.

6 The cylinder head and associated components may now be refitted as described in Part A, or B of this Chapter.

8.1 The exhaust valve stem seals are marked EX, and the inlet seals are marked IN

8.2 Lubricate the stems of the valves before inserting them in their guides

Use a dab of grease to retain the collets on the valve stems.

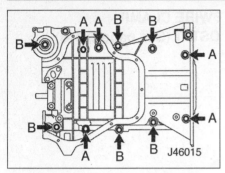

9.2a Lower crankcase retaining bolt locations – 2.0 litre engines post-August 2000

A   Long bolts   B   Short bolts

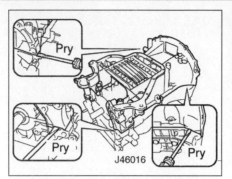

9.2b Removing the lower crankcase from the cylinder block – 2.0 litre engines post-August 2000

9.6a Unscrewing the nuts/bolts from No 1 piston big-end bearing cap

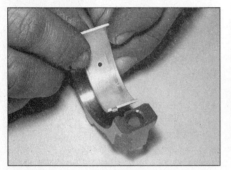

9.6b Recovering the bottom half bearing shell from the big-end bearing cap

9.8 Recovering the upper half bearing shell from the connecting rod

recover the bottom half bearing shell. If the bearing shells are to be re-used, tape the cap and the shell together **(see illustrations)**. Note that a complete set of new big-end bearing cap bolts/nuts will be required for reassembly.

7 Where necessary, to prevent the possibility of damage to the crankshaft bearing journals, tape over the connecting rod bolt threads or fit a length of plastic hose to them.

8 Using a hammer handle, push the piston up through the bore, and remove it from the top of the cylinder block. Recover the bearing shell, and tape it to the connecting rod for safe-keeping **(see illustration)**.

9 Loosely refit the big-end cap to the connecting rod, and secure with the nuts/bolts – this will help to keep the components in their correct order.

10 Remove No 4 piston assembly in the same way.

11 Turn the crankshaft through 180° to bring pistons 2 and 3 to BDC (bottom dead centre), and remove them in the same way.

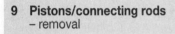

9   Pistons/connecting rods – removal

1 Remove the timing belt/chain, cylinder head, sump, oil pump pick-up tube, or oil pump and, where applicable, the oil cooler and water by-pass pipe, as described in Part A or Part B of this Chapter.

2 On 2.0 litre engines post-August 2000, gradually and evenly slacken and remove the eleven bolts securing the lower crankcase to the cylinder block, noting the different bolt lengths. Use a flat-bladed screwdriver to gently prise the lower crankcase from the cylinder block, at the cast-in leverage points **(see illustrations)**. Collect the O-ring from the joint face on the oil filter side, and remove the oil seal from the end of the crankshaft.

3 If there is a pronounced wear ridge at the top of any bore, it may be necessary to remove it with a scraper or ridge reamer, to avoid piston damage during removal. Such a ridge indicates excessive wear of the cylinder bore.

4 Each connecting rod and bearing cap should be identified for its respective cylinder, however the markings do not include the cylinder number. Make a note of the markings and the respective cylinders, or alternatively use a hammer and centre-punch, paint or similar, to mark each connecting rod and big-end bearing cap with its respective cylinder number on the flat machined surface provided.

5 Turn the crankshaft to bring pistons 1 and 4 to BDC (bottom dead centre).

6 Unscrew the nuts/bolts from No 1 piston big-end bearing cap. Take off the cap, and

10   Crankshaft – removal

1 Remove the timing belt/chain, sump, oil pump and pick-up tube and flywheel/driveplate with reference to Part A or Part B of this Chapter (the engine must be removed from the vehicle) then, where applicable, unbolt the rear engine plate and oil seal housing and recover the gasket **(see illustrations)**.

2 Remove the pistons and connecting rods,

10.1a Remove the rear engine plate (where fitted) . . .

10.1b . . . then unscrew the bolts . . .

10.1c . . . remove the oil seal housing . . .

10.1d . . . and recover the gasket –
pre-August 2000 engines

10.3 Checking the crankshaft endfloat
with a dial gauge

10.5 Checking the crankshaft endfloat
with feeler blades on the centre (No 3)
main bearing

as described in Section 9. **Note:** *If no work is to be done on the pistons and connecting rods, there is no need to remove the cylinder head, or to push the pistons out of the cylinder bores. The pistons should just be pushed far enough up the bores to position them clear of the crankshaft journals.*

3 Before the crankshaft is removed, check the endfloat. Mount a dial indicator with the stem in line with the crankshaft throws **(see illustration)**.

4 Push the crankshaft fully one way and zero the dial indicator. Next, lever the crankshaft the other way as far as possible and check the reading on the dial indicator. The distance that it moves is the endfloat. If it's greater than specified, check the crankshaft thrust surfaces for wear. If no wear is evident, new thrustwashers should correct the endfloat.

5 If a dial indicator isn't available, feeler gauges can be used. Gently pry or push the crankshaft fully one way. Slip feeler gauges between the crankshaft and the face of the number 3 (thrust) main bearing to determine the clearance **(see illustration)**.

All engines except 1.6 and 1.8 litre post-August 2000

6 Working in sequence, slacken the main bearing cap retaining bolts by a turn at a time **(see illustration)**. Once all bolts are loose, unscrew and remove them from the cylinder block. Note that the caps are normally numbered from the timing belt/chain end of the engine, and in addition an arrow points to the timing end **(see illustration)**. If identification markings are not evident, suitably mark them to indicate cap location and fitted direction. Note that on 2.0 litre engines post-August 2000, a complete set of new main bearing cap bolts will be required for reassembly.

7 Remove the main bearing caps and recover the lower main bearing shells. Tape each shell to its relevant cap for safe-keeping. Also recover the thrustwashers either side of the centre main bearing cap keeping them identified for position.

8 Carefully lift out the crankshaft, taking care not to displace the upper main bearing shells.

9 Recover the upper bearing shells from the cylinder block, and tape them to their respective positions on the main bearing caps.

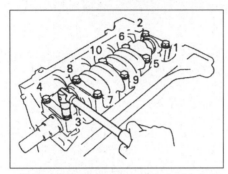

10.6a Main bearing cap bolt slackening
sequence

Remove the thrustwasher halves from the side of centre main bearing, and store them with the main bearing cap.

1.6 and 1.8 litre engines post-August 2000

10 Working in a diagonal sequence, gradually and evenly slacken and remove the ten hexagon-head bolts securing the main bearing ladder to the cylinder block **(see illustration)**. Note that it will be necessary to remove the oil filter union to access one of the bolts beneath.

11 Working in the **reverse** of the tightening sequence **(see illustration 16.19)**, gradually and evenly slacken and remove the ten central 12-point head bolts securing the main bearing ladder to the cylinder block **(see**

10.10 Removing the hexagon head bolts
securing the main bearing ladder to the
cylinder block – 1.6 and 1.8 litre engines
post-August 2000

10.6b Main bearing caps are numbered
and marked with an arrow towards the
timing end of the engine

illustration). Note that a complete set of new 12-point head bolts will be required for reassembly.

12 Use a flat-bladed screwdriver to gently prise the main bearing ladder from the cylinder block, at the cast-in leverage points. Ensure the lower bearing shells stay in their original positions in the bearing ladder.

13 Carefully lift out the crankshaft, taking care not to displace the upper main bearing shells. Remove the oil seal from the end of the crankshaft.

14 Recover the upper bearing shells from the cylinder block, and tape them to their respective positions on the main bearing ladder. Remove the thrustwasher halves from the side of centre main bearing, and store them with the main bearing ladder.

10.11 Removing the 12-point head bolts
securing the main bearing ladder to the
cylinder block – 1.6 and 1.8 litre engines
post-August 2000

11.1a Removing the oil pressure sensor from the cylinder block

11.1b Power steering pump lower mounting bracket

11.1c Alternator adjustment bracket on the right-hand end of the cylinder block

11 Cylinder block –
cleaning and inspection

Cleaning

1 Remove all external components and electrical switches/sensors from the block, and unbolt the alternator and power steering pump brackets as applicable **(see illustrations)**.
2 For complete cleaning, the core plugs should ideally be removed. Drill a small hole in the plugs, then insert a self-tapping screw into the hole. Pull out the plugs by pulling on the screw with a pair of grips, or by using a slide hammer.
3 Scrape all traces of sealant from the cylinder block/crankcase, taking care not to damage the gasket/sealing surfaces.
4 Remove all oil gallery plugs (where fitted). The plugs are usually very tight – they may have to be drilled out, and the holes retapped. Use new plugs when the engine is reassembled.
5 If any of the castings are extremely dirty, all should be steam-cleaned.
6 After the castings are returned, clean all oil holes and oil galleries one more time. Flush all internal passages with warm water until the water runs clear. Dry thoroughly, and apply a light film of oil to all mating surfaces and the cylinder bores, to prevent rusting. If you have access to compressed air, use it to speed up the drying process, and to blow out all the oil holes and galleries.

 Warning: Wear eye protection when using compressed air.

12.2 Carefully expand the rings from the top of the piston

7 If the castings are not very dirty, you can do an adequate cleaning job with hot, soapy water and a stiff brush. Take plenty of time, and do a thorough job. Regardless of the cleaning method used, be sure to clean all oil holes and galleries very thoroughly, and to dry all components well. Protect the cylinder bores as described above, to prevent rusting.
8 All threaded holes must be clean, to ensure accurate torque readings during reassembly. To clean the threads, run the correct-size tap into each of the holes to remove rust, corrosion, thread sealant or sludge, and to restore damaged threads. If possible, use compressed air to clear the holes of debris produced by this operation.

 Warning: Wear eye protection when cleaning out these holes in this way.

9 Apply suitable sealant to the new oil gallery plugs, and insert them into the holes in the block. Tighten them securely. Similarly use a suitable sealant on new core plugs and tap them into place using a close-fitting tube or socket.
10 If the engine is not going to be reassembled right away, cover it with a large plastic bag to keep it clean; protect all mating surfaces and the cylinder bores as described above, to prevent rusting.

Inspection

11 Visually check the block for cracks, rust and corrosion. Look for stripped threads in the threaded holes. It's also a good idea to have the block checked for hidden cracks by an engine reconditioning specialist that has the

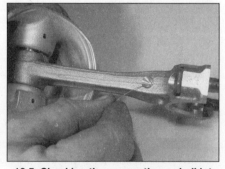

12.5 Checking the connecting rod oil jet hole for blockage

equipment to do this type of work, especially if the vehicle had a history of overheating or using coolant. If defects are found, have the block repaired, if possible, or renewed.
12 If in any doubt as to the condition of the cylinder block, have it inspected and measured by an engine reconditioning specialist. If the bores are worn or damaged, they will be able to carry out any necessary reboring (where possible), and supply appropriate oversized pistons, etc.

12 Pistons/connecting rods
– inspection

1 Before the inspection process can begin, the piston/connecting rod assemblies must be cleaned, and the original piston rings removed from the pistons. **Note:** *Always use new piston rings when the engine is reassembled.*
2 Carefully expand the old rings over the top of the pistons – note that the oil control ring assembly normally incorporates two rails and an expander. The use of two or three old feeler blades will be helpful in preventing the rings dropping into empty grooves **(see illustration)**. Be careful not to scratch the piston with the ends of the ring. The rings are brittle, and will snap if they are spread too far. They're also very sharp – protect your hands and fingers. Always remove the rings from the top of the piston.
3 Scrape away all traces of carbon from the top of the piston. A hand-held wire brush (or a piece of fine emery cloth) can be used, once the majority of the deposits have been scraped away.
4 Remove the carbon from the ring grooves in the piston, using an old ring. Break the ring in half to do this (be careful not to cut your fingers – piston rings are sharp). Be careful to remove only the carbon deposits – do not remove any metal, and do not nick or scratch the sides of the ring grooves.
5 Once the deposits have been removed, clean the piston/connecting rod assembly with paraffin or a suitable solvent, and dry thoroughly. Make sure that the oil return holes in the ring grooves are clear, and check that the oil jet holes are also clear **(see illustration)**.
6 If the pistons and cylinder walls aren't

damaged or worn excessively, and if the cylinder block is not rebored, new pistons won't be necessary. Normal piston wear appears as even vertical wear on the piston thrust surfaces and slight looseness of the top ring in its groove. New piston rings, however, should always be used when an engine is rebuilt.

7 Carefully inspect each piston for cracks around the skirt, around the gudgeon pin holes, and at the piston ring lands (between the ring grooves).

8 Look for scoring and scuffing on the thrust faces of the skirt, holes in the piston crown and burned areas at the edge of the crown. If the skirt is scored or scuffed, the engine may have been suffering from overheating and/or abnormal combustion, which caused excessively high operating temperatures. The cooling and lubrication systems should be checked thoroughly. A hole in the piston crown is an indication that abnormal combustion (pre-ignition) was occurring. Burned areas at the edge of the piston crown are usually evidence of spark knock (detonation). If any of the above problems exist, the causes must be corrected or the damage will occur again. The causes may include inlet air leaks, incorrect air/fuel mixture, incorrect ignition timing and EGR system malfunctions.

9 Corrosion of the piston, in the form of small pits, indicates that coolant is leaking into the combustion chamber and/or the crankcase. Again, the cause must be corrected or the problem may persist in the rebuilt engine.

10 If in any doubt as to the condition of the pistons and connecting rods, have them inspected and measured by an engine reconditioning specialist. If new parts are required, they will be able to supply appropriate-sized pistons/rings, and rebore (where possible) or hone the cylinder block.

13 Crankshaft – inspection

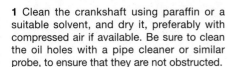

1 Clean the crankshaft using paraffin or a suitable solvent, and dry it, preferably with compressed air if available. Be sure to clean the oil holes with a pipe cleaner or similar probe, to ensure that they are not obstructed.

 Warning: Wear eye protection when using compressed air.

2 Check the main and big-end bearing journals for uneven wear, scoring, pitting and cracking.

3 Big-end bearing wear is accompanied by distinct metallic knocking when the engine is running (particularly noticeable when the engine is pulling from low speed) and some loss of oil pressure.

4 Main bearing wear is accompanied by severe engine vibration and rumble – getting progressively worse as engine speed increases – and again by loss of oil pressure.

5 Check the bearing journal for roughness by running a finger lightly over the bearing surface. Any roughness (which will be accompanied by obvious bearing wear) indicates that the crankshaft requires regrinding (where possible) or renewal.

6 If the crankshaft has been reground, check for burrs around the crankshaft oil holes (the holes are usually chamfered, so burrs should not be a problem unless regrinding has been carried out carelessly). Remove any burrs with a fine file or scraper, and thoroughly clean the oil holes as described previously.

7 Have the crankshaft journals measured by an engine reconditioning specialist. If the crankshaft is worn or damaged, they may be able to regrind the journals and supply suitable undersize bearing shells. If no undersize shells are available and the crankshaft has worn beyond the specified limits, it will have to be renewed. Consult your Toyota dealer or engine specialist for further information on parts availability.

14 Main and big-end bearings – inspection

1 Even though the main and big-end bearings should be renewed during the engine overhaul, the old bearings should be retained for close examination, as they may reveal valuable information about the condition of the engine.

2 Bearing failure can occur due to lack of lubrication, the presence of dirt or other foreign particles, overloading the engine, or corrosion. Regardless of the cause of bearing failure, the cause must be corrected (where applicable) before the engine is reassembled, to prevent it from happening again **(see illustration)**.

3 When examining the bearing shells, remove them from the cylinder block, the main bearing caps/ladder, the connecting rods and the connecting rod big-end bearing caps. Lay them out on a clean surface in the same general position as their location in the engine. This will enable you to match any bearing problems with the corresponding crankshaft journal. *Do not* touch any shell's bearing surface with your fingers while checking it, or the delicate surface may be scratched.

4 Dirt and other foreign matter gets into the engine in a variety of ways. It may be left in the engine during assembly, or it may pass through filters or the crankcase ventilation system. It may get into the oil, and from there into the bearings. Metal chips from machining operations and normal engine wear are often present. Abrasives are sometimes left in engine components after reconditioning, especially when parts are not thoroughly cleaned using the proper cleaning methods. Whatever the source, these foreign objects often end up embedded in the soft bearing material, and are easily recognised. Large particles will not embed in the bearing, and will score or gouge the bearing and journal.

The best prevention for this cause of bearing failure is to clean all parts thoroughly, and keep everything spotlessly-clean during engine assembly. Frequent and regular engine oil and filter changes are also recommended.

5 Lack of lubrication (or lubrication breakdown) has a number of interrelated causes. Excessive heat (which thins the oil), overloading (which squeezes the oil from the bearing face) and oil leakage (from excessive bearing clearances, worn oil pump or high engine speeds) all contribute to lubrication breakdown. Blocked oil passages, which usually are the result of misaligned oil holes in a bearing shell, will also oil-starve a bearing, and destroy it. When lack of lubrication is the cause of bearing failure, the bearing material is wiped or extruded from the steel backing of the bearing. Temperatures may increase to the point where the steel backing turns blue from overheating.

6 Driving habits can have a definite effect on bearing life. Full-throttle, low-speed operation (labouring the engine) puts very high loads on bearings, tending to squeeze out the oil film. These loads cause the bearings to flex, which produces fine cracks in the bearing face (fatigue failure). Eventually, the bearing material will loosen in pieces, and tear away from the steel backing.

7 Short-distance driving leads to corrosion of bearings, because insufficient engine heat is produced to drive off the condensed water and corrosive gases. These products collect in the engine oil, forming acid and sludge. As the oil is carried to the engine bearings, the acid attacks and corrodes the bearing material.

8 Incorrect bearing installation during engine assembly will lead to bearing failure as well. Tight-fitting bearings leave insufficient bearing running clearance, and will result in oil starvation. Dirt or foreign particles trapped

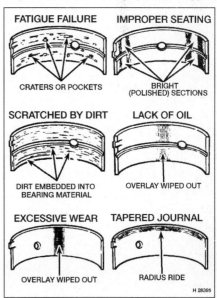

14.2 Typical bearing failures

16.5a Press the bearing shells into their correct locations in the cylinder block . . .

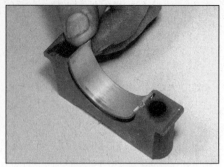

16.5b . . . and caps

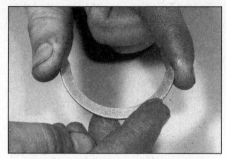

16.6 Use a dab of grease to hold the thrustwashers in position each side of the centre main bearing

behind a bearing shell result in high spots on the bearing, which lead to failure.

9 *Do not* touch any shell's bearing surface with your fingers during reassembly; there is a risk of scratching the delicate surface, or of depositing particles of dirt on it.

10 As mentioned at the beginning of this Section, the bearing shells should be renewed as a matter of course during engine overhaul; to do otherwise is false economy.

15 Engine overhaul – reassembly sequence

1 Before reassembly begins, ensure that all new parts have been obtained, and that all necessary tools are available. Read through the entire procedure, to familiarise yourself with the work involved, and to ensure that all items necessary for reassembly of the engine are at hand. In addition to all normal tools and materials, thread-locking compound will be needed. A suitable tube of liquid sealant will also be required for the joint faces that are fitted without gaskets; it is recommended that Toyota sealant (available from your Toyota dealer) is used.

2 In order to save time and avoid problems, engine reassembly can be carried out in the following order:

a) *Crankshaft (Section 16).*
b) *Piston/connecting rod assemblies (Sections 17 and 18).*
c) *Oil pump, oil pump pick-up tube and oil*

16.8 Make sure that the thrustwashers are correctly located each side of the centre main bearing cap

sea/housing *(see Part A or Part B of this Chapter).*
d) *Sump (see Part A or Part B of this Chapter).*
e) *Flywheel/driveplate (see Part A or Part B of this Chapter).*
f) *Cylinder head (see Part A or Part B of this Chapter).*
g) *Timing belt/chain, tensioner, sprockets and idler pulleys (see Part A or Part B of this Chapter).*
h) *Inlet and exhaust manifolds (Chapter 4A).*
i) *Engine external components.*

3 At this stage, all engine components should be absolutely clean and dry, with all faults repaired. The components should be laid out (or in individual containers) on a completely clean work surface.

16 Crankshaft – refitting

1 Crankshaft installation is the first major step in engine reassembly. It's assumed at this point that the engine block and crankshaft have been cleaned, inspected and repaired or reconditioned.

2 Position the engine with the bottom facing up.

All engines except 1.6 and 1.8 litre post-August 2000

3 Remove the main bearing cap bolts and lift out the caps. Lay the caps out in the proper order.

4 If they're still in place, remove the old

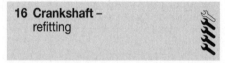

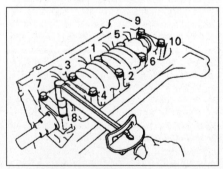

16.9 Main bearing cap tightening sequence

bearing shells from the block and the main bearing caps. Wipe the main bearing surfaces of the block and caps with a clean, lint-free cloth. They must be kept spotlessly clean.

5 Clean the back sides of the new main bearing shells and lay the bearing half with the oil groove in each main bearing saddle in the block **(see illustration)**. Note that on 2.0 litre engines pre-August 2000, the centre (No 3) upper and lower main bearing shells are 22.9 mm wide and all the others are 19.2 mm wide – ensure the shells are fitted accordingly. Lay the other bearing half from each bearing set in the corresponding main bearing cap **(see illustration)**. Make sure the tab on each bearing insert fits into the recess in the block or cap. Also, the oil holes in the block must line up with the oil holes in the bearing shell.

6 Position the thrustwashers on either side of the No 3 bearing position with the oil grooves facing outwards. If necessary, they can be held in position with a smear of grease **(see illustration)**.

7 Wipe clean the thrustwashers and bearing faces in the block and lubricate them thoroughly with clean engine oil.

8 Make sure the crankshaft journals are clean, then lay the crankshaft in place in the block. Clean the faces of the bearings in the caps, then lubricate them with clean engine oil. Install the caps in their respective positions with the arrows pointing toward the front of the engine. The tanged lower thrustwashers should be placed on the caps with their oil grooves facing outward and the tangs fitting into the cap slots **(see illustration)**.

9 Apply a light coat of oil to the bolt threads and the undersides of the bolt heads, then install them. Tighten all the main bearing cap bolts to the specified torque, in sequence **(see illustration)**.

10 Rotate the crankshaft a number of times by hand to check for any obvious binding.

11 Check the crankshaft endfloat with a feeler gauge or a dial indicator as described in Section 10. The endfloat should be correct if the crankshaft thrust faces aren't worn or damaged and new thrustwashers have been installed.

12 On all except 2.0 litre engines post-August 2000, install a new crankshaft oil seal, then refit the seal housing to the block – see Part A or Part B of this Chapter.

16.14a Fit the bearing shells with the oil grooves to the cylinder block . . .

16.14b . . . and fit the plain shells to the main bearing ladder – 1.6 and 1.8 litre engines post-August 2000

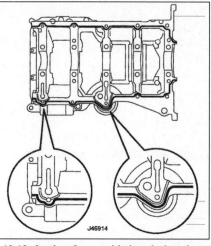

16.18 Apply a 2 mm wide bead of sealant to the main bearing ladder – 1.6 and 1.8 litre engines post-August 2000

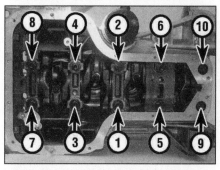

16.19 Main bearing ladder bolt tightening sequence – 1.6 and 1.8 litre engines post-August 2000

1.6 and 1.8 litre engines post-August 2000

13 If they're still in place, remove the old bearing shells from the block and the main bearing ladder. Wipe the main bearing surfaces of the block and ladder with a clean, lint-free cloth. They must be kept spotlessly clean.

14 Clean the back sides of the new main bearing shells and lay the bearing half with the oil groove in each main bearing saddle in the block. Lay the other bearing half from each bearing set in the corresponding main bearing ladder **(see illustrations)**. Make sure the tab on each bearing shell fits into the recess in the block or ladder. Also, the oil holes in the block must line up with the oil holes in the bearing shell.

15 Position the thrustwashers on either side of the No 3 bearing position with the oil grooves facing outwards. If necessary, they can be held in position with a smear of grease.

16 Wipe clean the thrustwashers and bearing faces in the block and lubricate them thoroughly with clean engine oil.

17 Make sure the crankshaft journals are clean, then lay the crankshaft in place in the block. Clean the faces of the bearings in the main bearing ladder, then lubricate them with clean engine oil.

18 Apply a 2 mm wide bead of sealant (Toyota No 08826-00080 or equivalent) to the main bearing ladder **(see illustration)**. Install the main bearing ladder within 3 minutes or the sealant will harden.

19 Refit the 12-point head main bearing ladder bolts (the inner row of 10), and tighten them in sequence to the Stage 1 torque setting, then to the Stage 2 setting **(see illustration)**. Again, working in sequence, tighten the bolts to the Stage 3 angle setting, followed by the Stage 4 angle setting, using an angle-tightening gauge.

20 Refit the remaining hexagon-head bolts to the main bearing ladder and progressively tighten them in a diagonal sequence to the specified torque.

21 Rotate the crankshaft a number of times by hand to check for any obvious binding.

22 Check the crankshaft endfloat with a feeler gauge or a dial indicator as described in Section 10. The endfloat should be correct if the crankshaft thrust faces aren't worn or damaged and new thrustwashers have been installed.

23 Install a new crankshaft oil seal with reference to Part B of this Chapter.

17 Piston rings – refitting

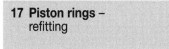

1 Before fitting the new piston rings, the ring end gaps must be checked.

2 Lay out the piston/connecting rod assemblies and the new ring sets so the ring sets will be matched with the same piston and cylinder during the end gap measurement and engine assembly.

3 Insert the top (number one) ring into the first cylinder and square it up with the cylinder walls by pushing it in with the top of the piston. The ring should be near the bottom of the cylinder, at the lower limit of ring travel.

4 To measure the end gap, slip feeler gauges between the ends of the ring until a gauge equal to the gap width is found **(see illustration)**. The feeler gauge should slide between the ring ends with a slight amount of drag. Compare the measurement to that given in the Specifications. If the gap is larger or smaller than specified, double-check to make sure you have the correct rings before proceeding.

5 If the gap is too small (unlikely if genuine Toyota parts are used), it must be enlarged, or the ring ends may contact each other during engine operation, causing serious damage. Ideally, new piston rings providing the correct end gap should be fitted. As a last resort, the end gap can be increased by filing the ring ends very carefully with a fine file. Mount the file in a vice with soft jaws, slip the ring over the file with the ends contacting the file face, and slowly move the ring to remove material from the ends. Take care, as piston rings are sharp, and are easily broken.

6 With new piston rings, it is unlikely that the end gap will be too large. If the gaps are too large, check that you have the correct rings for your engine and for the particular cylinder bore size.

7 Repeat the checking procedure for each ring in the first cylinder, and then for the rings in the remaining cylinders. Remember to keep rings, pistons and cylinders matched up.

8 Once the ring end gaps have been checked and if necessary corrected, the rings can be fitted to the pistons.

9 Fit the piston rings using the same technique as for removal. Fit the bottom (oil control) ring first, and work up. When fitting a three-piece oil control ring, first insert the expander, then fit the lower rail with its gap

17.4 With the piston ring square in the bore, measure the end gap with a feeler gauge

17.9a Fit the expander in the oil control ring groove . . .

17.9b . . . followed by the lower and upper rails

positioned 120° from the expander gap, then fit the upper rail with its gap positioned 120° from the lower rail **(see illustrations)**. When fitting a two-piece oil control ring, first insert the expander, then fit the control ring with its gap positioned 180° from the expander gap. Ensure that the second compression ring is fitted the correct way up, with its identification mark (either a dot of paint or the word TOP stamped on the ring surface) at the top, and the stepped surface at the bottom. Arrange the gaps of the top and second compression rings 120° either side of the oil control ring gap, but make sure that none of the ring gaps are positioned over the gudgeon pin hole. **Note:** *Always follow any instructions supplied with the new piston ring sets – different manufacturers may specify different procedures. Do not mix up the top and second compression rings, as they have different cross-sections.*

18 Pistons/connecting rods – refitting

1 Before installing the piston/connecting rod assemblies, the cylinder walls must be perfectly clean, the top edge of each cylinder must be chamfered, and the crankshaft must be in place.
2 Remove the cap from the end of the number one connecting rod (refer to the marks made during removal). Remove the original bearing shells and wipe the bearing surfaces of the connecting rod and cap with a clean, lint-free cloth. They must be kept spotlessly clean.
3 Clean the back side of the new upper bearing shell, then lay it in place in the connecting rod. Make sure the tab on the bearing fits into the recess in the rod so the oil holes line up. Don't hammer the bearing insert

into place and be very careful not to nick or gouge the bearing face.
4 Clean the back side of the other bearing shell and install it in the rod cap. Again, make sure the tab on the bearing fits into the recess in the cap, and don't apply any lubricant. It's critically important that the mating surfaces of the bearing and connecting rod are perfectly clean and oil-free when they're assembled.
5 Position the piston ring gaps at staggered intervals around the piston **(see illustrations)**.
6 Where applicable, slip a section of plastic or rubber hose over each connecting rod cap bolt to protect the cylinder bore.
7 Lubricate the piston and rings with clean engine oil and attach a piston ring compressor to the piston. Leave the skirt protruding about 8.0 mm to guide the piston into the cylinder. The rings must be compressed until they're flush with the piston.
8 Rotate the crankshaft until the number one connecting rod journal is at BDC (bottom dead centre) and apply a coat of engine oil to the cylinder wall.
9 Gently insert the piston/connecting rod assembly into the number one cylinder bore and rest the bottom edge of the ring compressor on the cylinder block. Ensure that the piston front marking (in the form of one or two indentations or a single protrusion) on the piston crown is toward the timing belt/chain end of the engine.
10 Tap the top edge of the ring compressor to ensure it's contacting the block around its entire circumference.
11 Gently tap on the top of the piston with the end of a wooden hammer handle **(see illustration)** while guiding the end of the connecting rod into place on the crankshaft journal. The piston rings may try to pop out of the ring compressor just before entering the cylinder bore, so keep some downward pressure on the ring compressor. Work slowly, and if any resistance is felt as the piston enters the cylinder, stop immediately. Find out what's binding and fix it before proceeding.
Caution: Do not, for any reason, force the piston into the cylinder – you might break a ring and/or the piston.
12 Make sure the bearing faces are perfectly clean, then lubricate them with clean engine oil.

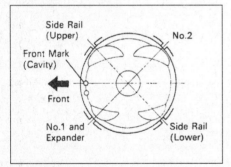

18.5a Piston ring end gap spacing – 1.6 and 1.8 litre engines pre-August 2000

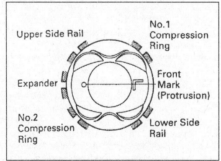

18.5b Piston ring end gap spacing – 2.0 litre engines pre-August 2000

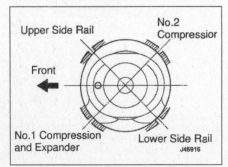

18.5c Piston ring end gap spacing – 1.6 and 1.8 litre engines post-August 2000

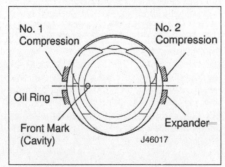

18.5d Piston ring end gap spacing – 2.0 litre engines post-August 2000

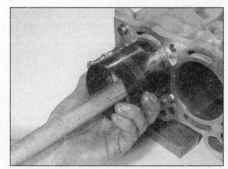

18.11 Using a hammer handle to tap the piston into its bore

13 Slide the connecting rod into place on the journal, remove the protective hoses from the rod cap bolts, and fit the bearing cap. Note that the faces with the identification marks must match (which means that the bearing shell locating tabs abut each other). Fit the nuts/bolts and tighten them to the specified torque.

14 Tighten the bearing cap retaining nuts/bolts to their Stage 1 torque setting, using a torque wrench and socket, then tighten them through the specified Stage 2 angle setting.

15 Rotate the crankshaft and check that it turns freely; some stiffness is to be expected if new components have been fitted, but there should be no signs of binding or tight spots.

16 Refit the remaining three piston/connecting rod assemblies in the same way.

2.0 litre engines post-August 2000

17 Ensure that the joint faces of the cylinder block and lower crankcase are thoroughly clean and dry, then place a new O-ring in the oil gallery groove on the cylinder block joint face.

18 Apply a 2.5 to 3.0 mm wide bead of sealant (Toyota No 08826-00080 or equivalent) to the lower crankcase **(see illustration)**. Install the lower crankcase within 3 minutes or the sealant will harden.

19 Refit the six short bolts and five long bolts in their correct positions, and tighten them all hand-tight **(see illustration 9.2a)**. Working in a diagonal sequence, progressively tighten the bolts to the specified torque.

20 Install a new crankshaft oil seal with reference to Part B of this Chapter.

All engines

21 Refit the oil pump, oil pump pick-up tube, sump, rear engine plate, cylinder head, timing belt/chain, flywheel/driveplate and the remainder of the external components with reference to Part A, Part B and earlier Sections of this Chapter.

19 Engine – initial start-up after overhaul

1 With the engine refitted in the vehicle, double-check the engine oil and coolant levels. Make a final check that everything has been reconnected, and that there are no tools or rags left in the engine compartment.

2 Remove the spark plugs and, on pre-August 2000 engines, disable the ignition system by disconnecting the wiring multiplug connectors at the ignition coils (see Chapter 5B).

3 Disable the fuel injection system by disconnecting the wiring connector from the fuel pump(s) as described in Chapter 4A, Section 2.

4 Turn the engine on the starter until the oil pressure warning light goes out. Refit the spark plugs, and reconnect the ignition and fuel injection system wiring connectors.

5 Start the engine, noting that this may take a little longer than usual, due to the fuel system components having been disturbed.

6 While the engine is idling, check for fuel, water and oil leaks. Don't be alarmed if there are some odd smells and smoke from parts getting hot and burning off oil deposits.

7 Assuming all is well, keep the engine idling

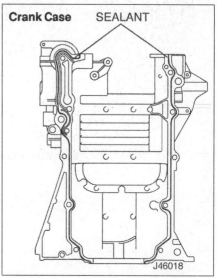

18.18 Apply a 2.5 to 3.0 mm wide bead of sealant to the lower crankcase – 2.0 litre engines post-August 2000

until hot water is felt circulating through the radiator top hose, then switch off the engine.

8 After a few minutes, recheck the oil and coolant levels as described in Chapter 1, and top-up as necessary.

9 If new pistons, rings or crankshaft bearings have been fitted, the engine must be treated as new, and run-in for the first 500 miles. Do not operate the engine at full-throttle, or allow it to labour at low engine speeds in any gear. It is recommended that the oil and filter be changed at the end of this period.

Notes

Chapter 3
Cooling, heating and air conditioning systems

Contents

Degrees of difficulty

Easy, suitable for novice with little experience	Fairly easy, suitable for beginner with some experience	Fairly difficult, suitable for competent DIY mechanic	Difficult, suitable for experienced DIY mechanic	Very difficult, suitable for expert DIY or professional

Specifications

General
Radiator cap opening pressure	0.75 to 1.05 bars
Coolant mixture type and capacity	See Chapter 1

Thermostat
Opening temperature.	80° to 84°C
Minimum valve lift at 95°C	8.0 mm

Engine coolant temperature sensor resistance
20°C.	2 to 3 k ohms
40°C.	0.9 to 1.3 k ohms
80°C.	0.2 to 0.4 k ohms

Air conditioning system
Refrigerant:
Type	R-134a
Quantity	450 ± 50g
Air conditioning compressor oil type	ND-Oil 8

Torque wrench settings

	Nm	lbf ft
Pre-August 2000 models		
Air conditioning compressor mounting bolts	25	18
Air conditioning refrigerant pipe retaining bolts	10	7
Coolant pump body to cover	9	7
Coolant pump elbow nuts	15	11
Coolant pump to cylinder block:		
1.6 and 1.8 litre engines	14	10
2.0 litre engines	8	6
Cylinder block drain plug:		
1.6 and 1.8 litre engines	34	25
2.0 litre engines	25	18
Thermostat cover/inlet	9	7
Post-August 2000 models		
Air conditioning compressor mounting bolts	25	18
Air conditioning refrigerant pipe retaining bolts	10	7
Coolant pump bolts/nuts:		
1.6 and 1.8 litre engines:		
Short bolts	9	7
Long bolts.	11	8
2.0 litre engines	9	7
Coolant pump pulley (2.0 litre engines)	26	19
Cylinder block drain plug	8	6
Thermostat cover/inlet	9	7

1 General information and precautions

Engine cooling system

All models covered by this manual use a pressurised engine cooling system with thermostatically-controlled coolant circulation. An impeller type coolant pump mounted on the front of the cylinder block pumps coolant through the engine. The coolant flows around each cylinder and toward the rear of the engine. Cast-in coolant passages direct coolant around the inlet and exhaust ports, near the spark plug areas and in proximity to the exhaust valve guides.

A wax-pellet type thermostat is located in the thermostat housing at the transmission end of the engine, or on the front face of the cylinder block. During warm-up, the closed thermostat prevents coolant from circulating through the radiator. When the engine reaches normal operating temperature, the thermostat opens and allows hot coolant to travel through the radiator, where it is cooled before returning to the engine.

The cooling system is sealed by a pressure-type radiator cap. This raises the boiling point of the coolant, and the higher boiling point of the coolant increases the cooling efficiency of the radiator. If the system pressure exceeds the cap pressure-relief value, the excess pressure in the system forces the spring-loaded valve inside the cap off its seat and allows the coolant to escape through the overflow tube into the coolant expansion tank. When the system cools, the excess coolant is automatically drawn from the expansion tank back into the radiator.

The coolant expansion tank does double duty as both the point at which fresh coolant is added to the cooling system to maintain the proper level, and as a holding tank for heated coolant.

This type of cooling system is known as a closed design because coolant that escapes past the pressure cap is saved and re-used.

Heating system

The heating system consists of a blower fan and heater matrix located within the heater assembly under the facia, the inlet and outlet hoses connecting the heater matrix to the engine cooling system, and the heater/air conditioning control panel on the facia. Engine coolant is circulated through the heater matrix. When the heater mode is activated, a flap door opens to expose the heater matrix to the passenger compartment. A fan switch on the control panel activates the blower motor, which forces air through the matrix, heating the air.

Air conditioning system

The air conditioning system consists of a condenser mounted in front of the radiator, an evaporator mounted adjacent to the heater matrix, a compressor mounted on the engine, and the pipework connecting all of the above.

A blower fan forces the warmer air of the passenger compartment through the evaporator matrix (sort of a radiator-in-reverse), transferring the heat from the air to the refrigerant. The liquid refrigerant boils off into low pressure vapour, taking the heat with it when it leaves the evaporator. The compressor keeps refrigerant circulating through the system, pumping the warmed refrigerant through the condenser where it is cooled and then circulated back to the evaporator.

Precautions

 Warning: Do not attempt to remove the radiator pressure cap, or to disturb any part of the cooling system, while the engine is hot, as there is a high risk of scalding. If the radiator pressure cap must be removed before the engine and radiator have fully cooled (even though this is not recommended), the pressure in the cooling system must first be relieved. Cover the cap with a thick layer of cloth, to avoid scalding, and slowly unscrew the pressure cap until a hissing sound is heard. When the hissing has stopped, indicating that the pressure has reduced, slowly unscrew the pressure cap until it can be removed; if more hissing sounds are heard, wait until they have stopped before unscrewing the cap completely. At all times, keep your face well away from the pressure cap opening, and protect your hands.

Warning: Do not allow antifreeze to come into contact with your skin, or with the painted surfaces of the vehicle. Rinse off spills immediately, with plenty of water. Never leave antifreeze lying around in an open container, or in a puddle in the driveway or on the garage floor. Children and pets are attracted by its sweet smell, but antifreeze can be fatal if ingested.

Warning: Refer to Section 10 for precautions to be observed when working on models equipped with air conditioning.

2 Cooling system hoses – disconnection and renewal

Note: *Refer to the warnings given in Section 1 of this Chapter before proceeding. Hoses should only be disconnected once the engine has cooled sufficiently to avoid scalding.*

1 If the checks described in Chapter 1 reveal a faulty hose, it must be renewed as follows.

2 First drain the cooling system (see Chapter 1). If the coolant is not due for renewal, it may be re-used if it is collected in a clean container. Squirt a little penetrating oil onto the hose clips if they are corroded.

3 To disconnect a hose, release its retaining clips, then move them along the hose, clear of the stubs. Carefully work the hose free. **Do not** attempt to disconnect any part of the system while it is still hot.

4 Note that the radiator stubs are fragile; do not use excessive force when attempting to remove the hoses. If a hose is difficult to remove, try to release it by twisting it.

 If all else fails, cut the hose with a sharp knife, then slit it so that it can be peeled off in two pieces. Although this may prove expensive if the hose is otherwise undamaged, it is preferable to buying a new radiator.

5 When fitting a hose, first slide the clips onto the centre of the hose, then engage the hose with its union. If clamp type clips were originally fitted and they have lost their tension, it is a good idea to update them with screw type clips when refitting the hose.

 If the hose is stiff, use a little soapy water as a lubricant, or soften the hose by soaking it in hot water. Do not use oil or grease, which may attack the rubber.

6 Work the hose fully into place, checking that it is correctly routed, then slide each clip along the hose until it passes over the flared end of the relevant outlet, before securing it in position.

3.7 Automatic transmission fluid cooler line on the radiator bottom tank

3.4 Disconnecting the top hose from the radiator

3.6a Disconnect the wiring connector at the main cooling fan . . .

7 Refill the cooling system with reference to Chapter 1.

8 Check thoroughly for leaks as soon as possible after disturbing any part of the cooling system.

3 Radiator – removal, inspection and refitting

Note: *Refer to the warnings given in Section 1 of this Chapter before starting work.*

 If leakage is the reason for removing the radiator, bear in mind that minor leaks can often be cured using a radiator sealant with the radiator in situ.

3.8 Unbolting the radiator upper mounting brackets from the crossmember

3.5 Disconnecting the expansion tank hose from the tank

3.6b . . . and at the air conditioning condenser cooling fan (if fitted)

Removal

1 Disconnect the battery negative terminal (refer to *Disconnecting the battery* in the Reference Chapter).

2 Firmly apply the handbrake, then jack up the front of the car and support it securely on axle stands (see *Jacking and vehicle support*).

3 Unbolt and remove the undershields from beneath the engine, then drain the cooling system as described in Chapter 1.

4 Disconnect the top and bottom hoses from the radiator **(see illustration)**.

5 Disconnect the hose from the expansion tank **(see illustration)**.

6 Disconnect the wiring to the cooling fan(s) at the connector(s) on the fan shroud(s) **(see illustrations)**.

7 On models with automatic transmission, disconnect the fluid cooler lines from the bottom of the radiator **(see illustration)**.

8 Unbolt the upper mounting brackets from the front engine compartment crossmember and remove them from the top of the radiator **(see illustration)**.

9 Lift the radiator and cooling fan assembly from the lower rubber mountings and remove it from the engine compartment **(see illustration)**.

10 If necessary remove the mounting rubbers from the front valance.

Inspection

11 If the radiator has been removed due to suspected blockage, reverse-flush it as described in Chapter 1. Clean dirt and debris from the radiator fins, using an air line (in which

3.9 Lifting the radiator and cooling fans from the engine compartment

case, wear eye protection) or a soft brush. Be careful, as the fins are sharp, and can also be easily damaged.

12 If necessary, a radiator specialist can perform a flow test on the radiator, to establish whether an internal blockage exists.

13 A leaking radiator must be referred to a specialist for permanent repair. Do not attempt to weld or solder a leaking radiator, as damage to the plastic components may result.

14 If the radiator is to be sent for repair, or is to be renewed, remove the cooling fan(s) (Section 5) and all hoses first.

15 Inspect the condition of the upper and lower radiator mounting rubbers, and renew them if necessary.

Refitting

16 Refitting is a reversal of removal but, on completion, refill and bleed the cooling system as described in Chapter 1.

4.8a Removing the thermostat cover/inlet – 1.6 and 1.8 litre engines pre-August 2000

4.9a The thermostat jiggle pin (arrowed) must face upwards

4 Thermostat – removal, testing and refitting

Note: *Refer to the warnings given in Section 1 of this Chapter before starting work.*

1 Before assuming the thermostat is to blame for a cooling system problem, check the coolant level, auxiliary drivebelt tension and condition (see Chapter 1), and temperature gauge operation.

2 If the engine seems to be taking a long time to warm-up (based on heater output or temperature gauge operation), the thermostat is probably stuck open. Renew the thermostat.

3 If the engine runs hot, use your hand to check the temperature of the radiator top hose. If the hose isn't hot, but the engine is, the thermostat is probably stuck closed, preventing the coolant inside the engine from escaping to the radiator – renew the thermostat.

Caution: Don't drive the vehicle without a thermostat. The lack of a thermostat will slow warm-up time. The engine management system's ECU will then stay in warm-up mode for longer than necessary, causing emissions and fuel economy to suffer.

4 If the radiator top hose is hot, it means that the coolant is flowing and the thermostat is open. Consult the *Fault finding* section at the end of this manual to assist in tracing possible cooling system faults.

4.8b Thermostat cover/inlet – 2.0 litre engines pre-August 2000

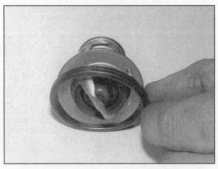

4.9b Removing the rubber sealing ring from the thermostat

Pre-August 2000 models

Removal

5 On 1.6 and 1.8 litre engines, the thermostat is located in a housing bolted to the transmission end of the cylinder head. On 2.0 litre engines it is located on the coolant pump at the front right-hand end of the cylinder block.

6 Drain the cooling system as described in Chapter 1.

7 Disconnect the radiator top hose from the thermostat cover/inlet.

8 Unscrew the nuts and remove the thermostat cover/inlet from the studs on the housing **(see illustrations)**.

9 Note that the jiggle pin on the thermostat is facing upwards, then withdraw the thermostat from the thermostat housing or cover/inlet. Ease the rubber sealing ring from the edge of the thermostat **(see illustrations)**.

Testing

10 Suspend the thermostat on a length of string in a container full of cold water. Heat the water to bring it to the boil – the thermostat must open by the time the water boils. If not, renew it.

11 If a thermometer is available, the opening temperature of the thermostat may be determined; compare with the figures given in the Specifications. The opening temperature is also marked on the thermostat.

12 If the thermostat fails to close as the water cools, it must be renewed.

Refitting

13 Commence refitting by thoroughly cleaning the mating faces and seating of the cover/inlet and the housing.

14 Fit a new rubber sealing ring to the thermostat.

15 Locate the thermostat in the housing or inlet (as applicable) making sure that the jiggle pin is facing upwards. On 2.0 litre engines the cover/inlet has a protrusion for aligning the jiggle pin.

16 Refit the cover/inlet on the studs and tighten the mounting nuts progressively to the specified torque.

17 Reconnect the radiator top hose.

18 Refill the cooling system as described in Chapter 1.

Post-August 2000 models

Removal

19 The thermostat is located at the front right-hand end of the cylinder block, below the alternator.

20 Remove the alternator as described in Chapter 5A.

21 Undo the two nuts and remove the thermostat cover **(see illustration)**.

22 Remove the thermostat, and ease the rubber sealing ring from the thermostat edge **(see illustration 4.9b)**.

Testing

23 Proceed as described in paragraphs 10 to 12.

Refitting

24 Fit a new seal to the thermostat, and fit it into position on the engine block, with the jiggle pin at the 12 o'clock position.

25 Refit the thermostat cover and tighten the nuts to the specified torque.

26 Refit the alternator as described in Chapter 5A.

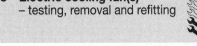

5 Electric cooling fan(s)
– testing, removal and refitting

Note: Refer to the warnings given in Section 1 of this Chapter before starting work.

Testing

1 The coolant temperature is monitored by the engine management electronic control unit, via the coolant temperature sensor. The fans are operated by the ECU, by energising the cooling fan relay(s).

2 If the fan does not appear to work, run the engine until normal operating temperature is reached, then allow it to idle. The fan should cut in within a few minutes (before the temperature gauge needle enters the red section).

3 The motor can be tested by disconnecting it from the wiring loom, and connecting a 12 volt supply directly to it. The motor should operate – if not, the motor or wiring is faulty.

4 If the motor operates when tested as described in paragraph 3, the fault must lie in the engine wiring harness, the relay, the coolant temperature sensor or the ECU. Any further fault diagnosis should be referred to a suitably-equipped Toyota dealer, or vehicle diagnostic specialist.

Removal

5 Make sure that the ignition is switched off, then disconnect the wiring to the relevant cooling fan at the connector on the fan shroud **(see illustrations 3.6a and 3.6b)**.

6 If the right-hand fan is to be removed, drain sufficient coolant to enable the upper radiator hose to be disconnected at the radiator (see Chapter 1).

6.2a Engine coolant temperature sensor location (arrowed) – 1.6 and 1.8 litre engines pre-August 2000

4.21 Undo the two nuts (arrowed) and remove the thermostat cover – post-August 2000 models

5.8 On Denso fans, undo the retaining nut (arrowed) and remove the fan from the motor shaft

7 Unscrew the mounting bolts securing the cooling fan shroud assembly to the rear of the radiator, then lift the assembly upwards taking care not to damage the radiator fins **(see illustration)**.

8 To remove the fan motor from the shroud, extract the retaining C-clip (Bosch fans) or undo the retaining nut (Denso fans) and remove the fan from the motor shaft **(see illustration)**.

9 Release the motor wiring from the clips on the shroud, then unscrew the three retaining nuts, or screws, and withdraw the fan motor **(see illustration)**.

Refitting

10 Refitting is a reversal of removal, but take care not to damage the radiator fins. Where applicable, top-up the cooling system as described in *Weekly checks*.

6.2b Engine coolant temperature sensor location (arrowed) – 2.0 litre engines pre-August 2000

5.7 Cooling fan shroud mounting bolts (arrowed)

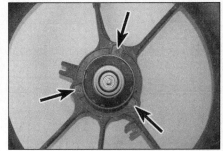

5.9 Unscrew the three retaining nuts or screws (arrowed) and withdraw the fan motor

6 Cooling system electrical sensors –
testing, removal and refitting

Note: Refer to the warnings given in Section 1 of this Chapter before starting work.

Coolant temperature sensor

Testing

1 The engine coolant temperature sensor provides information to the engine management electronic control unit to control the fuel and ignition systems.

2 On pre-August 2000 models, the sensor is located on the thermostat housing on the left-hand end of the cylinder head on 1.6 and 1.8 litre engines, and in the water outlet elbow on the left-hand end of the cylinder head on 2.0 litre engines **(see illustrations)**.

6.2c Engine coolant temperature sensor location (arrowed) – 1.6 and 1.8 litre engines post-August 2000

6.2d Engine coolant temperature sensor location (arrowed) – 2.0 litre engines post-August 2000

On post-August 2000 models, the sensor is located on the left-hand end of the cylinder head **(see illustrations)**. The sensor contains a thermistor – an electronic component whose electrical resistance decreases at a predetermined rate as its temperature rises.

3 The fuel injection/engine management ECU supplies the sensor with a set voltage and then, by measuring the current flowing in the sensor circuit, determines the engine temperature. This information is then used, in conjunction with other inputs, to control the fuel injection/engine management system.

4 If the sensor circuit should fail to provide adequate information, the ECU back-up facility will override the sensor signal. In this event, the ECU assumes a predetermined setting which will allow the fuel injection/ engine management system to run, albeit at reduced efficiency. When this occurs, the engine warning light on the instrument panel will come on, and the advice of a Toyota dealer should be sought. The sensor itself can be tested by removing it, and checking the resistances at various temperatures using an ohmmeter (heat the sensor in a container of water, and monitor the temperature with a thermometer). The resistance values are given in the Specifications. *Do not* attempt to test the circuit with the sensor fitted to the engine, and the wiring connector fitted, as there is a high risk of damaging the ECU.

5 Refer to Chapter 4A for further details of the fuel injection/engine management system.

Removal

6 For improved access, remove the air cleaner assembly and air inlet ducts as described in Chapter 4A.

7 Drain the cooling system as described in Chapter 1.

8 Disconnect the wiring plug from the sensor.

9 Unscrew the sensor from its location.

Refitting

10 Refitting is a reversal of removal, but tighten the sensor securely and refill the cooling system as described in Chapter 1.

Temperature gauge sender

Note: *The following procedures are only applicable to 1.6 and 1.8 litre engines pre-August 2000. On pre-August 2000, 2.0 litre engines, and all post-August 2000 engines, the*

6.11 Coolant temperature gauge sender location – 1.6 and 1.8 litre engines pre-August 2000

temperature gauge is controlled by the engine management electronic control unit using coolant temperature information provided by the engine coolant temperature sensor.

Testing

11 The sender is located on the coolant pump rear elbow **(see illustration)**.

12 The temperature gauge is fed with a voltage from the instrument panel feed (via the ignition switch and a fuse). The gauge earth is controlled by the sender. The sender contains a thermistor – an electronic component whose electrical resistance decreases at a predetermined rate as its temperature rises. When the coolant is cold, the sender resistance is high, current flow through the gauge is reduced, and the gauge needle points towards the cold end of the scale. As the coolant temperature rises and the sender resistance falls, current flow increases, and the gauge needle moves towards the upper end of the scale. If the sender is faulty, it must be renewed.

13 If the gauge develops a fault, first check the other instruments; if they do not work at all, or work erratically, check the instrument panel electrical feed. If the fault lies in the temperature gauge alone, check it as follows.

14 If the gauge needle remains at the cold end of the scale when the engine is hot, disconnect the sender wiring plug and earth the wire to the cylinder head. If the needle then deflects when the ignition is switched on, the sender unit is proved faulty, and should be renewed. If the needle still does not move,

7.10 Removing the bolt securing the power steering pump bracket to the cylinder head – 1.6 and 1.8 litre engines pre-August 2000

remove the instrument panel (Chapter 12) and check the continuity of the wire between the sender unit and the gauge, and the feed to the gauge unit. If continuity is shown, and the fault still exists, then the gauge is faulty, and the gauge should be renewed.

15 If the gauge needle remains at the hot end of the scale when the engine is cold, disconnect the sender wire. If the needle then returns to the cold end of the scale when the ignition is switched on, the sender unit is proved faulty, and should be renewed. If the needle still does not move, check the remainder of the circuit as described previously.

Removal and refitting

16 The procedure is similar to that described previously in this Section for the engine coolant temperature sensor.

---

7 Coolant pump – removal, inspection and refitting

Note: *Refer to the warnings given in Section 1 of this Chapter before starting work.*

1.6 and 1.8 litre engines pre-August 2000

Removal

1 Disconnect the battery negative terminal (refer to *Disconnecting the battery* in the Reference Chapter).

2 Drain the cooling system as described in Chapter 1.

3 Remove the camshaft cover as described in Chapter 2A.

4 Loosen the bolts securing the drive pulley to the coolant pump one or two turns – the bolts are easier to loosen before removing the drivebelt.

5 Firmly apply the handbrake, then jack up the front of the car and support it securely on axle stands (see *Jacking and vehicle support*). Remove the right-hand roadwheel, then unbolt and remove the undershield from under the right-hand side of the engine compartment.

6 Remove the auxiliary drivebelt(s) (alternator, power steering and air conditioning, as applicable), as described in Chapter 1.

7 Fully unscrew the bolts securing the pulley to the coolant pump. **Note:** *It is not possible to completely remove the pulley as there is insufficient room between the pulley and inner wing panel. The pulley is removed together with the pump, however, it must be moved to the rear as far as possible at this stage in order to remove the middle timing cover.*

8 Unbolt and remove the upper and middle timing belt covers with reference to Chapter 2A.

9 Unscrew the bolt securing the engine oil level dipstick tube to the coolant pump rear elbow, then withdraw the tube from the rear of the oil pump housing and remove from the engine compartment. Check that the O-ring is still located on the bottom end of the tube.

10 Unscrew the bolt securing the power steering pump bracket to the cylinder head, then loosen the pump mounting bolts and move the pump as far to the rear as possible **(see illustration)**.
11 Disconnect the wiring from the temperature gauge sender on the coolant pump-to-cylinder head elbow.
12 Unbolt and remove the support from the rear elbow.
13 Unscrew the two nuts securing the coolant pump rear elbow to the cylinder head, pull the elbow from the studs, and recover the gasket **(see illustrations)**.
14 Unscrew the bolts securing the coolant pump to the right-hand end of the cylinder block, then withdraw the assembly upwards while guiding it from behind the timing belt. Recover the coolant pump pulley then remove the O-ring from the cylinder block **(see illustrations)**.
15 With the assembly on the bench, release the clips and disconnect the elbow and hose from the rear of the coolant pump **(see illustration)**.
16 Unscrew the bolts and separate the rear cover from the coolant pump. Recover the gasket **(see illustrations)**.

Inspection

17 Check the pump body and impeller for signs of excessive corrosion. Turn the impeller and check for stiffness due to corrosion, or roughness due to excessive end play. If the pump bearings are worn excessively, it is possible to fit new bearings, however, this work is best entrusted to a Toyota dealer or overhaul specialist who will have a press required to both remove and fit the bearings.

Refitting

18 Refitting is a reversal of the removal procedure, however, always fit new gaskets to the cover and elbow, and fit a new O-ring to the cylinder block. The rear elbow gasket must be located on the studs with the protrusion facing upwards. Tighten all nuts and bolts to the specified torque settings (where given). *Do not* forget to locate the pulley on the coolant pump before refitting the pump to the cylinder block – tighten the pulley bolts moderately and fully tighten them after adjusting the auxiliary drivebelt as described in Chapter 1. Refit the camshaft cover with reference to Chapter 2A. Refill the cooling system with reference to Chapter 1, then start the engine and check all disturbed joints for leaks as soon as the engine is fully warmed-up.

2.0 litre engines pre-August 2000

Removal

19 Drain the cooling system as described in Chapter 1. Disconnect the radiator top hose from the thermostat cover elbow on the coolant pump.
20 Remove the timing belt and idler pulley(s) as described in Chapter 2A.

21 Remove the alternator as described in Chapter 5A, then unbolt the lower alternator mounting bracket.
22 Unscrew the two nuts securing the bypass pipe to the coolant pump on the front of the engine.

23 Unscrew the three mounting bolts securing the coolant pump to the cylinder block, then withdraw the pump from the bypass pipe and remove from the engine compartment. Recover the O-ring from the bypass pipe and the gasket from the cylinder block.

7.13a Removing the coolant pump rear elbow . . .

7.13b . . . and gasket – 1.6 and 1.8 litre engines pre-August 2000

7.14a Removing the coolant pump . . .

7.14b . . . and O-ring – 1.6 and 1.8 litre engines pre-August 2000

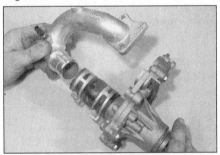

7.15 Removing the elbow and hose from the rear of the coolant pump – 1.6 and 1.8 litre engines pre-August 2000

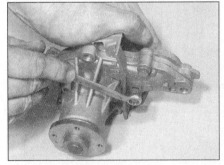

7.16a Unscrew the bolts . . .

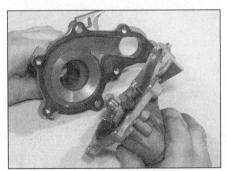

7.16b . . . separate the cover . . .

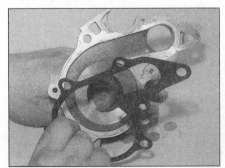

7.16c . . . and remove the gasket – 1.6 and 1.8 litre engines pre-August 2000

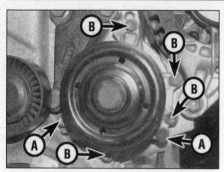

7.31 The bolts marked (A) are the short bolts, whilst the ones marked (B) are the long bolts – 1.6 and 1.8 litre engines post-August 2000

24 With the assembly on the bench, unbolt the coolant pump from the cover and recover the gasket. If necessary, remove the thermostat with reference to Section 4.

Inspection

25 Clean all mating surfaces thoroughly then inspect the coolant pump for wear and damage.
26 Check the pump body and impeller for signs of excessive corrosion. Turn the impeller and check for stiffness due to corrosion, or roughness due to excessive end play. Renew the pump if the bearings are worn excessively.

Refitting

27 Refitting is a reversal of removal, but fit a new O-ring and gaskets and tighten all nuts and bolts to the specified torque wrench settings (where given). Refit the timing belt as described in Chapter 2A, and adjust the alternator drivebelt with reference to Chapter 1. Refill the cooling system with reference to Chapter 1, then start the engine and check all disturbed joints for leaks as soon as the engine is fully warmed-up.

1.6 and 1.8 litre engines post-August 2000

Removal

28 Disconnect the battery negative terminal (refer to *Disconnecting the battery* in the Reference Chapter).
29 Drain the cooling system as described in Chapter 1.
30 Remove the auxiliary drivebelt as described in Chapter 1.
31 Undo the 6 bolts, noting their different lengths, and remove the coolant pump **(see illustration)**. Discard the O-ring seal, a new one must be fitted.

Inspection

32 Clean all mating surfaces thoroughly then inspect the coolant pump for wear and damage.
33 Check the pump body and impeller for signs of excessive corrosion. Turn the impeller and check for stiffness due to corrosion, or roughness due to excessive end play.

Renew the pump if the bearings are worn excessively.

Refitting

34 Refitting is a reversal of removal, but fit a new O-ring and tighten all bolts to the specified torque wrench settings. Refit the auxiliary drivebelt and refill the cooling system as described in Chapter 1. Start the engine and check all disturbed joints for leaks as soon as the engine is fully warmed-up.

2.0 litre engines post-August 2000

Removal

35 Disconnect the battery negative terminal (refer to *Disconnecting the battery* in the Reference Chapter).
36 Drain the cooling system as described in Chapter 1.
37 Remove the auxiliary drivebelt as described in Chapter 1.
38 Loosen the bolts securing the drive pulley to the coolant pump one or two turns. Use a screwdriver between two of the bolts to hold the pulley, while the remaining bolt is loosened, and repeat until all three are loose. Remove the bolts and the pulley.
39 Detach the cable clip securing the crankshaft position sensor wiring to the coolant pump, then release the wiring from the cable guide.
40 Undo the four bolts and two nuts securing the coolant pump to the cylinder block and lift off the crankshaft position sensor cable guide.
41 Use a flat-bladed screwdriver at the upper and lower leverage points to carefully prise the pump free, then remove the pump from the cylinder block. Take great care not to damage the sealing surfaces.

Inspection

42 Clean the mating surfaces of the pump and cylinder block thoroughly, ensuring that all traces of old sealant are removed.
43 Check the pump body and impeller for signs of excessive corrosion. Turn the impeller and check for stiffness due to corrosion, or roughness due to excessive end play. Renew the pump if the bearings are worn excessively.

Refitting

44 Apply a 2 mm (approximately) wide bead of Toyota sealant No 08826-00100, or equivalent, to the coolant pump flange, ensuring that the bead goes around the inside of the bolt holes. **Note:** *Refitting must be completed within 5 minutes once the sealer has been applied.*
45 Locate the pump on the cylinder block, place the cable guide over the mounting stud and refit the retaining nuts and bolts. Tighten the nuts and bolts to the specified torque.
46 Locate the crankshaft position sensor wiring in the cable guide, and attach the cable clip to the pump body.
47 Refit the coolant pump drive pulley and secure with the retaining bolts tightened to

the specified torque. Prevent the pulley from turning as the bolts are tightened, using the same method as for removal.
48 Refit the auxiliary drivebelt and refill the cooling system as described in Chapter 1. Start the engine and check all disturbed joints for leaks as soon as the engine is fully warmed-up.

8 Heating and ventilation system – general information

The heater/ventilation system consists of a blower motor (housed beneath the passenger's side of the facia), face level vents in the centre and at each end of the facia, and air ducts to the front footwells.

The control unit is located in the facia, and the controls operate flap valves to deflect and mix the air flowing through the various parts of the heating/ventilation system. The flap valves are contained in the main heater unit, which acts as a central distribution unit, passing air to the various ducts and vents.

Cold air enters the system through the grille at the rear of the engine compartment. If required, the airflow is boosted by the blower fan, and then flows through the various ducts, according to the settings of the controls. Stale air is expelled through ducts at the rear of the vehicle. If warm air is required, the cold air is passed over the heater matrix, which is heated by the engine coolant.

A recirculation switch enables the outside air supply to be closed off, while the air inside the vehicle is recirculated. This can be useful to prevent unpleasant odours entering from outside the vehicle, but should only be used briefly, as the recirculated air inside the vehicle will soon become stale.

9 Heating and ventilation system components – removal and refitting

Control panel

Removal – pre-August 2000 models

1 Disconnect the battery negative terminal (refer to *Disconnecting the battery* in the Reference Chapter).
2 Except on models with automatic air conditioning, remove the passenger's side lower facia panel and the glovebox, as described in Chapter 11.
3 On all models, remove the facia centre panel as described in Chapter 11.
4 Except on models with automatic air conditioning, release the clip securing the temperature control cable to the side of the heater assembly, and unhook the inner cable end fitting.
5 Undo the three retaining screws and pull the heater/ventilation control panel away from the facia.

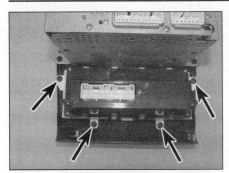

9.10 Undo the four screws (arrowed) and remove the heater/ventilation control panel from the facia centre panel – post-August 2000 models

6 Disconnect the wiring connectors at the rear of the panel. Note the fitted position of the recirculation and air distribution control cables, then release the retaining clips and unhook the inner cable end fittings. Withdraw the control panel from the facia, noting the routing of the temperature control cable as the panel is removed.

Refitting – pre-August 2000 models

7 Refitting is a reversal of removal. Reconnect the control cables in their previously noted positions and check their operation before finally refitting the control panel. If adjustment is necessary, reposition the outer cables in their retaining clips.

Removal – post-August 2000 models

8 Disconnect the battery negative terminal (refer to *Disconnecting the battery* in the Reference Chapter).
9 Remove the facia centre panel as described in Chapter 11.
10 Undo the four retaining screws and remove the heater/ventilation control panel from the rear of the facia centre panel **(see illustration)**.

Refitting – post-August 2000 models

11 Refitting is a reversal of removal.

Heater matrix

Removal

12 Disconnect the battery negative terminal (refer to *Disconnecting the battery* in the Reference Chapter).
13 Drain the cooling system as described in Chapter 1.
14 Undo the two screws and fold back the carpet on the driver's side.
15 Extract the two retaining clips and remove the cover panel from the side of the heater assembly **(see illustration)**.
16 Position cloth rags or absorbent material in the footwell to catch any spilt coolant.
17 Undo the screw(s) securing the heater pipe support bracket(s) to the side of the heater assembly **(see illustration)**.
18 Undo the two screws and remove the upper and lower clamps securing the heater pipes to the matrix **(see illustration)**. Carefully

9.15 Extract the two retaining clips and remove the cover panel from the side of the heater assembly

withdraw the pipes and recover the O-rings from the pipe ends. Note that new O-rings will be required for refitting.
19 Slide the matrix out of the side of the heater assembly.

Refitting

20 Refitting is a reversal of removal, using new O-rings on the heater pipes. On completion, refill the cooling system as described in Chapter 1.

Heater blower motor

Removal

21 Remove the passenger's side lower facia panel and the glovebox, as described in Chapter 11.
22 Disconnect the blower motor wiring connector **(see illustration)**.
23 Unscrew the three retaining screws and

9.18 Undo the screws (arrowed) and remove the upper and lower clamps securing the heater pipes to the matrix

9.23a Unscrew the three retaining screws (arrowed) . . .

9.17 Undo the screw (arrowed) securing the heater pipe support bracket to the side of the heater assembly

lower the blower motor out from under the facia **(see illustrations)**.

Refitting

24 Refitting is a reversal of removal.

Heater blower motor resistor

Removal

25 Remove the driver's side lower facia panel as described in Chapter 11.
26 Reach up under the facia and disconnect the resistor wiring connector.
27 Unscrew the two retaining screws and remove the resistor from the side of the heater assembly **(see illustration)**.

Heater assembly

⚠️ *Warning: On models with air conditioning, read the precautions given in Section 10, and have the*

9.22 Disconnect the blower motor wiring connector (arrowed)

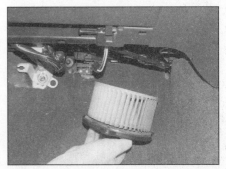

9.23b . . . and lower the blower motor out from under the facia

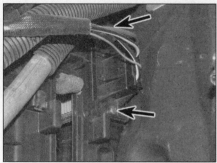

9.27 Unscrew the two retaining screws (arrowed) and remove the blower motor resistor from the side of the heater assembly

system discharged by a Toyota dealer or air conditioning specialist. Do not carry out the following work unless the system has been discharged.

Removal

28 Have the air conditioning system professionally discharged, on models so equipped.

29 Disconnect the battery negative terminal (refer to *Disconnecting the battery* in the Reference Chapter).

30 Drain the cooling system as described in Chapter 1.

31 Remove the complete facia assembly, including the reinforcement brace, as described in Chapter 11.

32 From within the engine compartment, release the clips and disconnect the two heater hoses from the pipe stubs on the bulkhead. Extract the sealing grommet from the bulkhead.

33 On models with air conditioning, disconnect the refrigerant pipes at the engine compartment bulkhead. The pipes clamps can be released using a very small flat-bladed screwdriver to press down the silver clip **(see**

Many car accessory shops sell one-shot air conditioning recharge aerosols. These generally contain refrigerant, compressor oil, leak sealer and system conditioner. Some also have a dye to help pinpoint leaks.

⚠️ **Warning: These products must only be used as directed by the manufacturer, and do not remove the need for regular maintenance.**

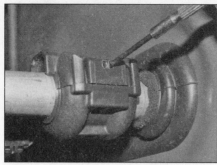

9.33 Use a small screwdriver to depress the silver clip and release the air conditioning pipe clamps

illustration). Discard the O-ring seals, new ones must be fitted. Plug or cover the ends of the pipes, and recover the grommet from the bulkhead.

34 Undo the two screws and remove the air duct from the side of the heater unit.

35 Disconnect the wiring connectors from the blower motor housing on the side of the heater assembly.

36 Disconnect the control cable, then undo the nut, bolt and two screws securing the blower motor housing to the side of the heater assembly and to the body. Withdraw the blower motor housing from its location and remove it from the car.

37 Fold the carpet back, away from the heater assembly as far as possible, then undo the retaining screw and remove the two rear compartment air ducts.

38 Position cloth rags or absorbent material in the footwell to catch any spilt coolant as the heater assembly is removed.

39 Check that all wiring has been disconnected from the heater assembly and moved clear. Undo the upper and lower retaining nuts and withdraw the assembly from inside the vehicle. Be prepared for some loss of coolant from the heater matrix stubs.

Refitting

40 Refitting is a reversal of removal, but note the following:

   a) Make sure that all wiring and cables are routed as noted during removal.

   b) Make sure that all air ducts are securely reconnected.

10.6 Air conditioning system high-pressure service port location (arrowed)

   c) On models with air conditioning, use new O-rings when reconnecting the refrigerant pipes.

   d) Refit the reinforcement brace and facia as described in Chapter 11.

   e) Refill the cooling system as described in Chapter 1.

   f) Have the air conditioning system recharged, on models so equipped.

10 Air conditioning system – general information and precautions

General information

1 An air conditioning system is available on certain models. It enables the temperature of incoming air to be lowered, and also dehumidifies the air, which makes for rapid demisting and increased comfort.

2 The cooling side of the system works in the same way as a domestic refrigerator. Refrigerant gas is drawn into a belt-driven compressor, and passes into a condenser mounted on the front of the radiator, where it loses heat and becomes liquid. The liquid passes through an expansion valve to an evaporator, where it changes from liquid under high pressure to gas under low pressure. This change is accompanied by a drop in temperature, which cools the evaporator. The refrigerant returns to the compressor, and the cycle begins again.

3 Air blown through the evaporator passes to the heater assembly, where it is mixed with hot air blown through the heater matrix to achieve the desired temperature in the passenger compartment.

4 The heating side of the system works in the same way as on models without air conditioning.

5 The system is electronically-controlled. Any problems with the system should be referred to a Toyota dealer, or air conditioning specialist **(see Tool tip)**.

Air conditioning service ports

6 The high-pressure service port is located in front of the condenser **(see illustration)**. On post-August 2000 models, it will be necessary to remove the plastic panel above the radiator grille for access **(see illustrations 11.8a, 11.8b and 11.8c)**.

7 On pre-August 2000 models, the low-pressure service port is located just in front of the air conditioning compressor **(see illustration)**.

8 On post-August 2000 models, the low-pressure service port is located on the left-hand side of the engine compartment, between the radiator and the battery **(see illustration)**.

Precautions

9 When an air conditioning system is fitted, it is necessary to observe special precautions whenever dealing with any part of the system, or its associated components. The refrigerant is potentially dangerous, and should only be handled by qualified persons. Uncontrolled discharging of the refrigerant is dangerous and damaging to the environment for the following reasons.

a) If it is splashed onto the skin, it can cause frostbite.

b) The refrigerant is heavier then air and so displaces oxygen. In a confined space which is not adequately ventilated this could lead to a risk of suffocation. The gas is odourless and colourless so there is no warning of its presence in the atmosphere.

c) Although not poisonous, in the presence of a naked flame (including a cigarette) it forms a noxious gas which causes headaches, nausea, etc.

⚠ **Warning: Never attempt to open any air conditioning system refrigerant pipe/hose union without first having the system fully discharged by a Toyota dealer or air conditioning specialist. On completion of work, have the system recharged by a dealer or air conditioning specialist.**

⚠ **Warning: Always seal disconnected refrigerant pipe unions as soon as they are disconnected to keep moisture and contamination out of the system. Also renew all sealing O-rings whenever they are disturbed.**

Caution: Do not operated the air conditioning system if it is known to be short of refrigerant as this could damage the compressor.

11 Air conditioning system components – removal and refitting

⚠ **Warning: Read the precautions given in Section 10, and have the system discharged by a Toyota dealer or air conditioning specialist. Do not carry out the following work unless the system has been discharged (where necessary).**

Compressor

Note: If the compressor is being removed as part of another procedure, it may not be necessary to have the system discharged. Usually, the compressor can be unbolted and tied to one side without the need to disturb the refrigerant lines.

Removal

1 Disconnect the battery negative terminal (refer to *Disconnecting the battery* in the Reference Chapter).

2 Firmly apply the handbrake, then jack up the front of the car and support it securely on axle stands (see *Jacking and vehicle support*). Remove the right-hand roadwheel,

10.7 Air conditioning system low-pressure service port location (arrowed) – pre-August 2000 models

then unbolt and remove the undershield from under the right-hand side of the engine compartment.

3 Remove the auxiliary drivebelt(s) (alternator, power steering and air conditioning, as applicable), as described in Chapter 1.

4 Disconnect the compressor wiring connector and release the wiring from the retaining clip(s) **(see illustration)**. Where applicable, undo the screw and disconnect the earth lead from the compressor body.

5 With the system discharged, undo the retaining bolts and disconnect the refrigerant pipes from the compressor **(see illustration)**. Discard the O-ring seals – new ones must be used when refitting. Cap the open fittings immediately to keep moisture and contamination out of the system.

6 Support the compressor, then remove the

11.4 Disconnect the compressor wiring connector and release the wiring from the retaining clip(s)

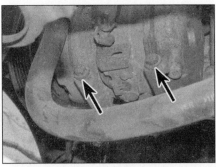

11.6a Air conditioning compressor lower mounting bolts (arrowed) . . .

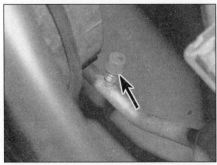

10.8 Air conditioning system low-pressure service port location (arrowed) – post-August 2000 models

mounting bolts (three or four, depending on engine type) **(see illustrations)**. Lower the compressor and remove it from under the car.

Refitting

7 Refitting is a reversal of removal, but note the following:

a) Use new O-rings coated with compressor oil, when reconnecting the refrigerant pipes.

b) Tighten the compressor mounting bolts to the specified torque.

c) Have the system professionally recharged and tested on completion.

Condenser

Removal

8 On post-August 2000 models, extract the

11.5 Undo the retaining bolts (arrowed) and disconnect the refrigerant pipes from the compressor

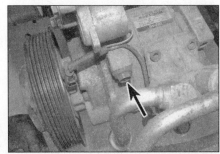

11.6b . . . and upper mounting bolt (arrowed) – 1.6 and 1.8 litre engines post-August 2000

11.8a On post-August 2000 models, extract the retaining clips . . .

11.8b . . . and the plastic rivets . . .

11.8c . . . and remove the plastic panel above the radiator grille

11.9a Disconnect the upper (arrowed) . . .

11.9b . . . and lower (arrowed) refrigerant pipes from the condenser

11.11 Undo the condenser upper mounting bracket nuts (arrowed) on each side

retaining clips and plastic rivets and remove the plastic panel above the radiator grille **(see illustrations)**.

9 With the system discharged, undo the retaining bolts and disconnect the refrigerant pipes from the condenser **(see illustrations)**. Discard the O-ring seals – new ones must be used when refitting. Cap the open fittings immediately to keep moisture and contamination out of the system.

10 Unbolt the radiator upper mounting brackets from the front engine compartment crossmember and remove them from the top of the radiator **(see illustration 3.8)**.

11 Undo the two condenser upper mounting bracket nuts **(see illustration)**.

12 Push the top of the radiator back towards the engine, push the condenser towards the radiator, then lift the condenser upwards from its location.

Refitting

13 Refitting is a reversal of removal, but note the following:

a) Use new O-rings coated with compressor oil, when reconnecting the refrigerant pipes.

b) Have the system professionally recharged and tested on completion.

Evaporator

Removal

14 Remove the heater assembly as described in Section 9.

15 On models with automatic air conditioning, disconnect the operating link, undo the retaining screws and remove the air temperature control motor from the side of the heater assembly.

16 Undo the eight screws and remove the evaporator cover, then pull the evaporator from its location.

Refitting

17 Refitting is a reversal of removal.

Chapter 4 Part A:
Fuel and exhaust systems

Contents

Degrees of difficulty

Easy, suitable for novice with little experience 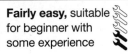	**Fairly easy,** suitable for beginner with some experience	**Fairly difficult,** suitable for competent DIY mechanic	**Difficult,** suitable for experienced DIY mechanic	**Very difficult,** suitable for expert DIY or professional

Specifications

General
System type . . . .   Toyota sequential multi-point fuel injection

Fuel system data

All except 2.0 litre engines post-August 2000
Idle speed. . . . .   700 ± 50 rpm
Fuel pump type . . . .   Electric, immersed in tank
Fuel system regulated pressure . . . .   3.0 to 3.4 bar

2.0 litre engines post-August 2000
Idle speed. . . . .   675 ± 50 rpm
Fuel pump type . . . .   Electric, immersed in tank, with additional engine-mounted, high-pressure fuel pump
Fuel system regulated pressure . . . .   3.7 to 4.2 bar
High-pressure fuel pump delivery pressure . . . .   95.2 to 104.8 bar

Inlet manifold
Maximum gasket face distortion . . . .   0.2 mm

Exhaust manifold
Maximum gasket face distortion . . . .   0.3 mm

Recommended fuel
All models. . . . .   95 RON unleaded

Torque wrench settings

	Nm	lbf ft
Pre-August 2000 models		
Exhaust manifold stay to cylinder block		
1.6 and 1.8 litre engines....................................	59	44
2.0 litre engines	42	31
Exhaust manifold stay to exhaust manifold:		
1.6 and 1.8 litre engines....................................	39	29
2.0 litre engines	42	31
Exhaust manifold to cylinder head:		
1.6 and 1.8 litre engines....................................	34	25
2.0 litre engines	49	36
Fuel inlet hose to fuel rail (1.6 and 1.8 litre engines)	29	21
Fuel rail bolts:		
1.6 and 1.8 litre engines....................................	10	7
2.0 litre engines	13	10
Fuel tank retaining strap bolts	35	26
Heat shield to exhaust manifold...................................	10	7
Inlet manifold nuts/bolts...	19	14
Inlet manifold support bracket (1.6 and 1.8 litre engines):		
Upper bolt...	19	14
Lower bolt...	39	29
Pulsation damper to fuel rail (2.0 litre engines	34	25
Throttle housing to inlet manifold:		
1.6 and 1.8 litre engines....................................	22	16
2.0 litre engines	19	14
Post-August 2000 models		
Camshaft position sensor	9	7
Crankshaft position sensor	9	7
Exhaust manifold stay to cylinder block:		
1.6 litre engines	37	27
1.8 litre engines:		
Right-hand bolt..	49	36
Left-hand bolt...	37	27
2.0 litre engines	40	30
Exhaust manifold to cylinder head...............................	37	27
Fuel pressure sensor (2.0 litre engines)	26	19
Fuel rail bolts	18	13
Fuel tank retaining strap bolts	35	26
Heat shield to exhaust manifold:		
1.6 and 1.8 litre engines....................................	18	13
2.0 litre engines	13	9
High-pressure fuel pump fuel outlet pipe union (2.0 litre engines).....	30	22
High-pressure fuel pump pulsation damper (2.0 litre engines)	33	24
High-pressure fuel pump to camshaft cover (2.0 litre engines)	25	18
Injector clamp bracket bolts (2.0 litre engines)	13	10
Inlet manifold nuts/bolts..	30	22
Throttle housing to inlet manifold:		
1.6 and 1.8 litre engines....................................	30	22
2.0 litre engines	10	7

1 General information and precautions

General information

The fuel supply system consists of a fuel tank (which is mounted under the rear of the car, with an electric fuel pump immersed in it), a fuel filter and fuel feed lines.

On all except 2.0 litre engines post-August 2000, the fuel pump supplies fuel to the fuel rail, which acts as a reservoir for the four fuel injectors which inject fuel into the inlet tracts.

On 2.0 litre engines post-August 2000, the in-tank fuel pump supplies fuel to a high-pressure fuel pump, mounted on the cylinder head. The high-pressure pump then supplies fuel to the fuel rail which acts as a reservoir for the four fuel injectors, which inject fuel directly into the combustion chambers in the cylinder head.

On all engines, a fuel filter is incorporated in the fuel supply line to ensure that the fuel supplied to the injectors is clean.

The electronic fuel injection system is controlled by the engine management electronic control unit; further information

on the emission control and ignition system components of these may be found in Chapters 4B and 5B respectively, while further information regarding the fuel injection/engine management system is given in Section 6.

Precautions

⚠️ **Warning: Petrol is extremely flammable – great care must be taken when working on any part of the fuel system. Do not smoke or allow any naked flames or uncovered light bulbs near the work area. Note that gas powered domestic appliances with pilot flames, such as heaters, boilers and** *tumble dryers, also present a fire hazard – bear this in mind if you are working in an area where such appliances are present. Always keep a suitable fire extinguisher close to the work area and familiarise yourself with its operation before starting work. Wear eye protection when working on fuel systems and wash off any fuel spilt on bare skin immediately with soap and water. Note that fuel vapour is just as dangerous as liquid fuel; a vessel that has just been emptied of liquid fuel will still contain vapour and can be potentially explosive. Petrol is a highly dangerous and volatile liquid, and the precautions necessary when handling it cannot be overstressed.*

• Many of the operations described in this Chapter involve the disconnection of fuel lines, which may cause an amount of fuel spillage. Before commencing work, refer to the above *Warning* and the information in *Safety first!* at the beginning of this manual.

• When working with fuel system components, pay particular attention to cleanliness – dirt entering the fuel system may cause blockages which will lead to poor running.

Note: *Residual pressure will remain in the fuel lines long after the vehicle was last used. When disconnecting any fuel line, first depressurise the fuel system as described in Section 7.*

2 Air cleaner and inlet ducts – removal and refitting

Removal

1 Remove the air filter element as described in Chapter 1.

2 Unscrew and remove the mounting bolts from inside the air cleaner base. Disconnect the air cleaner base from the inlet duct on the front left-hand side of the engine compartment and remove the base **(see illustrations)**.

Refitting

3 Refitting is a reversal of removal, ensuring that all clips and mounting bolts are tightened securely.

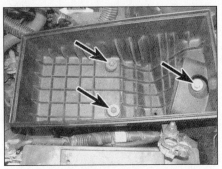

2.2a Unscrew and remove the air cleaner base mounting bolts (arrowed) . . .

3 Accelerator cable – removal, refitting and adjustment

Note: *An accelerator cable is not fitted to 2.0 litre models post-August 2000.*

Removal

1 Working in the engine compartment, turn the throttle valve segment on the throttle housing to release the tension on the accelerator inner cable, then disconnect the cable end fitting **(see illustration)**.

2 Loosen the locknuts on the threaded portion of the accelerator outer cable at the cable support bracket **(see illustration)**. Slip the outer cable out of the support bracket.

3 Release the outer cable from the relevant support clips.

4 Remove the driver's side lower facia panel as described in Chapter 11.

5 Squeeze together the ends of the retaining clip, and pull the plastic grommet/fitting from the accelerator pedal, then detach the cable **(see illustration)**. Remove the two bolts securing the cable retainer to the bulkhead.

6 From inside the vehicle, pull the cable through the bulkhead.

Refitting

7 Feed the cable through the bulkhead from inside the vehicle, then reconnect the inner cable to the top of the accelerator pedal and tighten the retainer plate bolts securely. Refit the lower facia panel as described in Chapter 11.

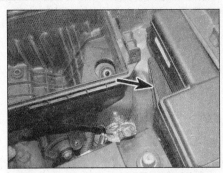

2.2b . . . then disconnect the air cleaner base from the inlet duct (arrowed)

8 In the engine compartment, locate the cable in the support clip and bracket and reconnect the inner cable end fitting to the throttle valve segment.

Adjustment

9 With both adjusting nuts loose check that the inner cable is slack. Unscrew the nut nearest the throttle valve segment several turns.

10 Tighten the nut furthest from the segment until the segment just starts to move, then back off the nut 1.5 to 2.0 turns to provide the correct amount of play. Tighten the locknut to retain the ferrule in this position.

11 Have an assistant depress the accelerator pedal, and check that the throttle valve segment opens fully and returns smoothly to its stop.

4 Accelerator pedal – removal and refitting

Removal

All except 2.0 litre models post-August 2000

1 Detach the accelerator cable from the pedal as described in the previous Section.

2 Unbolt the accelerator pedal from the bulkhead **(see illustration)**.

3 Examine the mounting bracket and pedal pivot for signs of wear, and renew as necessary.

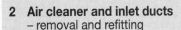

3.1 Disconnecting the accelerator cable from the throttle valve segment – typical arrangement shown

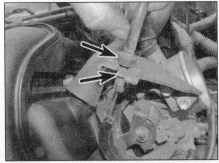

3.2 Loosen the locknuts (arrowed) on the accelerator outer cable at the cable support bracket – typical arrangement shown

3.5 Squeeze together the ends of the retaining clip (arrowed), and pull the plastic grommet/fitting from the accelerator pedal

2.0 litre models post-August 2000

4 Remove the driver's side lower facia panel as described in Chapter 11.

5 Disconnect the wiring connector from the accelerator pedal position sensor on the side of the mounting bracket.

6 Undo the upper bolt and lower nut(s) and remove the pedal assembly.

7 Examine the mounting bracket and pedal pivot for signs of wear, and renew as necessary.

Refitting

8 Refitting is a reversal of the removal procedure, applying a little multi-purpose grease to the pedal pivot. On completion, adjust the accelerator cable as described in Section 3 (where applicable).

5 Unleaded petrol – general information and usage

Note: *The information given in this Chapter is correct at the time of writing. If updated information is thought to be required, check with a Toyota dealer. If travelling abroad, consult one of the motoring organisations (or a similar authority) for advice on the fuel available.*

1 The fuel recommended by Toyota is given in the Specifications Section of this Chapter.

2 All models are designed to run on fuel with a minimum octane rating of 95 (RON). All models have a catalytic converter, and so must be run on unleaded fuel only. Under no circumstances should leaded/lead replacement fuel (UK 4-star/LRP) be used, as this may damage the converter.

3 Super unleaded petrol (98 octane) can also be used in all models if wished, though there is no advantage in doing so.

6 Fuel injection system – general information

Note: *The fuel injection ECU is of the 'self-learning' type, meaning that, as it operates, it also monitors and stores the settings which give optimum engine performance under all operating conditions. When the battery is disconnected, these settings are lost and the ECU reverts to the base settings programmed into its memory at the factory. On restarting, this may lead to the engine running/idling roughly for a short while, until the ECU has relearned the optimum settings. This process is best accomplished by taking the vehicle on a road test (for approximately 15 minutes), covering all engine speeds and loads, concentrating mainly in the 2500 to 3500 rpm region.*

All except 2.0 litre engines post-August 2000

The Electronic Control Unit (ECU), which

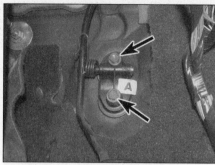

4.2 Accelerator pedal retaining bolts (arrowed) – all except 2.0 litre models post-August 2000

controls both the ignition system and electronic fuel injection functions of the engine management system, is located inside the vehicle, behind the facia on the passenger's side. In addition to its control of the fuel injection and ignition functions, the ECU also provides electronic control of the automatic transmission on models so equipped.

The ECU is supplied with data from sensors which monitor inlet manifold pressure or inlet air density, inlet air temperature, coolant temperature, engine speed, throttle valve opening angle, camshaft position and exhaust gas oxygen content. The data is compared with preprogrammed values stored in the ECU memory to determine the appropriate electrical signals to operate the injectors. The injectors are supplied with fuel at constant pressure by means of an electric fuel pump and a pressure regulator, therefore the quantity of fuel injected is determined by the time that the injectors remain open.

Under certain conditions, engine idle speed can be regulated by the idle speed control valve under the control of the ECU. The valve opens and closes an air passage to allow intake air to bypass the throttle valve in the throttle housing.

A fail-safe function is incorporated in the ECU so that if one of the sensors fails, a back-up circuit will take over to allow the vehicle to be driven, albeit at reduced power and efficiency. A Check Engine warning lamp will light to indicate that this condition is present, and a fault code will be stored in the ECU relating to the circuit affected. The fault codes can be accessed using suitable diagnostic equipment (see Section 13).

All 1.6 and 1.8 litre engines pre-August 2000 are equipped with the Toyota Lean Combustion System and are referred to as Lean-Burn engines. On these engines, modifications to the inlet manifold configuration and fuel injector positioning allow a lean air/fuel mixture ratio to be used without sacrificing engine performance. This arrangement enhances fuel economy and significantly reduces toxic exhaust emissions. Additionally, a vacuum-operated inlet air control valve assembly is incorporated in the inlet manifold. Under ECU control, the vacuum operated butterfly valves in the air

control valve assembly can be opened or closed, thus effectively altering the length of the inlet tract. This ensures that maximum engine torque is available under all engine speed and load conditions.

2.0 litre engines post-August 2000

The operation of the system is similar to that described previously, but with a number of significant differences.

An additional high-pressure fuel pump is used to supply the injectors with fuel at significantly higher pressure than in a conventional system. The electric pump mounted in the fuel tank acts as a 'pre-pump' and supplies fuel to the high-pressure pump mounted on the engine. The injectors are supplied with fuel at constant pressure by the high-pressure pump and a pressure regulator. As with the previously described system, the quantity of fuel injected is determined by the time that the injectors remain open.

A 'drive-by-wire' electronic throttle control system is used, under the direct control of an additional ECU known as an Electronic Driver Unit (EDU). A throttle control motor, integral with the throttle housing, alters the position of the throttle valve according to driver input. An accelerator pedal position sensor informs the EDU of the position, and rate of change, of the accelerator pedal, and the EDU then controls the throttle valve by means of the throttle control motor – no accelerator cable is fitted.

A vacuum-operated inlet air control valve assembly is also used, and operates as previously described for 1.6 and 1.8 litre engines pre-August 2000.

7 Fuel injection system – depressurisation

⚠️ *Warning: Refer to the warning in Section 1 before proceeding. The following procedure will merely relieve the pressure in the fuel system – remember that fuel will still be present in the system components, and take precautions accordingly before disconnecting any of them.*

1 The fuel system referred to in this Section consists of the tank-mounted fuel pump, the high-pressure fuel pump (where applicable), the fuel filter, the fuel rail and injectors, and the metal pipes and flexible hoses of the fuel lines between these components. All these contain fuel which will be under pressure while the engine is running and/or while the ignition is switched on. The pressure will remain for some time after the ignition has been switched off, and must be relieved before any of these components are disturbed for servicing work.

2 Remove the fuel filler cap – this will relieve any pressure built-up in the tank.

3 Remove the rear seat cushion as described in Chapter 11.

4 Fold back the carpet and prise up the fuel pump access cover **(see illustrations)**.

5 Disconnect the fuel pump/fuel gauge sender wiring connector from the top of the fuel pump assembly **(see illustration)**.

6 Start the engine, and allow it to run until it stalls.

7 Try to start the engine at least twice more, to ensure that all residual pressure has been relieved then switch off the ignition.

8 Reconnect the wiring to the fuel pump/fuel gauge sender and refit the cover, followed by the rear seat cushion. **Do not** switch on the ignition until completion of work.

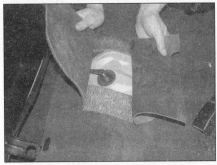
7.4a Fold back the carpet . . .

7.4b . . . and prise up the fuel pump access cover

8 Fuel pump – removal and refitting

⚠ **Warning: Refer to the warning in Section 1 before proceeding. Since a fuel tank drain plug is not provided, it is preferable to carry out this work when the tank is nearly empty.**

Note: *Two different types of fuel pump may be encountered – one type is manufactured by TMC (Toyota Motor Co), and the second type is manufactured by Bosch. Refer to the accompanying illustrations to identify the pump type being worked on, and proceed as described under the appropriate sub-heading below.*

Removal

1 Depressurise the fuel system as described in Section 7, paragraphs 2 to 7.

2 Disconnect the battery negative terminal (refer to *Disconnecting the battery* in the Reference Chapter).

TMC (Toyota Motor Co) pumps

3 Slacken the union bolt and disconnect the supply line from the fuel pump. Counterhold the union with a further spanner while loosening the bolt. Tape or cover the end of the line **(see illustration)**.

4 Where a fuel return hose is fitted, release the retaining clip then disconnect the return hose from the top of the fuel pump **(see illustrations)**.

5 Unscrew the crosshead screws securing the pump to the fuel tank **(see illustration)**.

6 Carefully withdraw the fuel pump/fuel gauge sender unit assembly from the top of the tank, taking care not to damage the float and arm **(see illustration)**.

7 Recover the gasket from the top of the fuel tank.

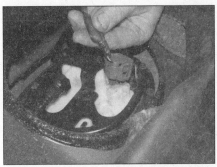
7.5 Disconnect the fuel pump/fuel gauge sender wiring connector from the top of the fuel pump assembly

8 Remove the fuel gauge sender unit with reference to Section 10, then release the clips securing the small hose to the pump **(see illustration)**.

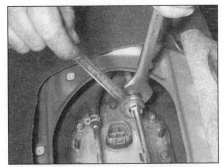
8.3 Disconnecting the fuel supply line union from the fuel pump – TMC fuel pumps

8.4a Release the clip . . .

8.4b . . . and disconnect the return hose (where fitted) from the top of the fuel pump – TMC fuel pumps

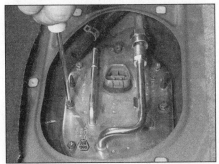
8.5 Unscrew the crosshead screws . . .

8.6 . . . and withdraw the fuel pump/fuel gauge sender unit assembly from the top of the fuel tank – TMC fuel pumps

8.8 Release the clips securing the small hose to the fuel pump – TMC fuel pumps

8.10 Release the pump from the bottom of the bracket, then pull it from the fuel hose – TMC fuel pumps

8.11 Depress the tabs on the quick-release fitting and disconnect the fuel supply line from the pump – Bosch fuel pumps

8.12 Unscrew the crosshead screws and withdraw the retaining plate from the top of the pump – Bosch fuel pumps

8.13a Withdraw the fuel pump/fuel gauge sender unit assembly from the top of the fuel tank . . .

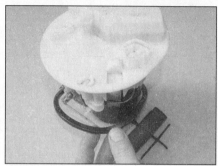

8.13b . . . and recover the O-ring seal from the underside of the pump flange – Bosch fuel pumps

9 Undo the screw and disconnect the earth lead from the side of the pump body.
10 Release the pump from the bottom of the bracket by moving it sideways, then pull it from the hose **(see illustration)**. Remove the hose and recover the seat from the bracket. If necessary, prise out the clip and remove the inlet filter from the pump.

Bosch pumps

11 Depress the tabs on the side of the quick-release fitting and disconnect the supply line from the fuel pump **(see illustration)**. Tape or cover the end of the line.
12 Unscrew the crosshead screws and withdraw the retaining plate from the top of the pump **(see illustration)**.
13 Carefully withdraw the fuel pump/fuel gauge sender unit assembly from the top of the tank, taking care not to damage the float and arm. Recover the O-ring seal from the underside of the pump flange **(see illustrations)**.
14 The fuel gauge sender unit can be removed as described in Section 10, but no further dismantling of the pump is possible.

Refitting

TMC (Toyota Motor Co) pumps

15 Refitting is a reversal of removal, but make sure the fuel pump is securely located in the bracket before tightening the hose clips. Always fit a new gasket. Before refitting the access cover, reconnect the wiring to the fuel pump/fuel gauge sender and reconnect the

battery. Switch on the ignition and check for fuel leaks at the supply and, where applicable, the return pipes.

Bosch pumps

16 Refitting is a reversal of removal, using a new sealing O-ring. Before refitting the access cover, reconnect the wiring to the fuel pump/fuel gauge sender and reconnect the battery. Switch on the ignition and check for fuel leaks at the supply pipe.

---

9 High-pressure fuel pump (2.0 litre engines post-August 2000) – removal and refitting

⚠️ *Warning: Refer to the warning in Section 1 before proceeding.*

9.4 High-pressure fuel pump pulsation damper (arrowed)

Removal

1 Depressurise the fuel system as described in Section 7.
2 Disconnect the battery negative terminal (refer to *Disconnecting the battery* in the Reference Chapter).
3 Undo the four nuts and remove the plastic cover from the top of the engine.
4 Unscrew the pulsation damper from the side of the pump and collect the washers on each side of the fuel inlet pipe banjo union **(see illustration)**. Note that new washers will be required for refitting.
5 Unscrew the union nut and disconnect the fuel outlet pipe from the pump.
6 Release the retaining clip and disconnect the fuel return hose from the pump.
7 Disconnect the wiring connector, then progressively slacken and unscrew the two pump retaining nuts.
8 Lift the pump off the camshaft cover and collect the insulator block.

Refitting

9 Refitting is a reversal of removal, using a new insulator block, and new washers on the fuel inlet pipe banjo union. Start the engine and check for fuel leaks before refitting the engine cover.

---

10 Fuel gauge sender unit – removal and refitting

⚠️ *Warning: Refer to the warning in Section 1 before proceeding. Since a fuel tank drain plug is not provided, it is preferable to carry out this work when the tank is nearly empty.*

Removal

1 Remove the fuel pump (see Section 8).
2 Disconnect the fuel gauge sender unit wiring connector **(see illustrations)**.
3 Unscrew the crosshead screws, and withdraw the fuel gauge sender unit from the side of the fuel pump assembly **(see illustrations)**.

Refitting

4 Refitting is a reversal of removal, but tighten

the crosshead screws securely. Refit the fuel pump with reference to Section 8.

11 Fuel tank –
removal, inspection and refitting

⚠️ *Warning: Refer to the warning in Section 1 before proceeding. Since a fuel tank drain plug is not provided, it is preferable to carry out this work when the tank is nearly empty.*

Removal

1 Depressurise the fuel system as described in Section 7, paragraphs 2 to 7.
2 Disconnect the battery negative terminal (refer to *Disconnecting the battery* in the Reference Chapter).
3 Disconnect the fuel pump supply and, where applicable, return lines as described in Section 8, according to pump type.
4 If the tank is not empty at this stage, remove the fuel pump completely (Section 8) and syphon or hand-pump the remaining fuel into a suitable container. Refit the fuel pump to prevent entry of dust and dirt.
5 Chock the front wheels then jack up the rear of the car and securely support it on axle stands (see *Jacking and vehicle support*).
6 Remove the exhaust system tailpipe with reference to Section 20.
7 Drill out the rivets and remove the heat shield from under the fuel tank.
8 Loosen the clip and disconnect the filler hose from the rear of the tank **(see illustration)**.
9 Loosen the clip and disconnect the breather hose from the tank **(see illustration)**.
10 Place a trolley jack with an interposed block of wood beneath the tank, then raise the jack until it is supporting the weight of the tank.
11 Unscrew and remove the tank retaining strap bolts, then move each strap away from the tank **(see illustration)**.
12 Slowly lower the fuel tank until any remaining fuel and vapour lines become accessible then disconnect them. Lower the tank to the ground, and remove it from underneath the vehicle.

Inspection

13 Whilst removed, the fuel tank can be inspected for damage or deterioration. Removal of the fuel pump (Section 8) will allow a partial inspection of the interior. If the tank is contaminated with sediment or water, swill it out with clean petrol. Do not under any circumstances undertake any repairs on a leaking or damaged fuel tank; this work must be carried out by a professional who has experience in this critical and potentially-dangerous work.
14 Whilst the fuel tank is removed from the vehicle, it should not be placed in an area

10.2a Disconnecting the fuel gauge sender unit wiring connector – TMC fuel pumps

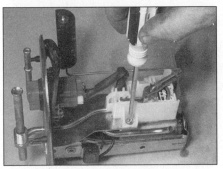
10.3a Undo the screws . . .

where sparks or open flames could ignite the fumes coming out of the tank. Be especially careful inside garages where a natural-gas type appliance is located, because the pilot light could cause an explosion.
15 If necessary, the filler and ventilation hoses

11.8 Fuel filler hose connection to the rear of the fuel tank

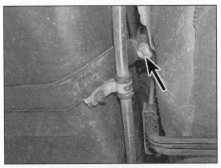
11.11 Fuel tank retaining strap bolt (arrowed)

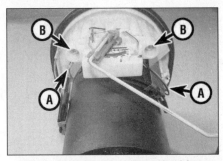
10.2b Fuel gauge sender unit wiring connectors (A) and attachment screws (B) – Bosch fuel pumps

10.3b . . . and withdraw the fuel gauge sender unit from the pump bracket – TMC fuel pumps

may be removed by unbolting the retaining clamp from the underbody, then unbolting the collar and plate from under the filler flap **(see illustration)**. Remove the mudguard and hose cover, then disconnect the hose from the collar.

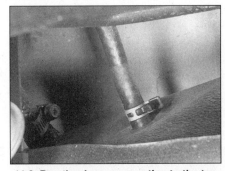
11.9 Breather hose connection to the top of the fuel tank

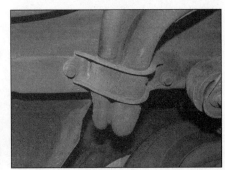
11.15 Fuel tank filler and ventilation hose retaining clamp on the underbody

12.7 Disconnecting the idle speed control valve wiring

12.8 Disconnecting a coolant hose from the bottom of the throttle housing

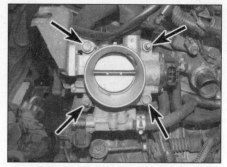

12.9a Typical throttle housing retaining nut/bolt locations (arrowed) . . .

12.9b . . . remove the throttle housing . . .

12.9c . . . and recover the flat gasket . . .

12.9d . . . or rubber type gasket, according to engine type

Refitting

16 Refitting is a reversal of the removal procedure, noting the following points:

a) *When lifting the tank back into position, take care to ensure that the various hoses are not trapped between the tank and vehicle body. Tighten the fuel tank mounting bolts to the specified torque setting.*

b) *Ensure that all pipes and hoses are correctly routed, and securely held in position with their retaining clips.*

c) *On completion refill the tank with fuel, run the engine, and check for signs of leakage prior to taking the vehicle on the road.*

12 Throttle housing –
removal and refitting

 Warning: Refer to the warning in Section 1 before proceeding.

Removal

All except 2.0 litre engines post-August 2000

1 Disconnect the battery negative terminal (refer to *Disconnecting the battery* in the Reference Chapter).

2 Where applicable, undo the nuts, prise out the two rear fasteners, and remove the plastic cover from the top of the engine.

3 Working as described in Chapter 1, remove the air cleaner lid and air filter element, then drain the cooling system.

4 Turn the segment on the throttle housing to open the throttle, then disconnect the inner accelerator cable. On automatic transmission models, also disconnect the kickdown cable.

5 Where applicable, unbolt the accelerator cable support bracket and move it to one side (the accelerator cable can remain attached to the bracket).

6 Disconnect the wiring from the throttle position sensor on the side of the throttle housing.

7 Disconnect the wiring from the idle speed control valve on the lower front of the throttle housing **(see illustration)**.

8 Identify the positions of the vacuum, coolant, air and, where fitted, the evaporative emission and EGR hoses, then disconnect them **(see illustration)**.

9 Progressively unscrew the throttle housing mounting bolts/nuts. Where an additional support bracket is fitted, undo the lower mounting bolt and remove the bracket. Withdraw the throttle housing from the inlet manifold and recover the gasket **(see illustrations)**.

2.0 litre engines post-August 2000

10 Disconnect the battery negative terminal (refer to *Disconnecting the battery* in the Reference Chapter).

11 Undo the four nuts and remove the plastic cover from the top of the engine.

12 Working as described in Chapter 1, remove the air cleaner lid and air filter element, then drain the cooling system.

13 Disconnect the wiring connector from the throttle control motor.

14 Identify the positions of the coolant and evaporative emission hoses, then disconnect them.

15 Undo the two nuts and two bolts and remove the throttle housing support bracket. Recover the two washers from the support bracket attachment to the throttle housing.

16 Progressively unscrew the four throttle housing mounting bolts. Withdraw the throttle housing from the inlet manifold and recover the gasket.

Refitting

17 Refitting is a reversal of the removal procedure, noting the following points:

a) *Clean the mating surfaces and fit a new gasket to the throttle housing. On post-August 2000 engines, ensure that the gasket is fitted with the protruding tab uppermost.*

b) *Tighten the retaining nuts/bolts to the specified torque.*

c) *Where applicable, adjust the accelerator cable (Section 3), and on automatic transmission models the kickdown cable (Chapter 7B).*

d) *Refill the cooling system (Chapter 1).*

13 Fuel injection system –
fault diagnosis

1 If a fault appears in the fuel injection/ignition system, first ensure that all the system wiring connectors are securely connected and free of corrosion. Ensure that the fault is not due to

poor maintenance; ie, check that the air cleaner filter element is clean, the spark plugs are in good condition and correctly gapped, the cylinder compression pressures are correct and that the engine breather hoses are clear and undamaged, referring to Chapters 1, 2A, 2B and 5B for further information.

2 If these checks fail to reveal the cause of the problem, the vehicle should be taken to a suitably-equipped Toyota dealer or engine management diagnostic specialist for testing. A diagnostic socket is located on the passenger's compartment fusebox, to which a fault code reader or other suitable test equipment can be connected **(see illustration)**. By using the code reader or test equipment, the engine management ECU can be interrogated, and any stored fault codes can be retrieved. Live data can also be captured from the various system sensors and actuators, indicating their operating parameters. This will allow the fault to be quickly and simply traced, alleviating the need to test all the system components individually, which is a time-consuming operation that carries a risk of damaging the ECU.

14 Fuel injection system components (pre-August 2000 engines) – removal and refitting

⚠️ *Warning: Refer to the warning in Section 1 before proceeding.*

Fuel rail and injectors

Note: *If a faulty injector is suspected, before condemning the injector it is worth trying the effect of one of the proprietary injector-cleaning treatments.*

1.6 and 1.8 litre engines

1 Depressurise the fuel system as described in Section 7.
2 Disconnect the battery negative terminal (refer to *Disconnecting the battery* in the Reference Chapter).
3 Disconnect the crankcase ventilation hoses from the camshaft cover and inlet manifold.
4 On right-hand drive models, turn the segment on the throttle housing to open the throttle, then disconnect the inner accelerator cable. On automatic transmission models, also disconnect the kickdown cable. Unbolt the accelerator cable support bracket from the inlet manifold.
5 Unscrew the union bolt and disconnect the fuel inlet hose from the left-hand end of the fuel rail. Recover the two washers **(see illustration)**. Note that new washers will be required for refitting.
6 Disconnect the wiring connectors from the injectors **(see illustration)**.
7 Unscrew the three mounting bolts and carefully remove the fuel rail together with the injectors **(see illustration)**. Recover the spacers from the cylinder head.
8 Extract the retaining clips and withdraw the injectors from the fuel rail. Remove the two O-

ring seals from each injector **(see illustration)**. Discard the seals; new ones must be used on refitting.
9 Refitting is a reverse of the removal procedure, noting the following points:
 a) Fit new O-ring seals to all the injectors.
 b) Apply a smear of engine oil to the O-rings to aid installation, then ease the injectors into the fuel rail. Secure each injector with its retaining clip.
 c) Fit the three spacers to the cylinder head, then ease the injectors and fuel rail assembly into position. Insert the mounting bolts and tighten to the specified torque.
 d) Use new washers when refitting the fuel inlet hose union bolt, and tighten the bolt to the specified torque.
 e) On right-hand drive models, adjust the accelerator cable as described in Section 3 and, where applicable, the kickdown cable as described in Chapter 7B.
 f) On completion, start the engine and check for fuel leaks.

2.0 litre engines

10 Depressurise the fuel system as described in Section 7.
11 Disconnect the battery negative terminal (refer to *Disconnecting the battery* in the Reference Chapter).
12 Turn the segment on the throttle housing to open the throttle, then disconnect the inner accelerator cable. On automatic transmission models, also disconnect the kickdown cable. Unbolt the accelerator cable support bracket from the inlet manifold.

14.5 Removing the fuel inlet hose – 1.6 and 1.8 litre engines

14.7 Removing the fuel rail and injectors – 1.6 and 1.8 litre engines

13.2 Diagnostic socket location (arrowed) on the passenger's compartment fusebox

13 Remove the camshaft cover as described in Chapter 2A.
14 Unscrew the pulsation damper and disconnect the fuel inlet hose from the left-hand end of the fuel rail. Recover the two washers. Note that new washers will be required for refitting.
15 Disconnect the wiring connectors from the injectors.
16 Unscrew the two bolts securing the fuel rail to the cylinder head and carefully remove the fuel rail together with the injectors. Recover the two fuel rail spacers, and the insulator from each injector location in the cylinder head. Discard the insulators; new ones must be used on refitting.
17 Withdraw the injectors from the fuel rail and remove the O-ring seal and the grommet from the top of each injector. Discard the O-ring seals and grommets; new ones must be used on refitting.

14.6 Disconnecting the wiring connectors from the injectors – 1.6 and 1.8 litre engines

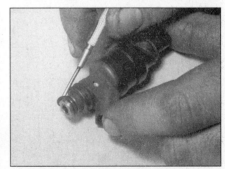

14.8 Remove the O-ring seals from each injector – 1.6 and 1.8 litre engines

18 Refitting is a reverse of the removal procedure, noting the following points:

a) *Fit a new grommet and O-ring to each injector, and fit new injector insulators to the cylinder head.*

b) *Apply a smear of engine oil to the O-rings to aid installation, then ease the injectors into the fuel rail.*

c) *Fit the two spacers, then ease the injectors and fuel rail assembly into position on cylinder head. Insert the mounting bolts and tighten to the specified torque.*

d) *Use new washers when refitting the fuel hose and pulsation damper, and tighten the damper to the specified torque.*

e) *Refit the camshaft cover as described in Chapter 2A.*

f) *Adjust the accelerator cable as described in Section 3 and, where applicable, the kickdown cable as described in Chapter 7B.*

g) *On completion, start the engine and check for fuel leaks.*

Fuel pressure regulator

19 Remove the fuel pump as described in Section 8.

20 Undo the retaining screw and withdraw the sub-filter from the base of the pressure regulator. Remove the sealing O-ring from the regulator pipe stub. Discard the O-ring; a new one must be used on refitting.

21 Disconnect the fuel hose and withdraw the pressure regulator from the base of the fuel pump assembly.

22 Refitting is a reverse of the removal procedure, noting the following points:

a) *Fit a new O-ring to the pressure regulator pipe stub. Apply a smear of engine oil to the O-ring, then ease the sub-filter into position.*

b) *Refit the fuel pump as described in Section 8.*

Throttle position sensor

23 Disconnect the throttle position sensor wiring connector.

24 Undo the two retaining screws then remove the throttle position sensor along with its gasket (where fitted).

25 Fit a new gasket (where necessary) to the throttle position sensor and refit the sensor to the throttle housing.

26 Refit and tighten the two retaining screws, then reconnect the wiring connector.

Throttle opener

2.0 litre engines

27 Remove the throttle housing as described in Section 12.

28 Disconnect the vacuum hose at the throttle opener.

29 Undo the bolts securing the throttle opener mounting bracket to the base of the throttle housing then remove the throttle opener and bracket.

30 Refit the throttle opener and mounting bracket to the throttle housing and tighten its retaining bolts securely, then refit the throttle housing as described in Section 12.

14.47 Disconnecting the wiring from the MAP sensor

31 On completion of refitting, check the throttle opener adjustment as follows.

32 Start the engine and warm it up to normal operating temperature.

33 Switch the engine off and connect a tachometer in accordance with the maker's instructions.

34 Start the engine again and allow it to idle. Disconnect the vacuum hose at the throttle opener and plug its end.

35 Increase the engine speed to 2500 rpm then release the throttle. The throttle opener should hold the engine speed at 1300 to 1500 rpm when the throttle is released. If the engine speed is not as specified, slacken the locknut, then turn the adjusting screw on the throttle opener plunger to set the engine speed at 1400 rpm. Tighten the locknut, reconnect the vacuum hose and check that the engine speed returns to the idle speed setting given in the Specifications.

36 Switch the engine off and disconnect the tachometer.

Idle speed control valve

37 Remove the throttle housing as described in Section 12.

38 Undo the screws securing the valve to the base of the throttle housing then remove the valve, noting the correct fitted position of its gasket.

39 Ensure the mating surfaces are clean then fit a new gasket to the valve.

40 Refit the idle speed control valve to the throttle housing and tighten its retaining screws securely, then refit the throttle housing as described in Section 12.

14.49 Withdraw the inlet air temperature sensor from the air cleaner housing grommet

Vacuum solenoid valve

1.6 and 1.8 litre engines

41 The inlet manifold air control valve assembly is controlled by a vacuum solenoid valve located at the rear of the engine, beneath the inlet manifold.

42 Remove the knock sensor as described in Chapter 5B.

43 Disconnect the wiring connector, then note the location of the hoses and disconnect them.

44 Undo the two bolts and remove the valve mounting bracket from the inlet manifold.

45 Unbolt the valve from the mounting bracket.

46 Refitting is a reverse of removal.

Manifold absolute pressure sensor

47 The MAP sensor is mounted on the engine compartment bulkhead. Disconnect the vacuum hose and wiring connector and remove the mounting bracket retaining bolt **(see illustration)**.

48 Refitting is a reverse of the removal procedure.

Inlet air temperature sensor

49 Disconnect the wiring connector and withdraw the sensor from the air cleaner housing grommet **(see illustration)**.

50 Refitting is a reverse of the removal procedure.

Coolant temperature sensor

51 Refer to Chapter 3.

Knock sensor

52 Refer to Chapter 5B.

Crankshaft position sensor

1.6 and 1.8 litre engines

53 The sensor is located adjacent to the crankshaft pulley at the rear of the engine.

54 Firmly apply the handbrake, then jack up the front of the car and support it securely on axle stands (see *Jacking and vehicle support*).

55 Trace the wiring back from the sensor and disconnect the wiring connector.

56 Undo the retaining bolt and withdraw the sensor from its location.

57 Refitting is a reverse of the removal procedure.

2.0 litre engines

58 The crankshaft position sensor is located adjacent to the crankshaft pulley at the front of the engine.

59 Firmly apply the handbrake, then jack up the front of the car and support it securely on axle stands (see *Jacking and vehicle support*). Remove the right-hand roadwheel, then unbolt and remove the undershield from under the right-hand side of the engine compartment.

60 Remove the auxiliary drivebelt(s) (alternator, power steering and air conditioning, as applicable), as described in Chapter 1.

61 Remove the right-hand engine/transmission mounting as described in Chapter 2A.
62 Remove the alternator as described in Chapter 5A.
63 The crankshaft must now be held stationary while the crankshaft pulley bolt is loosened. Toyota technicians use a special tool bolted to the crankshaft pulley to hold the crankshaft, and a similar tool can be fabricated out of flat metal bar. Alternatively, on manual transmission models have an assistant engage top gear and depress the brake pedal. On automatic transmission models, remove the starter motor (Chapter 5A) and use a wide-bladed screwdriver engaged with the starter ring gear to hold the crankshaft stationary.
64 Unscrew the crankshaft pulley bolt and slide the pulley off of the end of the crankshaft. If it is tight, use a suitable puller to remove it.
65 Unbolt and remove the upper and lower timing belt covers and, where fitted, recover the gaskets.
66 Slide the outer timing belt guide from the crankshaft.
67 Trace the wiring back from the sensor and disconnect the wiring connector.
68 Release the wiring connector from the alternator adjustment link bracket, then free the wiring from the retaining clips on the front of the engine.
69 Undo the retaining bolt and withdraw the sensor from its location.
70 Refitting is a reverse of the removal procedure. Refer to the Chapters indicated in the removal procedure when refitting components disturbed for access. Tighten the crankshaft pulley retaining bolt to the specified torque (Chapter 2A).

Camshaft position sensor

1.6 and 1.8 litre engines

71 The camshaft position sensor is located at the left-hand end of the cylinder head, at the rear of the exhaust camshaft **(see illustration)**.
72 Disconnect the wiring connector, then undo the retaining bolt and withdraw the sensor from its location.
73 Refitting is a reverse of the removal procedure.

2.0 litre engines

74 The camshaft position sensor is located at the right-hand end of the cylinder head, below the inlet camshaft timing belt sprocket.
75 Disconnect the wiring connector, then undo the retaining bolt and withdraw the sensor from its location.
76 Refitting is a reverse of the removal procedure.

Electronic Control Unit (ECU)

77 The ECU is located behind the facia on the passenger's side. For access, remove the passenger's side lower facia panel and the glovebox, as described in Chapter 11.
78 Disconnect the battery negative terminal (refer to *Disconnecting the battery* in the Reference Chapter). **Note:** *Disconnecting the*

14.71 Camshaft position sensor location (arrowed) – 1.6 and 1.8 litre engines

battery will erase any fault codes stored in the ECU. It is recommended that the ECU is interrogated using diagnostic test equipment prior to battery disconnection. Entrust this task to a Toyota dealer or suitably-equipped specialist.
79 Disconnect the wiring connectors then unscrew the nuts securing the ECU mounting bracket to the bulkhead. Withdraw the ECU and mounting bracket from under the facia.
80 Refitting is a reverse of the removal procedure. **Note:** *If a new ECU has been fitted, it may be necessary to be recode it using special test equipment. Entrust this task to a Toyota dealer or suitably-equipped specialist. After reconnecting the battery, the vehicle must be driven for several miles so that the ECU can learn its basic settings. If the engine still runs erratically, the basic settings may be reinstated by a Toyota dealer or specialist using special diagnostic equipment.*

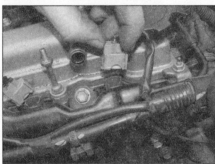

15.5 Disconnect the wiring connectors from the injectors . . .

15.8a Remove the plastic locking collar . . .

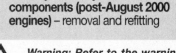

15 Fuel injection system components (post-August 2000 engines) – removal and refitting

⚠️ *Warning: Refer to the warning in Section 1 before proceeding.*

Fuel rail and injectors

Note: *If a faulty injector is suspected, before condemning the injector it is worth trying the effect of one of the proprietary injector-cleaning treatments.*

1.6 and 1.8 litre engines

1 Depressurise the fuel system as described in Section 7.
2 Disconnect the battery negative terminal (refer to *Disconnecting the battery* in the Reference Chapter).
3 Undo the two nuts at the front, prise out the two plastic fasteners at the rear and remove the plastic cover from the top of the engine.
4 Disconnect the crankcase ventilation hose from the front of the camshaft cover.
5 Disconnect the wiring connectors from the injectors **(see illustration)**.
6 Release the three retaining clips and move the wiring harness clear of the fuel rail **(see illustration)**.
7 Undo the bolt securing the fuel supply pipe to the left-hand end of the cylinder head.
8 Disconnect the fuel supply hose at the fuel filter by first removing the plastic locking collar. Squeeze the tabs on the side of the quick-release fitting and pull the fitting off the filter **(see illustrations)**.

15.6 . . . then release the retaining clips and move the wiring harness clear of the fuel rail – 1.6 and 1.8 litre engines

15.8b . . . then squeeze the tabs on the side of the fuel supply hose fitting to release it – 1.6 and 1.8 litre engines

15.9a Undo the two mounting bolts . . .

15.9b . . . lift off the fuel rail complete with injectors . . .

15.9c . . . and recover the spacers from the cylinder head – 1.6 and 1.8 litre engines

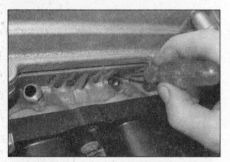

15.10 Hook out the grommet from each injector location in the cylinder head – 1.6 and 1.8 litre engines

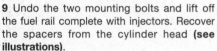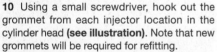

15.11a Remove the O-ring from the top of each injector . . .

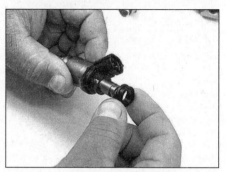

15.11b . . . and, on 1.6 litre engines, also remove the grommet

9 Undo the two mounting bolts and lift off the fuel rail complete with injectors. Recover the spacers from the cylinder head **(see illustrations)**.

10 Using a small screwdriver, hook out the grommet from each injector location in the cylinder head **(see illustration)**. Note that new grommets will be required for refitting.

11 Carefully pull the injectors out of the fuel rail, then remove the O-ring and, on 1.6 litre engines, the grommet, from the upper end of each injector **(see illustrations)**. Note that new O-rings and grommets will be required for refitting.

12 Refitting is a reverse of the removal procedure, noting the following points:
 a) *Fit new O-ring seals and, where applicable, new grommets to all the injectors.*
 b) *Apply a smear of petrol or spindle oil to the O-rings to aid installation, then ease the injectors into the fuel rail using a twisting motion.*
 c) *Fit a new grommet to each injector location in the cylinder head.*
 d) *Fit the two spacers to the cylinder head, then ease the injectors and fuel rail assembly into position. Insert the mounting bolts and tighten to the specified torque.*
 e) *On completion, start the engine and check for fuel leaks.*

2.0 litre engines

13 Depressurise the fuel system as described in Section 7.
14 Disconnect the battery negative terminal

(refer to *Disconnecting the battery* in the Reference Chapter).

15 Undo the four nuts and remove the plastic cover from the top of the engine.
16 Remove the inlet manifold and inlet air control valve assembly as described in Section 17.
17 Disconnect the wiring connectors from the injectors.
18 Disconnect the wiring connector from the knock sensor, then remove the heat insulator from the rear of the cylinder block.
19 Unscrew the union nuts and disconnect the fuel outlet pipe from the high-pressure fuel pump and fuel rail.
20 Release the retaining clips and disconnect the fuel return hoses from the high-pressure fuel pump and fuel rail.
21 Disconnect the wiring connector from the fuel pressure sensor on the fuel rail.
22 Undo the five bolts securing the fuel rail to the cylinder head.
23 Undo the retaining bolt and remove the clamp bracket from each injector.
24 Lift off the fuel rail complete with injectors. Using a small screwdriver, hook out the large gasket and the small gasket from each injector location in the cylinder head. Note that new gaskets will be required for refitting.
25 Carefully pull the injectors out of the fuel rail. Extract the circlip, then remove the outer washer, O-ring, centre washer and inner washer from each injector. Note the size and position of each washer as it is removed, as a guide to reassembly. Note that new circlips, O-rings and washers will be required for refitting.

26 Refitting is a reverse of the removal procedure, noting the following points:
 a) *Fit a new inner washer, centre washer, O-ring, outer washer and circlip to each injector.*
 b) *Apply a smear of petrol or spindle oil to the O-rings to aid installation, then ease the injectors into the fuel rail using a twisting motion.*
 c) *Fit a new small gasket and large gasket to each injector location in the cylinder head, noting that the small gaskets must be fitted with their chamfered side facing away from the cylinder head (ie, towards the injector).*
 d) *Ease the injectors and fuel rail assembly into position on cylinder head. Refit the injector clamp brackets and tighten the bolts to the specified torque, then insert and tighten the fuel rail mounting bolts to the specified torque.*
 e) *Refit the inlet manifold and inlet air control valve assembly as described in Section 17.*

Fuel pressure regulator

27 The fuel pressure regulator is part of the fuel pump/fuel gauge sender unit assembly located in the fuel tank. On fuel pumps manufactured by Bosch, the regulator is integral with the pump and cannot be renewed separately. On pumps manufactured by TMC (Toyota Motor Co), the pressure regulator is a renewable component and removal and refitting procedures are contained in Section 14.

Throttle position sensor

Note: *On 2.0 litre engines, the throttle position*

15.29 Disconnect the throttle position sensor wiring connector – 1.6 and 1.8 litre engines

15.34 Idle speed control valve mounting screws (arrowed) – 1.6 and 1.8 litre engines

15.37 Vacuum solenoid valve location (arrowed) – 2.0 litre engines

sensor is an integral part of the throttle housing and cannot be individually renewed.

1.6 and 1.8 litre engines

28 Undo the two nuts at the front, prise out the two plastic fasteners at the rear and remove the plastic cover from the top of the engine.
29 Disconnect the throttle position sensor wiring connector **(see illustration)**.
30 Undo the two retaining screws then remove the throttle position sensor along with its gasket (where fitted).
31 Fit a new gasket (where necessary) to the throttle position sensor and refit the sensor to the throttle housing.
32 Refit and tighten the two retaining screws, then reconnect the wiring connector.

Idle speed control valve

Note: *On 2.0 litre engines, a throttle control motor, integral with the throttle housing, performs the idle speed control function.*

1.6 and 1.8 litre engines

33 Remove the throttle housing as described in Section 12.
34 Undo the screws securing the valve to the base of the throttle housing then remove the valve, noting the correct fitted position of its gasket **(see illustration)**.
35 Ensure the mating surfaces are clean then fit a new gasket to the valve.
36 Refit the idle speed control valve to the throttle housing and tighten its retaining screws securely, then refit the throttle housing as described in Section 12.

Vacuum solenoid valve

2.0 litre engines

37 The inlet manifold air control valve assembly is controlled by a vacuum solenoid valve located on the right-hand side of the inlet manifold **(see illustration)**.
38 Undo the four nuts and remove the plastic cover over the engine.
39 Disconnect the wiring connector, then note the location of the hoses and disconnect them.
40 Undo the retaining bolt and remove the vacuum solenoid valve from the inlet manifold.
41 Refitting is a reverse of removal.

Manifold absolute pressure sensor

2.0 litre engines

42 The MAP sensor is located below the left-hand side of the inlet manifold.
43 Undo the four nuts and remove the plastic cover from the top of the engine.
44 Disconnect the vacuum hose and wiring connector, then unbolt the sensor from its location.
45 Refitting is a reverse of the removal procedure.

Inlet air temperature sensor

2.0 litre engines

46 Disconnect the wiring connector and withdraw the sensor from the air cleaner housing grommet **(see illustration)**.

47 Refitting is a reverse of the removal procedure.

Coolant temperature sensor

48 Refer to Chapter 3.

Knock sensor

49 Refer to Chapter 5B.

Crankshaft position sensor

1.6 and 1.8 litre engines

50 The crankshaft position sensor is located adjacent to the crankshaft pulley at the front of the engine.
51 Undo the two nuts at the front, prise out the two plastic fasteners at the rear and remove the plastic cover from the top of the engine.
52 Firmly apply the handbrake, then jack up the front of the car and support it securely on axle stands (see *Jacking and vehicle support*).
53 Remove the alternator as described in Chapter 5A.
54 Trace the wiring back from the sensor to the connector attached to the engine oil dipstick support bracket. Disconnect the wiring connector, noting that due to the limited access available, it is beneficial to unclip the connector from the bracket **(see illustration)**.
55 Undo the bolt securing the sensor wiring loom retaining bracket to the timing chain cover **(see illustration)**.
56 Undo the retaining bolt and withdraw the sensor from the timing chain cover **(see illustration)**. Discard the sensor O-ring, a new one will be required for refitting.

15.46 Disconnect the wiring connector (arrowed) and withdraw the inlet air temperature sensor – 2.0 litre engines

15.54 Disconnect the crankshaft position sensor wiring connector – 1.6 and 1.8 litre engines

15.55 Undo the bolt (arrowed) securing the wiring loom bracket to the timing chain cover . . .

15.56 . . . then unbolt and remove the crankshaft position sensor – 1.6 and 1.8 litre engines

57 Refitting is a reverse of the removal procedure, using a new sensor O-ring.

2.0 litre engines

58 The crankshaft position sensor is located adjacent to the crankshaft pulley at the front of the engine.

59 Undo the four nuts and remove the plastic cover from the top of the engine.

60 Firmly apply the handbrake, then jack up the front of the car and support it securely on axle stands (see *Jacking and vehicle support*).

61 Trace the wiring back from the sensor to the connector attached to a support bracket at the top of the timing chain cover **(see illustration)**. Disconnect the wiring connector, and unclip the connector from the bracket.

62 Remove the alternator as described in Chapter 5A.

63 Detach the cable clip securing the crankshaft position sensor wiring to the coolant pump, then release the wiring from the cable guide.

64 Undo the retaining bolt and withdraw the sensor from the timing chain cover. Discard the sensor O-ring, a new one will be required for refitting.

65 Refitting is a reverse of the removal procedure, using a new sensor O-ring.

Camshaft position sensor

1.6 and 1.8 litre engines

66 The camshaft position sensor is located at the left-hand end of the cylinder head, on the forward facing side.

67 Undo the two nuts at the front, prise

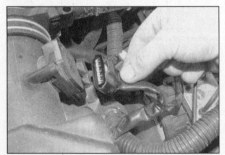

15.82 Disconnect the wiring connector from the airflow meter – 1.6 and 1.8 litre engines

15.61 Disconnect the crankshaft position sensor wiring connector (arrowed), and unclip the connector from the bracket – 2.0 litre engines

out the two plastic fasteners at the rear and remove the plastic cover from the top of the engine.

68 Disconnect the wiring connector, then undo the retaining bolt and withdraw the sensor from its location **(see illustration)**. Discard the sensor O-ring, a new one will be required for refitting.

69 Refitting is a reverse of the removal procedure, using a new sensor O-ring.

2.0 litre engines

70 The camshaft position sensor is located at the left-hand end of the cylinder head, at the rear of the inlet camshaft.

71 Undo the four nuts and remove the plastic cover from the top of the engine.

72 Disconnect the wiring connector, then undo the retaining bolt and withdraw the sensor from its location.

73 Refitting is a reverse of the removal procedure.

Accelerator pedal position sensor

2.0 litre engines

74 The sensor is an integral part of the accelerator pedal assembly and cannot be renewed separately (see Section 4).

Fuel pressure sensor

2.0 litre engines

75 The fuel pressure sensor is located in the centre of the fuel rail.

76 Depressurise the fuel system as described in Section 7.

77 Disconnect the battery negative terminal

15.87 Undo the two bolts and remove the anti-theft bracket over the ECU wiring connectors

15.68 Undo the retaining bolt and remove the camshaft position sensor – 1.6 and 1.8 litre engines

(refer to *Disconnecting the battery* in the Reference Chapter).

78 Undo the four nuts and remove the plastic cover from the top of the engine.

79 Remove the inlet manifold and inlet air control valve assembly as described in Section 17.

80 Disconnect the wiring connector from the pressure sensor, then unscrew the sensor from the fuel rail and collect the sealing washer. Discard the sealing washer, a new one will be required for refitting.

81 Refitting is a reverse of the removal procedure. Use a new sealing washer and tighten the sensor to the specified torque.

Airflow meter

1.6 and 1.8 litre engines

82 Disconnect the wiring connector from the airflow meter located on the side of the air cleaner lid **(see illustration)**.

83 Undo the two screws and withdraw the sensor from the air cleaner lid. Discard the sensor O-ring, a new one will be required for refitting.

84 Refitting is a reverse of the removal procedure, using a new sensor O-ring.

Electronic Control Unit (ECU)

85 The ECU is located behind the facia on the passenger's side. For access, remove the passenger's side lower facia panel and the glovebox, as described in Chapter 11.

86 Disconnect the battery negative terminal (refer to *Disconnecting the battery* in the Reference Chapter). **Note:** *Disconnecting the battery will erase any fault codes stored in the ECU. It is recommended that the ECU is interrogated using diagnostic test equipment prior to battery disconnection. Entrust this task to a Toyota dealer or suitably-equipped specialist.*

87 Undo the two bolts and remove the anti-theft bracket over the ECU wiring connectors **(see illustration)**. On later models, the anti-theft bracket retaining bolts are of the tamperproof type and, ideally, a Toyota special tool is required to remove them. In the absence of the special tool, it is just possible to unscrew them by tapping them anti-clockwise using a hammer and small punch.

For refitting, either obtain new tamperproof bolts or use conventional bolts instead.

88 Release the glovebox damper cable from the ECU lower mounting bracket **(see illustration)**.

89 Disconnect the wiring connectors then unscrew the nuts securing the ECU mounting bracket to the bulkhead. The lower nut may also be of the tamperproof type and can be removed as described in paragraph 87.

90 Withdraw the ECU and mounting bracket from under the facia **(see illustration)**.

91 Refitting is a reverse of the removal procedure. **Note:** *If a new ECU has been fitted, it may be necessary to be recode it using special test equipment. Entrust this task to a Toyota dealer or suitably-equipped specialist. After reconnecting the battery, the vehicle must be driven for several miles so that the ECU can learn its basic settings. If the engine still runs erratically, the basic settings may be reinstated by a Toyota dealer or specialist using special diagnostic equipment.*

Electronic Driver Unit (EDU)

2.0 litre engines

92 The EDU controls the operation of the electronic throttle control system and is mounted in the engine compartment on the left-hand suspension strut turret (right-hand drive models), or on the right-hand suspension strut turret (left-hand drive models).

93 Disconnect the battery negative terminal (refer to *Disconnecting the battery* in the Reference Chapter).

94 Disconnect the wiring connectors then unscrew the two bolts securing the EDU mounting bracket to the strut turret **(see illustration)**. Withdraw the unit from the engine compartment.

95 Refitting is a reverse of the removal procedure.

---

16 Inlet manifold (pre-August 2000 engines) – removal and refitting

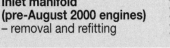 **Warning: Refer to the warning in Section 1 before proceeding.**

1.6 and 1.8 litre engines

Removal

1 Remove the throttle housing as described in Section 12.

2 Disconnect the two positive crankcase ventilation hoses from the inlet manifold.

3 Disconnect the wiring connector from the vacuum solenoid valve on the underside of the inlet manifold.

4 Release the wiring harness from the inlet manifold rear support bracket, then unbolt the bracket from the manifold and cylinder block.

5 Unscrew the two nuts and seven bolts securing the inlet manifold to the cylinder head. Withdraw the manifold from the studs

15.88 Release the glovebox damper cable from the ECU lower mounting bracket

and remove it from the engine compartment. Recover the gasket.

6 If required, disconnect the vacuum hoses and unbolt the vacuum solenoid valve assembly from the underside of the manifold.

7 Clean the surfaces of the inlet manifold and cylinder head and check the inlet manifold for distortion using a straight-edge and feeler blade. If the distortion exceeds the specified maximum, renew the manifold.

Refitting

8 Refitting is a reverse of the removal procedure. Use a new gasket and tighten the mounting nuts and bolts to the specified torque.

2.0 litre engines

Removal

9 Remove the throttle housing as described in Section 12.

10 Remove the fuel rail and injectors as described in Section 14.

11 Remove the EGR valve, vacuum modulator and vacuum solenoid valve as described in Chapter 4B.

12 Disconnect the remaining wiring connections and the air and vacuum hoses, labelling them for reconnection.

13 Undo the two nuts and six bolts securing the manifold to the cylinder head. Withdraw the manifold from the studs and remove it from the engine compartment. Recover the gasket.

14 Clean the surfaces of the inlet manifold and cylinder head and check the inlet manifold

17.3 Undo the two bolts (arrowed) and remove the inlet manifold upper support bracket – 1.6 and 1.8 litre engines

15.90 Withdraw the ECU and mounting bracket from under the facia

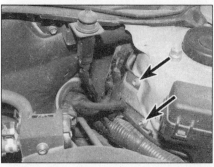

15.94 EDU mounting bracket retaining bolts (arrowed) – 2.0 litre engines

for distortion using a straight-edge and feeler blade. If the distortion exceeds the specified maximum, renew the manifold.

Refitting

15 Refitting is a reverse of the removal procedure. Use a new gasket and tighten the mounting nuts and bolts to the specified torque.

---

17 Inlet manifold (post-August 2000 engines) – removal and refitting

 Warning: Refer to the warning in Section 1 before proceeding.

1.6 and 1.8 litre engines

Removal

1 Remove the throttle housing as described in Section 12.

2 Release the clips securing the engine wiring harness to the two brackets on the top of the manifold. Disconnect the camshaft position sensor wiring connector and move the harness to one side.

3 Undo the two bolts and release the upper support bracket from the manifold **(see illustration)**.

4 Disconnect the brake servo vacuum hose and the positive crankcase ventilation hose from the manifold **(see illustration)**.

5 Undo the three bolts and two nuts, and collect the two wiring harness brackets. Withdraw the inlet manifold from the cylinder head and release the wiring harness clip as

17.4 Disconnect the two hoses (arrowed) from the inlet manifold – 1.6 and 1.8 litre engines

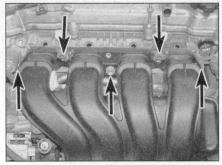

17.5a Undo the nuts and bolts (arrowed) and remove the inlet manifold . . .

17.5b . . . then remove the manifold O-ring seals – 1.6 and 1.8 litre engines

the manifold is removed. Recover the inlet manifold O-ring seals **(see illustrations)**.
6 Thoroughly clean the surfaces of the inlet manifold and cylinder head prior to refitting.

Refitting

7 Refitting is a reverse of the removal procedure. Use new O-ring seals and tighten the mounting nuts and bolts to the specified torque.

18.3 Separating the exhaust downpipe from the exhaust manifold

18.4a Unscrew the bolts . . .

18.4b . . . and remove the heat shield from the exhaust manifold

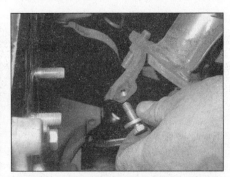

18.5 Removing the bolt from the exhaust manifold stay

18.6a Progressively loosen the mounting nuts . . .

18.6b . . . then remove the nuts . . .

2.0 litre engines

Removal

8 Remove the throttle housing as described in Section 12.
9 Label and disconnect the positive crankcase ventilation hoses and vacuum hoses from the inlet manifold and inlet air control valve assembly.
10 Undo the five bolts and two nuts securing the inlet manifold and inlet air control valve assembly to the cylinder head. Lift the inlet manifold off the inlet air control valve assembly and recover the gasket. Lift the inlet air control valve assembly off the cylinder head and recover the second gasket.
11 Thoroughly clean the surfaces of the inlet manifold, inlet air control valve assembly and cylinder head prior to refitting.

Refitting

12 Refitting is a reverse of the removal procedure. Use new gaskets and tighten the mounting nuts and bolts to the specified torque.

18 Exhaust manifold (pre-August 2000 engines) – removal and refitting

Removal

1 Firmly apply the handbrake, then jack up the front of the car and support it securely on axle stands (see *Jacking and vehicle support*).
2 Disconnect the lean mixture sensor, or oxygen sensor, wiring connector.
3 Unscrew the nuts (or bolts) securing the exhaust front downpipe to the exhaust manifold and, where fitted, recover the compression springs. Lower the downpipe and remove the gasket **(see illustration)**. It may difficult to lower the downpipe as it often jams on the studs, therefore disconnection can be left until the manifold is removed.
4 Unbolt and remove the heat shield **(see illustrations)**.
5 Unbolt and remove the exhaust manifold stay **(see illustration)**.
6 Progressively unscrew the mounting nuts, and withdraw the exhaust manifold from the studs on the cylinder head **(see illustrations)**. Remove the gasket.

7 Where a heat shield is fitted underneath, unbolt it from the manifold.
8 Clean the surfaces of the exhaust manifold and cylinder head and check the exhaust manifold for distortion using a straight-edge and feeler blade. If the distortion exceeds the specified maximum, renew the manifold.

Refitting

9 Refitting is a reverse of the removal procedure, but fit new gaskets to the cylinder head and exhaust front downpipe, and tighten the mounting nuts/bolts to the specified torque (where given).

19 Exhaust manifold (post-August 2000 engines) – removal and refitting

1.6 litre engines

Removal

1 Firmly apply the handbrake, then jack up the front of the car and support it securely on axle stands (see *Jacking and vehicle support*).
2 Remove the oxygen sensor from the exhaust manifold as described in Chapter 4B.
3 Unscrew the two bolts securing the exhaust front downpipe to the exhaust manifold, and recover the compression springs **(see illustration)**. Lower the downpipe and remove the gasket.
4 Unbolt and remove the heat shield.
5 Undo the two bolts securing the exhaust manifold stay to the cylinder block.
6 Progressively unscrew the five mounting nuts, and withdraw the exhaust manifold from the studs on the cylinder head. Remove the gasket.
7 Clean the surfaces of the exhaust manifold and cylinder head and check the exhaust manifold for distortion using a straight-edge and feeler blade. If the distortion exceeds the specified maximum, renew the manifold.

Refitting

8 Refitting is a reverse of the removal procedure, but fit new gaskets to the cylinder head and exhaust front downpipe, and tighten the mounting nuts/bolts to the specified torque (where given).

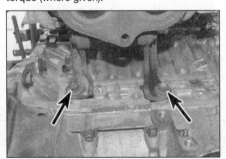

19.13 Undo the bolts (arrowed) securing the exhaust manifold stays to the cylinder block – 1.8 litre engines

18.6c . . . and withdraw the exhaust manifold from the cylinder head studs

1.8 litre engines

Note: *The exhaust manifold also incorporates the two front catalytic converters.*

Removal

9 Firmly apply the handbrake, then jack up the front of the car and support it securely on axle stands (see *Jacking and vehicle support*).
10 Remove the two oxygen sensors from the exhaust manifold as described in Chapter 4B.
11 Unscrew the three nuts securing the exhaust front downpipe to the exhaust manifold. Lower the downpipe and remove the two gaskets.
12 Unbolt and remove the upper heat shield **(see illustration)**.
13 Undo the bolts securing the left-hand and right-hand exhaust manifold stays to the cylinder block **(see illustration)**.
14 Progressively unscrew the five mounting nuts, and withdraw the exhaust manifold from

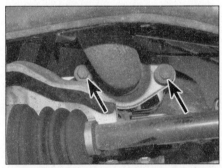

19.3 Exhaust front downpipe-to-manifold bolts (arrowed) – 1.6 litre engines

19.14a Withdraw the exhaust manifold from the studs on the cylinder head . . .

the studs on the cylinder head. Remove the gasket **(see illustrations)**.
15 Clean the surfaces of the exhaust manifold and cylinder head and check the exhaust manifold for distortion using a straight-edge and feeler blade. If the distortion exceeds the specified maximum, renew the manifold.

Refitting

16 Refitting is a reverse of the removal procedure, but fit new gaskets to the cylinder head and exhaust front downpipe, and tighten the mounting nuts/bolts to the specified torque (where given).

2.0 litre engines

Note: *The exhaust manifold also incorporates the two front catalytic converters.*

Removal

17 Firmly apply the handbrake, then jack up the front of the car and support it securely on axle stands (see *Jacking and vehicle support*).
18 Remove the upper right-hand oxygen sensor from the exhaust manifold as described in Chapter 4B. Disconnect the wiring connectors for the upper left-hand oxygen sensor and the two lower oxygen sensors.
19 Unscrew the two nuts securing the exhaust front downpipe to the exhaust manifold. Lower the downpipe and remove the gasket.
20 Unbolt and remove the upper heat shield **(see illustration)**.
21 Undo the bolts securing the left-hand and right-hand exhaust manifold stays to the cylinder block.
22 Progressively unscrew the five mounting

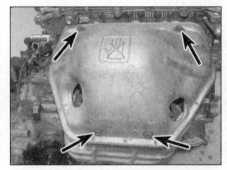

19.12 Upper heat shield retaining bolts (arrowed) – 1.8 litre engines

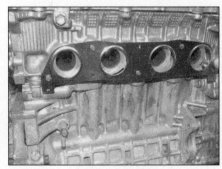

19.14b . . . then remove the gasket – 1.8 litre engines

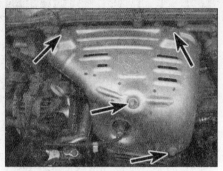

19.20 Upper heat shield retaining bolts (arrowed) – 2.0 litre engines

nuts, and withdraw the exhaust manifold from the studs on the cylinder head. Remove the gasket. If necessary, unbolt and remove the inner and outer lower heat shields.

23 Clean the surfaces of the exhaust manifold and cylinder head and check the exhaust manifold for distortion using a straight-edge and feeler blade. If the distortion exceeds the specified maximum, renew the manifold.

Refitting

24 Refitting is a reverse of the removal procedure, but fit new gaskets to the cylinder head and exhaust front downpipe, and tighten the mounting nuts/bolts to the specified torque (where given).

20 Exhaust system – general information, removal and refitting

General information

1 The exhaust system consists of multiple sections that include the front downpipe, catalytic converter, intermediate pipe, and the tailpipe with resonator and rear silencer. Depending on model year and engine type, a catalytic converter may be incorporated in the front downpipe, or it may be part of the intermediate pipe. On 1.8 and 2.0 litre engines post-August 2000, two catalytic converters are incorporated in the exhaust manifold, and a third catalytic converter is located in the front downpipe or intermediate pipe.

2 The system is suspended throughout its entire length by rubber mountings, and all exhaust sections are joined by flanged joints which are secured together by studs and nuts.

Removal

 Warning: The catalytic converter operates at very high temperatures – make sure it is cool before working on the exhaust system.

3 Each exhaust section can be removed individually or, alternatively, the complete system can be removed as a unit.

4 First jack up the vehicle, and support it on axle stands (see *Jacking and vehicle support*). Alternatively, position the car over an inspection pit, or on car ramps.

Front downpipe

5 Where the exhaust gas oxygen sensor is located in the downpipe, trace the wiring back to the connector and disconnect it. On later models, the sensor wiring connector is located inside the car in the footwell.

6 Unscrew the nuts/bolts securing the downpipe to the exhaust manifold and, where applicable, recover the compression springs. Lower the downpipe and recover the gasket(s).

7 Unbolt the downpipe from the intermediate pipe or tailpipe, and remove it from under the vehicle. Recover the gasket from the flanged joint.

Intermediate pipe

8 Unbolt the front downpipe from the intermediate pipe.

9 Unbolt the intermediate pipe from the tailpipe.

10 Support the intermediate pipe and release it from the mounting rubbers. Remove the intermediate pipe from under the vehicle and collect the gaskets from the flanged joints.

Tailpipe

11 Unbolt the front downpipe or intermediate pipe from the tailpipe.

12 Support the tailpipe and release it from the mounting rubbers. Remove the tailpipe from under the vehicle and collect the gasket from the flanged joint.

Complete system

13 Unscrew the nuts/bolts securing the front downpipe to the exhaust manifold and, where applicable, recover the compression springs. Lower the downpipe and recover the gasket(s).

14 Support the exhaust system, then release the rubber mountings and lower the system to the ground.

Heat shields

15 Heat shields are riveted to the underbody and may be removed by drilling out the securing rivets. In most instances there is sufficient clearance to carry out this operation with the exhaust system in place.

Refitting

16 Each section is refitted by a reverse of the removal sequence, noting the following points:

a) *Ensure that all traces of corrosion have been removed from the flanges, and renew the gasket(s).*

b) *Inspect the rubber mountings for signs of damage or deterioration, and renew as necessary.*

c) *Prior to tightening the exhaust system fasteners, ensure that all rubber mountings are correctly located, and that there is adequate clearance between the exhaust system and vehicle underbody/ suspension components, etc.*

d) *When refitting the heat shields, use new pop rivets to secure them to the underbody.*

Chapter 4 Part B:
Emission control systems

Contents

Degrees of difficulty

Easy, suitable for novice with little experience	Fairly easy, suitable for beginner with some experience	Fairly difficult, suitable for competent DIY mechanic	Difficult, suitable for experienced DIY mechanic	Very difficult, suitable for expert DIY or professional

Specifications

Torque wrench settings	Nm	lbf ft
Lean mixture sensor	20	15
Oxygen sensor	44	32

1 General information

1 Models covered in this manual are fitted with the following emission control systems.
   a) Crankcase emission control.
   b) Catalytic converter.
   c) Evaporative emission control.
   d) Exhaust gas recirculation (2.0 litre engines pre-August 2000 only).
The systems operate as follows.

Crankcase emission control

2 To reduce the emission of unburned hydrocarbons from the crankcase into the atmosphere, the engine is sealed, and the blow-by gases and oil vapour are drawn from inside the crankcase, through the Positive Crankcase Ventilation (PCV) valve, into the inlet manifold, to be burned by the engine during normal combustion.

3 Under conditions of high manifold vacuum, the gases will be sucked positively out of the crankcase. Under conditions of low manifold vacuum, the gases are forced out of the crankcase by the (relatively) higher crankcase pressure; if the engine is worn, the raised crankcase pressure (due to increased blow-by) will cause some of the flow to return under all manifold conditions.

Catalytic converter

4 To minimise the amount of pollutants which escape into the atmosphere, a catalytic converter is fitted in the exhaust system front downpipe, or intermediate pipe. Additionally, on 1.8 and 2.0 litre engines post-August 2000, two further catalytic converters are incorporated in the exhaust manifold. The system is of closed-loop type, in which exhaust gas oxygen sensor(s) (or lean mixture sensor on 1.6 and 1.8 litre engines pre-August 2000) provides the engine management ECU with constant feedback, enabling the unit to adjust the mixture to provide the best possible conditions for the converter to operate.

5 The sensor's tip is sensitive to oxygen, and sends the control unit a varying voltage depending on the amount of oxygen in the exhaust gases; if the intake air/fuel mixture is too rich, the sensor sends a high-voltage signal. The voltage falls as the mixture weakens. Peak conversion efficiency of all major pollutants occurs if the intake air/fuel mixture is maintained at the chemically-correct ratio for the complete combustion of petrol – 14.7 parts (by weight) of air to 1 part of fuel (the stoichiometric ratio). The sensor output voltage alters in a large step at this point, the control unit using the signal change as a reference point, and correcting the intake air/fuel mixture accordingly by altering the fuel injector pulse width (injector opening time). The sensor has a built-in heating element (controlled by the ECU), to quickly bring the sensor's tip to an efficient operating temperature.

Evaporative emission control

6 An evaporative emission control system is fitted in order to minimise the escape of unburned hydrocarbons into the atmosphere. The fuel tank filler cap is sealed, and a carbon canister collects the petrol vapours generated in the fuel tank when the car is stationary. It stores the vapours until they can be cleared into the inlet manifold when the engine is running. To ensure that the engine runs correctly when it is cold and/or idling, and to protect the catalytic converter from the effects of an over-rich mixture, the system is designed to operate only when the engine has warmed-up and is under load.

7 On pre-August 2000 engines, the system is operated by a Bi-metal Vacuum Switching Valve (BVSV) located on the left-hand end of the cylinder head. At coolant temperatures below 35°C the valve is closed and the system is disabled, however at temperatures above 54°C the valve is open and the system is enabled.

8 On post-August 2000 engines, the system is operated by a Vacuum Solenoid Valve (VSV) mounted on the air cleaner assembly, and controlled by the engine management ECU.

Exhaust Gas Recirculation

9 An Exhaust Gas Recirculation (EGR) system is fitted to 2.0 litre engines pre-August 2000. This reduces the level of nitrogen oxides produced during combustion by introducing a proportion of the exhaust gas back into the inlet manifold under certain engine operating conditions. The system is controlled by a Vacuum Solenoid Valve (VSV) via the engine management ECU. The VSV supplies vacuum to the EGR valve which then opens and allows a proportion of exhaust gases to flow into the inlet manifold. With the throttle valve closed the system is inactive since there is no vacuum available to open the EGR valve, however, when the throttle valve is opened initially the first vacuum port is opened and the EGR valve will open provided that the ECU has energised the VSV. Further opening of the throttle valve causes a second vacuum port to be influenced by engine vacuum. This causes the vacuum modulator to increase the amount of exhaust gases entering the engine. The modulator has an internal diaphragm which is subject to exhaust gas pressure on one side, and to atmospheric pressure through a filter on the other side.

2.6 Disconnecting the lean mixture sensor wiring connector

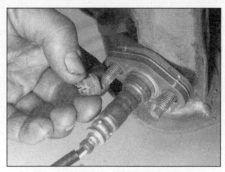

2.7a Unscrew the mounting nuts . . .

2.7b . . . then remove the lean mixture sensor . . .

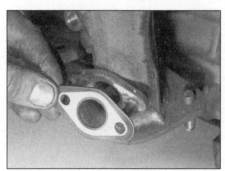

2.7c . . . and gasket

2 Emission control systems – testing and component renewal

Crankcase emission control

1 Disconnect the crankcase ventilation hoses and check that they are clear and undamaged, then refit them.

2 To check the PCV valve, pull it out of the grommet in the camshaft cover (pre-August 2000 engines), or unscrew it from the cover (post-August 2000 engines) and shake the valve. It should rattle, indicating that it's not clogged with deposits. If the valve does not rattle, renew it.

3 Start the engine and allow it to idle, then place your finger over the valve opening – vacuum should be felt. If no vacuum is felt,

the PCV valve may be defective or the hose may be blocked. Also check for vacuum leaks at the valve, filler cap and all the hoses.

Catalytic converter

Testing

4 If the CO level at the tailpipe is too high, the operation of the exhaust gas oxygen sensor(s)/lean mixture sensor should be tested by a Toyota dealer or engine diagnostic specialist.

Renewal

5 Refer to Chapter 4A.

Lean mixture sensor

Note: *The sensor is delicate, and it will not work if it is dropped or knocked, if its power supply is disrupted, or if any cleaning materials are used on it.*

Renewal

6 On 1.6 and 1.8 litre engines pre-August 2000, a lean mixture sensor is located in the exhaust manifold. First trace the wiring back to the connector and disconnect it **(see illustration)**.

7 Unscrew the mounting nuts, then remove the sensor and recover the gaskets **(see illustrations)**.

8 Refitting is a reversal of the removal procedure, but prior to installing the sensor, apply a smear of high-temperature grease to the sensor mounting stud threads. Tighten the nuts to the specified torque. Check that the wiring is correctly routed, and in no danger of contacting either the exhaust system or the engine.

Oxygen sensor

Note: *The sensor is delicate, and it will not work if it is dropped or knocked, if its power supply is disrupted, or if any cleaning materials are used on it.*

Renewal

9 On all except 1.6 and 1.8 litre engines pre-August 2000, exhaust gas oxygen sensors are located in the exhaust system front downpipe/intermediate pipe, and/or exhaust manifold. According to engine type and number of sensors fitted, the sensors monitor exhaust CO level after the gasses have passed through the catalytic converter(s), or before *and* after the gasses have passed through the catalytic converter(s).

10 Trace the wiring back from the relevant oxygen sensor(s), (which are screwed into the exhaust front downpipe, intermediate pipe, or into the exhaust manifold). Disconnect the wiring connectors and free the wiring from any relevant retaining clips or ties. Note that on later models, the wiring connector for the front downpipe mounted sensor is located inside the car, in the footwell.

11 Unscrew the sensor from the exhaust system front downpipe/intermediate pipe, or manifold and remove it along with its sealing washer (where fitted) **(see illustrations)**.

12 Refitting is a reverse of the removal procedure using a new sealing washer (where applicable). Prior to installing the sensor apply a smear of high temperature grease to the sensor threads. Ensure the sensor is securely

2.11a Exhaust gas oxygen sensor location (arrowed) in the exhaust downpipe on 2.0 litre engines pre-August 2000 . . .

2.11b . . . and in the exhaust manifold (arrowed) on 1.8 litre engines post-August 2000 . . .

2.11c . . . and in the top (arrowed) . . .

tightened and that the wiring is correctly routed and in no danger of contacting either the exhaust system or engine.

Evaporative emission control

Testing

13 To test the system, disconnect the hoses between the carbon canister (see below), BVSV (left-hand end of the cylinder head) or VSV (on the air cleaner assembly) and throttle housing, and check that they are clear by blowing through them **(see illustrations)**.

14 Check the fuel tank filler cap for a deformed or damaged seal.

15 Using low air pressure on the carbon canister port with the long stub, check that air flows through the canister freely and exits through the short stub.

16 Using air pressure on the carbon canister port with the short stub, check that no air flows from the long stub.

17 The BVSV valve may be tested by immersing it in water being heated. Connect an air supply to one of the outlets. At temperatures below 35°C the valve should be closed, however, at temperatures above 54°C it should be open.

Carbon canister

Renewal

18 On pre-August 2000 engines, the canister is located under the left-hand wheel arch on right-hand drive models, or under the right-hand wheel arch on left-hand drive models. Refer to Chapter 11 and remove the relevant wheel arch liner for access. On post-August 2000 models, the canister is located at the rear of the fuel tank.

19 According to model, jack up the front or rear of the car and support it securely on axle stands (see *Jacking and vehicle support*).

20 Make a note of the correct fitted location of each hose on the canister.

21 Release the retaining clips (where fitted) and disconnect the hoses from the canister.

2.11d . . . and side (arrowed) of the exhaust manifold on 2.0 litre engines post-August 2000 . . .

2.13a The BVSV is located on the left-hand end of the cylinder head – 2.0 litre engine pre-August 2000

22 Free the canister from its mounting bracket, and remove it from its location.

23 Refitting is a reverse of the removal procedure, ensuring that the hoses are correctly reconnected.

Exhaust gas recirculation

Testing

24 Detailed testing of the exhaust gas recirculation system should be entrusted to a Toyota dealer or engine diagnostic specialist.

Removal

25 To remove the EGR vacuum modulator,

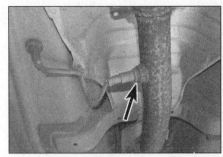

2.11e . . . and in the exhaust front downpipe/intermediate pipe (arrowed) on various engines

2.13b On later engines, the VSV (arrowed) is located on the air cleaner assembly

identify the hoses and disconnect them from the unit which is located on the top of the inlet manifold **(see illustration)**. Unscrew the mountings and remove the modulator.

26 To remove the EGR valve, identify the hoses and disconnect them from the unit which is located on the left-hand rear of the inlet manifold. Undo the two bolts and separate the EGR tube from the valve. Recover the gasket. Undo the two nuts and remove the EGR valve from the manifold. Recover the gasket.

27 The VSV is located on the engine compartment bulkhead **(see illustration)**. Identify the hoses then disconnect them from

2.25 EGR system vacuum modulator (A) and EGR valve (B) – 2.0 litre engines pre-August 2000

2.27 EGR vacuum solenoid valve location (arrowed) – 2.0 litre engines pre-August 2000

the valve. Disconnect the wiring plug, then unbolt the valve and bracket.

Refitting

28 Refitting is a reversal of removal, but make sure that the hoses are correctly refitted.

3 Catalytic converter –
general information
and precautions

The catalytic converter is a reliable and simple device which needs no maintenance in itself, but there are some facts of which an owner should be aware to ensure the converter functions properly for its full service life.

a) *DO NOT use leaded petrol (or LRP) in a vehicle with a catalytic converter – the lead will coat the precious metals, reducing their converting efficiency, and will eventually destroy the converter.*

b) *Always keep the ignition and fuel systems well-maintained in accordance with the manufacturer's schedule.*

c) *If the engine develops a misfire, do not drive the car at all (or at least as little as possible) until the fault is cured.*

d) *DO NOT push- or tow-start the car – this will soak the catalytic converter in unburned fuel, causing it to overheat when the engine does start.*

e) *DO NOT switch off the ignition at high engine speeds.*

f) *DO NOT use fuel or engine oil additives – these may contain substances harmful to the catalytic converter.*

g) *DO NOT continue to use the car if the engine burns oil to the extent of leaving a visible trail of blue smoke.*

h) *Remember that the catalytic converter operates at very high temperatures. DO NOT, therefore, park the car in dry undergrowth, over long grass, or over piles of dead leaves, after a long run.*

i) *Remember that the catalytic converter is FRAGILE – do not strike it with tools during servicing work.*

Chapter 5 Part A:
Starting and charging systems

Contents

Degrees of difficulty

Easy, suitable for novice with little experience	Fairly easy, suitable for beginner with some experience	Fairly difficult, suitable for competent DIY mechanic	Difficult, suitable for experienced DIY mechanic	Very difficult, suitable for expert DIY or professional

Specifications

General

System type	12 volt, negative earth

Battery

Type	Low-maintenance or maintenance-free
Charge condition:	
Poor	11.5 volts
Normal	12.0 volts
Good	12.5 volts

Torque wrench settings	Nm	lbf ft
Alternator mounting bolts:		
Pre-August 2000 models:		
Alternator-to-mounting bracket bolts	54	40
Alternator to adjustment link	19	14
Post-August 2000 models:		
14 mm head bolt	54	40
12 mm head bolt	25	18
Alternator pulley nut:		
Nippondenso	110	81
Bosch	65	48
Starter mounting bolts	39	29

1 General information, precautions and battery disconnection

General information

The engine electrical system consists mainly of the charging and starting systems. Because of their engine-related functions, these components are covered separately from the body electrical devices such as the lights, instruments, etc (which are covered in Chapter 12). Refer to Part B of this Chapter for information on the ignition system.

The electrical system is of 12 volt negative earth type.

The battery is of low-maintenance or maintenance-free (sealed for life) type, and is charged by the alternator, which is belt-driven from the crankshaft pulley.

The starter motor is of pre-engaged type incorporating an integral solenoid. On starting, the solenoid moves the drive pinion into engagement with the flywheel/driveplate ring gear before the starter motor is energised. Once the engine has started, a one-way clutch prevents the motor armature being driven by the engine until the pinion disengages.

Further details of the various systems are given in the relevant Sections of this Chapter. While some repair procedures are given, the usual course of action is to renew the component concerned. The owner whose interest extends beyond mere component renewal should obtain a copy of the *Automotive Electrical & Electronic Systems Manual*, available from the publishers of this manual.

Precautions

It is necessary to take extra care when working on the electrical system to avoid damage to semi-conductor devices (diodes and transistors), and to avoid the risk of personal injury. In addition to the precautions given in *Safety first!* at the beginning of this manual, observe the following when working on the system:

• Always remove rings, watches, etc, before working on the electrical system. Even with the battery disconnected, capacitive discharge could occur if a component's live terminal is earthed through a metal object. This could cause a shock or nasty burn.

• Do not reverse the battery connections. Components such as the alternator, electronic control units, or any other components having semi-conductor circuitry could be irreparably damaged.

• If the engine is being started using jump leads and a slave battery, connect the batteries positive-to-positive and negative-to-negative (see *Jump starting*). This also applies when connecting a battery charger but in this case both of the battery terminals should first be disconnected.

• Never disconnect the battery terminals, the alternator, any electrical wiring or any test instruments when the engine is running.

• Do not allow the engine to turn the alternator when the alternator is not connected.

• Never test for alternator output by flashing the output lead to earth.

• Never use an ohmmeter of the type incorporating a hand-cranked generator for circuit or continuity testing.

• Always ensure that the battery negative lead is disconnected when working on the electrical system.

• Before using electric-arc welding equipment on the car, disconnect the battery, alternator and components such as the fuel injection/ignition electronic control unit to protect them from the risk of damage.

Battery disconnection

Refer to the precautions listed in *Disconnecting the battery* in the Reference Chapter.

2 Electrical fault finding – general information

Refer to Chapter 12.

3 Battery – testing and charging

Testing

Standard and low maintenance battery

1 If the vehicle covers a small annual mileage, it is worthwhile checking the specific gravity of the electrolyte every three months to determine the state of charge of the battery. Use a hydrometer to make the check and compare the results with the following table. Note that the specific gravity readings assume an electrolyte temperature of 15ºC; for every 10ºC below 15ºC subtract 0.007. For every 10ºC above 15ºC add 0.007.

	Above 25ºC	Below 25ºC
Fully-charged	1.210 to 1.230	1.270 to 1.290
70% charged	1.170 to 1.190	1.230 to 1.250
Discharged	1.050 to 1.070	1.110 to 1.130

2 If the battery condition is suspect, first check the specific gravity of electrolyte in each cell. A variation of 0.040 or more between any cells indicates loss of electrolyte or deterioration of the internal plates.

3 If the specific gravity variation is 0.040 or more, the battery should be renewed. If the cell variation is satisfactory but the battery is discharged, it should be charged as described later in this Section.

Maintenance-free battery

4 In cases where a sealed for life maintenance-free battery is fitted, topping-up and testing of the electrolyte in each cell is not possible. The condition of the battery can therefore only be tested using a battery condition indicator or a voltmeter.

5 Some models may be fitted with a maintenance-free battery with a built-in charge condition indicator. The indicator is located in the top of the battery casing, and indicates the condition of the battery from its colour. Consult your battery supplier for specific information concerning charge condition indicator colours according to battery type.

All battery types

6 If testing the battery using a voltmeter, connect the voltmeter across the battery and compare the result with those given in the Specifications under charge condition. The test is only accurate if the battery has not been subjected to any kind of charge for the previous six hours. If this is not the case, switch on the headlights for 30 seconds, then wait four to five minutes before testing the battery after switching off the headlights. All other electrical circuits must be switched off, so check that the doors and tailgate are fully shut when making the test.

7 If the voltage reading is less than 12.0 volts, then the battery is discharged.

8 If the battery is to be charged, remove it from the vehicle (Section 4) and charge it as described later in this Section.

Charging

Note: *The following is intended as a guide only. Always refer to the manufacturer's recommendations (often printed on a label attached to the battery), and always disconnect both terminal leads before charging a battery.*

Standard and low maintenance battery

9 Charge the battery at a rate of 3.5 to 4 amps and continue to charge the battery at this rate until no further rise in specific gravity is noted over a four hour period.

10 Alternatively, a trickle charger charging at the rate of 1.5 amps can safely be used overnight.

11 Specially rapid boost charges which are claimed to restore the power of the battery in 1 to 2 hours are not recommended, as they can cause serious damage to the battery plates through overheating.

12 While charging the battery, note that the temperature of the electrolyte should never exceed 38ºC.

Maintenance-free battery

13 This battery type takes considerably longer to fully recharge than the standard type, the time taken being dependent on the extent of discharge, but it can take anything up to three days.

14 A constant voltage type charger is required, to be set, when connected, to 13.9 to 14.9 volts with a charger current below 25 amps. Using this method, the battery should be usable within three hours, giving a voltage reading of 12.5 volts, but this is for a partially discharged battery and, as mentioned, full charging can take considerably longer.

15 If the battery is to be charged from a fully discharged state (condition reading less than 12.2 volts), have it recharged by your local automotive electrician, as the charge rate is higher and constant supervision during charging is necessary.

4 Battery – removal and refitting

Note: *Refer to the warnings and precautions given in 'Safety first!' and in Section 1 of this Chapter before proceeding.*

Removal

1 The battery is located in the left-hand front corner of the engine compartment.

2 Loosen the clamp bolt, and disconnect the earth lead from the battery negative terminal **(see illustration)**.

3 Lift the insulation cover and disconnect the lead from positive terminal in the same way **(see illustration)**.

4.2 Loosen the clamp bolt, and disconnect the earth lead from the battery negative terminal

4.3 Lift the insulation cover and disconnect the lead from positive terminal in the same way

4 Unscrew the bolt, and remove the retaining clamp securing the battery to the battery platform **(see illustration)**.
5 Lift the battery out of the engine compartment, and if necessary remove the plastic tray from the battery platform **(see illustration)**.

Refitting

6 Refitting is a reversal of removal; always reconnect the positive lead first followed by the negative lead.
7 Smear petroleum jelly on the terminals after reconnecting the leads to prevent corrosion – corroded connections are amongst the most frequent causes of electrical system faults.

5 Charging system – testing

Note: *Refer to the warnings and precautions given in 'Safety first!' and in Section 1 of this Chapter before proceeding.*
1 If the ignition warning light fails to illuminate when the ignition is switched on, first check the alternator wiring connections for security. If satisfactory, check that the warning light bulb has not blown, and that the bulbholder is secure in its location in the instrument panel. If the light still fails to illuminate, check the continuity of the warning light feed wire from the alternator to the bulbholder. If all is satisfactory, the alternator is at fault and should be renewed or taken to an auto-electrician for testing and repair.
2 If the ignition warning light illuminates when the engine is running, stop the engine and check that the drivebelt is intact and correctly tensioned (see Chapter 1) and that the alternator connections are secure. If all is so far satisfactory, have the alternator checked by an auto-electrician.
3 If the alternator output is suspect even though the warning light functions correctly, the regulated voltage may be checked as follows.
4 Connect a voltmeter across the battery terminals and start the engine.
5 Increase the engine speed until the voltmeter reading remains steady; the reading should be approximately 12 to 13 volts, and no more than 14.2 volts.
6 Switch on as many electrical accessories (eg, the headlights, heated rear window and heater blower) as possible, and check that the alternator maintains the regulated voltage at around 13 to 14 volts.
7 If the regulated voltage is not as stated, the fault may be due to worn brushes, weak brush springs, a faulty voltage regulator, a faulty diode, a severed phase winding or worn or damaged slip-rings. The alternator should be renewed or taken to an auto-electrician for testing and repair.

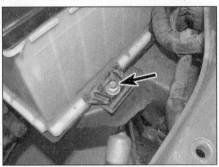

4.4 Unscrew the bolt (arrowed), and remove the battery retaining clamp

6 Alternator – removal and refitting

Note: *Refer to the warnings and precautions given in 'Safety first!' and in Section 1 of this Chapter before proceeding.*

Removal

Pre-August 2000 models

1 Disconnect the battery negative terminal (refer to *Disconnecting the battery* in the Reference Chapter).
2 Loosen the auxiliary drivebelt tension with reference to Chapter 1, and disengage it from the alternator pulley **(see illustration)**.
3 Note the location of the wiring on the rear of the alternator, then disconnect it.
4 Unscrew and remove the alternator lower

6.2 Disconnecting the auxiliary drivebelt from the alternator – pre-August 2000 models

6.5a . . . upper mounting bolt . . .

4.5 Lift the battery out, and if necessary remove the plastic tray

mounting bolt from the adjustment link bracket **(see illustration)**.
5 Unscrew and remove the upper mounting bolt, then withdraw the alternator from the engine compartment **(see illustrations)**.

Post-August 2000 models

6 Disconnect the battery negative terminal (refer to *Disconnecting the battery* in the Reference Chapter).
7 Remove the auxiliary drivebelt as described in Chapter 1.
8 Note the location of the wiring on the rear of the alternator, then disconnect it **(see illustration)**.
9 On models fitted with air conditioning, disconnect the wiring connector on the air conditioning compressor **(see illustration)**.
10 Undo the bolt and detach the wiring harness support bracket from the alternator **(see illustration)**.

6.4 Remove the lower mounting bolt . . .

6.5b . . . and withdraw the alternator – pre-August 2000 models

11 Unscrew and remove the upper and lower mounting bolts, then withdraw the alternator from the engine **(see illustration)**.

Refitting

12 Refitting is a reversal of removal ensuring all mounting bolts are tightened to the specified torque. Refit and, where applicable, tension the auxiliary drivebelt as described in Chapter 1.

7 Alternator – testing and overhaul

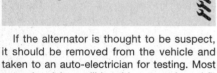

If the alternator is thought to be suspect, it should be removed from the vehicle and taken to an auto-electrician for testing. Most auto-electricians will be able to supply and fit brushes at a reasonable cost. However, check on the cost of repairs before proceeding as it may prove more economical to obtain a new or exchange alternator.

8 Starting system – testing

Note: *Refer to the warnings and precautions given in 'Safety first!' and in Section 1 of this Chapter before proceeding.*

1 If the starter motor fails to operate when the ignition key is turned to the appropriate position, the following possible causes may be to blame.

  a) *The battery is faulty.*
  b) *The electrical connections between the switch, solenoid, battery and starter motor are somewhere failing to pass the necessary current from the battery through the starter to earth.*
  c) *The solenoid is faulty.*
  d) *The starter motor is mechanically or electrically defective.*

6.8 Disconnect the wiring at the rear of the alternator – post-August 2000 models

6.9 Disconnect the wiring connector on the air conditioning compressor – post-August 2000 models

2 To check the battery, switch on the headlights. If they dim after a few seconds, this indicates that the battery is discharged – recharge (see Section 2) or renew the battery. If the headlights glow brightly, operate the starter motor on the ignition switch and observe the lights. If they dim, then this indicates that current is reaching the starter motor, therefore the fault must lie in the starter motor. If the lights continue to glow brightly (and no clicking sound can be heard from the starter motor solenoid), this indicates that there is a fault in the circuit or solenoid – see following paragraphs. If the starter motor turns slowly when operated, but the battery is in good condition, then this indicates that either the starter motor is faulty, or there is considerable resistance somewhere in the circuit.

3 If a fault in the circuit is suspected, disconnect the battery leads (including the earth connection to the body), the starter/solenoid wiring and the engine/transmission earth strap. Thoroughly clean the connections, and reconnect the leads and wiring, then use a voltmeter or test lamp to check that full battery voltage is available at the battery positive lead connection to the solenoid, and that the earth is sound. Smear

petroleum jelly around the battery terminals to prevent corrosion – corroded connections are amongst the most frequent causes of electrical system faults.

4 If the battery and all connections are in good condition, check the circuit by disconnecting the trigger wire from the starter solenoid blade terminal. Connect a voltmeter or test lamp between the wire end and a good earth (such as the battery negative terminal), and check that the wire is live when the ignition switch is turned to the start position. If it is, then the circuit is sound – if not, the circuit wiring can be checked as described in Chapter 12.

5 The solenoid contacts can be checked by connecting a voltmeter or test lamp across the solenoid. When the ignition switch is turned to the start position, there should be a reading or lighted bulb, as applicable. If there is no reading or lighted bulb, the solenoid is faulty and should be renewed.

6 If the circuit and solenoid are proved sound, the fault must lie in the starter motor. In this event, it may be possible to have the starter motor overhauled by a specialist, but check on the cost of spares before proceeding, as it may prove more economical to obtain a new or exchange motor.

6.10 Undo the bolt and detach the wiring harness support bracket from the alternator – post-August 2000 models

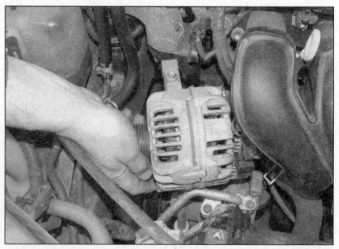

6.11 Unscrew the upper and lower mounting bolts, then withdraw the alternator from the engine – post-August 2000 models

9.6 Disconnect the battery lead and the trigger wire from the starter solenoid terminals

9.8 Starter motor mounting bolts (arrowed) – 1.6 and 1.8 litre post-August 2000 models

9 Starter motor – removal and refitting

Note: *Refer to the warnings and precautions given in 'Safety first!' and in Section 1 of this Chapter before proceeding.*

Removal

1 The starter motor is located at the rear of the engine on 1.6 and 1.8 litre models pre-August 2000, and at the front of the engine on all other models.

2 Disconnect the battery negative terminal (refer to *Disconnecting the battery* in the Reference Chapter).

3 Remove the air cleaner assembly and inlet air duct as described in Chapter 4A.

4 Firmly apply the handbrake, then jack up the front of the car and support it securely on axle stands (see *Jacking and vehicle support*).

5 Where necessary, remove the engine compartment undershield on the left-hand side, with reference to Chapter 11.

6 Disconnect the battery lead and the trigger wire from the starter solenoid terminals **(see illustration)**.

7 On 1.6 and 1.8 litre engines post-August 2000, undo the bolts and remove the throttle housing support bracket.

8 Unscrew the mounting bolts and manoeuvre the starter motor from the engine compartment **(see illustration)**.

Refitting

9 Refitting is a reversal of removal but tighten the mounting bolts to the specified torque.

10 Starter motor – testing and overhaul

If the starter motor is thought to be suspect, it should be removed from the vehicle and taken to an auto-electrician for testing. Most auto-electricians will be able to supply and fit brushes at a reasonable cost. However, check on the cost of repairs before proceeding as it may prove more economical to obtain a new or exchange motor.

Chapter 5 Part B:
Ignition system

Contents

Degrees of difficulty

Easy, suitable for novice with little experience	**Fairly easy,** suitable for beginner with some experience	**Fairly difficult,** suitable for competent DIY mechanic	**Difficult,** suitable for experienced DIY mechanic	**Very difficult,** suitable for expert DIY or professional

Specifications

General

Ignition system type:

Pre-August 2000 models . . . . Static (distributorless) ignition system controlled by engine management ECU

Post-August 2000 models . . . . Direct ignition system (DIS) with one ignition coil per cylinder, controlled by engine management ECU

Firing order. . . . . 1–3–4–2 (No 1 cylinder at timing belt/chain end)

Ignition coil resistance (pre-August 2000 models):

Primary resistance . . . . Not available

Secondary resistance:

Cold (below 50°C). . . . . 9.7 to 16.7 k ohms

Hot (above 50°C) . . . . 12.4 to 19.6 k ohms

HT lead resistance . . . . 25 k ohms (maximum)

Torque wrench settings

	Nm	lbf ft
Pre-August 2000 models		
Ignition coil mounting bracket to cylinder head:		
1.6 and 1.8 litre engines.	18	13
2.0 litre engines:		
14 mm head bolt.	42	31
12 mm head bolt/nut	21	15
Ignition coil to mounting bracket	10	7
Knock sensor	44	32
Post-August 2000 models		
Ignition coil mounting bolts	10	7
Knock sensor:		
1.6 and 1.8 litre engines.	39	29
2.0 litre engines.	44	32

2.2 Diagnostic socket location (arrowed) on the passenger's compartment fusebox

1 General information and precautions

General information

The ignition system is integrated with the fuel system, to form a combined engine management system which is controlled by the engine electronic control unit (ECU).

Two types of ignition systems are fitted to models covered by this manual.

The first type, fitted to pre-August 2000 engines, is a static, distributorless ignition system. Here the crankshaft speed and position is monitored by a sensor fitted adjacent to the crankshaft pulley at the right-hand end of the engine. Camshaft position is monitored by a sensor fitted to the left-hand end of the cylinder head adjacent to the exhaust camshaft (1.6 and 1.8 litre engines) or at the right-hand end of the cylinder head adjacent to the inlet camshaft (2.0 litre engines). The engine management ECU calculates the optimum moment to trigger the spark, then interrupts the primary signal to one of the two ignition coils bolted to the left-hand end of the cylinder head. The positive and negative ends of secondary coils are connected to the spark plugs on cylinders 1 and 4, and 2 and 3. When the primary current is interrupted, the secondary coil generates a spark at the two cylinders it's connected to. However, only one of these sparks occurs at the correct combustion phase and causes ignition, the other spark occurs harmlessly

during the exhaust stroke, and is known as a 'wasted' spark. A knock sensor is also fitted, to monitor for any signs of pre-ignition. Should any be detected, the ECU will gradually retard the ignition timing until the symptoms disappear.

The second type, fitted to post-August 2000 engines, is a direct ignition system and has one ignition coil per cylinder, fitted directly above each spark plug. The engine management ECU uses information from the crankshaft and camshaft position sensors to calculate the optimum time to generate a spark at each cylinder sequentially. A knock sensor is also fitted, to monitor for any signs of pre-ignition. Should any be detected, the ECU will gradually retard the ignition timing until the symptoms disappear.

Precautions

Refer to the precautions given in Chapter 5A, Section 1, and the following:

a) *Do not keep the ignition switch on for more than 10 minutes with the engine stopped.*
b) *Never connect the ignition coil terminals to earth. This could result in damage to the coil and/or the ECU.*
c) *Do not disconnect the battery when the engine is running.*
d) *Refer to the warning at the beginning of the next Section concerning HT voltage.*

2 Ignition system – testing

⚠️ *Warning: Due to the high voltages produced by the electronic ignition system, extreme care must be taken when working on the system with the ignition switched on. Persons with surgically-implanted cardiac pacemaker devices should keep well clear of the ignition circuits, components and test equipment.*

1 If a fault appears in the engine management system, first ensure that all the system wiring connectors are securely connected and free of corrosion. Ensure that the fault is not due to poor maintenance; ie, check that the air cleaner filter element is clean, the spark plugs

are in good condition and correctly gapped, the cylinder compression pressures are correct and that the engine breather hoses are clear and undamaged, referring to Chapters 1, 2A and 2B for further information.

2 If these checks fail to reveal the cause of the problem, the vehicle should be taken to a suitably-equipped Toyota dealer or engine management diagnostic specialist for testing. A diagnostic socket is located on the passenger's compartment fusebox, to which a fault code reader or other suitable test equipment can be connected **(see illustration)**. By using the code reader or test equipment, the engine management ECU can be interrogated, and any stored fault codes can be retrieved. This will allow the fault to be quickly and simply traced, alleviating the need to test all the system components individually, which is a time-consuming operation that carries a risk of damaging the ECU.

3 The only ignition system checks which can be carried out by the home mechanic are those described in Chapter 1 relating to the spark plugs and, on pre-August 2000 models, the ignition coil secondary resistances as described in Section 3.

3 Ignition coils – testing and renewal

Testing

Pre-August 2000 models

1 Ensure the ignition is switched off, then note their fitted positions, and disconnect the HT leads from the ignition coils.

2 Using an ohmmeter, measure the secondary resistance between the positive and negative HT terminals of each coil **(see illustration)**.

3 If the resistances measured for either coil is outside those given in the Specifications, the coil(s) may be defective.

Post-August 2000 models

4 At the time of writing, no testing specifications were available for these engines.

Renewal

1.6 and 1.8 litre engines pre-August 2000

5 Ensure the ignition is switched off, then disconnect the wiring connector from the relevant coil **(see illustration)**.

6 Make a note of the correct fitted positions of the HT leads then disconnect them from the coil terminals **(see illustration)**.

7 Undo the two retaining bolts securing the relevant coil to its mounting bracket and remove it from the engine compartment **(see illustration)**.

8 If required, undo the bolt securing the coil mounting bracket(s) to the cylinder head and remove the relevant bracket.

9 Refitting is a reversal of removal.

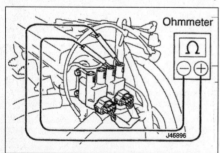

3.2 Measure the secondary resistance between the positive and negative HT terminals of each coil

3.5 Disconnect the ignition coil wiring connector . . .

3.6 . . . and the HT leads . . .

3.7 . . . then undo the bolts (arrowed) and remove the coil from the mounting bracket – 1.6 and 1.8 litre engines pre-August 2000

3.20 disconnect the wiring connectors from the ignition coils . . .

3.21 . . . undo the two bolts and move the plastic wiring harness protector to one side . . .

3.22 . . . then undo the bolts and pull the ignition coils off the spark plugs – 1.6 and 1.8 litre engines post-August 2000

2.0 litre engines pre-August 2000

10 Disconnect the battery negative terminal (refer to *Disconnecting the battery* in the Reference Chapter).
11 Remove the throttle housing as described in Chapter 4A.
12 Disconnect the wiring connector from each ignition coil.
13 Make a note of the correct fitted positions of the HT leads then disconnect them from the coil terminals.
14 Release the retaining clip and free the wiring harness from the ignition coil mounting bracket.
15 Undo the two nuts and two bolts securing the coil mounting bracket to the cylinder head and inlet manifold. Note the location of the earth lead on the upper mounting stud.
16 Withdraw the mounting bracket complete with the two ignition coils from the engine.
17 Undo the two bolts and remove the relevant coil from the mounting bracket. If both coils are to be removed, suitably identify them so they can be refitted in their original positions (left or right).
18 Refitting is a reversal of removal.

1.6 and 1.8 litre engines post-August 2000

19 Undo the two nuts, prise out the two plastic fasteners at the rear, and remove the plastic cover from the top of the engine.
20 Ensure the ignition is switched off, then disconnect the wiring connectors from the ignition coils **(see illustration)**.
21 Undo the two bolts securing the plastic wiring harness protector to the camshaft cover and move the harness to one side **(see illustration)**.
22 Undo the bolts and pull the ignition coils from the top of the spark plugs **(see illustration)**. Recover the dust seal from the ignition coil body.
23 Refitting is a reversal of removal.

2.0 litre engines post-August 2000

24 Undo the four nuts and remove the plastic cover from the top of the engine.
25 Ensure the ignition is switched off, then disconnect the wiring connectors from the ignition coils.
26 Undo the bolts and pull the ignition coils from the top of the spark plugs. Recover the dust seal from the ignition coil body.
27 Refitting is a reversal of removal.

4 Ignition system sensors – removal and refitting

Crankshaft position sensor
1 Refer to Chapter 4A.

Camshaft position sensor
2 Refer to Chapter 4A.

Knock sensor
3 On post-August 2000 engines, the knock sensor is located on the front face of the cylinder block (1.6 and 1.8 litre engines) or rear face of the cylinder block (2.0 litre engines). To gain access it will be necessary to remove the

inlet manifold as described in Chapter 4A. On all other engines, the sensor is located on the rear face of the cylinder block and access is possible with the inlet manifold still in place.
4 Disconnect the knock sensor wiring connector, then unscrew the sensor from the engine.
5 Refitting is a reversal of removal, but ensure that the sensor is tightened to the specified torque. Where applicable, refit the inlet manifold as described in Chapter 4A.

5 Ignition timing – checking and adjustment

Due to the nature of the ignition system, the ignition timing is constantly being monitored and adjusted by the engine management ECU.
The only way in which the ignition timing can be checked is by using specialist diagnostic test equipment, connected to the engine management system diagnostic socket (located adjacent to the passenger's compartment fusebox). No adjustment of the ignition timing is possible. Should the ignition timing be incorrect, then a fault is likely to be present in the engine management system.

Chapter 6
Clutch

Contents

Degrees of difficulty

Easy, suitable for novice with little experience	Fairly easy, suitable for beginner with some experience	Fairly difficult, suitable for competent DIY mechanic	Difficult, suitable for experienced DIY mechanic	Very difficult, suitable for expert DIY or professional

Specifications

General

Type	Diaphragm spring, single dry plate, hydraulic operation
Minimum clutch disc rivet head depth	0.3 mm

Clutch pedal height (from pedal pad to asphalt sheet):

Pre-August 2000 right-hand drive models:
1.6 and 1.8 litre engines	148.7 to 158.7 mm
2.0 litre engines	157.4 to 167.4 mm

Pre-August 2000 left-hand drive models:
1.6 and 1.8 litre engines	139.7 to 149.7 mm
2.0 litre engines	148.3 to 158.3 mm

Post-August 2000 right-hand drive models:
1.6 and 1.8 litre engines	144.3 to 154.3 mm
2.0 litre engines	152.9 to 162.9 mm

Post-August 2000 left-hand drive models:
1.6 and 1.8 litre engines	139.7 to 149.7 mm
2.0 litre engines	148.3 to 158.3 mm

Clutch pedal free play	1.0 to 5.0 mm
Master cylinder pushrod play	5.0 to 15.0 mm

Torque wrench settings

	Nm	lbf ft
Clutch cover-to-flywheel bolts	19	14
Hydraulic pipe union nuts	15	11
Master cylinder to bulkhead	12	9
Release lever pivot stud:		
1.6 and 1.8 litre engines	37	27
2.0 litre engines	39	29
Slave cylinder bleed screw	8	6
Slave cylinder to transmission	12	9

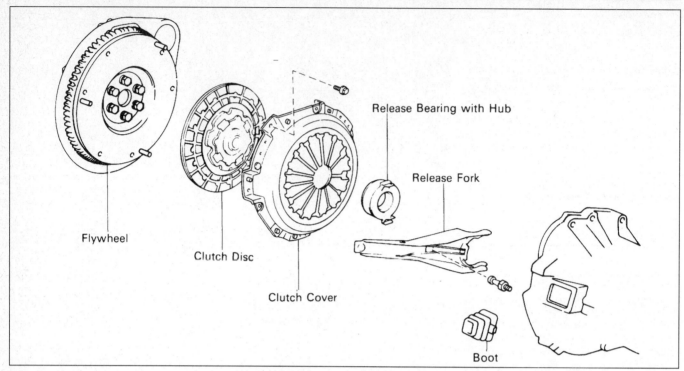

1.1 Typical clutch assembly details

Flywheel

Clutch Disc

Clutch Cover

Release Bearing with Hub

Release Fork

Boot

1 General information

All manual transmission models are equipped with an hydraulically-operated single dry plate diaphragm spring clutch assembly. The unit consists of a clutch disc (or driven plate), a steel cover (doweled and bolted to the rear face of the flywheel, it contains the pressure plate and diaphragm spring) and a release mechanism **(see illustration)**.

The clutch disc is free to slide along the splines of the transmission input shaft, and is held in position, between the flywheel and the pressure plate, by the pressure exerted on the pressure plate by the diaphragm spring. Friction lining material is riveted to the clutch disc, which has a spring-cushioned hub to absorb transmission shocks and help ensure a smooth take-up of the drive.

2.2 If the original clutch is to be refitted, mark the relationship of the clutch cover to the flywheel

The diaphragm spring is mounted on pins, and is held in place in the cover by annular fulcrum rings.

The release bearing is located on a guide sleeve at the front of the transmission, and the bearing is free to slide on the sleeve, under the action of the release lever which pivots inside the clutch bellhousing.

The release mechanism is operated by the clutch pedal, using hydraulic pressure. The pedal acts on the hydraulic master cylinder pushrod, and a slave cylinder, mounted on the transmission bellhousing, operates the clutch release lever via a pushrod.

When the clutch pedal is depressed, the release lever pushes the release bearing forwards, to bear against the centre of the diaphragm spring, thus pushing the centre of the diaphragm spring inwards. The diaphragm spring acts against the fulcrum rings in the cover, and so, as the centre of the spring is pushed in, the outside of the spring is pushed out, allowing the pressure plate to move backwards away from the clutch disc.

When the clutch pedal is released, the diaphragm spring forces the pressure plate into contact with the friction linings on the clutch disc, and simultaneously pushes the disc forwards on its splines, forcing it against the flywheel. The clutch disc is now firmly sandwiched between the pressure plate and the flywheel, and drive is taken up.

The clutch is self-adjusting. As wear takes place on the clutch disc friction linings over a period of time, the pressure plate automatically moves closer to the clutch disc to compensate.

2 Clutch assembly – removal, inspection and refitting

⚠ *Warning: Dust created by clutch wear and deposited on the clutch components may contain asbestos, which is a health hazard. DO NOT blow it out with compressed air, or inhale any of it. DO NOT use petrol (or petroleum-based solvents) to clean off the dust. Brake system cleaner or methylated spirit should be used to flush the dust into a suitable receptacle. After the clutch components are wiped clean with rags, dispose of the contaminated rags and cleaner in a sealed, marked container.*

Removal

1 Remove the transmission, as described in Chapter 7A.

2 If the original clutch is to be refitted, make alignment marks between the clutch cover and the flywheel, so that the clutch can be refitted in its original position **(see illustration)**.

3 Unscrew and remove the clutch cover retaining bolts, working in a diagonal sequence and slackening the bolts only a few turns at a time. If necessary, the flywheel may be held stationary using a wide-bladed screwdriver, inserted in the teeth of the starter ring gear and resting against a suitable bolt or part of the cylinder block.

4 Ease the clutch cover off its locating dowels. Be prepared to catch the clutch disc, which will drop out as the cover is removed. Note which way round the disc is fitted.

Inspection

5 With the clutch assembly removed, clean off all traces of dust using a dry cloth. Although most clutch discs now have asbestos-free linings, some do not, and it is wise to take suitable precautions; *asbestos dust is harmful, and must not be inhaled.*

6 Examine the friction linings of the clutch disc for wear and loose rivets, and the disc for distortion, cracks, broken or weak cushioning springs and worn splines. The surface of the friction linings may be highly glazed, but, as long as the friction material pattern can be clearly seen, this is satisfactory. If there is any sign of oil contamination, indicated by a continuous, or patchy, shiny black discolouration, the disc must be renewed. The source of the contamination must be traced and rectified before fitting new clutch components; typically, a leaking crankshaft oil seal or transmission input shaft oil seal – or both – will be to blame (renewal procedures are given Chapter 2A, 2B and Chapter 7A respectively). The disc must also be renewed if the lining thickness has worn down to, or just above, the level of the rivet heads. Check that the rivet head depth is greater than the minimum figure given in the Specifications.

7 Check the machined faces of the flywheel and pressure plate. If either is grooved, or heavily scored, renewal is necessary. The pressure plate must also be renewed if any cracks are apparent, or if the diaphragm spring is damaged or its pressure suspect.

8 With the clutch removed, it is advisable to check the condition of the release bearing, as described in Section 3.

Refitting

9 If new clutch components are to be fitted, where applicable, ensure that all anti-corrosion preservative is cleaned from the contact surfaces of the pressure plate.

10 It is important to ensure that no oil or grease gets onto the clutch disc linings, or the pressure plate and flywheel faces. It is advisable to refit the clutch assembly with clean hands, and to wipe down the pressure plate and flywheel faces with a clean, dry rag before assembly begins.

11 Begin reassembly by placing the clutch disc against the flywheel, the two sides of the disc may be marked *Engine side* and/or *Transmission side*. If no identification markings are visible, the greater projecting side of the cushioning springs (not the splined hub) on the clutch disc must face away from the flywheel **(see illustration)**.

12 Hold the clutch disc against the flywheel and fit the clutch cover assembly, where applicable aligning the marks on the flywheel and cover **(see illustration)**. Ensure that the clutch cover locates over the dowels on the flywheel. Insert the securing bolts and tighten them finger-tight, so that the clutch disc is gripped, but can still be moved.

13 The clutch disc must now be centralised, so that, when the engine and transmission are

2.11 Position the clutch disc with the greater projecting side of the cushioning springs facing away from the flywheel

mated, the transmission input shaft splines will pass through the splines in the clutch disc hub.

14 Centralisation can be carried out by inserting a round bar or a long screwdriver through the hole in the centre of the clutch disc, so that the end of the bar rests in the hole in the end of the crankshaft. Moving the bar sideways or up and down, as necessary, move the clutch disc in whichever direction is necessary to achieve centralisation. With the bar removed, view the clutch disc hub in relation to the hole in the centre of the crankshaft and the circle created by the ends of the diaphragm spring fingers. When the hub appears exactly in the centre, all is correct.

15 An alternative and more accurate method of centralisation is to use a commercially-available clutch-aligning tool, obtainable from most accessory shops. The tool must be of the type that locates on the ends of the diaphragm spring fingers.

16 Once the clutch is centralised, progressively tighten the cover bolts in a diagonal sequence to the torque setting given in the Specifications. Remove the alignment tool, if used.

17 Ensure that the input shaft splines, clutch disc splines and release bearing guide sleeve are clean. Apply a thin smear of molybdenum disulphide grease to the input shaft splines and the release bearing guide sleeve. Only use a very small amount of grease, otherwise the excess will inevitably find its way onto the friction linings when the vehicle is in use.

18 Refit the transmission (see Chapter 7A).

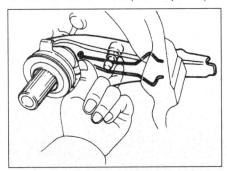

3.2 Disengage the release lever from the ball-stud by pulling on the retention spring, then remove the lever and bearing

2.12 Hold the clutch disc against the flywheel and fit the clutch cover assembly, where applicable aligning the marks on the flywheel and cover

3 Clutch release bearing and lever – removal, inspection and refitting

Note: *Refer to the warning at the beginning of Section 2 before proceeding.*

Removal

1 Remove the transmission, as described in Chapter 7A.

2 Release the spring clip securing the release lever to the pivot stud, then withdraw the release lever, complete with the bearing, from the guide sleeve in the transmission bellhousing **(see illustration)**. Recover the rubber dust cover if it is loose.

3 Slide the release bearing from the lever and the retaining spring clips **(see illustration)**.

4 If desired, the release lever pivot stud can be unscrewed from the bellhousing.

Inspection

5 Spin the release bearing, and check it for excessive roughness. Hold the outer race, and attempt to move it laterally against the inner race. If any excessive movement or roughness is evident, renew the bearing.

 HAYNES HiNT *If a new clutch has been fitted, it is wise to renew the release bearing as a matter of course.*

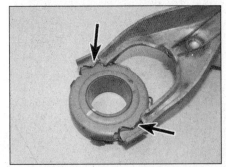

3.3 Slide the release bearing from the lever and the retaining spring clips (arrowed)

3.9 Push the clutch release lever onto the ball-stud until it's firmly seated

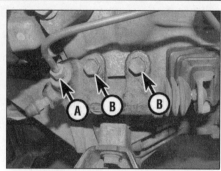

4.4 Clutch slave cylinder fluid pipe union (A) and mounting bolts (B)

Refitting

6 Where applicable, screw the pivot stud into position in the bellhousing and tighten to the specified torque.

7 Lightly lubricate the release bearing and slave cylinder pushrod contact surfaces on the release lever, the release bearing guide sleeve, the transmission input shaft splines, and the release lever pivot stud with molybdenum disulphide grease.

8 Locate the release bearing into position in the lever, ensuring that the forked ends of the lever engage under the spring clips on the bearing.

9 Slide the release bearing onto the transmission guide sleeve while passing the end of the release lever through the opening in the bellhousing. Push the clutch release lever onto the ball-stud until it's firmly seated **(see illustration)**.

10 Refit the transmission as described in Chapter 7A.

4 Clutch slave cylinder – removal, overhaul and refitting

⚠️ *Warning: Hydraulic fluid is poisonous; wash off immediately and thoroughly in the case of skin contact, and seek immediate medical advice if any fluid is swallowed or gets into the eyes. Certain types of hydraulic fluid are inflammable, and may ignite when allowed into contact with hot components; when servicing any hydraulic system, it is safest to assume that the fluid is inflammable, and to take precautions against the risk of fire as though it is petrol that is being handled. Hydraulic fluid is also an effective paint stripper, and will attack plastics; if any is spilt, it should be washed off immediately, using copious quantities of fresh water. Finally, it is hygroscopic (it absorbs moisture from the air) – old fluid may be contaminated and unfit for further use. When topping-up or renewing the fluid, always use the recommended type, and ensure that it comes from a freshly-opened sealed container.*

Removal

1 The slave cylinder is located on the transmission bellhousing at the front.

2 Where applicable, unscrew the bolt(s) securing the hydraulic fluid pipe support bracket to the cylinder or transmission.

3 Place a suitable container beneath the slave cylinder to catch escaping hydraulic fluid.

4 Unscrew the fluid pipe union, and disconnect the fluid pipe from the slave cylinder **(see illustration)**. Once the fluid had drained, plug the open ends of the pipe and slave cylinder to prevent dirt ingress.

5 Unscrew the two bolts securing the slave cylinder to the transmission bellhousing, then withdraw the cylinder, complete with the pushrod, and the pipe bracket, where applicable.

Overhaul

Note: *Before attempting to overhaul the assembly, check on the price and availability of spare parts, and the price of a new unit, as overhaul may not be viable on economic grounds alone.*

6 Remove the pushrod and rubber boot, then unscrew the bleed screw from the cylinder body **(see illustration)**.

7 Apply compressed air (from a foot pump or bicycle tyre pump) to the bleed screw hole, to force the piston from the cylinder. The piston will be ejected with the spring.

8 Wash all the parts in clean hydraulic fluid, then lay them out for inspection.

9 Examine the cylinder bore and piston carefully for signs of scoring or wear ridges. If these are apparent, renew the complete slave cylinder. If the condition of the components appears satisfactory, a repair kit containing

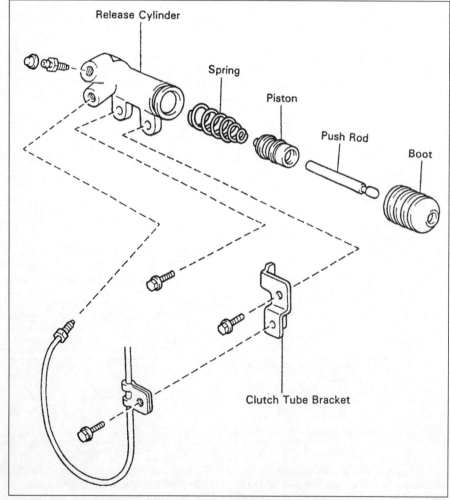

4.6 Typical clutch slave (release) cylinder components

Release Cylinder, Spring, Piston, Push Rod, Boot, Clutch Tube Bracket new rubber seals should be obtained. Never re-use the old seals. Depending on manufacturer, the repair kit may be supplied as a new piston with seals already fitted.

10 Where applicable, remove the old seals from the piston, noting the orientation of the seal lips to aid fitting of the new seals.

11 Fit new seals to the piston, using the fingers only. To ease fitting of the seals, lubricate them with clean hydraulic fluid of the specified type (see *Lubricants and fluids*). Ensure that the sealing lip edge of the main seal is towards the spring end of the piston.

12 Lubricate the cylinder bore with clean hydraulic fluid and insert the spring, with the larger coils towards fluid union end of the cylinder.

13 Carefully insert the piston, engaging the locating lug into the centre of the spring.

14 If necessary, fit a new rubber boot to the pushrod, then insert the pushrod assembly into the cylinder. The notched end of the pushrod should face away from the piston. Ensure that the rubber boot locates in the groove in the end of the cylinder.

15 Refit the bleed screw to the cylinder body.

Refitting

16 Offer the slave cylinder into position on the transmission bellhousing, and engage the pushrod with the recess in the clutch release lever. Refit and tighten the cylinder securing bolts.

17 Reconnect the fluid pipe to the cylinder and tighten the union.

18 Where applicable, refit and tighten the bolt(s) securing the hydraulic fluid pipe bracket to the cylinder or transmission.

19 Bleed the clutch hydraulic system as described in Section 6.

5 Clutch master cylinder – removal, overhaul and refitting

Note: *Refer to the warning at the beginning of Section 4 before proceeding.*

Removal

1 The clutch master cylinder is located on the engine compartment bulkhead, next to the brake servo/master cylinder assembly.

2 To reduce fluid loss, draw off as much fluid as possible from the clutch hydraulic fluid reservoir.

 HAYNES HiNT *An ideal way to remove fluid from the master cylinder reservoir is to use a clean syringe or an old poultry baster.*

3 On left-hand-drive models, disconnect the fluid reservoir hose connecting the reservoir to the master cylinder **(see illustration)**. If necessary, unclip the reservoir from its bracket to improve access.

4 Place a suitable container beneath the master cylinder fluid pipe union to catch escaping fluid, then unscrew the union and disconnect the fluid pipe from the cylinder.

5 Remove the lower facia panel on the driver's side as described in Chapter 11.

6 Working in the driver's footwell, reach up behind the pedals and pull the securing clip from the clutch pedal-to-master cylinder pushrod clevis pin. Slide out the clevis pin.

7 Again working in the footwell, unscrew the two nuts securing the master cylinder to the bulkhead.

8 Withdraw the master cylinder from the engine compartment.

Overhaul

Note: *Before attempting to overhaul the assembly, check on the price and availability of spare parts, and the price of a new unit, as overhaul may not be viable on economic grounds alone. New seals will be required on reassembly. On right-hand-drive models, a new fluid reservoir seal and reservoir securing roll-pin will also be required on reassembly.*

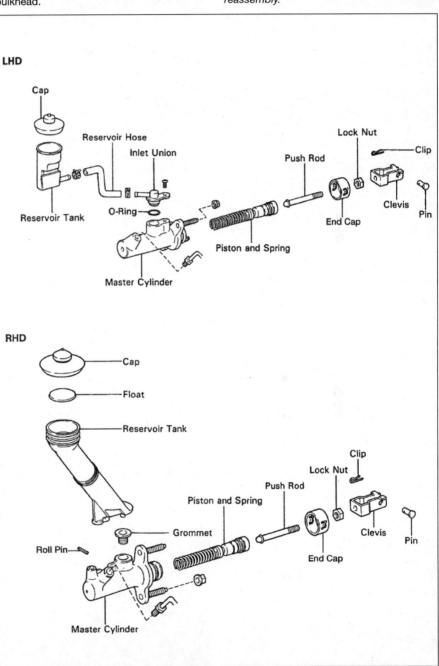

5.3 Exploded view of the clutch master cylinder (early type shown)

Upper assembly – Left-hand-drive models   *Lower assembly – Right-hand-drive models*

9 With the master cylinder removed, proceed as follows.

10 On right-hand-drive models, remove the fluid reservoir from the top of the master cylinder as follows.

a) *Using a pin-punch and hammer, drive out the roll-pin.*

b) *Slide the reservoir from the master cylinder, and recover the rubber seal. Discard the seal, a new one must be used on refitting.*

11 On left-hand-drive models, proceed as follows.

a) *Disconnect the fluid reservoir connecting hose from the master cylinder, if not already done.*

b) *Remove the securing screw, and withdraw the fluid inlet union from the master cylinder. Recover the O-ring seal.*

12 On early models, prise up the locking tabs, using a small screwdriver, and pull the end cap from the pushrod end of the master cylinder. Note that a new end cap should be used on refitting. Where applicable, recover the spacer ring.

13 On later models, pull back the rubber boot from the pushrod end of the master cylinder. Using circlip pliers, extract the circlip, then remove the pushrod and washer.

14 Withdraw the piston and spring assembly from the master cylinder bore. Wash all components in clean hydraulic fluid, then lay them out for inspection.

15 Examine the cylinder bore and piston carefully for signs of scoring or wear ridges. If these are apparent, renew the complete master cylinder. If the condition of the components appears satisfactory, a repair kit containing new rubber seals and a new end cap or rubber boot should be obtained. Never re-use the old seals. Depending on manufacturer, the repair kit may be supplied as a new piston with seals already fitted.

16 Where applicable, remove the old seals from the piston, noting the orientation of the seal lips to aid fitting of the new seals.

17 Fit new seals to the piston, using the fingers only. To ease fitting of the seals, lubricate them with clean hydraulic fluid of the specified type (see *Lubricants and fluids*). Ensure that the sealing lip edge of each seal is towards the spring end of the piston.

18 Lubricate the cylinder bore and the piston with clean hydraulic fluid, then insert the spring and piston assembly into the bore.

19 To renew the end cap or rubber boot on the pushrod, first accurately mark the position of the clevis locknut using quick-drying paint, such as correction fluid. Hold the clevis, slacken the locknut, then unscrew the clevis and locknut from the pushrod.

20 Remove the original end cap or rubber boot and slide the new components over the pushrod. Screw the locknut onto the pushrod, up to the position marked on removal. Refit the clevis and tighten the locknut to secure.

21 On early models, insert the pushrod into the cylinder bore, then fit the end cap to the cylinder, ensuring that the locking tabs lock the cap in position.

22 On later models, insert the pushrod into the cylinder bore, locate the washer in position and refit the retaining circlip. Ensure that the circlip is fully seated in its internal groove in the cylinder bore.

23 On left-hand-drive models, refit the fluid reservoir as follows.

a) *Examine the O-ring and renew if necessary, then refit the fluid inlet union, and tighten the securing screw.*

b) *Reconnect the fluid hose to the master cylinder. Note that the end of the hose with the yellow mark connects to the master cylinder, and the yellow mark should face upwards.*

24 On right-hand-drive models, fit a new rubber seal to the master cylinder fluid inlet, then refit the fluid reservoir, and secure with a new roll-pin.

Refitting

25 Refitting is a reversal of removal, bearing in mind the following points.

a) *Ensure that the master cylinder pushrod clevis pin and securing clip are correctly refitted.*

b) *On left-hand-drive models, note that when reconnecting the fluid hose to the reservoir, the white mark on the hose should face upwards.*

c) *On completion, bleed the clutch hydraulic system as described in Section 6, and check the clutch pedal adjustment as described in Section 7.*

6 Hydraulic system – bleeding

Note: *Refer to the warning at the beginning of Section 4 before proceeding.*

1 The correct operation of any hydraulic system is only possible after removing all air from the components and circuit; this is achieved by bleeding the system.

2 During the bleeding procedure, add only clean, unused hydraulic fluid of the specified type (see *Lubricants and fluids*); never re-use fluid that has already been bled from the

6.9 Clutch slave cylinder bleed screw (arrowed)

system. Ensure that sufficient fluid is available before starting work.

3 If there is any possibility of incorrect fluid being already in the system, the clutch hydraulic components and circuit must be flushed completely with uncontaminated, correct fluid, and new seals should be fitted to the various components.

4 If hydraulic fluid has been lost from the system, or air has entered because of a leak, ensure that the fault is cured before proceeding further.

5 Unscrew the clutch fluid reservoir cap, and top up the reservoir to the MAX level line. Refit the cap loosely, and remember to maintain the fluid level at least above the MIN level line throughout the procedure, otherwise there is a risk of further air entering the system.

6 There is a number of one-man, do-it-yourself, hydraulic bleeding kits currently available from motor accessory shops. It is recommended that one of these kits is used wherever possible, as they greatly simplify the bleeding operation, and also reduce the risk of expelled air and fluid being drawn back into the system. If such a kit is not available, the basic (two-man) method must be used, which is described in detail below.

7 If a one-man kit is to be used, prepare the vehicle as described previously, and follow the kit manufacturer's instructions, as the procedure may vary according to the type being used; generally, they are as outlined below in the relevant sub-section.

Bleeding

Basic (two-man) method

8 Collect a clean glass jar and a suitable length of plastic or rubber tubing, which is a tight fit over the bleed screw on the slave cylinder, and a ring spanner to fit the screw. The help of an assistant will also be required.

9 Where applicable, remove the dust cap from the bleed screw and fit the bleed tube to the screw **(see illustration)**.

10 Immerse the other end of the bleed tube in the jar, which should contain enough fluid to cover the end of the tube.

11 Ensure that the reservoir fluid level is maintained at least above the MIN level line throughout the procedure.

12 Open the bleed screw approximately half a turn, and have your assistant depress the clutch pedal with a smooth steady stroke down to the floor, and then hold it there. When the flow of fluid through the tube stops, tighten the bleed screw and have your assistant release the pedal slowly.

13 Repeat this operation (paragraph 12) until clean fluid, free from air bubbles, can be seen flowing from the end of the tube.

14 When no more air bubbles appear, tighten the bleed screw, remove the bleed tube and refit the dust cap (where applicable). Check that the clutch pedal feels firm when depressed.

Using a one-way valve kit

15 As their name implies, these kits consist of a length of tubing with a one-way valve fitted, to prevent expelled air and fluid being drawn back into the system; some kits incorporate a translucent container, which can be positioned so that the air bubbles can be more easily seen flowing from the end of the tube.

16 The kit is connected to the bleed screw, which is then opened. The user returns to the driver's seat, depresses the clutch pedal with a smooth steady stroke, and slowly releases it; this is repeated until the expelled fluid is clear of air bubbles.

17 Note that these kits simplify work so much that it is easy to forget the reservoir fluid level; ensure that this is maintained at least above the MIN level line at all times.

Using a pressure-bleeding kit

18 These kits are usually operated by the reserve of pressurised air contained in the spare tyre. However, note that it will probably be necessary to reduce the pressure to a lower level than normal; refer to the instructions supplied with the kit.

19 By connecting a pressurised, fluid-filled container to the fluid reservoir, bleeding is then carried out by simply opening the bleed screw and allowing the fluid to run out, rather like turning on a tap, until no air bubbles can be seen in the expelled fluid.

20 This method has the advantage that the large reservoir of fluid provides an additional safeguard against air being drawn into the system during bleeding.

All methods

21 When bleeding is completed, check and top-up the fluid level in the reservoir.

22 Check the feel of the clutch pedal. If it feels at all spongy, air must still be present in the system, and further bleeding is indicated. Failure to bleed satisfactorily after a reasonable repetition of the bleeding operations may be due to worn master cylinder seals.

23 Discard hydraulic fluid which has been bled from the system; it will not be fit for re-use.

7 Clutch pedal – removal, refitting and adjustment

Removal

1 Disconnect the battery negative terminal (refer to *Disconnecting the battery* in the Reference Chapter).

2 Remove the lower facia panel on the driver's side as described in Chapter 11.

3 Detach the helper spring from the upper part of the pedal arm.

4 Disconnect the pushrod from the pedal arm by removing the clevis pin securing clip and the clevis pin.

5 Unscrew the nut from the end of the pedal pivot bolt and remove the washer. Remove the bolt then withdraw the pedal arm.

Refitting

6 Refitting is the reverse of the removal procedure, but carry out the following adjustments before refitting the lower facia panel.

Adjustment

Pedal height

7 Peel back the carpet below the pedals and measure the clutch pedal height **(see illustration)**. Note that the measurement should be taken from the upper face of the pedal rubber to the asphalt sheet on the floorpan. If the height is not within the specified tolerance range, slacken the pedal height adjusting bolt locknut and turn the adjusting bolt until the correct height is achieved. Tighten the locknut on completion and refit the carpet.

8 Once the pedal height is correct, check the free play as follows.

Pedal free play and pushrod play

9 While gently depressing the clutch pedal with the fingers, measure the pedal travel (at the pedal pad) until the resistance increases

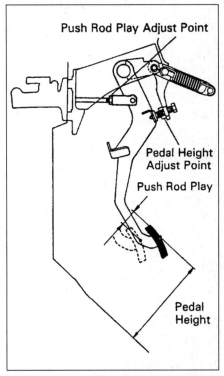

7.7 Clutch pedal adjustment details

very slightly. This measurement is the pedal free play. Now depress the pedal further until the beginning of clutch resistance is felt. This second measurement, from the pedal at rest position to the beginning of clutch resistance is the master cylinder pushrod play.

10 Compare the measurements obtained with those given in the Specifications. If adjustment is required, slacken the clevis locknut and turn the pushrod until the settings are correct. Recheck the pedal height on completion and repeat the adjustment procedures if necessary. When all is correct, tighten the clevis locknut.

11 Refit the lower facia panel, then reconnect the battery if not already done.

Chapter 7 Part A:
Manual transmission

Contents

Degrees of difficulty

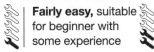

Easy, suitable for novice with little experience	**Fairly easy,** suitable for beginner with some experience	**Fairly difficult,** suitable for competent DIY mechanic	**Difficult,** suitable for experienced DIY mechanic	**Very difficult,** suitable for expert DIY or professional

Specifications

General

Type	Five forward speeds and reverse, synchromesh on all forward gears, final drive integral with transmission
Application:	
1.6 and 1.8 litre engines	C50 or C250
2.0 litre engines	S50, S54 or S55

Torque wrench settings

	Nm	lbf ft
Engine-to-transmission lower attachment bolts:		
Pre-August 2000 models	43	32
Post-August 2000 models	23	17
Engine-to-transmission reinforcing plate bolts:		
C50 and C250 transmissions	43	32
S50, S54 and S55 transmissions:		
M8 bolts	21	15
M10 bolts	44	32
Nuts	44	32
Engine-to-transmission upper attachment bolts	64	47
Engine/transmission longitudinal crossmember bolts	73	54
Front engine/transmission mounting to crossmember	72	53
Gear lever housing to floor	12	9
Left-hand engine/transmission mounting bracket through-bolt	87	64
Left-hand engine/transmission mounting bracket to transmission	52	38
Oil filler/level and drain plugs:		
C50 and C250 transmissions	39	29
S50, S54 and S55 transmissions	49	36
Rear engine/transmission mounting bracket through-bolt	87	64
Rear engine/transmission mounting bracket to transmission	64	47
Roadwheel nuts	103	76
Starter mounting bolts	39	29
Towing eye to longitudinal crossmember	39	29

2.2 Manual transmission oil filler/level plug (arrowed)

1 General information

All manual transmission models are fitted with a 5-speed transmission contained in a casing bolted to the left-hand end of the engine. All the transmission types are similar, the main differences being in the gear selector mechanism, gear ratios, and the casing design to suit the different engines in the range.

Drive is transmitted from the crankshaft via the clutch to the transmission input shaft, which has a splined extension to accept the clutch disc hub. The input shaft runs parallel to the mainshaft, and the input shaft and mainshaft gears are in constant mesh. Selection of gears is by sliding synchromesh hubs, which lock the appropriate mainshaft gears to the mainshaft.

3.4a Prise out the retaining clip . . .

3.4b . . . and remove the washer securing each gearchange control inner cable end to the transmission levers

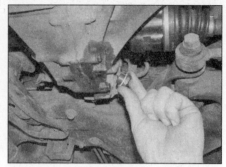

2.3 Unscrew the manual transmission oil drain plug

The 5th speed components are located in an extension housing at the end of the transmission.

Reverse gear is obtained by sliding an idler gear into mesh with two straight-cut gears on the input shaft and mainshaft.

All the forward gear teeth are helically cut, to reduce noise and improve wear characteristics.

The differential is mounted in the main transmission casing, and drive is transmitted to the differential by a pinion gear on the end of the mainshaft. The inboard ends of the driveshafts locate directly into the differential.

Gear selection is by a floor-mounted gearchange lever, via two control cables.

2 Manual transmission oil – draining and refilling

Draining

1 To improve access, jack up the vehicle and support on axle stands (see *Jacking and vehicle support*), but ensure that the vehicle is level. Remove the engine compartment undershield on the left-hand side, with reference to Chapter 11.
2 Working at the front of the transmission, unscrew the filler/level plug from the forward facing side of the transmission casing **(see illustration)**.
3 Position a suitable container beneath the oil drain plug, located below the left-hand driveshaft constant velocity joint, then unscrew the drain plug **(see illustration)**. Try to hold the plug in as it is unscrewed the last

3.5 Extract the retainers securing the gearchange control outer cables to the bracket

few turns, then move it away sharply so that the oil flows into the container and not up your sleeve.
4 Once the oil has drained fully (it may be necessary to reposition the container as the flow slows down), refit the drain plug, using a new sealing washer (where applicable), and tighten it securely.

Filling

5 Fill the transmission with the specified type and quantity of oil through the filler/level hole. Add the oil slowly until it begins to trickle out of the hole.
6 Allow the oil to settle, then refit and tighten the filler/level plug.
7 Refit the engine compartment undershield, then lower the vehicle to the ground.

3 Gearchange components – removal, refitting and adjustment

Gearchange control cables

Removal

1 Two control cables are used: the select control cable and the shift control cable. Both cables are removed and refitted together as an assembly.
2 Disconnect the battery negative terminal (refer to *Disconnecting the battery* in the Reference Chapter).
3 Remove the air cleaner assembly, and the air intake duct, as described in Chapter 4A.
4 Working at the transmission end of the cables, extract the retaining clip, and remove the washer securing each inner cable end to the gearchange levers on the transmission **(see illustrations)**.
5 Extract the two outer cable retainers securing the cables to the transmission bracket **(see illustration)**.
6 Working inside the vehicle, remove the centre console as described in Chapter 11.
7 Prise out the clip, and remove the washer securing the select control cable inner cable end to the bellcrank on the side of the gear lever housing. Extract the retainer securing the outer cable to the gear lever housing **(see illustrations)**.

3.7a Prise out the clip, remove the washer and disconnect the select control cable inner cable from the gear lever bellcrank

3.7b Extract the retainer securing the outer cable to the gear lever housing

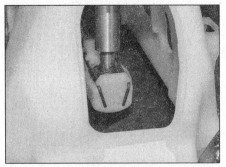

3.8 Extract the clip and disconnect the shift control cable inner cable end at the bottom of the gear lever

3.10 Undo the two bolts (arrowed) and release the cable support bracket from the underbody

8 Unbolt the gear lever housing from the floor, and lift it for access to the shift control cable inner cable end at the bottom of the gear lever **(see illustration)**. Disconnect the cable as described previously for the select control cable.
9 Firmly apply the handbrake, then jack up the front of the car and support it securely on axle stands (see *Jacking and vehicle support*).
10 Undo the two bolts securing the cable support bracket to the underbody **(see illustration)**.
11 Refer to Chapter 4A and remove the exhaust system front pipe and the heat shield below the gear lever housing.
12 Undo the bolts and remove the retaining plate and weatherproofing grommet from the underbody. Pull the cable assembly through the grommet and remove the cables from under the car.

Refitting
13 Refitting is a reversal of removal.

Gearchange lever mechanism

Removal
14 Disconnect the battery negative terminal (refer to *Disconnecting the battery* in the Reference Chapter).
15 Remove the centre console as described in Chapter 11.
16 Prise out the clip, and remove the washer securing the select control cable inner cable end to the bellcrank on the side of the gear lever housing **(see illustrations 3.7a and 3.7b)**. Extract the retainer securing the outer cable to the gear lever housing.

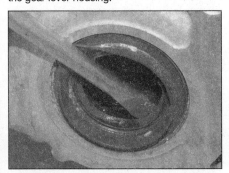

4.2 Using a screwdriver to prise out the driveshaft oil seal from the transmission

17 Unbolt the gear lever housing from the floor, and lift it for access to the shift control cable inner cable end at the bottom of the gear lever **(see illustration 3.8)**. Disconnect the cable as described previously for the select control cable, then remove the housing from the car.

Refitting
18 Refitting is a reversal of removal.

---

4 Oil seals – renewal

Driveshaft oil seals

1 Remove the relevant driveshaft as described in Chapter 8.
2 Note the fitted depth of the seal then, using a screwdriver, carefully prise out the oil seal, taking care not to damage the seal housing **(see illustration)**.
3 Thoroughly clean the oil seal housing in the transmission.
4 Dip the new oil seal in clean transmission oil, then press it into the housing as far as possible by hand.
5 Using a tube or socket of suitable diameter, carefully tap the seal into place, to the fitted depth noted during removal **(see illustration)**. Ensure that the seal is fitted square, and take care not to damage the seal lip.
6 Refit the driveshaft as described in Chapter 8.

4.5 Tap the new seal into position using a tube or socket of suitable diameter

Input shaft oil seal

Note: *The transmissions fitted to many 1.6 and 1.8 litre post-August 2000 models have an integral release bearing guide sleeve, and an oil seal fitted to the inside of the transmission casing. As the transmission must be disassembled to change the seal, entrust this task to a Toyota dealer or suitably-equipped specialist.*

7 With the transmission removed as described in Section 6, remove the clutch release lever and bearing, as described in Chapter 6.
8 Unbolt the guide sleeve from the bellhousing, then carefully prise out the seal, taking care not to scratch the seal housing.
9 Thoroughly clean the oil seal housing.
10 Wrap tape around the input shaft splines, to protect the lips of the new seal as it is installed.
11 Dip the new seal in clean transmission oil, then use a tube or socket of suitable diameter to tap the seal into position. Ensure that the seal is fitted square, and take care not to damage the seal lip.
12 Remove the tape from the input shaft, then refit the guide sleeve and tighten the securing bolts.
13 Refit the clutch release lever and bearing as described in Chapter 6, then refit the transmission as described in Section 6.

---

5 Reversing light switch – testing, removal and refitting

Testing

1 The reversing light circuit is controlled by a plunger-type switch located on top of the transmission casing in the engine compartment. If a fault develops in the circuit, first ensure that the circuit fuse has not blown.
2 To test the switch, remove the air cleaner assembly and intake duct as described in Chapter 4A. Disconnect the wiring connector, and use a multimeter (set to the resistance function) or a battery-and-bulb test circuit to check that there is continuity between the switch terminals only when reverse gear is selected. If this is not the case, and there

6.4 Disconnect the wiring plug from the reversing light switch

6.5 Unbolt the earth lead from the transmission

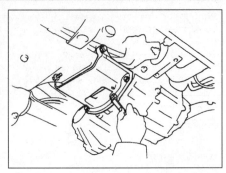

6.14 Removing the engine-to-transmission reinforcing plate

are no obvious breaks or other damage to the wires, the switch is faulty, and must be renewed.

Removal

3 Disconnect the battery negative terminal (refer to *Disconnecting the battery* in the Reference Chapter).
4 Remove the air cleaner assembly and intake duct as described in Chapter 4A.
5 Disconnect the switch wiring plug **(see illustration 6.4)**.
6 Unscrew the switch from the transmission.

Refitting

7 Refitting is a reversal of removal.

6 Manual transmission – removal and refitting

Removal

1 Disconnect the battery negative terminal (refer to *Disconnecting the battery* in the Reference Chapter).
2 Remove the battery and battery tray as described in Chapter 5A.
3 Remove the air cleaner assembly, and the air intake duct, as described in Chapter 4A.
4 Disconnect the wiring plug from the reversing light switch **(see illustration)**.
5 Unbolt the earth lead from the transmission **(see illustration)**. Undo the wiring harness support bracket bolt and release the harness from the top of the transmission.
6 Unscrew the bolt(s) securing the hydraulic

fluid pipe support bracket to the clutch slave cylinder and transmission.
7 With reference to Chapter 6, unscrew the two bolts securing the clutch slave cylinder to the transmission bellhousing, then withdraw the cylinder, complete with the pushrod. Wrap a cable tie around the cylinder and pushrod to prevent the cylinder piston from being ejected.
8 Disconnect the gearchange control cables from the transmission, as described in Section 3.
9 On models without ABS, disconnect the wiring connector from the vehicle speed sensor at the rear of the transmission.
10 Working at the top of the transmission casing, unscrew the upper engine-to-transmission mounting bolts, and the upper starter motor mounting bolt.
11 Firmly apply the handbrake, then jack up the front of the car and support it securely on axle stands (see *Jacking and vehicle support*). Remove the front roadwheels.
12 Remove the engine compartment undershields, with reference to Chapter 11.
13 Drain the transmission oil as described in Section 2.
14 Unscrew the securing bolts and remove the engine-to-transmission reinforcing plate (where fitted) **(see illustration)**.
15 Where applicable, unscrew the securing bolts, and remove the clutch bellhousing cover plate.
16 With reference to Chapter 4A, disconnect the exhaust front pipe from the manifold (engines with the exhaust manifold at the rear) or remove the front and intermediate pipes completely (engines with the exhaust manifold at the front).

17 Remove the driveshafts as described in Chapter 8.
18 Connect a hoist and lifting tackle to the engine lifting bracket at the left-hand end of the cylinder head, and raise the hoist to just take the weight of the engine.
19 Remove the engine/transmission longitudinal crossmember as follows **(see illustration)**.
  a) *Unscrew the two securing bolts, and remove the towing eye from the crossmember.*
  b) *Prise out the cover plugs, and unscrew the two bolts securing the front engine/transmission mounting to the crossmember.*
  c) *Where applicable, unscrew the securing bolt and release the air conditioning pipe clamp from the crossmember.*
  d) *Prise out the rear cover plug and unscrew the five securing bolts, two at the front and three at the rear, and remove the crossmember.*
20 Disconnect the wiring from the starter motor.
21 Unscrew the lower securing bolt, and remove the starter motor.
22 Unscrew the through-bolt securing the rear engine/transmission mounting bracket to the mounting rubber.
23 Unscrew the three bolts securing the rear engine/transmission mounting bracket to the transmission.
24 Unscrew the nuts and bolts, and remove the left-hand engine/transmission mounting bracket from the transmission **(see illustrations)**.

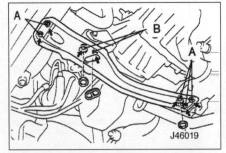

6.19 Longitudinal crossmember retaining bolts (A) and front engine/transmission mounting bracket bolts (B)

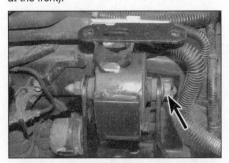

6.24a Unscrew the left-hand engine/ transmission mounting through-bolt (arrowed) . . .

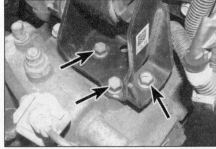

6.24b . . . and the mounting bracket bolts (arrowed) and remove the mounting bracket

25 Support the transmission using a jack, and a block of wood, then unscrew the lower engine-to-transmission bolts.

26 Lower the engine and transmission, then slide the transmission from the engine, taking care not to allow the transmission to hang on the input shaft. Lower the transmission from under the vehicle.

Refitting

27 Before attempting to refit the transmission, ensure that the clutch disc is centralised, as described in Chapter 6.

28 Further refitting is a reversal of removal, bearing in mind the following points.

  a) *Tighten all fixings to the specified torque, where applicable.*
  b) *Refit the driveshafts as described in Chapter 8.*
  c) *Reconnect/refit the exhaust front/ intermediate pipe as described in Chapter 4A.*
  d) *Fill the transmission with oil as described in Section 2.*

---

7   Manual transmission overhaul –
general information

Overhauling a manual transmission is a difficult and involved job for the DIY home mechanic. In addition to dismantling and reassembling many small parts, clearances must be precisely measured and, if necessary, changed by selecting shims and spacers. Internal transmission components are also often difficult to obtain, and, in many instances, extremely expensive. Because of this, if the transmission develops a fault or becomes noisy, the best course of action is to have the unit overhauled by a specialist repairer, or to obtain an exchange reconditioned unit. Be aware that some transmission repairs can be carried out with the transmission in the car.

Nevertheless, it is not impossible for the more experienced mechanic to overhaul the transmission, provided the special tools are available, and the job is done in a deliberate step-by-step manner, so that nothing is overlooked.

The tools necessary for an overhaul include internal and external circlip pliers, bearing pullers, a slide hammer, a set of pin punches, a dial test indicator, and possibly a hydraulic press. In addition, a large, sturdy workbench and a vice will be required.

During dismantling of the transmission, make careful notes of how each component is fitted, to make reassembly easier and more accurate.

Before dismantling the transmission, it will help if you have some idea what area is malfunctioning. Certain problems can be closely related to specific areas in the transmission, which can make component examination and renewal easier. Refer to the *Fault finding* Section at the end of this manual for more information.

Chapter 7 Part B:
Automatic transmission

Contents

Degrees of difficulty

| **Easy,** suitable for novice with little experience | **Fairly easy,** suitable for beginner with some experience | **Fairly difficult,** suitable for competent DIY mechanic | **Difficult,** suitable for experienced DIY mechanic | **Very difficult,** suitable for expert DIY or professional |

Specifications

General

Type . . . . Fully electronic, four-speed with torque converter lock-up
Application:
  Pre-August 2000 models:
    1.8 litre engines . . . . A245E or A246E
    2.0 litre engines A241E
  Post-August 2000 models:
    1.8 litre engines A246E
    2.0 litre engines U240E

Torque converter fitted position

Distance from bellhousing face to torque converter retaining bolt lugs:
  Pre-August 2000 models:
    A241E transmissions . . . . 12.75 mm (minimum)
    A245E and A246E transmissions . . . . 22.8 mm (minimum)
  Post-August 2000 models:
    A246E transmissions . . . . 15.5 mm (minimum)
    U240E transmissions . . . . 12.75 mm (minimum)

Torque wrench settings

	Nm	lbf ft
Engine-to-transmission lower attachment bolts:		
Pre-August 2000 models	43	32
Post-August 2000 models:		
A246E transmissions:		
At rear of bellhousing	46	34
At base of bellhousing	23	17
U240E transmissions	46	34
Engine-to-transmission reinforcing plate bolts:		
A241E transmissions:		
M8 bolts	21	15
M10 bolts	44	32
Nuts	44	32
A245E and A246E transmissions	43	32
Engine-to-transmission upper attachment bolts	64	47
Engine/transmission longitudinal crossmember bolts	73	54
Front engine/transmission mounting to crossmember	72	53
Left-hand engine/transmission mounting bracket through-bolt	87	64
Left-hand engine/transmission mounting bracket to transmission	52	38
Rear engine/transmission mounting bracket through-bolt	87	64
Rear engine/transmission mounting bracket to transmission	64	47
Roadwheel nuts	103	76
Starter mounting bolts	39	29
Torque converter to driveplate:		
A241E, A245E and A246E transmissions	27	20
U240E transmissions	41	30
Towing eye to longitudinal crossmember	39	29
Transmission fluid drain plug	17	13

1 General information

A four-speed, fully electronic, automatic transmission is available as an option on 1.8 litre and 2.0 litre engine models.

The transmission comprises a torque converter, an epicyclic geartrain, hydraulically-operated clutches and brakes, and an electronic control system controlled by the engine management electronic control unit (ECU).

Drive is taken from the engine to the transmission by a torque converter. This is a type of fluid-coupling between engine and transmission, which acts as a clutch and also provides a degree of torque multiplication when accelerating. The torque converter is mechanically locked to the engine, under the control of the ECU, when the transmission is operating in certain gear selector positions, thus eliminating losses due to slip, and improving fuel economy.

The epicyclic geartrain provides either of the four forward or one reverse gear ratio, according to which of its component parts are held stationary or allowed to turn. The components of the geartrain are held or released by brakes and clutches which are hydraulically-activated. A fluid pump within the transmission provides the necessary hydraulic pressure to operate the brakes and clutches.

Driver control of the transmission is by a selector lever and three, two-position switches. The selector lever has a drive position, and a hold facility on 1st and 2nd gear. The drive position (D) provides automatic changing throughout the range of all forward gear ratios, and is the position selected for normal driving. An automatic kickdown facility shifts the transmission down a gear if the accelerator pedal is fully depressed. The hold facility is similar to the drive position, but limits the number of gear ratios available – ie, when the selector lever is in the 2 position, only the first two ratios can be selected; and in the L position, only the first ratio can be selected. The lower ratio hold (L) is useful when travelling down steep gradients, or for preventing unwanted selection of high gears on twisty roads.

Two driving programs are provided for selection by the driving pattern selector switch; normal or power. With the switch released, the transmission will use the normal program, and will change gear at an engine speed which is biased towards fuel economy. With the switch depressed, the transmission will use the power program and gearchanges will take place at a higher engine speed, giving improved acceleration. The PWR indicator light on the instrument panel will illuminate when the power program is selected.

A snow mode selector switch is also provided to reduce the effects of engine torque in arduous road conditions. With the switch depressed, the transmission starts off in 2nd gear and the power driving program (if selected) is cancelled. The SNOW indicator light on the instrument panel will illuminate when snow mode is selected.

The transmission also has an overdrive switch which allows the transmission to operate as a four-speed or a three-speed transmission. When the overdrive switch is in the 'on' position, the transmission will use all four speeds for greater economy. With the switch in the 'off' position, only the first three speeds will be selected. The O/D OFF indicator light on the transmission will illuminate when the switch is in the 'off' position. Note that when the engine coolant temperature is low, only the first three speeds can be selected, even if the overdrive switch is in the 'on' position.

Later transmissions are additionally equipped with a shift lock system incorporated into the selector lever assembly. Besides the conventional selector lever lock button (to inhibit shifting into R, P, 2 and L positions) the shift lock system prevents the lever being moved from P until the ignition is switched on and the brake pedal is depressed.

Automatic control of the transmission is by the engine management ECU which receives signal inputs from the engine management sensors relating to engine and transmission operating conditions. From this data, the ECU can establish the optimum gear shifting speeds and lock-up engagement points according to transmission mode selected, and driver inputs.

In addition to control of the engine management system and transmission, the ECU incorporates a built-in fault diagnosis facility. A fault is signalled to the driver by the flashing of the O/D OFF indicator light on the instrument panel. If a fault of this nature does occur, the ECU stores a series of signals (or fault codes) for subsequent read-out during fault diagnosis.

Due to the complexity of the automatic

transmission, any repair or overhaul work must be left to a Toyota dealer or automatic transmission specialist with the necessary equipment for fault diagnosis and repair. The contents of the following Sections are therefore confined to supplying general information, and any service information and instructions that can be used by the owner.

2 Automatic transmission fluid – draining and refilling

Draining

1 To improve access, jack up the car and support it on axle stands (see *Jacking and vehicle support*), but ensure that it is level.
2 If necessary, remove the engine compartment undershields, with reference to Chapter 11.
3 Position a suitable container beneath the transmission fluid drain plug, then wipe clean the area all around the plug and unscrew it **(see illustration)**. Try to hold the plug in as it is unscrewed the last few turns, then move it away sharply so that the fluid flows into the container and not up your sleeve.
Caution: If the vehicle has just been run, the transmission fluid may be very hot.
4 Once the fluid has drained fully, refit the drain plug, using a new sealing washer (where applicable), and tighten it to the specified torque.

Filling

5 Where applicable, refit the engine compartment undershields, then lower the car to the ground.
6 Open the bonnet and remove the transmission fluid dipstick from its tube **(see illustration)**.
7 Slowly fill the transmission with the specified fluid (see *Lubricants and fluids*) through the dipstick tube, using a clean funnel if necessary. On early transmissions, continue filling the transmission until the level reaches the upper of the two notches on the dipstick, either side of the word COOL. On later transmissions, continue filling the transmission until the level reaches the upper line on the dipstick, just below the word COOL **(see illustrations)**.
8 Refit the dipstick to its tube then, with the handbrake applied and the selector lever in the P position, start the engine. While the engine is idling, depress the brake pedal and move the selector lever through all the gear positions, beginning and ending in P.
9 With the engine still idling, recheck the fluid level. Add further fluid as necessary to bring the level up to the upper of the two notches on the dipstick, either side of the word COOL, or the upper line on the dipstick, just below the word COOL.
10 Final checking of the fluid level should be carried out after the car has been driven for approximately 10 miles, and with reference to the procedures contained in Chapter 1.

2.3 Automatic transmission fluid drain plug location on the sump pan

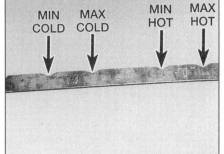

2.7a Transmission fluid level markings on the early type dipstick . . .

3 Gear selector cable – adjustment, removal and refitting

Adjustment

1 Move the gear selector lever through the full range of positions, and check that the gear position indicator correctly indicates the relevant gear position. If the indicator is not aligned with the correct position, carry out the following adjustment procedure.
2 Firmly apply the handbrake, then jack up the front of the car and support it securely on axle stands (see *Jacking and vehicle support*). Remove the engine compartment undershield on the left-hand side, with reference to Chapter 11.
3 Working at the gear selector lever on the transmission, loosen the nut securing the cable to the selector lever **(see illustration)**.

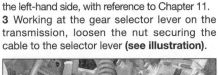

3.3 Loosen the nut securing the selector cable to the transmission selector lever

2.6 Depress the retaining tab and withdraw the transmission fluid dipstick from its tube

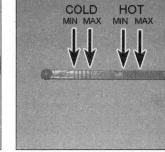

2.7b . . . and on the later type dipstick

4 Rotate the transmission selector lever anti-clockwise as far as it will go.
5 Move the lever back two notches to the neutral position.
6 Move the gear selector lever inside the vehicle to the N position.
7 Hold the transmission selector lever lightly towards the R side of N, then tighten the securing nut.
8 Refit the undershield, then lower the car to the ground.

Removal

9 Firmly apply the handbrake, then jack up the front of the car and support it securely on axle stands (see *Jacking and vehicle support*). Remove the engine compartment undershield on the left-hand side, with reference to Chapter 11.
10 Unscrew the retaining nut and disconnect the selector cable from the transmission selector lever **(see illustration 3.3)**.

3.11 Extract the retaining clip to disconnect the selector outer cable from the bracket

3.14 Prise the selector inner cable end fitting (arrowed) from the selector lever

11 Extract the retaining clip and disconnect the selector outer cable from the support bracket **(see illustration)**.

12 Working backwards along the cable until it enters the passenger compartment, release it from its securing clips.

13 Remove the centre console as described in Chapter 11.

14 Prise the selector inner cable end fitting from the lower end of the selector lever **(see illustration)**.

15 Extract the clip securing the outer cable to the selector lever base and withdraw the cable **(see illustration)**.

16 Release the cable grommet and retaining plate (where fitted) on the bulkhead, and remove the cable assembly from the engine compartment.

Refitting

17 Refitting is the reversal of removal, but adjust the cable as described previously before tightening the cable-to-transmission selector lever retaining nut.

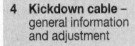

4 Kickdown cable –
general information
and adjustment

General information

1 The kickdown cable (or more precisely, the throttle valve control cable) connects the throttle linkage on the engine with the valve block inside the transmission, thus regulating the opening of the valve block fluid passages according to throttle position.

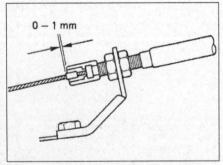

4.4 Kickdown cable stopper protrusion

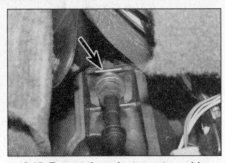

3.15 Extract the selector outer cable retaining clip (arrowed) and withdraw the cable

2 The lower end of the cable is connected to a cam inside the transmission which actuates the valves in the valve block. To gain access to the attachment, it is necessary to remove the transmission sump pan and valve block assembly, together with other transmission internal components. As this work carries a very high risk of dirt entry and possible future transmission malfunction if not carried out under scrupulously clean conditions, removal, refitting or complete cable renewal should be entrusted to a Toyota dealer.

Adjustment

3 Ensure that the accelerator cable is correctly adjusted as described in Chapter 4A.

4 With the accelerator pedal released (throttle fully closed) check that the crimped metal stopper on the inner cable protrudes from the end of the rubber sleeve on the outer cable by between 0 and 1.0 mm **(see illustration)**.

5 If the stopper protrusion is incorrect, slacken the outer cable locknuts at the support bracket and adjust the position of the outer cable as necessary **(see illustration)**. Tighten the locknuts on completion.

5 Starter inhibitor switch
– removal, refitting
and adjustment

Removal

1 Firmly apply the handbrake, then jack up the front of the car and support it securely on axle stands (see *Jacking and vehicle support*).

4.5 Slacken the outer cable locknuts (arrowed) to adjust the kickdown cable

2 Remove the engine compartment undershield on the left-hand side, with reference to Chapter 11.

3 Disconnect the starter inhibitor switch wiring connector.

4 Working at the gear selector lever on the transmission, unscrew the nut securing the gear selector cable to the selector lever, and disconnect the cable **(see illustration 3.3)**.

5 Unscrew the securing nut, recover the washer, and remove the gear selector lever from the switch.

6 Using a screwdriver, prise back the tab on the lockwasher under the nut securing the switch to the valve shaft.

7 Unscrew the nut, and recover the lockwasher and shim(s).

8 Unscrew the two securing bolts, and withdraw the switch from the transmission.

Refitting

9 Offer the switch into position over the valve shaft, then refit the shim(s), lockwasher, and securing nut. Tighten the securing nut and bend over the lockwasher tab.

10 Temporarily refit the gear selector lever to the switch. Rotate the gear selector lever anti-clockwise as far as it will go, then turn it back, clockwise, by two notches.

11 Remove the gear selector lever.

12 Align the groove in the valve shaft with the neutral basic line marked on the switch body, then refit and tighten the switch securing bolts **(see illustration)**.

13 Refit the gear selector lever, washer and securing nut, and tighten the nut securely.

14 Reconnect the switch wiring, then refit and adjust the selector cable as described in Section 3.

15 Refit the undershield, then lower the car to the ground.

Adjustment

16 If the engine can be started with the transmission selector lever in any position other than N or P, the starter inhibitor switch requires adjustment.

17 Firmly apply the handbrake, then jack up the front of the car and support it securely on axle stands (see *Jacking and vehicle support*). Remove the engine compartment undershield on the left-hand side, with reference to Chapter 11.

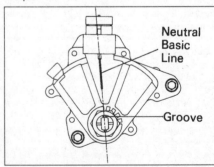

5.12 Setting the starter inhibitor switch

18 Loosen the two starter inhibitor switch securing bolts.

19 Set the transmission selector lever to the N position.

20 Align the groove in the valve shaft with the neutral basic line marked on the switch body, then refit and tighten the switch securing bolts (**see illustration 5.12**).

21 Refit the undershield, then lower the car to the ground.

6 Oil seals – renewal

Driveshaft oil seals

1 Remove the relevant driveshaft as described in Chapter 8.

2 Using a screwdriver, carefully prise out the oil seal, taking care not to damage the seal housing (**see illustration**).

3 Thoroughly clean the oil seal housing in the transmission.

4 Dip the new oil seal in clean transmission oil, then press it into the housing as far as possible by hand.

5 Using a tube or socket of suitable diameter, carefully tap the seal into place (**see illustration**). Drive it into the bore squarely and make sure it's completely seated. When the seals are fully-seated, they should be recessed in their bores by the following amount:

Transmission	Left-hand seal	Right-hand seal
A241E	5.2 mm	Flush
A245E	5.3 mm	3.1 mm
A246E	5.3 mm	3.1 mm
U240E	2.7 mm	Flush

6 Refit the driveshaft as described in Chapter 8.

Vehicle speed sensor O-ring

7 The speed sensor is located on the transmission housing. Look for lubricant around the sensor housing to determine if the O-ring is leaking.

8 Disconnect the wiring connector and unbolt the vehicle speed sensor from the transmission (**see illustration**).

9 Using a scribe or a small screwdriver, remove the O-ring from the sensor (**see illustration**) and install a new O-ring. Lubricate the new O-ring with automatic transmission fluid to protect it during refitting of the sensor.

10 Refitting is the reverse of removal.

7 Automatic transmission – removal and refitting

Removal

1 Disconnect the battery negative terminal (refer to *Disconnecting the battery* in the Reference Chapter).

6.2 Lever the driveshaft oil seal from the transmission casing

6.8 Disconnect the speed sensor wiring connector (arrowed), remove the bolt (arrowed) and remove the speed sensor

2 Remove the battery and battery tray as described in Chapter 5A.

3 Remove the air cleaner assembly, and the air intake duct, as described in Chapter 4A.

4 Turn the segment on the throttle housing to open the throttle, then disconnect the kickdown cable end. Unscrew the locknut and release the outer cable from the bracket.

5 Firmly apply the handbrake, then jack up the front of the car and support it securely on axle stands (see *Jacking and vehicle support*). Remove the front roadwheels.

6 Remove the engine compartment undershields, with reference to Chapter 11.

7 Drain the transmission fluid as described in Section 2.

8 With reference to Chapter 4A, disconnect the exhaust front pipe from the manifold (engines with the exhaust manifold at the rear)

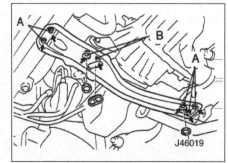

7.15 Longitudinal crossmember retaining bolts (A) and front engine/transmission mounting bracket bolts (B)

6.5 Drive the seal into place using a tubular drift or socket that bears only on the hard, outer edge of the seal

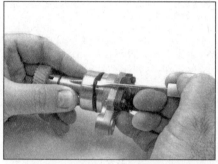

6.9 Using a scribe or a small screwdriver, remove the O-ring from the sensor

or remove the front and intermediate pipes completely (engines with the exhaust manifold at the front).

9 Remove the driveshafts as described in Chapter 8.

10 Remove the starter motor as described in Chapter 5A.

11 Connect a suitable hoist and lifting tackle to the engine lifting brackets, and raise the hoist to just take the weight of the engine and transmission.

12 Working at the left-hand end of the transmission, unscrew the nuts and bolts securing the transmission mounting to the transmission.

13 Disconnect the transmission earth cable from the transmission.

14 Release the kickdown cable from the clamp.

15 Remove the engine/transmission longitudinal crossmember as follows (**see illustration**).

a) *Unscrew the two securing bolts, and remove the towing eye from the crossmember.*

b) *Prise out the cover plugs, and unscrew the two bolts securing the front engine/transmission mounting to the crossmember.*

c) *Where applicable, unscrew the securing bolt and release the air conditioning pipe clamp from the crossmember.*

d) *Prise out the rear cover plug and unscrew the five securing bolts, two at the front and three at the rear, and remove the crossmember.*

7.23 Mark the relationship of the torque converter to the driveplate as an aid to refitting

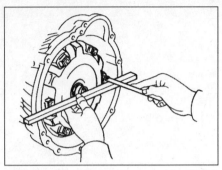

7.30 Checking the torque converter fitted position

16 Disconnect the vehicle speed sensor, and the starter inhibitor switch wiring connectors from the transmission. Note their fitted positions, then disconnect all remaining electrical connectors from the transmission. Detach the wiring harness clamps from the transmission and set the wiring harnesses aside.

17 Disconnect the gear selector cable from the selector lever on the transmission as described in Section 3.

18 Place a container beneath the fluid cooler hose connections at the transmission, then release the securing clips, and disconnect the hoses from the transmission.

19 Where fitted, unscrew the securing bolts and remove the engine-to-transmission reinforcing plate.

20 Unscrew the through-bolt securing the rear engine/transmission mounting bracket to the mounting rubber.

21 Unscrew the three bolts securing the rear engine/transmission mounting bracket to the transmission.

22 Where applicable, remove the cover at the base of the bellhousing for access to the torque converter-to-driveplate bolts.

23 Using a spanner on the crankshaft pulley bolt, turn the engine for access to each torque converter-to-driveplate bolt in turn. Mark the relationship of the torque converter to the driveplate so they can be installed in the same position, then unscrew the six torque converter-to-driveplate bolts **(see illustration)**.

24 Support the transmission, using a jack and block of wood.

25 Work around the transmission bellhousing, and unscrew the engine-to-transmission bolts.

26 According to model, unscrew the remaining transmission mounting bolts.

27 Carefully manipulate the transmission away from the engine, then lower the assembly, and withdraw it from under the car. As the transmission is removed, take great care not to allow the torque converter to fall out.

28 To prevent the torque converter from falling out of the transmission after removal, bolt a metal plate or bar across the end of the bellhousing.

Refitting

29 Commence refitting by removing the plate used to retain the torque converter on the transmission.

30 Check the torque converter fitted position as follows:

a) *Place a straight-edge across the end of the transmission bellhousing.*

b) *Using a steel rule or calipers, measure the distance between the straight-edge and the torque converter-to-driveplate bolt lugs at the edge of the torque converter* **(see illustration)**.

c) *The distance measured should be as given in the Specifications. If the distance is less than the minimum specified, it is probable that the torque converter is not fully engaged with the transmission. Try pushing the torque converter further into the bellhousing.*

31 Turn the torque converter so that, when the transmission is installed, the torque converter-to-driveplate bolt holes in the torque converter align with the corresponding bolt holes in the driveplate. Ensure also that the match marks on the torque converter and driveplate, made during paragraph 23, will be aligned.

32 Lift the transmission into position, and offer it up to the engine.

33 Refit the engine-to-transmission bolts, and tighten them to the specified torque.

34 Refit and tighten the transmission mounting retaining bolts.

35 Refit the torque converter-to-driveplate bolts, and tighten them evenly to the specified torque.

36 Where applicable, refit the engine-to-transmission reinforcing plate.

37 Further refitting is a reversal of removal, bearing in mind the following points.

a) *Tighten all fixings to the specified torque where given.*

b) *Refit the starter motor with reference to Chapter 5A.*

c) *Reconnect and adjuster the gear selector cable as described in Section 3.*

d) *Reconnect/refit the exhaust front/ intermediate pipe as described in Chapter 4A.*

e) *Refit the driveshafts as described in Chapter 8.*

f) *Reconnect the kickdown cable then adjust it as described in Section 4.*

g) *Fill the transmission with fluid as described in Section 2.*

8 Automatic transmission overhaul – general information

In the event of a fault occurring with the transmission, it is first necessary to determine whether it is of an electrical, mechanical or hydraulic nature, and to do this special test equipment is required. It is therefore essential to have the work carried out by a Toyota dealer or automatic transmission specialist, if a transmission fault is suspected.

Do not remove the transmission from the vehicle for repair before professional fault diagnosis has been carried out, since most tests require the transmission to be in the vehicle.

Chapter 8
Driveshafts

Contents

Degrees of difficulty

Easy, suitable for novice with little experience	Fairly easy, suitable for beginner with some experience	Fairly difficult, suitable for competent DIY mechanic	Difficult, suitable for experienced DIY mechanic	Very difficult, suitable for expert DIY or professional

Specifications

General

Type . . . . Unequal length steel with constant velocity (CV) joint at each end

Overhaul

Standard length setting dimension:
  1.6 and 1.8 litre engine models pre-August 2000:
    Left-hand driveshaft . . . . 544.7 ± 2.0 mm
    Right-hand driveshaft . . . . 859.3 ± 2.0 mm
  2.0 litre engine models pre-August 2000:
    Left-hand driveshaft . . . . 554.0 ± 2.0 mm
    Right-hand driveshaft . . . . 840.7 ± 2.0 mm
  1.6 litre engine models post-August 2000:
    Left-hand driveshaft . . . . 655.7 ± 0.8 mm
    Right-hand driveshaft . . . . 944.7 ± 0.8 mm
  1.8 litre engine models post-August 2000:
    With manual transmission:
      Left-hand driveshaft . . . . 655.7 ± 0.8 mm
      Right-hand driveshaft . . . . 943.6 ± 1.0 mm
    With automatic transmission:
      Left-hand driveshaft . . . . 653.2 ± 0.8 mm
      Right-hand driveshaft . . . . 943.6 ± 1.0 mm
  2.0 litre engine models post-August 2000:
    Left-hand driveshaft . . . . 650.8 ± 0.7 mm
    Right-hand driveshaft . . . . 922.6 ± 1.0 mm
Dust cover setting dimension:
  1.8 litre engine models:
    With manual transmission. . . . . 86 to 87 mm
    With automatic transmission . . . . 83 to 84 mm
  2.0 litre engine models:
    Pre-August 2000. . . . . 86 to 87 mm
    Post-August 2000 . . . . 87 to 88 mm
Lubricant type . . . . Special grease supplied with gaiter repair kits – joints are otherwise prepacked with grease, and sealed
Lubricant quantity:
  Pre-August 2000 models:
    Inner CV joints . . . . 125.5 to 135.5 g
    Outer CV joints . . . . 85.0 to 105.0 g
  Post-August 2000 models:
    Inner CV joints:
      1.6 litre engine models . . . . 125.5 to 135.5 g
      1.8 litre engine models . . . . 140.0 to 150.0 g
      2.0 litre engine models . . . . 120.0 to 130.0 g
    Outer CV joints . . . . 85.0 to 105.0 g

Torque wrench settings

	Nm	lbf ft
ABS wheel speed sensor bolt	8	6
Driveshaft intermediate bearing housing-to-bracket bolts	64	47
Hub/driveshaft retaining nut	216	159
Roadwheel nuts	103	76
Suspension lower balljoint to lower arm	127	94
Track rod end balljoint to hub carrier	49	36

1 General information

Drive is transmitted from the differential to the front wheels by means of two unequal length steel driveshafts incorporating constant velocity (CV) joints at each end.

On all models, the driveshafts are fitted with ball-and-cage-type constant velocity joints at their outer ends. These outer joints cannot be dismantled. Each joint has an outer member, which is splined at its outer end to accept the wheel hub, and is threaded so that the hub can be fastened by a large nut.

On all models, tripod-type inner constant velocity joints are used. The outer members of the inner joints are splined, and engage directly with the differential sunwheels.

On 1.8 litre engine models post-August 2000 and all 2.0 litre engine models, the inner section of the right-hand driveshaft is supported by an intermediate bearing located in a bracket bolted to the engine.

2.2a Extract the hub/driveshaft retaining nut split pin . . .

2.2b . . . and remove the locking cap over the nut

2 Driveshaft – removal and refitting

Warning: Do not allow the vehicle to rest on its wheels with one or both driveshafts removed, as damage to the wheel bearing(s) may result. If moving the vehicle is unavoidable, temporarily insert the outer ends of the driveshaft(s) in the hub(s) and tighten the hub nut(s). In this case the inner end(s) of the driveshaft(s) must be supported, for example by suspending with string from the vehicle underbody.

Right-hand driveshaft – 1.8 litre post-August 2000 and all 2.0 litre models

Removal

Note: *A new hub/driveshaft retaining nut split pin, track rod end balljoint nut split pin, and CV joint snap-ring must be used on refitting.*

1 Firmly apply the handbrake, then jack up the front of the car and support it securely on axle stands (see *Jacking and vehicle support*). Remove the relevant front roadwheel.

2 Extract the hub/driveshaft retaining nut split pin and remove the locking cap over the nut **(see illustrations)**.

3 Have an assistant firmly depress the brake pedal to prevent the front hub from rotating. Using a socket and a long extension bar, slacken and remove the hub/driveshaft retaining nut. Alternatively, a tool can be

TOOL TiP

A tool to hold the front hub stationary whilst the driveshaft retaining nut is slackened can be fabricated from two lengths of steel strip (one long, one short) and a nut and bolt; the nut and bolt forming the pivot of a forked tool.

fabricated from two lengths of steel strip (one long, one short) and a nut and bolt; the nut and bolt forming the pivot of a forked tool. Bolt the tool to the hub using two wheel nuts, and hold the tool to prevent the hub from rotating as the hub/driveshaft retaining nut is undone **(see Tool Tip)**. This nut is very tight; make sure that there is no risk of pulling the car off the axle stands.

4 Undo the retaining bolt and withdraw the ABS wheel speed sensor from the hub carrier **(see illustration)**.

5 Drain the transmission oil/fluid as described in Chapter 7A or 7B as applicable.

6 Extract the split pin from the track rod end balljoint, and unscrew the balljoint nut as far as the end of the balljoint shank threads **(see illustration)**. Using a balljoint separator tool, release the track rod end balljoint tapered shank. Once the taper has separated, unscrew the nut and detach the track rod end from the hub carrier.

7 Unscrew the bolt and two nuts, and disconnect the suspension lower balljoint from the lower arm **(see illustration)**.

2.4 Undo the retaining bolt and withdraw the ABS wheel speed sensor from the hub carrier

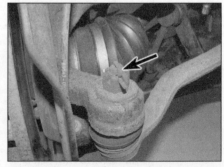

2.6 Extract the split pin (arrowed) from the track rod end balljoint

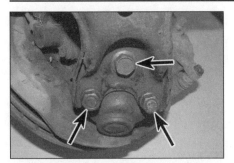

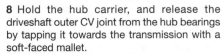

2.7 Unscrew the bolt and two nuts (arrowed), and disconnect the suspension lower balljoint from the lower arm

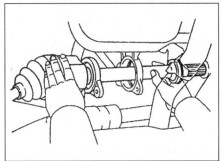

2.10 Removing the right-hand driveshaft on models with an intermediate bearing

2.17 Removing the driveshaft outer CV joint from the hub carrier

8 Hold the hub carrier, and release the driveshaft outer CV joint from the hub bearings by tapping it towards the transmission with a soft-faced mallet.
9 Unscrew the two bolts securing the driveshaft intermediate bearing housing to the bracket on the engine.
10 Pull the hub carrier and suspension strut assembly outwards and withdraw the driveshaft outer CV joint from the hub carrier. Pull the inner end of the driveshaft from the transmission, and withdraw the driveshaft through the bearing housing bracket, complete with the intermediate bearing assembly **(see illustration)**.

Refitting

11 Before installing the driveshaft, examine the driveshaft oil seal in the transmission for signs of damage or deterioration and, if necessary, renew it, referring to the appropriate Part of Chapter 7 for further information. (Having got this far it is worth renewing the seal as a matter of course.)
12 Coat the driveshaft oil seal with a little grease, then slide the inner end of the driveshaft into the differential, simultaneously engaging the intermediate bearing with the bracket on the engine. Take care not to damage the differential oil seal.
13 Refit the bolts securing the driveshaft intermediate bearing housing to the bracket, and tighten them to the specified torque.
14 Proceed as described in paragraphs 24 to 31.

All other driveshafts

Removal

15 Proceed as described in paragraphs 1 to 8.
16 Using a metal lever, prise the driveshaft inner CV joint from the transmission. Locate the lever on the lug provided on the side of the joint.
17 Once the inner CV joint has been released from the transmission, withdraw the outer joint from the hub carrier and remove the driveshaft from under the vehicle **(see illustration)**.
18 Remove the snap-ring from the splined end of the inner CV joint **(see illustration)**. **Note:** *This snap-ring must be renewed each time the driveshaft is withdrawn from the transmission. The hub/driveshaft retaining nut split pin and*

the track rod end balljoint nut split pin must also be renewed when refitting the driveshaft.

Refitting

19 Before installing the driveshaft, examine the driveshaft oil seal in the transmission for signs of damage or deterioration and, if necessary, renew it, referring to the appropriate Part of Chapter 7 for further information. (Having got this far it is worth renewing the seal as a matter of course.)
20 Thoroughly clean the driveshaft splines, and the apertures in the transmission and hub assembly. Apply a thin film of grease to the oil seal lips, and to the driveshaft splines and shoulders. Check that all gaiter clips are securely fastened.
21 Fit a new snap-ring to the splined end of the inner CV joint.
22 With the opening in the snap-ring facing downwards, offer the inner end of the driveshaft up to the opening in the transmission then, using a soft metal drift, and a hammer, tap the CV joint into position until the snap-ring engages with the differential.
23 Check that the inner CV joint is fully engaged with the differential by pulling on the joint. There should be 2 to 3 mm of movement, but it should not be possible to pull the joint out by hand.
24 Engage the driveshaft outer CV joint with the hub carrier, then reconnect the suspension lower balljoint to the lower arm. Secure with the bolt and two nuts, tightened to the specified torque.
25 Engage the track rod end balljoint shank with the hub carrier, and screw on the balljoint

2.18 Remove the snap-ring from the splined end of the inner CV joint

nut. Tighten the nut to the specified torque, fit a new split pin and bend over the split pin legs to secure. If the castellations in the nut do not line up with the hole in the balljoint shank, tighten the nut a little more until the split pin can be fitted.
26 Refit the hub/driveshaft retaining nut and, using the method employed on removal to prevent the hub from rotating, tighten the hub/driveshaft retaining nut to the specified torque. Check that the hub rotates freely.
27 Refit the hub/driveshaft nut locking cap, fit a new split pin and bend over the split pin legs to secure **(see illustration)**.
28 Refit the ABS wheel speed sensor and secure with the retaining bolt, tightened to the specified torque.
29 Refill the transmission with oil/fluid as described in the relevant Part of Chapter 7.
30 Refit the roadwheel, and lower the vehicle to the ground.
31 On completion, have the front wheel alignment checked at the earliest opportunity (see Chapter 10).

3 Driveshaft rubber gaiters – renewal

Inner CV joint gaiter

Note: *Before proceeding, obtain a suitable gaiter repair kit which should include grease, new gaiter securing clips, and new CV joint circlips.*

1 With the driveshaft removed as described in Section 2, proceed as follows.

2.27 Fit a new split pin to the hub/driveshaft retaining nut and bend over the legs to secure

3.6 Make alignment marks on the driveshaft, tripod and driveshaft joint outer member

3.7 Removing the tripod retaining circlip

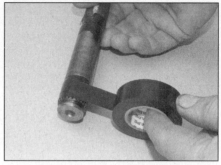

3.13 Tape over the driveshaft splines to prevent damage to the new gaiter

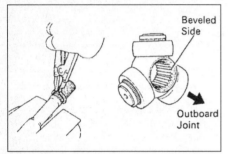

3.15 Fit a new circlip then fit the tripod with its bevelled side toward the outer (roadwheel) end of the driveshaft

3.16 Tap the tripod into position on the splines using a hammer and soft metal drift

2 Release the rubber gaiter inner and outer retaining clips by cutting through them using a junior hacksaw. Spread the clips and remove them from the gaiter.

3 Slide the gaiter back from the joint along the driveshaft.

4 Using quick-drying paint, make alignment marks on the driveshaft and the driveshaft joint outer member. **Do not** use a punch to make the marks.

5 Slide the joint outer member from the driveshaft.

6 Make alignment marks on the driveshaft tripod and the end of the driveshaft **(see illustration)**. Again, do not use a punch to make the marks.

7 Using a pair of circlip pliers, remove the circlip from the end of the driveshaft **(see illustration)**.

8 Similarly, release the circlip located behind the joint tripod, and slide it down the driveshaft, away from the tripod.

9 Using a hammer and a soft metal drift, tap the tripod from the end of the driveshaft.

10 Slide the circlip from the driveshaft.

11 Slide the gaiter from the driveshaft, complete with the securing clips.

12 Wipe away as much of the old grease as possible (do not use any solvent) to allow the joint components to be inspected. Examine the tripod, bearing rollers and outer member

for any signs of scoring or wear, and for smoothness of movement of the rollers on the tripod stems. If any of the components are found to be worn or damaged, it will be necessary to renew the complete joint assembly.

13 Wrap a little tape over the driveshaft splines to prevent damage to the new gaiter as it is fitted, then slide the new gaiter, complete with the securing clips onto the inner end of the driveshaft **(see illustration)**.

14 Remove the tape from the driveshaft splines.

15 Fit a new circlip to the driveshaft groove nearest the gaiter. Align the marks made on the joint tripod and the end of the driveshaft before removal. Note that the bevelled edge of the tripod hub must face towards the outer end of the driveshaft **(see illustration)**.

16 Tap the tripod into position on the splines using a hammer and soft metal drift **(see illustration)**. Tap on the tripod hub, **not** the rollers.

17 Fit a new circlip to secure the tripod **(see illustration)**.

18 Pack the joint outer member with the grease supplied in the repair kit **(see illustration)**. Use any surplus grease to pack the gaiter.

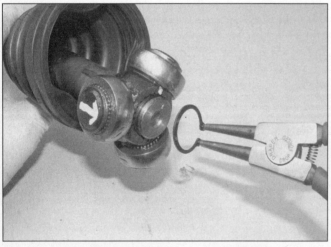

3.17 Fit a new circlip to secure the tripod

3.18 Pack the joint outer member with the grease supplied in the repair kit

3.20 Slide the clip in place and compress the raised portion using pincers or side-cutters

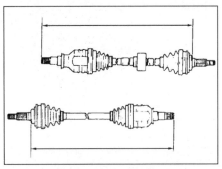

3.21a Measuring points for setting driveshaft standard length (models without an intermediate bearing)

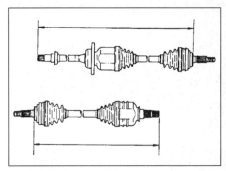

3.21b Measuring points for setting driveshaft standard length (models with an intermediate bearing)

19 Align the marks made on the joint outer member and the driveshaft before removal, then slide the outer member over the tripod.

20 Slide the gaiter over the joint outer member, and secure it using the larger clip **(see illustration)**.

21 Move the joints in or out slightly to set the driveshaft to the standard length setting dimension as given in the Specifications **(see illustrations)**. Ensure that the gaiter is located in its grooves and not stretched or contracted. Secure the smaller end to the driveshaft using the new clip.

Outer CV joint gaiter

Note: *Do not attempt to dismantle the driveshaft outer CV joints. Before proceeding, obtain a suitable gaiter repair kit which should include grease and new gaiter securing clips. New CV joint circlips and a new snap-ring (where applicable) will be required for the inner joint.*

22 Remove the inner joint gaiter as described previously in this Section.

23 If working on the right-hand driveshaft of a model fitted with a vibration damper, mark the position of the damper, then prise up the locking tab, and remove the metal clip securing the damper **(see illustration)**. Note which way round the damper is fitted to ensure correct refitting, then slide the damper from the end of the driveshaft.

24 Release the rubber gaiter inner and outer retaining clips by cutting through them using a junior hacksaw. Spread the clips and remove them from the gaiter.

25 Slide the gaiter along the driveshaft, and remove it from the inner end. **Do not** attempt to dismantle the outer driveshaft CV joint.

26 Using old rags, clean away as much of the old grease as possible from the outer CV joint. Do not use any solvents to clean the joint.

27 Move the inner splined driving member from side-to-side, to expose each ball in turn at the top of its track. Examine the balls for cracks, flat spots, or signs of surface pitting.

28 Inspect the ball tracks on the inner and outer members. If the tracks have widened, the balls will no longer be a tight fit. At the same time, check the ball cage windows for wear or cracking between the windows. If any of the constant velocity

joint components are found to be worn or damaged, it will be necessary to renew the complete driveshaft, as the outer joint is not supplied separately.

29 Fill the driveshaft joint with the new grease supplied in the repair kit. Save any surplus grease to push into the new gaiter.

30 Wind a little tape around the driveshaft inner CV joint splines to protect the gaiter as it is fitted.

31 Slide the new gaiter onto the inner end of the driveshaft, along with the securing clips, then slide it along the driveshaft.

32 Remove the tape from the driveshaft splines.

33 Secure the gaiter to the outer CV joint using the larger clip, then move the joints in or out slightly to set the driveshaft to the standard length **(see illustrations 3.21a and 3.21b)**. Ensure that the gaiter is located in its grooves and not stretched or contracted. Secure it to the driveshaft using the smaller clip.

34 Where applicable, refit the vibration damper, ensuring that it is fitted in its original position (align the marks made before removal). Secure the damper using a new clip.

35 Refit the inner joint gaiter as described previously in this Section.

4 Driveshaft overhaul – general information

1 If any of the checks described in Chapter 1 reveal wear in a driveshaft constant velocity joint, first check that the hub/driveshaft retaining nut is still correctly tightened with reference to the procedures contained in Section 2 relating to removal and refitting of the hub/driveshaft nut.

2 Road test the vehicle, and listen for a metallic clicking from the front as the vehicle is driven slowly in a circle on full-lock. If a clicking noise is heard, this indicates wear in the outer constant velocity joint.

3 If vibration, consistent with roadspeed, is felt through the vehicle when accelerating, there is a possibility of wear in the inner constant velocity joints.

4 Inner constant velocity joints can be

dismantled and inspected for wear as described in Section 3. Check on the availability of components before dismantling a joint. Outer joints are only supplied as an assembly complete with the relevant driveshaft.

5 Driveshaft intermediate bearing – renewal

Note 1: *An intermediate bearing is only fitted to 1.8 litre engine models post-August 2000 and all 2.0 litre engine models.*

Note 2: *A suitable press will be required for this operation. A new bearing securing snap-ring will be required on refitting.*

1 Remove the right-hand driveshaft as described in Section 2, then proceed as follows.

2 Remove the driveshaft inner CV joint outer member as described in Section 3.

3 Support the differential dust cover at the inner end of the driveshaft on a suitable metal plate, then press the end of the driveshaft from the dust cover.

4 Using a screwdriver at the outer end of the bearing housing, prise out the snap-ring securing the bearing in the bearing housing.

5 Support the bearing housing on a metal plate, then press the driveshaft from the bearing housing.

6 Similarly, support the bearing dust cover, and press the driveshaft from the dust cover.

7 Using circlip pliers, release the circlip

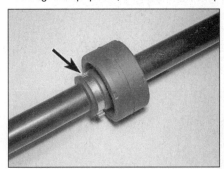

3.23 Right-hand driveshaft vibration damper and retaining clip (arrowed)

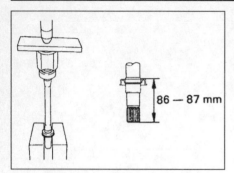

5.15 Dust cover fitting and setting (refer to the Specifications for the correct dimension according to model)

86 — 87 mm

securing the intermediate bearing to the driveshaft.

8 Support the bearing, and press the driveshaft from the bearing. Alternatively, it may be possible to use a long-reach bearing puller.

9 Thoroughly clean the bearing housing, and the contact faces of the driveshaft.

10 Using a press, with a suitable adapter to push on the outer bearing race, press the new bearing into the bearing housing.

11 Fit a new snap-ring to secure the bearing in the housing.

12 Support the bearing housing using a suitable tube or socket then, using a soft metal mandrel resting on the inner surface of

the driveshaft joint outer member, press the end of the driveshaft into the bearing.

13 Fit a new circlip to secure the assembly to the driveshaft.

14 Support the bearing dust cover, then press the end of the driveshaft into the dust cover, using the mandrel on the joint outer member, as described previously.

15 Similarly, press the driveshaft into the differential dust cover, to achieve the dimension given in the Specifications between the outer face of the dust cover and the end of the driveshaft splines **(see illustration)**.

16 Refit the driveshaft inner joint outer member as described in Section 3, then refit the driveshaft as described in Section 2.

Chapter 9
Braking system

Contents

Degrees of difficulty

Easy, suitable for novice with little experience 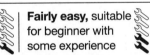 | **Fairly easy,** suitable for beginner with some experience | **Fairly difficult,** suitable for competent DIY mechanic | **Difficult,** suitable for experienced DIY mechanic | **Very difficult,** suitable for expert DIY or professional

Specifications

Front brakes
Type . . . . Ventilated disc, with single piston sliding calipers
Minimum disc thickness. . . . . 23.0 mm
Maximum disc run-out (disc fitted). . . . . 0.05 mm
Minimum brake pad thickness . . . . 2.0 mm

Rear drum brakes
Type . . . . Drum with leading and trailing shoes and automatic adjusters
Maximum drum diameter. . . . . 229.6 mm
Minimum brake lining thickness. . . . . 1.0 mm
Brake shoe-to-drum clearance . . . . 0.6 mm

Rear disc brakes
Type . . . . Solid disc with single piston sliding calipers
Minimum disc thickness. . . . . 9.0 mm
Maximum disc run-out (disc fitted). . . . . 0.15 mm
Minimum brake pad thickness. . . . . 1.0 mm

Handbrake (rear disc brake models)
Handbrake shoe minimum thickness. . . . . 1.0 mm

Brake pedal

Brake pedal height (from pedal pad to asphalt sheet):
  Pre-August 2000 models:
    Right-hand drive models .... 149.5 to 159.5 mm
    Left-hand drive models............................. 139.8 to 149.8 mm
  Post-August 2000 models:
    Right-hand drive models .... 149.5 to 159.5 mm
    Left-hand drive models............................. 147.0 to 157.0 mm
Brake pedal free play .... 1.0 to 6.0 mm
Brake pedal reserve travel (minimum):
  Pre-August 2000 models:
    Right-hand drive models .... 80.0 mm
    Left-hand drive models............................. 70.0 mm
  Post-August 2000 models:
    Right-hand drive models .... 75.0 mm
    Left-hand drive models............................. 55.0 mm

Torque wrench settings

	Nm	lbf ft
ABS hydraulic modulator to mounting bracket	13	10
ABS hydraulic modulator mounting bracket to body:		
Bolts..	19	14
Nuts	13	10
ABS wheel speed sensor bolts	8	6
Brake hose banjo union bolts..........................	30	22
Brake pipe union nuts	15	11
Front brake caliper:		
Anchor bracket to hub carrier.......................	94	69
Guide pin bolts..................................	34	25
Master cylinder to servo unit	25	18
Rear brake caliper:		
Anchor bracket bolts	47	35
Lower guide bolt.................................	20	15
Upper guide pin	27	20
Rear wheel cylinder to backplate.......................	13	10
Roadwheel nuts	103	76
Vacuum servo unit to bulkhead	13	10

1 General information

The braking system is of the dual-circuit hydraulic type, with servo assistance to the front disc brakes and rear drum/disc brakes. The dual-circuit hydraulic system is a safety feature – in the event of a malfunction somewhere in one of the hydraulic circuits, the other circuit continues to operate, providing at least some braking effort. Under normal circumstances, both brake circuits operate in unison, to provide efficient braking.

The front brakes are of the ventilated disc type on all models. The front brake calipers are of single piston sliding type mounted on the front hub carriers each side.

Rear drum brakes are fitted to pre-August 2000 models, while later models are equipped with rear disc brakes.

On drum brake models, each rear brake shoe assembly is operated by a twin-piston wheel cylinder. To take up the brake adjustment as the linings wear, each rear brake assembly incorporates an automatic adjuster mechanism.

The handbrake operates the rear brake shoes by means of a floor-mounted lever and two cables.

On models fitted with rear disc brakes, the brake calipers are of single piston sliding type, with handbrake operation by means of separate handbrake shoes operating within a drum-in-disc arrangement.

An anti-lock braking system is fitted as standard or optional equipment on all models, and has many of the components in common with the conventional braking system. Further details on ABS can be found later in this Chapter.

Note: *When servicing any part of the system, work carefully and methodically; also observe scrupulous cleanliness when overhauling any part of the hydraulic system. Always renew components (in axle sets, where applicable) if in doubt about their condition, and use only genuine Toyota parts, or at least those of known good quality. Note the warnings given in 'Safety first!' and at relevant points in this Chapter concerning the dangers of asbestos dust and hydraulic fluid.*

2 Hydraulic system – bleeding

⚠️ *Warning: Hydraulic fluid is poisonous; wash off immediately and thoroughly in the case of skin contact, and seek immediate medical advice if any fluid is swallowed or gets into the eyes. Certain types of hydraulic fluid are inflammable, and may ignite when allowed into contact with hot components; when servicing any hydraulic system, it is safest to assume that the fluid IS inflammable, and to take precautions against the risk of fire as though it is petrol that is being handled. Hydraulic fluid is also an effective paint stripper, and will attack plastics; if any is spilt, it should be washed off immediately, using copious quantities of clean water. Finally, it is hygroscopic (it absorbs moisture from the air). The more moisture is absorbed by the fluid, the lower its boiling point becomes, leading to a dangerous loss of braking under hard use. Old fluid may be contaminated and unfit for further use. When topping-up or renewing the fluid, always use the recommended type, and ensure that it comes from a freshly-opened sealed container.*

General

1 The correct functioning of the brake hydraulic system is only possible after removing all air from the components and circuit; this is achieved by bleeding the system.

2 During the bleeding procedure, add only

Braking system 9•3

clean, fresh hydraulic fluid of the specified type (see *Lubricants and fluids*); never re-use fluid that has already been bled from the system. Ensure that sufficient fluid is available before starting work.

3 If there is any possibility of incorrect fluid being used in the system, the brake lines and components must be completely flushed with uncontaminated fluid and new seals fitted to the components.

4 If brake fluid has been lost from the master cylinder due to a leak in the system, ensure that the cause is traced and rectified before proceeding further.

5 Park the car on level ground, switch off the ignition and select first gear (manual transmission) or Park (automatic transmission) then chock the wheels and release the handbrake.

6 Check that all pipes and hoses are secure, unions tight, and bleed screws closed. Remove the dust caps and clean any dirt from around the bleed screws.

7 Unscrew the master cylinder reservoir cap, and top up the reservoir to the MAX level line. Refit the cap loosely, and remember to maintain the fluid level at least above the MIN level line throughout the procedure, otherwise there is a risk of further air entering the system.

8 There is a number of one-man, do-it-yourself, brake bleeding kits currently available from motor accessory shops. It is recommended that one of these kits is used wherever possible, as they greatly simplify the bleeding operation, and also reduce the risk of expelled air and fluid being drawn back into the system. If such a kit is not available, the basic (two-man) method must be used, which is described in detail below.

9 If a kit is to be used, prepare the car as described previously, and follow the kit manufacturer's instructions, as the procedure may vary slightly according to the type being used; generally, they are as outlined below in the relevant sub-section.

10 Whichever method is used, the same sequence must be followed (paragraphs 11 and 12) to ensure the removal of all air from the system. Note that if the master cylinder has been disconnected or if the fluid reservoir has been emptied, the master cylinder should be bled first.

Bleeding sequence

11 If the hydraulic system has only been partially disconnected and suitable precautions were taken to minimise fluid loss, it should only be necessary to bleed that part of the system (ie, the primary or secondary circuit).

12 If the complete system is to be bled, then it should be done in the following sequence:
   a) *Master cylinder**.
   b) *Left-hand rear brake.*
   c) *Right-hand front brake.*
   d) *Right-hand rear brake.*
   e) *Left-hand front brake.*

* Only necessary if the master cylinder has been disconnected or if the fluid reservoir has been emptied.

Bleeding master cylinder

13 The master cylinder must be bled if it has been disconnected or if the fluid reservoir has been emptied.

14 Take adequate precautions to ensure that hydraulic fluid is not ejected with force from the master cylinder (which could cause damage or injury) during the following procedure.

15 Disconnect the hydraulic pipes from the master cylinder and place a container under it to catch the fluid that will be ejected. Use plenty of clean rags to prevent fluid spraying on to surrounding components. Ensure that the reservoir is topped-up with clean fluid of the specified type and engage the help of an assistant.

16 Have your assistant **slowly** depress the brake pedal and hold it down. Cover the master cylinder fluid outlets with your fingers and have your assistant slowly release the brake pedal so that fluid is drawn forcibly from the reservoir and into the cylinder body. Repeat this procedure three or four times to expel all air from the master cylinder, topping-up the reservoir as necessary throughout.

17 When the master cylinder is completely primed, have your assistant hold the pedal down, and, while it is held down, reconnect the hydraulic pipes to the master cylinder fluid outlets and tighten them securely.

18 Top-up the reservoir and continue bleeding the hydraulic circuits using the following procedures.

Bleeding system

Basic (two-man) method

19 Collect a clean glass jar of reasonable size and a suitable length of plastic or rubber tubing, which is a tight fit over the bleed screw, and a ring spanner to fit the screws. The help of an assistant will also be required.

20 If not already done, remove the dust cap from the bleed screw of the first wheel to be bled and fit the spanner and bleed tube to the screw. Place the other end of the tube in the jar, and pour in sufficient fluid to cover the end of the tube.

21 Ensure that the master cylinder reservoir fluid level is maintained at least above the MIN level line throughout the procedure.

22 Have the assistant fully depress the brake pedal several times to build-up pressure, then maintain it on the final downstroke.

23 While pedal pressure is maintained, unscrew the bleed screw (approximately one turn) and allow the compressed fluid and air to flow into the jar. The assistant should maintain pedal pressure, following it down to the floor if necessary, and should not release it until instructed to do so. When the flow stops, tighten the bleed screw again have the assistant release the pedal slowly, and recheck the reservoir fluid level.

2.28 One-way valve brake bleeding kit connected to a rear wheel cylinder bleed screw

24 Repeat the steps given in paragraphs 22 and 23) until the fluid emerging from the bleed screw is free from air bubbles.

25 When no more air bubbles appear, tighten the bleed screw securely, remove the tube and spanner and refit the dust cap. **Do not overtighten the bleed screw**.

26 Repeat these procedures on the remaining calipers in sequence until all air is removed from the system and the brake pedal feels firm again.

Using a one-way valve kit

27 As their name implies, these kits consist of a length of tubing with a one-way valve fitted, to prevent expelled air and fluid being drawn back into the system; some kits include a translucent container, which can be positioned so that the air bubbles can be more easily seen flowing from the end of the tube.

28 The kit is connected to the bleed screw, which is then opened **(see illustration)**. The user returns to the driver's seat, depresses the brake pedal with a smooth steady stroke, and slowly releases it; this is repeated until the expelled fluid is clear of air bubbles.

29 Note that these kits simplify work so much that it is easy to forget the master cylinder fluid level; ensure that this is maintained at least above the MIN level line at all times.

Using a pressure-bleeding kit

30 These kits are usually operated by the reserve of pressurised air contained in the spare tyre. However, note that it will probably be necessary to reduce the pressure to a lower level than normal; refer to the instructions supplied with the kit.

31 By connecting a pressurised, fluid-filled container to the master cylinder reservoir, bleeding is then carried out by simply opening each bleed screw in turn (in the specified sequence) and allowing the fluid to run out, until no more air bubbles can be seen in the expelled fluid.

32 This method has the advantage that the large reservoir of fluid provides an additional safeguard against air being drawn into the system during bleeding.

33 Pressure bleeding is particularly effective when bleeding difficult systems, or when bleeding the complete system at the time of routine fluid renewal.

All methods

34 When bleeding is complete, and firm pedal feel is restored, wash off any spilt fluid, tighten the bleed screws securely, and refit their dust caps.
35 Check the hydraulic fluid level in the master cylinder reservoir and top-up if necessary.
36 Discard any hydraulic fluid that has been bled from the system; it will not be fit for re-use.
37 Check the feel of the brake pedal. If it feels at all spongy, air must still be present in the system, and further bleeding is required. Failure to bleed satisfactorily after a reasonable repetition of the bleeding operations may be due to worn master cylinder seals.

3 Hydraulic pipes and hoses – renewal

Note: *Before starting work, refer to the warning at the beginning of Section 2 concerning the dangers of hydraulic fluid.*
1 If any pipe or hose is to be renewed, minimise hydraulic fluid loss by removing the master cylinder reservoir cap, placing a piece of plastic film over the reservoir and sealing it with an elastic band. Alternatively, flexible hoses can be sealed, if required, using a proprietary brake hose clamp; metal brake pipe unions can be plugged (if care is taken not to allow dirt into the system) or capped immediately they are disconnected. Place a wad of rag under any union that is to be disconnected, to catch any spilt fluid.

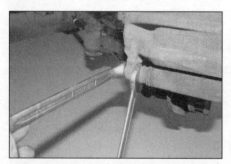
4.3a Unscrew the caliper lower guide pin bolt while counterholding the guide pin with a second spanner

4.3c . . . and swing the caliper upwards to allow access to the brake pads

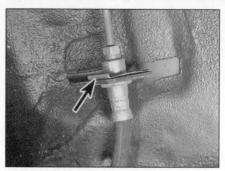
3.2a Brake flexible hose spring clip attachment (arrowed) . . .

2 If a flexible hose is to be disconnected, unscrew the brake pipe union nut before removing the spring clip or undoing the hose support bracket retaining bolts which secure the hose to its mounting **(see illustrations)**.
3 To unscrew the union nuts, it is preferable to obtain a brake pipe spanner of the correct size; these are available from most large motor accessory shops. Failing this, a close-fitting open-ended spanner will be required, though if the nuts are tight or corroded, their flats may be rounded-off if the spanner slips. In such a case, a self-locking wrench is often the only way to unscrew a stubborn union, but it follows that the pipe and the damaged nuts must be renewed on reassembly. Always clean a union and surrounding area before disconnecting it. If disconnecting a component with more than one union, make a careful note of the connections before disturbing any of them.
4 If a brake pipe is to be renewed, it can be

4.3b Remove the guide pin bolt . . .

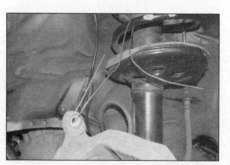
4.3d Tie the caliper up in the raised position using a length of wire or string from the coil spring

3.2b . . . and hose support bracket attachment bolt (arrowed)

obtained, cut to length and with the union nuts and end flares in place from Toyota dealers. All that is then necessary is to bend it to shape, following the line of the original, before fitting it to the car. Alternatively, most motor accessory shops can make up brake pipes from kits, but this requires very careful measurement of the original, to ensure that the new one is of the correct length. The safest answer is usually to take the original to the shop as a pattern.
5 Before refitting, blow through the new pipe or hose with dry compressed air. Do not overtighten the union nuts. It is not necessary to exercise brute force to obtain a sound joint.
6 If flexible rubber hoses are renewed, ensure that the pipes and hoses are correctly routed, with no kinks or twists, and that they are secured in the clips or brackets provided.
7 After fitting, bleed the hydraulic system as described in Section 2, wash off any spilt fluid, and check carefully for fluid leaks.

4 Front brake pads – renewal

⚠ *Warning: Disc brake pads must be renewed on both front wheels at the same time – never renew the pads on only one wheel as uneven braking may result. Dust created by wear of the pads may contain asbestos, which is a health hazard. Never blow it out with compressed air and do not inhale any of it. DO NOT use petroleum-based solvents to clean brake parts. Use brake cleaner or methylated spirit only. DO NOT allow any brake fluid, oil or grease to contact the brake pads or disc. Also refer to the warning at the start of Section 2 concerning the dangers of hydraulic fluid.*
1 Firmly apply the handbrake, then jack up the front of the car and support it securely on axle stands (see *Jacking and vehicle support*).
2 Push in the caliper piston by sliding the caliper body towards the outside of the vehicle by hand.
3 Follow the accompanying photos **(illustrations 4.3a to 4.3m)** for the actual pad renewal procedure, bearing in mind the additional points listed below. Be sure to stay in order and read the caption under

4.3e Withdraw the outer brake pad and shims . . .

4.3f . . . and inner brake pad and shims, from the anchor bracket . . .

4.3g . . . then remove the two anti-squeal shims from each brake pad

4.3h Remove the four brake pad support plates from their locations in the anchor bracket

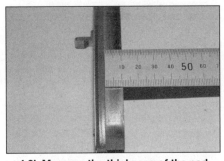

4.3i Measure the thickness of the pad friction material. If any are worn down to the specified minimum, or fouled with oil or grease, all four pads must be renewed

4.3j Check the caliper guide pins slide easily and the rubber gaiters are not damaged

each illustration. Note that if the old pads are to be refitted, ensure that they are identified so that they can be returned to their original positions.

4 With the old pads removed, brush the dust and dirt from the caliper, piston and disc.

⚠ *Warning: Take great care not to inhale the dust as it is injurious to health.*

5 Inspect the dust cover around the piston for damage and for evidence of fluid leaks, which if found will necessitate caliper overhaul as described in Section 5. Inspect the disc for signs of cracks, scoring or severe abrasions with reference to Section 6.

6 If new brake pads are to be fitted, the caliper piston must be pushed back into the cylinder to allow for the extra pad thickness. Either use a G-clamp or similar tool, or use suitable pieces of wood as levers. Clamp off

the flexible brake hose leading to the caliper then connect a brake bleeding kit to the caliper bleed screw. Open the bleed screw as the piston is retracted, the surplus brake fluid will then be collected in the bleed kit vessel **(see illustration 4.3k)**. Close the bleed screw just before the caliper piston is pushed fully into the caliper. This should ensure no air enters the hydraulic system. **Note:** *The ABS unit contains hydraulic components that are very sensitive to impurities in the brake fluid. Even the smallest particles can cause the system to fail through blockage. The pad retraction method described here prevents any debris in the brake fluid expelled from the caliper from being passed back to the ABS hydraulic unit, as well as preventing any chance of damage to the master cylinder seals.*

7 Repeat the above procedure on the opposite front brake.

8 Before lowering the vehicle, check the that the fluid level in the brake master cylinder reservoir is up to the Maximum level mark, and top-up with the specified fluid type if required (see *Weekly checks*). Depress the brake pedal a few times to position the pads against the disc, then recheck the fluid level in the reservoir and further top-up the fluid level if necessary.

9 Refit the roadwheels, then lower the vehicle to the ground. Tighten the roadwheel retaining nuts to the specified torque.

Caution: New pads will not give full braking efficiency until they have bedded-in. Be prepared for this, and avoid hard braking as far as possible for the first hundred miles or so after pad renewal.

4.3k If new pads have been fitted, before refitting the caliper, push back the caliper piston whilst opening the bleed screw

4.3l Remove the pad wear indicator (arrowed) off the old inner brake pad and transfer it to the new inner pad

4.3m Fit the pad support plates, and the inner and outer pads together with their shims. Lower the caliper into position and secure with the guide pin bolt tightened to the specified torque

5.4 Unscrew the brake hose-to-caliper banjo union bolt (arrowed), and recover the copper sealing washers

5.7a Unscrew the two anchor bracket mounting bolts . . .

5.7b . . . and withdraw the anchor bracket from the hub carrier

5 Front brake caliper –
removal, overhaul and refitting

Note: *Before starting work, refer to the warning at the beginning of Section 2 concerning the dangers of hydraulic fluid, and to the warning at the beginning of Section 4 concerning the dangers of asbestos dust.*

Removal

1 Firmly apply the handbrake, then jack up the front of the car and support it securely on axle stands (see *Jacking and vehicle support*). Remove the relevant front roadwheel.

2 Push in the caliper piston slightly by sliding the caliper body towards the outside of the vehicle by hand.

3 To minimise fluid loss, unscrew the master cylinder reservoir filler cap and place a piece of polythene over the filler neck. Secure the polythene with an elastic band ensuring that an airtight seal is obtained. Alternatively, use a brake hose clamp, a G-clamp, or a similar tool with protected jaws, to clamp the front flexible hydraulic hose.

4 Unscrew the brake hose-to-caliper banjo union bolt, then recover the copper sealing washers **(see illustration)**. Note that new washers will be needed for refitting. Cover or plug the open hydraulic unions to keep them clean.

5 Unscrew the caliper upper and lower guide pin bolts using a ring spanner while counter-holding the guide pins with an open-ended spanner **(see illustrations 4.3a and 4.3b)**. Remove the guide pin bolts and lift the caliper off the brake pads and anchor bracket.

6 To remove the caliper anchor bracket, first remove the brake pads with reference to Section 4. If they are likely to be re-used, mark them for identification (inner and outer, right- or left-hand as applicable) to ensure that they are installed in their original locations when refitting.

7 Unscrew the two anchor bracket mounting bolts, and withdraw the anchor bracket from the hub carrier **(see illustrations)**.

Overhaul

8 With the caliper removed, clean it externally with methylated spirit and a soft brush.

9 Remove the bleed screw and empty any remaining hydraulic fluid out of the caliper.

10 Remove the piston dust boot and pull the piston out of the caliper bore. If the piston is reluctant to move, apply **low** air pressure (eg, from a foot pump) to the fluid inlet, but note that the piston may be ejected with some force.

11 Hook out the piston seal from the bore using a blunt instrument.

12 Withdraw the two guide pins from the anchor bracket then remove the guide pin dust boots by tapping them off using a screwdriver and small hammer.

13 Clean the piston and caliper bore with a lint-free rag and some clean brake fluid or methylated spirit. Slight imperfections may be polished out with steel wool. If any pitting, scoring or wear ridges are evident, the caliper must be renewed.

14 Renew all rubber components (seals and dust boots) as a matter of course. Blow through the fluid inlet and bleed screw hole with compressed air.

15 Fit the new guide pin dust boots to the anchor bracket by tapping them into place using a hammer and suitable socket bit. Lubricate the guide pins sparingly with high-melting-point brake grease and insert them through the dust boots into the anchor bracket. Note that the pin with the guide bush locates in the bottom hole.

16 Lubricate the new piston seal with clean brake fluid. Insert the seal into the groove in the bore, using your fingers only.

17 Lubricate the piston and bore with clean brake fluid, then install the piston in the caliper.

6.4 Check the brake disc run-out using a dial test indicator

18 Fit a new dust boot to the piston and caliper, seating it correctly in its groove.

19 Refit the caliper bleed screw.

Refitting

20 If removed, refit the caliper anchor bracket and tighten the bolts to the specified torque.

21 Refit the brake pads to the anchor bracket with reference to Section 4.

22 Place the caliper over the brake pads and screw in the guide pin bolts. Hold the guide pins with a spanner and tighten the guide pin bolts to the specified torque.

23 Reconnect the flexible hydraulic hose banjo union using new copper washers and ensuring that the hose is not kinked. Tighten the union bolt to the specified torque.

24 Remove the brake hose clamp or polythene, where fitted, and bleed the hydraulic system as described in Section 2.

25 Apply the footbrake two or three times to settle the pads then refit the roadwheel and lower the car. Tighten the wheel nuts to the specified torque.

6 Front brake disc –
inspection, removal and refitting

Note: *Before starting work, refer to the warning at the beginning of Section 4 concerning the dangers of asbestos dust.*

Inspection

Note: *If either disc requires renewal, BOTH should be renewed at the same time, to ensure even and consistent braking. New brake pads should also be fitted.*

1 Remove the front brake pads as described in Section 4.

2 With the brake pads removed, temporarily secure the disc to the wheel hub using three wheel nuts with suitable packing washers.

3 Inspect the disc friction surfaces for cracks or deep scoring (light grooving is normal and may be ignored). A cracked disc must be renewed; a scored disc can be reclaimed by machining, provided that the thickness is not reduced below the specified minimum.

4 Check the disc run-out using a dial test indicator with its probe positioned 10.0 mm from the outer edge of the disc **(see illustration)**. If

6.5 Using a micrometer to measure the disc thickness

the run-out exceeds the figures given in the Specifications, check the axial play of the hub bearings as described in Chapter 10. If the hub bearings are satisfactory, reposition the disc on the wheel hub, one fifth of a turn from its original position. Secure with three wheel nuts and repeat the run-out check. Continue repositioning the disc, one fifth of a turn at a time, checking the run-out in each position. If the run-out is still excessive after all disc positions have been tried, machining may be possible, otherwise disc renewal will be necessary.

 If a dial test indicator is not available, check the run-out by positioning a fixed pointer near the outer edge, in contact with the disc face. Rotate the disc and measure the maximum displacement of the pointer with feeler blades.

5 Excessive disc thickness variation can also cause judder. Check this using a micrometer **(see illustration)**. If the thickness variation exceeds the figures given in the Specifications, machining may be possible, otherwise disc renewal will be necessary.

Removal

6 If not already done, firmly apply the handbrake, then jack up the front of the car and support it securely on axle stands (see *Jacking and vehicle support*).

7 If the brake pads have not been removed, push in the caliper piston slightly by sliding the caliper body towards the outside of the vehicle by hand.

8 Undo the two bolts securing the brake caliper anchor bracket to the hub carrier. Withdraw the caliper and anchor bracket, complete with brake pads and suspend the caliper from the front suspension coil spring using string or wire, but take care not to stretch or kink the flexible brake hydraulic hose.

9 Check whether the position of the disc in relation to the hub is marked, and if not, make your own mark as an aid to refitting. Where applicable, remove the wheel nuts temporarily fitted to hold the disc during the inspection procedure, and lift off the disc **(see illustration)**.

Refitting

10 Ensure that the hub and disc mating faces are spotlessly clean. Clean rustproofing compound off a new disc with methylated spirit and a rag.
11 Locate the disc on the hub with the orientation marks made on removal aligned (where applicable).
12 Refit the brake caliper and anchor bracket and tighten the bolts to the specified torque.
13 Apply the footbrake two or three times to settle the pads then refit the roadwheel and lower the car. Tighten the wheel nuts to the specified torque.

---

7 Rear brake drum – removal, inspection and refitting

Note: *Before starting work, refer to the warning at the beginning of Section 8 concerning the dangers of asbestos dust.*

Removal

1 Chock the front wheels then jack up the rear of the car and support it on axle stands (see *Jacking and vehicle support*). Remove the appropriate rear roadwheel, and release the handbrake.
2 It should now be possible to slide the drum off the rear hub and brake shoes. If the drum is tight on the hub or wheel studs due to corrosion, insert two suitable screws or bolts into the threaded holes on the drum face. Tighten the bolts evenly, a little at a time until the drum releases **(see illustration)**. If the brake drum is stuck on the brake shoes due to a severe internal wear ridge, first check that the handbrake is fully released, then proceed as follows.
3 Remove the centre console as described in Chapter 11. Slacken the locknut, then back off the handbrake cable adjusting nut so the cable is slack **(see illustration 19.4)**.
4 Remove the rubber access plug from the rear of the brake backplate, behind the trailing brake shoe.
5 Cut a length of stiff wire (welding rod or similar, approximately 2 mm diameter) to a length of approximately 60 mm, and bend the last 10 mm of one end through 90° to make a hooked tool.
6 Insert the bent end of the wire through the access hole in the backplate, and hook it over the handbrake lever on the trailing brake shoe. Pull the wire to lift the handbrake lever away from the shoe, allowing the stop-peg on the lever to pass behind the shoe. This will enable the brake shoes to retract further, providing sufficient clearance for the brake drum to be removed. Withdraw the drum and refit the rubber plug to the access hole.
7 With the brake drum removed, brush or wipe the dust from the drum, brake shoes, wheel cylinder and backplate.

 Warning: Take great care not to inhale the dust as it is injurious to health.

6.9 Front brake disc removal

Inspection

Note: *If a brake drum requires renewal, BOTH rear drums should be renewed at the same time to ensure even and consistent braking. New brake shoes should also be fitted.*
8 Examine the internal surface of the brake drum for signs of scoring, cracks or a severe wear ridge. If any deterioration of the friction surface is evident, it may be possible to reclaim it by machining provided that the drum diameter does not exceed the specified maximum. If any cracks are apparent, the drum must be renewed.

Refitting

9 If a new brake drum is to be installed, use a suitable solvent to remove any preservative coating that may have been applied to its interior. Note that it may also be necessary to shorten the adjuster strut length, by rotating the strut wheel, to allow the drum to pass over the brake shoes.
10 Ensure that the handbrake lever stop-peg is correctly repositioned against the edge of the brake shoe web, then locate the brake drum on the stub axle.
11 Depress the footbrake repeatedly to operate the self-adjusting mechanism. Whilst depressing the pedal, have an assistant listen to the rear drums, to check that the adjuster strut is functioning correctly; if so, a clicking sound will be emitted by the strut as the pedal is depressed.
12 Repeat the above procedure on the remaining rear brake assembly (where necessary), then check and, if necessary, adjust the handbrake as described in Section 19.

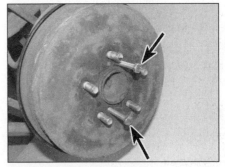

7.2 If the rear drum is tight on the hub, use two bolts (arrowed) to help release it

13 On completion, refit the roadwheel(s), then lower the vehicle to the ground and tighten the wheel nuts to the specified torque.

14 Where applicable, refit the centre console as described in Chapter 11.

8 Rear brake shoes – renewal

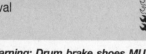

⚠ **Warning: Drum brake shoes MUST be renewed on both rear wheels at the same time – NEVER renew the shoes on only one wheel, as uneven braking may result. Also, the dust created by wear of the shoes may contain asbestos, which is a health hazard. Never blow it out with compressed air, and don't inhale any of it. An approved filtering mask should be worn when working on the brakes. DO NOT use petroleum-based solvents to clean brake parts – use brake cleaner or methylated spirit only.**

1 Remove the rear brake drum as described in Section 7.

2 Working carefully, and taking the necessary precautions, remove all traces of brake dust from the brake drum, backplate and shoes.

3 Measure the thickness of the friction material of each brake shoe at several points; if either shoe is worn at any point to the specified minimum thickness or less, all four shoes must be renewed as a set. The shoes should also

8.6a Remove the shoe hold-down springs and pins by depressing the spring and sliding it off the pin while holding the pin from behind. Remove the pins from the rear of the backplate

be renewed if any are fouled with oil or grease; there is no satisfactory way of degreasing friction material, once contaminated.

4 If any of the brake shoes are worn unevenly, or fouled with oil or grease, trace and rectify the cause before reassembly.

5 Note the location and orientation of all components before disassembly as an aid to reassembly.

6 Follow the accompanying photos (illustrations 8.6a to 8.6t) for the actual brake shoe renewal procedure, bearing in mind the additional points listed below. Be sure to stay in order and read the caption under each illustration.

7 With the brake shoes removed, clean the adjuster mechanism and its associated

8.6b Ease the trailing brake shoe from the bottom anchor, and disconnect the lower return spring from both shoes

components, then lay all the parts out and check them thoroughly for signs of wear and loss of tension or distortion of any of the springs.

8 Once the brake shoes have been refitted, turn the strut adjuster wheel, using a screwdriver, to expand the shoes until the brake drum just slides over the shoes.

9 Refit the brake drum as described in Section 7.

10 Repeat the above procedure on the remaining rear brake.

Caution: New brake shoes will not give full braking efficiency until they have bedded-in. Be prepared for this, and avoid hard braking as far as possible for the first hundred miles or so after shoe renewal.

8.6c Move the bottom ends of the brake shoes towards each other, then disconnect the tops of the shoes from the wheel cylinder. Manoeuvre the shoe assembly over the hub

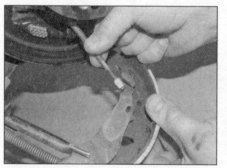

8.6d Turn the shoe assembly over, force back the spring, and disengage the handbrake cable from the brake lever

8.6e Fit a strong elastic band around the wheel cylinder pistons to retain them

8.6f With the assembly on the bench remove the upper return spring, adjuster lever and spring and the adjuster strut

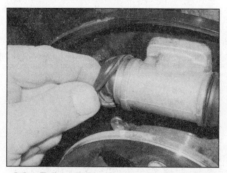

8.6g Before fitting the new brake shoes, peel back the wheel cylinder rubber boots to check for leaks

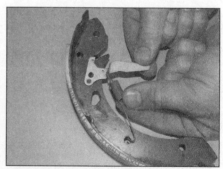

8.6h Place the adjuster lever over the pin on the leading shoe and reconnect the spring

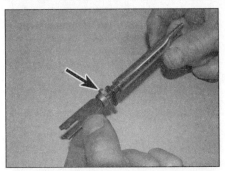

8.6i Rotate the adjuster wheel (arrowed) to set the adjuster strut at its shortest possible length

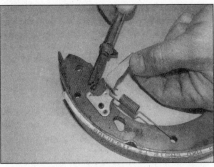

8.6j Engage the adjuster strut with the slot on the leading shoe web and with the adjuster lever

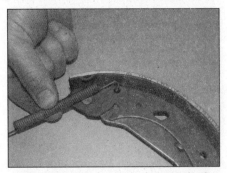

8.6k Fit the upper return spring to both brake shoes . . .

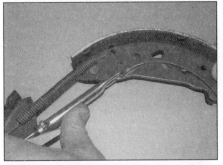

8.6l . . . then engage the other end of the adjuster strut with the slot in the trailing shoe

8.6m Move the lower ends of the shoes together . . .

8.6n . . . and fit the lower return spring

8.6o Check that the adjuster strut, adjuster lever and all the springs are correctly fitted and engaged

8.6p Apply a little high-melting-point grease to the shoe contact points on the backplate (arrowed), the lower anchor, and the wheel cylinder pistons

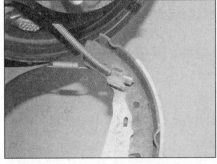

8.6q Turn the brake shoe assembly over and connect the handbrake cable to the brake lever

8.6r Manoeuvre the brake shoe assembly over the hub and engage the upper ends of the shoes with the wheel cylinder pistons. Cut off the elastic band used to retain the wheel cylinder pistons

8.6s Engage the leading shoe with the bottom anchor (arrowed), then pull the trailing shoe out and engage it with the bottom anchor too

8.6t Insert the hold-down spring pins from the rear of the backplate, then depress the hold-down springs and slide them under the ends of the pins

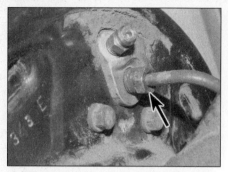

9.3 Unscrew the brake pipe union nut (arrowed) at the rear of the wheel cylinder

9.4 Unscrew the two retaining bolts and withdraw the wheel cylinder from the backplate

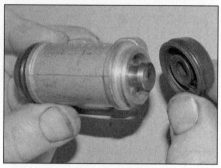

9.5 Pull the rubber boots from each end of the wheel cylinder

9 Rear wheel cylinder – removal, overhaul and refitting

Note: *Before starting work, refer to the warning at the beginning of Section 2 concerning the dangers of hydraulic fluid.*

Removal

1 Remove the rear brake drum as described in Section 7.
2 Using a brake hose clamp or self-locking wrench with protected jaws, clamp the flexible brake hose near its support bracket on the underbody. This will minimise brake fluid loss during subsequent operations.
3 Wipe away all traces of dirt around the brake pipe union at the rear of the wheel cylinder, then unscrew the union nut **(see illustration)**.
4 Unscrew the two retaining bolts and withdraw the wheel cylinder from the backplate **(see illustration)**. Plug the brake pipe, to prevent the possible ingress of dirt and to minimise further fluid loss whilst the cylinder is detached from it.

Overhaul

5 Clean the external surfaces of the cylinder, then pull free the rubber boots from each end of the cylinder **(see illustration)**.
6 The pistons and spring will probably shake out; if not, use a foot pump to apply air pressure through the hydraulic union and eject them.
7 Remove the cup seals from the pistons then clean the pistons and the cylinder by washing in fresh brake fluid or methylated spirits (not petrol, paraffin or any other mineral-based fluid). Examine the surfaces of the pistons and the cylinder bores. Look for any signs of rust, scoring or metal-to-metal rubbing which, if

evident, will necessitate renewal of the wheel cylinder.
8 Lubricate the piston seals with clean brake fluid, then fit them to the pistons **(see illustrations)**.
9 Smear a little clean brake fluid onto the cylinder bore, pistons and seals, then insert the spring, followed by the pistons, into the cylinder bore **(see illustrations)**. Ease the piston seals into the bore using a thumbnail, or blunt plastic tool.
10 Fit the rubber boots, and check the pistons can move freely in their bores.

Refitting

11 Wipe clean the backplate, and remove the plug from the end of the hydraulic pipe. Place the wheel cylinder in position and engage the pipe union. Screw the union nut in by a few turns to ensure that the threads engage.
12 Refit the two retaining bolts and tighten to the specified torque.
13 Tighten the brake pipe union nut securely.
14 Refit the brake drum as described in Section 7.
15 Remove the clamp from the flexible brake hose then bleed the brake hydraulic system as described in Section 2. Providing suitable precautions were taken to minimise loss of fluid, it should only be necessary to bleed the relevant rear brake.

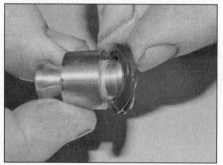

9.8a Manoeuvre the seal . . .

9.8b . . . onto the piston

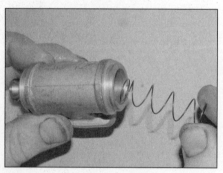

9.9a Fit the spring . . .

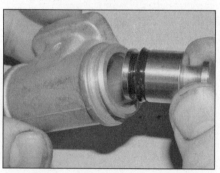

9.9b . . . followed by the piston

10 Rear brake pads – renewal

Warning: Disc brake pads must be renewed on both rear wheels at the same time – never renew the pads on only one wheel as uneven braking may result. Dust created by wear of the pads may contain asbestos, which is a health hazard. Never blow it out with compressed air and do not inhale any of it. DO NOT use petroleum-based solvents to clean brake parts. Use brake cleaner or methylated spirit only. DO NOT allow any brake fluid, oil or grease to contact the brake pads or disc. Also refer to the warning at the start of Section 2 concerning the dangers of hydraulic fluid.

1 Chock the front wheels then jack up the rear

10.3a Unscrew the brake caliper lower guide bolt and remove the bolt from the caliper

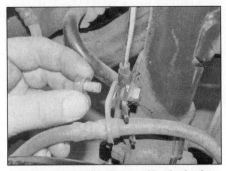

10.3b Undo the bolt securing the brake hydraulic hose support bracket to the rear suspension strut

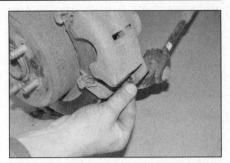

10.3c Swing the caliper upwards to allow access to the brake pads, and tie the caliper in the raised position using a length of wire or string from the coil spring

10.3d Withdraw the outer brake pad and shims . . .

10.3e . . . and inner brake pad and shims, from the anchor bracket . . .

10.3f . . . then remove the two anti-squeal shims from each brake pad

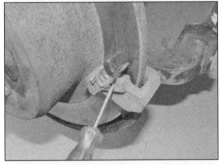

10.3g Remove the four brake pad support plates from their locations in the anchor bracket

of the car and support it on axle stands (see *Jacking and vehicle support*). Remove the rear roadwheels.

2 Push in the caliper piston by sliding the caliper body towards the outside of the vehicle by hand.

3 Follow the accompanying photos **(illustrations 10.3a to 10.3i)** for the actual pad renewal procedure, bearing in mind the additional points listed below. Be sure to stay in order and read the caption under each illustration. Note that if the old pads are to be refitted, ensure that they are identified so that they can be returned to their original positions.

4 With the old pads removed, brush the dust and dirt from the caliper, piston and disc.

 Warning: Take great care not to inhale the dust as it is injurious to health.

10.3h Measure the thickness of the pad friction material. If any are worn down to the specified minimum, or fouled with oil or grease, all four pads must be renewed

5 Inspect the dust cover around the piston for damage and for evidence of fluid leaks, which if found will necessitate caliper overhaul as described in Section 11. Inspect the disc for signs of cracks, scoring or severe abrasions with reference to Section 12.

6 If new brake pads are to be fitted, the caliper piston must be pushed back into the cylinder to allow for the extra pad thickness. Either use a G-clamp or similar tool, or use suitable pieces of wood as levers. Clamp off the flexible brake hose leading to the caliper then connect a brake bleeding kit to the caliper bleed screw. Open the bleed screw as the piston is retracted, the surplus brake fluid will then be collected in the bleed kit vessel **(see illustration 4.3k)**. Close the bleed screw just before the caliper piston is pushed fully into the caliper. This should ensure no air enters the hydraulic system. **Note:** *The ABS unit*

10.3i Fit the pad support plates, and the inner and outer pads together with their shims. Lower the caliper into position and secure with the guide bolt tightened to the specified torque. Refit the brake hydraulic hose support bracket to the rear suspension strut

contains hydraulic components that are very sensitive to impurities in the brake fluid. Even the smallest particles can cause the system to fail through blockage. The pad retraction method described here prevents any debris in the brake fluid expelled from the caliper from being passed back to the ABS hydraulic unit, as well as preventing any chance of damage to the master cylinder seals.

7 Repeat the above procedure on the opposite rear brake.

8 Before lowering the vehicle, check the that the fluid level in the brake master cylinder reservoir is up to the Maximum level mark, and top-up with the specified fluid type if required (see *Weekly checks*). Depress the

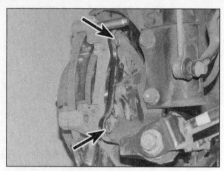

11.7 Rear brake caliper anchor bracket mounting bolts (arrowed)

brake pedal a few times to position the pads against the disc, then recheck the fluid level in the reservoir and further top-up the fluid level if necessary.

9 Refit the roadwheels, then lower the vehicle to the ground. Tighten the roadwheel retaining nuts to the specified torque.

Caution: New pads will not give full braking efficiency until they have bedded-in. Be prepared for this, and avoid hard braking as far as possible for the first hundred miles or so after pad renewal.

11 Rear brake caliper –
removal, overhaul and refitting

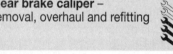

Note: *Before starting work, refer to the warning at the beginning of Section 2 concerning the dangers of hydraulic fluid, and to the warning at the beginning of Section 10 concerning the dangers of asbestos dust.*

Removal

1 Chock the front wheels then jack up the rear of the car and support it on axle stands (see *Jacking and vehicle support*). Remove the relevant rear roadwheel.

2 Push in the caliper piston slightly by sliding the caliper body towards the outside of the vehicle by hand.

3 To minimise fluid loss, unscrew the master cylinder reservoir filler cap and place a piece of polythene over the filler neck. Secure the polythene with an elastic band ensuring that an airtight seal is obtained. Alternatively, use a

12.5a Remove the access plug from the disc . . .

brake hose clamp, a G-clamp, or a similar tool with protected jaws, to clamp the front flexible hydraulic hose.

4 Unscrew the brake hose-to-caliper banjo union bolt, and recover the copper sealing washers. Note that new washers will be needed for refitting. Cover or plug the open hydraulic unions to keep them clean.

5 Unscrew the caliper lower guide bolt **(see illustration 10.3a)**, swing the caliper upwards clear of the brake pads, then slide it off the upper guide pin.

6 To remove the caliper anchor bracket, first remove the brake pads with reference to Section 10. If they are likely to be re-used, mark them for identification (inner and outer, right- or left-hand, as applicable) to ensure that they are installed in their original locations when refitting.

7 Unscrew the two anchor bracket mounting bolts, and withdraw the anchor bracket from the rear axle carrier **(see illustration)**.

Overhaul

8 This is essentially the same procedure as that described for the front caliper (see Section 5) except that the guide pin dust boots and bushings are a simple push-fit in their caliper locations.

Refitting

9 If removed, refit the caliper anchor bracket and tighten the bolts to the specified torque.

10 Refit the brake pads to the anchor bracket with reference to Section 10.

11 Engage the caliper with the upper guide pin, lower it down over the brake pads and screw in the lower guide bolt. Tighten the guide bolt to the specified torque.

12 Reconnect the flexible hydraulic hose banjo union using new copper washers and ensuring that the hose is not kinked. Tighten the union bolt to the specified torque. Refit and tighten the bolt securing the brake hydraulic hose support bracket to the rear suspension strut.

13 Remove the brake hose clamp or polythene, where fitted, and bleed the hydraulic system as described in Section 2.

14 Apply the footbrake two or three times to settle the pads then refit the roadwheel and lower the car. Tighten the wheel nuts to the specified torque.

12.5b . . . and insert a screwdriver through the hole to turn the handbrake shoe adjuster wheel

12 Rear brake disc –
inspection, removal and refitting

Note: *Before starting work, refer to the warning at the beginning of Section 10 concerning the dangers of asbestos dust.*

Inspection

Note: *If either disc requires renewal, BOTH should be renewed at the same time, to ensure even and consistent braking. New brake pads should also be fitted.*

1 With the rear brake pads removed (Section 10), the inspection procedures are the same as for the front brake disc, and reference should be made to Section 6, paragraphs 2 to 5 inclusive. Additionally, after removal, check the condition of the handbrake drums. The drums are unlikely to wear unless the handbrake is habitually used to stop the car.

Removal

2 If not already done, chock the front wheels then jack up the rear of the car and support it on axle stands (see *Jacking and vehicle support*). Remove the relevant roadwheel and release the handbrake.

3 If the brake pads have not been removed, push in the caliper piston slightly by sliding the caliper body towards the outside of the vehicle by hand.

4 Undo the two bolts securing the brake caliper anchor bracket to the rear axle carrier **(see illustration 11.7)**. Withdraw the caliper and anchor bracket, complete with brake pads, and suspend the caliper from the rear suspension coil spring using string or wire, but take care not to stretch or kink the flexible brake hydraulic hose. If necessary, undo the bolt securing the brake hydraulic hose support bracket to the rear suspension strut.

5 Check whether the position of the disc in relation to the hub is marked, and if not, make your own mark as an aid to refitting. Where applicable, remove the wheel nuts, temporarily fitted to hold the disc during the inspection procedure, and lift off the disc. If the disc is tight due to it binding on the handbrake shoes, remove the access plug from the disc and turn the disc so that the access hole is at the bottom. Insert a screwdriver through the hole and turn the handbrake shoe adjuster wheel to back off the shoe adjustment **(see illustrations)**.

6 Insert two suitable bolts into the threaded holes on the disc face. Tighten the bolts evenly, a little at a time until the disc releases **(see illustration)**.

Refitting

7 Ensure that the hub and disc mating faces are spotlessly clean. Clean rustproofing compound off a new disc with methylated spirit and a rag.

8 Locate the disc on the hub with the

12.6 Using two bolts to release the rear brake disc

orientation marks made on removal aligned (where applicable).
9 Refit the brake caliper and anchor bracket and tighten the bolts to the specified torque. If removed, refit the bolt securing the brake hydraulic hose support bracket to the rear suspension strut.
10 Apply the footbrake two or three times to settle the pads then adjust the handbrake as described in Section 19.
11 Refit the roadwheel and lower the car. Tighten the wheel nuts to the specified torque.

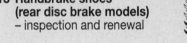

13 Handbrake shoes (rear disc brake models) – inspection and renewal

Inspection

1 Remove the rear brake disc as described in Section 12.

13.6c Prise the shoes apart at the bottom and remove the adjuster and lower return spring

13.6f Push the handbrake cable spring back and disengage the cable end from the lever on the rear shoe

13.6a Unhook the two handbrake shoe upper return springs from the anchor post and from the shoes

2 Working carefully, and taking the necessary precautions, remove all traces of brake dust from the brake disc, backplate and handbrake shoes.
3 Measure the thickness of the friction material of each handbrake brake shoe at several points; if either shoe is worn at any point to the specified minimum thickness or less, all four shoes must be renewed as a set. The shoes should also be renewed if any are fouled with oil or grease; there is no satisfactory way of degreasing friction material, once contaminated.
4 If any of the handbrake shoes are worn unevenly, or fouled with oil or grease, trace and rectify the cause before reassembly.
5 Note the location and orientation of all components before disassembly as an aid to reassembly.

Renewal

6 Follow the accompanying photos

13.6d Lift the inner hold-down cup to disengage the locating tab, then remove the front brake shoe

13.6g Turn the outer hold-down cups as necessary and remove the outer cups, springs, inner cups and pins

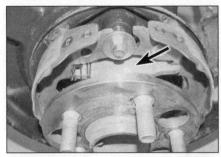

13.6b Spread the shoes at the top and remove the shoe strut and spring (arrowed)

(illustrations 13.6a to 13.6s) for the actual shoe renewal procedure, bearing in mind the additional points listed below. Be sure to stay in order and read the caption under each illustration.
7 With the handbrake shoes removed, clean the backplate, the inside of the brake disc and the adjuster mechanism. Lay all the parts out and check them thoroughly for signs of wear and loss of tension or distortion of any of the springs. Make sure that the adjuster wheel turns freely on its threads.
8 It will be necessary to transfer the handbrake lever on the old rear shoe to the new rear shoe. Prise off the retaining C-clip, withdraw the shim, then remove the handbrake lever from the rear shoe. Attach the handbrake lever to the new rear shoe, fit the shim and secure with the C-clip. Using feeler blades check that the clearance between the handbrake lever and the shoe web is less than 0.35 mm. If the

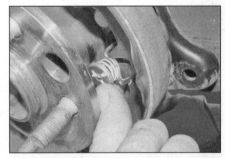

13.6e Disengage the hold-down cup from the rear brake shoe in the same way and slide out the shoe

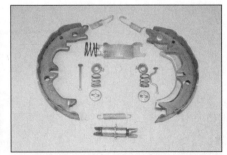

13.6h Clean all the parts check them thoroughly for signs of wear and loss of tension or distortion of any of the springs

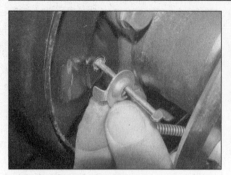

13.6i Fit the hold-down pins and inner hold-down cups . . .

13.6j . . . springs . . .

13.6k . . . and outer hold-down cups to the backplate, noting that the straight pin is for the front shoe and the cranked pin for the rear shoe

14 Brake master cylinder – removal, overhaul and refitting

Note: *Before starting work, refer to the warning at the beginning of Section 2 concerning the dangers of hydraulic fluid.*

Removal

1 Disconnect the wiring connector from the fluid level warning indicator. Unscrew the filler cap and remove the brake fluid from the reservoir.

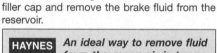

HAYNES HiNT *An ideal way to remove fluid from the reservoir is to use a clean syringe or an old poultry baster.*

13.6l Push the handbrake cable spring back and connect the cable end to the lever on the rear shoe

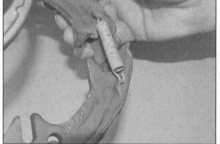

13.6m Connect the lower return spring to both handbrake shoes

clearance is excessive, obtain a new shim, noting that different thicknesses are available.
9 Prior to refitting, apply a smear of high-melting-point grease to the shoe contact areas on the brake backplate, and to the threads of the adjuster mechanism.

10 On completion turn the adjuster wheel to fully retract the adjuster, then refit the brake disc as described in Section 12.
11 Repeat the above procedure on the remaining rear brake.

13.6n Lift the inner hold-down cups and locate the shoes on the backplate

13.6o Make sure that the tag on each inner hold-down cup (arrowed) locates in the hole in the brake shoe

13.6p Prise the shoes apart at the bottom and refit the adjuster (arrowed)

13.6q Spread the shoes at the top and refit the shoe strut and spring

13.6r Fit the upper return springs to the brake shoes . . .

13.6s . . . then locate them in position on the anchor post

2 Identify each brake pipe and its connection to the master cylinder **(see illustration)**. Unscrew the brake pipe union nuts and disconnect the pipes. Plug the connections and tape over the pipe ends, to prevent the entry of dust and dirt.

3 Unscrew the mounting nuts and withdraw the brake pipe bracket and master cylinder from the servo unit.

Overhaul

4 With the master cylinder removed, empty any remaining fluid from it, and clean it externally.

5 Using a screwdriver, prise off the seal from the end of the master cylinder body.

6 Undo the retaining screw at the base of the hydraulic fluid reservoir, then withdraw the reservoir from the top of the master cylinder.

7 Extract the reservoir O-ring seals from the top face of the master cylinder.

8 Turn the master cylinder over so that the reservoir inlet ports are facing downward. Push the pistons in all the way with a screwdriver until the secondary piston retaining pin drops out of the reservoir inlet port.

9 Mount the cylinder in a soft-jawed vice, push the pistons in again, and extract the piston retaining snap-ring from the cylinder bore.

10 Release the pistons and remove the three spacers from the end of the cylinder bore and primary piston.

11 Remove the cylinder from the vice and pull free the primary piston and spring assembly from the master cylinder bore. Pull the piston straight out, not at an angle, otherwise there is a risk of scoring the cylinder bore.

12 Extract the secondary piston and spring assembly by shaking or lightly tapping the cylinder body on a block of wood.

13 Wash all components of the cylinder in methylated spirit or clean hydraulic brake fluid of the specified type. Do not use any other type of cleaning fluid.

14 Inspect the master cylinder and piston assemblies for any signs of excessive wear or damage. Deep scoring in the cylinder bore and/or on the piston surfaces will necessitate a new master cylinder being fitted.

15 If the cylinder is in a serviceable condition, obtain a cylinder repair kit which comprises pre-assembled primary and secondary piston assemblies, together with new seals and O-rings.

16 Check that all components are perfectly clean before they refitted. Smear them in new brake fluid of the specified type as they are assembled. *Do not allow grease, old fluid or any other lubricant to contact the components during reassembly.*

17 Lubricate the pistons before refitting them to the cylinder and as they are inserted, use a twisting action to assist in pushing them into position. Ensure that the secondary piston is inserted with the slot for the retaining pin facing upwards.

18 With the secondary and primary pistons in position, fit the three spacers and the snap-ring, while pushing the pistons into the bore as was done for removal.

19 With the pistons still pushed in, fit the secondary piston retaining pin through the reservoir inlet port.

20 Using new seals, refit the reservoir and secure with the retaining screw.

21 Fit the new seal to the end of the master cylinder body.

Refitting

22 Refitting is a reversal of removal. Tighten the master cylinder retaining nuts to the specified torque and bleed the hydraulic system as described in Section 2 on completion.

15 Brake pedal – check and adjustment

Pedal height

1 Peel back the carpet below the pedals and measure the brake pedal height **(see illustration)**. Note that the measurement should be taken from the upper face of the pedal rubber to the asphalt sheet on the floorpan.

2 If the height is not within the specified tolerance range, remove the driver's side lower facia panel as described in Chapter 11 for access to the top of the pedal.

3 Disconnect the wiring connector at the stop-light switch, then slacken the locknut and unscrew the switch. Slacken the brake pedal (vacuum servo unit) pushrod locknut and turn the pushrod until the correct height is achieved. Tighten the locknut.

4 With the pedal height correctly set, refit the stop-light switch and locknut and screw in the switch until it just contacts the pedal stopper.

5 Unscrew the stop-light switch one turn, reconnect the wiring connector and check that the stop-lights come on when the pedal is depressed between 5 and 15 mm. If necessary, disconnect the wiring connector, reposition the switch and check the stop-light operation again. Continue this procedure until the correct setting is obtained, then tighten the switch locknut. Check the stop-light operation once more and make sure the lights go out when the pedal is released.

6 Once the pedal height and stop-light switch adjustment are correct, check the free play as follows.

Pedal free play

7 With the engine switched-off, depress the brake pedal several times to exhaust the vacuum in the servo unit.

8 While gently depressing the brake pedal with the fingers, measure the pedal travel (at the pedal pad) until the resistance is felt to increase. This measurement, from the pedal at rest position to the beginning of firm resistance is the pedal free play.

9 Compare the measurement obtained with

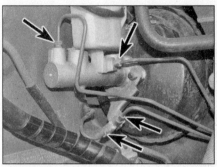

14.2 Brake pipe connections at the master cylinder

that given in the Specifications. If the stop-light switch has been correctly adjusted, the pedal free play should also be correct. If the clearance is not as specified, recheck the pedal height and stop-light switch adjustments as described previously. If the clearance is still incorrect, it is likely that there is either air in the hydraulic system which should be bled out as described in Section 2, or a fault in the master cylinder or vacuum servo unit.

Pedal reserve travel

10 Chock the rear wheels then start the engine and release the handbrake.

11 Depress the brake pedal a few times then press down hard and hold it.

12 Pedal reserve travel is measured from the upper face of the pedal rubber to the asphalt sheet on the floorpan with the pedal depressed. Compare the measurement taken with the figures given in the Specifications.

13 If the reserve travel is less than specified, check the pedal height as previously described and check the adjustment of the rear brakes (Sections 8 and 10). If the brake pedal feels spongy when depressed, bleed the hydraulic system as described in Section 2.

14 When all the checks and adjustments are complete, refit the facia lower panel.

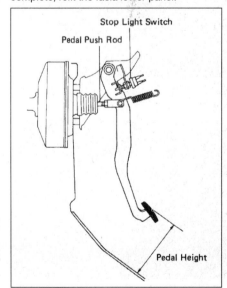

15.1 Brake pedal height adjustment details

16.4 Vacuum servo unit pushrod clevis pin attachment (arrowed) at the brake pedal

16 Brake pedal –
removal and refitting

Removal

1 Disconnect the battery negative terminal (refer to *Disconnecting the battery* in the Reference Chapter).
2 Remove the driver's side lower facia panel as described in Chapter 11
3 Detach the return spring from the upper part of the pedal arm.
4 Disconnect the brake pedal (vacuum servo unit) pushrod from the pedal arm by removing the clevis pin securing clip and the pin **(see illustration)**.
5 Unscrew the nut from the end of the pedal pivot bolt and remove the washer. Remove the bolt then withdraw the pedal arm.

Refitting

6 Refitting is the reverse of the removal procedure, but carry out the checks and adjustments described in Section 15 before refitting the facia lower panel.

17 Brake vacuum servo unit
– testing, removal and refitting

Testing

1 To test the operation of the servo unit, depress the footbrake several times to exhaust the vacuum, then start the engine whilst

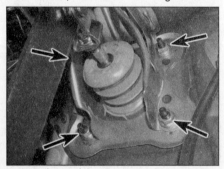

17.13 Vacuum servo unit mounting nuts (arrowed)

keeping the pedal firmly depressed. As the engine starts, there should be a noticeable 'give' in the brake pedal as the vacuum builds-up. Allow the engine to run for at least two minutes, then switch it off. If the brake pedal is now depressed it should feel normal, but further applications should result in the pedal feeling firmer, with the pedal stroke decreasing with each application.
2 If the servo does not operate as described, first inspect the servo unit check valve as described in Section 18.
3 If the servo unit still fails to operate satisfactorily, the fault lies within the unit itself. Repairs to the unit are not possible – if faulty, the servo unit must be renewed.

Removal

4 Disconnect the battery negative terminal (refer to *Disconnecting the battery* in the Reference Chapter).
5 Remove the brake master cylinder as described in Section 14.
6 On right-hand drive models with manual transmission, remove the clutch master cylinder as described in Chapter 6.
7 On left-hand drive models with anti-lock brakes, remove the ABS hydraulic modulator as described in Section 25.
8 Disconnect the vacuum hose at the connection on the servo unit.
9 According to model, detach any additional cables and brackets in the engine compartment likely to impede removal of the servo unit.
10 Remove the driver's side lower facia panel as described in Chapter 11
11 Detach the return spring from the upper part of the brake pedal arm.
12 Disconnect the brake pedal (vacuum servo unit) pushrod from the brake pedal arm by removing the clevis pin securing clip and the clevis pin.
13 Undo the four nuts then remove the servo from the engine compartment **(see illustration)**. Recover the gasket between the servo and the bulkhead.

Refitting

14 Refitting is a reversal of removal bearing in mind the following points:
  a) *Ensure that the servo-to-bulkhead gasket is in position before fitting the servo.*

19.4 Slacken the handbrake cable locknut (the upper nut) while holding the adjuster nut

  b) *Tighten all nuts and bolts to the specified torque.*
  c) *Refit the brake master cylinder as described in Section 14.*
  d) *Where applicable, refit the ABS hydraulic modulator assembly as described in Section 25, and the clutch master cylinder as described in Chapter 6.*
  e) *Bleed the hydraulic system as described in Section 2.*
  f) *Carry out the brake pedal check and adjustment as described in Section 15.*

18 Brake vacuum servo unit check valve
– removal, testing and refitting

Removal

1 Disconnect the vacuum hose at the connection on the servo unit.
2 Withdraw the valve from its rubber sealing grommet, using a pulling and twisting motion.

Testing

3 Examine the check valve for signs of damage, and renew if necessary. The valve may be tested by blowing through it in both directions. Air should flow through the valve in one direction only – when blown through from the servo unit end of the valve. Renew the valve if this is not the case.
4 Examine the rubber sealing grommet and flexible vacuum hose for signs of damage or deterioration, and renew as necessary.

Refitting

5 Carefully ease the check valve into position, taking great care not to displace or damage the grommet. Reconnect the vacuum hose to the valve.
6 On completion, start the engine and check for air leaks from the check valve-to-servo unit connection.

19 Handbrake –
adjustment

1 The handbrake lever, when correctly adjusted, should travel four to seven clicks of the ratchet when a moderate pulling force is applied. If it travels less than the specified number of clicks (see Chapter 1), there is a possibility that the handbrake may not release completely and the brake shoes may drag on the drum. If the lever can be pulled up more than the specified amount the handbrake may not hold properly on a slope.

Rear drum brake models

2 Chock the rear wheels and release the handbrake.
3 Remove the centre console as described in Chapter 11.
4 Locate the handbrake cable adjuster on the side of the handbrake lever and slacken

the locknut (the upper nut) while holding the adjuster nut (see illustration).

5 Turn the adjuster nut as necessary until the desired lever travel is obtained then tighten the locknut.

6 Refit the centre console.

Rear disc brake models

7 To adjust the handbrake shoe clearance, chock the front wheels then jack up the rear of the car and support it on axle stands (see *Jacking and vehicle support*). Remove the rear roadwheels and temporarily refit three wheel nuts (with suitable spacers) each side to hold the brake discs in place.

8 Remove the plug from the access hole on each rear disc (see illustration 12.5a). With the handbrake fully released, turn one of the rear discs until the access hole is in its lowest position and the handbrake shoe internal adjuster wheel can be seen through the hole. Insert a screwdriver through the hole and turn the adjuster wheel as necessary until the disc is locked (see illustration 12.5b). Now back off the adjuster wheel by 8 notches until the disc is again free to turn without any trace of binding. Refit the access plug then repeat this procedure on the other rear brake.

9 Refit the roadwheels and lower the car to the ground. Tighten the wheel nuts to the specified torque.

10 Settle the handbrake shoes by driving the car slowly on a safe quiet road for about 400 metres with the handbrake lightly applied. This will clean any rust and deposits from the handbrake shoes and drum. Release the handbrake then apply it again and repeat the procedure.

11 With the handbrake shoe clearance correctly set, adjust the handbrake lever travel as described above in paragraphs 2 to 6.

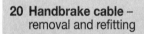

20 Handbrake cable –
removal and refitting

Removal

1 Chock the front wheels then jack up the rear of the car and support it on axle stands (see *Jacking and vehicle support*).

2 Remove the exhaust tailpipe and silencer and the heat shield below the handbrake lever as described in Chapter 4A.

Primary cable

3 Remove the centre console as described in Chapter 11.

4 With the handbrake releaased, unscrew the cable locknut and adjuster nut on the side of the handbrake lever (see illustration 19.4). Detach the primary cable from the lever.

5 From under the car, turn the primary cable end through 90° and disconnect it from the equaliser yoke (see illustration).

6 Extract the cable entry grommet from the floorpan and pull the cable out through the hole.

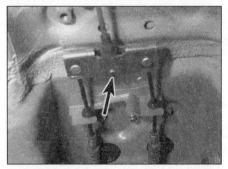

20.5 Handbrake primary cable attachment (arrowed) at the equaliser yoke

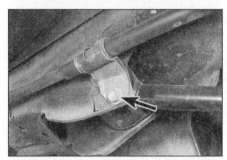

20.9a Undo the secondary cable support bracket from the suspension components (arrowed) . . .

Secondary cable

7 Remove the rear brake shoes (drum brake models) or handbrake shoes (disc brake models) on the relevant side as described in Section 8 or 13 respectively.

8 Undo the cable retaining bolts from the brake backplate and pull the cable end through the backplate (see illustration).

9 Undo the cable support bracket nuts and bolts from the suspension components and underbody (see illustrations).

10 Pull the nylon bushing out of the front mounting bracket and disconnect the cable from the equaliser.

Refitting

11 Refitting is a reversal of removal, but adjust the handbrake as described in Section 19 on completion.

21 Handbrake lever –
removal and refitting

Removal

1 Remove the centre console as described in Chapter 11.

2 With the rear wheels chocked and the handbrake off, unscrew the cable locknut and adjuster nut on the side of the handbrake lever (see illustration 19.4). Detach the primary cable from the lever.

3 Disconnect the wiring connector from the handbrake warning light switch.

20.8 Handbrake secondary cable retaining bolts (arrowed) on the brake backplate

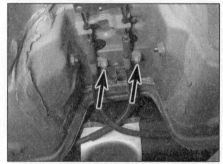

20.9b . . . and the underbody attachments (arrowed)

4 Undo the warning light switch mounting screw and remove the switch.

5 Undo the bolts securing the lever assembly to the floor and remove the lever from the car.

Refitting

6 Refitting is a reversal of removal. Adjust the handbrake as described in Section 19 on completion.

22 Handbrake warning
light switch –
removal and refitting

Removal

1 Remove the centre console as described in Chapter 11.

2 Disconnect the wiring connector from the warning light switch on the side of the handbrake lever bracket (see illustration).

22.2 Handbrake warning light switch location (arrowed) on the side of the handbrake lever bracket

23.2 Brake stop-light switch location on the brake pedal bracket

3 Undo the switch mounting screw and remove the switch.

Refitting

4 Refitting is a reversal of removal.

23 Stop-light switch – removal and refitting

Removal

1 Remove the driver's side lower facia panel as described in Chapter 11.
2 Disconnect the wiring connector at the stop-light switch located on the brake pedal bracket, then slacken the locknut and unscrew the switch **(see illustration)**.

Refitting

3 Refitting of the switch is carried out as part of the brake pedal check and adjustment procedures contained in Section 15.

24 Anti-lock braking system (ABS) – general information

The anti-lock braking system comprises a hydraulic modulator unit and the four wheel speed sensors. The modulator unit contains the electronic control unit (ECU), the hydraulic solenoid valves and the electrically-driven return pump. The purpose of the system is to prevent the wheel(s) locking during heavy

braking. This is achieved by automatic release of the brake on the relevant wheel, followed by re-application of the brake.

The solenoid valves are controlled by the ECU, which itself receives signals from the four wheel speed sensors which monitor the speed of rotation of each wheel. By comparing these signals, the ECU can determine the speed at which the vehicle is travelling. It can then use this speed to determine when a wheel is decelerating at an abnormal rate, compared to the speed of the vehicle, and therefore predicts when a wheel is about to lock. During normal operation, the system functions in the same way as a non-ABS braking system.

If the ECU senses that a wheel is about to lock, it closes the relevant outlet solenoid valves in the hydraulic unit, which then isolates the relevant brake(s) on the wheel(s) which is/are about to lock from the master cylinder, effectively sealing-in the hydraulic pressure.

If the speed of rotation of the wheel continues to decrease at an abnormal rate, the ECU opens the inlet solenoid valves on the relevant brake(s), and operates the electrically-driven return pump which pumps the hydraulic fluid back into the master cylinder, releasing the brake. Once the speed of rotation of the wheel returns to an acceptable rate, the pump stops; the solenoid valves switch again, allowing the hydraulic master cylinder pressure to return to the caliper or wheel cylinder, which then re-applies the brake. This cycle can be carried out many times a second.

The action of the solenoid valves and return pump creates pulses in the hydraulic circuit. When the ABS system is functioning, these pulses can be felt through the brake pedal.

The operation of the ABS system is entirely dependent on electrical signals. To prevent the system responding to any inaccurate signals, a built-in safety circuit monitors all signals received by the ECU. If an inaccurate signal or low battery voltage is detected, the ABS system is automatically shut-down, and the warning light on the instrument panel is illuminated, to inform the driver that the ABS system is not operational. Normal braking should still be available, however.

Later models may also equipped with additional safety features built around the ABS

system. These systems include electronic brake force distribution, which automatically apportions braking effort between the front and rear wheels, emergency brake assist, which guarantees full braking effort in the event of an emergency stop by monitoring the rate at which the brake pedal is depressed and (on some models) an electronic stability program which monitors the vehicle's cornering forces and steering wheel angle, then applies the braking force to the appropriate roadwheel to enhance the stability of the vehicle.

Should a fault develop in the system, the ECU illuminates a warning light on the instrument panel constantly. To facilitate fault diagnosis, the system is provided with an on-board diagnostic facility. In the event of a fault, the ECU stores a series of fault codes for subsequent read-out and diagnosis. If the instrument panel warning light remains on after the engine has been started, the vehicle must be taken to a Toyota dealer or suitably-equipped diagnostic specialist for fault diagnosis and repair.

25 Anti-lock braking system (ABS) components – removal and refitting

Removal

Front wheel speed sensor

1 Firmly apply the handbrake, then jack up the front of the car and support it securely on axle stands (see *Jacking and vehicle support*).
2 Remove the front wheel arch liner (see Chapter 11) and disconnect the wheel sensor wiring connector. Undo the bolts or release the supports securing the wiring to the suspension components **(see illustrations)**.
3 Undo the bolt securing the sensor to the hub carrier and withdraw the sensor **(see illustration)**.

Rear wheel speed sensor

4 Chock the front wheels then jack up the rear of the car and support it on axle stands (see *Jacking and vehicle support*). Remove the roadwheel.
5 Undo the bolts which secure the sensor

25.2a Wheel speed sensor wiring connector (arrowed) under the front wheel arch

25.2b Wheel speed sensor wiring attachments (arrowed) on the front suspension components

25.3 Undo the retaining bolt and withdraw the wheel speed sensor from the hub carrier

25.5 Undo the bolt securing the wheel speed sensor to the rear hub carrier

to the rear hub carrier, the wiring support bracket to the rear suspension strut, and wiring support clip under the wheel arch **(see illustration)**.

6 Release the wiring and grommet from the cable entry point under the wheel arch.

7 Remove the rear seat base and seat back as described in Chapter 11.

8 Trace the wiring back until the connector inside the car is located then disconnect it.

9 Pull the wiring through the cable entry point and remove the sensor from under the wheel arch.

Hydraulic modulator

Note: *Before starting work, refer to the warning at the beginning of Section 2 concerning the dangers of hydraulic fluid.*

10 Disconnect the battery negative terminal (refer to *Disconnecting the battery* in the Reference Chapter). For improved access, remove the air cleaner and inlet ducts as described in Chapter 4A.

11 Wipe clean all the brake pipe unions at the hydraulic modulator then unscrew the union nuts and carefully ease the pipes clear. Place absorbent rags beneath the pipe unions to catch any spilled fluid and label the pipes as an aid to refitting.

12 Pull out the locking catch and disconnect the wiring connector from the ECU on the front of the modulator.

13 Undo the bolts securing the hydraulic modulator mounting bracket and remove the modulator, complete with bracket, from the engine compartment. Undo the two nuts and separate the modulator from the mounting bracket.

14 Note that the modulator is a sealed precision assembly and must not under any circumstances be dismantled.

Electronic control unit (ECU)

15 The ECU is essentially an integral part of the hydraulic modulator assembly. Although removal and refitting is possible, this work should be entrusted to a Toyota dealer or ABS specialist.

Refitting

16 In all cases, refitting is a reversal of the removal operations but note the following points:

a) *Clean off all dirt from the wheel speed sensors and mounting locations before refitting and also clean the pulse wheels with a stiff brush.*

b) *Bleed the hydraulic system as described in Section 2 after refitting the hydraulic modulator.*

Chapter 10
Suspension and steering

Contents

Degrees of difficulty

Easy, suitable for novice with little experience	Fairly easy, suitable for beginner with some experience	Fairly difficult, suitable for competent DIY mechanic	Difficult, suitable for experienced DIY mechanic	Very difficult, suitable for expert DIY or professional

Specifications

Front wheel alignment and steering angles

Toe setting	1.0 ± 2.0 mm toe-in
Camber	−0°21 ± 45'
Castor (non-adjustable)	1°20' ± 45'
Steering axis inclination (non-adjustable)	13°22' ± 45'

Rear wheel alignment

Toe setting	2.0 ± 2.0 mm toe-in
Camber (non-adjustable):	
Saloon and Hatchback models	−0°31' ± 30'
Estate models	−0°25' ± 30'

Torque wrench settings

	Nm	lbf ft
Front suspension		
ABS wheel speed sensor bolt	8	6
Anti-roll bar clamp plates	19	14
Anti-roll bar drop link to anti-roll bar	44	32
Anti-roll bar drop link to suspension lower arm	44	32
Brake caliper anchor bracket to hub carrier	94	69
Brake hose bracket to suspension strut	29	21
Engine/transmission longitudinal crossmember bolts	73	54
Engine/transmission mounting bracket to subframe	72	53
Hub/driveshaft retaining nut	216	159
Lower balljoint to hub carrier	103	76
Lower balljoint to lower arm	127	94
Subframe brace to body	146	108
Subframe to body	206	152
Suspension lower arm control link outer bolt	84	62
Suspension lower arm front pivot bolt	127	94
Suspension lower arm rear mounting bolt	145	107
Suspension strut piston rod nut	47	35
Suspension strut to hub carrier	255	188
Suspension strut upper mounting to body	80	59

Torque wrench settings (continued)

	Nm	lbf ft
Rear suspension		
ABS wheel speed sensor bolt	8	6
Anti-roll bar clamp plates	19	14
Anti-roll bar drop link to anti-roll bar	44	32
Anti-roll bar drop link to suspension strut	44	32
Fuel tank retaining strap bolts	35	26
Hub carrier to rear axle carrier	80	59
Longitudinal link mounting bolts/nuts	113	83
Subframe brace:		
Outer bolts	64	47
Inner bolts	5	4
Subrame stiffener plates to body	56	41
Subframe to body	64	47
Suspension strut piston rod nut	49	36
Suspension strut to rear axle carrier	255	188
Suspension strut upper mounting to body	39	29
Transverse link mounting bolts/nuts	118	87
Steering		
Hydraulic pipe flare union nuts	44	32
Hydraulic pipe union banjo bolts	51	38
Steering column mounting nuts/bolts	25	19
Steering gear mounting bolts/nuts	78	58
Steering pump mounting and adjustment bolts:		
Pre-August 2000 models:		
1.6 and 1.8 litre models:		
Mounting bolt	62	46
Adjustment bolt	39	29
2.0 litre models:		
Mounting bolt	62	46
Adjustment bolt	43	32
Post-August 2000 models:		
1.6 and 1.8 litre models:		
Mounting bolts	37	27
2.0 litre models:		
Mounting bolts	50	37
Steering shaft universal joint clamp bolt	35	26
Steering wheel to column shaft nut	34	25
Track rod end balljoint to hub carrier	49	36
Roadwheel nuts		
All models	103	76

1 General information

The front suspension is of the conventional MacPherson strut type, incorporating coil springs and integral telescopic shock absorbers. The MacPherson struts are located by transverse lower suspension arms, which utilise rubber inner mounting bushes and incorporate a balljoint at the outer ends. The front hub carriers, which carry the hub bearings, brake calipers and the hub/disc assemblies, are bolted to the MacPherson struts and connected to the lower arms via the balljoints. The anti-roll bar is rubber-mounted onto the subframe, and connects both the lower arms, via drop links.

The rear suspension is of the MacPherson strut type, incorporating coil springs and integral telescopic shock absorbers. The MacPherson struts are located laterally by two transverse links each side, bolted to the subframe at their inner ends, and longitudinally by a single longitudinal link each side. The rear transverse links are adjustable to enable wheel alignment adjustment. The rear hub carriers, which carry the hub bearings, and drum/disc assemblies are bolted to the rear axle carriers which carry the rear brake shoes or disc brake calipers. These are in turn bolted to the MacPherson struts and connected to the transverse and longitudinal links. The rear anti-roll bar is rubber-mounted onto the chassis sidemembers, and connects both the suspension struts via drop links.

The steering column shaft lower universal joint is connected to the steering gear pinion by means of a clamp bolt.

The steering gear is mounted on the front subframe. It is connected by two track rods and track rod ends to the steering arms projecting rearwards from the hub carriers. The track rod ends are threaded to enable wheel alignment adjustment.

Power steering is fitted to all models. The power steering pump is belt-driven from the crankshaft pulley or coolant pump pulley according to engine type.

2 Front hub carrier – removal and refitting

Note: *A new hub/driveshaft retaining nut split pin, and track rod end balljoint nut split pin must be used on refitting.*

Removal

1 Firmly apply the handbrake, then jack up the front of the car and support it securely on axle stands (see *Jacking and vehicle support*). Remove the relevant front roadwheel.
2 On models with ABS, remove the ABS wheel speed sensor, as described in Chapter 9, to avoid any possibility of damage during the removal procedure.

2.3a Extract the hub/driveshaft retaining nut split pin . . .

2.3b . . . and remove the locking cap over the nut

2.5 Brake caliper anchor bracket retaining bolts (arrowed)

3 Extract the hub/driveshaft retaining nut split pin and remove the locking cap over the nut **(see illustrations)**.

4 Have an assistant firmly depress the brake pedal to prevent the front hub from rotating. Using a socket and a long extension bar, slacken and remove the hub/driveshaft retaining nut. Alternatively, a tool can be fabricated to prevent the hub from rotating (see Chapter 8, Section 2). This nut is very tight; make sure that there is no risk of pulling the car off the axle stands.

5 Undo the two bolts securing the brake caliper anchor bracket to the hub carrier **(see illustration)**. Withdraw the caliper and anchor bracket, complete with brake pads and suspend the assembly from a suitable place under the wheel arch using string or wire. To avoid straining the flexible brake hose or metal pipes, unbolt the flexible hose support bracket from the suspension strut.

6 Mark the relationship of the brake disc to the wheel hub with quick-drying paint then remove the disc.

7 Loosen the nuts securing the suspension strut to the hub carrier, while counterholding the bolts **(see illustration 4.3)**. Do not remove the bolts at this stage.

8 Extract the split pin from the track rod end balljoint nut, and unscrew the nut as far as the end of the balljoint shank threads **(see illustration)**. Using a balljoint separator tool, release the track rod end balljoint tapered shank. Once the taper has separated, unscrew the nut and detach the track rod end from the hub carrier.

9 Unscrew the bolt and two nuts, and disconnect the suspension lower balljoint from the lower arm **(see illustration)**.

10 Hold the hub carrier, and release the driveshaft outer CV joint from the hub bearings by tapping it towards the transmission with a soft-faced mallet.

11 Unscrew the nuts securing the hub carrier to the suspension strut, then withdraw the bolts, and remove the hub carrier.

Refitting

12 Refitting is a reversal of removal, bearing in mind the following points.

a) Tighten all fixings to the specified torque.

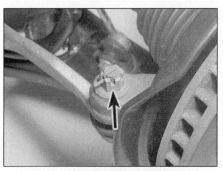

2.8 Track rod end balljoint retaining nut and split pin (arrowed)

b) Do not fully tighten the hub carrier-to-suspension strut nuts until the lower arm and track rod end balljoints have been reconnected.

c) Use new split pins to secure the track rod end balljoint nut, and the hub/driveshaft nut and locking cap, and bend over the split pin legs to secure.

d) When refitting the brake disc, align the marks made on removal.

e) Refit the ABS wheel speed sensor, as described in Chapter 9.

f) On completion, have the front wheel alignment checked at the earliest opportunity.

3 Front hub bearing – checking and renewal

Checking

1 Firmly apply the handbrake, then jack up the front of the car and support it securely on axle stands (see *Jacking and vehicle support*).

2 Undo the two bolts securing the brake caliper anchor bracket to the hub carrier **(see illustration 2.5)**. Withdraw the caliper and anchor bracket, complete with brake pads, and suspend the assembly from a suitable place under the wheel arch using string or wire. To avoid straining the flexible brake hose or metal pipes, unbolt the flexible hose support bracket from the suspension strut.

3 Mark the relationship of the brake disc to

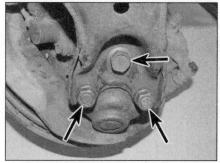

2.9 Unscrew the bolt and two nuts (arrowed), and disconnect the suspension lower balljoint from the lower arm

the wheel hub with quick-drying paint then remove the disc.

4 Wear in the front hub bearings can be checked by measuring the amount of side play present. To do this, a dial gauge should be fixed so that its probe is in contact with the disc contact face of the wheel hub, near the centre of the hub. The axial play should be between 0 and 0.05 mm. If the play is greater than specified, the bearings are worn excessively and must be renewed.

5 At the same time, check the run-out of the wheel hub by repositioning the dial gauge probe towards the outside edge of the hub. Rotate the hub, and observe the deviation in the reading. If the run-out is greater than 0.07 mm, the wheel hub should be renewed.

Renewal

Note: *The front hub bearings should only be removed from the hub carrier if they are to be renewed. The removal procedure renders the bearings unserviceable, and they must not be re-used. Prior to dismantling, it should be noted that a hub/bearing puller, and an assortment of metal tubes of various diameters (and preferably, a press) will be required. Unless these tools are available, the renewal of the hub bearings will have to be entrusted to a Toyota dealer or suitably-equipped garage.*

6 Remove the hub carrier as described in Section 2.

7 The wheel hub must now be removed from the bearing inner races. It is preferable to use a press to do this, but it is possible to drive out

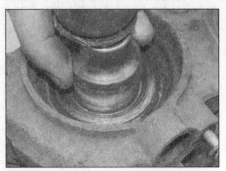

3.7 Drive the wheel hub from the bearing using a suitable tube or drift

3.8 Using a puller to remove the bearing inner race from the wheel hub

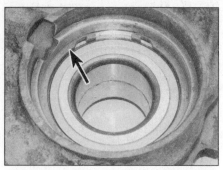

3.9 Extract the bearing circlip (arrowed) from the hub carrier

the hub using a length of metal tube/socket of suitable diameter **(see illustration)**.

8 Part of the bearing inner race will remain on the wheel hub as it is removed, and this should be removed using a chisel and suitable puller **(see illustration)**.

9 Using circlip pliers, extract the bearing retaining circlip from the inboard side of the hub carrier **(see illustration)**.

10 Remove the split pin from the hub carrier lower balljoint nut. Loosen the balljoint nut, and unscrew it as far as the end of the threads on the balljoint. Using a suitable balljoint separator tool, disconnect the balljoint from the hub carrier.

11 Unscrew the securing bolts, and remove the brake disc shield from the hub carrier.

12 Support the inboard side of the hub carrier, then drive or press out the bearing, using a socket or tube acting on the bearing outer race.

13 Thoroughly clean the bearing contact face of the hub carrier.

14 Support the outboard side of the hub carrier, then drive or press in the new bearing up to the shoulder in the hub carrier, using a socket or tube acting on the bearing outer race. Do not apply any pressure to the inner race.

15 Secure the bearing using a new retaining circlip, ensuring that the circlip locates fully in its groove.

16 Refit the brake disc shield, and securely tighten the three bolts.

17 Support the outboard side of the wheel hub (do not support the hub on the wheel studs), then press or drive the hub carrier onto the wheel hub, using a socket or tube acting on the bearing inner race.

18 Refit the lower balljoint to the hub carrier, then refit the nut, and tighten it to the specified torque. Insert a new split pin and bend over the split pin legs to secure the nut.

19 Refit the hub carrier as described in Section 2.

4 Front suspension strut – removal, overhaul and refitting

Removal

1 Firmly apply the handbrake, then jack up the front of the car and support it securely on axle stands (see *Jacking and vehicle support*). Remove the relevant front roadwheel.

2 Unscrew the bolt(s) securing the flexible brake hose support bracket and, where applicable, the ABS wheel speed sensor wiring support bracket to the suspension strut. Also release the wheel speed sensor wiring clip from the hub carrier **(see illustrations)**.

3 Undo and remove the nuts securing the suspension strut to the hub carrier, while counterholding the bolts. Do not remove the bolts at this stage **(see illustration)**.

4 Working in the engine compartment, unscrew the three nuts securing the top of the suspension strut to the vehicle body. Remove the nuts and, where fitted, the stiffener plate. Withdraw the suspension strut-to-hub carrier bolts and remove the strut from under the wheel arch **(see illustrations)**.

Overhaul

⚠️ *Warning: Before attempting to dismantle the suspension strut, a suitable tool to hold the coil spring in compression must be obtained.*

4.2a Unscrew the bolts (arrowed) securing the brake hose and wiring support brackets to the suspension strut . . .

4.2b . . . and release the wiring clip (arrowed) from the hub carrier

4.3 Remove the nuts securing the suspension strut to the hub carrier

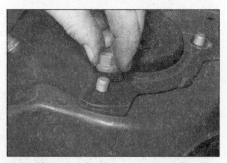

4.4a Unscrew the three nuts securing the top of the suspension strut to the vehicle body . . .

4.4b . . . then remove the nuts and the stiffener plate

4.6 Fit the compressor and compress the spring until all tension is relieved from the upper mounting

4.8 Unscrew the central piston rod nut while holding the upper spring seat

4.10a Lift off the upper mounting . . .

4.10b . . . the dust seal . . .

4.10c . . . the upper spring seat . . .

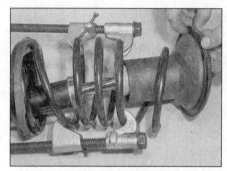

4.10d . . . and the upper mounting rubber

Adjustable coil spring compressors which can be positively secured to the spring coils are readily available, and are recommended for this operation. Any attempt to dismantle the strut without such a tool is likely to result in damage or personal injury.

5 With the strut removed from the car as described previously, clean away all external dirt.

6 Fit the spring compressor tool and compress the coil spring until all tension is relieved from the upper mounting **(see illustration)**.

7 Prise off the dust cap from the top of the strut, then securely clamp the upper spring seat using a pair of grips or similar reaction tool so that it cannot rotate in relation to the strut.

8 Unscrew the central piston rod nut **(see illustration)**.

9 Note the orientation and location of all components to aid refitting.

10 Lift off the upper mounting, dust seal, upper spring seat, and upper mounting rubber **(see illustrations)**.

11 Lift off the spring and compressor tool **(see illustration)**. Do not remove the tool from the spring unless the spring is to be renewed.

12 Withdraw the bump rubber and the lower mounting rubber **(see illustrations)**.

13 With the strut assembly now completely dismantled, examine all the components for wear, damage or deformation. Check the rubbers for cracks and splits. Renew any of the components as necessary.

14 Examine the strut for signs of fluid leakage. Check the strut piston rod for signs of pitting along its entire length and check the strut body for signs of damage or elongation of the mounting bolt holes. Test the operation of the strut, while holding it in an upright position, by moving the piston rod through a full stroke and then through short strokes of 50 to 100 mm.

In both cases the resistance felt should be smooth and continuous. If the resistance is jerky, or uneven, or if there is any visible sign of wear or damage to the strut, renewal is necessary.

15 If any doubt exists about the condition of the coil spring, gradually release the spring compressor, and check the spring for distortion and signs of cracking. Since no minimum free length is specified by Toyota, the only way to check the tension of the spring is to compare it to a new component. Renew the spring if it is damaged or distorted, or if there is any doubt as to its condition.

16 Inspect all other components for signs of damage or deterioration, and renew any that are suspect.

17 Reassembly is a reversal of dismantling, bearing in mind the following points.

a) *If a new strut is being fitted, prime the strut before refitting the spring, by*

4.11 Withdraw the spring and compressor tool . . .

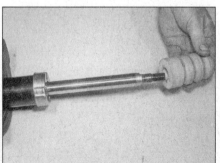

4.12a . . . followed by the bump rubber . . .

4.12b . . . and lower mounting rubber

compressing and extending the piston rod several times.

b) *Ensure that all components are correctly orientated and positioned, as noted before dismantling.*

c) *Ensure that the locating lug on the lower mounting rubber engages with the corresponding cut-out in the lower spring seat.*

d) *Make sure that the spring ends are correctly located in the upper and lower seats.*

e) *Ensure that the upper spring seat is correctly orientated, with the arrow and OUT marking positioned on the outboard side of the strut.*

f) *Tighten the piston rod nut to the specified torque.*

g) *Pack grease around the top of the piston rod before refitting the dust cap.*

Refitting

18 Refitting is a reversal of removal, but tighten all fixings to the specified torque and, on completion, have the front wheel alignment checked at the earliest opportunity (see Section 25).

5 Front suspension lower arm – removal and refitting

Note: *If removing the left-hand lower arm on models equipped with automatic transmission, it will be necessary to remove the front subframe as described in Section 8; the left-hand lower arm can then be detached once the subframe is removed.*

Removal

1 Firmly apply the handbrake, then jack up the front of the car and support it securely on axle stands (see *Jacking and vehicle support*). Remove the relevant front roadwheel.

2 Unscrew the securing nut, and disconnect the anti-roll bar drop link from the bracket on the lower arm **(see illustration)**. Note that it may be necessary to counterhold the drop link pin using an Allen key or bit.

3 Unscrew the bolt and two nuts, and disconnect the suspension lower balljoint from the lower arm **(see illustration 2.9)**.

4 Undo the bolt and remove the nut securing

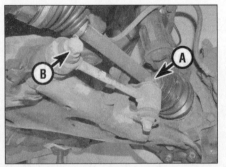

5.4 Control link-to-lower arm retaining bolt (A) and lower arm front pivot bolt (B)

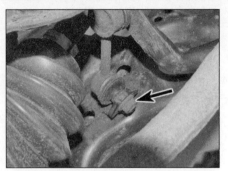

5.2 Unscrew the nut (arrowed) and disconnect the anti-roll bar drop link from the lower arm bracket

the outer end of the control link to the lower arm **(see illustration)**. **Note:** *On models with automatic transmission, a control link is only fitted to the right-hand lower arm.*

5 Unscrew the lower arm front pivot bolt and the rear mounting bolt **(see illustration)**. Remove the control link, then withdraw the lower arm from the subframe.

6 If the mounting and pivot bushes are found to be in poor condition, the complete arm must be renewed. The suspension arm must also be renewed if it has suffered any form of structural damage.

Refitting

7 Locate the lower arm in position in the subframe. Engage the control link with the lower arm and fit the lower arm front pivot bolt and rear mounting bolt. Tighten the bolts moderately tight only at this stage. Refit and moderately tighten the control link outer end securing bolt and nut.

8 Reconnect the suspension lower balljoint to the lower arm and secure with the bolt and two nuts, tightened to the specified torque.

9 Reconnect the anti-roll bar drop link, then tighten the securing nut to the specified torque, counterholding the drop link pin as during removal, if necessary.

10 Refit the roadwheel, and lower the vehicle to the ground. Tighten the wheel nuts to the specified torque.

11 Bounce the car up and down several times to allow the suspension to settle.

12 Tighten the lower arm pivot and mounting bolts to the specified torque, starting with the

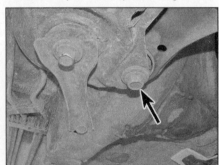

5.5 Lower arm rear mounting bolt (arrowed)

front pivot bolt, then the rear mounting bolt. Tighten the control link outer end retaining bolt nut to the specified torque.

13 On completion, have the wheel alignment checked as soon as possible (see Section 25).

6 Front suspension lower balljoint – renewal

Removal

1 Remove the front hub carrier as described in Section 2.

2 With the hub carrier on the bench, extract the split pin and unscrew the nut securing the lower balljoint to the hub carrier.

3 Using a small two-legged puller, release the taper of the balljoint shank and separate the balljoint from the hub carrier.

4 Move the balljoint shank from side-to-side and check for any signs of excessive stiffness, binding or free play. Also check the condition of the rubber boot. Renew the balljoint if any defects are found.

Refitting

5 Refitting is a reversal of removal, bearing in mind the following points:

a) *Tighten the balljoint-to-hub carrier retaining nut to the specified torque and insert a new split pin. Bend over the split pin legs to secure.*

b) *Refit the hub carrier as described in Section 2.*

7 Front anti-roll bar components – removal and refitting

Removal

1 Remove the front subframe as described in Section 8.

2 Unscrew the securing nut, and disconnect the anti-roll bar drop links from the brackets on the lower suspension arms **(see illustration 5.2)**. Note that it may be necessary to counterhold the drop link pin using an Allen key or bit.

3 Undo the bolts securing the two clamp plates to the subframe, lift off the plates and remove the anti-roll bar. Remove the two rubber bushes from the anti-roll bar.

4 If required, the drop links can be removed from the anti-roll bar after undoing their retaining nuts.

5 Inspect the condition of the rubber bushes and renew if any signs of deterioration are visible. Check the condition of the drop link balljoints and renew the drop links if the balljoints are worn.

Refitting

6 Refitting is a reversal of removal, tightening all nuts and bolts to the specified torque. With the anti-roll bar in position on the subframe, refit the subframe as described in Section 8.

8 Front subframe –
removal and refitting

Removal

1 Firmly apply the handbrake, then jack up the front of the car and support it securely on axle stands (see *Jacking and vehicle support*). Remove the front roadwheels.
2 Remove the engine compartment undershields, with reference to Chapter 11.
3 Unscrew the securing nuts, and disconnect the anti-roll bar drop links from the brackets on the lower suspension arms **(see illustration 5.2)**. Note that it may be necessary to counterhold the drop link pins using an Allen key or bit.
4 Extract the split pin from the left-hand track rod end balljoint nut, and unscrew the nut as far as the end of the balljoint shank threads **(see illustration 2.8)**. Using a balljoint separator tool, release the track rod end balljoint tapered shank. Once the taper has separated, unscrew the nut and detach the track rod end from the hub carrier. Repeat this operation on the right-hand track rod end balljoint.
5 Unscrew the bolt and two nuts each side, and disconnect the suspension lower balljoint from each lower suspension arm **(see illustration 2.9)**.
6 Disconnect the fluid return hose from the power steering fluid reservoir and allow the fluid to drain into a suitable container.
7 Clean the area around the power steering pressure and return pipe unions on the steering gear pinion housing. Unscrew the pipe union nuts or banjo union bolts and, where fitted, recover the sealing washers. Note that new sealing washers must be obtained for refitting.
8 Make alignment marks on the steering column shaft universal joint and the steering gear pinion shaft to ensure correct alignment when refitting. Undo the universal joint clamp bolt and separate the joint from the steering gear pinion shaft **(see illustration)**.
9 Refer to Chapter 4A and remove the exhaust front downpipe, or downpipe and intermediate section, as necessary.
10 Disconnect the power steering return hose at the support bracket above the steering gear.
11 Connect a hoist and lifting tackle to the engine lifting bracket at the left-hand end of the cylinder head, and raise the hoist to just take the weight of the engine.
12 From under the car, remove the engine/transmission longitudinal crossmember as follows **(see illustration)**.
a) Unscrew the two securing bolts, and remove the towing eye from the crossmember.
b) Prise out the cover plugs, and unscrew the two bolts securing the front engine/transmission mounting to the crossmember.

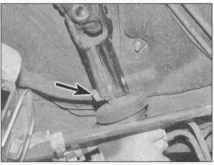

8.8 Steering column shaft lower universal joint clamp bolt (arrowed)

c) Where applicable, unscrew the securing bolt and release the air conditioning pipe clamp from the crossmember.
d) Prise out the rear cover plug and unscrew the five securing bolts, two at the front and three at the rear, and remove the crossmember.
13 Undo the nuts and bolts securing the rear engine/transmission mounting bracket to the subframe.
14 Position a jack under the subframe and just take the subframe weight.
15 Slacken, but do not remove at this stage, the suspension lower arm front pivot bolt and the rear mounting bolt on each side **(see illustrations)**.
16 Working through the holes in the suspension lower arms, undo and remove the mounting nuts at the front of the subframe. Undo the two rear mounting bolts each side, securing the subframe and subframe braces, and remove the braces. Slowly lower the subframe, steering gear and suspension lower arm assemblies to the ground. Withdraw the unit from under the car for further dismantling.
17 If required, the suspension lower arm(s) and steering gear can be unbolted from the subframe and removed, with reference to the relevant Sections of this Chapter.

Refitting

18 Refit the steering gear and suspension lower arm(s) to the subframe, with reference to the relevant Sections of this Chapter. Tighten the steering gear mounting bolts to the specified torque, but only tighten the suspension lower arm bolts moderately tight

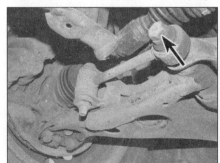

8.15a Slacken the suspension lower arm front pivot bolt (arrowed) . . .

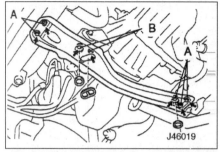

8.12 Longitudinal crossmember retaining bolts (A) and front engine/transmission mounting bracket bolts (B)

at this stage. Final tightening is carried out with the weight of the car on its roadwheels.
19 Manoeuvre the subframe assembly into position on the car and refit the retaining nuts and bolts. Tighten the mountings to the specified torque.
20 Refit the engine/transmission mounting bracket nuts/bolts and tighten to the specified torque.
21 Refit the engine/transmission longitudinal crossmember and refit the retaining bolts, cover plugs and related components in the reverse of the removal sequence given in paragraph 12. Tighten all fastenings to the specified torque. Remove the hoist and lifting tackle once the crossmember is secure.
22 Reconnect the power steering return hose at the support bracket above the steering gear.
23 Refit the exhaust sections as described in Chapter 4A.
24 Attach the steering column intermediate shaft universal joint to the steering gear pinion shaft ensuring that the marks made on removal are aligned. If new components have been fitted and no marks are present, set the roadwheels, steering gear and steering wheel in the straight-ahead position, then reconnect the universal joint. Refit the clamp bolt and tighten to the specified torque.
25 Reconnect the power steering pressure and return pipe unions to the pinion housing using new sealing washers where applicable.
26 Reconnect the fluid return hose to the power steering fluid reservoir.
27 Reconnect the suspension lower balljoints to the lower arms and secure with the bolt and

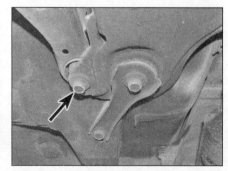

8.15b . . . and rear mounting bolt (arrowed) on each side

two nuts each side, tightened to the specified torque.

28 Reconnect the anti-roll bar drop links, then tighten the securing nuts to the specified torque, counterholding the drop link pins as during removal if necessary.

29 Engage the track-rod end balljoint shank with the hub carrier on each side, and screw on the balljoint nuts. Tighten the nuts to the specified torque, fit new split pins and bend over the split pin legs to secure. If the castellations in the nuts do not line up with the holes in the balljoint shanks, tighten the nuts a little more until the split pins can be fitted.

30 Refit the engine compartment undershields.

31 Refit the roadwheel, and lower the vehicle to the ground. Tighten the roadwheel nuts to the specified torque.

32 Bounce the car up and down several times to allow the suspension to settle.

33 Tighten the lower arm pivot and mounting bolts to the specified torque, starting with the front pivot bolt, then the rear mounting bolt.

34 Fill the power steering fluid reservoir with the specified fluid (see *Lubricants and fluids*) then bleed the power steering gear as described in Section 22.

35 On completion, have the front wheel alignment checked at the earliest opportunity (see Section 25).

9 Rear hub bearing – checking and renewal
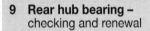

Checking

1 Chock the front wheels then jack up the rear of the car and support it on axle stands (see *Jacking and vehicle support*). Remove the rear roadwheels.

2 Refer to Chapter 9 and remove the rear brake drum or rear brake disc, as applicable.

3 Wear in the rear hub bearings can be checked by measuring the amount of side play present. To do this, a dial gauge should be fixed so that its probe is in contact with the drum or disc contact face of the wheel hub, near the centre of the hub. The axial play should be between 0 and 0.05 mm.

10.3 Two of the four hub carrier-to-rear axle carrier retaining bolts (arrowed)

If the play is greater than specified, the bearings are worn excessively and must be renewed.

4 At the same time, check the run-out of the wheel hub by repositioning the dial gauge probe towards the outside edge of the hub. Rotate the hub, and observe the deviation in the reading. If the run-out is greater than 0.07 mm, the wheel hub and bearings should be renewed.

Renewal

5 If renewal of the hub bearings is necessary a complete rear hub carrier and wheel hub assembly must be obtained (see Section 10). The assembly cannot be dismantled and the bearing is not available separately.

10 Rear hub carrier – removal and refitting

Removal

1 Chock the front wheels then jack up the rear of the car and support it on axle stands (see *Jacking and vehicle support*). Remove the relevant rear roadwheel.

2 Refer to Chapter 9 and remove the rear brake drum or rear brake disc, as applicable.

3 Undo the four bolts securing the hub carrier to the rear axle carrier **(see illustration)**. The bolts can be accessed by inserting a socket and extension bar through the hole in the wheel hub.

4 Withdraw the hub carrier assembly from the axle carrier and recover the sealing O-ring.

Refitting

5 Refitting is a reversal of removal, bearing in mind the following points:
a) Use a new sealing O-ring lightly lubricated with multi-purpose grease.
b) Tighten the hub carrier retaining bolts to the specified torque.
c) Refit the rear brake drum or disc as described in Chapter 9.

11 Rear axle carrier – removal and refitting

Removal

1 Remove the rear hub carrier as described in Section 10.

2 Withdraw the brake backplate from the axle carrier and tie the backplate to the rear coil spring using string or wire. To avoid straining the flexible brake hydraulic hose, disconnect it from the support bracket on the suspension strut.

3 On models with anti-lock brakes, undo the retaining bolt and remove the ABS wheel speed sensor from the axle carrier.

4 Slacken, but do not remove at this stage, the two nuts and bolts securing the suspension strut to the axle carrier **(see illustration)**.

5 Undo the two nuts and two bolts and disconnect the two transverse links from the axle carrier **(see illustration)**.

6 Undo the nut and bolt and disconnect the longitudinal link from the base of the axle carrier **(see illustration)**.

7 Remove the two previously-slackened suspension strut-to-axle carrier nuts and bolts and remove the axle carrier from the car.

Refitting

8 Connect the suspension strut, transverse links and longitudinal link to the axle carrier and tighten the nuts and bolts moderately tight only at this stage.

9 With the carrier in place, tighten the suspension strut-to-axle carrier nuts and bolts to the specified torque. The transverse and longitudinal link securing nuts are tightened when the weight of the car is standing on its roadwheels.

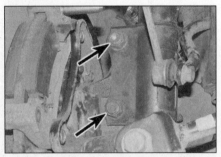

11.4 Slacken the two nuts (arrowed) securing the suspension strut to the rear axle carrier

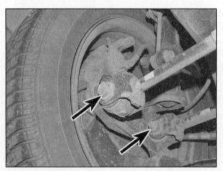

11.5 Transverse link attachments (arrowed) at the rear axle carrier

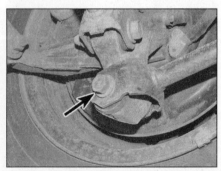

11.6 Longitudinal link attachment at the base of the rear axle carrier

10 Where applicable, refit the ABS wheel speed sensor and secure with the retaining bolt.

11 Place the brake backplate in position then refit the rear hub carrier (see Section 9).

12 Reconnect the brake hose support bracket to the suspension strut.

13 Refit the roadwheel, and lower the car to the ground. Tighten the wheel nuts to the specified torque.

14 Bounce the car up and down several times to allow the suspension to settle.

15 Tighten the longitudinal link and transverse link securing nuts and bolts to the specified torque.

12 Rear suspension strut – removal, overhaul and refitting

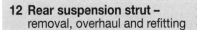

Removal

1 Refer to Chapter 11 and remove the relevant rear interior trim panels for access to the suspension strut upper mounting.

2 Chock the front wheels then jack up the rear of the car and support it on axle stands (see *Jacking and vehicle support*). Remove the relevant rear roadwheel.

3 Undo the support bracket bolts and remove the flexible brake hydraulic hose and the ABS speed sensor wiring from the suspension strut **(see illustrations)**.

4 Unscrew the securing nut, and disconnect the anti-roll bar drop link from the suspension strut **(see illustration)**. It will be necessary to counterhold the drop link pin using an Allen key or hexagon bit as the nut is unscrewed.

5 Slacken the two nuts and bolts securing the suspension strut to the rear axle carrier **(see illustration)**.

6 Position a jack under the rear axle carrier and raise the jack to just take the weight of the suspension assembly.

7 Working in the luggage compartment, lift off the protective cap from the centre of the strut mounting then unscrew the three nuts securing the top of the suspension strut to the vehicle body **(see illustrations)**.

8 Lower the jack under the rear axle carrier then remove the previously-slackened nuts and bolts securing the strut to the axle carrier. Remove the suspension strut assembly from under the wheel arch.

Overhaul

⚠️ *Warning: Before attempting to dismantle the suspension strut, a suitable tool to hold the coil spring in compression must be obtained. Adjustable coil spring compressors which can be positively secured to the spring coils are readily available, and are recommended for this operation. Any attempt to dismantle the strut without such a tool is likely to result in damage or personal injury.*

9 With the strut removed from the car as

12.3a Undo the support bracket bolts and remove the flexible brake hydraulic hose . . .

12.3b . . . and the ABS wheel speed sensor wiring from the suspension strut

12.4 Unscrew the securing nut, and disconnect the anti-roll bar drop link from the suspension strut

described previously, clean away all external dirt.

10 Fit the spring compressor tool and compress the coil spring until all tension is relieved from the upper mounting.

11 Securely clamp the upper spring seat

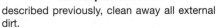
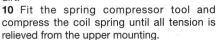

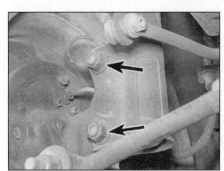

12.5 Suspension strut-to-rear axle carrier retaining bolts (arrowed)

using a pair of grips so that it cannot rotate in relation to the strut.

12 Unscrew the central piston rod nut and remove the nut and collar **(see illustrations)**.

13 Note the orientation and location of all components to aid refitting.

12.7a Lift off the protective cap from the centre of the strut mounting . . .

12.7b . . . then unscrew the three nuts (arrowed) securing the top of the suspension strut to the vehicle body

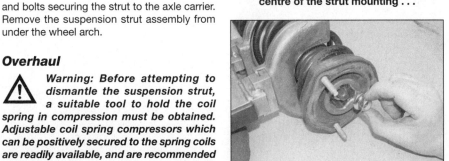

12.12a Unscrew the central piston rod nut . . .

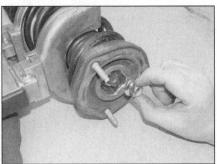

12.12b . . . and remove the nut and collar

12.14a Lift off the upper mounting and upper spring seat . . .

12.14b . . . followed by the bump rubber

12.15 Withdraw the spring and compressor tool . . .

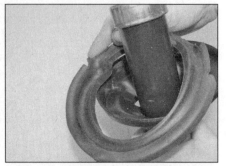

12.16 . . . followed by the lower mounting rubber

12.21 Fit the upper mounting with the pointed edge (arrowed) positioned toward the outboard side of the strut

14 Lift off the upper mounting and upper spring seat, followed by the bump rubber **(see illustrations)**.
15 Withdraw the spring and compressor tool. Do not remove the tool from the spring unless the spring is to be renewed **(see illustration)**.
16 Withdraw the lower mounting rubber **(see illustration)**.
17 With the strut assembly now completely dismantled, examine all the components for wear, damage or deformation. Check the rubbers for cracks and splits. Renew any of the components as necessary.
18 Examine the strut for signs of fluid leakage. Check the strut piston rod for signs of pitting along its entire length and check the strut body for signs of damage or elongation of the mounting bolt holes. Test the operation of the strut, while holding it in an upright position, by moving the piston rod through a full stroke and then through short strokes of 50 to 100 mm. In both cases the resistance felt should be smooth

and continuous. If the resistance is jerky, or uneven, or if there is any visible sign of wear or damage to the strut, renewal is necessary.
19 If any doubt exists about the condition of the coil spring, gradually release the spring compressor, and check the spring for distortion and signs of cracking. Since no minimum free length is specified by Toyota, the only way to check the tension of the spring is to compare it to a new component. Renew the spring if it is damaged or distorted, or if there is any doubt as to its condition.
20 Inspect all other components for signs of damage or deterioration, and renew any that are suspect.
21 Reassembly is a reversal of dismantling, bearing in mind the following points.
a) If a new strut is being fitted, prime the strut before refitting the spring, by compressing and extending the piston rod several times.
b) Ensure that all components are correctly

orientated and positioned, as noted before dismantling.
c) Make sure that the spring ends are correctly located in the upper and lower seats.
d) Ensure that the upper spring seat is correctly orientated, with the pointed edge of the upper mounting positioned toward the outboard side of the strut (see illustration).
e) Tighten the piston rod nut to the specified torque.

Refitting
22 Refitting is a reversal of removal, tightening all fixings to the specified torque.

13 Rear suspension longitudinal links – removal and refitting

Removal
1 Chock the front wheels then jack up the rear of the car and support it on axle stands (see *Jacking and vehicle support*). Remove the relevant rear roadwheel.
2 Undo the handbrake cable support bracket bolt and move the cable to one side **(see illustration)**.
3 Undo the nut and bolt and disconnect the longitudinal link from the base of the axle carrier **(see illustration 11.6)**.
4 Undo the nut and bolt and disconnect the longitudinal link from its forward chassis mounting then remove the link from car **(see illustration)**.

Refitting
5 Engage the link in its chassis and axle carrier locations, fit the mounting nuts and bolts and tighten the nuts moderately tight only at this stage.
6 Refit the roadwheel, and lower the car to the ground. Tighten the wheel nuts to the specified torque.
7 Bounce the car up and down several times to allow the suspension to settle.
8 Tighten the longitudinal link mounting nuts and bolts to the specified torque, then refit the handbrake cable support bracket.

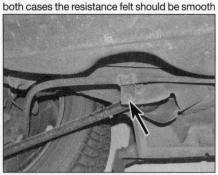

13.2 Handbrake cable support bracket bolt (arrowed)

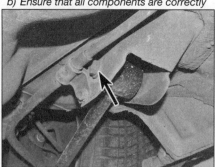

13.4 Longitudinal link front mounting bolt (arrowed)

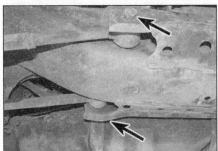

14.6 Left-hand side transverse link attachments (arrowed) at the rear subframe

14.8 Subframe brace outer attachment bolt (arrowed)

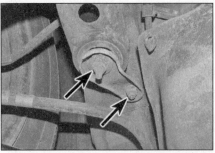

14.9 Undo the two nuts each side (arrowed) securing the subframe and stiffener plates to the underbody

14 Rear suspension transverse links – removal and refitting

Removal

1 Remove both rear suspension longitudinal links as described in Section 13.

2 Undo the nut and bolt each side and disconnect the adjustable transverse links from the base of the axle carrier.

3 Undo the bolt each side, disconnect the adjustable transverse links from the rear subframe then remove the links from under car.

4 Refer to Chapter 4A and remove the exhaust tailpipe.

5 Undo the nut and bolt each side and disconnect the transverse links from the base of the axle carrier **(see illustration 11.5)**.

6 Slacken, but do not remove at this stage, the bolt securing each transverse link to the subframe **(see illustration)**.

7 Place a jack under the centre of the rear subframe and raise the jack until it just contacts the subframe.

8 Undo the two outer bolts and the two inner bolts and remove the subframe brace **(see illustration)**.

9 Undo the two nuts each side securing the subframe and stiffener plates to the underbody **(see illustration)**. Remove the stiffener plates.

10 Slowly lower the jack and subframe assembly until sufficient clearance exists for the transverse link inner mounting bolts to be withdrawn.

11 Remove the mounting bolts securing the transverse links to the subframe, then remove the links from under the car.

12 To dismantle the adjustable transverse links, slacken the locknuts and unscrew the two link ends from the centre section.

13 Check the condition of all components and renew any that show evidence of damage or distortion. Note that if the mounting bushes in the links are worn, a new link must be obtained; the bushes are not available separately.

14 Prior to refitting, measure the length of the adjustable transverse links between the centres of the mounting bolt holes. Set the length of each link to 420.0 ± 1.5 mm by slackening the locknuts and turning the centre section. Once the link length is set, check that there are the same number of exposed threads visible next to the locknuts on each side. If not, turn the links themselves in relation to the centre section, as necessary, until the length is correct and the same number of threads are visible each side. Tighten the locknuts when all is correct.

Refitting

15 Refitting is a reversal of removal, bearing in mind the following points:

a) *Secure the links with the mounting bolts/nuts, but only tighten the bolts/nuts moderately tight at this stage. Final tightening is carried out with the weight of the car on its roadwheels.*

b) *Locate the subframe, stiffenr plates and subframe brace in position and tighten the mounting bolts and nuts to the specified torque.*

c) *Refit the longitudinal links as described in Section 13.*

d) *Refit the exhaust tailpipe as described in Chapter 4A.*

e) *With the car on its roadwheels, bounce it up and down several times to allow the suspension to settle then tighten the longitudinal link and transverse link mounting nuts and bolts to the specified torque.*

f) *On completion have the rear wheel alignment checked at the earliest opportunity (see Section 25).*

15 Rear anti-roll bar components – removal and refitting

Removal

1 Chock the front wheels then jack up the rear of the car and support it on axle stands (see *Jacking and vehicle support*). Remove the rear roadwheels.

2 Refer to Chapter 4A and remove the exhaust tailpipe.

3 Unscrew the securing nuts, and disconnect the anti-roll bar drop links from the rear

suspension struts **(see illustration)**. Note that it may be necessary to counterhold the drop link pins using an Allen key or bit.

4 Disconnect the drop links from the anti-roll bar in the same way and remove the links.

5 Place a jack under the centre of the rear subframe and raise the jack until it just contacts the subframe.

6 Undo the two outer bolts and the two inner bolts and remove the subframe brace **(see illustration 14.8)**.

7 Undo the two nuts each side securing the subframe and stiffener plates to the underbody **(see illustration 14.9)**. Remove the stiffener plates.

8 Slowly lower the jack and subframe assembly until sufficient clearance exists to gain access to the anti-roll bar clamp plates.

9 Undo the bolts securing the two anti-roll bar clamp plates to the chassis members each side and lift off the plates.

10 Place a second jack with an interposed block of wood beneath the fuel tank, then raise the jack until it is supporting the weight of the tank.

11 Unscrew and remove the two fuel tank retaining strap rear bolts.

12 Slowly lower the jack and fuel tank slightly, then turn the anti-roll bar as necessary and manoeuvre it out from under the left-hand side of the car. Withdraw the two bushes from the anti-roll bar after removal.

13 Inspect the condition of the rubber bushes and renew if any signs of deterioration are visible. Check the condition of the drop link balljoints and renew the drop links if the balljoints are worn.

15.3 Rear anti-roll bar drop link attachment (arrowed) to the rear suspension strut

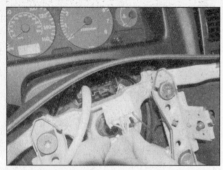

17.4 Disconnect the horn wiring at the steering wheel connector

17.5a Make alignment marks (arrowed) between the steering wheel and column shaft . . .

17.5b . . . then slacken the steering wheel retaining nut

17.6 If the wheel is tight, use a suitable puller to release the taper

17.7 Centralise the airbag rotary connector and align the pointers (arrowed) on the connector face

6 Grip the wheel each side, and pull it to release it from the taper on the column shaft. If the wheel is tight, use a suitable puller. Threaded holes are provided in the steering wheel hub for this purpose **(see illustration)**. Once the wheel has released, undo the nut and withdraw the wheel from the column shaft.

Refitting

7 Make sure that the front wheels are in the straight-ahead position. Turn the airbag rotary connector assembly at the top of the column behind the steering wheel location anti-clockwise until it becomes tight. Now turn it clockwise two complete turns and align the pointers on the lower left of the connector face **(see illustration)**.
8 Align the marks on the steering wheel and column shaft made on removal and locate the wheel in position.
9 Refit the retaining nut and tighten it to the specified torque.
10 Reconnect the horn wiring connector.
11 Refit the airbag unit as described in Chapter 12.

Refitting

14 Refitting is a reversal of removal, tightening all nuts and bolts to the specified torque.

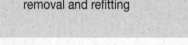

16 Rear subframe –
removal and refitting

Rear subframe removal and refitting is part of the rear transverse link removal and refitting operations. Refer to Section 14 for the full procedure.

17 Steering wheel –
removal and refitting

Note: *All models are equipped with a driver's airbag.*

18.4 Combination switch upper securing screws (arrowed)

⚠️ **Warning: Refer to the airbag precautions given in Chapter 12 before proceeding.**

Removal

1 Turn the ignition key to release the steering lock, then set the front roadwheels in the straight-ahead position. Move the ignition key to the 'off' position.
2 Disconnect the battery negative terminal (refer to *Disconnecting the battery* in the Reference Chapter).
3 Remove the airbag unit from the centre of the steering wheel as described in Chapter 12.
4 Disconnect the horn wiring at the connector at the top of the steering wheel **(see illustration)**.
5 Mark the position of the steering wheel in relation to the column shaft using quick-drying paint, then slacken the steering wheel retaining nut two or three turns **(see illustrations)**.

18.5 Release the retaining clip (arrowed) and withdraw the rubber dust cover from the floor

18 Steering column –
removal and refitting

Removal

1 Remove the steering wheel as described in Section 17.
2 Remove the driver's side lower facia panel and the steering column shrouds as described in Chapter 11.
3 Unclip the large wiring connector from the steering column then disconnect the combination switch, ignition switch, airbag and anti-theft system transponder wiring connectors.
4 Undo the two upper screws, and single lower screw securing the combination switch, and remove the switch from the steering column **(see illustration)**.
5 Fold back the carpet, release the retaining clip, and withdraw the steering column shaft rubber dust cover from the floor **(see illustration)**.
6 Working in the engine compartment, make

19.3 Carefully unclip the anti-theft system transponder from the ignition switch

19.5a Depress the lock barrel securing plunger . . .

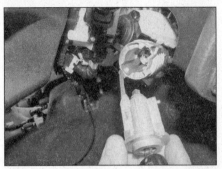

19.5b . . . while pulling the key to withdraw the lock barrel

alignment marks on the steering gear pinion shaft and column shaft lower universal joint using quick-drying paint. Undo the clamp bolt securing the lower universal joint to the pinion shaft **(see illustration 8.8)**. Carefully lever the lower universal joint up and off the pinion shaft.

7 Undo the two upper bolts and two lower nuts securing the steering column to its mounting under the facia and remove the steering column assembly from the car.

Refitting

8 Refitting is a reversal of removal, bearing in mind the following points:
  a) *Tighten all nuts and bolts to the specified torque (where given).*
  b) *Ensure that the alignment marks made during removal between the steering gear pinion shaft and lower universal joint are aligned.*
  c) *Refit the steering column shrouds and lower facia panel as described in Chapter 11.*
  d) *Refit the steering wheel as described in Section 17.*

19 Ignition switch/ steering column lock – removal and refitting

Removal

1 Disconnect the battery negative terminal (refer to *Disconnecting the battery* in the Reference Chapter).
2 Remove the driver's side lower facia panel and the steering column shrouds as described in Chapter 11.

Key lock barrel

3 Using a small screwdriver, carefully unclip the anti-theft system transponder from the ignition switch **(see illustration)**.
4 Insert the ignition key into the lock and turn it to the ACC position.
5 Depress the lock barrel securing plunger, using a small screwdriver inserted through the access hole in the lock housing, while pulling the key to withdraw the lock barrel **(see illustrations)**.

Ignition/starter switch

Caution: Do not remove the ignition/

starter switch whilst the key lock barrel is removed
6 Disconnect the switch wiring connectors.
7 Remove the two screws securing the switch to the rear of the lock barrel housing and remove the switch.
8 Installation is the reverse of removal.

Refitting

9 Refitting is a reversal of removal. Ensure that the lock barrel is correctly aligned so that its shaft engages with the ignition/starter switch, and ensure that the plunger secures it positively. Refit the steering column shrouds and lower facia panel as described in Chapter 11 on completion.

20 Steering gear assembly – removal and refitting

Removal

1 Remove the front subframe as described in Section 8.
2 Undo the steering gear mounting bolts and nuts and remove the steering gear from the subframe **(see illustrations)**.

Refitting

3 Refitting is a reversal of removal. Tighten the steering gear mounting nuts and bolts to the specified torque then refit the subframe as described in Section 8.

20.2a Typical steering gear-to-subframe left-hand mounting . . .

20.2b . . . and right-hand mounting (right-hand drive version shown)

21 Steering gear rubber gaiters – renewal

1 Remove the track rod end from the track rod as described in Section 24.
2 Count and record the number of exposed threads from the back of the track rod end locknut to the beginning of the threaded portion of the track rod. Now unscrew the locknut.
3 Release the rubber gaiter retaining clips and withdraw the gaiter from the steering gear and track rod.
4 Liberally apply power steering fluid to the rack teeth, bush and track rod inner balljoint.
5 Fit the new gaiter and its new inner clip to the steering gear ensuring that they are correctly located, then fasten the clip to secure. Secure the small end of the gaiter with a new outer clip.
6 Screw the track rod end locknut back onto the track rod positioning it in the exact location as noted during removal.
7 Refit the track rod end as described in Section 24.

22 Power steering hydraulic system – bleeding

1 This will normally only be required if any part of the hydraulic system has been disconnected.

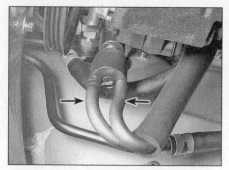

23.5 Where fitted, disconnect the two hoses (arrowed) from the power steering pump – pre-August 2000 models

2 Referring to *Weekly checks*, remove the fluid reservoir filler cap, and top-up with the specified fluid to the maximum level mark.
3 Firmly apply the handbrake, then jack up the front of the car and support it securely on axle stands (see *Jacking and vehicle support*).
4 With the engine switched off, slowly turn the steering wheel from lock-to-lock several times.
5 Lower the car to the ground, start the engine and allow it to idle for a few minutes. With the engine still idling, turn the steering wheel to full left, or full right lock and hold it there for two or three seconds. Now turn the steering to full lock in the other direction and again hold it there for a few seconds. Repeat this procedure several times.
6 Stop the engine, recheck the fluid level and top-up if necessary.

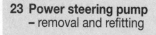

23 Power steering pump
– removal and refitting

Removal

Pre-August 2000 models

1 Remove the auxiliary (power steering pump) drivebelt as described in Chapter 1.
2 On 2.0 litre models, remove the right-hand driveshaft as described in Chapter 8.
3 Slacken the hose clip and disconnect the fluid return hose from the pump. Allow the fluid to drain into a suitable container.
4 Undo the banjo union bolt and disconnect the fluid feed (pressure) pipe from the pump,

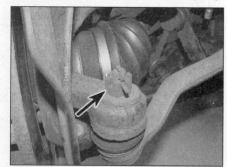

24.4 Track rod end balljoint retaining nut and split pin (arrowed)

23.8 Release the clip and disconnect the fluid return hose from the power steering pump – post-August 2000 models

collecting the sealing washers as the union is disconnected. Note that new sealing washers will be required for refitting.
5 Where applicable, disconnect the pressure switch wiring connector, or the small bore hoses from the air control valve **(see illustration)**.
6 Undo the pump mounting bolt and adjuster bolt and remove the pump assembly from the engine.

Post-August 2000 models

7 Remove the auxiliary drivebelt as described in Chapter 1.
8 Slacken the hose clip and disconnect the fluid return hose from the pump **(see illustration)**. Allow the fluid to drain into a suitable container.
9 On 1.6 and 1.8 litre models, undo the bolt securing the fluid feed (pressure) pipe support bracket from the pump. Unscrew the feed pipe union nut and disconnect the pipe.
10 On 2.0 litre models, undo the banjo union bolt and disconnect the fluid feed (pressure) pipe from the pump, collecting the sealing washers as the union is disconnected. Note that new sealing washers will be required for refitting.
11 Disconnect the pressure switch wiring connector **(see illustration)**.
12 Undo the pump mounting bolt and adjuster bolt and remove the pump assembly from the engine.
13 Turn the pump pulley so that the two pump mounting bolts are accessible through the slots in the pulley. Hold the bolts with a socket and extension, while unscrewing the nuts at the rear.
14 Withdraw the bolts and remove the pump assembly from the engine.

Refitting

15 Refitting is a reversal of removal, bearing in mind the following points:
  a) *Tighten all fastenings to the specified torque.*
  b) *Use new sealing washers on the fluid feed pipe banjo union.*
  c) *Where applicable, refit the driveshaft as described in Chapter 8.*
  d) *Refit and adjust the auxiliary drivebelt as described in Chapter 1.*
  e) *On completion, bleed the power steering hydraulic system as described in Section 22.*

23.11 Disconnect the power steering pressure switch wiring connector from the pump – post-August 2000 models

24 Track rod end –
removal and refitting

Removal

1 Firmly apply the handbrake, then jack up the front of the car and support it securely on axle stands (see *Jacking and vehicle support*). Remove the relevant front roadwheel.
2 Use a wire brush to scrub clean the exposed track rod threads, then use a straight-edge and a scriber, or similar, to mark the relationship of the track rod end to the track rod.
3 Holding the track rod end, unscrew its locknut by one quarter of a turn.
4 Extract the split pin from the track rod end balljoint nut and unscrew the nut as far as the end of the balljoint shank threads **(see illustration)**. Using a balljoint separator tool, release the track rod end balljoint tapered shank. Once the taper has separated, unscrew the nut and detach the track rod end from the hub carrier.
5 Counting the exact number of turns necessary to do so, unscrew the track rod end from the track rod.

Refitting

6 Screw the track rod end onto the track rod the number of turns noted during removal. This should return the track rod end to within a quarter turn of the locknut and, if the original component is being refitted, bring the marks made on removal into alignment. Now tighten the locknut while holding the track rod end securely.
7 Engage the shank of the track rod end balljoint with the hub carrier, and refit the retaining nut. Tighten the nut to the specified torque then fit a new split pin. If the castellations in the nut do not line up with the holes in the balljoint shank, tighten the nut a little more until the split pin can be fitted. Bend over the split pin legs to secure.
8 Refit the roadwheel, and lower the car to the ground. Tighten the wheel nuts to the specified torque.
9 Finally, have the front wheel alignment checked (see Section 25).

25 Wheel alignment and steering angles – general information

Definitions

1 A car's steering and suspension geometry is defined in four basic settings; the steering axis is defined as an imaginary line drawn through the axis of the suspension strut, extended where necessary to contact the ground.

2 **Camber** is the angle between each roadwheel and a vertical line drawn through its centre and tyre contact patch, when viewed from the front or rear of the car. Positive camber is when the roadwheels are tilted outwards from the vertical at the top; negative camber is when they are tilted inwards. The front camber angle is adjustable by using suspension strut-to-hub carrier retaining bolts of different diameters. The rear camber angle is not adjustable.

3 **Castor** is the angle between the steering axis and a vertical line drawn through each roadwheel's centre and tyre contact patch, when viewed from the side of the car. Positive castor is when the steering axis is tilted so that it contacts the ground ahead of the vertical; negative castor is when it contacts the ground behind the vertical. The castor angle is not adjustable.

4 **Toe** is the difference, viewed from above, between lines drawn through the roadwheel centres and the car's centre-line. 'Toe-in' is when the roadwheels point inwards, towards each other at the front, while 'toe-out' is when they splay outwards from each other at the front.

5 The front wheel toe setting is adjusted by screwing the track rod in or out of its balljoints, to alter the effective length of the track rod assembly.

6 Rear wheel toe setting is adjusted by altering the length of the rear suspension adjustable transverse links.

Checking and adjustment

7 Due to the special measuring equipment necessary to check the wheel alignment and steering angles, and the skill required to use it properly, the checking and adjustment of these settings is best left to a Toyota dealer or similar expert. Note that most tyre-fitting shops now possess sophisticated checking equipment.

Notes

Chapter 11
Bodywork and fittings

Contents

Degrees of difficulty

Easy, suitable for novice with little experience	**Fairly easy,** suitable for beginner with some experience	**Fairly difficult,** suitable for competent DIY mechanic	**Difficult,** suitable for experienced DIY mechanic	**Very difficult,** suitable for expert DIY or professional

Specifications

Torque wrench settings	Nm	lbf ft
Boot lid to hinge.	8	6
Door hinge bolts.	26	19
Front seat belts:		
Inertia reel mounting bolts	44	32
Anchor bolts.	44	32
Seat belt stalk.	42	31
Front seat mounting bolts	37	27
Hinge to tailgate	13	10
Passenger's airbag mounting bolts	21	15
Rear seat belts (all mountings).	65	48
Rear seat mounting bolts:		
Saloon models	37	27
Hatchback and Estate models	21	15
Tailgate hinge to body	21	15

1 General information

The bodyshell is made of pressed-steel sections, and is available in 4-door Saloon, 5-door Hatchback and 5-door Estate versions. Most components are welded together, but some use is made of structural adhesives, and the front wings are bolted on.

The front and rear body sections incorporate crumple zones and the doors are fitted with side bars. The lower areas of the body and doors are coated with an anti-stone chipping protective material.

Extensive use is made of plastic materials, mainly in the interior, but also in exterior components. The outer sections of the front and rear bumpers are injection-moulded from a synthetic material which is very strong, and yet light. Plastic components such as wheel arch liners are fitted to the underside of the vehicle, to improve the body's resistance to corrosion.

2 Maintenance – bodywork and underframe

The general condition of a vehicle's bodywork is the one thing that significantly affects its value. Maintenance is easy, but needs to be regular. Neglect, particularly after minor damage, can lead quickly to further deterioration and costly repair bills. It is important also to keep watch on those parts of the vehicle not immediately visible, for instance the underside, inside all the wheel arches, and the lower part of the engine compartment.

The basic maintenance routine for the bodywork is washing – preferably with a lot of water, from a hose. This will remove all the loose solids which may have stuck to the vehicle. It is important to flush these off in such a way as to prevent grit from scratching the finish. The wheel arches and underframe need washing in the same way, to remove any accumulated mud, which will retain moisture and tend to encourage rust. Paradoxically enough, the best time to clean the underframe and wheel arches is in wet weather, when the mud is thoroughly wet and soft. In very wet weather, the underframe is usually cleaned of large accumulations automatically, and this is a good time for inspection.

Periodically, except on vehicles with a wax-based underbody protective coating, it is a good idea to have the whole of the underframe of the vehicle steam-cleaned, engine compartment included, so that a thorough inspection can be carried out to see what minor repairs and renovations are necessary. Steam-cleaning is available at many garages, and is necessary for the removal of the accumulation of oily grime, which sometimes is allowed to become thick in certain areas. If steam-cleaning facilities are not available, there are some excellent grease solvents available which can be brush-applied; the dirt can then be simply hosed off. Note that these methods should not be used on vehicles with wax-based underbody protective coating, or the coating will be removed. Such vehicles should be inspected annually, preferably just prior to Winter, when the underbody should be washed down, and any damage to the wax coating repaired. Ideally, a completely fresh coat should be applied. It would also be worth considering the use of such wax-based protection for injection into door panels, sills, box sections, etc, as an additional safeguard against rust damage, where such protection is not provided by the vehicle manufacturer.

After washing paintwork, wipe off with a chamois leather to give an unspotted clear finish. A coat of clear protective wax polish will give added protection against chemical pollutants in the air. If the paintwork sheen has dulled or oxidised, use a cleaner/polisher combination to restore the brilliance of the shine. This requires a little effort, but such dulling is usually caused because regular washing has been neglected. Care needs to be taken with metallic paintwork, as special non-abrasive cleaner/polisher is required to avoid damage to the finish. Always check that the door and ventilator opening drain holes and pipes are completely clear, so that water can be drained out. Brightwork should be treated in the same way as paintwork. Windscreens and windows can be kept clear of the smeary film which often appears, by the use of proprietary glass cleaner. Never use any form of wax or other body or chromium polish on glass.

3 Maintenance – upholstery and carpets

Mats and carpets should be brushed or vacuum-cleaned regularly, to keep them free of grit. If they are badly stained, remove them from the vehicle for scrubbing or sponging, and make quite sure they are dry before refitting. Seats and interior trim panels can be kept clean by wiping with a damp cloth. If they do become stained (which can be more apparent on light-coloured upholstery), use a little liquid detergent and a soft nail brush to scour the grime out of the grain of the material. Do not forget to keep the headlining clean in the same way as the upholstery. When using liquid cleaners inside the vehicle, do not over-wet the surfaces being cleaned. Excessive damp could get into the seams and padded interior, causing stains, offensive odours or even rot.

> **HAYNES HINT** *If the inside of the vehicle gets wet accidentally, it is worthwhile taking some trouble to dry it out properly, particularly where carpets are involved. Do not leave oil or electric heaters inside the vehicle for this purpose.*

4 Minor body damage – repair

Minor scratches in bodywork

If the scratch is very superficial, and does not penetrate to the metal of the bodywork, repair is very simple. Lightly rub the area of the scratch with a paintwork renovator, or a very fine cutting paste, to remove loose paint from the scratch, and to clear the surrounding bodywork of wax polish. Rinse the area with clean water.

Apply touch-up paint to the scratch using a fine paint brush; continue to apply fine layers of paint until the surface of the paint in the scratch is level with the surrounding paintwork. Allow the new paint at least two weeks to harden, then blend it into the surrounding paintwork by rubbing the scratch area with a paintwork renovator or a very fine cutting paste. Finally, apply wax polish.

Where the scratch has penetrated right through to the metal of the bodywork, causing the metal to rust, a different repair technique is required. Remove any loose rust from the bottom of the scratch with a penknife, then apply rust-inhibiting paint to prevent the formation of rust in the future. Using a rubber or nylon applicator, fill the scratch with bodystopper paste. If required, this paste can be mixed with cellulose thinners to provide a very thin paste which is ideal for filling narrow scratches. Before the stopper-paste in the scratch hardens, wrap a piece of smooth cotton rag around the top of a finger. Dip the finger in cellulose thinners, and quickly sweep it across the surface of the stopper-paste in the scratch; this will ensure that the surface of the stopper-paste is slightly hollowed. The scratch can now be painted over as described earlier in this Section.

Dents in bodywork

When deep denting of the vehicle's bodywork has taken place, the first task is to pull the dent out, until the affected bodywork almost attains its original shape. There is little point in trying to restore the original shape completely, as the metal in the damaged area will have stretched on impact, and cannot be reshaped fully to its original contour. It is better to bring the level of the dent up to a point which is about 3 mm below the level of the surrounding bodywork. In cases where the dent is very shallow anyway, it is not worth trying to pull it out at all. If the underside of the dent is accessible, it can be hammered out gently from behind, using a mallet with a wooden or plastic head. Whilst doing this, hold a suitable block of wood firmly against the outside of the panel, to absorb the impact from the hammer blows and thus prevent a large area of the bodywork from being belled-out.

Should the dent be in a section of the bodywork which has a double skin, or some other factor making it inaccessible from behind, a different technique is called for. Drill several small holes through the metal inside the area – particularly in the deeper section. Then screw long self-tapping screws into the holes, just sufficiently for them to gain a good purchase in the metal. Now the dent can be pulled out by pulling on the protruding heads of the screws with a pair of pliers.

The next stage of the repair is the removal of the paint from the damaged area, and from an inch or so of the surrounding sound bodywork. This is accomplished most easily by using a wire brush or abrasive pad on a power drill, although it can be done just as effectively by hand, using sheets of abrasive paper. To complete the preparation for filling, score the surface of the bare metal with a screwdriver or the tang of a file, or alternatively, drill small holes in the affected area. This will provide a really good key for the filler paste.

To complete the repair, see the Section on filling and respraying.

Rust holes or gashes

Remove all paint from the affected area, and from an inch or so of the surrounding sound bodywork, using an abrasive pad or a wire brush on a power drill. If these are not available, a few sheets of abrasive paper will do the job most effectively. With the paint removed, you will be able to judge the severity of the corrosion, and therefore decide whether to renew the whole panel (if this is possible) or to repair the affected area. New body panels are not as expensive as most people think, and it is often quicker and more satisfactory to fit a new panel than to attempt to repair large areas of corrosion.

Remove all fittings from the affected area, except those which will act as a guide to the original shape of the damaged bodywork (eg headlight shells etc). Then, using tin snips or a hacksaw blade, remove all loose metal and any other metal badly affected by corrosion. Hammer the edges of the hole inwards, in order to create a slight depression for the filler paste.

Wire-brush the affected area to remove the powdery rust from the surface of the remaining metal. Paint the affected area with rust-inhibiting paint, if the back of the rusted area is accessible, treat this also.

Before filling can take place, it will be necessary to block the hole in some way. This can be achieved by the use of aluminium or plastic mesh, or aluminium tape.

Aluminium or plastic mesh, or glass-fibre matting, is probably the best material to use for a large hole. Cut a piece to the approximate size and shape of the hole to be filled, then position it in the hole so that its edges are below the level of the surrounding bodywork. It can be retained in position by several blobs of filler paste around its periphery.

Aluminium tape should be used for small or very narrow holes. Pull a piece off the roll, trim it to the approximate size and shape required, then pull off the backing paper (if used) and stick the tape over the hole; it can be overlapped if the thickness of one piece is insufficient. Burnish down the edges of the tape with the handle of a screwdriver or similar, to ensure that the tape is securely attached to the metal underneath.

Filling and respraying

Before using this Section, see the Sections on dent, deep scratch, rust holes and gash repairs.

Many types of bodyfiller are available, but generally speaking, those proprietary kits which contain a tin of filler paste and a tube of resin hardener are best for this type of repair. A wide, flexible plastic or nylon applicator will be found invaluable for imparting a smooth and well-contoured finish to the surface of the filler.

Mix up a little filler on a clean piece of card or board – measure the hardener carefully (follow the maker's instructions on the pack), otherwise the filler will set too rapidly or too slowly. Using the applicator, apply the filler paste to the prepared area; draw the applicator across the surface of the filler to achieve the correct contour and to level the surface. As soon as a contour that approximates to the correct one is achieved, stop working the paste – if you carry on too long, the paste will become sticky and begin to pick-up on the applicator. Continue to add thin layers of filler paste at 20-minute intervals, until the level of the filler is just proud of the surrounding bodywork.

Once the filler has hardened, the excess can be removed using a metal plane or file. From then on, progressively-finer grades of abrasive paper should be used, starting with a 40-grade production paper, and finishing with a 400-grade wet-and-dry paper. Always wrap the abrasive paper around a flat rubber, cork, or wooden block – otherwise the surface of the filler will not be completely flat. During the smoothing of the filler surface, the wet-and-dry paper should be periodically rinsed in water. This will ensure that a very smooth finish is imparted to the filler at the final stage.

At this stage, the dent should be surrounded by a ring of bare metal, which in turn should be encircled by the finely feathered edge of the good paintwork. Rinse the repair area with clean water, until all of the dust produced by the rubbing-down operation has gone.

Spray the whole area with a light coat of primer – this will show up any imperfections in the surface of the filler. Repair these imperfections with fresh filler paste or bodystopper, and once more smooth the surface with abrasive paper. Repeat this spray-and-repair procedure until you are satisfied that the surface of the filler, and the feathered edge of the paintwork, are perfect. Clean the repair area with clean water, and allow to dry fully.

HAYNES HiNT *If bodystopper is used, it can be mixed with cellulose thinners to form a really thin paste which is ideal for filling small holes.*

The repair area is now ready for final spraying. Paint spraying must be carried out in a warm, dry, windless and dust-free atmosphere. This condition can be created artificially if you have access to a large indoor working area, but if you are forced to work in the open, you will have to pick your day very carefully. If you are working indoors, dousing the floor in the work area with water will help to settle the dust which would otherwise be in the atmosphere. If the repair area is confined to one body panel, mask off the surrounding panels; this will help to minimise the effects of a slight mis-match in paint colours. Bodywork fittings (eg chrome strips, door handles etc) will also need to be masked off. Use genuine masking tape, and several thicknesses of newspaper, for the masking operations.

Before commencing to spray, agitate the aerosol can thoroughly, then spray a test area (an old tin, or similar) until the technique is mastered. Cover the repair area with a thick coat of primer; the thickness should be built up using several thin layers of paint, rather than one thick one. Using 400-grade wet-and-dry paper, rub down the surface of the primer until it is really smooth. While doing this, the work area should be thoroughly doused with water, and the wet-and-dry paper periodically rinsed in water. Allow to dry before spraying on more paint.

Spray on the top coat, again building up the thickness by using several thin layers of paint. Start spraying at one edge of the repair area, and then, using a side-to-side motion, work until the whole repair area and about 2 inches of the surrounding original paintwork is covered. Remove all masking material 10 to 15 minutes after spraying on the final coat of paint.

Allow the new paint at least two weeks to harden, then, using a paintwork renovator, or a very fine cutting paste, blend the edges of the paint into the existing paintwork. Finally, apply wax polish.

Plastic components

With the use of more and more plastic body components by the vehicle manufacturers (eg bumpers. spoilers, and in some cases major body panels), rectification of more serious damage to such items has become a matter of either entrusting repair work to a specialist in this field, or renewing complete components. Repair of such damage by the DIY owner is not really feasible, owing to the cost of the equipment and materials required for effecting such repairs. The basic technique involves making a groove along the line of the crack in the plastic, using a rotary burr in a power drill. The damaged part is then welded back together, using a hot-air gun to heat up and fuse a plastic filler rod into the groove. Any excess plastic is then removed, and the area rubbed down to a smooth finish. It is important that a filler rod of the correct plastic is used, as body components can be made of a variety of different types (eg polycarbonate, ABS, polypropylene).

Damage of a less serious nature (abrasions, minor cracks etc) can be repaired by the DIY owner using a two-part epoxy filler repair material. Once mixed in equal proportions, this is used in similar fashion to the bodywork filler used on metal panels. The filler is usually cured in twenty to thirty minutes, ready for sanding and painting.

If the owner is renewing a complete component himself, or if he has repaired it with epoxy filler, he will be left with the problem of finding a suitable paint for finishing which is compatible with the type of plastic used. At one time, the use of a universal paint was not possible, owing to the complex range of plastics encountered in body component applications. Standard paints, generally speaking, will not bond to plastic or rubber satisfactorily. However, it is now possible to obtain a plastic body parts finishing kit which consists of a pre-primer treatment, a primer and coloured top coat. Full instructions are normally supplied with a kit, but basically, the method of use is to first apply the pre-primer to the component concerned, and allow it to dry for up to 30 minutes. Then the primer is applied, and left to dry for about an hour before finally applying the special-coloured

top coat. The result is a correctly-coloured component, where the paint will flex with the plastic or rubber, a property that standard paint does not normally possess.

5 Major body damage – repair

Where serious damage has occurred, or large areas need renewal due to neglect, it means that complete new panels will need welding-in, and this is best left to professionals. If the damage is due to impact, it will also be necessary to check the alignment of the bodyshell, and this can only be carried out accurately by a Toyota dealer using special jigs. If the body is left misaligned, it is primarily dangerous, as the car will not handle properly, and secondly, uneven stresses will be imposed on the steering, suspension and possibly transmission, causing abnormal wear, or complete failure, particularly to such items as the tyres.

6 Bumpers – removal and refitting

Front bumper

Pre-August 2000 models

1 Firmly apply the handbrake, then jack up the front of the car and support it securely on

axle stands (see *Jacking and vehicle support*).
2 Remove the engine compartment undershields, with reference to Section 23.
3 Remove the radiator grille as described in Section 7.
4 Remove the front direction indicator light units as described in Chapter 12.
5 Where applicable, disconnect the foglight wiring connectors, and disconnect the headlight washer hoses.
6 Undo the two screws each side securing the bumper upper trim strips below the headlights. Release the outer edge of each trim strip by depressing the tab to disengage the locating clip. Remove both trim strips from the bumper **(see illustrations)**.
7 Working under the front wheel arches, unscrew the screw(s) securing the wheel arch liners to the underbody. Carefully pull out the liner slightly for access to the bolts securing the rear of the front bumper to the body. Unscrew and remove the bolts.
8 Unscrew and remove the bolts securing the bottom of the front bumper to the underbody.
9 Support the front bumper then unscrew and remove the upper expanding rivet **(see illustration)**.
10 Release the remaining retaining clips and withdraw the front bumper from the body taking care not to damage the paintwork.
11 Refitting is a reversal of removal.

Post-August 2000 models

12 Firmly apply the handbrake, then jack up the front of the car and support it securely on axle stands (see *Jacking and vehicle support*).
13 Remove the engine compartment undershields, with reference to Section 23.
14 Remove the front direction indicator light units as described in Chapter 12.
15 Extract the retaining clips and plastic rivets and remove the plastic panel above the radiator grille **(see illustrations)**.
16 Working under the front wheel arches, unscrew the screw(s) securing the wheel arch liners to the underbody. Carefully pull out the liner slightly for access to the bolts securing the rear of the front bumper to the front wing. Unscrew and remove the bolts **(see illustration)**.
17 Where applicable, disconnect the foglight wiring connectors, and disconnect the headlight washer hoses.

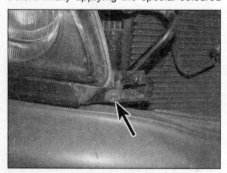

6.6a Undo the inner screw (arrowed) . . .

6.6b . . . and outer screw (arrowed) securing the bumper upper trim strips below the headlights

6.6c Release the outer edge of each trim strip by depressing the tab to disengage the locating clip

6.9 Unscrew and remove the bumper upper expanding rivet (arrowed)

6.15a On post-August 2000 models, extract the retaining clips . . .

6.15b . . . and the plastic rivets . . .

6.15c . . . and remove the plastic panel above the radiator grille

6.16 Unscrew the bolts securing the rear of the front bumper to the front wing

6.18 Unscrew and remove the bolts securing the bottom of the front bumper to the underbody

6.19a Unscrew and remove the bumper upper mounting bolt on the inside (arrowed) . . .

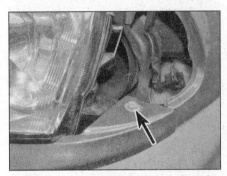

6.19b . . . and outside (arrowed) of each headlight . . .

18 Unscrew and remove the bolts securing the bottom of the front bumper to the underbody **(see illustration)**.

19 Support the front bumper then unscrew and remove the upper mounting bolts on either side of each headlight, and at the top of the radiator grille **(see illustrations)**.

20 Carefully withdraw the front bumper from the body taking care not to damage the paintwork **(see illustration)**.

21 Refitting is a reversal of removal.

Rear bumper

22 To improve access chock the front wheels, then jack up the rear of the vehicle and support on axle stands (see *Jacking and vehicle support*).

23 Refer to Section 26 and remove the boot lid/tailgate aperture lower panel and, on Saloon models, the luggage compartment rear trim panel. On Hatchback and Estate models,

remove the luggage compartment lower side trim panels.

24 On Saloon models, extract the retaining clips and remove the rear light cluster bulb access panel on each side.

6.19c . . . and at the top of the radiator grille (arrowed)

25 Undo the three screws and remove the rear mudguard on each side **(see illustrations)**.

26 Extract the clips securing the rear wheel arch liners to the rear bumper **(see illustration)**.

6.20 Withdraw the front bumper from the body taking care not to damage the paintwork

6.25a Undo the lower screw (arrowed) . . .

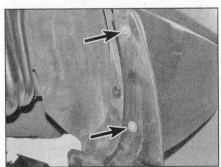

6.25b . . . and the two side screws (arrowed) and remove the rear mudguard

6.26 Extract the clips securing the rear wheel arch liners to the rear bumper

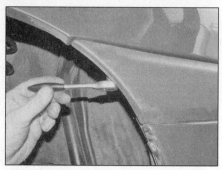

6.27 Unscrew the mounting bolts from the front upper edge of the rear bumper

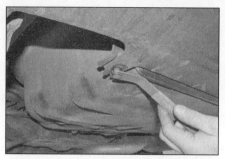

6.28 From under the car extract the clips from the front lower edge of the rear bumper

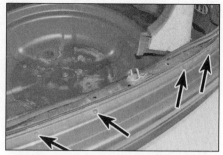

6.29 Undo and remove the four screws (arrowed) securing the upper edge of the rear bumper

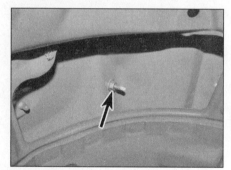

6.30 From inside the luggage compartment, undo the nut each side (arrowed) securing the bumper to the body

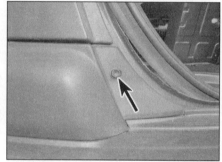

6.31 On Estate models, undo the bolt (arrowed) on each side of the tailgate aperture

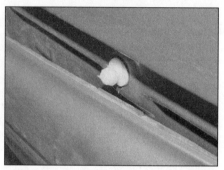

6.33 When refitting, ensure that the slot on each side of the bumper engages correctly with the stud on the body

27 Carefully pull back the liners and unscrew the mounting bolts from the front upper edge of the rear bumper **(see illustration)**.

28 From under the car extract the clips from the front lower edge of the rear bumper **(see illustration)**.

29 Undo and remove the four screws securing the upper edge of the bumper below the luggage compartment aperture **(see illustration)**.

30 From inside the luggage compartment, undo the nut each side securing the rear corner of the bumper to the body **(see illustration)**. On Saloon models, the nut is accessible through the rear light cluster bulb access aperture.

31 On Estate models, undo the bolt on each side of the tailgate aperture **(see illustration)**.

32 Withdraw the rear bumper from the body taking care not to damage the paintwork.

33 Refitting is a reversal of removal, but

ensure that the slot on each side of the bumper engages correctly with the stud on the body **(see illustration)**.

7 Radiator grille – removal and refitting

Note: *The following procedure is only applicable to pre-August 2000 models. On later models, the radiator grille is integral with the front bumper.*

Removal

1 Open the bonnet and unscrew the retaining screw from the upper centre of the radiator grille **(see illustration)**.

2 Pull the radiator grille forward to disengage the two retaining clips each side remove it from the body **(see illustration)**.

Refitting

3 Refitting is a reversal of removal.

8 Bonnet – removal, refitting and adjustment

Removal

1 Open the bonnet and have an assistant support it. Using a pencil or felt tip pen, mark the outline of each bonnet hinge relative to the bonnet, to use as a guide on refitting.

2 Disconnect the windscreen washer fluid supply hose from the connector under the bonnet, and release it from the clips.

3 Unscrew the bolts securing the bonnet to the hinges and, with the help of an assistant, carefully lift the bonnet clear. Store the bonnet out of the way in a safe place.

4 Inspect the bonnet hinges for signs of wear and free play at the pivots, and if necessary renew.

Refitting

5 With the aid of an assistant, offer up the bonnet, and loosely fit the retaining bolts. Align the hinges with the marks made on removal, then tighten the retaining bolts securely.

6 Reconnect the windscreen washer fluid supply hose.

7 Adjust the alignment of the bonnet as follows.

7.1 Unscrew the retaining screw (arrowed) from the upper centre of the radiator grille

7.2 Pull the radiator grille forward to disengage the two retaining clips each side (arrowed) then remove the grille

Adjustment

8 Close the bonnet, and check for alignment with the adjacent panels. If necessary, slacken the hinge bolts and re-align the bonnet to suit. Note that one of the hinge bolts each side is a centering bolt and full adjustment may not be possible with this bolt in place. If difficulty is experienced, substitute the centering bolt with a standard bolt and washer. Once the bonnet is correctly aligned, tighten the relevant hinge bolts securely.

9 Once the bonnet is correctly aligned, check that the bonnet fastens and releases in a satisfactory manner. If adjustment is necessary, slacken the bonnet lock retaining bolts, and adjust the position of the lock to suit. Once the lock is operating correctly, securely tighten its retaining bolts. Make sure that the bonnet striker enters the lock centrally.

10 If necessary, align the front edge of the bonnet with the wing panels by turning the rubbers screwed into the body front panel, to raise or lower the front edge as required.

9 Bonnet lock and release cable – removal and refitting

Removal

1 For improved access on pre-August 2000 models, remove the radiator grille as described in Section 7. On post-August 2000 models, extract the retaining clips and plastic rivets and remove the plastic panel above the radiator grille (see illustrations 6.15a, 6.15b and 6.15c).

2 Unscrew the three securing bolts, and remove the lock assembly from the front engine compartment crossmember (see illustration).

3 Unhook the end of the bonnet release cable from the lock lever. Withdraw the lock assembly from the vehicle.

4 Firmly apply the handbrake, then jack up the front of the car and support it securely on axle stands (see *Jacking and vehicle support*). Remove the front wheel arch liner on the driver's side as described in Section 23.

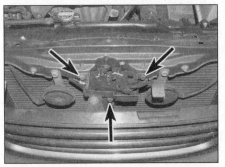
9.2 Unscrew the three bolts (arrowed), and remove the bonnet lock assembly from the engine compartment crossmember

5 Release the cable from the clips in the engine compartment.

6 Remove the driver's side lower facia panel as described in Section 26.

7 Disconnect the outer cable and the inner cable end fitting from the bonnet release lever (see illustration).

8 Working inside the vehicle on the driver's side, remove the screws securing the lower trim panel to the facia and remove the panel. Free the bonnet release lever from the lower trim panel.

9 Note the routing of the cable, and release it from the clips under the wheel arch and in the engine compartment. Feed the cable through the bulkhead grommet into the vehicle interior. On some models, it may be necessary to move certain components in the engine compartment to one side to gain access to the cable clips. It is advisable to tie a length of string to the cable before removal, to aid fitting. Pull the cable through the bulkhead, then untie the string and leave it in place until the cable is to be fitted.

Refitting

10 Refitting is a reversal of removal, but use the string to pull the cable into position, and ensure that the bulkhead grommet is securely located. Make sure that the cable is routed as noted before removal, and reposition the cable in its securing clips under the wheel arch and in the engine compartment. Check the bonnet release mechanism for correct operation on completion.

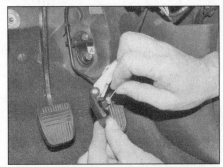
9.7 Disconnect the outer cable and the inner cable end fitting from the bonnet release lever

10 Door – removal, refitting and adjustment

Removal

1 Disconnect the battery negative terminal (refer to *Disconnecting the battery* in the Reference Chapter).

2 If the door is to be dismantled, remove the relevant door inner trim panel (Section 11). Disconnect, and draw out the wiring to the electrical components inside the door; also ensure that the earth lead wiring is disconnected. If the door is being removed intact, the wiring can be disconnected by extracting the rubber grommet from the door pillar, then disconnecting the wiring connector (see illustrations).

3 Drive out the roll-pin securing the door check arm to its body bracket.

4 Use a marker pen to mark around the door hinge positions as an aid to correct refitting (see illustration).

5 With the aid of an assistant to support the door, remove the bolts and detach the door. If necessary, the door hinges can be unbolted from the body.

Refitting

6 Refitting is the reverse of the removal procedure, noting the following points.

a) Align the hinges with the marks made on removal and lightly tighten the hinge bolts, then gently close the door and check that it fits correctly in its aperture,

10.2a Extract the rubber grommet from the door pillar . . .

10.2b . . . and disconnect the wiring connector

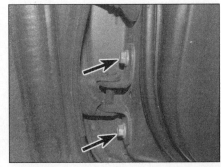
10.4 Front door hinge lower retaining bolts (arrowed)

10.8 Door striker retaining screws (arrowed)

with equal gaps at all points between it and the surrounding bodywork; if adjustment is required see below. Securely tighten the bolts.

b) When the door fits correctly in its aperture, check that it fits flush with the surrounding bodywork; if adjustment is required, move the striker (see below).

Adjustment

7 To adjust the doors in a forwards, rearwards and/or vertical direction slacken the hinge-to-body bolts; to adjust them in a left, right and/or vertical direction slacken the hinge-to-door bolts. Securely tighten the bolts when the fit is correct.

8 The striker alignment should be checked after either the door or the lock has been disturbed. To adjust a striker, slacken its screws, reposition it and securely tighten the screws **(see illustration)**.

11.2 Prise free the top of the exterior mirror trim panel, tip it out at the top, then disengage the lower lugs

11 Door inner trim panel
– removal and refitting

Front door trim panel

Removal

1 Disconnect the battery negative terminal (refer to *Disconnecting the battery* in the Reference Chapter).

2 Using a screwdriver, carefully prise free the top of the exterior mirror trim panel to release the upper retaining clip. Disengage the lower lugs and remove the panel **(see illustration)**.

3 Lift up the trim cap and undo the screw securing the inner trim panel to the interior door handle. Slide the panel forward to disengage it from the handle **(see illustrations)**.

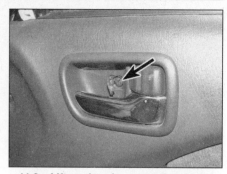

11.3a Lift up the trim cap and undo the screw (arrowed) . . .

4 Lift up the trim cap and undo the screw at the base of the door pull **(see illustration)**.

5 Lift the rear of the door pull and electric window switch assembly, then slide it rearwards to disengage the front retaining plate **(see illustrations)**. Disconnect the wiring connector and remove the assembly.

6 At the edge of the door pull aperture, undo the two screws securing the trim panel to the inner bracket **(see illustration)**.

7 Undo the centre screw of the six expanding rivets securing the front and rear edges of the trim panel to the door, then extract the rivet body. Pull the base of the panel away from the door to release the two inner retaining clips, then lift it upwards and off the door **(see illustrations)**.

Refitting

8 Refitting is a reversal of removal.

11.3b . . . then slide the trim panel forward to disengage it from the handle

11.4 Lift up the trim cap and undo the screw at the base of the door pull

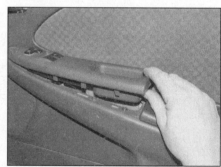

11.5a Lift the rear of the door pull and electric window switch assembly . . .

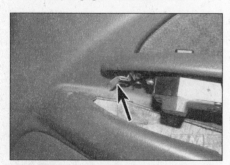

11.5b . . . then slide it rearwards to disengage the front retaining plate (arrowed)

11.6 Undo the two screws securing the trim panel to the inner bracket

11.7a Undo the screws from the expanding rivets securing the edges of the trim panel to the door . . .

11.7b . . . pull the base of the panel away from the door, then lift it upwards and off the door

11.9a Use a rag to release the regulator handle retaining clip . . .

11.9b . . . then withdraw the handle and refit the spring clip to the handle

11.11a Lift up the trim cap and undo the screw . . .

11.11b . . . then slide the trim panel forward to disengage it from the handle

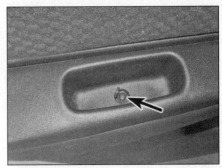

11.12 Lift up the trim cap and undo the screw (arrowed) at the base of the armrest

Rear door trim panel

Removal

9 On models with manual windows, slide a clean rag between the window regulator handle and the trim panel. Move the rag from side-to-side while pulling upwards to release the regulator handle retaining spring clip. Once the clip releases, withdraw the handle from the regulator shaft and refit the spring clip to the handle (see illustrations). Remove the regulator handle plastic washer from the regulator shaft.

10 On models with electric windows, prise out the switch panel and disconnect the wiring.

11 Lift up the trim cap and undo the screw securing the inner trim panel to the interior door

handle. Slide the panel forward to disengage it from the handle (see illustrations).

12 Lift up the trim cap and undo the screw at the base of the armrest (see illustration).

13 Extract the seven expanding rivets around the trim panel periphery by unscrewing the centre section, then removing the rivet body (see illustrations).

14 Using a wide-blade screwdriver, carefully prise the trim panel from the door to release the inner retaining clips, then lift the panel upwards and off the door.

Refitting

15 Refitting is a reversal of removal, but on manual window models make sure that the regulator handle is pointing upwards, and at 30° to the rear, with the window fully closed.

12 Door handle and lock components
– removal and refitting

Interior door handle

Removal

1 Remove the door inner trim panel as described in Section 11.

2 Using a small screwdriver, release the retaining clip at the front of the handle, then slide the handle forward to disengage the retaining lugs (see illustration).

3 Withdraw the handle from the door and disconnect the operating rods (see illustration).

11.13a Unscrew the centre section of the expanding rivets . . .

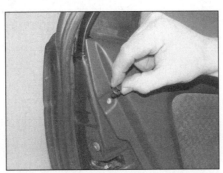

11.13b . . . then remove the rivet body

12.2 Release the retaining clip at the front of the interior door handle, then slide the handle forward to remove

12.3 Withdraw the handle from the door and disconnect the operating rods

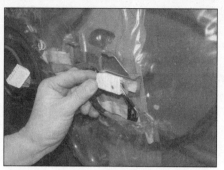

12.7a Unclip the wiring harness connector from the trim panel support bracket . . .

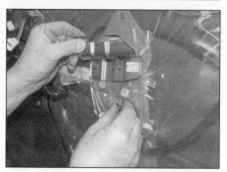

12.7b . . . then unbolt the bracket from the door

12.8 Release the door mirror and loudspeaker wiring connectors from the door, then disconnect the connectors

12.9 Using a sharp knife, carefully release the plastic sealing sheet from the adhesive bead

12.10 Release the wiring harness from the door stiffener plate, then undo the three bolts and remove the plate

Refitting

4 Refitting is a reversal of removal.

Front door lock assembly

Note: *Due to limited access, it is preferable to remove the door lock and lock cylinder together. The following procedure therefore covers removal and refitting of the door lock, lock cylinder and exterior handle.*

Removal

5 Remove the door inner trim panel as described in Section 11.

6 Remove the interior door handle as described previously in this Section.

7 Unclip the wiring harness connector from the inner trim panel support bracket, then unbolt the bracket from the door **(see illustrations)**.

8 Release the door exterior mirror and loudspeaker tweeter wiring connectors from their clips on the door, then disconnect the connectors **(see illustration)**.

9 Using a sharp knife, carefully release the plastic sealing sheet from the adhesive bead and remove the sheet from the door **(see illustration)**.

10 Release the wiring harness retaining clip from the door stiffener plate, then undo the three mounting bolts and remove the plate **(see illustration)**.

11 Remove the grommets from the access holes at the rear of the door **(see illustration)**.

12 Disconnect the two operating rods from the lock, and release the long rod from the bellcrank **(see illustration)**.

13 Undo the bolt securing the window glass lower rear guide channel to the door. Disengage the upper end of the guide channel from the window frame and remove the channel from the door **(see illustrations)**.

14 Working through the aperture in the door, disconnect the lock operating rod from the door exterior handle **(see illustration)**.

15 Working through the apertures in the door, undo the bolt securing the lock cylinder to the

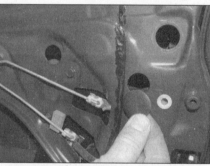

12.11 Remove the grommets from the access holes at the rear of the door

12.12 Disconnect the two operating rods from the lock, and release the long rod from the bellcrank

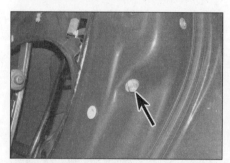

12.13a Undo the bolt (arrowed) securing the window glass lower rear guide channel to the door

12.13b Disengage the upper end of the guide channel (arrowed) from the window frame . . .

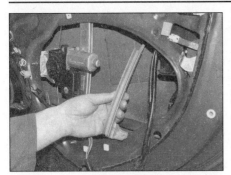

12.13c . . . and remove the channel from the door

12.14 Disconnect the lock operating rod from the door exterior handle

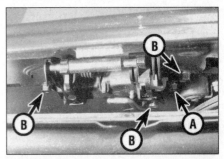

12.15a Undo the bolt (A) securing the lock cylinder to the exterior handle, and the bolts (B) securing the handle to the door

12.15b Tip the exterior handle outwards at the bottom and remove it from the door

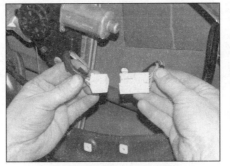

12.16 Disconnect the door lock motor wiring connector

12.17a Undo the two bolts (arrowed) securing the door lock frame to the door inner panel . . .

exterior handle, and the three bolts securing the exterior handle to the door. Tip the exterior handle outwards at the bottom and remove it from the door (see illustrations).

16 Disconnect the door lock motor wiring connector (see illustration).

17 Undo the two bolts securing the door lock frame to the door inner panel, and the three screws securing the lock to the outer edge of the door (see illustrations).

18 Manipulate the door lock and frame, complete with lock cylinder, out through the door aperture (see illustration).

19 Disconnect the operating rod and remove the lock cylinder (see illustration).

Refitting

20 Refitting is a reversal of removal, bearing in mind the following points:
- a) *Check the operation of the door lock components before refitting the plastic sealing sheet.*
- b) *If the plastic sealing sheet was in any way damaged during removal, a new sheet must be fitted.*
- c) *Make sure all the relevant wiring connectors and operating rods are pulled through the openings in the plastic sealing sheet before fitting the sheet.*

Rear door lock

Removal

21 Remove the door inner trim panel as described in Section 11.

22 Remove the interior door handle as described previously in this Section.

23 Undo the two bolts and remove the inner

trim panel support bracket from the door stiffener plate (see illustration).

24 Disconnect the door lock wiring harness connector then, using a sharp knife, carefully release the plastic sealing sheet from the

adhesive bead and remove the sheet from the door (see illustrations).

25 Release the door lock wiring harness support clips from the door stiffener plate (see illustration).

12.17b . . . and the three screws (arrowed) securing the lock to the outer edge of the door

12.18 Manipulate the door lock and frame, complete with lock cylinder, out through the door aperture

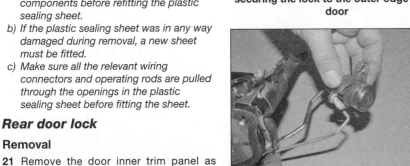

12.19 Disconnect the operating rod and remove the lock cylinder

12.23 Undo the two bolts (arrowed) and remove the inner trim panel support bracket from the door stiffener plate

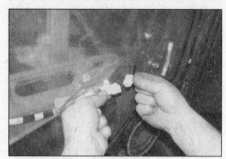

12.24 Disconnect the door lock wiring harness connector then carefully release the plastic sealing sheet

12.25 Release the wiring harness support clips from the door stiffener plate

12.26 Disconnect the two operating rods from the door lock levers

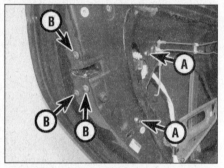

12.27 Undo the bolts (A) securing the door lock frame to the door panel, and the screws (B) securing the lock to the outer edge of the door

26 Disconnect the two operating rods from the door lock levers (see illustration).
27 Undo the two bolts securing the door lock frame to the door inner panel, and the three

12.28 Manipulate the door lock and frame out through the door aperture

screws securing the lock to the outer edge of the door (see illustration).
28 Manipulate the door lock and frame out through the door aperture (see illustration).

Refitting

29 Refitting is a reversal of removal, bearing in mind the following points:
a) *Check the operation of the door lock components before refitting the plastic sealing sheet.*
b) *If the plastic sealing sheet was in any way damaged during removal, a new sheet must be fitted.*
c) *Make sure all the relevant wiring connectors and operating rods are pulled through the openings in the plastic sealing sheet before fitting the sheet.*

Rear door exterior handle

Removal

30 Remove the rear door lock as described in paragraphs 21 to 28 of this Section.
31 Using a socket inserted through the aperture in the door panel, unscrew the two bolts securing the exterior handle to the door. Withdraw the handle and lever assembly taking care not to damage the paintwork (see illustrations).

Refitting

32 Refitting is a reversal of removal.

13 Door window glass and regulator – removal and refitting

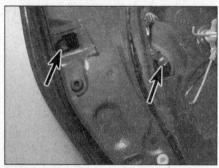

12.31a Unscrew the two bolts (arrowed) securing the exterior handle to the door . . .

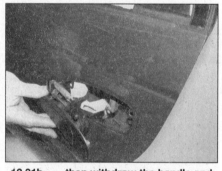

12.31b . . . then withdraw the handle and lever assembly

Front door window glass

Removal

1 Proceed as described in Section 12, paragraphs 5 to 10.
2 Temporarily reconnect the electric window switch, and the battery negative lead. Position the window so that the two bolts securing the base of the window glass to the window regulator lifting bracket are accessible.
3 Undo the two bolts securing the base of the window glass to the window regulator lifting bracket (see illustration).
4 Lift the window glass upward slightly at the rear, and remove the glass from the outside of the door (see illustration).

Refitting

5 Refitting is a reversal of removal, bearing in mind the following points:

13.3 Undo the two bolts (arrowed) securing the window glass to the regulator lifting bracket

13.4 Lift the glass upward at the rear, and remove it from the outside of the door

13.9a Disconnect the regulator motor wiring connector . . .

13.9b . . . undo the four regulator retaining nuts (arrowed) . . .

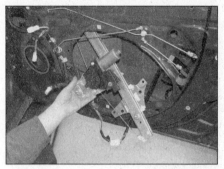

13.9c . . . and remove the regulator assembly through the door aperture

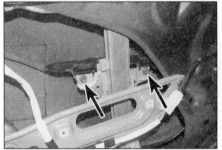

13.13 Undo the two bolts (arrowed) securing the window glass to the regulator lifting bracket

a) *Check the operation of all components before refitting the plastic sealing sheet.*
b) *If the plastic sealing sheet was in any way damaged during removal, a new sheet must be fitted.*
c) *Make sure all the relevant wiring connectors and operating rods are pulled through the openings in the plastic sealing sheet before fitting the sheet.*

Front door window regulator

Removal

6 Proceed as described in Section 12, paragraphs 5 to 10.
7 Temporarily reconnect the electric window switch, and the battery negative lead. Position the window so that the two bolts securing the base of the window glass to the window regulator lifting bracket are accessible.
8 Undo the two bolts securing the base of the window glass to the window regulator lifting bracket **(see illustration 13.3)**. Slide the window glass upward to the closed position and secure it with masking tape over the top of the door frame.
9 Disconnect the regulator motor wiring connector, then undo the four regulator retaining nuts. Remove the regulator assembly through the door aperture **(see illustrations)**.

Refitting

10 Refitting is a reversal of removal, bearing in mind the following points:
  a) *Check the operation of all components before refitting the plastic sealing sheet.*
  b) *If the plastic sealing sheet was in any way*

13.14 Carefully remove the window aperture channel seal from the top and rear of the door frame

damaged during removal, a new sheet must be fitted.
  c) *Make sure all the relevant wiring connectors and operating rods are pulled through the openings in the plastic sealing sheet before fitting the sheet.*

Rear door window glass

Removal

11 Proceed as described in Section 12, paragraphs 21 to 24.
12 Position the window so that the two bolts securing the base of the window glass to the window regulator lifting bracket are accessible. Temporarily refit the window regulator handle, or reconnect the electric window switch, and the battery negative lead as applicable, to allow the window to be positioned.
13 Undo the two bolts securing the base of the window glass to the window regulator lifting bracket **(see illustration)**. Release the

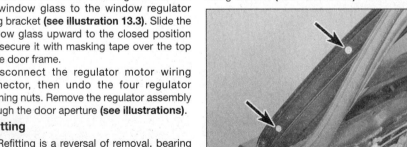

13.18a On Hatchback and Estate models, undo the two screws (arrowed) at the rear of the door frame . . .

13.15 Carefully prise up and remove the outer waist seal from the door

glass from the lifting bracket and carefully lower the glass to the bottom of the door.
14 Beginning at the rear upper corner, carefully remove the window aperture channel seal from the top and rear of the door frame **(see illustration)**.
15 Using a screwdriver, carefully prise up and remove the outer waist seal from the door **(see illustration)**. Take care not to scratch the door or bend the waist seal.
16 Release the sealing weatherstrip from the side and top of the door frame.
17 On Saloon models, undo the two bolts on the inner door panel and the single bolt at the top of the door frame and remove the rear window guide channel from the door.
18 On Hatchback and Estate models, undo the two screws at the rear of the door frame, and the bolt and screw on the inner door panel and remove the rear window guide channel **(see illustrations)**.

13.18b . . . and the bolt and screw (arrowed) on the inner door panel . . .

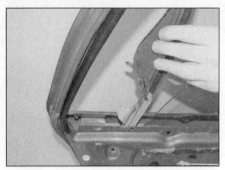

13.18c . . . then remove the rear window guide channel

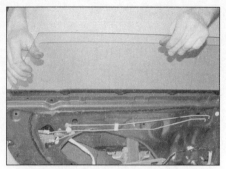

13.19 Lift the window glass up and manipulate it out from the door

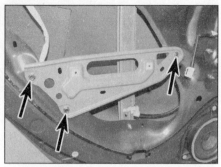

13.26 Undo the three mounting bolts (arrowed) and remove the stiffener plate

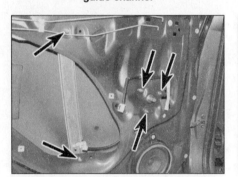

13.28a Undo the five nuts (arrowed) securing the regulator to the door . . .

13.28b . . . then remove the regulator assembly through the door aperture

19 Lift the window glass up and manipulate it out from the door **(see illustration)**.

20 On Saloon models, if required, remove the rear quarterlight glass and weatherstrip from the door frame.

Refitting

21 Refitting is a reversal of removal, bearing in mind the following points:

a) *Check the operation of all components before refitting the plastic sealing sheet.*

b) *If the plastic sealing sheet was in any way damaged during removal, a new sheet must be fitted.*

c) *Make sure all the relevant wiring connectors and operating rods are pulled through the openings in the plastic sealing sheet before fitting the sheet.*

Rear door window regulator

Removal

22 Proceed as described in Section 12, paragraphs 21 to 24.

23 Position the window so that the two bolts securing the base of the window glass to the window regulator lifting bracket are accessible. Temporarily refit the window regulator handle, or reconnect the electric window switch and the battery negative lead, as applicable, to allow the window to be positioned.

24 Undo the two bolts securing the base of the window glass to the window regulator lifting bracket **(see illustration 13.13)**. Slide the window glass upward to the closed position and secure it with masking tape over the top of the door frame.

25 Release the door lock wiring harness

support clips from the door stiffener plate **(see illustration 12.25)**.

26 Undo the three mounting bolts and remove the stiffener plate **(see illustration)**.

27 On models with electric windows, disconnect the regulator motor wiring connector.

28 Undo the five nuts securing the regulator to the door, then remove the regulator assembly through the door aperture **(see illustrations)**.

Refitting

29 Refitting is a reversal of removal, bearing in mind the following points:

a) *Check the operation of all components before refitting the plastic sealing sheet.*

b) *If the plastic sealing sheet was in any way damaged during removal, a new sheet must be fitted.*

c) *Make sure all the relevant wiring connectors and operating rods are pulled through the openings in the plastic sealing sheet before fitting the sheet.*

---

14 Boot lid –
removal, refitting and adjustment

Removal

1 Disconnect the battery negative terminal (refer to *Disconnecting the battery* in the Reference Chapter).

2 Open the boot and disconnect the wiring from the rear lighting (see Chapter 12).

3 Use a marker pen to mark around the boot hinge positions as an aid to correct refitting.

4 With the aid of an assistant, undo the

bolts securing the boot lid to its hinges, then remove the boot lid. **Do not** attempt to remove the hinges until the torsion bars have been removed (Section 15).

Refitting

5 Refitting is a reversal of removal, but if necessary adjust the position of the boot as follows.

Adjustment

6 Close the boot and ensure that it sits flush with the surrounding panels and that there is an equal gap between the boot lid and each rear wing; the lid should close smoothly and positively, with no excessive force being applied. If this is not the case, loosen the bolts securing the boot lid to its hinges, then reposition the boot and tighten the bolts.

7 Check that the boot lock engages centrally with the striker on the rear panel. If necessary, remove the trim and loosen the striker screws, then reposition the striker and tighten the screws.

---

15 Boot lid torsion bar –
removal and refitting

Note: *A Toyota special tool is recommended for carrying out the following procedure, as the torsion bars may whip out and cause injury or damage if attempts are made to remove them without it; if this tool is not available, or an alternative cannot be fabricated from a long bar with a cranked, padded end, the task is best entrusted to your Toyota dealer.*

Removal

1 Refer to Section 26 and remove the luggage compartment trim panels for access to the boot lid torsion bars.

2 Release the torsion bars from the centre bracket.

3 Have an assistant support the boot lid, then attach the special tool to the first torsion bar and press down to release the bar from the hinge extension.

4 Release the special tool slowly then disengage the torsion bar from the anchor-end bracket. Withdraw the bar from the luggage compartment.

5 Repeat the procedure on the second torsion bar and withdraw it from the luggage compartment.

Refitting

6 Refitting is the reverse of the removal procedure.

16 Boot lid lock and lock cylinder – removal and refitting

Removal

1 Open the boot lid, then remove the trim panel (Section 26) for access to the lock.
2 Disconnect the lock cylinder operating rod from the lock.
3 Unbolt the lock and withdraw it from the boot lid.
4 Undo the two lock cylinder retaining nuts and remove the cylinder together with the operating rod.

Refitting

5 Refitting is a reversal of removal.

17 Fuel filler flap release mechanism – removal and refitting

Removal

1 The mechanism is cable-operated, with a lever mounted on the floor next to the driver's seat and release catches on the fuel filler flap.
2 To remove the lever unit, peel up the carpet, unscrew the mounting bolt and release the unit's locating tag. Withdraw the unit and disconnect the cable.
3 The cable is routed through the inside of the vehicle, and crossing over to the opposite side. Remove the rear seat and trim components and peel back the carpet as necessary to reach the cable if it is to be renewed.
4 To remove the fuel filler flap release catch, open the flap and unscrew the retaining nut, then remove the relevant interior trim and withdraw the catch into the luggage compartment. Disconnect the cable and remove the catch.

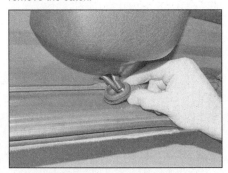

18.4 Withdraw the grommet/protector from the top centre of the tailgate

5 To remove the boot lid/tailgate release catch open the boot lid/tailgate and remove, where fitted, the trim panel covering the lock striker. Unscrew the striker bolts, withdraw the striker/catch assembly and disconnect the cable.

Refitting

6 Refitting is the reverse of the removal procedure.

18 Tailgate and support struts – removal, refitting and adjustment

Tailgate

Removal

1 Disconnect the battery negative terminal (refer to *Disconnecting the battery* in the Reference Chapter).
2 Using a screwdriver, carefully prise the tailgate washer jet from its location and disconnect the washer hose **(see illustration)**.
3 Refer to Chapter 12 and remove the high-mounted stop-light bulbholder. Disconnect the wiring connector from the bulbholder.
4 Withdraw the grommet/protector from the top centre of the tailgate, and pull out the washer hose and high-mounted stop-light wiring **(see illustration)**.
5 Remove the tailgate trim panel (Section 26), then disconnect the tailgate wiring and attach drawstrings to the multi-plugs; withdraw the remaining grommet/protector from the top left-hand side of the tailgate and remove the wiring, leaving the drawstrings in place in the tailgate **(see illustration)**.
6 With an assistant supporting the tailgate, disconnect the support struts as described later in this Section.
7 With the aid of an assistant, unbolt the tailgate from its hinges and remove it **(see illustration)**.

Refitting

8 Refitting is the reverse of the removal procedure, but check that the tailgate sits flush with the surrounding panels when closed and that there is an equal gap between it and

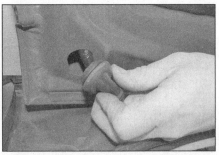

18.5 Withdraw the remaining grommet/protector from the top left-hand side of the tailgate

18.2 Carefully prise the tailgate washer jet from its location and disconnect the washer hose

each rear wing. If necessary, adjust the tailgate as follows.

Adjustment

9 To adjust the tailgate in right, left and vertical directions, slacken the bolts securing the tailgate to its hinges. Reposition the tailgate and tighten the bolts. Note that one of the hinge bolts each side is a centering bolt and full adjustment may not be possible with this bolt in place. If difficulty is experienced, substitute the centering bolt with a standard bolt and washer.
10 To adjust the tailgate in forward, rearward and vertical directions, remove the luggage compartment upper side trim panel (Section 26). Carefully prise the rear section of the headlining away from the clips on the roof.
11 Loosen the tailgate hinge mounting nuts slightly, then reposition the tailgate as necessary and tighten the nuts.
12 Slowly close the tailgate and check that the lock engages with the striker centrally. If not, remove the trim from the rear luggage compartment, then loosen the mounting bolts and reposition the striker. Tighten the mounting bolts on completion, and refit the headlining and removed trim.

Support strut

Removal

13 Open the tailgate and support it using suitable wooden props.
14 Note which way round the strut is fitted – the piston rod end is located on the tailgate.
15 Using a small screwdriver, release the

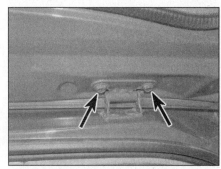

18.7 Tailgate-to-hinge retaining bolts (arrowed)

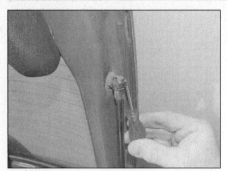

18.15 Release the spring clips, and pull the support strut from its balljoints

spring clip, and pull the support strut from its balljoint on the tailgate **(see illustration)**.
16 Similarly, release the strut from the balljoint on the body, and withdraw the strut from the vehicle.

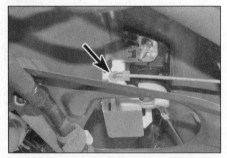

19.2 Disconnect the tailgate lock operating rod at its attachment on the lock cylinder (arrowed)

19.3b . . . then disconnect the tailgate lock wiring connector

19.8 Undo the two nuts and remove the lock cylinder from the tailgate

Refitting

17 Refitting is a reversal of removal, but ensure the spring clips are correctly engaged.

19 Tailgate lock components
– removal and refitting

Tailgate lock
Removal
1 Open the tailgate then remove the trim panel (see Section 26).
2 Disconnect the tailgate lock operating rod at its attachment on the lock cylinder **(see illustration)**.
3 Release the wiring support clip from the inner panel, then disconnect the tailgate lock wiring connector **(see illustration)**.

19.3a Release the wiring support clip from the inner panel (arrowed) . . .

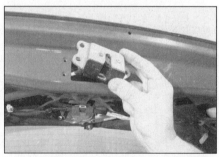

19.4 Undo the three retaining bolts and remove the lock and operating rod from the tailgate

19.11 Disconnect the lock actuator operating rod at its attachment on the lock cylinder

4 Undo the three retaining bolts and remove the lock and operating rod from the base of the tailgate **(see illustration)**.
Refitting
5 Refitting is a reversal of removal, but make sure that operating rod is securely connected and check the lock operation before refitting the trim panel.

Tailgate lock cylinder
Removal
6 Open the tailgate then remove the trim panel (see Section 26).
7 Working through the aperture in the inner panel, disconnect the two operating rods from the lock cylinder **(see illustration)**.
8 Undo the two nuts and remove the lock cylinder from the tailgate **(see illustration)**.
Refitting
9 Refitting is a reversal of removal, but make sure that operating rods are securely connected and check the lock operation before refitting the trim panel.

Tailgate lock actuator
Removal
10 Open the tailgate then remove the trim panel (see Section 26).
11 Disconnect the lock actuator operating rod at its attachment on the lock cylinder **(see illustration)**.
12 Undo the two retaining bolts and withdraw the actuator through the tailgate aperture. Disconnect the wiring connector and remove the actuator **(see illustration)**.

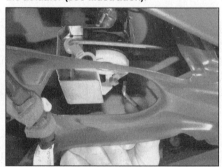

19.7 Disconnect the two operating rods from the lock cylinder

19.12 Undo the two retaining bolts, withdraw the actuator, and disconnect the wiring connector

19.16 Tailgate lock striker retaining screws (arrowed)

Refitting

13 Refitting is a reversal of removal, but make sure that operating rod is securely connected and check the lock operation before refitting the trim panel.

Tailgate lock striker

Removal

14 Remove the trim panel from the rear of the luggage compartment (see Section 26).
15 Using a marker pen, mark the position of the lock striker as a guide for refitting.
16 Unscrew the mounting screws, and remove the striker (see illustration).

Refitting

17 Refitting is a reversal of removal. If necessary adjust the position of the lock striker with reference to Section 18.

20 Exterior mirror and glass – removal and refitting

Mirror assembly

Removal

1 Remove the front door inner trim panel as described in Section 11.
2 Disconnect the wiring connectors for the electric mirror and loudspeaker tweeter.
3 Undo the three mirror retaining bolts. Lift off the tweeter and remove the mirror assembly from the door (see illustration).

Refitting

4 Refitting is a reversal of removal.

Mirror glass

Removal

5 Operate the mirror control so that the outer edge of the glass is fully away from the mirror body.
6 Slide the mirror glass slightly to the outside (away from the car), then pull the outer edge rearwards, and remove it (see illustrations).
7 Disconnect the mirror heater wiring connectors (where applicable) as the mirror is withdrawn (see illustration).

20.3 Undo the three retaining bolts, lift off the tweeter and remove the mirror assembly from the door

20.6b ... then pull the outer edge rearwards, and remove it

Refitting

8 Where applicable, reconnect the wires to the rear of the mirror glass, then push the glass into position to engage the securing clips.

21 Windscreen, tailgate/rear window and fixed side window glass – general information

These areas of glass are secured by the tight fit of the weatherstrip in the body aperture, and are bonded in position with a special adhesive. Renewal of such fixed glass is a difficult, messy and time-consuming task, which is considered beyond the scope of the home mechanic. It is difficult, unless one has plenty of practice, to obtain a secure, waterproof fit. Furthermore, the task carries a high risk of breakage; this applies especially to the laminated glass windscreen. In view of this, owners are strongly advised to have this sort of work carried out by one of the many specialist windscreen fitters.

22 Sunroof components – general information

Due to the complexity of the sunroof mechanism, considerable expertise is required to repair, renew or adjust the sunroof components successfully. Removal of the roof first requires the headlining to be removed, which is a tedious operation,

20.6a Slide the mirror glass slightly to the outside (away from the car) ...

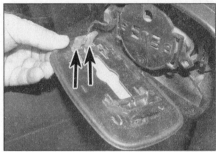

20.7 Disconnect the mirror heater wiring connectors (arrowed) as the mirror glass is withdrawn

and not a task to be undertaken lightly. Any problems with the sunroof should be referred to a Toyota dealer.

23 Body exterior fittings – removal and refitting

Engine undershields

Removal

1 Firmly apply the handbrake, then jack up the front of the car and support it securely on axle stands (see Jacking and vehicle support).
2 Unscrew the mounting bolts and remove the undershields from the underbody (see illustrations).

Refitting

3 Refitting is a reversal of removal.

23.2a Undo the engine undershield retaining bolt ...

23.2b ... and screw under the wheel arch ...

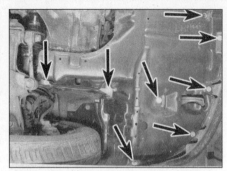

23.2c ... then undo the bolts (arrowed) on the underbody

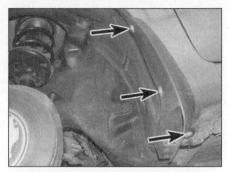

23.4a Undo the screws (arrowed) and remove the mudguard ...

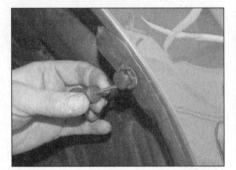

23.4b ... then extract the expanding rivets ...

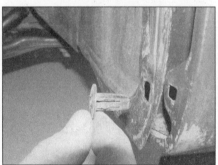

23.4c ... and the retaining clips ...

23.4d ... and remove the wheel arch liner

Wheel arch liners

4 The wheel arch liners are secured by a combination of bolts self-tapping screws and plastic clips, and the removal/refitting procedure is self-evident **(see illustrations)**.

At the front it will also be necessary to partially release the relevant engine compartment undershield, where the panels overlap.

Body trim strips and badges

5 The various body trim strips and badges are held in position with a special adhesive tape. Removal requires the trim/badge to be heated, to soften the adhesive, and then cut away from the surface. Due to the high risk of damage to the vehicle paintwork during this operation, it is recommended that this task should be entrusted to a Toyota dealer.

24 Seats – removal and refitting

Removal

Front seats

⚠ *Warning: The front seats are equipped with side airbags built into the outer sides of the seats. Refer to Chapter 12 for the precautions which should be observed when dealing with an airbag system. Do not tamper with the airbag unit in any way, and do not attempt to test any airbag system components. Note that the airbag is triggered if the mechanism is supplied with an electrical current (including via an ohmmeter), or if the assembly is subjected to a temperature of greater than 100°C.*

1 De-activate the airbag system (see Chapter 12) before attempting to remove the seat.
2 Slide the seat fully forward and remove the reclining adjustment knob from the side of the seat base **(see illustration)**.
3 Carefully prise off the seat lower side trim panel and undo the seat belt anchor bolt from the side of the seat **(see illustrations)**.

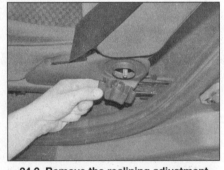

24.2 Remove the reclining adjustment knob from the side of the front seat base

24.3a Prise off the seat lower side trim panel ...

24.3b ... and undo the seat belt anchor bolt (arrowed) from the side of the seat

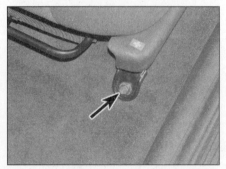

24.4 Slide the seat back and unbolt the seat runner forward ends (arrowed)

24.5 Slide the seat forward, then remove the covers and unbolt the seat runner rear ends

24.8 Disconnect the airbag wiring connector and release the wiring from the clips on the seat base

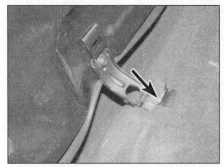

24.11 On Hatchback and Estate models, unscrew the mounting bolts (arrowed) and remove the rear seat base

4 Slide the seat as far back as possible, then unbolt the seat runner forward ends **(see illustration)**.
5 Slide the seat as far forward as possible, then remove the covers from the seat runner rear ends **(see illustration)**.
6 Unbolt the seat runner rear ends from the floor, then tip the seat backwards for access to the underside.
7 Release the trim panel or storage net from the seat base.
8 Disconnect the airbag wiring connector and release the airbag wiring from the clips on the seat base **(see illustration)**. It may be found that the wiring is also secured to the retaining clips with insulation tape. If so, very carefully cut through the tape, taking great care not to damage the wiring.

9 Where fitted, disconnect the seat heater wiring connector and free the wiring from the retaining clips.
10 Remove the seat from inside the car.

Rear seats

11 The seat base is secured at its forward edge by sockets on Saloon models and by bolts on Hatchback and Estate models. On Saloon models lift the front edge of the seat base and remove it. On Hatchback and Estate models, unscrew the mounting bolts and remove the seat base **(see illustration)**.
12 The seat back can be removed by first folding it forward and detaching the luggage compartment carpet panel (the panel is retained by clips that push into the seat back).

Undo the seat back hinge securing bolts at the centre of the car, then undo the seat back-to-hinge securing bolt at the side. The relevant seat back can then be removed **(see illustrations)**.
13 The rear seat side cushions can be removed by first removing the seat base, then pulling back the carpet and unscrewing the lower mounting bolt. Lift the side cushion upwards to disengage the wire hook and remove the relevant side cushion **(see illustrations)**.

Refitting

14 Refitting is the reverse of the removal procedure, but tighten the mounting bolts to the specified torque.

24.12a Detach the luggage compartment carpet panel . . .

24.12b . . . undo the centre seat back hinge securing bolts at the rear . . .

24.12c . . . and at the front . . .

24.12d . . . then undo the seat back-to-hinge securing bolt at the side

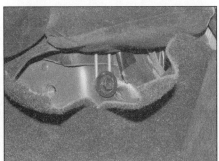

24.13a Unscrew the side cushion lower mounting bolt . . .

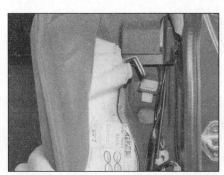

24.13b . . . then lift the cushion upwards to disengage the wire hook

25.4 Disconnect the wiring connector from the inertia reel pretensioner unit

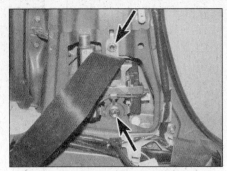

25.5a Undo the inertia reel mounting bolts (arrowed) . . .

25.5b . . . and withdraw the inertia reel from the door pillar

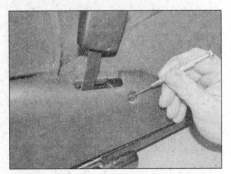

25.6a Extract the seat side trim panel securing stud . . .

25.6b . . . then pull the side trim panel from its location

25.7 Undo the retaining bolt (arrowed) and remove the seat belt stalk from the seat frame

25 Seat belt components – removal and refitting

Note: *Note of the positions of any washers and spacers on the seat belt anchors, and ensure that they are refitted in their original positions.*

Removal

Front seat belt

⚠ *Warning: The front seat belt inertia reels are equipped with a pyrotechnic pretensioner mechanism. Refer to the airbag system precautions contained in Chapter 12 which apply equally to the seat belt pretensioners. Do not tamper with the pretensioner unit in any way, and do not attempt to test the*

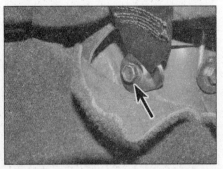

25.10 Rear seat belt inertia reel retaining bolt (arrowed)

unit. Note that the unit is triggered if the mechanism is supplied with an electrical current (including via an ohmmeter), or if the assembly is subjected to a temperature of greater than 100°C. Once removed from the car the pyrotechnic components should be stored in a suitable area in accordance with applicable safety regulations.

1 De-activate the airbag system (which will also de-activate the pyrotechnic pretensioner mechanism) as described in Chapter 12 before attempting to remove the seat belt.

2 Remove the relevant front seat as described in Section 24.

3 Remove the B-pillar trim panels as described in Section 26.

4 Disconnect the wiring connector from the inertia reel pretensioner unit (see illustration).

5 Undo the inertia reel mounting bolts, withdraw the inertia reel from the door pillar,

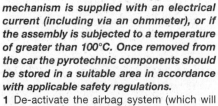
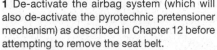

25.12 Rear seat belt anchor bolt (arrowed) at the base of the rear seat side cushion

and remove the seat belt assembly from the car (see illustrations).

6 To remove the seat belt stalk from the seat, extract the side trim panel securing stud, then pull the side trim panel from its location (see illustration).

7 Undo the retaining bolt and remove the seat belt stalk from the seat frame (see illustration).

Rear seat belts

8 On Saloon models, remove the parcel shelf trim panel and the rear upper side panel on the relevant side as described in Section 26.

9 On Hatchback and Estate models, remove the luggage compartment lower side panel cover as described in Section 26.

10 On all models, undo the inertia reel retaining bolt (see illustration).

11 Lift up or remove the rear seat base, as applicable.

12 Undo the seat belt anchor bolt at the base of the rear seat side cushion (see illustration). Remove the seat belt assembly from the car.

13 To remove the belt buckles, note their locations then unbolt them from the floor.

14 Removal of the rear seat centre belt requires complete dismantling of the rear seat back and this work should be entrusted to a Toyota dealer.

Refitting

15 Refitting is the reverse of the removal procedure, but make sure that the belts are correctly routed and tighten the mounting bolts to the specified torque.

26.2 Prise the weatherstrip from the front door aperture in the vicinity of the A-pillar

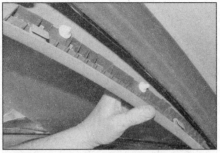

26.4 Carefully pull the trim away from the A-pillar, to release the internal retaining lugs

26.5 Lift the trim up to disengage it from the side of the facia

26 Interior trim panels – general information

Note: *Take extra care when removing plastic clips from interior trim panels, as the clips and panels are easily damaged or broken.*

Door inner trim

1 Refer to Section 11.

A-pillar trim

⚠ **Warning:** *Later models may be equipped with curtain shield airbags, the lower section of which is located behind the A-pillar trim. Refer to the airbag system precautions contained in Chapter 12. Do not tamper with the airbag unit in any way, and use extreme caution when working near the A-pillars of vehicles so equipped.*

2 Prise the weatherstrip from the front door aperture in the vicinity of the A-pillar **(see illustration)**.
3 On models equipped with curtain shield airbags, lift the trim cap and undo the A-pillar trim retaining screw.
4 Starting at the top, carefully pull the trim away from the A-pillar, to release the internal retaining lugs **(see illustration)**.
5 Lift the trim up to disengage it from the side of the facia and remove it from the vehicle **(see illustration)**.
6 Refitting is a reversal of removal, but ensure that all retaining clips are fully engaged and that the weatherstrip is fully seated.

Lower B-pillar trim

7 Remove the relevant front seat as described in Section 24.
8 Prise the weatherstrip from the front and rear door apertures in the vicinity of the B-pillar.

9 Carefully prise free the front and rear sill trim panels adjacent to the B-pillar to enable the lower trim to be removed.
10 Carefully prise the lower trim panel away from the base of the pillar to release the internal clips, then similarly release the panel from the upper B-pillar trim **(see illustrations)**. Remove the trim panel from the car.
11 Refitting is a reversal of removal, but ensure that all retaining clips are fully engaged and that the weatherstrip is fully seated.

Upper B-pillar trim

12 Remove the lower B-pillar trim as described previously.
13 Remove the trim cap, then unscrew the front seat belt upper mounting bolt **(see illustrations)**.
14 Undo the trim lower retaining screw, then carefully prise the trim panel away from the pillar, to release the internal clips **(see illustrations)**.

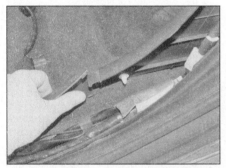

26.10a Carefully prise the lower B-pillar trim panel away from the base of the pillar . . .

26.10b . . . then release the panel from the upper B-pillar trim

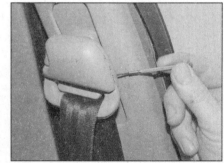

26.13a Remove the trim cap . . .

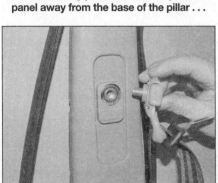

26.13b . . . then unscrew the front seat belt upper mounting bolt

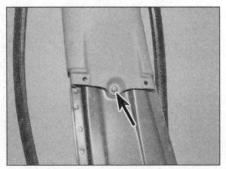

26.14a Undo the trim lower retaining screw (arrowed) . . .

26.14b . . . then carefully prise the upper B-pillar trim away from the pillar

26.20 Unscrew the plastic nut, then pull the footwell kick panel away from the door pillar

15 Refitting is a reversal of removal, but ensure that all retaining clips are fully engaged and that the weatherstrip is fully seated.

Sill trim

16 Prise the weatherstrip from the lower edge of the relevant door aperture.
17 Carefully prise the door sill trim away from the sill to release its retaining clips and remove it from the car.
18 Refitting is a reversal of removal, but ensure that all retaining clips are fully engaged and that the weatherstrip is fully seated.

Footwell kick panels

19 Remove the sill trim on the relevant side, as described previously.
20 Unscrew the plastic nut securing the front of the panel to the floor. Pull the panel away from the door pillar to release the retaining clips, and remove the panel from the car (see illustration).

26.37 Remove the cover panel at the seat belt entry point

26.40a Undo the two screws (arrowed) at the front . . .

21 Refitting is a reversal of removal

Parcel shelf trim panel

Saloon models

22 Remove the high-mounted stop-light as described in Chapter 12.
23 Remove the rear seat side cushions as described in Section 24.
24 Extract the two stud fasteners each side securing the front of the panel to the body. Lift the panel to disengage the retaining clips, then remove the panel from the car.
25 Refitting is a reversal of removal

Rear upper side panel

Saloon models

26 Remove the rear seat side cushions as described in Section 24.
27 Prise the weatherstrip from the rear door aperture in the vicinity of the upper side panel.

26.33 Extract the stud fastener securing the lower rear corner of the luggage compartment lower side panel

26.38 On Estate models, prise up and remove the upper section of the lower side panel cover

26.40b . . . then disengage the clip at the rear and remove the side panel cover lower section

26.34 Pull the panel away from the body to release the retaining clips

28 Undo the retaining screw (or stud fastener) at the front lower corner of the upper side panel.
29 Carefully prise the upper side panel from its location to release the four retaining clips and remove it from the car.
30 Refitting is a reversal of removal.

Luggage compartment lower side panel

Hatchback and Estate models

31 Remove the rear seat side cushions as described in Section 24.
32 Remove the boot lid/tailgate aperture lower panel as described later in this Section.
33 Extract the stud fastener securing the lower rear corner of the panel (see illustration).
34 Pull the panel away from the body to release the retaining clips and remove the panel from the car (see illustration).
35 Refitting is a reversal of removal.

Luggage compartment lower side panel cover

Hatchback and Estate models

36 Remove the luggage compartment lower side panel as described previously.
37 Remove the cover panel at the seat belt entry point in side panel cover (see illustration).
38 On Estate models, carefully prise up and remove the upper section of the lower side panel cover, over the rear seat belt inertia reel (see illustration).
39 Remove the luggage compartment upper side panel as described later in this Section.
40 Undo the two screws at the front, disengage the clip at the rear and remove the side panel cover lower section (see illustrations).
41 Refitting is a reversal of removal.

Luggage compartment upper side panel

Hatchback and Estate models

42 Remove the rear seat side cushions as described in Section 24.
43 On Estate models, carefully prise up and remove the upper section of the lower side panel cover, over the rear seat belt inertia reel (see illustration 26.38).

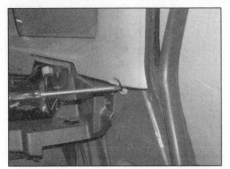

26.45 Undo the screw securing the lower front corner of the upper side panel

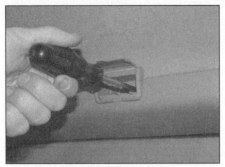

26.46a On Estate models undo the upper screw . . .

26.46b . . . and rear retaining screw

44 Prise the weatherstrip from the rear door aperture in the vicinity of the upper side panel.
45 Undo the screw securing the lower front corner of the upper side panel **(see illustration)**.
46 On Estate models undo the upper and rear retaining screws **(see illustrations)**.
47 Pull the panel away from the body to release the retaining clips and remove the panel from the car **(see illustration)**.
48 Refitting is a reversal of removal.

Luggage compartment trim

Saloon models

49 The luggage compartment side and rear trim panels are secured by a combination of stud fasteners and internal clips. Extract the fasteners, then withdraw the relevant panel to release the clips.

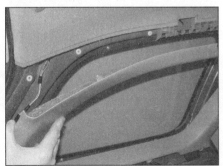

26.47 Pull the panel away from the body to release the retaining clips

26.53 Prise the panel upwards to release its retaining clips and remove it from the car

50 Refitting is a reversal of removal.

Boot lid/tailgate aperture lower panel

51 Prise the weatherstrip from the tailgate aperture in the vicinity of the lower panel.
52 Extract the stud fasteners securing the panel to the rear body panel **(see illustration)**.
53 Carefully prise the panel upwards to release its retaining clips and remove it from the car **(see illustration)**.
54 Refitting is a reversal of removal.

Boot lid/tailgate trim panel

55 On Hatchback models, disengage the parcel shelf cords from the lifting pins.
56 On Hatchback and Estate models, undo the retaining screw in the tailgate pull recess **(see illustration)**.
57 On Saloon models, unscrew the centre

26.52 Extract the stud fasteners securing the boot lid/tailgate aperture lower panel to the rear body panel

26.56 Undo the retaining screw in the tailgate pull recess

screws then remove all the plastic rivets. On Hatchback and Estate models, starting at the lower edge, carefully lever the trim panel away from the boot lid/tailgate to release the internal plastic clips **(see illustration)**.
58 Remove the panel from the boot lid/tailgate.
59 Refitting is a reversal of removal, but ensure that all retaining clips are fully engaged.

Headlining

60 The headlining is clipped to the roof and can be withdrawn only once all fittings such as the grab handles, sunvisors, sunroof (if fitted), windscreen, rear quarter windows and related trim panels have been removed, and the door, tailgate and sunroof aperture sealing strips have been prised clear.
61 Note that headlining removal and refitting requires considerable skill and experience if it is to be carried out without damage and is therefore best entrusted to an expert.

27 Centre console – removal and refitting

Removal

1 On manual transmission models, unscrew and remove the gear lever knob **(see illustration)**.
2 Undo the retaining screw and remove the trim cover from the handbrake lever **(see illustrations)**.

26.57 Carefully lever the trim panel away from the boot lid/tailgate

27.1 On manual transmission models, unscrew and remove the gear lever knob

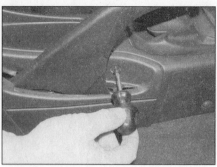

27.2a Undo the retaining screw . . .

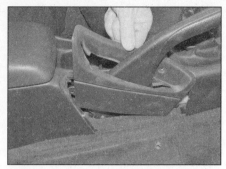

27.2b . . . and remove the trim cover from the handbrake lever

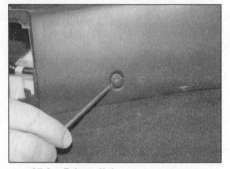

27.3a Prise off the screw caps . . .

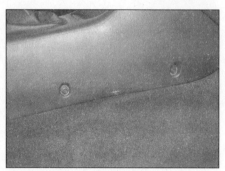

27.3b . . . and undo the two console front mounting screws each side

27.4a Remove the CD rack base from the console box . . .

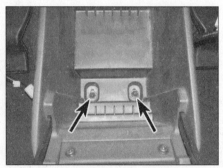

27.4b . . . and undo the two screws (arrowed)

3 Prise off the screw caps and undo the two console front mounting screws each side **(see illustrations)**.

4 Open the console box lid and remove the CD rack base. Undo the two screws now exposed **(see illustrations)**.

27.5 Lift the centre console up and over the handbrake lever and remove it from the car

5 Lift the console up and over the handbrake lever and remove it from the car **(see illustration)**.

Refitting

6 Refitting is a reversal of removal.

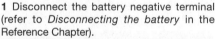

28 Facia panel components – removal and refitting

Facia centre panel

1 Disconnect the battery negative terminal (refer to *Disconnecting the battery* in the Reference Chapter).

2 The centre panel is retained by six clips, two along the lower edge, one on each side, and two at the top. Using a screwdriver, carefully prise the panel from the facia to release the clips. Once the panel is free, lift it upwards and withdraw it from the facia **(see illustration)**.

3 Disconnect the radio aerial and the multiplug connectors from the components attached to the panel **(see illustration)**.

4 Refitting is a reversal of removal.

Lower facia panel

Driver's side

5 Disconnect the battery negative terminal (refer to *Disconnecting the battery* in the Reference Chapter).

6 Undo the two screws securing the bonnet release handle to the lower facia panel **(see illustration)**.

7 Undo the screw at each lower corner of the panel. Lower the base of the panel to disengage the upper locating lugs then withdraw the panel from the facia **(see illustrations)**.

8 Separate the bonnet release handle from the panel, then detach the air conditioning

28.2 Prise free the facia centre panel, then lift it upwards and withdraw it from the facia

28.3 Disconnect the radio aerial and the multiplug connectors from the panel components

28.6 Undo the two screws securing the bonnet release handle to the lower facia panel

28.7a Undo the screw at each lower corner of the panel . . .

28.7b . . . then lower the panel to disengage the upper locating lugs (arrowed)

28.8a Separate the bonnet release handle from the panel . . .

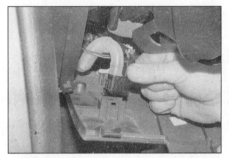

28.8b . . . then detach the air conditioning temperature sensor from its support bracket

28.9 Where applicable, disconnect the wiring connector from the satellite navigation system receiver/amplifier

temperature sensor from its support bracket **(see illustrations)**.

9 On models fitted with a satellite navigation system, disconnect the wiring connector from the receiver/amplifier **(see illustration)**.

10 Remove the panel from the driver's footwell.

11 Refitting is a reversal of removal.

Passenger's side

12 Using a small screwdriver carefully prise the upper edge of the panel away from the facia to release the three retaining clips **(see illustration)**.

13 Disengage the lower edge of the panel from its location and remove it from the passenger's footwell.

14 Refitting is a reversal of removal.

Glovebox

15 Remove the passenger's side lower facia panel as described previously.

16 Release the glovebox damper cable from the floor-mounted bracket **(see illustration)**.

17 Pull out the two hinge pins and remove the glovebox from the facia **(see illustration)**.

18 Refitting is a reversal of removal.

Driver's switch/ventilation panel

19 Remove the driver's side lower facia panel as described previously.

20 Pull the switch/ventilation panel outward at the bottom to release the two lower retaining clips **(see illustration)**.

21 Using a small screwdriver, carefully prise the upper edge of the panel away from the facia to release the upper and side

retaining clips. Disconnect the switch wiring connectors then remove the panel **(see illustrations)**.

22 Refitting is a reversal of removal.

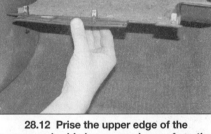

28.12 Prise the upper edge of the passenger's side lower panel away from the facia to release the three retaining clips

28.17 Pull out the two hinge pins and remove the glovebox from the facia

Steering column shrouds

23 Remove the driver's side lower facia panel as described previously.

24 Turn the steering wheel as necessary

28.16 Release the glovebox damper cable from the floor-mounted bracket

28.20 Pull the switch/ventilation panel outward at the bottom to release the two lower retaining clips

28.21a Prise the upper edge of the panel away from the facia to release the upper and side retaining clips . . .

28.21b . . . then withdraw the panel and disconnect the wiring connectors

28.24 Undo the two retaining screws on the face of the steering column lower shroud

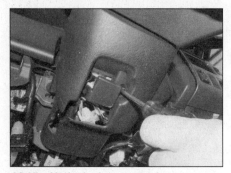

28.25a Undo the lower retaining screw . . .

28.25b . . . and lift off the lower shroud

28.27 Lift the upper shroud to release the locating peg, then manipulate the shroud up and off the column

for access, then undo the two retaining screws on the face of the lower shroud (see illustration).

25 Undo the lower retaining screw and lift off the lower shroud (see illustrations).

26 Release the tilt lever and lower the steering column as far as possible.

27 Lift the upper shroud to release the locating peg, then manipulate the shroud up and off the column, toward the outside of the car (see illustration). Clearance between the shroud and the base of the instrument panel surround is extremely limited, but with patience it is just possible to remove the shroud.

28 Refitting is a reversal of removal.

Instrument panel

29 Refer to Chapter 12.

Complete facia assembly

Note: *This is an involved operation entailing the removal of numerous components and assemblies, and the disconnection of a multitude of wiring connectors. Make notes of the location of all disconnected wiring, or attach labels to the connectors, to avoid confusion when refitting.*

 Warning: Refer to the airbag system precautions given in Chapter 12 before proceeding.

30 Disconnect the battery negative terminal (refer to *Disconnecting the battery* in the Reference Chapter).

31 Set the steering wheel in the straight-ahead position, and engage the steering lock.

Move the front seats as far back as possible or, for improved access, remove them as described in Section 24.

32 Remove the following facia panels as described previously in this Section:
  a) *Facia centre panel.*
  b) *Driver's side lower facia panel.*
  c) *Passenger's side lower facia panel.*
  d) *Glovebox.*
  e) *Driver's switch/ventilation panel.*
  f) *Steering column shrouds.*

33 Remove the following interior trim panels as described in Section 26:
  a) *A-pillar trim.*
  b) *Front sill trim.*
  c) *Footwell kick panels.*

34 Remove the centre console as described in Section 27.

35 Remove the steering wheel as described in Chapter 10.

28.38a Undo the screw (arrowed) at each lower outer corner of the facia

36 Remove the instrument panel as described in Chapter 12.

37 The main facia wiring harness is removed together with the facia. Working methodically, trace the facia wiring harness and disconnect all the wiring connectors, noting their fitted positions. It will also be necessary to disconnect the airbag wiring connector at the control unit under the centre console location, and to separate the Scotch-lock type connectors for the satellite navigation system (where fitted). Label all disconnected wiring and take notes to aid refitting.

38 Undo the facia attachments as follows (see illustrations):
  a) *Two screws, one at each lower outer corner of the facia.*
  b) *One screw at the base of the glovebox aperture.*
  c) *One nut and two passenger's airbag*

28.38b Undo the screw at the base of the glovebox aperture

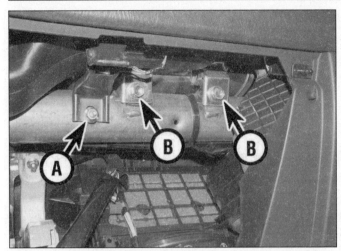

28.38c Undo the nut (A) and two passenger's airbag retaining bolts (B) on the reinforcement brace

28.38d Undo the two screws (arrowed) in the centre panel aperture

28.38e Undo the two nuts (arrowed) in the instrument panel aperture

28.38f Undo the screw (arrowed) on the reinforcement brace support strut

28.39 Check that everything is disconnected and moved clear, then remove the facia from the car

retaining bolts on the reinforcement brace.

d) Two screws in the centre panel aperture.
e) Two nuts in the instrument panel aperture.
f) One screw on the reinforcement brace support strut.

39 With the help of an assistant, lift the facia from its location and move it rearward. As soon as sufficient clearance exists, check that everything is disconnected and moved clear, then remove the facia from the car **(see illustration)**.

40 If the reinceforcement brace is to be removed, it will be necessary to first remove and disconnect all components attached to it. Make notes and label all removed or disconnected components. Once everything has been removed, undo the nuts and bolts securing the support strut to the reinceforcement brace, then undo the nuts and bolts securing the brace to the body. Remove the brace from the car.

41 Refitting is a reversal of removal ensuring that all wiring is correctly reconnected and all mountings securely tightened.

Chapter 12
Body electrical systems

Contents

Degrees of difficulty

Easy, suitable for novice with little experience	**Fairly easy,** suitable for beginner with some experience	**Fairly difficult,** suitable for competent DIY mechanic	**Difficult,** suitable for experienced DIY mechanic	**Very difficult,** suitable for expert DIY or professional

Specifications

General
System type .... 12 volt, negative earth
Fuses .... See wiring diagrams at end of Chapter
and stickers on fusebox lids for specific vehicle details

Bulb ratings
Watts

Direction indicator	21 bayonet
Direction indicator side repeater	5 wedge
Front foglight	55 H7
Front sidelight	5 wedge
Glovebox light	1.4 wedge
Headlight	55 H7
Interior light	10 festoon
Luggage compartment light:	
Hatchback and Estate	5 festoon
Saloon	3.8 wedge
Number plate light	5 wedge
Personal light	5 bayonet
Rear foglight	21 bayonet
Reversing light	21 bayonet
Stop/tail lights (Estate models)	21/5 bayonet
Stop-lights (Saloon and Hatchback models)	21 bayonet
Tail lights (Saloon and Hatchback models)	5 bayonet

Torque wrench settings

	Nm	lbf ft
Airbag control unit	20	15
Airbag front impact sensors	20	15
Airbag side impact sensors	20	15
Driver's airbag bolts	9	6
Wiper arm retaining nut:		
Windscreen wiper	20	15
Tailgate wiper	18	13

1 General information

⚠️ **Warning: Before carrying out any work on the electrical system, read through the precautions given in 'Safety first!' at the beginning of this manual, and in Chapter 5A.**

The electrical system is of 12 volt negative earth type. Power for the lights and all electrical accessories is supplied by a lead-acid type battery, which is charged by the alternator.

This Chapter covers repair and service procedures for the various electrical components not associated with the engine. Information on the battery, alternator and starter motor can be found in Chapter 5A.

It should be noted that, prior to working on any component in the electrical system, the battery negative terminal should first be disconnected, to prevent the possibility of electrical short-circuits and/or fires.

2 Electrical fault finding
– general information

Note: *Refer to the precautions given in 'Safety first!' and in Chapter 5A before starting work. The following tests relate to testing of the main electrical circuits, and should not be used to test delicate electronic circuits, particularly where an electronic control unit is used.*

General

1 A typical electrical circuit consists of an electrical component, any switches, relays, motors, fuses, fusible links or circuit breakers related to that component, and the wiring and connectors which link the component to both the battery and the bodyshell. To help pinpoint a problem in an electrical circuit, wiring diagrams are included at the end of this chapter.

2 Before attempting to diagnose an electrical fault, first study the appropriate wiring diagram, to obtain a more complete understanding of the components included in the particular circuit concerned. The possible sources of a fault can be narrowed down by noting whether other components related to the circuit are operating properly. If several components or circuits fail at one time, the problem is likely to be related to a shared fuse or earth connection.

3 Electrical problems usually stem from simple causes, such as loose or corroded connections, a faulty earth connection, a blown fuse, a melted fusible link, or a faulty relay (refer to Section 3 for details of testing relays). Visually inspect the condition of all fuses, wires and connections in a problem circuit before testing the components. Use the wiring diagrams to determine which terminal connections will need to be checked, in order to pinpoint the trouble-spot.

4 The basic tools required for electrical fault-finding include a circuit tester or voltmeter (a 12 volt bulb with a set of test leads can also be used for certain tests); a self-powered test light (sometimes known as a continuity tester); an ohmmeter (to measure resistance); a battery and set of test leads; and a jumper wire, preferably with a circuit breaker or fuse incorporated, which can be used to bypass suspect wires or electrical components. Before attempting to locate a problem with test instruments, use the wiring diagram to determine where to make the connections.

⚠️ **Warning: Under no circumstances may live measuring instruments such as ohmmeters, voltmeters or a bulb and test leads be used to test any of the airbag and pyrotechnical seat belt circuitry. Any testing of these components must be left to a Toyota dealer, as there is a danger of activating the system if the correct procedures are not followed.**

5 To find the source of an intermittent wiring fault (usually due to a poor or dirty connection, or damaged wiring insulation), a wiggle test can be performed on the wiring. This involves wiggling the wiring by hand, to see if the fault occurs as the wiring is moved. It should be possible to narrow down the source of the fault to a particular section of wiring. This method of testing can be used in conjunction with any of the tests described in the following sub-Sections.

6 Apart from problems due to poor connections, two basic types of fault can occur in an electrical circuit – open-circuit, or short-circuit.

7 Open-circuit faults are caused by a break somewhere in the circuit, which prevents current from flowing. An open-circuit fault will prevent a component from working, but will not cause the relevant circuit fuse to blow.

8 Short-circuit faults are caused by a short somewhere in the circuit, which allows the current flowing in the circuit to escape along an alternative route, usually to earth. Short-circuit faults are normally caused by a breakdown in wiring insulation, which allows a feed wire to touch either another wire, or an earthed component such as the bodyshell. A short-circuit fault will normally cause the relevant circuit fuse to blow.

Finding an open-circuit

9 To check for an open-circuit, connect one lead of a circuit tester or voltmeter to either the negative battery terminal or a known good earth.

10 Connect the other lead to a connector in the circuit being tested, preferably nearest to the battery or fuse.

11 Switch on the circuit, bearing in mind that some circuits are live only when the ignition switch is moved to a particular position.

12 If voltage is present (indicated either by the tester bulb lighting or a voltmeter reading, as applicable), this means that the section of the circuit between the relevant connector and the battery is problem-free.

13 Continue to check the remainder of the circuit in the same fashion.

14 When a point is reached at which no voltage is present, the problem must lie between that point and the previous test point with voltage. Most problems can be traced to a broken, corroded or loose connection.

Finding a short-circuit

15 To check for a short-circuit, first disconnect the load(s) from the circuit (loads are the components which draw current from a circuit, such as bulbs, motors, heating elements, etc).

16 Remove the relevant fuse from the circuit, and connect a circuit tester or voltmeter to the fuse connections.

17 Switch on the circuit, bearing in mind that some circuits are live only when the ignition switch is moved to a particular position.

18 If voltage is present (indicated either by the tester bulb lighting or a voltmeter reading, as applicable), this means that there is a short-circuit.

19 If no voltage is present, but the fuse still blows with the load(s) connected, this indicates an internal fault in the load(s).

Finding an earth fault

20 The battery negative terminal is connected to earth – the metal of the engine/transmission and the car body – and most systems are wired so that they only receive a positive feed, the current returning via the metal of the car body. This means that the component mounting and the body form part of that circuit. Loose or corroded mountings can therefore cause a range of electrical faults, ranging from total failure of a circuit, to a puzzling partial fault. In particular, lights may shine dimly (especially when another circuit sharing the same earth point is in operation), motors (eg, wiper motors or the radiator cooling fan motor) may run slowly, and the operation of one circuit may have an apparently-unrelated effect on another. Note that on many vehicles, earth straps are used between certain components, such as the engine/transmission and the body, usually where there is no metal-to-metal contact between components, due to flexible rubber mountings, etc.

21 To check whether a component is properly earthed, disconnect the battery, and connect one lead of an ohmmeter to a known good earth point. Connect the other lead to the wire or earth connection being tested. The resistance reading should be zero; if not, check the connection as follows.

22 If an earth connection is thought to be faulty, dismantle the connection, and clean back to bare metal both the bodyshell and the wire terminal or the component earth connection mating surface. Be careful to remove all traces of dirt and corrosion, then use a knife to trim away any paint, so that a clean metal-to-metal joint is made.

3.3a For access to the facia-mounted fuses, open the storage box and remove the box from the facia . . .

3.3b . . . the fuse locations and ratings are shown on a label at the rear of the box

3.3c For access to the engine compartment fuses, remove the fuse/relay box cover. The fuse locations and ratings are shown on a label inside the cover

On reassembly, tighten the joint fasteners securely; if a wire terminal is being refitted, use serrated washers between the terminal and the bodyshell, to ensure a clean and secure connection. When the connection is remade, prevent the onset of corrosion in the future by applying a coat of petroleum jelly or silicone-based grease, or by spraying on (at regular intervals) a proprietary ignition sealer.

3 Fuses, fusible links and relays – general information

Fuses

1 Fuses are designed to break a circuit when a predetermined current is reached, in order to protect the components and wiring which could be damaged by excessive current flow. Any excessive current flow will be due to a fault in the circuit, usually a short-circuit.
2 Fuses and relays are located behind the driver's side of the facia, and in the fuse/relay box in the left-hand side of the engine compartment next to the battery. According to model and equipment fitted, additional fuses may be located in a fuse/relay box in the engine compartment above the radiator.
3 For access to the facia-mounted fuses, open the storage box and remove the box from the facia. The fuse locations and ratings are shown on a label attached to the rear of the box. For access to the fuses in the engine compartment, unclip and remove the fuse/relay box cover. The fuse locations and ratings are shown on a label attached to the inside of the cover **(see illustrations)**.
4 A blown fuse can be recognised from its melted or broken wire.
5 To remove a fuse, first ensure that the relevant circuit is switched off.
6 To remove a standard current fuse, use the plastic tweezers supplied and pull the fuse from its location **(see illustration)**. To remove a medium current fuse (30 and 40 amp) simply pull the fuse from its socket.
7 Spare fuses are provided in the fusebox.
8 Before renewing a blown fuse, trace and rectify the cause, and always use a fuse of the correct rating (fuse ratings are specified on the

inside of the fusebox cover). Never substitute a fuse of a higher rating, or make temporary repairs using wire or metal foil; more serious damage, or even fire, could result.

Fusible links

9 The fusible links are located in the fuse/relay box in the left-hand side of the engine compartment next to the battery. The links are designed to melt in the event of a serious wiring fault, thus protecting the main wiring loom from damage; in the event of a link melting, the fault must be traced and rectified before the link is renewed. When renewing a fusible link, use **only** a genuine Toyota part.

Relays

10 A relay is an electrically-operated switch, which is used for the following reasons:
a) A relay can switch a heavy current remotely from the circuit in which the current is flowing, therefore allowing the use of lighter-gauge wiring and switch contacts.
b) A relay can receive more than one control input, unlike a mechanical switch.
c) A relay can have a timer function – for example, the intermittent wiper relay.
11 The various relays are located behind the driver's side of the facia, and in the fuse/relay box in the left-hand side of the engine compartment next to the battery. The fuel pump relay for the fuel injection system is located behind the footwell kick panel on the passenger's side **(see illustration)**, and

additional relays may be located in a fuse/relay box in the engine compartment above the radiator.
12 If a circuit or system controlled by a relay develops a fault, and the relay is suspect, operate the system. If the relay is functioning, it should be possible to hear it click as it is energised. If this is the case, the fault lies with the components or wiring of the system. If the relay is not being energised, then either the relay is not receiving a main supply or a switching voltage, or the relay itself is faulty. Testing is by the substitution of a known good unit, but be careful – while some relays are identical in appearance and in operation, others look similar but perform different functions.
13 To remove a relay, first ensure that the relevant circuit is switched off. The relay can then simply be pulled out from the socket, and pushed back into position.

4 Switches – removal and refitting

Note: *Disconnect the battery negative terminal (refer to 'Disconnecting the battery' in the Reference Chapter) before removing any switch, and reconnect the lead after refitting the switch.*

Ignition switch/steering lock

1 Refer to Chapter 10.

3.6 Use the plastic tweezers supplied and pull the fuse from its location

3.11 Fuel pump relay location (arrowed)

4.3 Steering column combination switch retaining screws (arrowed)

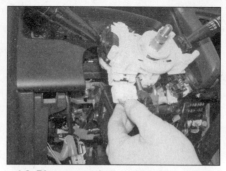

4.6 Disconnect the combination switch wiring connectors

4.7a Undo the two upper screws (arrowed) . . .

4.7b . . . and single lower screw . . .

4.7c . . . and remove the combination switch from the steering column

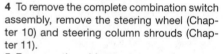

4.10 Undo the two screws (arrowed) and remove the switch panel from the facia centre panel

Steering column switches

Removal

2 To remove the two switches individually from the combination switch assembly, remove the steering column shrouds as described in Chapter 11.

3 Disconnect the switch wiring connector, then undo the two screws and remove the relevant switch **(see illustration)**.

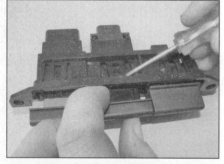

4.11a Lift the locking tab . . .

4.11b . . . and withdraw the relevant switch from the panel

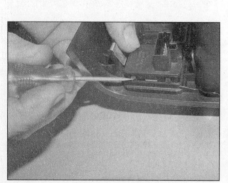

4.14a Depress the retaining lugs . . .

4.14b . . . and push the relevant switch out of the switch/ventilation panel

4 To remove the complete combination switch assembly, remove the steering wheel (Chapter 10) and steering column shrouds (Chapter 11).

5 Remove the airbag rotary connector as described in Section 20.

6 Disconnect the combination switch wiring connectors **(see illustration)**.

7 Undo the two upper screws, and single lower screw, and remove the combination switch from the steering column **(see illustrations)**.

Refitting

8 Refitting is a reversal of removal.

Facia centre panel switches

Removal

9 Remove the facia centre panel as described in Chapter 11.

10 Undo the two screws securing the switch panel to the top of the facia centre panel **(see illustration)**. Withdraw the switch panel.

11 Lift the locking tab and withdraw the relevant switch from the panel **(see illustrations)**.

Refitting

12 Refitting is a reversal of removal.

Driver's side switch/ ventilation panel switches

Removal

13 Remove the driver's side switch/ventilation panel as described in Chapter 11.

14 Depress the retaining lugs on the side of the relevant switch and push the switch out of the panel **(see illustrations)**.

4.19 Lift up the trim cap and undo the screw at the base of the door pull

4.20a Lift the rear of the door pull and electric window switch assembly . . .

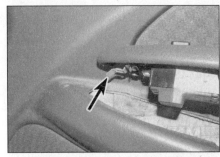

4.20b . . . then slide it rearwards to disengage the front retaining plate (arrowed)

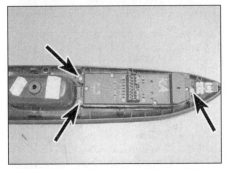

4.21a Undo the three screws (arrowed) . . .

4.21b . . . and remove the switch assembly from the door pull

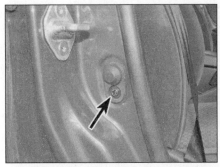

4.24 Courtesy light/door ajar warning switch retaining screw (arrowed)

Refitting

15 Refitting is a reversal of removal.

Centre console switches

Removal

16 Remove the centre console (see Chapter 11).
17 Release the securing clips, then push the relevant switch out of the centre console.

Refitting

18 Refitting is a reversal of removal.

Electric window switches

Removal

19 Lift up the trim cap and undo the screw at the base of the door pull **(see illustration)**.
20 Lift the rear of the door pull and electric window switch assembly, then slide it rearwards to disengage the front retaining plate **(see illustrations)**. Disconnect the wiring connector and remove the assembly.
21 Undo the three screws and remove the switch assembly from the door pull **(see illustrations)**.

Refitting

22 Refitting is a reversal of removal.

Courtesy light/ door ajar warning switch

Removal

23 Open the door to expose the switch in the door pillar.
24 Remove the securing bolt, then withdraw the switch from the door pillar and remove the

rubber gaiter **(see illustration)**. Disconnect the wiring connector as it becomes accessible.

> **HAYNES HiNT** *Tape the wiring to the door pillar, or tie a length of string to the wiring to retrieve it if it falls back into the door pillar.*

Refitting

25 Refitting is a reversal of removal.

Audio remote control switch

Removal

26 Using a small screwdriver, carefully prise out the trim cap at the front of the switch **(see illustration)**.
27 Undo the retaining screw, then push the switch toward the steering wheel to release the retaining lugs. Withdraw the switch from

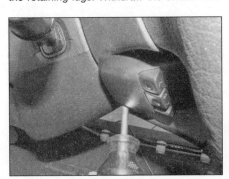

4.27a Undo the retaining screw . . .

the steering wheel and disconnect the wiring connector **(see illustrations)**.

Refitting

28 Refitting is a reversal of removal.

4.26 Carefully prise out the trim cap at the front of the audio remote control switch

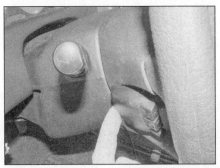

4.27b . . . then push the switch toward the steering wheel to release the retaining lugs

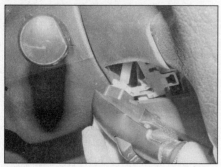

4.27c Withdraw the switch and disconnect the wiring connector

Handbrake warning light switch

29 Refer to Chapter 9.

Stop-light switch

30 Refer to Chapter 9.

5.2 Pull the relevant rubber dust cover from the rear of the headlight unit

5.3 Disconnect the wiring connector from the headlight bulb

5.5 ... and withdraw the bulb from the headlight

4.31a Carefully prise the automatic transmission mode control switch from the selector lever housing ...

Automatic transmission mode control switch

Removal

31 Using a small screwdriver, carefully prise the switch from the selector lever housing and disconnect the wiring connector **(see illustrations)**.

Refitting

32 Refitting is a reversal of removal.

5 Bulbs (exterior lights) – renewal

General

1 Whenever a bulb is renewed, note the following points:

5.4 Release the spring clip from the rear of the bulb ...

5.8 Pull the outer rubber dust cover from the rear of the headlight unit

4.31b ... withdraw the switch and disconnect the wiring connector

a) Make sure the electrical circuit is switched off.
b) Remember that, if the light has just been in use, the bulb may be extremely hot.
c) Always check the bulb contacts and holder, ensuring that there is clean metal-to-metal contact between the bulb and its live contact(s) and earth. Clean off any corrosion or dirt before fitting a new bulb.
d) Wherever bayonet-type bulbs are fitted, ensure that the live contact(s) bear firmly against the bulb contact.
e) Always ensure that the new bulb is of the correct rating (see Specifications), and that it is completely clean before fitting.

Headlight

2 Open the bonnet and pull the relevant rubber dust cover from the rear of the headlight unit **(see illustration)**.
3 Disconnect the wiring connector from the rear of the relevant headlight bulb **(see illustration)**.
4 Squeeze the retaining spring clip ends, and release the clip from the rear of the bulb **(see illustration)**.
5 Withdraw the bulb from the headlight **(see illustration)**.
6 When handling the new bulb, use a tissue or clean cloth, to avoid touching the glass with the fingers; moisture and grease from the skin can cause blackening and rapid failure of this type of bulb.

> **HAYNES HINT** *If the headlight bulb glass is accidentally touched, wipe it clean using methylated spirit.*

7 Install the new bulb, ensuring that its locating tabs are located in the light unit cut-outs. Secure the bulb in position with the retaining clip, then refit the wiring connector and dust cover.

Front sidelight

8 Open the bonnet and pull the outer rubber dust cover from the rear of the headlight unit **(see illustration)**.
9 Twist the sidelight bulbholder and remove it from the headlight unit **(see illustration)**.

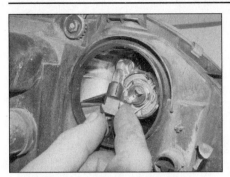

5.9 Twist the sidelight bulbholder and remove it from the headlight unit

5.10 Pull the wedge-type bulb from the bulbholder

5.14a Insert a long thin screwdriver through the gap at the side of the headlight unit . . .

5.14b . . . to depress this retaining catch (arrowed) on the direction indicator unit

5.15a Twist the bulbholder and remove it from the indicator unit . . .

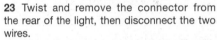

5.15b . . . then twist the bulb to remove it from the holder

10 Pull the wedge-type bulb from the bulbholder **(see illustration)**.
11 Push the new bulb into the bulbholder, then insert the bulbholder in the headlight unit and twist to secure.
12 Refit the dust cover.

Front direction indicator

13 Open the bonnet.
14 Insert a long thin screwdriver through the gap at the side of the headlight unit. While pulling outward on the direction indicator unit, depress the retaining catch with the screwdriver to release the unit from its location **(see illustrations)**.
15 Withdraw the direction indicator from the front wing, then twist the bulbholder and remove it from the unit. Twist the bulb to remove it from the holder **(see illustrations)**.
16 Fit the new bulb using a reversal of the removal procedure.

Direction indicator side repeater

17 Using a small screwdriver, push the front direction indicator side repeater lens rearwards, and release the unit from the front wing **(see illustrations)**.
18 Twist the bulbholder from the unit, then pull out the wedge-type bulb **(see illustrations)**.
19 Fit the new bulb using a reversal of the removal procedure.

Front foglight

20 Where fitted, the front foglights are located in the front bumper. Remove the engine compartment undershield on the relevant side with reference to Chapter 11.

21 Unscrew the retaining screw located on the inner upper corner of the light unit. Withdraw the unit from the location pins on the front bumper.
22 Disconnect the wiring plug and remove the light unit from the vehicle.

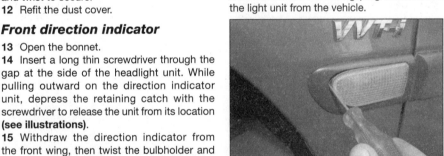

5.17a Push the front direction indicator side repeater lens rearwards . . .

5.17b . . . and release the unit from the front wing

23 Twist and remove the connector from the rear of the light, then disconnect the two wires.
24 Squeeze the spring ends and pivot the spring away from the bulb. Remove the bulb.
25 Fit the new bulb using a reversal of the

5.18a Twist the bulbholder from the unit . . .

5.18b . . . then pull out the wedge-type bulb

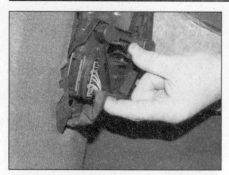

5.33 Squeeze the two plastic tabs together and withdraw the rear light cluster bulbholder – Hatchback models

removal procedure. If necessary, the light beam may be adjusted by turning the screw located on the inner lower corner.

Rear light cluster bulbs

Saloon models

26 Open the boot lid.
27 Extract the retaining clips and remove the rear light cluster bulb access panel.
28 Squeeze the two plastic retaining tabs together and withdraw the bulbholder assembly from the light unit.
29 Depress and twist the relevant bulb and remove it from the bulbholder.
30 Fit the new bulb using a reversal of the removal procedure.

Hatchback models

31 Open the tailgate.
32 Open the rear light cluster bulb access

5.39 Depress and twist the relevant bulb and remove it from the bulbholder – Estate models

5.43 Squeeze the two plastic tabs together and withdraw the bulbholder from the light unit – Estate models

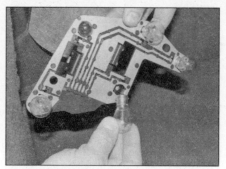

5.34 Depress and twist the relevant bulb and remove it from the bulbholder – Hatchback models

panel in the luggage compartment rear trim panel.
33 Reach through the aperture, squeeze the two plastic retaining tabs together and withdraw the bulbholder assembly from the light unit **(see illustration)**.
34 Depress and twist the relevant bulb and remove it from the bulbholder **(see illustration)**.
35 Fit the new bulb using a reversal of the removal procedure.

Rear direction indicator and stop/tail light bulbs

Estate models

36 Open the tailgate.
37 Open the rear light cluster bulb access panel in the luggage compartment rear trim panel.
38 Reach through the aperture and lift up the bulbholder retaining catch, then withdraw the bulbholder from the light unit **(see illustration)**.

5.42 Release the bulb access panel in the tailgate trim panel – Estate models

5.44 Depress and twist the relevant bulb and remove it from the bulbholder – Estate models

5.38 Lift up the bulbholder retaining catch (arrowed), then withdraw the bulbholder from the light unit – Estate models

39 Depress and twist the relevant bulb and remove it from the bulbholder **(see illustration)**.
40 Fit the new bulb using a reversal of the removal procedure.

Reversing light and rear foglight bulbs

Estate models

41 Open the tailgate.
42 Using a small screwdriver if necessary, release the bulb access panel in the tailgate trim panel **(see illustration)**.
43 Squeeze the two plastic retaining tabs together and withdraw the bulbholder assembly from the light unit **(see illustration)**.
44 Depress and twist the relevant bulb and remove it from the bulbholder **(see illustration)**.
45 Fit the new bulb using a reversal of the removal procedure.

Rear number plate light

Saloon models

46 Remove the boot lid trim panel as described in Chapter 11.
47 Twist and remove the bulbholder then pull out the wedge-type bulb.
48 Fit the new bulb using a reversal of the removal procedure.

Hatchback and Estate models

49 Open the tailgate.
50 Using a small screwdriver, release the bulb access panel in the tailgate trim panel **(see illustration)**.

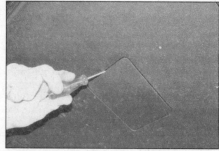

5.50 Release the bulb access panel in the tailgate trim panel – Hatchback and Estate models

5.51a Twist and remove the number plate light bulbholder . . .

5.51b . . . then pull out the wedge-type bulb – Hatchback and Estate models

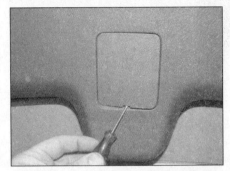

5.56 Release the bulb access panel in the tailgate trim panel – Hatchback models

5.57a Twist and remove the high-mounted stop-light bulbholder . . .

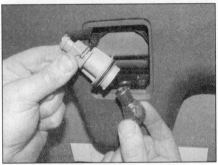

5.57b . . . then depress and twist the bulb to remove it – Hatchback models

5.59 Depress the base of the high-mounted stop-light cover then withdraw the cover from the light unit – Estate models

51 Twist and remove the bulbholder, then pull out the wedge-type bulb **(see illustrations)**.
52 Fit the new bulb using a reversal of the removal procedure.

High-mounted stop-light

Saloon models

53 Push the stop-light unit towards the rear window and lift up the front edge. Disengage the rear locating lug and withdraw the unit.
54 Twist and remove the bulbholder, then depress and twist the bulb to remove it.
55 Fit the new bulb using a reversal of the removal procedure.

Hatchback models

56 Using a small screwdriver, release the bulb access panel in the tailgate trim panel **(see illustration)**.
57 Twist and remove the bulbholder, then

depress and twist the bulb to remove it **(see illustrations)**.
58 Fit the new bulb using a reversal of the removal procedure.

Estate models

59 Depress the base of the stop-light cover then withdraw the cover from the light unit **(see illustration)**.
60 Twist and remove the bulbholder, then depress and twist the bulb to remove it **(see illustration)**.

6	Bulbs (interior lights) – renewal

General

1 Refer to Section 5, paragraph 1.

Roof front console light

2 Open the roof console box lid and undo the two retaining screws **(see illustration)**.
3 Withdraw the console from the roof and disconnect the wiring connector **(see illustration)**. Remove the console from the car.
4 Depress the retaining tab and withdraw the bulbholder and switch plate. Depress and twist the bulb to remove it **(see illustration)**.

Interior and luggage area lights

5 Using a small screwdriver, prise the lens from the light unit **(see illustration)**.
6 Remove the festoon-type bulb from the light contacts **(see illustration)**.
7 Fit the new bulb using a reversal of the removal procedure, but make sure the bulb is held firmly between the contacts. Bend the contacts if necessary.

5.60 Twist and remove the bulbholder, then depress and twist the bulb to remove it – Estate models

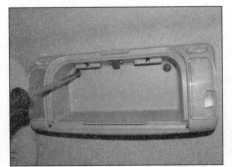

6.2 Open the roof console box lid and undo the two retaining screws

6.3 Withdraw the console from the roof and disconnect the wiring connector

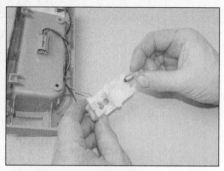

6.4 Depress and twist the front console bulb to remove it

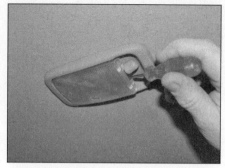

6.5 Prise the lens from the interior light unit

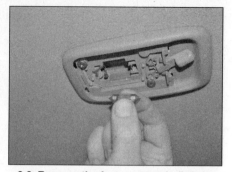

6.6 Remove the festoon-type bulb from the light contacts

6.9 Twist the relevant bulbholder anticlockwise to remove it from the rear of the instrument panel

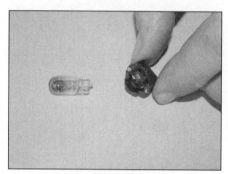

6.10 Pull the wedge-type bulb from the bulbholder

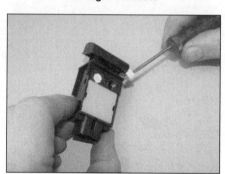

6.17 Twist the bulbholder anti-clockwise to remove it from the switch

Instrument panel lights

8 Remove the instrument panel, as described in Section 8.
9 Twist the relevant bulbholder anti-clockwise to remove it from the rear of the instrument panel **(see illustration)**.
10 Pull the wedge-type bulb from the bulbholder **(see illustration)**.
11 Fit the new bulb using a reversal of the removal procedure, with reference to Section 8 when refitting the instrument panel.

Heater control panel bulbs

12 Remove the heater/ventilation control panel as described in Chapter 3.
13 Twist the relevant bulbholder anti-clockwise, and withdraw the bulbholder.
14 Pull the wedge-type bulb from the bulbholder. On later models, the bulbs are integral with the bulbholders.

15 Fit the new bulb using a reversal of the removal procedure.

Switch illumination bulb

16 Remove the relevant switch as described in Section 4.
17 Twist the bulbholder anti-clockwise to remove it from the switch. The bulb is integral with the bulbholder **(see illustration)**.
18 Fit the new bulb using a reversal of the removal procedure.

Automatic transmission selector panel illumination

19 Remove the centre console as described in Chapter 11.
20 Twist the bulbholder anti-clockwise then pull it from the selector housing.
21 Pull the wedge type bulb from the holder.
22 Fit the new bulb using a reversal of the removal procedure.

7 Exterior light units – removal and refitting

Headlight unit

Pre-August 2000 models

1 Remove the front direction indicator light as described later in this Section.
2 Remove the radiator grille as described in Chapter 11.
3 Referring to the procedures contained in Chapter 11, Section 6, remove the front bumper upper trim strips below the headlights.
4 Disconnect the headlight wiring from the rear of the headlight unit.
5 Unscrew the upper mounting bolts **(see illustration 7.9b)**.
6 Unscrew the lower mounting bolts and withdraw the headlight unit from the front of the vehicle.
7 Refitting is a reversal of removal.

Post-August 2000 models

8 Remove the front bumper as described in Chapter 11.
9 Disconnect the headlight wiring connectors, then unscrew the headlight upper mounting bolts **(see illustrations)**.
10 Insert a screwdriver beneath the headlight to compress the tabs of the lower mounting, while at the same time pulling out the headlight unit **(see illustration)**. Once the lower mounting has been released, withdraw

7.9a Disconnect the headlight wiring connectors ...

7.9b ... then unscrew the headlight upper mounting bolts (arrowed)

7.10 Insert a screwdriver beneath the headlight to compress the tabs of the lower mounting (shown with headlight removed)

the headlight unit from the front of the vehicle.

11 Refitting is a reversal of removal.

Front direction indicator

12 The procedure is described as part of the bulb renewal procedure in Section 5.

Direction indicator side repeater

13 The procedure is described as part of the bulb renewal procedure in Section 5.

Front foglight

14 The procedure is described as part of the bulb renewal procedure in Section 5.

Rear light cluster

Saloon models

15 Remove the rear light cluster bulbholder as described in Section 5.

7.27 Undo the three retaining nuts and remove the reversing light and rear foglight unit from the tailgate – Estate models

7.30 Undo the retaining nuts and remove the exterior trim surround

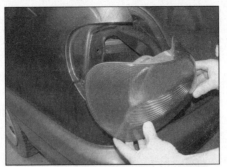

7.20 Undo the three retaining nuts and remove the light unit from the body – Hatchback models

16 Refer to Chapter 11 and remove the relevant luggage compartment trim for access to the light unit retaining nuts.

17 Undo the retaining nuts and remove the light unit from the body.

18 Refitting is a reversal of removal.

Hatchback models

19 Remove the rear light cluster bulbholder as described in Section 5.

20 Working through the access panel in the luggage compartment rear trim panel, undo the three retaining nuts and remove the light unit from the body **(see illustration)**.

21 Refitting is a reversal of removal.

Rear direction indicator and stop/tail light unit

Estate models

22 Remove the rear light cluster bulbholder as described in Section 5.

23 Working through the access panel in the luggage compartment rear trim panel, undo the three retaining nuts and remove the light unit from the body **(see illustration)**.

24 Refitting is a reversal of removal.

Reversing light and rear foglight unit

Estate models

25 Remove the tailgate trim panel as described in Chapter 11.

26 Remove the reversing light and rear foglight bulbholder as described in Section 5.

27 Undo the retaining nuts and remove the light unit from the tailgate **(see illustration)**.

7.31 Depress the retaining lug (arrowed) and withdraw the rear number plate light unit from its location

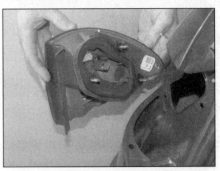

7.23 Undo the three retaining nuts and remove the direction indicator and stop/tail light unit from the body – Estate models

28 Refitting is a reversal of removal.

Rear number plate light unit

29 Open the boot lid/tailgate and remove the trim panel as described in Chapter 11.

30 Working through the access holes in the boot lid/tailgate, undo the retaining nuts and remove the exterior trim surround **(see illustration)**.

31 Disconnect the wiring connector, then depress the retaining lug on the side of the light unit, and withdraw the unit from its location **(see illustration)**.

32 Refitting is a reversal of removal.

---

8 Instrument panel – removal and refitting

Removal

1 Disconnect the battery negative terminal (refer to *Disconnecting the battery* in the Reference Chapter).

2 Using the tilt mechanism, lower the steering column as far as possible.

3 Undo the instrument panel surround upper retaining screws **(see illustration)**.

4 Pull the surround outward and release the lower retaining clips. On models with satellite navigation, release the aerial from the top of the surround. The aerial is located on a magnetic pad, but it may additionally be retained with masking tape. Remove the surround.

5 Undo the three screws securing

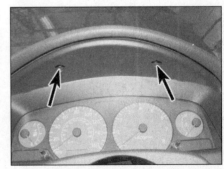

8.3 Instrument panel surround upper retaining screws (arrowed)

8.5 Undo the three screws (arrowed) securing the instrument panel to the facia

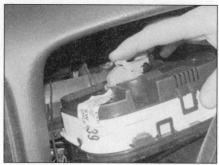

8.6 Lift the locking levers and disconnect the wiring connectors at the rear of the instrument panel

the instrument panel to the facia (see illustration).
6 Withdraw the instrument panel, then lift the locking levers and disconnect the wiring connectors at the rear of the panel (see illustration). Remove the instrument panel from the car.

Refitting
7 Refitting is a reversal of removal, but make sure that the wiring connectors are fully engaged.

9 Instrument panel components – removal and refitting

1 The instrument panel warning and illumination bulbs can be renewed as described in Section 6.

10.2a On post-August 2000 models, extract the retaining clips . . .

10.2c . . . and remove the plastic panel above the radiator grille

2 At the time of writing it would appear that only the bulbs can be renewed, and the printed circuit and instruments are not available separately. Consult a Toyota dealer for further information on component availability.

10 Horn – removal and refitting

Removal
1 Disconnect the battery negative terminal (refer to *Disconnecting the battery* in the Reference Chapter).
2 On post-August 2000 models, extract the retaining clips and plastic rivets and remove the plastic panel above the radiator grille (see illustrations).
3 Unscrew the horn mounting bracket bolt,

10.2b . . . and the plastic rivets . . .

10.3 Horn mounting bracket retaining bolt (arrowed)

withdraw the horn and disconnect the wiring connector (see illustration).

Refitting
4 Refitting is a reversal of removal.

11 Wiper arm – removal and refitting

Removal
1 Operate the wiper motor, then switch it off so that the wiper arm returns to the parked position.
2 Stick a piece of tape along the edge of the wiper blade, to use as an alignment aid on refitting.
3 Lift up the wiper arm spindle nut cover, then slacken, but do not remove, the spindle nut.
4 Using a small puller, release the wiper arm from the spindle (see illustration). Once the arm is free, remove the puller, unscrew the spindle nut and remove the wiper arm.
5 If both windscreen wiper arms are removed, note their locations, as different arms are fitted to the driver's and passenger's sides.

Refitting
6 Refitting is a reversal of removal, but ensure that the wiper arm and spindle splines are clean and dry, and align the blades with the tape fitted before removal.

12 Windscreen wiper motor and linkage – removal and refitting

Removal
1 Remove the wiper arms as described in Section 11.
2 Open the bonnet. Make sure the ignition is switched off.
3 Using a screwdriver to release the clips, remove the weatherstrip from the front edge of the bulkhead cowl panel (see illustration).
4 Unscrew and remove the screws and remove the cowl panel (see illustration).
5 Disconnect the wiring at the motor connector (see illustration).

11.4 Using a puller to release the wiper arm from the spindle

6 Unscrew the mounting bolts and withdraw the windscreen wiper motor and linkage from the bulkhead (see illustration).

7 If necessary disconnect the operating rods from the crank arm, then unscrew the retaining screws and remove the motor from the linkage bracket.

Refitting

8 Refitting is a reversal of removal, but apply a little grease to the crank arm ball before reconnecting the linkage and refer to Section 11 when refitting the wiper arms.

13 Tailgate wiper motor – removal and refitting

Removal

1 Remove the wiper arm as described in Section 11.

2 Open the tailgate and remove the inner trim panel as described in Chapter 11.

3 Disconnect the wiring at the connector.

4 Unscrew the mounting bolts and withdraw the wiper motor from the tailgate (see illustration).

Refitting

5 Refitting is a reversal of removal.

14 Washer system components – removal and refitting

Washer fluid reservoir

Removal

1 The washer fluid reservoir is located under the wheel arch on the right-hand side. To gain access, remove the wheel arch liner as described in Chapter 11.

2 Disconnect the wiring connectors from the washer pumps, then disconnect the fluid hoses. Be prepared for fluid spillage. Plug the washer pump outlets as soon as the hoses have been disconnected.

3 Undo the front and rear mounting bolts and remove the reservoir from under the wheel arch (see illustrations).

12.3 Remove the weatherstrip from the front edge of the bulkhead cowl panel

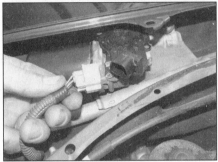
12.5 Disconnect the wiring at the windscreen wiper motor connector

Refitting

4 Refitting is a reversal of removal.

Washer pump(s)

Removal

5 Proceed as described in paragraphs 1 and 2.

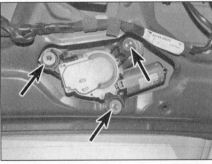
13.4 Tailgate wiper motor mounting bolts (arrowed)

12.4 Undo the screws and remove the bulkhead cowl panel

12.6 Unscrew the mounting bolts and withdraw the windscreen wiper motor and linkage from the bulkhead

6 Using a small screwdriver, depress the retaining catch and remove the washer pump retaining collar (see illustrations).

7 Pull the washer pump(s) from the reservoir, and recover the grommet. If the reservoir still contains fluid, be prepared for fluid spillage.

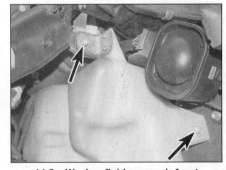
14.3a Washer fluid reservoir front mounting bolts (arrowed) . . .

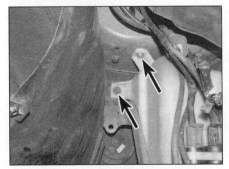
14.3b . . . and rear mounting bolts (arrowed)

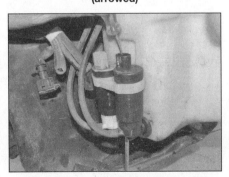
14.6a Depress the retaining catch with a screwdriver . . .

14.6b . . . and remove the washer pump retaining collar

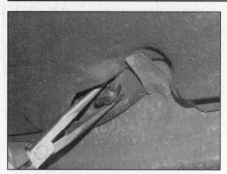

14.10 Release the windscreen washer jet securing tabs using long-nosed pliers, then push the jet from the bonnet

Refitting

8 Refitting is a reversal of removal.

Windscreen washer jet

Removal

9 Open the bonnet.
10 Working under the bonnet, release the securing tabs using long-nosed pliers, then push the jet from the bonnet **(see illustration)**. Disconnect the fluid hose, and withdraw the jet.

Refitting

11 Refitting is a reversal of removal. Adjust the jet nozzle(s) using a pin so that liquid is sprayed onto the centre of the glass.

Tailgate washer jet

Removal

12 Open the tailgate and, using a screwdriver, carefully prise the tailgate washer jet from its location and disconnect the washer hose **(see illustration)**.

Refitting

13 Refitting is a reversal of removal. Adjust the jet nozzle using a pin so that liquid is sprayed onto the centre of the glass.

15 Audio unit –
removal and refitting

Caution: If the audio unit fitted to the vehicle is one with an anti-theft security code, refer to the information given in the Reference Section at the rear of this manual before disconnecting the battery.
Note: *Various audio systems are fitted to Avensis vehicles, according to model year and trim level. The following Section depicts audio unit removal on a later, medium specification vehicle. The procedure will differ for other models.*

Removal

1 Disconnect the battery negative terminal (refer to *Disconnecting the battery* in the Reference Chapter).
2 Remove the facia centre panel as described in Chapter 11.

14.12 Carefully prise the tailgate washer jet from its location and disconnect the washer hose

3 Undo the retaining screws and remove the audio unit from the facia centre panel **(see illustration)**.

Refitting

4 Refitting is a reversal of removal.

16 Loudspeakers –
removal and refitting

Front door-mounted tweeters

1 To remove the tweeter speaker, proceed as described in Chapter 11, Section 20.

Door-mounted loudspeakers

Removal

2 To remove the door mounted loudspeakers, remove the front or rear door inner trim panel as described in Chapter 11.
3 Drill out the retaining rivets and withdraw the speaker from the door **(see illustration)**. Disconnect the wiring connector and remove the speaker.

Refitting

4 Refitting is a reversal of removal, using new rivets to secure the speaker.

17 Anti-theft alarm system
– general information

All models are fitted with the Toyota Vehicle

16.3 Loudspeaker retaining rivets (arrowed)

15.3 Undo the retaining screws (arrowed) each side, and remove the audio unit from the facia centre panel

Security System (TVSS) which is controlled by an ECU located beneath the facia on the passenger's side.
Any suspected faults with the system should be referred to a Toyota dealer.

18 Heated front seat
components –
general information

Certain models are fitted with heated front seats. The seats are heated by electrical elements built into the seat cushions. For access to the heating elements, the seats must be dismantled, and this work should be entrusted to a Toyota dealer.

19 Airbag and Supplementary
Restraint System – general
information and precautions

General information

1 An airbag and seat belt Supplementary Restraint System (SRS) is fitted to all models to prevent serious chest, head and side injuries during various accident situations. The driver's airbag is fitted in the steering wheel centre pad, and the passenger's airbag is fitted in the top of the facia panel. Side airbags are also fitted to the front seats. Pyrotechnic seat belt pretensioners are fitted, which automatically tighten the seat belts in the event of an accident. The pretensioners form part of the seat belt inertia reel mechanism. Later models may also be fitted with curtain shield airbags to inhibit occupant injury in the event of a side-on collision.
2 The SRS system is armed when the ignition key is in the 'on' or 'start' positions, and is activated by impact sensors located in strategic points within the body. The system airbag ECU is located beneath the rear of the centre console, and the side airbag impact sensors are located in the B-pillars. The front impact sensors are located on the chassis members each side, in the engine compartment.
3 The airbags are inflated by a gas generator, which forces the bag out from its location in the steering wheel, facia, front seat or headlining.

20.3 Undo the Torx screw each side of the steering wheel boss securing the airbag

20.4a Release the wiring connector locking clip . . .

20.4b . . . then disconnect the wiring connector and remove the airbag

Precautions

 Warning: Before carrying out any operations on the airbag or supplementary restraint system, disconnect the battery (see 'Disconnecting the battery' in the Reference Chapter) and wait at least two minutes. Make sure no one is inside the vehicle when the battery is reconnected then, with the driver's door open, switch the ignition on from outside vehicle and check the operation of the airbag warning light.

 Warning: Do not subject the area of the body around the control unit to any form of shock which could trigger the system.

Warning: Note that the airbags must not be subjected to temperatures in excess of 100°C. When the airbag is removed, ensure that it is stored with the pad upwards to prevent possible inflation.

Warning: Do not allow any solvents or cleaning agents to contact the airbag assemblies. They must be cleaned using only a damp cloth.

Warning: The airbags and control unit are both sensitive to impact. If either is dropped or damaged they should be renewed.

Warning: Disconnect the airbag control unit wiring connector prior to using arc welding equipment on the vehicle.

20 Airbag system components
– removal and refitting

 Warning: Refer to the precautions given in Section 19 before carrying out the following operations.

Driver's airbag

Removal

1 Disconnect the battery negative terminal (refer to *Disconnecting the battery* in the Reference Chapter). Wait at least two minutes before proceeding, to allow any residual electrical energy to dissipate.

2 Remove the audio remote control switch from the steering wheel as described in Section 4.
3 Undo the Torx screw each side of the steering wheel boss securing the airbag. There is no need to remove the screws, simply undo them to the 'released' position **(see illustration)**.
4 Withdraw the airbag from the steering wheel and release the wiring connector locking clip using a small screwdriver. Disconnect the wiring connector and remove the airbag **(see illustrations)**.

 Warning: Do not knock or drop the airbag unit and store it with its padded surface uppermost.

Refitting

5 Securely reconnect the wiring connector then seat the airbag unit in the steering wheel, ensuring the wiring does not become trapped.
6 Tighten the airbag retaining screws to the specified torque, then refit the audio remote control switch to the steering wheel as described in Section 4.
7 Make sure no one is inside the vehicle then reconnect the battery. With the driver's door open, switch the ignition on from outside vehicle and check the operation of the warning light.

Passenger's airbag

Removal

8 Disconnect the battery negative terminal (refer to *Disconnecting the battery* in the Reference Chapter). Wait at least two minutes

before proceeding, to allow any residual electrical energy to dissipate.
9 Remove the complete facia assembly as described in Chapter 11.
10 Release the locking clip using a small screwdriver, then disconnect the airbag wiring connector.
11 Undo the four nuts and remove the airbag unit from the underside of the facia **(see illustration)**.

Refitting

12 Refitting is a reversal of removal.
13 On completion, make sure no one is inside the vehicle, then reconnect the battery. With the driver's door open, switch the ignition on from outside vehicle and check the operation of the warning light.

Airbag rotary connector

Removal

14 Remove the airbag unit as described previously.
15 Remove the steering wheel as described in Chapter 10, and the steering column shrouds as described in Chapter 11.
16 Taking care not to rotate the unit, undo the four retaining screws and remove it from the steering column switch assembly. Disconnect the wiring connectors **(see illustrations)**.

Refitting

17 If a new rotary connector unit is being fitted, cut the cable-tie, or remove the seal, fitted to prevent the unit accidentally rotating.
18 A new rotary connector should be supplied in the centralised position – if not, or there is a

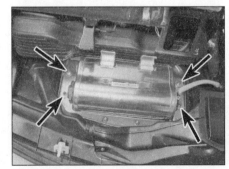

20.11 Passenger's airbag retaining nuts (arrowed)

20.16a Undo the four rotary connector retaining screws (arrowed) . . .

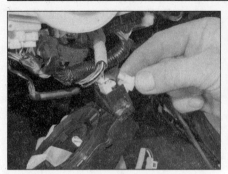

20.16b . . . then remove it from the steering column switch assembly and disconnect the wiring connectors

20.24 Release the retaining clip and disconnect the wiring connectors from the airbag control unit

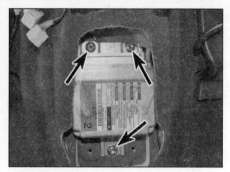

20.25 Airbag control unit retaining nuts (arrowed)

chance the unit is not centralised, proceed as follows.

19 Turn the rotary connector, anti-clockwise until it becomes tight. Now turn it clockwise two complete turns and align the pointers on the lower left of the connector face.

20 Reconnect the wiring then fit the unit to the steering column switch assembly and securely tighten its retaining screws.

21 Refit the steering column shrouds (Chapter 11) and steering wheel (Chapter 10), then refit the airbag unit as described above.

Airbag control unit

Removal

22 Disconnect the battery negative terminal (refer to *Disconnecting the battery* in the Reference Chapter). Wait at least two minutes before proceeding, to allow any residual electrical energy to dissipate.

23 Remove the centre console as described in Chapter 11.

24 Release the retaining clip and disconnect the wiring connectors from the airbag control unit **(see illustration)**.

25 Unscrew the retaining nuts then remove the control unit from the vehicle **(see illustration)**.

Refitting

26 Refitting is a reversal of removal.

27 On completion, make sure no one is inside the vehicle, then reconnect the battery. With the driver's door open, switch the ignition on

from outside vehicle and check the operation of the warning light.

Side airbag

28 Removal and refitting of the side airbag units should be entrusted to a Toyota dealer. The seat must be dismantled to enable the airbag unit to removed/refitted.

Curtain shield airbag

29 Removal and refitting of the curtain shield airbag units should be entrusted to a Toyota dealer. The headlining must be partially removed to enable the airbag unit to removed/refitted.

Side impact sensors

Removal

30 Disconnect the battery negative terminal (refer to *Disconnecting the battery* in the Reference Chapter). Wait at least two minutes before proceeding, to allow any residual electrical energy to dissipate.

31 The side impact sensors are fitted to the vehicle B-pillars (between the driver's and passenger's doors).

32 Remove the front seat belt inertia reel units as described in Chapter 11.

33 Release the clip and disconnect the wiring connector from the sensor.

34 Undo the nut and two bolts and remove the sensor.

Refitting

35 Refitting is a reversal of removal.

36 On completion, make sure no one is inside the vehicle, then reconnect the battery. With the driver's door open, switch the ignition on from outside vehicle and check the operation of the warning light.

Front impact sensors

37 Disconnect the battery negative terminal (refer to *Disconnecting the battery* in the Reference Chapter). Wait at least two minutes before proceeding, to allow any residual electrical energy to dissipate.

Left-hand sensor removal

38 Remove the battery and battery tray as described in Chapter 5A. The sensor is located beneath the battery support frame.

39 Disconnect the sensor wiring connector, undo the two nuts and remove the sensor.

Right-hand sensor removal

40 The sensor is located on the chassis member behind the right-hand headlight.

41 Disconnect the sensor wiring connector, undo the two nuts and remove the sensor.

Refitting

42 Refitting is a reversal of removal.

43 On completion, make sure no one is inside the vehicle, then reconnect the battery. With the driver's door open, switch the ignition on from outside vehicle and check the operation of the warning light.

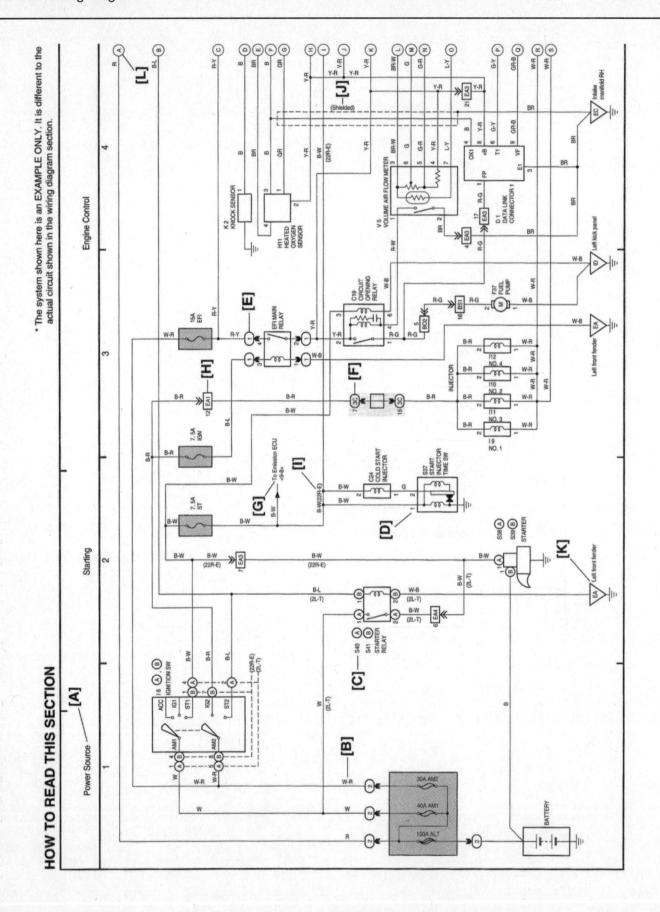

[A] : System Title

[B] : Indicates the wiring color.

Wire colors are indicated by an alphabetical code.

B = Black	W = White	BR = Brown
L = Blue	V = Voilet	SB = Sky Blue
R = Red	G = Green	LG = Light Green
P = Pink	Y = Yellow	GR = Gray
O = Orange		

The first letter indicates the basic wire color and the second letter indicates the color of the stripe.

Example: L – Y

L – Y (Yellow)

L – (Blue)

[C] : The position of the parts is the same as shown in the wiring diagram and wire routing.

[D] : Indicates the pin number of the connector.

The numbering system is different for female and male connectors.

Example: Numbered in order from upper left to lower right

Numbered in order from upper right to lower left

Female   Male

The numbering system for the overall wiring diagram is the same as above.

[E] : Indicates a Relay Block. No shading is used and only the Relay Block No. is shown to distinguish it from the J/B.

Example: ① Indicates Relay Block No.1

[F] : Junction Block (The number in the circle is the J/B No. and the connector code is shown beside it). Junction Blocks are shaded to clearly separate them from other parts.

Example:

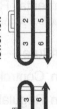

3C indicates that it is inside Junction Block No.3

[G] : Indicates related system.

[H] : Indicates the wiring harness and wiring harness connector. The wiring harness with male terminal is shown with arrows (≫).

Outside numerals are pin numbers.

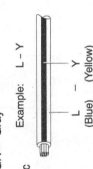

Male (≫)

Female

[I] : ( ) is used to indicate different wiring and connector, etc. when the vehicle model, engine type, or specification is different.

[J] : Indicates a shielded cable.

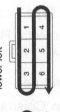

[K] : Indicates and located on ground point.

[L] : The same code occuring on the next page indicates that the wire harness is continuous.

HINT :

Junction connector in this manual include a short terminal which is connected to a number of wire harnesses. Always perform inspection with the short terminal installed. (When installing the wire harnesses, the harnesses can be connected to any position within the short terminal grouping. Accordingly, in other vehicles, the same position in the short terminal may be connected to a wire harness from a different part.)

Wire harness sharing the same short terminal grouping have the same color.

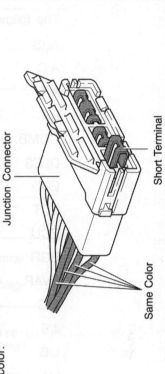

Junction Connector

Short Terminal

Same Color

Note: Only diagrams relevant to the specific coverage of this manual are included, so these do not follow a complete numerical sequence (non-applicable diagrams have been omitted). Consequently some diagrams contain cross-references to others which are not included here.

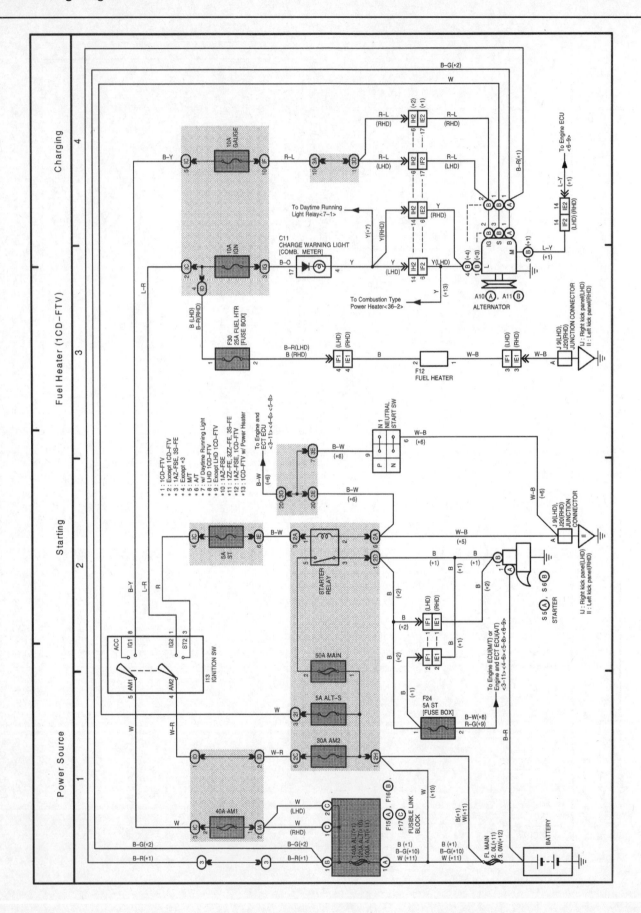

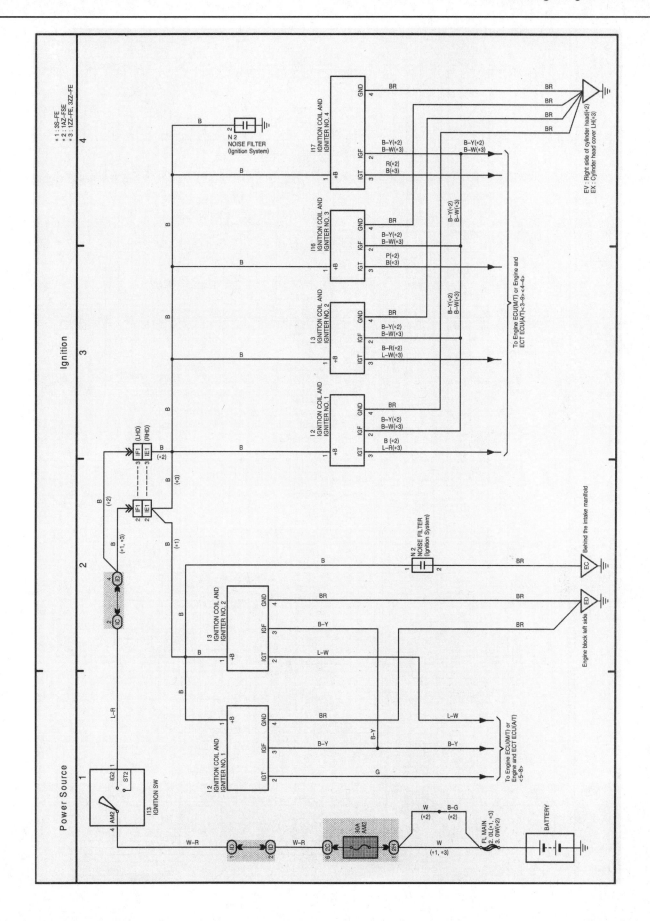

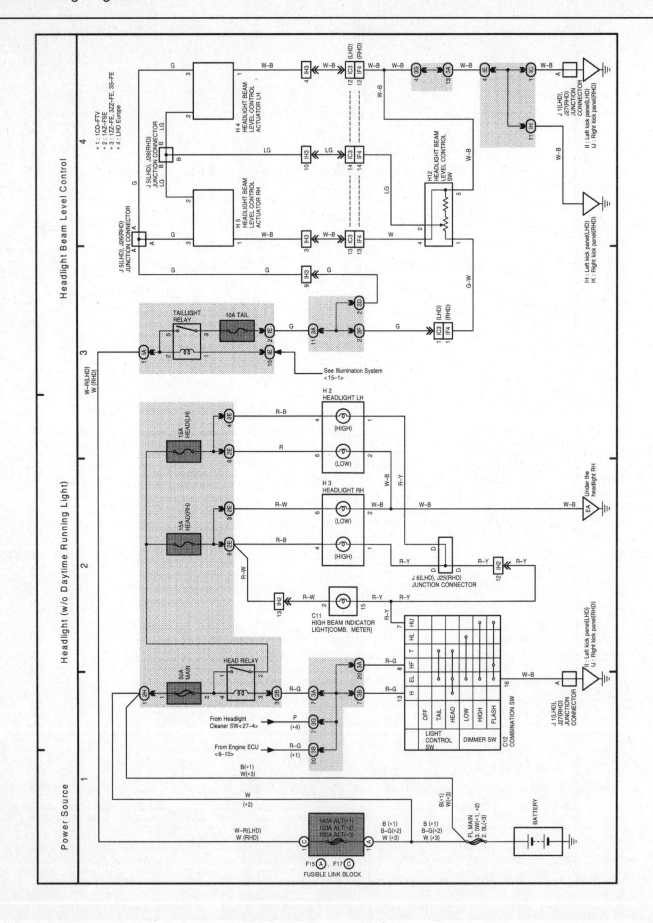

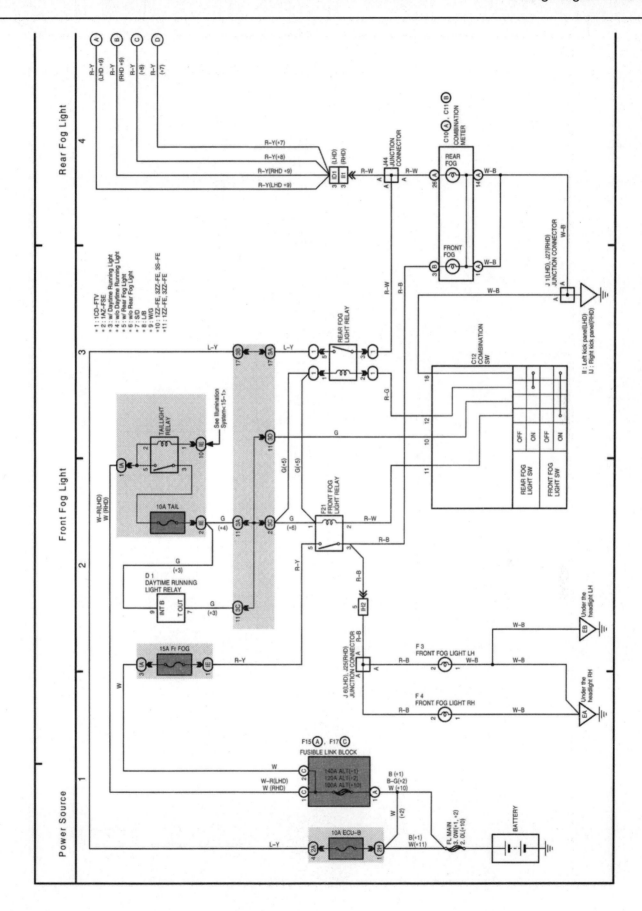

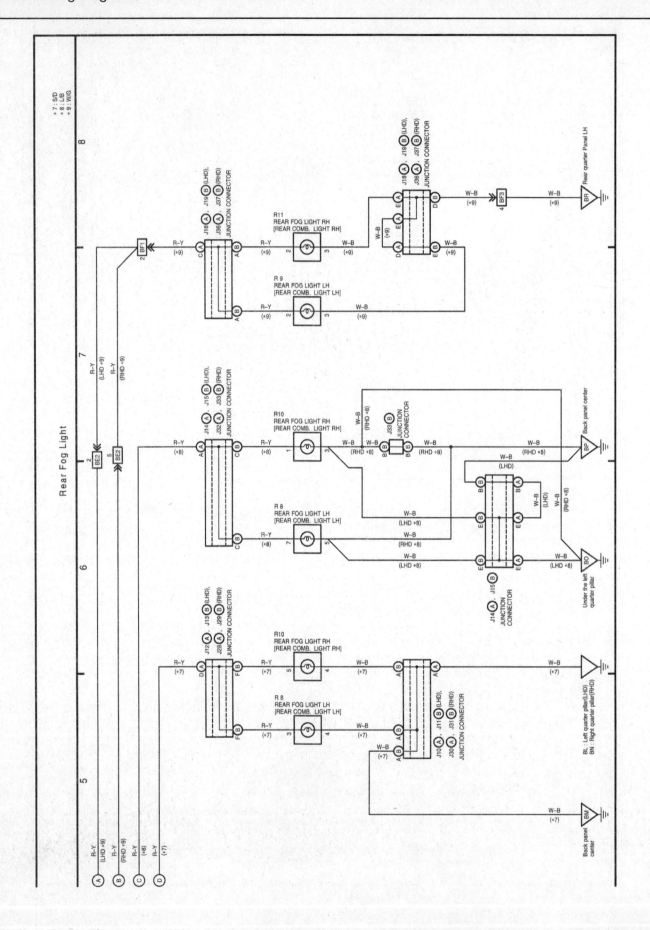

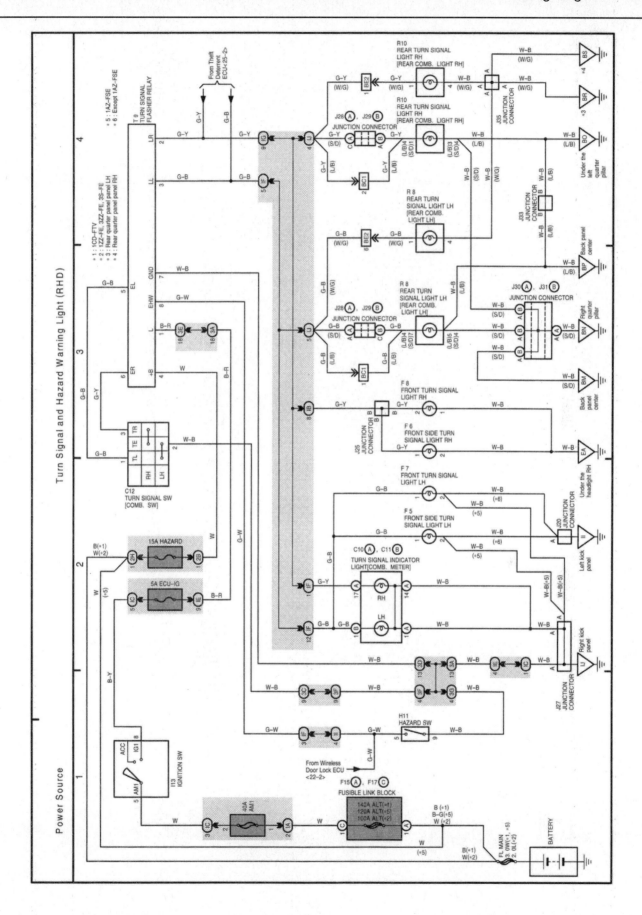

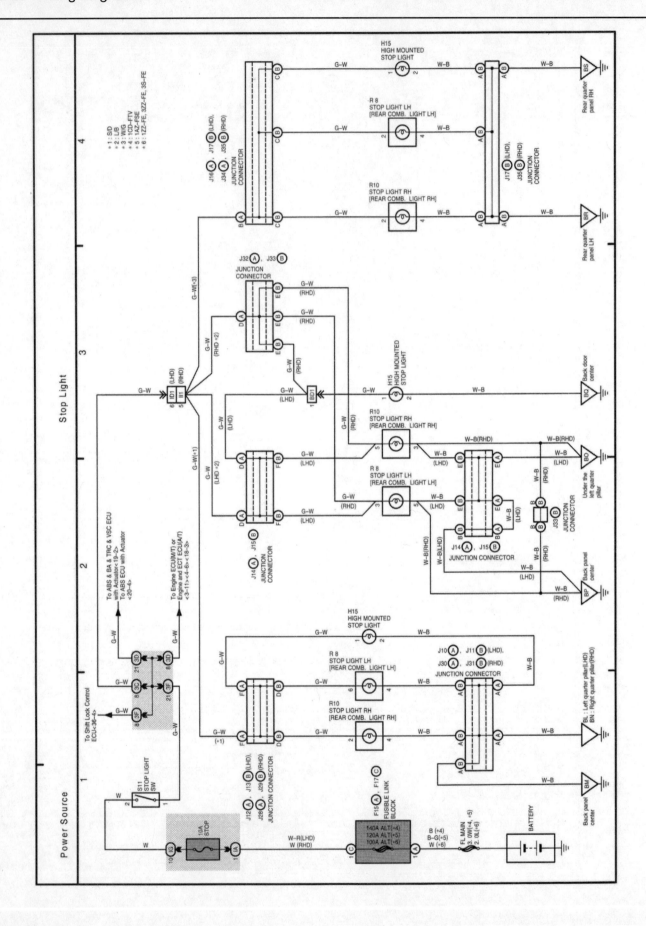

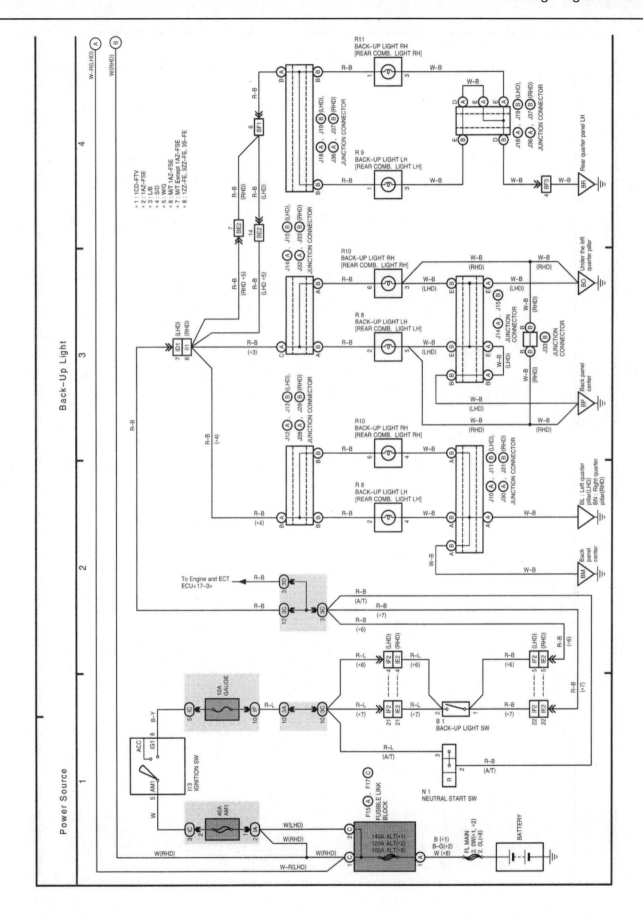

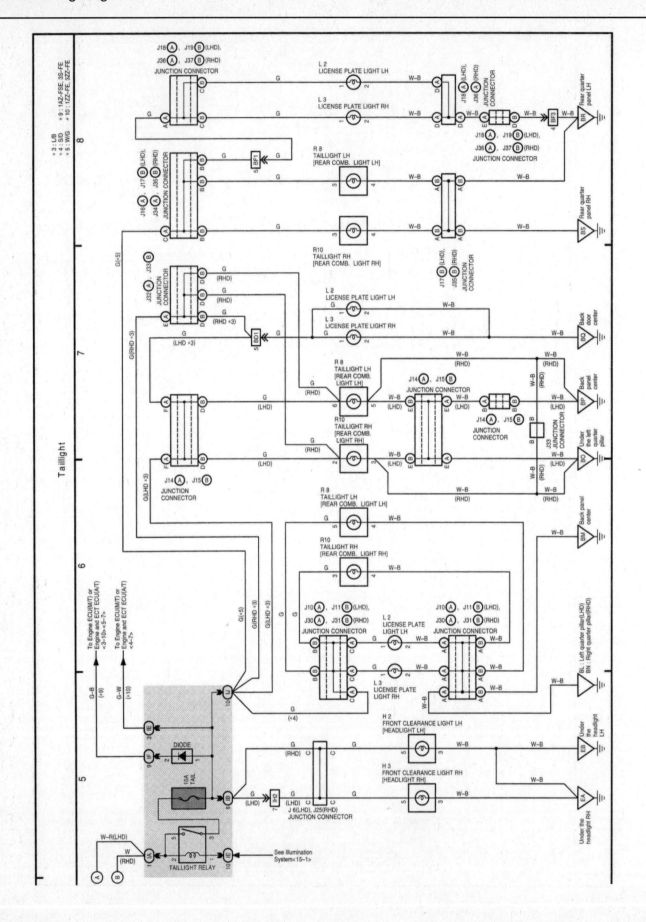

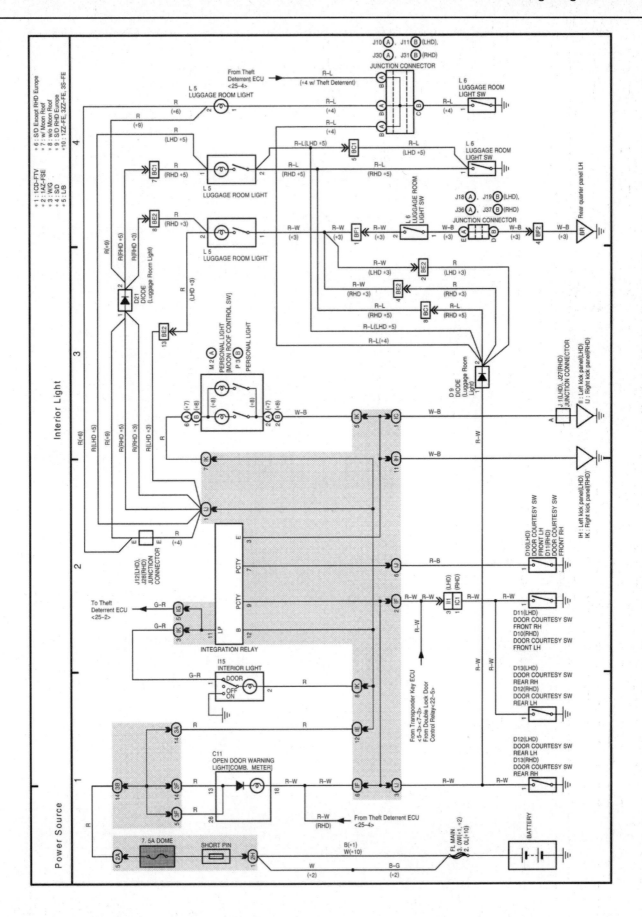

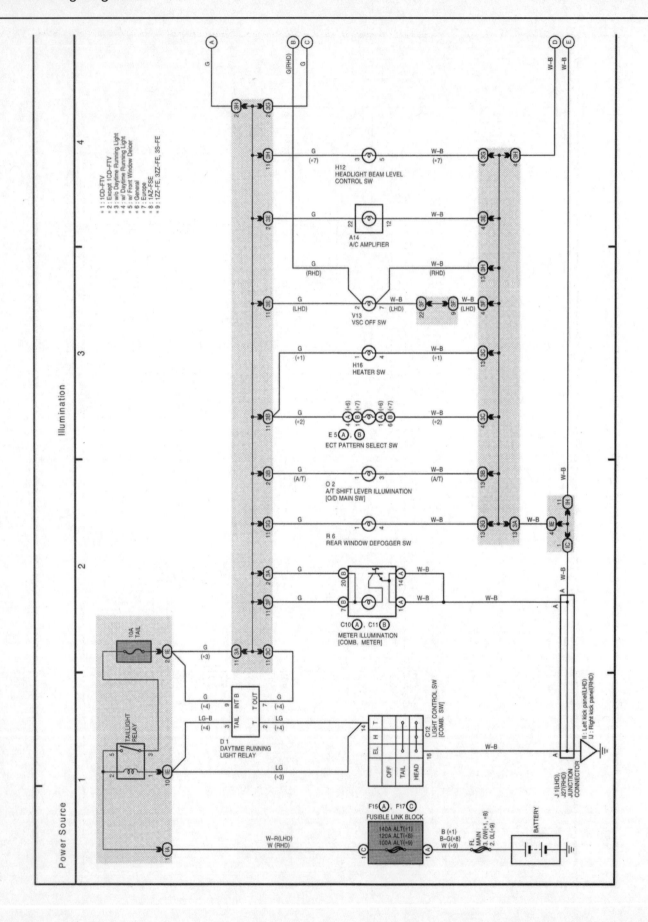

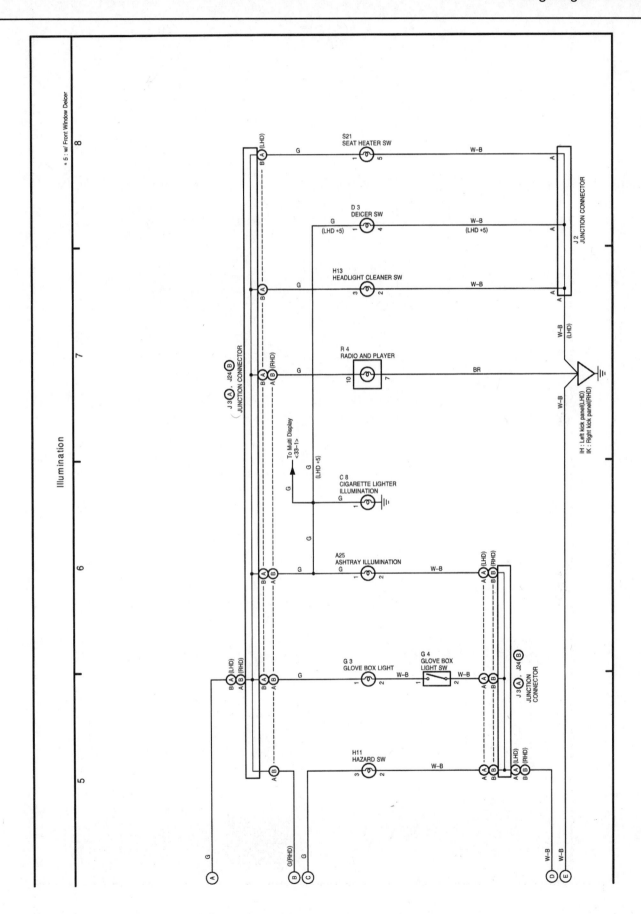

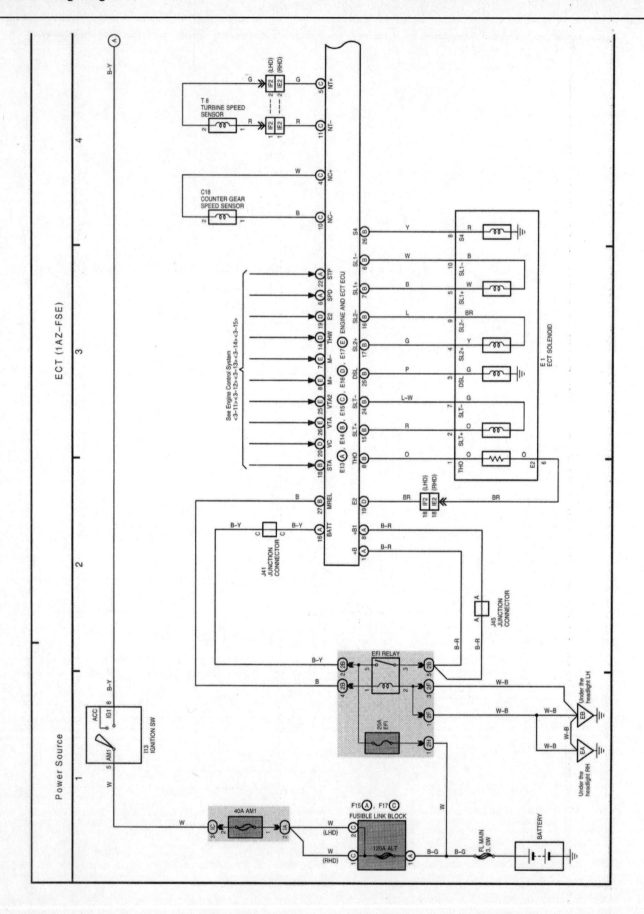

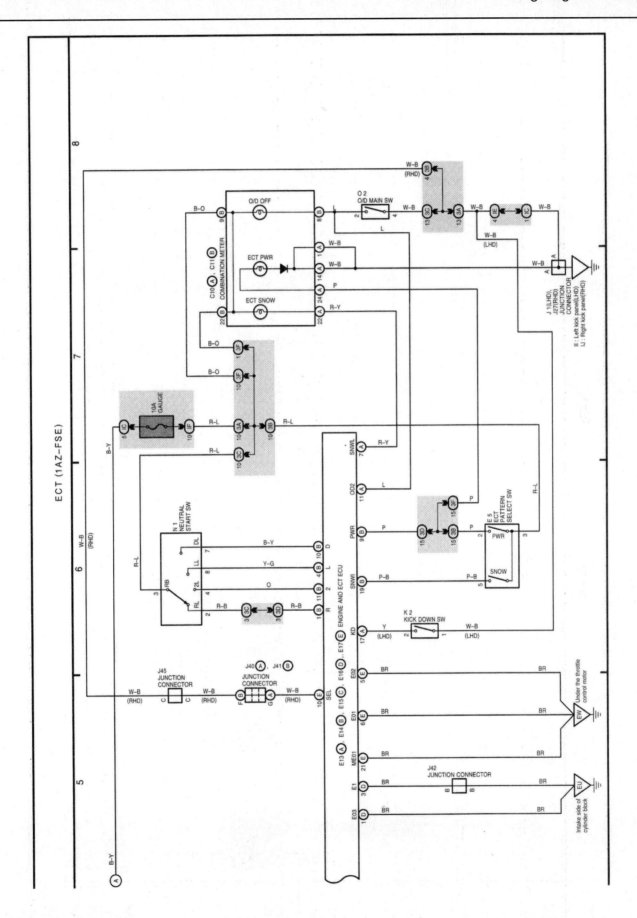

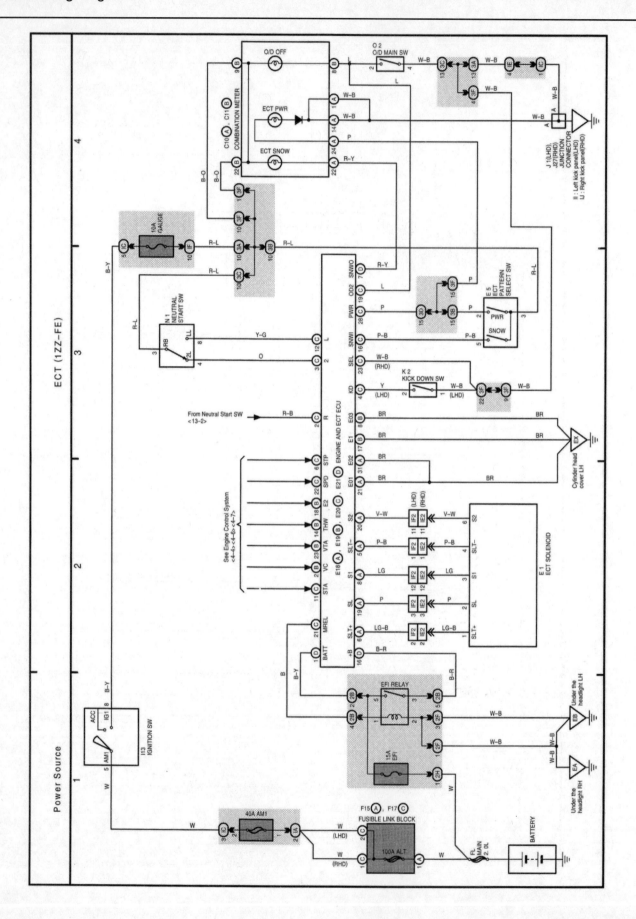

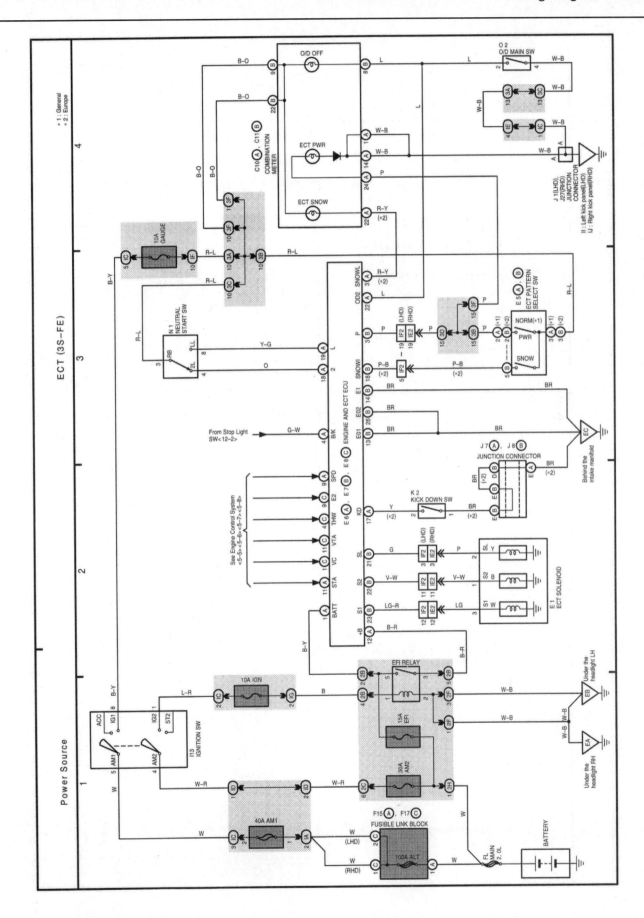

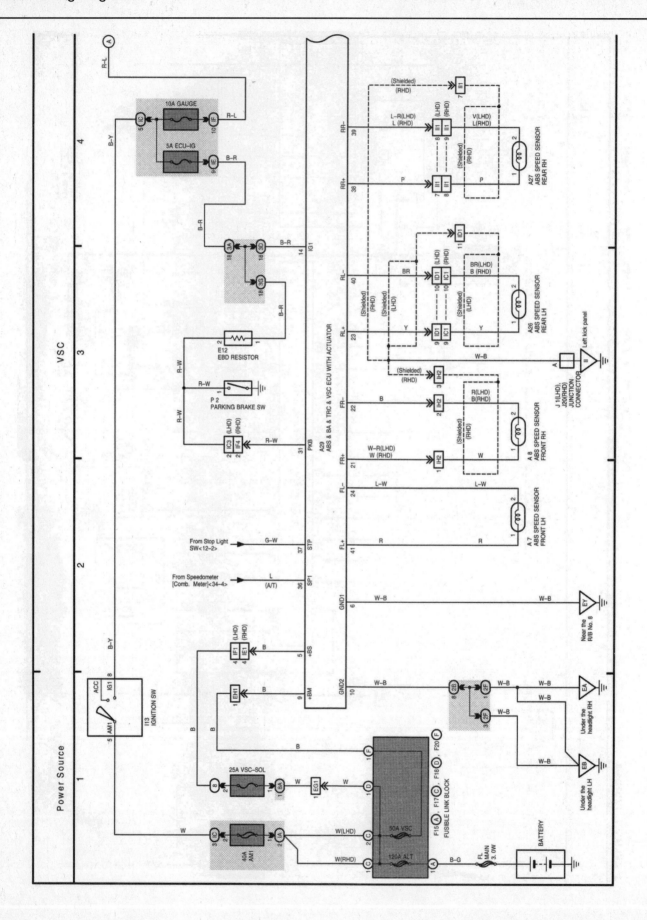

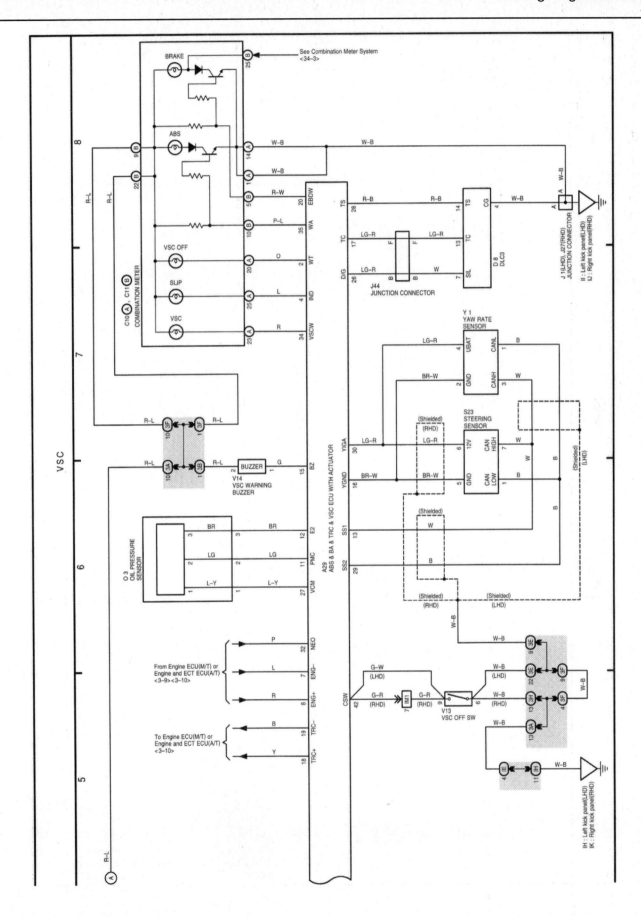

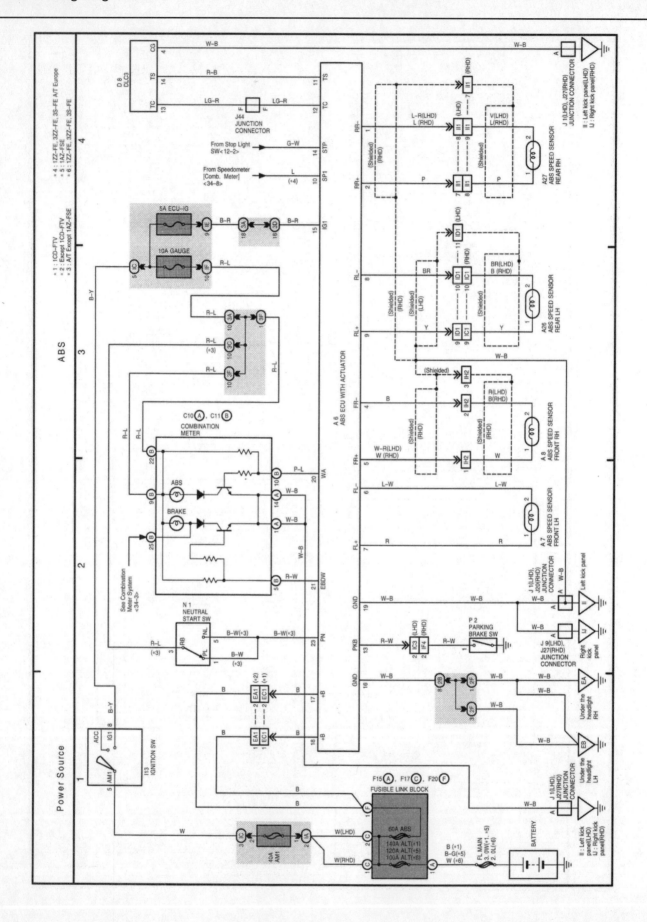

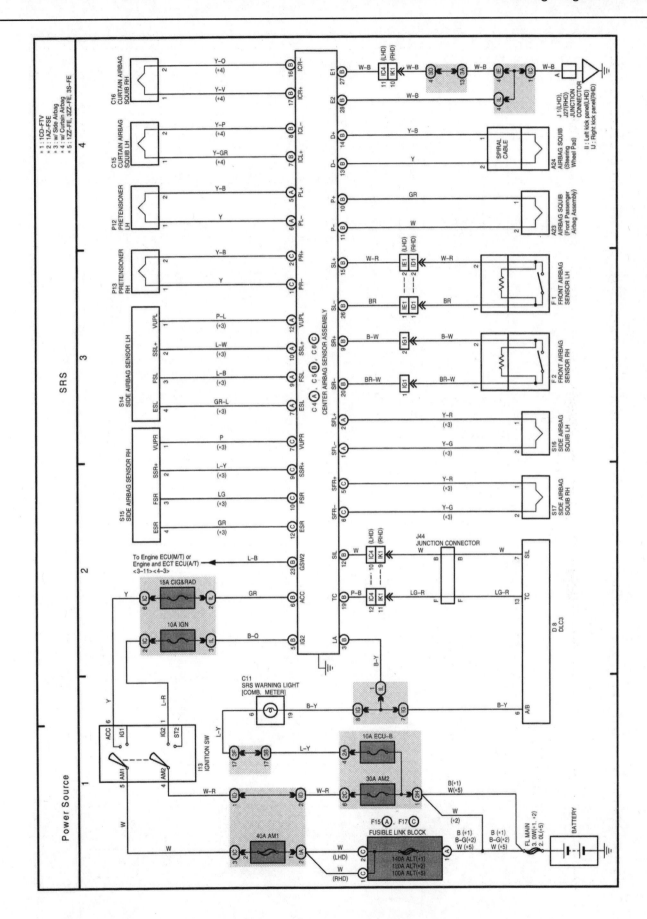

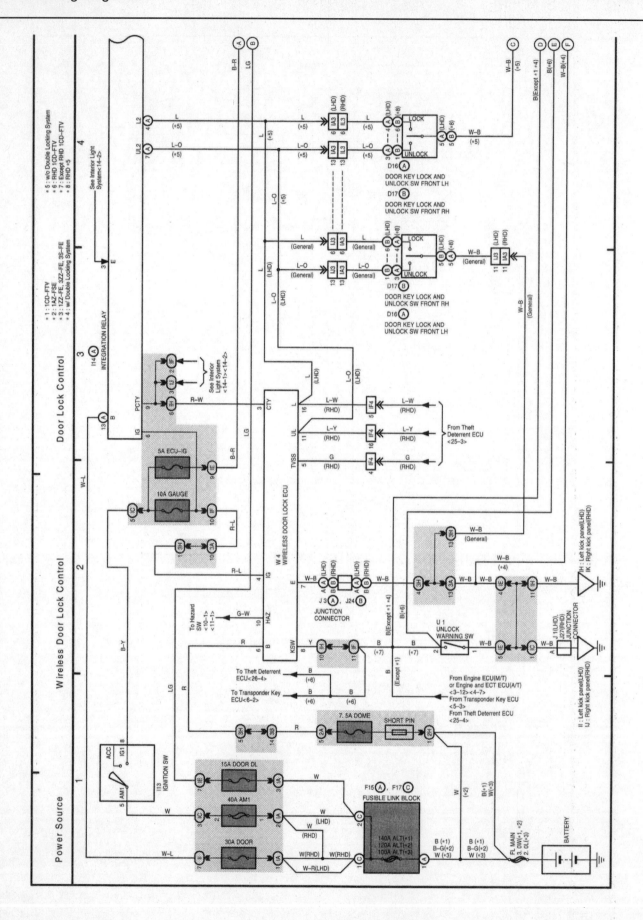

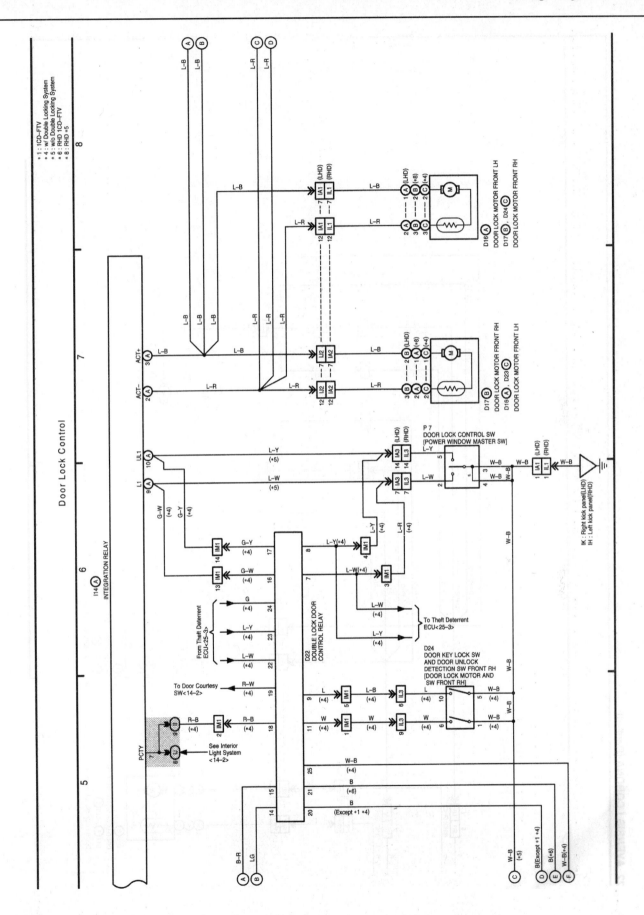

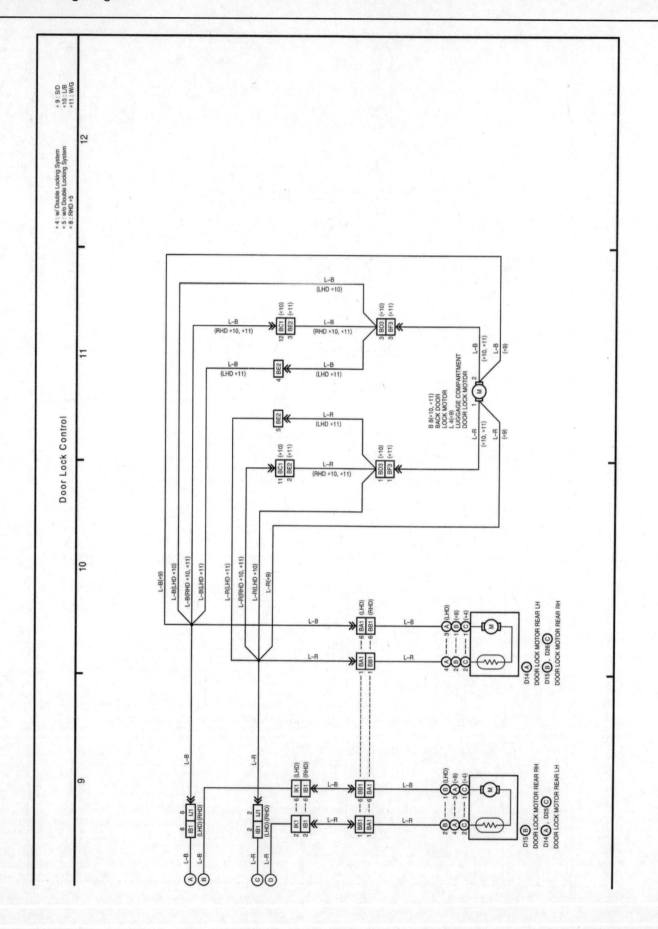

Door Lock Control

*4 : w/ Double Locking System
*5 : w/o Double Locking System
*8 : RHD *5

*9 : S/D
*10 : L/B
*11 : W/G

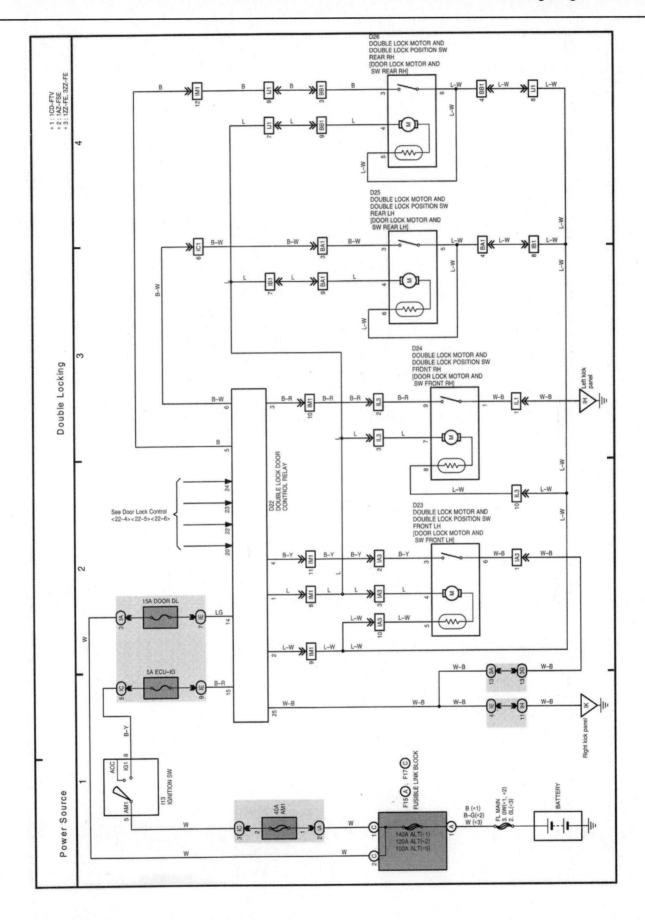

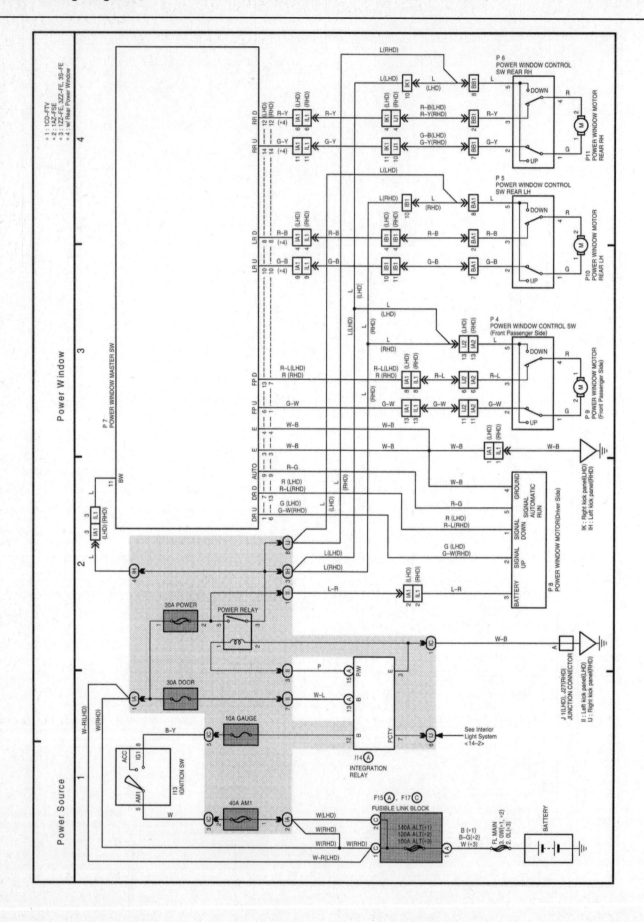

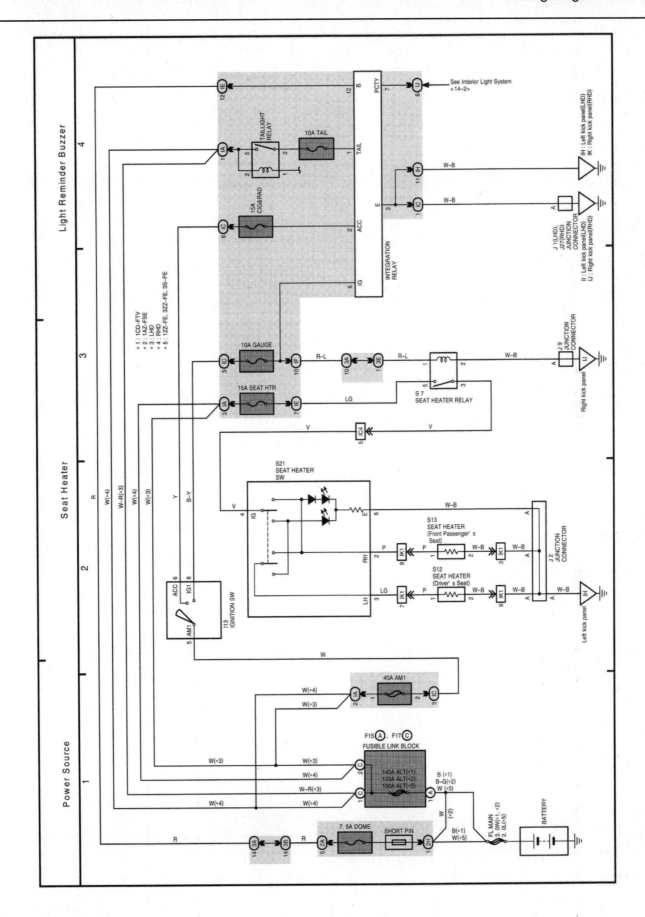

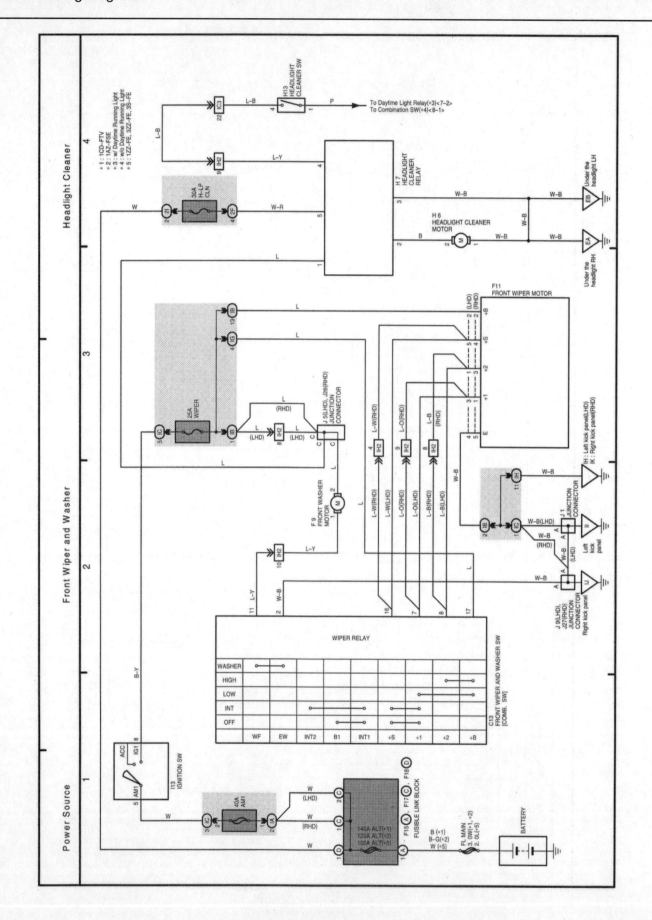

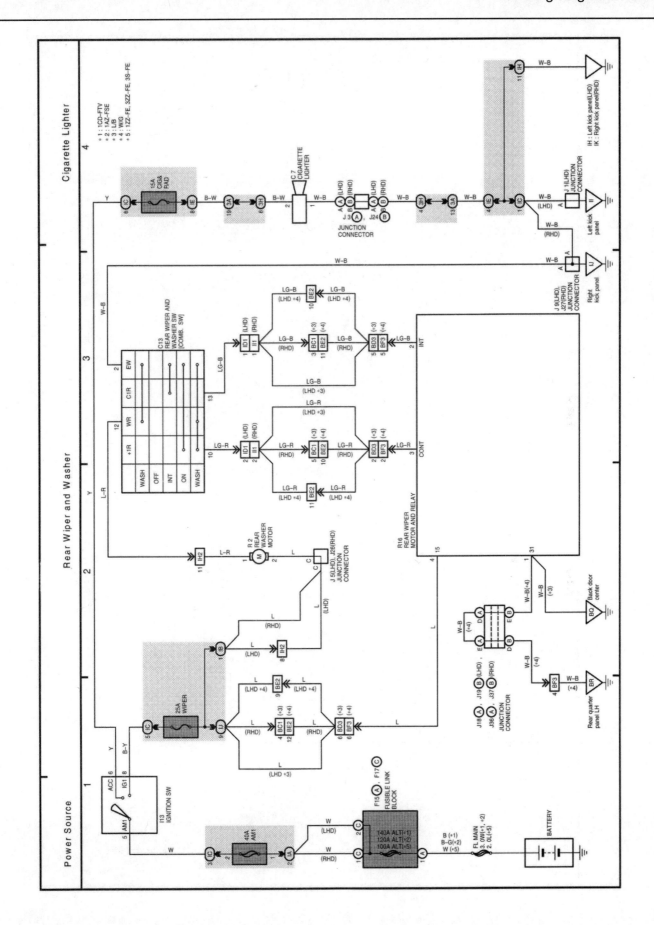

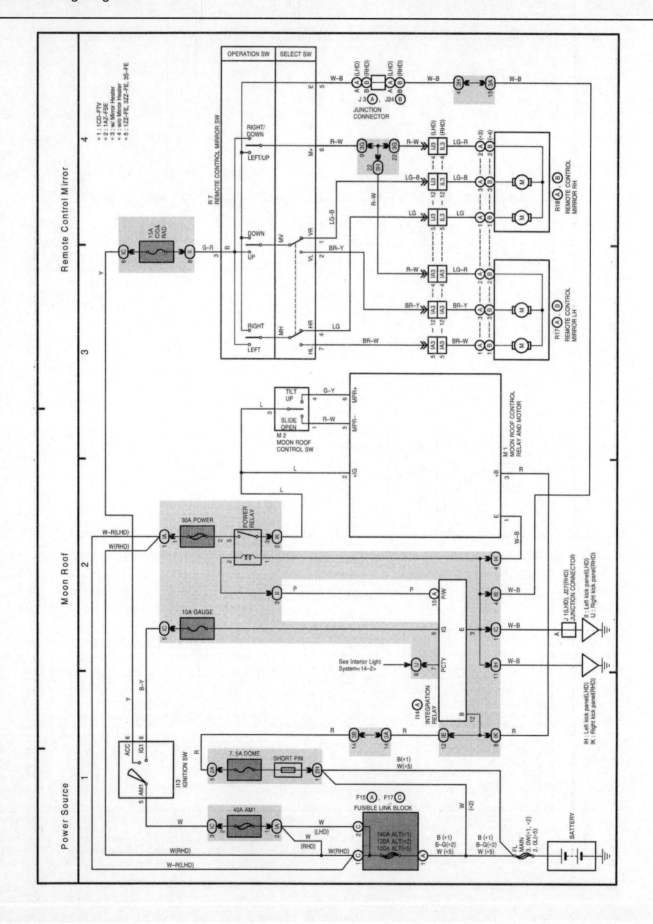

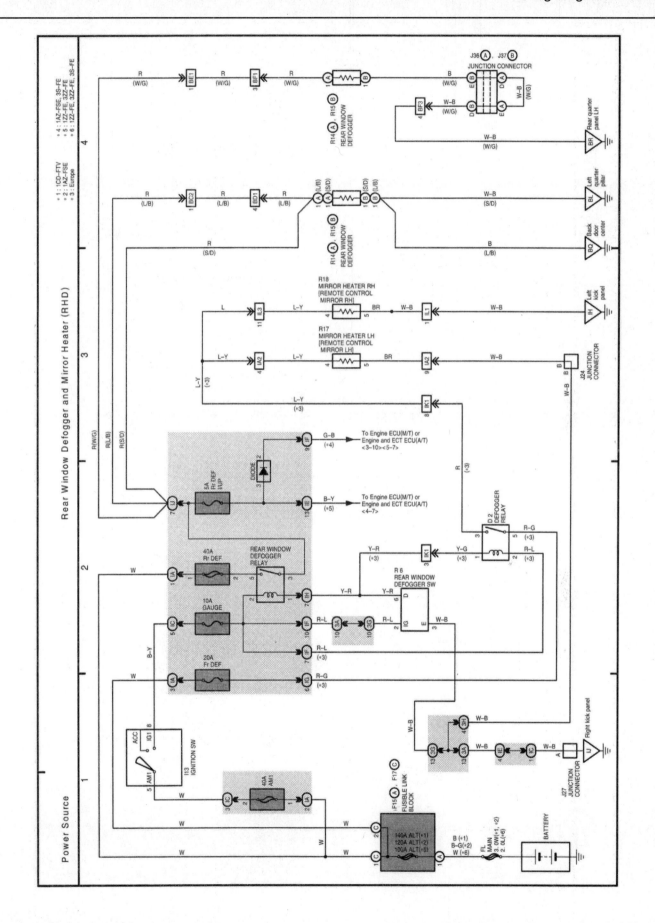

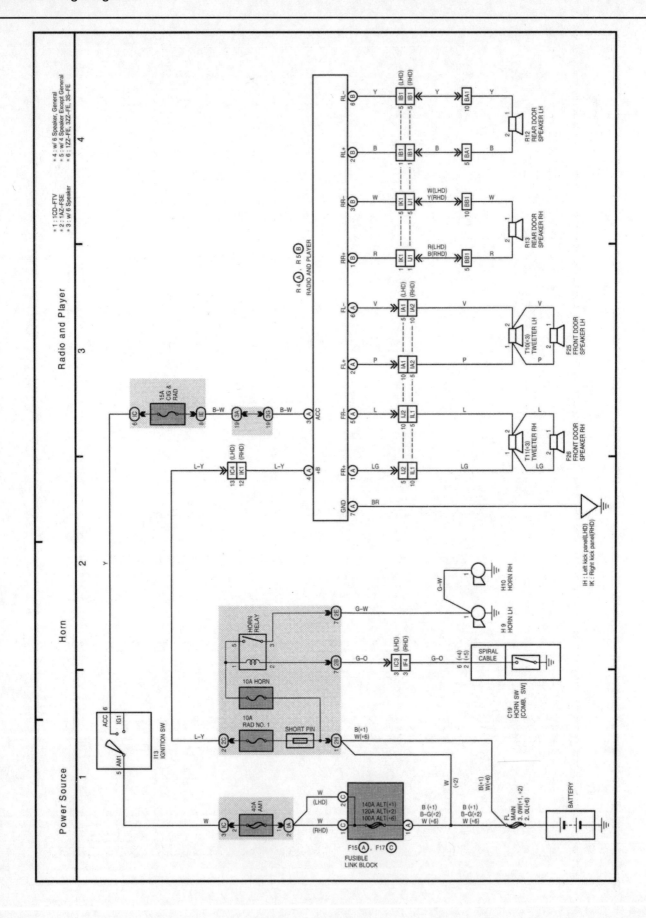

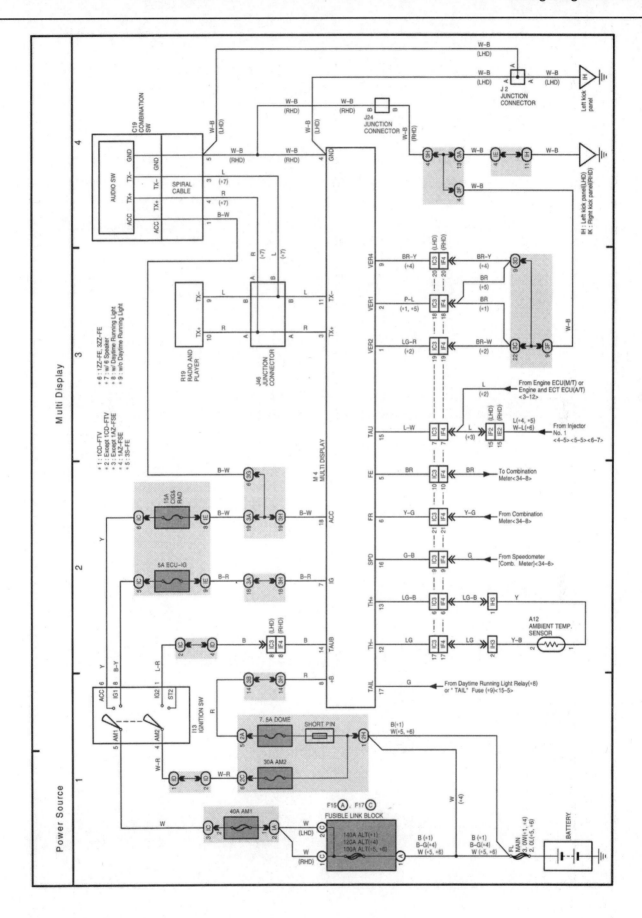

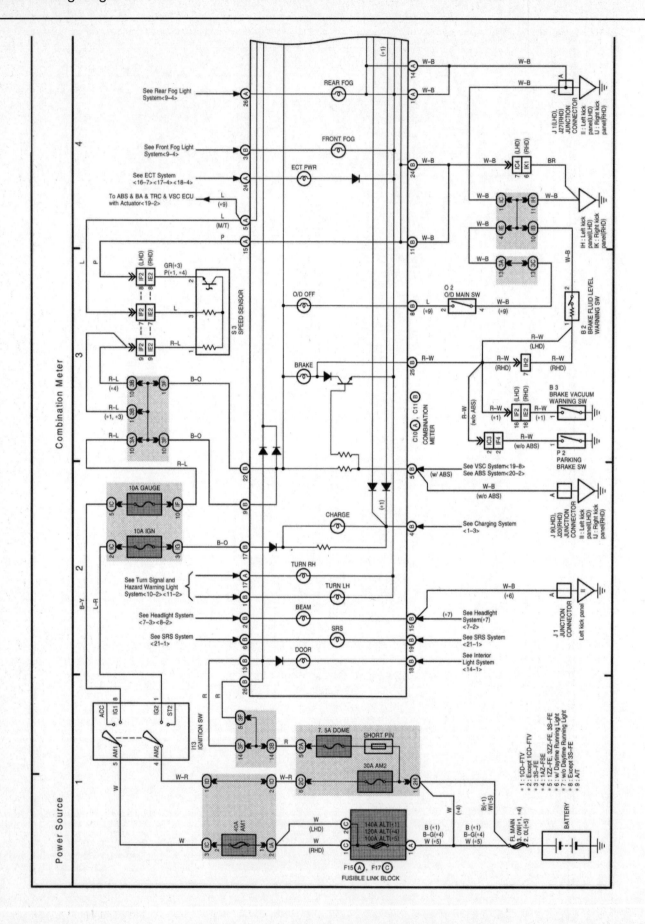

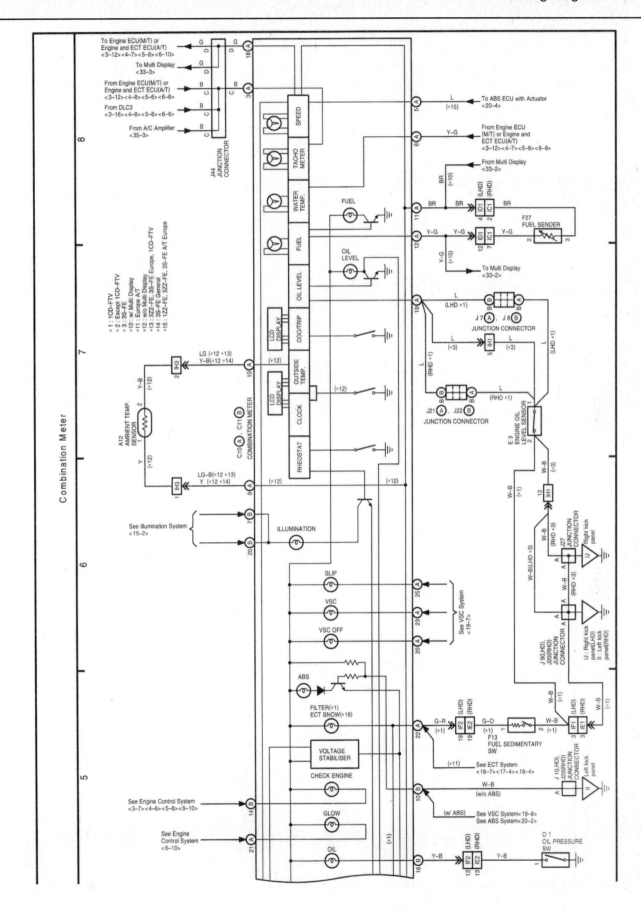

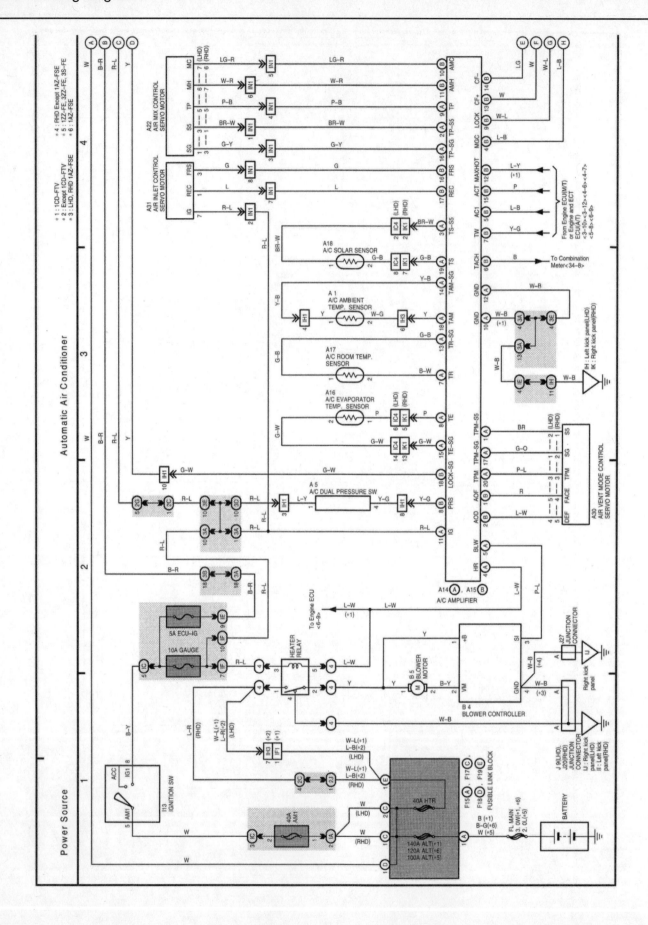

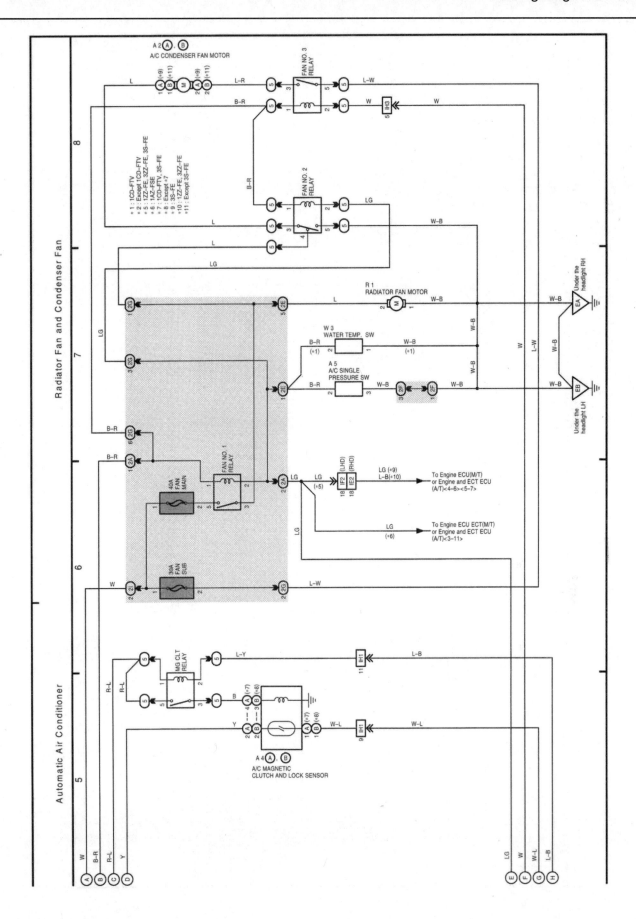

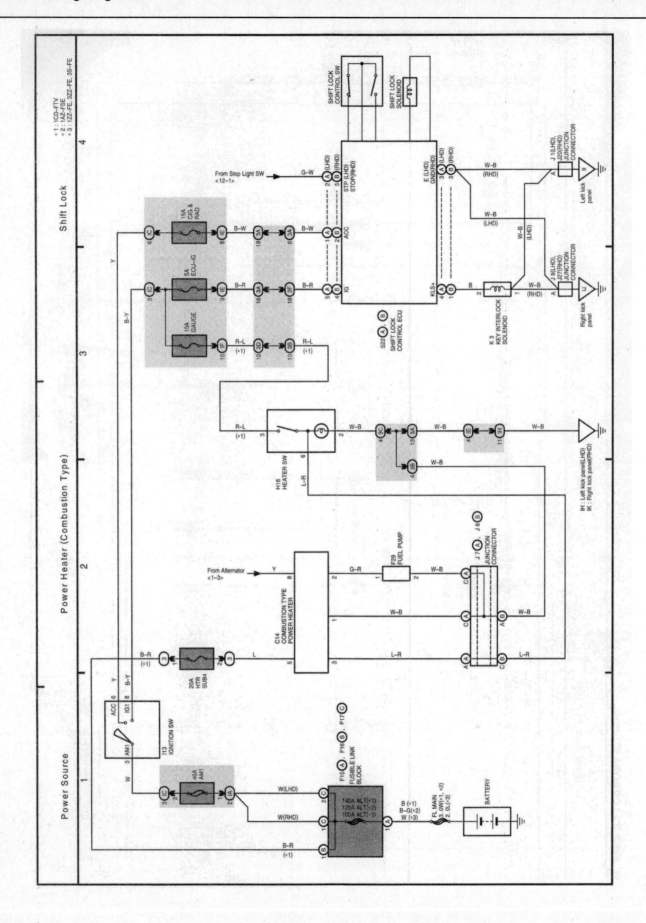

Dimensions and weights

Note: *All figures are approximate, and may vary according to model. Refer to manufacturer's data for exact figures.*

Dimensions

Overall length:
  Pre-August 2000 models:

Saloon and Hatchback	4490 mm
Estate	4570 mm

  Post-August 2000 models:

Saloon and Hatchback	4520 mm
Estate	4600 mm
Overall width.	1710 mm

Overall height:

Saloon and Hatchback	1425 mm
Estate	1500 mm
Wheelbase	2630 mm
Front track	1480 mm
Rear track	1450 mm

Weights

Kerb weight	1185 to 1290 kg
Towing weight.	1300 kg

Length (distance)

Inches (in)	x 25.4	= Millimetres (mm)	x 0.0394	= Inches (in)	
Feet (ft)	x 0.305	= Metres (m)	x 3.281	= Feet (ft)	
Miles	x 1.609	= Kilometres (km)	x 0.621	= Miles	

Volume (capacity)

Cubic inches (cu in; in^3)	x 16.387	= Cubic centimetres (cc; cm^3)	x 0.061	= Cubic inches (cu in; in^3)	
Imperial pints (Imp pt)	x 0.568	= Litres (l)	x 1.76	= Imperial pints (Imp pt)	
Imperial quarts (Imp qt)	x 1.137	= Litres (l)	x 0.88	= Imperial quarts (Imp qt)	
Imperial quarts (Imp qt)	x 1.201	= US quarts (US qt)	x 0.833	= Imperial quarts (Imp qt)	
US quarts (US qt)	x 0.946	= Litres (l)	x 1.057	= US quarts (US qt)	
Imperial gallons (Imp gal)	x 4.546	= Litres (l)	x 0.22	= Imperial gallons (Imp gal)	
Imperial gallons (Imp gal)	x 1.201	= US gallons (US gal)	x 0.833	= Imperial gallons (Imp gal)	
US gallons (US gal)	x 3.785	= Litres (l)	x 0.264	= US gallons (US gal)	

Mass (weight)

Ounces (oz)	x 28.35	= Grams (g)	x 0.035	= Ounces (oz)	
Pounds (lb)	x 0.454	= Kilograms (kg)	x 2.205	= Pounds (lb)	

Force

Ounces-force (ozf; oz)	x 0.278	= Newtons (N)	x 3.6	= Ounces-force (ozf; oz)	
Pounds-force (lbf; lb)	x 4.448	= Newtons (N)	x 0.225	= Pounds-force (lbf; lb)	
Newtons (N)	x 0.1	= Kilograms-force (kgf; kg)	x 9.81	= Newtons (N)	

Pressure

Pounds-force per square inch (psi; lbf/in^2; lb/in^2)	x 0.070	= Kilograms-force per square centimetre (kgf/cm^2; kg/cm^2)	x 14.223	= Pounds-force per square inch (psi; lbf/in^2; lb/in^2)
Pounds-force per square inch (psi; lbf/in^2; lb/in^2)	x 0.068	= Atmospheres (atm)	x 14.696	= Pounds-force per square inch (psi; lbf/in^2; lb/in^2)
Pounds-force per square inch (psi; lbf/in^2; lb/in^2)	x 0.069	= Bars	x 14.5	= Pounds-force per square inch (psi; lbf/in^2; lb/in^2)
Pounds-force per square inch (psi; lbf/in^2; lb/in^2)	x 6.895	= Kilopascals (kPa)	x 0.145	= Pounds-force per square inch (psi; lbf/in^2; lb/in^2)
Kilopascals (kPa)	x 0.01	= Kilograms-force per square centimetre (kgf/cm^2; kg/cm^2)	x 98.1	= Kilopascals (kPa)
Millibar (mbar)	x 100	= Pascals (Pa)	x 0.01	= Millibar (mbar)
Millibar (mbar)	x 0.0145	= Pounds-force per square inch (psi; lbf/in^2; lb/in^2)	x 68.947	= Millibar (mbar)
Millibar (mbar)	x 0.75	= Millimetres of mercury (mmHg)	x 1.333	= Millibar (mbar)
Millibar (mbar)	x 0.401	= Inches of water (inH_2O)	x 2.491	= Millibar (mbar)
Millimetres of mercury (mmHg)	x 0.535	= Inches of water (inH_2O)	x 1.868	= Millimetres of mercury (mmHg)
Inches of water (inH_2O)	x 0.036	= Pounds-force per square inch (psi; lbf/in^2; lb/in^2)	x 27.68	= Inches of water (inH_2O)

Torque (moment of force)

Pounds-force inches (lbf in; lb in)	x 1.152	= Kilograms-force centimetre (kgf cm; kg cm)	x 0.868	= Pounds-force inches (lbf in; lb in)
Pounds-force inches (lbf in; lb in)	x 0.113	= Newton metres (Nm)	x 8.85	= Pounds-force inches (lbf in; lb in)
Pounds-force inches (lbf in; lb in)	x 0.083	= Pounds-force feet (lbf ft; lb ft)	x 12	= Pounds-force inches (lbf in; lb in)
Pounds-force feet (lbf ft; lb ft)	x 0.138	= Kilograms-force metres (kgf m; kg m)	x 7.233	= Pounds-force feet (lbf ft; lb ft)
Pounds-force feet (lbf ft; lb ft)	x 1.356	= Newton metres (Nm)	x 0.738	= Pounds-force feet (lbf ft; lb ft)
Newton metres (Nm)	x 0.102	= Kilograms-force metres (kgf m; kg m)	x 9.804	= Newton metres (Nm)

Power

Horsepower (hp)	x 745.7	= Watts (W)	x 0.0013	= Horsepower (hp)

Velocity (speed)

Miles per hour (miles/hr; mph)	x 1.609	= Kilometres per hour (km/hr; kph)	x 0.621	= Miles per hour (miles/hr; mph)

Fuel consumption*

Miles per gallon, Imperial (mpg)	x 0.354	= Kilometres per litre (km/l)	x 2.825	= Miles per gallon, Imperial (mpg)
Miles per gallon, US (mpg)	x 0.425	= Kilometres per litre (km/l)	x 2.352	= Miles per gallon, US (mpg)

Temperature

Degrees Fahrenheit = (°C x 1.8) + 32   Degrees Celsius (Degrees Centigrade; °C) = (°F - 32) x 0.56

It is common practice to convert from miles per gallon (mpg) to litres/100 kilometres (l/100km), where mpg x l/100 km = 282

Spare parts are available from many sources, including maker's appointed garages, accessory shops, and motor factors. To be sure of obtaining the correct parts, it may sometimes be necessary to quote the vehicle identification number. If possible, it can also be useful to take the old parts along for positive identification. Items such as starter motors and alternators may be available under a service exchange scheme - any parts returned should always be clean.

Our advice regarding spare part sources is as follows.

Officially-appointed garages

This is the best source of parts which are peculiar to your car, and are not otherwise generally available (eg, badges, interior trim, certain body panels, etc). It is also the only place at which you should buy parts if the vehicle is still under warranty.

Accessory shops

These are very good places to buy materials and components needed for the maintenance of your car (oil, air and fuel filters, spark plugs, light bulbs, drivebelts, oils and greases, brake pads, touch-up paint, etc). Parts like this sold by a reputable shop are of the same standard as those used by the car manufacturer.

Motor factors

Good factors will stock all the more important components which wear out comparatively quickly and can sometimes supply individual components needed for the overhaul of a larger assembly. They may also handle work such as cylinder block reboring, crankshaft regrinding and balancing, etc.

Tyre and exhaust specialists

These outlets may be independent or members of a local or national chain. They

frequently offer competitive prices when compared with a main dealer or local garage, but it will pay to obtain several quotes before making a decision. Also ask what extras may be added to the quote - for instance, fitting a new valve and balancing the wheel are both often charged on top of the price of a new tyre.

Other sources

Beware of parts or materials obtained from market stalls, car boot sales or similar outlets. Such items are not invariably sub-standard, but there is little chance of compensation if they do prove unsatisfactory. In the case of safety-critical components such as brake pads there is the risk not only of financial loss but also of an accident causing injury or death.

Second-hand components or assemblies obtained from a car breaker can be a good buy in some circumstances, but this sort of purchase is best made by the experienced DIY mechanic.

Vehicle identification

Modifications are a continuing and unpublicised process in vehicle manufacture, quite apart from major model changes. Spare parts lists are compiled upon a numerical basis, the individual vehicle identification numbers being essential to correct identification of the component concerned.

When ordering spare parts, always give as much information as possible. Quote the car model, year of manufacture, vehicle and engine numbers, as appropriate.

The *Vehicle Identification Number* (VIN) is stamped into the right-hand side of the engine compartment bulkhead **(see illustration)**. This number, together with vehicle weight information is also contained on a label attached to the outside of the B-pillar, on the left-hand side of the car.

The *Engine number* is stamped on a machined surface on the cylinder block in the following locations:

Pre-August 2000 engines

1.6 and 1.8 litre engines:
Front left-hand side of the cylinder block, at the flywheel end

2.0 litre engines:
Left-hand end of the cylinder block, over the transmission

Post-August 2000 engines

1.6 and 1.8 litre engines:
Left-hand end of the cylinder block, over the transmission

2.0 litre engines:
Front left-hand side of the cylinder block, at the flywheel end

The VIN is stamped into the engine compartment bulkhead

Whenever servicing, repair or overhaul work is carried out on the car or its components, observe the following procedures and instructions. This will assist in carrying out the operation efficiently and to a professional standard of workmanship.

Joint mating faces and gaskets

When separating components at their mating faces, never insert screwdrivers or similar implements into the joint between the faces in order to prise them apart. This can cause severe damage which results in oil leaks, coolant leaks, etc upon reassembly. Separation is usually achieved by tapping along the joint with a soft-faced hammer in order to break the seal. However, note that this method may not be suitable where dowels are used for component location.

Where a gasket is used between the mating faces of two components, a new one must be fitted on reassembly; fit it dry unless otherwise stated in the repair procedure. Make sure that the mating faces are clean and dry, with all traces of old gasket removed. When cleaning a joint face, use a tool which is unlikely to score or damage the face, and remove any burrs or nicks with an oilstone or fine file.

Make sure that tapped holes are cleaned with a pipe cleaner, and keep them free of jointing compound, if this is being used, unless specifically instructed otherwise.

Ensure that all orifices, channels or pipes are clear, and blow through them, preferably using compressed air.

Oil seals

Oil seals can be removed by levering them out with a wide flat-bladed screwdriver or similar implement. Alternatively, a number of self-tapping screws may be screwed into the seal, and these used as a purchase for pliers or some similar device in order to pull the seal free.

Whenever an oil seal is removed from its working location, either individually or as part of an assembly, it should be renewed.

The very fine sealing lip of the seal is easily damaged, and will not seal if the surface it contacts is not completely clean and free from scratches, nicks or grooves. If the original sealing surface of the component cannot be restored, and the manufacturer has not made provision for slight relocation of the seal relative to the sealing surface, the component should be renewed.

Protect the lips of the seal from any surface which may damage them in the course of fitting. Use tape or a conical sleeve where possible. Lubricate the seal lips with oil before fitting and, on dual-lipped seals, fill the space between the lips with grease.

Unless otherwise stated, oil seals must be fitted with their sealing lips toward the lubricant to be sealed.

Use a tubular drift or block of wood of the appropriate size to install the seal and, if the seal housing is shouldered, drive the seal down to the shoulder. If the seal housing is unshouldered, the seal should be fitted with its face flush with the housing top face (unless otherwise instructed).

Screw threads and fastenings

Seized nuts, bolts and screws are quite a common occurrence where corrosion has set in, and the use of penetrating oil or releasing fluid will often overcome this problem if the offending item is soaked for a while before attempting to release it. The use of an impact driver may also provide a means of releasing such stubborn fastening devices, when used in conjunction with the appropriate screwdriver bit or socket. If none of these methods works, it may be necessary to resort to the careful application of heat, or the use of a hacksaw or nut splitter device.

Studs are usually removed by locking two nuts together on the threaded part, and then using a spanner on the lower nut to unscrew the stud. Studs or bolts which have broken off below the surface of the component in which they are mounted can sometimes be removed using a stud extractor. Always ensure that a blind tapped hole is completely free from oil, grease, water or other fluid before installing the bolt or stud. Failure to do this could cause the housing to crack due to the hydraulic action of the bolt or stud as it is screwed in.

When tightening a castellated nut to accept a split pin, tighten the nut to the specified torque, where applicable, and then tighten further to the next split pin hole. Never slacken the nut to align the split pin hole, unless stated in the repair procedure.

When checking or retightening a nut or bolt to a specified torque setting, slacken the nut or bolt by a quarter of a turn, and then retighten to the specified setting. However, this should not be attempted where angular tightening has been used.

For some screw fastenings, notably cylinder head bolts or nuts, torque wrench settings are no longer specified for the latter stages of tightening, "angle-tightening" being called up instead. Typically, a fairly low torque wrench setting will be applied to the bolts/nuts in the correct sequence, followed by one or more stages of tightening through specified angles.

Locknuts, locktabs and washers

Any fastening which will rotate against a component or housing during tightening should always have a washer between it and the relevant component or housing.

Spring or split washers should always be renewed when they are used to lock a critical component such as a big-end bearing retaining bolt or nut. Locktabs which are folded over to retain a nut or bolt should always be renewed.

Self-locking nuts can be re-used in non-critical areas, providing resistance can be felt when the locking portion passes over the bolt or stud thread. However, it should be noted that self-locking stiffnuts tend to lose their effectiveness after long periods of use, and should then be renewed as a matter of course.

Split pins must always be replaced with new ones of the correct size for the hole.

When thread-locking compound is found on the threads of a fastener which is to be re-used, it should be cleaned off with a wire brush and solvent, and fresh compound applied on reassembly.

Special tools

Some repair procedures in this manual entail the use of special tools such as a press, two or three-legged pullers, spring compressors, etc. Wherever possible, suitable readily-available alternatives to the manufacturer's special tools are described, and are shown in use. In some instances, where no alternative is possible, it has been necessary to resort to the use of a manufacturer's tool, and this has been done for reasons of safety as well as the efficient completion of the repair operation. Unless you are highly-skilled and have a thorough understanding of the procedures described, never attempt to bypass the use of any special tool when the procedure described specifies its use. Not only is there a very great risk of personal injury, but expensive damage could be caused to the components involved.

Environmental considerations

When disposing of used engine oil, brake fluid, antifreeze, etc, give due consideration to any detrimental environmental effects. Do not, for instance, pour any of the above liquids down drains into the general sewage system, or onto the ground to soak away. Many local council refuse tips provide a facility for waste oil disposal, as do some garages. If none of these facilities are available, consult your local Environmental Health Department, or the National Rivers Authority, for further advice.

With the universal tightening-up of legislation regarding the emission of environmentally-harmful substances from motor vehicles, most vehicles have tamperproof devices fitted to the main adjustment points of the fuel system. These devices are primarily designed to prevent unqualified persons from adjusting the fuel/air mixture, with the chance of a consequent increase in toxic emissions. If such devices are found during servicing or overhaul, they should, wherever possible, be renewed or refitted in accordance with the manufacturer's requirements or current legislation.

OIL CARE
FOLLOW THE CODE

OIL BANK LINE
0800 66 33 66
www.oilbankline.org.uk

Note: It is antisocial and illegal to dump oil down the drain. To find the location of your local oil recycling bank, call this number free.

The jack supplied with the vehicle tool kit should only be used for changing the roadwheels - see *Wheel changing* at the front of this manual. When carrying out any other kind of work, raise the vehicle using a hydraulic (or trolley) jack, and always supplement the jack with axle stands positioned under the vehicle jacking points **(see illustration)**.

When using a hydraulic jack or axle stands, always position the jack head or axle stand head under one of the relevant jacking points (note that the jacking points for use with the vehicle jack are different from those for a hydraulic trolley jack). When jacking up the front of the vehicle with a hydraulic jack, position the jack head under the longitudinal crossmember beneath the engine compartment. When jacking up the rear of the vehicle, position the jack head under the rear subframe between the inner ends of the rear suspension links. **Do not** jack the vehicle under the sump.

Never work under, around, or near a raised vehicle, unless it is adequately supported on stands.

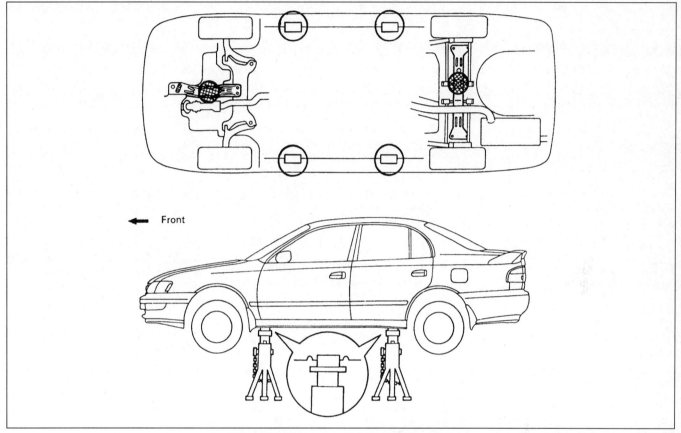

Front

Jacking and vehicle support points on the underbody

Disconnecting the battery

Numerous systems fitted to the vehicle require battery power to be available at all times, either to ensure their continued operation (such as the clock) or to maintain control unit memories which would be erased if the battery were to be disconnected. Whenever the battery is to be disconnected therefore, first note the following, to ensure that there are no unforeseen consequences of this action:

a) First, it is a wise precaution to remove the key from the ignition, and to keep it with you, so that it does not get locked in if the central locking should engage accidentally when the battery is reconnected.

b) All models covered in this manual are equipped with a Toyota anti-theft alarm system. When reconnecting the battery after disconnection, the alarm may be automatically activated. If so, use the remote transmitter to turn off the alarm, or turn off the alarm manually by switching on the ignition. To fully reactivate the system once the battery is reconnected, lock then unlock the vehicle using the remote transmitter; the alarm will be functional again the next time the vehicle is locked with the remote transmitter.

c) If a security-coded audio unit is fitted, and the unit and/or the battery is disconnected, the unit will not function again on reconnection until the correct security code is entered. Details of this procedure, which varies according to the unit fitted, are given in the vehicle owner's handbook. Ensure you have the correct code before you disconnect the battery. If you do not have the code or details of the correct procedure, but can supply proof of ownership and a legitimate reason for wanting this information, a Toyota dealer may be able to help.

d) On all engines, the engine management electronic control unit is of the 'self-learning' type, meaning that as it operates, it also monitors and stores the settings which give optimum engine performance under all operating conditions. When the battery is disconnected, these settings are lost and the ECU reverts to the base settings programmed into its memory at the factory. On restarting, this may lead to the engine running/idling roughly for a short while, until the ECU has re-learned the optimum settings. This process is best accomplished by taking the vehicle on a road test (for approximately 15 minutes), covering all engine speeds and loads, concentrating mainly in the 2500 to 3500 rpm region.

e) On all models, when reconnecting the battery after disconnection, switch on the ignition and wait 10 seconds to allow the electronic vehicle systems to stabilise and re-initialise.

Introduction

A selection of good tools is a fundamental requirement for anyone contemplating the maintenance and repair of a motor vehicle. For the owner who does not possess any, their purchase will prove a considerable expense, offsetting some of the savings made by doing-it-yourself. However, provided that the tools purchased meet the relevant national safety standards and are of good quality, they will last for many years and prove an extremely worthwhile investment.

To help the average owner to decide which tools are needed to carry out the various tasks detailed in this manual, we have compiled three lists of tools under the following headings: *Maintenance and minor repair*, *Repair and overhaul*, and *Special*. Newcomers to practical mechanics should start off with the *Maintenance and minor repair* tool kit, and confine themselves to the simpler jobs around the vehicle. Then, as confidence and experience grow, more difficult tasks can be undertaken, with extra tools being purchased as, and when, they are needed. In this way, a *Maintenance and minor repair* tool kit can be built up into a *Repair and overhaul* tool kit over a considerable period of time, without any major cash outlays. The experienced do-it-yourselfer will have a tool kit good enough for most repair and overhaul procedures, and will add tools from the *Special* category when it is felt that the expense is justified by the amount of use to which these tools will be put.

Maintenance and minor repair tool kit

The tools given in this list should be considered as a minimum requirement if routine maintenance, servicing and minor repair operations are to be undertaken. We recommend the purchase of combination spanners (ring one end, open-ended the other); although more expensive than open-ended ones, they do give the advantages of both types of spanner.

☐ *Combination spanners:*
  Metric - 8 to 19 mm inclusive
☐ *Adjustable spanner - 35 mm jaw (approx.)*
☐ *Spark plug spanner (with rubber insert) - petrol models*
☐ *Spark plug gap adjustment tool - petrol models*
☐ *Set of feeler gauges*
☐ *Brake bleed nipple spanner*
☐ *Screwdrivers:*
  Flat blade - 100 mm long x 6 mm dia
  Cross blade - 100 mm long x 6 mm dia
  Torx - various sizes (not all vehicles)
☐ *Combination pliers*
☐ *Hacksaw (junior)*
☐ *Tyre pump*
☐ *Tyre pressure gauge*
☐ *Oil can*
☐ *Oil filter removal tool*
☐ *Fine emery cloth*
☐ *Wire brush (small)*
☐ *Funnel (medium size)*
☐ *Sump drain plug key (not all vehicles)*

Repair and overhaul tool kit

These tools are virtually essential for anyone undertaking any major repairs to a motor vehicle, and are additional to those given in the *Maintenance and minor repair* list. Included in this list is a comprehensive set of sockets. Although these are expensive, they will be found invaluable as they are so versatile - particularly if various drives are included in the set. We recommend the half-inch square-drive type, as this can be used with most proprietary torque wrenches.

The tools in this list will sometimes need to be supplemented by tools from the *Special* list:

☐ *Sockets (or box spanners) to cover range in previous list (including Torx sockets)*
☐ *Reversible ratchet drive (for use with sockets)*
☐ *Extension piece, 250 mm (for use with sockets)*
☐ *Universal joint (for use with sockets)*
☐ *Flexible handle or sliding T "breaker bar" (for use with sockets)*
☐ *Torque wrench (for use with sockets)*
☐ *Self-locking grips*
☐ *Ball pein hammer*
☐ *Soft-faced mallet (plastic or rubber)*
☐ *Screwdrivers:*
  Flat blade - long & sturdy, short (chubby), and narrow (electrician's) types
  Cross blade – long & sturdy, and short (chubby) types
☐ *Pliers:*
  Long-nosed
  Side cutters (electrician's)
  Circlip (internal and external)
☐ *Cold chisel - 25 mm*
☐ *Scriber*
☐ *Scraper*
☐ *Centre-punch*
☐ *Pin punch*
☐ *Hacksaw*
☐ *Brake hose clamp*
☐ *Brake/clutch bleeding kit*
☐ *Selection of twist drills*
☐ *Steel rule/straight-edge*
☐ *Allen keys (inc. splined/Torx type)*
☐ *Selection of files*
☐ *Wire brush*
☐ *Axle stands*
☐ *Jack (strong trolley or hydraulic type)*
☐ *Light with extension lead*
☐ *Universal electrical multi-meter*

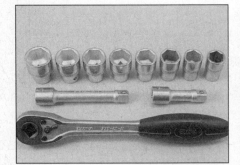

Sockets and reversible ratchet drive

Brake bleeding kit

Torx key, socket and bit

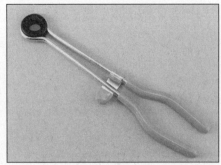

Hose clamp

Angular-tightening gauge

Special tools

The tools in this list are those which are not used regularly, are expensive to buy, or which need to be used in accordance with their manufacturers' instructions. Unless relatively difficult mechanical jobs are undertaken frequently, it will not be economic to buy many of these tools. Where this is the case, you could consider clubbing together with friends (or joining a motorists' club) to make a joint purchase, or borrowing the tools against a deposit from a local garage or tool hire specialist. It is worth noting that many of the larger DIY superstores now carry a large range of special tools for hire at modest rates.

The following list contains only those tools and instruments freely available to the public, and not those special tools produced by the vehicle manufacturer specifically for its dealer network. You will find occasional references to these manufacturers' special tools in the text of this manual. Generally, an alternative method of doing the job without the vehicle manufacturers' special tool is given. However, sometimes there is no alternative to using them. Where this is the case and the relevant tool cannot be bought or borrowed, you will have to entrust the work to a dealer.

- ☐ Angular-tightening gauge
- ☐ Valve spring compressor
- ☐ Valve grinding tool
- ☐ Piston ring compressor
- ☐ Piston ring removal/installation tool
- ☐ Cylinder bore hone
- ☐ Balljoint separator
- ☐ Coil spring compressors (where applicable)
- ☐ Two/three-legged hub and bearing puller
- ☐ Impact screwdriver
- ☐ Micrometer and/or vernier calipers
- ☐ Dial gauge
- ☐ Stroboscopic timing light
- ☐ Dwell angle meter/tachometer
- ☐ Fault code reader
- ☐ Cylinder compression gauge
- ☐ Hand-operated vacuum pump and gauge
- ☐ Clutch plate alignment set
- ☐ Brake shoe steady spring cup removal tool
- ☐ Bush and bearing removal/installation set
- ☐ Stud extractors
- ☐ Tap and die set
- ☐ Lifting tackle
- ☐ Trolley jack

Buying tools

Reputable motor accessory shops and superstores often offer excellent quality tools at discount prices, so it pays to shop around.

Remember, you don't have to buy the most expensive items on the shelf, but it is always advisable to steer clear of the very cheap tools. Beware of 'bargains' offered on market stalls or at car boot sales. There are plenty of good tools around at reasonable prices, but always aim to purchase items which meet the relevant national safety standards. If in doubt, ask the proprietor or manager of the shop for advice before making a purchase.

Care and maintenance of tools

Having purchased a reasonable tool kit, it is necessary to keep the tools in a clean and serviceable condition. After use, always wipe off any dirt, grease and metal particles using a clean, dry cloth, before putting the tools away. Never leave them lying around after they have been used. A simple tool rack on the garage or workshop wall for items such as screwdrivers and pliers is a good idea. Store all normal spanners and sockets in a metal box. Any measuring instruments, gauges, meters, etc, must be carefully stored where they cannot be damaged or become rusty.

Take a little care when tools are used. Hammer heads inevitably become marked, and screwdrivers lose the keen edge on their blades from time to time. A little timely attention with emery cloth or a file will soon restore items like this to a good finish.

Working facilities

Not to be forgotten when discussing tools is the workshop itself. If anything more than routine maintenance is to be carried out, a suitable working area becomes essential.

It is appreciated that many an owner-mechanic is forced by circumstances to remove an engine or similar item without the benefit of a garage or workshop. Having done this, any repairs should always be done under the cover of a roof.

Wherever possible, any dismantling should be done on a clean, flat workbench or table at a suitable working height.

Any workbench needs a vice; one with a jaw opening of 100 mm is suitable for most jobs. As mentioned previously, some clean dry storage space is also required for tools, as well as for any lubricants, cleaning fluids, touch-up paints etc, which become necessary.

Another item which may be required, and which has a much more general usage, is an electric drill with a chuck capacity of at least 8 mm. This, together with a good range of twist drills, is virtually essential for fitting accessories.

Last, but not least, always keep a supply of old newspapers and clean, lint-free rags available, and try to keep any working area as clean as possible.

Micrometers

Dial test indicator ("dial gauge")

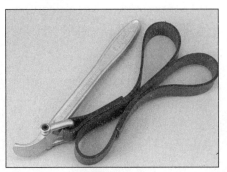

Strap wrench

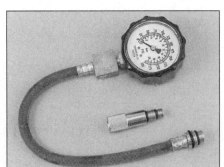

Compression tester

Fault code reader

This is a guide to getting your vehicle through the MOT test. Obviously it will not be possible to examine the vehicle to the same standard as the professional MOT tester. However, working through the following checks will enable you to identify any problem areas before submitting the vehicle for the test.

Where a testable component is in borderline condition, the tester has discretion in deciding whether to pass or fail it. The basis of such discretion is whether the tester would be happy for a close relative or friend to use the vehicle with the component in that condition. If the vehicle presented is clean and evidently well cared for, the tester may be more inclined to pass a borderline component than if the vehicle is scruffy and apparently neglected.

It has only been possible to summarise the test requirements here, based on the regulations in force at the time of printing. Test standards are becoming increasingly stringent, although there are some exemptions for older vehicles.

An assistant will be needed to help carry out some of these checks.

The checks have been sub-divided into four categories, as follows:

1 Checks carried out **FROM THE DRIVER'S SEAT**

2 Checks carried out **WITH THE VEHICLE ON THE GROUND**

3 Checks carried out **WITH THE VEHICLE RAISED AND THE WHEELS FREE TO TURN**

4 Checks carried out on **YOUR VEHICLE'S EXHAUST EMISSION SYSTEM**

1 Checks carried out **FROM THE DRIVER'S SEAT**

Handbrake

☐ Test the operation of the handbrake. Excessive travel (too many clicks) indicates incorrect brake or cable adjustment.
☐ Check that the handbrake cannot be released by tapping the lever sideways. Check the security of the lever mountings.

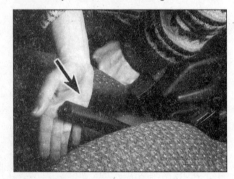

Footbrake

☐ Depress the brake pedal and check that it does not creep down to the floor, indicating a master cylinder fault. Release the pedal, wait a few seconds, then depress it again. If the pedal travels nearly to the floor before firm resistance is felt, brake adjustment or repair is necessary. If the pedal feels spongy, there is air in the hydraulic system which must be removed by bleeding.

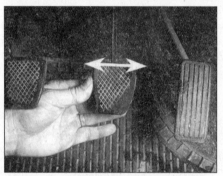

☐ Check that the brake pedal is secure and in good condition. Check also for signs of fluid leaks on the pedal, floor or carpets, which would indicate failed seals in the brake master cylinder.
☐ Check the servo unit (when applicable) by operating the brake pedal several times, then keeping the pedal depressed and starting the engine. As the engine starts, the pedal will move down slightly. If not, the vacuum hose or the servo itself may be faulty.

Steering wheel and column

☐ Examine the steering wheel for fractures or looseness of the hub, spokes or rim.
☐ Move the steering wheel from side to side and then up and down. Check that the steering wheel is not loose on the column, indicating wear or a loose retaining nut. Continue moving the steering wheel as before, but also turn it slightly from left to right.
☐ Check that the steering wheel is not loose on the column, and that there is no abnormal

movement of the steering wheel, indicating wear in the column support bearings or couplings.

Windscreen, mirrors and sunvisor

☐ The windscreen must be free of cracks or other significant damage within the driver's field of view. (Small stone chips are acceptable.) Rear view mirrors must be secure, intact, and capable of being adjusted.

290mm

☐ The driver's sunvisor must be capable of being stored in the "up" position.

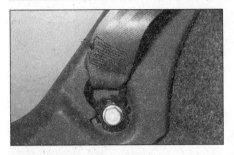

Seat belts and seats

Note: *The following checks are applicable to all seat belts, front and rear.*

☐ Examine the webbing of all the belts (including rear belts if fitted) for cuts, serious fraying or deterioration. Fasten and unfasten each belt to check the buckles. If applicable, check the retracting mechanism. Check the security of all seat belt mountings accessible from inside the vehicle.

☐ Seat belts with pre-tensioners, once activated, have a "flag" or similar showing on the seat belt stalk. This, in itself, is not a reason for test failure.

☐ The front seats themselves must be securely attached and the backrests must lock in the upright position.

Doors

☐ Both front doors must be able to be opened and closed from outside and inside, and must latch securely when closed.

2 Checks carried out WITH THE VEHICLE ON THE GROUND

Vehicle identification

☐ Number plates must be in good condition, secure and legible, with letters and numbers correctly spaced – spacing at (A) should be at least twice that at (B).

☐ The VIN plate and/or homologation plate must be legible.

Electrical equipment

☐ Switch on the ignition and check the operation of the horn.

☐ Check the windscreen washers and wipers, examining the wiper blades; renew damaged or perished blades. Also check the operation of the stop-lights.

☐ Check the operation of the sidelights and number plate lights. The lenses and reflectors must be secure, clean and undamaged.

☐ Check the operation and alignment of the headlights. The headlight reflectors must not be tarnished and the lenses must be undamaged.

☐ Switch on the ignition and check the operation of the direction indicators (including the instrument panel tell-tale) and the hazard warning lights. Operation of the sidelights and stop-lights must not affect the indicators - if it does, the cause is usually a bad earth at the rear light cluster.

☐ Check the operation of the rear foglight(s), including the warning light on the instrument panel or in the switch.

☐ The ABS warning light must illuminate in accordance with the manufacturers' design. For most vehicles, the ABS warning light should illuminate when the ignition is switched on, and (if the system is operating properly) extinguish after a few seconds. Refer to the owner's handbook.

Footbrake

☐ Examine the master cylinder, brake pipes and servo unit for leaks, loose mountings, corrosion or other damage.

☐ The fluid reservoir must be secure and the fluid level must be between the upper (**A**) and lower (**B**) markings.

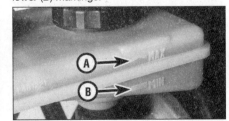

☐ Inspect both front brake flexible hoses for cracks or deterioration of the rubber. Turn the steering from lock to lock, and ensure that the hoses do not contact the wheel, tyre, or any part of the steering or suspension mechanism. With the brake pedal firmly depressed, check the hoses for bulges or leaks under pressure.

Steering and suspension

☐ Have your assistant turn the steering wheel from side to side slightly, up to the point where the steering gear just begins to transmit this movement to the roadwheels. Check for excessive free play between the steering wheel and the steering gear, indicating wear or insecurity of the steering column joints, the column-to-steering gear coupling, or the steering gear itself.

☐ Have your assistant turn the steering wheel more vigorously in each direction, so that the roadwheels just begin to turn. As this is done, examine all the steering joints, linkages, fittings and attachments. Renew any component that shows signs of wear or damage. On vehicles with power steering, check the security and condition of the steering pump, drivebelt and hoses.

☐ Check that the vehicle is standing level, and at approximately the correct ride height.

Shock absorbers

☐ Depress each corner of the vehicle in turn, then release it. The vehicle should rise and then settle in its normal position. If the vehicle continues to rise and fall, the shock absorber is defective. A shock absorber which has seized will also cause the vehicle to fail.

Exhaust system

□ Start the engine. With your assistant holding a rag over the tailpipe, check the entire system for leaks. Repair or renew leaking sections.

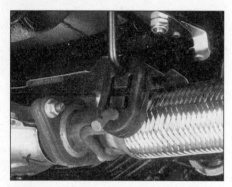

3 Checks carried out
WITH THE VEHICLE RAISED AND THE WHEELS FREE TO TURN

Jack up the front and rear of the vehicle, and securely support it on axle stands. Position the stands clear of the suspension assemblies. Ensure that the wheels are clear of the ground and that the steering can be turned from lock to lock.

Steering mechanism

□ Have your assistant turn the steering from lock to lock. Check that the steering turns smoothly, and that no part of the steering mechanism, including a wheel or tyre, fouls any brake hose or pipe or any part of the body structure.

□ Examine the steering rack rubber gaiters for damage or insecurity of the retaining clips. If power steering is fitted, check for signs of damage or leakage of the fluid hoses, pipes or connections. Also check for excessive stiffness or binding of the steering, a missing split pin or locking device, or severe corrosion of the body structure within 30 cm of any steering component attachment point.

Front and rear suspension and wheel bearings

□ Starting at the front right-hand side, grasp the roadwheel at the 3 o'clock and 9 o'clock positions and rock gently but firmly. Check for free play or insecurity at the wheel bearings, suspension balljoints, or suspension mountings, pivots and attachments.

□ Now grasp the wheel at the 12 o'clock and 6 o'clock positions and repeat the previous inspection. Spin the wheel, and check for roughness or tightness of the front wheel bearing.

□ If excess free play is suspected at a component pivot point, this can be confirmed by using a large screwdriver or similar tool and levering between the mounting and the component attachment. This will confirm whether the wear is in the pivot bush, its retaining bolt, or in the mounting itself (the bolt holes can often become elongated).

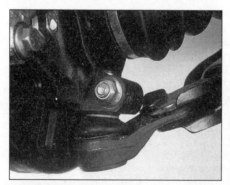

□ Carry out all the above checks at the other front wheel, and then at both rear wheels.

Springs and shock absorbers

□ Examine the suspension struts (when applicable) for serious fluid leakage, corrosion, or damage to the casing. Also check the security of the mounting points.

□ If coil springs are fitted, check that the spring ends locate in their seats, and that the spring is not corroded, cracked or broken.

□ If leaf springs are fitted, check that all leaves are intact, that the axle is securely attached to each spring, and that there is no deterioration of the spring eye mountings, bushes, and shackles.

□ The same general checks apply to vehicles fitted with other suspension types, such as torsion bars, hydraulic displacer units, etc. Ensure that all mountings and attachments are secure, that there are no signs of excessive wear, corrosion or damage, and (on hydraulic types) that there are no fluid leaks or damaged pipes.

□ Inspect the shock absorbers for signs of serious fluid leakage. Check for wear of the mounting bushes or attachments, or damage to the body of the unit.

Driveshafts
(fwd vehicles only)

□ Rotate each front wheel in turn and inspect the constant velocity joint gaiters for splits or damage. Also check that each driveshaft is straight and undamaged.

Braking system

□ If possible without dismantling, check brake pad wear and disc condition. Ensure that the friction lining material has not worn excessively, (A) and that the discs are not fractured, pitted, scored or badly worn (B).

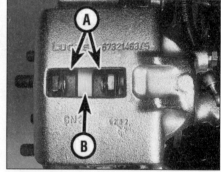

□ Examine all the rigid brake pipes underneath the vehicle, and the flexible hose(s) at the rear. Look for corrosion, chafing or insecurity of the pipes, and for signs of bulging under pressure, chafing, splits or deterioration of the flexible hoses.

□ Look for signs of fluid leaks at the brake calipers or on the brake backplates. Repair or renew leaking components.

□ Slowly spin each wheel, while your assistant depresses and releases the footbrake. Ensure that each brake is operating and does not bind when the pedal is released.

☐ Examine the handbrake mechanism, checking for frayed or broken cables, excessive corrosion, or wear or insecurity of the linkage. Check that the mechanism works on each relevant wheel, and releases fully, without binding.

☐ It is not possible to test brake efficiency without special equipment, but a road test can be carried out later to check that the vehicle pulls up in a straight line.

Fuel and exhaust systems

☐ Inspect the fuel tank (including the filler cap), fuel pipes, hoses and unions. All components must be secure and free from leaks.

☐ Examine the exhaust system over its entire length, checking for any damaged, broken or missing mountings, security of the retaining clamps and rust or corrosion.

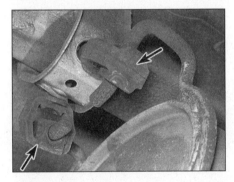

Wheels and tyres

☐ Examine the sidewalls and tread area of each tyre in turn. Check for cuts, tears, lumps, bulges, separation of the tread, and exposure of the ply or cord due to wear or damage. Check that the tyre bead is correctly seated on the wheel rim, that the valve is sound and properly seated, and that the wheel is not distorted or damaged.

☐ Check that the tyres are of the correct size for the vehicle, that they are of the same size

and type on each axle, and that the pressures are correct.

☐ Check the tyre tread depth. The legal minimum at the time of writing is 1.6 mm over at least three-quarters of the tread width. Abnormal tread wear may indicate incorrect front wheel alignment.

Body corrosion

☐ Check the condition of the entire vehicle structure for signs of corrosion in load-bearing areas. (These include chassis box sections, side sills, cross-members, pillars, and all suspension, steering, braking system and seat belt mountings and anchorages.) Any corrosion which has seriously reduced the thickness of a load-bearing area is likely to cause the vehicle to fail. In this case professional repairs are likely to be needed.

☐ Damage or corrosion which causes sharp or otherwise dangerous edges to be exposed will also cause the vehicle to fail.

4 Checks carried out on YOUR VEHICLE'S EXHAUST EMISSION SYSTEM

Petrol models

☐ The engine should be warmed up, and running well (ignition system in good order, air filter element clean, etc).

☐ Before testing, run the engine at around 2500 rpm for 20 seconds. Let the engine drop to idle, and watch for smoke from the exhaust. If the idle speed is too high, or if dense blue or black smoke emerges for more than 5 seconds, the vehicle will fail. Typically, blue smoke signifies oil burning (engine wear); black smoke means unburnt fuel (dirty air cleaner element, or other fuel system fault).

☐ An exhaust gas analyser for measuring carbon monoxide (CO) and hydrocarbons (HC) is now needed. If one cannot be hired or borrowed, have a local garage perform the check.

CO emissions (mixture)

☐ The MOT tester has access to the CO limits for all vehicles. The CO level is measured at idle speed, and at 'fast idle' (2500 to 3000 rpm). The following limits are given as a general guide:

   At idle speed – Less than 0.5% CO
   At 'fast idle' – Less than 0.3% CO
   Lambda reading – 0.97 to 1.03

☐ If the CO level is too high, this may point to poor maintenance, a fuel injection system problem, faulty lambda (oxygen) sensor or catalytic converter. Try an injector cleaning treatment, and check the vehicle's ECU for fault codes.

HC emissions

☐ The MOT tester has access to HC limits for all vehicles. The HC level is measured at 'fast idle' (2500 to 3000 rpm). The following limits are given as a general guide:

   At 'fast idle' – Less then 200 ppm

☐ Excessive HC emissions are typically caused by oil being burnt (worn engine), or by a blocked crankcase ventilation system ('breather'). If the engine oil is old and thin, an oil change may help. If the engine is running badly, check the vehicle's ECU for fault codes.

Diesel models

☐ The only emission test for diesel engines is measuring exhaust smoke density, using a calibrated smoke meter. The test involves accelerating the engine at least 3 times to its maximum unloaded speed.

Note: *On engines with a timing belt, it is VITAL that the belt is in good condition before the test is carried out.*

☐ With the engine warmed up, it is first purged by running at around 2500 rpm for 20 seconds. A governor check is then carried out, by slowly accelerating the engine to its maximum speed. After this, the smoke meter is connected, and the engine is accelerated quickly to maximum speed three times. If the smoke density is less than the limits given below, the vehicle will pass:

   Non-turbo vehicles: 2.5m-1
   Turbocharged vehicles: 3.0m-1

☐ If excess smoke is produced, try fitting a new air cleaner element, or using an injector cleaning treatment. If the engine is running badly, where applicable, check the vehicle's ECU for fault codes. Also check the vehicle's EGR system, where applicable. At high mileages, the injectors may require professional attention.

Engine

- [ ] Engine fails to rotate when attempting to start
- [ ] Engine rotates, but will not start
- [ ] Engine difficult to start when cold
- [ ] Engine difficult to start when hot
- [ ] Starter motor noisy or excessively-rough in engagement
- [ ] Engine starts, but stops immediately
- [ ] Engine idles erratically
- [ ] Engine misfires at idle speed
- [ ] Engine misfires throughout the driving speed range
- [ ] Engine hesitates on acceleration
- [ ] Engine stalls
- [ ] Engine lacks power
- [ ] Engine backfires
- [ ] Oil pressure warning light on with engine running
- [ ] Engine runs-on after switching off
- [ ] Engine noises

Cooling system

- [ ] Overheating
- [ ] Overcooling
- [ ] External coolant leakage
- [ ] Internal coolant leakage
- [ ] Corrosion

Fuel and exhaust systems

- [ ] Excessive fuel consumption
- [ ] Fuel leakage and/or fuel odour
- [ ] Excessive noise or fumes from exhaust system

Clutch

- [ ] Pedal travels to floor – no pressure or very little resistance
- [ ] Clutch fails to disengage (unable to select gears)
- [ ] Clutch slips (engine speed rises, with no increase in vehicle speed)
- [ ] Judder as clutch is engaged
- [ ] Noise when depressing or releasing clutch pedal

Transmission

- [ ] Noisy in neutral with engine running
- [ ] Noisy in one particular gear
- [ ] Difficulty engaging gears
- [ ] Jumps out of gear
- [ ] Vibration
- [ ] Lubricant leaks

Driveshafts

- [ ] Clicking or knocking noise on turns (at slow speed on full-lock)
- [ ] Vibration when accelerating or decelerating

Braking system

- [ ] Vehicle pulls to one side under braking
- [ ] Noise (grinding or high-pitched squeal) when brakes applied
- [ ] Excessive brake pedal travel
- [ ] Brake pedal feels spongy when depressed
- [ ] Excessive brake pedal effort required to stop vehicle
- [ ] Judder felt through brake pedal or steering wheel when braking
- [ ] Brakes binding
- [ ] Rear wheels locking under normal braking

Suspension and steering systems

- [ ] Vehicle pulls to one side
- [ ] Wheel wobble and vibration
- [ ] Excessive pitching and/or rolling around corners, or during braking
- [ ] Wandering or general instability
- [ ] Excessively-stiff steering
- [ ] Excessive play in steering
- [ ] Lack of power assistance
- [ ] Tyre wear excessive

Electrical system

- [ ] Battery will not hold a charge for more than a few days
- [ ] Ignition/no-charge warning light stays on with engine running
- [ ] Ignition/no-charge warning light fails to come on
- [ ] Lights inoperative
- [ ] Instrument readings inaccurate or erratic
- [ ] Horn inoperative, or unsatisfactory in operation
- [ ] Windscreen/tailgate wipers failed, or unsatisfactory in operation
- [ ] Windscreen/tailgate washers failed, or unsatisfactory in operation
- [ ] Electric windows inoperative, or unsatisfactory in operation
- [ ] Central locking system inoperative, or unsatisfactory in operation

Introduction

The vehicle owner who does his or her own maintenance according to the recommended service schedules should not have to use this section of the manual very often. Modern component reliability is such that, provided those items subject to wear or deterioration are inspected or renewed at the specified intervals, sudden failure is comparatively rare. Faults do not usually just happen as a result of sudden failure, but develop over a period of time. Major mechanical failures in particular are usually preceded by characteristic symptoms over hundreds or even thousands of miles. Those components which do occasionally fail without warning are often small and easily carried in the vehicle.

With any fault-finding, the first step is to decide where to begin investigations. Sometimes this is obvious, but on other occasions, a little detective work will be necessary. The owner who makes half a dozen haphazard adjustments or replacements may be successful in curing a fault (or its symptoms), but will be none the wiser if the fault recurs, and ultimately may have spent more time and money than was necessary. A calm and logical approach will be found to be more satisfactory in the long run. Always take into account any warning signs or abnormalities that may have been noticed in the period preceding the fault – power loss, high or low gauge readings, unusual smells, etc – and remember that failure of components such as fuses or spark plugs may only be pointers to some underlying fault.

The pages which follow provide an easy-reference guide to the more common problems which may occur during the operation of the vehicle. These problems and their possible causes are grouped under headings denoting various components or systems, such as Engine, Cooling system, etc. The general Chapter which deals with the problem is also shown in brackets; refer to the relevant part of that Chapter for system-specific information. Whatever the fault, certain basic principles apply. These are as follows:

Verify the fault. This is simply a matter of being sure that you know what the symptoms are before starting work. This is particularly important if you are investigating a fault for someone else, who may not have described it very accurately.

Don't overlook the obvious. For example, if the vehicle won't start, is there fuel in the tank? (Don't take anyone else's word on this particular point, and don't trust the fuel gauge either!) If an electrical fault is indicated, look for loose or broken wires before digging out the test gear.

Cure the disease, not the symptom. Substituting a flat battery with a fully-charged one will get you off the hard shoulder, but if the underlying cause is not attended to, the new battery will go the same way. Similarly, changing oil-fouled spark plugs for a new set will get you moving again, but remember that the reason for the fouling (if it wasn't simply an incorrect grade of plug) will have to be found and corrected.

Don't take anything for granted. Particularly, don't forget that a 'new' component may itself be defective (especially if it's been rattling around in the boot for months), and don't leave components out of a fault diagnosis sequence just because they are new or recently-fitted. When you do finally diagnose a difficult fault, you'll probably realise that all the evidence was there from the start.

Engine

Engine fails to rotate when attempting to start

☐ Battery terminal connections loose or corroded (Weekly checks).
☐ Battery discharged or faulty (Chapter 5).
☐ Broken, loose or disconnected wiring in the starting circuit (Chapter 5).
☐ Defective starter motor (Chapter 5).
☐ Starter pinion or flywheel ring gear teeth loose or broken (Chapter 2 and 5).
☐ Engine earth strap broken or disconnected (Chapter 5 and 12).

Engine rotates, but will not start

☐ Fuel tank empty.
☐ Battery discharged (engine rotates slowly) (Chapter 5).
☐ Battery terminal connections loose or corroded (Weekly checks).
☐ Worn, faulty or incorrectly-gapped spark plugs (Chapter 1).
☐ Engine management system fault (Chapter 4).
☐ Low cylinder compressions (Chapter 2).
☐ Major mechanical failure (eg camshaft drive) (Chapter 2).

Engine (continued)

Engine difficult to start when cold

- ☐ Battery discharged (Chapter 5).
- ☐ Battery terminal connections loose or corroded (*Weekly checks*).
- ☐ Worn, faulty or incorrectly-gapped spark plugs (Chapter 1).
- ☐ Engine management system fault (Chapter 4).
- ☐ Low cylinder compressions (Chapter 2).

Engine difficult to start when hot

- ☐ Engine management system fault (Chapter 4).
- ☐ Low cylinder compressions (Chapter 2).

Starter motor noisy or excessively-rough in engagement

- ☐ Starter pinion or flywheel ring gear teeth loose or broken (Chapter 2 and 5).
- ☐ Starter motor mounting bolts loose or missing (Chapter 5).
- ☐ Defective starter motor (Chapter 5).

Engine starts, but stops immediately

- ☐ Vacuum leak at the throttle housing/inlet manifold(Chapter 4).
- ☐ Engine management system fault (Chapter 4).

Engine idles erratically

- ☐ Vacuum leak at the throttle housing/inlet manifold (Chapter 4).
- ☐ Worn, faulty or incorrectly-gapped spark plugs (Chapter 1).
- ☐ Engine management system fault (Chapter 4).
- ☐ Uneven or low cylinder compressions (Chapter 2).
- ☐ Camshaft lobes worn (Chapter 2).
- ☐ Timing belt/chain incorrectly fitted (Chapter 2).

Engine misfires at idle speed

- ☐ Worn, faulty or incorrectly-gapped spark plugs (Chapter 1).
- ☐ Vacuum leak at the throttle housing/inlet manifold (Chapter 4).
- ☐ Engine management system fault (Chapter 4).
- ☐ Uneven or low cylinder compressions (Chapter 2).
- ☐ Disconnected, leaking, or perished crankcase ventilation hoses (Chapter 4).

Engine misfires throughout the driving speed range

- ☐ Fuel filter blocked (Chapter 1).
- ☐ Fuel pump faulty (Chapter 4).
- ☐ Fuel tank vent blocked, or fuel pipes restricted (Chapter 4).
- ☐ Worn, faulty or incorrectly-gapped spark plugs (Chapter 1).
- ☐ Vacuum leak at the throttle housing/inlet manifold (Chapter 4).
- ☐ Engine management system fault (Chapter 4).
- ☐ Faulty ignition HT coil (Chapter 5).
- ☐ Uneven or low cylinder compressions (Chapter 2).

Engine hesitates on acceleration

- ☐ Worn, faulty or incorrectly-gapped spark plugs (Chapter 1).
- ☐ Vacuum leak at the throttle housing/inlet manifold (Chapter 4).
- ☐ Engine management system fault (Chapter 4).

Engine stalls

- ☐ Fuel filter blocked (Chapter 1).
- ☐ Fuel pump faulty (Chapter 4).
- ☐ Fuel tank vent blocked, or fuel pipes restricted (Chapter 4).
- ☐ Worn, faulty or incorrectly-gapped spark plugs (Chapter 1).
- ☐ Vacuum leak at the throttle housing/inlet manifold (Chapter 4).
- ☐ Engine management system fault (Chapter 4).

Engine lacks power

- ☐ Timing belt/chain incorrectly fitted (Chapter 2).
- ☐ Fuel filter blocked (Chapter 1).
- ☐ Fuel pump faulty (Chapter 4).
- ☐ Uneven or low cylinder compressions (Chapter 2).
- ☐ Worn, faulty or incorrectly-gapped spark plugs (Chapter 1).
- ☐ Vacuum leak at the throttle housing/inlet manifold (Chapter 4).
- ☐ Engine management system fault (Chapter 4).
- ☐ Brakes binding (Chapter 1 and 9).
- ☐ Clutch slipping (Chapter 6).

Engine backfires

- ☐ Timing belt/chain incorrectly fitted (Chapter 2).
- ☐ Vacuum leak at the throttle housing/inlet manifold (Chapter 4).
- ☐ Engine management system fault (Chapter 4).

Oil pressure warning light on with engine running

- ☐ Low oil level, or incorrect oil grade (*Weekly checks*).
- ☐ Faulty oil pressure warning light switch (Chapter 5).
- ☐ Worn engine bearings and/or oil pump (Chapter 2).
- ☐ High engine operating temperature (Chapter 3).
- ☐ Oil pressure relief valve defective (Chapter 2).
- ☐ Oil pick-up strainer clogged (Chapter 2).

Engine runs-on after switching off

- ☐ Excessive carbon build-up in engine (Chapter 2).
- ☐ High engine operating temperature (Chapter 3).
- ☐ Engine management system fault (Chapter 4).

Engine noises

Pre-ignition (pinking) or knocking during acceleration or under load

- ☐ Engine management system fault (Chapter 4).
- ☐ Incorrect grade of spark plug (Chapter 1).
- ☐ Incorrect grade of fuel (Chapter 4).
- ☐ Vacuum leak at the throttle housing/inlet manifold (Chapter 4).
- ☐ Excessive carbon build-up in engine (Chapter 2).

Whistling or wheezing noises

- ☐ Leaking inlet manifold or throttle housing gasket (Chapter 4).
- ☐ Leaking vacuum hose (Chapter 4 and 9).
- ☐ Blowing cylinder head gasket (Chapter 2).

Tapping or rattling noises

- ☐ Worn valve gear or camshaft (Chapter 2).
- ☐ Ancillary component fault (coolant pump, alternator, etc) (Chapters 3, 5, etc).

Knocking or thumping noises

- ☐ Worn big-end bearings (regular heavy knocking, perhaps less under load) (Chapter 2).
- ☐ Worn main bearings (rumbling and knocking, perhaps worsening under load) (Chapter 2).
- ☐ Piston slap (most noticeable when cold) (Chapter 2).
- ☐ Ancillary component fault (coolant pump, alternator, etc) (Chapters 3, 5, etc).

Cooling system

Overheating

- [ ] Insufficient coolant in system (*Weekly checks*).
- [ ] Thermostat faulty (stuck closed) (Chapter 3).
- [ ] Radiator core blocked, or grille restricted (Chapter 3).
- [ ] Electric cooling fan or sensor faulty (Chapter 3).
- [ ] Pressure cap faulty (Chapter 3).
- [ ] Inaccurate temperature gauge/sensor (Chapter 3).
- [ ] Airlock in cooling system (Chapter 1).
- [ ] Engine management system fault (Chapter 4).

Overcooling

- [ ] Thermostat faulty (stuck open) (Chapter 3).
- [ ] Inaccurate temperature gauge/sensor (Chapter 3).

External coolant leakage

- [ ] Deteriorated or damaged hoses or hose clips (Chapter 1).
- [ ] Radiator core or heater matrix leaking (Chapter 3).
- [ ] Pressure cap faulty (Chapter 3).
- [ ] Coolant pump leaking (Chapter 3).
- [ ] Boiling due to overheating (Chapter 3).
- [ ] Core plug leaking (Chapter 2).

Internal coolant leakage

- [ ] Leaking cylinder head gasket (Chapter 2).
- [ ] Cracked cylinder head or cylinder bore (Chapter 2).

Corrosion

- [ ] Infrequent draining and flushing (Chapter 1).
- [ ] Incorrect coolant mixture or inappropriate coolant type (Chapter 1).

Fuel and exhaust systems

Excessive fuel consumption

- [ ] Air filter element dirty or clogged (Chapter 1).
- [ ] Engine management system fault (Chapter 4).
- [ ] Tyres under-inflated (*Weekly checks*).
- [ ] Brakes binding (Chapters 1 and 9).

Fuel leakage and/or fuel odour

- [ ] Damaged or corroded fuel tank, pipes or connections (Chapter 4).

Excessive noise or fumes from exhaust system

- [ ] Leaking exhaust system or manifold joints (Chapters 1 and 4).
- [ ] Leaking, corroded or damaged silencers or pipe (Chapters 1 and 4).
- [ ] Broken mountings causing body or suspension contact (Chapters 1 and 4).

Clutch

Pedal travels to floor – no pressure or very little resistance

☐ Hydraulic fluid level low/air in the hydraulic system (see *Weekly checks*).
☐ Broken clutch release bearing or fork (Chapter 6).
☐ Broken diaphragm spring in clutch pressure plate (Chapter 6).

Clutch fails to disengage (unable to select gears)

☐ Clutch disc sticking on gearbox input shaft splines (Chapter 6).
☐ Clutch disc sticking to flywheel or pressure plate (Chapter 6).
☐ Faulty pressure plate assembly (Chapter 6).
☐ Clutch release mechanism worn or incorrectly assembled (Chapter 6).

Clutch slips (engine speed rises, with no increase in vehicle speed)

☐ Clutch disc linings excessively worn (Chapter 6).
☐ Clutch disc linings contaminated with oil or grease (Chapter 6).
☐ Faulty pressure plate or weak diaphragm spring (Chapter 6).

Judder as clutch is engaged

☐ Clutch disc linings contaminated with oil or grease (Chapter 6).
☐ Clutch disc linings excessively worn (Chapter 6).
☐ Faulty or distorted pressure plate or diaphragm spring (Chapter 6).
☐ Worn or loose engine or gearbox mountings (Chapter 2).
☐ Clutch disc hub or gearbox input shaft splines worn (Chapter 6).

Noise when depressing or releasing clutch pedal

☐ Worn clutch release bearing (Chapter 6).
☐ Worn or dry clutch pedal bushes (Chapter 6).
☐ Faulty pressure plate assembly (Chapter 6).
☐ Pressure plate diaphragm spring broken (Chapter 6).
☐ Broken clutch disc cushioning springs (Chapter 6).

Manual transmission

Noisy in neutral with engine running

☐ Input shaft bearings worn (noise apparent with clutch pedal released, but not when depressed) (Chapter 7).*
☐ Clutch release bearing worn (noise apparent with clutch pedal depressed, possibly less when released) (Chapter 6).

Noisy in one particular gear

☐ Worn, damaged or chipped gear teeth (Chapter 7).*

Difficulty engaging gears

☐ Clutch fault (Chapter 6).
☐ Worn or damaged gear selector mechanism (Chapter 7).
☐ Worn synchroniser units (Chapter 7).*

Jumps out of gear

☐ Worn or damaged gear selector mechanism (Chapter 7).
☐ Worn synchroniser units (Chapter 7).*
☐ Worn selector forks (Chapter 7).*

Vibration

☐ Lack of oil (Chapter 1 and 7).
☐ Worn bearings (Chapter 7).*

Lubricant leaks

☐ Leaking differential output oil seal (Chapter 7).
☐ Leaking housing joint (Chapter 7).*
☐ Leaking input shaft oil seal (Chapter 7).

Although the corrective action necessary to remedy the symptoms described is beyond the scope of the home mechanic, the above information should be helpful in isolating the cause of the condition, so that the owner can communicate clearly with a professional mechanic.

Automatic transmission

Note: *Due to the complexity of the automatic transmission, it is difficult for the home mechanic to properly diagnose and service this unit. For problems other than the following, the vehicle should be taken to a dealer service department or automatic transmission specialist.*

Fluid leakage

☐ Automatic transmission fluid is usually deep red in colour. Fluid leaks should not be confused with engine oil, which can easily be blown onto the transmission by air flow.

☐ To determine the source of a leak, first remove all built-up dirt and grime from the transmission housing and surrounding areas, using a degreasing agent or by steam-cleaning. Drive the vehicle at low speed, so that air flow will not blow the leak far from its source. Raise and support the vehicle, and determine where the leak is coming from. The following are common areas of leakage.

a) Oil pan (Chapter 7B).
b) Dipstick tube (Chapter 7B).
c) Transmission-to-fluid cooler fluid pipes/unions (Chapter 7B).

Transmission will not downshift (kickdown) with accelerator pedal fully depressed

☐ Low transmission fluid level (see Chapter 1).
☐ Incorrect selector cable adjustment (Chapter 7B).
☐ Incorrect kickdown cable adjustment (Chapter 7B).

General gear selection problems

☐ The most likely cause of gear selection problems is a faulty or poorly-adjusted gear selector mechanism. The following are common problems associated with a faulty selector mechanism.
a) Engine starting in gears other than Park or Neutral.
b) Indicator on gear selector lever pointing to a gear other than the one actually being used.
c) Vehicle moves when in Park or Neutral.
d) Poor gear shift quality, or erratic gear changes.
☐ Refer any problems to a Toyota dealer, or an automatic transmission specialist.

Engine will not start in any gear, or starts in gears other than Park or Neutral

☐ Incorrect starter inhibitor switch adjustment (Chapter 7B).
☐ Incorrect selector cable adjustment (Chapter 7B).

Transmission slips, shifts roughly, is noisy, or has no drive in forward or reverse gears

☐ There are many probable causes for the above problems, but the home mechanic should be concerned with only one possibility - fluid level. Before taking the vehicle to a dealer or transmission specialist, check the fluid level and condition of the fluid as described in Chapter 1. Correct the fluid level as necessary, or change the fluid if needed. If the problem persists, professional help will be necessary.

Driveshafts

Clicking or knocking noise on turns (at slow speed on full-lock)

☐ Lack of constant velocity joint lubricant, possibly due to damaged gaiter (Chapter 8).
☐ Worn outer constant velocity joint (Chapter 8).

Vibration when accelerating or decelerating

☐ Worn inner constant velocity joint (Chapter 8).
☐ Bent or distorted driveshaft (Chapter 8).
☐ Worn intermediate bearing (where fitted) (Chapter 8).

Braking system

Note: *Before assuming that a brake problem exists, make sure that the tyres are in good condition and correctly inflated, that the front wheel alignment is correct, and that the vehicle is not loaded with weight in an unequal manner. Apart from checking the condition of all pipe and hose connections, any faults occurring on the anti-lock braking system should be referred to a Toyota dealer for diagnosis.*

Vehicle pulls to one side under braking

- ☐ Worn, defective, damaged or contaminated brake pads/shoes on one side (Chapter 9).
- ☐ Seized or partially-seized front brake caliper (Chapter 9).
- ☐ A mixture of brake pad/shoe materials fitted between sides (Chapter 9).
- ☐ Brake caliper mounting bolts loose (Chapter 9).
- ☐ Worn or damaged steering or suspension components (Chapter 1 and 10).

Noise (grinding or high-pitched squeal) when brakes applied

- ☐ Brake pad/shoe material worn down to metal backing (Chapter 1 and 9).
- ☐ Excessive corrosion of brake disc/drum. May be apparent after the vehicle has been standing for some time (Chapter 9).
- ☐ Foreign object (stone chipping, etc) trapped between brake disc and shield (Chapter 9).

Excessive brake pedal travel

- ☐ Faulty master cylinder (Chapter 9).
- ☐ Air in hydraulic system (Chapter 9).
- ☐ Faulty vacuum servo unit (Chapter 9).

Brake pedal feels spongy when depressed

- ☐ Air in hydraulic system (Chapter 9).
- ☐ Deteriorated flexible rubber hydraulic hoses (Chapter 1 and 9).
- ☐ Master cylinder mounting nuts loose (Chapter 9).
- ☐ Faulty master cylinder (Chapter 9).

Excessive brake pedal effort required to stop vehicle

- ☐ Faulty vacuum servo unit (Chapter 9).
- ☐ Disconnected, damaged or insecure brake servo vacuum hose (Chapter 9).
- ☐ Primary or secondary hydraulic circuit failure (Chapter 9).
- ☐ Seized brake caliper or wheel cylinder (Chapter 9).
- ☐ Brake pads/shoes incorrectly fitted (Chapter 9).
- ☐ Incorrect grade of brake pads/shoes fitted (Chapter 9).
- ☐ Brake pads/shoes contaminated (Chapter 9).

Judder felt through brake pedal or steering wheel when braking

- ☐ Excessive run-out or distortion of discs or drums (Chapters 9).
- ☐ Brake pads/shoes worn (Chapters 1 or and 9).
- ☐ Brake caliper mounting bolts loose (Chapter 9).
- ☐ Wear in suspension or steering components or mountings (Chapter 1 and 10).

Brakes binding

- ☐ Seized brake caliper or wheel cylinder (Chapter 9).
- ☐ Incorrectly-adjusted handbrake mechanism (Chapter 9).
- ☐ Faulty master cylinder (Chapter 9).

Rear wheels locking under normal braking

- ☐ Rear brake shoes contaminated (Chapter 1 and 9).
- ☐ Faulty or incorrectly adjusted rear brake pressure-regulating valve – models without ABS (Chapter 9).
- ☐ ABS system fault (Chapter 9).

Suspension and steering

Note: *Before diagnosing suspension or steering faults, be sure that the trouble is not due to incorrect tyre pressures, mixtures of tyre types, or binding brakes.*

Vehicle pulls to one side

- ☐ Defective tyre (*Weekly checks*).
- ☐ Excessive wear in suspension or steering components (Chapter 1 and 10).
- ☐ Incorrect front/rear wheel alignment (Chapter 10).
- ☐ Damage to steering or suspension components (Chapter 1 and 10).

Wheel wobble and vibration

- ☐ Front roadwheels out of balance (vibration felt mainly through the steering wheel) (*Weekly checks*).
- ☐ Rear roadwheels out of balance (vibration felt throughout the vehicle) (*Weekly checks*).
- ☐ Roadwheels damaged or distorted (*Weekly checks*).
- ☐ Faulty or damaged tyre (*Weekly checks*).
- ☐ Worn steering or suspension joints, bushes or components (Chapter 1 and 10).
- ☐ Wheel nuts loose (Chapter 1 and 10).

Excessive pitching and/or rolling around corners, or during braking

- ☐ Defective shock absorbers (Chapter 1 and 10).
- ☐ Broken or weak spring and/or suspension part (Chapter 1 and 10).
- ☐ Worn or damaged anti-roll bar or mountings (Chapter 10).

Wandering or general instability

- ☐ Incorrect front/rear wheel alignment (Chapter 10).
- ☐ Worn steering or suspension joints, bushes or components (Chapter 1 and 10).
- ☐ Roadwheels out of balance (*Weekly checks*).
- ☐ Faulty or damaged tyre (*Weekly checks*).
- ☐ Wheel nuts loose (Chapter 1 and 10).
- ☐ Defective shock absorbers (Chapter 1 and 10).

Excessively-stiff steering

- ☐ Broken or incorrectly-adjusted auxiliary drivebelt (Chapter 1).
- ☐ Faulty power steering pump (Chapter 10).
- ☐ Seized track rod end balljoint or suspension balljoint (Chapter 1 and 10).
- ☐ Incorrect front/rear wheel alignment (Chapter 10).
- ☐ Steering rack or column bent or damaged (Chapter 10).

Excessive play in steering

- ☐ Worn steering column universal joint (Chapter 10).
- ☐ Worn steering track rod end balljoints (Chapter 1 and 10).
- ☐ Worn steering rack (Chapter 10).
- ☐ Worn steering or suspension joints, bushes or components (Chapter 1 and 10).

Lack of power assistance

- ☐ Broken or incorrectly-adjusted auxiliary drivebelt (Chapter 1).
- ☐ Faulty power steering pump (Chapter 10).
- ☐ Restriction in power steering fluid hoses (Chapter 1).
- ☐ Faulty steering rack (Chapter 10).

Tyre wear excessive

Tyre treads exhibit feathered edges

- ☐ Incorrect toe setting (Chapter 10).

Tyres worn in centre of tread

- ☐ Tyres over-inflated (*Weekly checks*).

Tyres worn on inside and outside edges

- ☐ Tyres under-inflated (*Weekly checks*).

Tyres worn on inside or outside edges

- ☐ Incorrect camber/castor angles (wear on one edge only) (Chapter 10).
- ☐ Worn steering or suspension joints, bushes or components (Chapter 1 and 10).
- ☐ Excessively-hard cornering.
- ☐ Accident damage.

Tyres worn unevenly

- ☐ Tyres/wheels out of balance (*Weekly checks*).
- ☐ Excessive wheel or tyre run-out (Chapter 1).
- ☐ Worn shock absorbers (Chapter 1 and 10).
- ☐ Faulty tyre (*Weekly checks*).

Electrical system

Note: *For problems associated with the starting system, refer to the faults listed under 'Engine' earlier in this Section.*

Battery won't hold a charge for more than a few days

- ☐ Battery defective internally (Chapter 5).
- ☐ Battery terminal connections loose or corroded (*Weekly checks*).
- ☐ Auxiliary drivebelt broken, worn or incorrectly adjusted (Chapter 1).
- ☐ Alternator not charging at correct output (Chapter 5).
- ☐ Alternator or voltage regulator faulty (Chapter 5).
- ☐ Short-circuit causing continual battery drain (Chapter 5 and 12).

Ignition/no-charge warning light stays on with engine running

- ☐ Auxiliary drivebelt broken, worn, or incorrectly adjusted (Chapter 1).
- ☐ Internal fault in alternator or voltage regulator (Chapter 5).
- ☐ Broken, disconnected, or loose wiring in charging circuit (Chapter 5).

Ignition/no-charge warning light fails to come on

- ☐ Warning light bulb blown (Chapter 12).
- ☐ Broken, disconnected, or loose wiring in warning light circuit (Chapter 12).
- ☐ Alternator faulty (Chapter 5).

Lights inoperative

- ☐ Bulb blown (Chapter 12).
- ☐ Corrosion of bulb or bulbholder contacts (Chapter 12).
- ☐ Blown fuse (Chapter 12).
- ☐ Faulty relay (Chapter 12).
- ☐ Broken, loose, or disconnected wiring (Chapter 12).
- ☐ Faulty switch (Chapter 12).

Instrument readings inaccurate or erratic

Fuel or temperature gauges give no reading

- ☐ Faulty gauge sensor/sender unit (Chapter 3 or 4).
- ☐ Wiring open-circuit (Chapter 12).
- ☐ Faulty gauge (Chapter 12).

Fuel or temperature gauges give continuous maximum reading

- ☐ Faulty gauge sensor/sender unit (Chapter 3 or 4).
- ☐ Wiring short-circuit (Chapter 12).
- ☐ Faulty gauge (Chapter 12).

Horn inoperative, or unsatisfactory in operation

Horn operates all the time

- ☐ Horn push either earthed or stuck down (Chapter 12).
- ☐ Horn cable-to-horn push earthed (Chapter 12).

Horn fails to operate

- ☐ Blown fuse (Chapter 12).
- ☐ Cable or cable connections loose, broken or disconnected (Chapter 12).
- ☐ Faulty horn (Chapter 12).

Horn emits intermittent or unsatisfactory sound

- ☐ Cable connections loose (Chapter 12).
- ☐ Horn mountings loose (Chapter 12).
- ☐ Faulty horn (Chapter 12).

Windscreen/tailgate wipers failed, or unsatisfactory in operation

Wipers fail to operate, or operate very slowly

- ☐ Wiper blades stuck to screen, or linkage seized or binding (Chapter 1 and 12).
- ☐ Blown fuse (Chapter 12).
- ☐ Cable or cable connections loose, broken or disconnected (Chapter 12).
- ☐ Faulty wiper motor (Chapter 12).

Wiper blades sweep over too large or too small an area of the glass

- ☐ Wiper arms incorrectly positioned on spindles (Chapter 12).
- ☐ Excessive wear of wiper linkage (Chapter 12).
- ☐ Wiper motor or linkage mountings loose or insecure (Chapter 12).

Wiper blades fail to clean the glass effectively

- ☐ Wiper blade rubbers worn or perished (*Weekly checks*).
- ☐ Wiper arm tension springs broken, or arm pivots seized (Chapter 12).
- ☐ Insufficient windscreen washer additive to adequately remove road film (*Weekly checks*).

Electrical system (continued)

Windscreen/tailgate washers failed, or unsatisfactory in operation

One or more washer jets inoperative

☐ Blocked washer jet (*Weekly checks*).
☐ Disconnected, kinked or restricted fluid hose (Chapter 12).
☐ Insufficient fluid in washer reservoir (*Weekly checks*).

Washer pump fails to operate

☐ Broken or disconnected wiring or connections (Chapter 12).
☐ Blown fuse (Chapter 12).
☐ Faulty washer switch (Chapter 12).
☐ Faulty washer pump (Chapter 12).

Electric windows inoperative, or unsatisfactory in operation

Window glass will only move in one direction

☐ Faulty switch (Chapter 12).

Window glass slow to move

☐ Regulator seized or damaged, or in need of lubricant (Chapter 11).
☐ Door internal components or trim fouling regulator (Chapter 11).
☐ Faulty motor (Chapter 11).

Window glass fails to move

☐ Blown fuse (Chapter 12).
☐ Broken or disconnected wiring or connections (Chapter 12).
☐ Faulty motor (Chapter 11).

Central locking system inoperative, or unsatisfactory in operation

Complete system failure

☐ Blown fuse (Chapter 12).
☐ Broken or disconnected wiring or connections (Chapter 12).
☐ Faulty central locking actuator (Chapter 11).

Door/tailgate locks but will not unlock, or unlocks but will not lock

☐ Broken or disconnected link rod(s) (Chapter 11).
☐ Faulty central locking actuator (Chapter 11).

One lock fails to operate

☐ Broken or disconnected wiring or connections (Chapter 12).
☐ Faulty central locking actuator (Chapter 11).
☐ Broken, binding or disconnected link rod(s) (Chapter 11).

A

ABS (Anti-lock brake system) A system, usually electronically controlled, that senses incipient wheel lockup during braking and relieves hydraulic pressure at wheels that are about to skid.

Air bag An inflatable bag hidden in the steering wheel (driver's side) or the dash or glovebox (passenger side). In a head-on collision, the bags inflate, preventing the driver and front passenger from being thrown forward into the steering wheel or windscreen.

Air cleaner A metal or plastic housing, containing a filter element, which removes dust and dirt from the air being drawn into the engine.

Air filter element The actual filter in an air cleaner system, usually manufactured from pleated paper and requiring renewal at regular intervals.

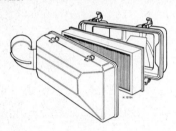

Air filter

Allen key A hexagonal wrench which fits into a recessed hexagonal hole.

Alligator clip A long-nosed spring-loaded metal clip with meshing teeth. Used to make temporary electrical connections.

Alternator A component in the electrical system which converts mechanical energy from a drivebelt into electrical energy to charge the battery and to operate the starting system, ignition system and electrical accessories.

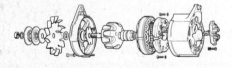

Alternator (exploded view)

Ampere (amp) A unit of measurement for the flow of electric current. One amp is the amount of current produced by one volt acting through a resistance of one ohm.

Anaerobic sealer A substance used to prevent bolts and screws from loosening. Anaerobic means that it does not require oxygen for activation. The Loctite brand is widely used.

Antifreeze A substance (usually ethylene glycol) mixed with water, and added to a vehicle's cooling system, to prevent freezing of the coolant in winter. Antifreeze also contains chemicals to inhibit corrosion and the formation of rust and other deposits that

would tend to clog the radiator and coolant passages and reduce cooling efficiency.

Anti-seize compound A coating that reduces the risk of seizing on fasteners that are subjected to high temperatures, such as exhaust manifold bolts and nuts.

Anti-seize compound

Asbestos A natural fibrous mineral with great heat resistance, commonly used in the composition of brake friction materials. Asbestos is a health hazard and the dust created by brake systems should never be inhaled or ingested.

Axle A shaft on which a wheel revolves, or which revolves with a wheel. Also, a solid beam that connects the two wheels at one end of the vehicle. An axle which also transmits power to the wheels is known as a live axle.

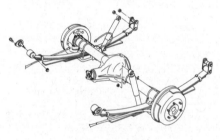

Axle assembly

Axleshaft A single rotating shaft, on either side of the differential, which delivers power from the final drive assembly to the drive wheels. Also called a driveshaft or a halfshaft.

B

Ball bearing An anti-friction bearing consisting of a hardened inner and outer race with hardened steel balls between two races.

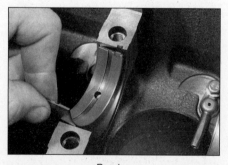

Bearing

Bearing The curved surface on a shaft or in a bore, or the part assembled into either, that permits relative motion between them with minimum wear and friction.

Big-end bearing The bearing in the end of the connecting rod that's attached to the crankshaft.

Bleed nipple A valve on a brake wheel cylinder, caliper or other hydraulic component that is opened to purge the hydraulic system of air. Also called a bleed screw.

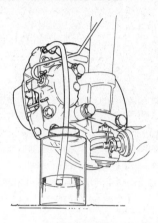

Brake bleeding

Brake bleeding Procedure for removing air from lines of a hydraulic brake system.

Brake disc The component of a disc brake that rotates with the wheels.

Brake drum The component of a drum brake that rotates with the wheels.

Brake linings The friction material which contacts the brake disc or drum to retard the vehicle's speed. The linings are bonded or riveted to the brake pads or shoes.

Brake pads The replaceable friction pads that pinch the brake disc when the brakes are applied. Brake pads consist of a friction material bonded or riveted to a rigid backing plate.

Brake shoe The crescent-shaped carrier to which the brake linings are mounted and which forces the lining against the rotating drum during braking.

Braking systems For more information on braking systems, consult the *Haynes Automotive Brake Manual*.

Breaker bar A long socket wrench handle providing greater leverage.

Bulkhead The insulated partition between the engine and the passenger compartment.

C

Caliper The non-rotating part of a disc-brake assembly that straddles the disc and carries the brake pads. The caliper also contains the hydraulic components that cause the pads to pinch the disc when the brakes are applied. A caliper is also a measuring tool that can be set to measure inside or outside dimensions of an object.

Camshaft A rotating shaft on which a series of cam lobes operate the valve mechanisms. The camshaft may be driven by gears, by sprockets and chain or by sprockets and a belt.

Canister A container in an evaporative emission control system; contains activated charcoal granules to trap vapours from the fuel system.

Canister

Carburettor A device which mixes fuel with air in the proper proportions to provide a desired power output from a spark ignition internal combustion engine.

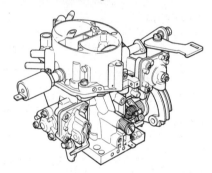

Carburettor

Castellated Resembling the parapets along the top of a castle wall. For example, a castellated balljoint stud nut.

Castellated nut

Castor In wheel alignment, the backward or forward tilt of the steering axis. Castor is positive when the steering axis is inclined rearward at the top.

Catalytic converter A silencer-like device in the exhaust system which converts certain pollutants in the exhaust gases into less harmful substances.

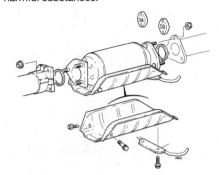

Catalytic converter

Circlip A ring-shaped clip used to prevent endwise movement of cylindrical parts and shafts. An internal circlip is installed in a groove in a housing; an external circlip fits into a groove on the outside of a cylindrical piece such as a shaft.

Clearance The amount of space between two parts. For example, between a piston and a cylinder, between a bearing and a journal, etc.

Coil spring A spiral of elastic steel found in various sizes throughout a vehicle, for example as a springing medium in the suspension and in the valve train.

Compression Reduction in volume, and increase in pressure and temperature, of a gas, caused by squeezing it into a smaller space.

Compression ratio The relationship between cylinder volume when the piston is at top dead centre and cylinder volume when the piston is at bottom dead centre.

Constant velocity (CV) joint A type of universal joint that cancels out vibrations caused by driving power being transmitted through an angle.

Core plug A disc or cup-shaped metal device inserted in a hole in a casting through which core was removed when the casting was formed. Also known as a freeze plug or expansion plug.

Crankcase The lower part of the engine block in which the crankshaft rotates.

Crankshaft The main rotating member, or shaft, running the length of the crankcase, with offset "throws" to which the connecting rods are attached.

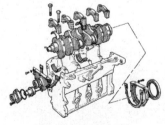

Crankshaft assembly

Crocodile clip See Alligator clip

D

Diagnostic code Code numbers obtained by accessing the diagnostic mode of an engine management computer. This code can be used to determine the area in the system where a malfunction may be located.

Disc brake A brake design incorporating a rotating disc onto which brake pads are squeezed. The resulting friction converts the energy of a moving vehicle into heat.

Double-overhead cam (DOHC) An engine that uses two overhead camshafts, usually one for the intake valves and one for the exhaust valves.

Drivebelt(s) The belt(s) used to drive accessories such as the alternator, water pump, power steering pump, air conditioning compressor, etc. off the crankshaft pulley.

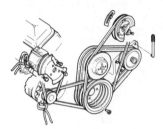

Accessory drivebelts

Driveshaft Any shaft used to transmit motion. Commonly used when referring to the axleshafts on a front wheel drive vehicle.

Driveshaft

Drum brake A type of brake using a drum-shaped metal cylinder attached to the inner surface of the wheel. When the brake pedal is pressed, curved brake shoes with friction linings press against the inside of the drum to slow or stop the vehicle.

Drum brake assembly

E

EGR valve A valve used to introduce exhaust gases into the intake air stream.

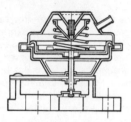

EGR valve

Electronic control unit (ECU) A computer which controls (for instance) ignition and fuel injection systems, or an anti-lock braking system. For more information refer to the *Haynes Automotive Electrical and Electronic Systems Manual.*

Electronic Fuel Injection (EFI) A computer controlled fuel system that distributes fuel through an injector located in each intake port of the engine.

Emergency brake A braking system, independent of the main hydraulic system, that can be used to slow or stop the vehicle if the primary brakes fail, or to hold the vehicle stationary even though the brake pedal isn't depressed. It usually consists of a hand lever that actuates either front or rear brakes mechanically through a series of cables and linkages. Also known as a handbrake or parking brake.

Endfloat The amount of lengthwise movement between two parts. As applied to a crankshaft, the distance that the crankshaft can move forward and back in the cylinder block.

Engine management system (EMS) A computer controlled system which manages the fuel injection and the ignition systems in an integrated fashion.

Exhaust manifold A part with several passages through which exhaust gases leave the engine combustion chambers and enter the exhaust pipe.

Exhaust manifold

F

Fan clutch A viscous (fluid) drive coupling device which permits variable engine fan speeds in relation to engine speeds.

Feeler blade A thin strip or blade of hardened steel, ground to an exact thickness, used to check or measure clearances between parts.

Feeler blade

Firing order The order in which the engine cylinders fire, or deliver their power strokes, beginning with the number one cylinder.

Flywheel A heavy spinning wheel in which energy is absorbed and stored by means of momentum. On cars, the flywheel is attached to the crankshaft to smooth out firing impulses.

Free play The amount of travel before any action takes place. The "looseness" in a linkage, or an assembly of parts, between the initial application of force and actual movement. For example, the distance the brake pedal moves before the pistons in the master cylinder are actuated.

Fuse An electrical device which protects a circuit against accidental overload. The typical fuse contains a soft piece of metal which is calibrated to melt at a predetermined current flow (expressed as amps) and break the circuit.

Fusible link A circuit protection device consisting of a conductor surrounded by heat-resistant insulation. The conductor is smaller than the wire it protects, so it acts as the weakest link in the circuit. Unlike a blown fuse, a failed fusible link must frequently be cut from the wire for replacement.

G

Gap The distance the spark must travel in jumping from the centre electrode to the side

Adjusting spark plug gap

electrode in a spark plug. Also refers to the spacing between the points in a contact breaker assembly in a conventional points-type ignition, or to the distance between the reluctor or rotor and the pickup coil in an electronic ignition.

Gasket Any thin, soft material - usually cork, cardboard, asbestos or soft metal - installed between two metal surfaces to ensure a good seal. For instance, the cylinder head gasket seals the joint between the block and the cylinder head.

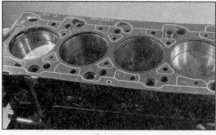

Gasket

Gauge An instrument panel display used to monitor engine conditions. A gauge with a movable pointer on a dial or a fixed scale is an analogue gauge. A gauge with a numerical readout is called a digital gauge.

H

Halfshaft A rotating shaft that transmits power from the final drive unit to a drive wheel, usually when referring to a live rear axle.

Harmonic balancer A device designed to reduce torsion or twisting vibration in the crankshaft. May be incorporated in the crankshaft pulley. Also known as a vibration damper.

Hone An abrasive tool for correcting small irregularities or differences in diameter in an engine cylinder, brake cylinder, etc.

Hydraulic tappet A tappet that utilises hydraulic pressure from the engine's lubrication system to maintain zero clearance (constant contact with both camshaft and valve stem). Automatically adjusts to variation in valve stem length. Hydraulic tappets also reduce valve noise.

I

Ignition timing The moment at which the spark plug fires, usually expressed in the number of crankshaft degrees before the piston reaches the top of its stroke.

Inlet manifold A tube or housing with passages through which flows the air-fuel mixture (carburettor vehicles and vehicles with throttle body injection) or air only (port fuel-injected vehicles) to the port openings in the cylinder head.

J

Jump start Starting the engine of a vehicle with a discharged or weak battery by attaching jump leads from the weak battery to a charged or helper battery.

L

Load Sensing Proportioning Valve (LSPV) A brake hydraulic system control valve that works like a proportioning valve, but also takes into consideration the amount of weight carried by the rear axle.

Locknut A nut used to lock an adjustment nut, or other threaded component, in place. For example, a locknut is employed to keep the adjusting nut on the rocker arm in position.

Lockwasher A form of washer designed to prevent an attaching nut from working loose.

M

MacPherson strut A type of front suspension system devised by Earle MacPherson at Ford of England. In its original form, a simple lateral link with the anti-roll bar creates the lower control arm. A long strut - an integral coil spring and shock absorber - is mounted between the body and the steering knuckle. Many modern so-called MacPherson strut systems use a conventional lower A-arm and don't rely on the anti-roll bar for location.

Multimeter An electrical test instrument with the capability to measure voltage, current and resistance.

N

NOx Oxides of Nitrogen. A common toxic pollutant emitted by petrol and diesel engines at higher temperatures.

O

Ohm The unit of electrical resistance. One volt applied to a resistance of one ohm will produce a current of one amp.

Ohmmeter An instrument for measuring electrical resistance.

O-ring A type of sealing ring made of a special rubber-like material; in use, the O-ring is compressed into a groove to provide the sealing action.

O-ring

Overhead cam (ohc) engine An engine with the camshaft(s) located on top of the cylinder head(s).

Overhead valve (ohv) engine An engine with the valves located in the cylinder head, but with the camshaft located in the engine block.

Oxygen sensor A device installed in the engine exhaust manifold, which senses the oxygen content in the exhaust and converts this information into an electric current. Also called a Lambda sensor.

P

Phillips screw A type of screw head having a cross instead of a slot for a corresponding type of screwdriver.

Plastigage A thin strip of plastic thread, available in different sizes, used for measuring clearances. For example, a strip of Plastigage is laid across a bearing journal. The parts are assembled and dismantled; the width of the crushed strip indicates the clearance between journal and bearing.

Plastigage

Propeller shaft The long hollow tube with universal joints at both ends that carries power from the transmission to the differential on front-engined rear wheel drive vehicles.

Proportioning valve A hydraulic control valve which limits the amount of pressure to the rear brakes during panic stops to prevent wheel lock-up.

R

Rack-and-pinion steering A steering system with a pinion gear on the end of the steering shaft that mates with a rack (think of a geared wheel opened up and laid flat). When the steering wheel is turned, the pinion turns, moving the rack to the left or right. This movement is transmitted through the track rods to the steering arms at the wheels.

Radiator A liquid-to-air heat transfer device designed to reduce the temperature of the coolant in an internal combustion engine cooling system.

Refrigerant Any substance used as a heat transfer agent in an air-conditioning system. R-12 has been the principle refrigerant for many years; recently, however, manufacturers have begun using R-134a, a non-CFC substance that is considered less harmful to the ozone in the upper atmosphere.

Rocker arm A lever arm that rocks on a shaft or pivots on a stud. In an overhead valve engine, the rocker arm converts the upward movement of the pushrod into a downward movement to open a valve.

Rotor In a distributor, the rotating device inside the cap that connects the centre electrode and the outer terminals as it turns, distributing the high voltage from the coil secondary winding to the proper spark plug. Also, that part of an alternator which rotates inside the stator. Also, the rotating assembly of a turbocharger, including the compressor wheel, shaft and turbine wheel.

Runout The amount of wobble (in-and-out movement) of a gear or wheel as it's rotated. The amount a shaft rotates "out-of-true." The out-of-round condition of a rotating part.

S

Sealant A liquid or paste used to prevent leakage at a joint. Sometimes used in conjunction with a gasket.

Sealed beam lamp An older headlight design which integrates the reflector, lens and filaments into a hermetically-sealed one-piece unit. When a filament burns out or the lens cracks, the entire unit is simply replaced.

Serpentine drivebelt A single, long, wide accessory drivebelt that's used on some newer vehicles to drive all the accessories, instead of a series of smaller, shorter belts. Serpentine drivebelts are usually tensioned by an automatic tensioner.

Serpentine drivebelt

Shim Thin spacer, commonly used to adjust the clearance or relative positions between two parts. For example, shims inserted into or under bucket tappets control valve clearances. Clearance is adjusted by changing the thickness of the shim.

Slide hammer A special puller that screws into or hooks onto a component such as a shaft or bearing; a heavy sliding handle on the shaft bottoms against the end of the shaft to knock the component free.

Sprocket A tooth or projection on the periphery of a wheel, shaped to engage with a chain or drivebelt. Commonly used to refer to the sprocket wheel itself.

Starter inhibitor switch On vehicles with an automatic transmission, a switch that prevents starting if the vehicle is not in Neutral or Park.

Strut See MacPherson strut.

T

Tappet A cylindrical component which transmits motion from the cam to the valve stem, either directly or via a pushrod and rocker arm. Also called a cam follower.

Thermostat A heat-controlled valve that regulates the flow of coolant between the cylinder block and the radiator, so maintaining optimum engine operating temperature. A thermostat is also used in some air cleaners in which the temperature is regulated.

Thrust bearing The bearing in the clutch assembly that is moved in to the release levers by clutch pedal action to disengage the clutch. Also referred to as a release bearing.

Timing belt A toothed belt which drives the camshaft. Serious engine damage may result if it breaks in service.

Timing chain A chain which drives the camshaft.

Toe-in The amount the front wheels are closer together at the front than at the rear. On rear wheel drive vehicles, a slight amount of toe-in is usually specified to keep the front wheels running parallel on the road by offsetting other forces that tend to spread the wheels apart.

Toe-out The amount the front wheels are closer together at the rear than at the front. On front wheel drive vehicles, a slight amount of toe-out is usually specified.

Tools For full information on choosing and using tools, refer to the *Haynes Automotive Tools Manual*.

Tracer A stripe of a second colour applied to a wire insulator to distinguish that wire from another one with the same colour insulator.

Tune-up A process of accurate and careful adjustments and parts replacement to obtain the best possible engine performance.

Turbocharger A centrifugal device, driven by exhaust gases, that pressurises the intake air. Normally used to increase the power output from a given engine displacement, but can also be used primarily to reduce exhaust emissions (as on VW's "Umwelt" Diesel engine).

U

Universal joint or U-joint A double-pivoted connection for transmitting power from a driving to a driven shaft through an angle. A U-joint consists of two Y-shaped yokes and a cross-shaped member called the spider.

V

Valve A device through which the flow of liquid, gas, vacuum, or loose material in bulk may be started, stopped, or regulated by a movable part that opens, shuts, or partially obstructs one or more ports or passageways. A valve is also the movable part of such a device.

Valve clearance The clearance between the valve tip (the end of the valve stem) and the rocker arm or tappet. The valve clearance is measured when the valve is closed.

Vernier caliper A precision measuring instrument that measures inside and outside dimensions. Not quite as accurate as a micrometer, but more convenient.

Viscosity The thickness of a liquid or its resistance to flow.

Volt A unit for expressing electrical "pressure" in a circuit. One volt that will produce a current of one ampere through a resistance of one ohm.

W

Welding Various processes used to join metal items by heating the areas to be joined to a molten state and fusing them together. For more information refer to the *Haynes Automotive Welding Manual*.

Wiring diagram A drawing portraying the components and wires in a vehicle's electrical system, using standardised symbols. For more information refer to the *Haynes Automotive Electrical and Electronic Systems Manual*.

Note: *References throughout this index are in the form "**Chapter number**" • "**Page number**". So, for example, 2C•15 refers to page 15 of Chapter 2C.*

Note: *References throughout this index are in the form "**Chapter number**" • "**Page number**". So, for example, 2C•15 refers to page 15 of Chapter 2C.*

Note: *References throughout this index are in the form* "**Chapter number**" • "**Page number**". *So, for example, 2C•15 refers to page 15 of Chapter 2C.*

Haynes Manuals – The Complete UK Car List

Title	Book No.
ALFA ROMEO Alfasud/Sprint (74 - 88) up to F *	0292
Alfa Romeo Alfetta (73 - 87) up to E *	0531
AUDI 80, 90 & Coupe Petrol (79 - Nov 88) up to F	0605
Audi 80, 90 & Coupe Petrol (Oct 86 - 90) D to H	1491
Audi 100 & 200 Petrol (Oct 82 - 90) up to H	0907
Audi 100 & A6 Petrol & Diesel (May 91 - May 97) H to P	3504
Audi A3 Petrol & Diesel (96 - May 03) P to 03	4253
Audi A4 Petrol & Diesel (95 - Feb 00) M to V	3575
AUSTIN A35 & A40 (56 - 67) up to F *	0118
Austin/MG/Rover Maestro 1.3 & 1.6 Petrol (83 - 95) up to M	0922
Austin/MG Metro (80 - May 90) up to G	0718
Austin/Rover Montego 1.3 & 1.6 Petrol (84 - 94) A to L	1066
Austin/MG/Rover Montego 2.0 Petrol (84 - 95) A to M	1067
Mini (59 - 69) up to H *	0527
Mini (69 - 01) up to X	0646
Austin/Rover 2.0 litre Diesel Engine (86 - 93) C to L	1857
Austin Healey 100/6 & 3000 (56 - 68) up to G *	0049
BEDFORD CF Petrol (69 - 87) up to E	0163
Bedford/Vauxhall Rascal & Suzuki Supercarry (86 - Oct 94) C to M	3015
BMW 316, 320 & 320i (4-cyl) (75 - Feb 83) up to Y *	0276
BMW 320, 320i, 323i & 325i (6-cyl) (Oct 77 - Sept 87) up to E	0815
BMW 3- & 5-Series Petrol (81 - 91) up to J	1948
BMW 3-Series Petrol (Apr 91 - 99) H to V	3210
BMW 3-Series Petrol (Sept 98 - 03) S to 53	4067
BMW 520i & 525e (Oct 81 - June 88) up to E	1560
BMW 525, 528 & 528i (73 - Sept 81) up to X *	0632
BMW 5-Series 6-cyl Petrol (April 96 - Aug 03) N to 03	4151
BMW 1500, 1502, 1600, 1602, 2000 & 2002 (59 - 77) up to S *	0240
CHRYSLER PT Cruiser Petrol (00 - 03) W to 53	4058
CITROËN 2CV, Ami & Dyane (67 - 90) up to H	0196
Citroën AX Petrol & Diesel (87 - 97) D to P	3014
Citroën Berlingo & Peugeot Partner Petrol & Diesel (96 - 05) P to 55	4281
Citroën BX Petrol (83 - 94) A to L	0908
Citroën C15 Van Petrol & Diesel (89 - Oct 98) F to S	3509
Citroën C3 Petrol & Diesel (02 - 05) 51 to 05	4197
Citroën CX Petrol (75 - 88) up to F	0528
Citroën Saxo Petrol & Diesel (96 - 04) N to 54	3506
Citroën Visa Petrol (79 - 88) up to F	0620
Citroën Xantia Petrol & Diesel (93 - 01) K to Y	3082
Citroën XM Petrol & Diesel (89 - 00) G to X	3451
Citroën Xsara Petrol & Diesel (97 - Sept 00) R to W	3751
Citroën Xsara Picasso Petrol & Diesel (00 - 02) W to 52	3944
Citroën ZX Diesel (91 - 98) J to S	1922
Citroën ZX Petrol (91 - 98) H to S	1881
Citroën 1.7 & 1.9 litre Diesel Engine (84 - 96) A to N	1379
FIAT 126 (73 - 87) up to E *	0305
Fiat 500 (57 - 73) up to M *	0090
Fiat Bravo & Brava Petrol (95 - 00) N to W	3572
Fiat Cinquecento (93 - 98) K to R	3501
Fiat Panda (81 - 95) up to M	0793
Fiat Punto Petrol & Diesel (94 - Oct 99) L to V	3251
Fiat Punto Petrol (Oct 99 - July 03) V to 03	4066
Fiat Regata Petrol (84 - 88) A to F	1167
Fiat Tipo Petrol (88 - 91) E to J	1625
Fiat Uno Petrol (83 - 95) up to M	0923
Fiat X1/9 (74 - 89) up to G *	0273
FORD Anglia (59 - 68) up to G *	0001
Ford Capri II (& III) 1.6 & 2.0 (74 - 87) up to E *	0283
Ford Capri II (& III) 2.8 & 3.0 V6 (74 - 87) up to E	1309
Ford Cortina Mk III 1300 & 1600 (70 - 76) up to P *	0070
Ford Escort Mk I 1100 & 1300 (68 - 74) up to N *	0171
Ford Escort Mk I Mexico, RS 1600 & RS 2000 (70 - 74) up to N *	0139
Ford Escort Mk II Mexico, RS 1800 & RS 2000 (75 - 80) up to W *	0735
Ford Escort (75 - Aug 80) up to V *	0280
Ford Escort Petrol (Sept 80 - Sept 90) up to H	0686
Ford Escort & Orion Petrol (Sept 90 - 00) H to X	1737
Ford Escort & Orion Diesel (Sept 90 - 00) H to X	4081
Ford Fiesta (76 - Aug 83) up to Y	0334
Ford Fiesta Petrol (Aug 83 - Feb 89) A to F	1030
Ford Fiesta Petrol (Feb 89 - Oct 95) F to N	1595
Ford Fiesta Petrol & Diesel (Oct 95 - Mar 02) N to 02	3397
Ford Fiesta Petrol & Diesel (Apr 02 - 05) 02 to 54	4170
Ford Focus Petrol & Diesel (98 - 01) S to Y	3759
Ford Focus Petrol & Diesel (Oct 01 - 04) 51 to 54	4167
Ford Galaxy Petrol & Diesel (95 - Aug 00) M to W	3984
Ford Granada Petrol (Sept 77 - Feb 85) up to B *	0481
Ford Granada & Scorpio Petrol (Mar 85 - 94) B to M	1245
Ford Ka (96 - 02) P to 52	3570
Ford Mondeo Petrol (93 - Sept 00) K to X	1923
Ford Mondeo Petrol & Diesel (Oct 00 - Jul 03) X to 03	3990
Ford Mondeo Diesel (93 - 96) L to N	3465
Ford Orion Petrol (83 - Sept 90) up to H	1009
Ford Sierra 4-cyl Petrol (82 - 93) up to K	0903
Ford Sierra V6 Petrol (82 - 91) up to J	0904
Ford Transit Petrol (Mk 2) (78 - Jan 86) up to C	0719
Ford Transit Petrol (Mk 3) (Feb 86 - 89) C to G	1468
Ford Transit Diesel (Feb 86 - 99) C to T	3019
Ford 1.6 & 1.8 litre Diesel Engine (84 - 96) A to N	1172
Ford 2.1, 2.3 & 2.5 litre Diesel Engine (77 - 90) up to H	1606
FREIGHT ROVER Sherpa Petrol (74 - 87) up to E	0463
HILLMAN Avenger (70 - 82) up to Y	0037
Hillman Imp (63 - 76) up to R *	0022
HONDA Civic (Feb 84 - Oct 87) A to E	1226
Honda Civic (Nov 91 - 96) J to N	3199
Honda Civic Petrol (Mar 95 - 00) M to X	4050
HYUNDAI Pony (85 - 94) C to M	3398
JAGUAR E Type (61 - 72) up to L *	0140
Jaguar MkI & II, 240 & 340 (55 - 69) up to H *	0098
Jaguar XJ6, XJ & Sovereign; Daimler Sovereign (68 - Oct 86) up to D	0242
Jaguar XJ6 & Sovereign (Oct 86 - Sept 94) D to M	3261
Jaguar XJ12, XJS & Sovereign; Daimler Double Six (72 - 88) up to F	0478
JEEP Cherokee Petrol (93 - 96) K to N	1943
LADA 1200, 1300, 1500 & 1600 (74 - 91) up to J	0413
Lada Samara (87 - 91) D to J	1610
LAND ROVER 90, 110 & Defender Diesel (83 - 95) up to N	3017
Land Rover Discovery Petrol & Diesel (89 - 98) G to S	3016
Land Rover Discovery Diesel (99 - 04) S to 54	4606
Land Rover Freelander Petrol & Diesel (97 - 02) R to 52	3929
Land Rover Series IIA & III Diesel (58 - 85) up to C	0529
Land Rover Series II, IIA & III 4-cyl Petrol (58 - 85) up to C	0314
MAZDA 323 (Mar 81 - Oct 89) up to G	1608
Mazda 323 (Oct 89 - 98) G to R	3455
Mazda 626 (May 83 - Sept 87) up to E	0929
Mazda B1600, B1800 & B2000 Pick-up Petrol (72 - 88) up to F	0267
Mazda RX-7 (79 - 85) up to C *	0460
MERCEDES-BENZ 190, 190E & 190D Petrol & Diesel (83 - 93) A to L	3450
Mercedes-Benz 200D, 240D, 240TD, 300D & 300TD 123 Series Diesel (Oct 76 - 85) up to C	1114
Mercedes-Benz 250 & 280 (68 - 72) up to L *	0346
Mercedes-Benz 250 & 280 123 Series Petrol (Oct 76 - 84) up to B *	0677
Mercedes-Benz 124 Series Petrol & Diesel (85 - Aug 93) C to K	3253
Mercedes-Benz C-Class Petrol & Diesel (93 - Aug 00) L to W	3511
MGA (55 - 62) *	0475
MGB (62 - 80) up to W	0111
MG Midget & Austin-Healey Sprite (58 - 80) up to W *	0265
MINI Petrol (July 01 - 05) Y to 05	4273
MITSUBISHI Shogun & L200 Pick-Ups Petrol (83 - 94) up to M	1944
MORRIS Ital 1.3 (80 - 84) up to B	0705
Morris Minor 1000 (56 - 71) up to K	0024
NISSAN Almera Petrol (95 - Feb 00) N to V	4053
Nissan Bluebird (May 84 - Mar 86) A to C	1223
Nissan Bluebird Petrol (Mar 86 - 90) C to H	1473
Nissan Cherry (Sept 82 - 86) up to D	1031
Nissan Micra (83 - Jan 93) up to K	0931
Nissan Micra (93 - 02) K to 52	3254
Nissan Primera Petrol (90 - Aug 99) H to T	1851
Nissan Stanza (82 - 86) up to D	0824
Nissan Sunny Petrol (May 82 - Oct 86) up to D	0895
Nissan Sunny Petrol (Oct 86 - Mar 91) D to H	1378
Nissan Sunny Petrol (Apr 91 - 95) H to N	3219
OPEL Ascona & Manta (B Series) (Sept 75 - 88) up to F *	0316
Opel Ascona Petrol (81 - 88)	3215
Opel Astra Petrol (Oct 91 - Feb 98)	3156
Opel Corsa Petrol (83 - Mar 93)	3160
Opel Corsa Petrol (Mar 93 - 97)	3159
Opel Kadett Petrol (Nov 79 - Oct 84) up to B	0634
Opel Kadett Petrol (Oct 84 - Oct 91)	3196
Opel Omega & Senator Petrol (Nov 86 - 94)	3157
Opel Rekord Petrol (Feb 78 - Oct 86) up to D	0543
Opel Vectra Petrol (Oct 88 - Oct 95)	3158
PEUGEOT 106 Petrol & Diesel (91 - 04) J to 53	1882
Peugeot 205 Petrol (83 - 97) A to P	0932
Peugeot 206 Petrol & Diesel (98 - 01) S to X	3757
Peugeot 206 Petrol & Diesel (01 - 06) Y to 56	4613
Peugeot 306 Petrol & Diesel (93 - 02) K to 02	3073
Peugeot 307 Petrol & Diesel (01 - 04) Y to 54	4147
Peugeot 309 Petrol (86 - 93) C to K	1266
Peugeot 405 Petrol (88 - 97) E to P	1559
Peugeot 405 Diesel (88 - 97) E to P	3198
Peugeot 406 Petrol & Diesel (96 - Mar 99) N to T	3394
Peugeot 406 Petrol & Diesel (Mar 99 - 02) T to 52	3982
Peugeot 505 Petrol (79 - 89) up to G	0762
Peugeot 1.7/1.8 & 1.9 litre Diesel Engine (82 - 96) up to N	0950
Peugeot 2.0, 2.1, 2.3 & 2.5 litre Diesel Engines (74 - 90) up to H	1607
PORSCHE 911 (65 - 85) up to C	0264
Porsche 924 & 924 Turbo (76 - 85) up to C	0397
PROTON (89 - 97) F to P	3255
RANGE ROVER V8 Petrol (70 - Oct 92) up to K	0606

Title	Book No.
RELIANT Robin & Kitten (73 - 83) up to A *	0436
RENAULT 4 (61 - 86) up to D *	0072
Renault 5 Petrol (Feb 85 - 96) B to N	1219
Renault 9 & 11 Petrol (82 - 89) up to F	0822
Renault 18 Petrol (79 - 86) up to D	0598
Renault 19 Petrol (89 - 96) F to N	1646
Renault 19 Diesel (89 - 96) F to N	1946
Renault 21 Petrol (86 - 94) C to M	1397
Renault 25 Petrol & Diesel (84 - 92) B to K	1228
Renault Clio Petrol (91 - May 98) H to R	1853
Renault Clio Diesel (91 - June 96) H to N	3031
Renault Clio Petrol & Diesel (May 98 - May 01) R to Y	3906
Renault Clio Petrol & Diesel (June 01 - 04) Y to 54	4168
Renault Espace Petrol & Diesel (85 - 96) C to N	3197
Renault Laguna Petrol & Diesel (94 - 00) L to W	3252
Renault Laguna Petrol & Diesel (Feb 01 - Feb 05) X to 54	4283
Renault Mégane & Scénic Petrol & Diesel (96 - 98) N to R	3395
Renault Mégane & Scénic Petrol & Diesel (Apr 99 - 02) T to 52	3916
Renault Megane Petrol & Diesel (Oct 02 - 05) 52 to 55	4284
Renault Scenic Petrol & Diesel (Sept 03 - 06) 53 to 06	4297
ROVER 213 & 216 (84 - 89) A to G	1116
Rover 214 & 414 Petrol (89 - 96) G to N	1689
Rover 216 & 416 Petrol (89 - 96) G to N	1830
Rover 211, 214, 216, 218 & 220 Petrol & Diesel (Dec 95 - 99) N to V	3399
Rover 25 & MG ZR Petrol & Diesel (Oct 99 - 04) V to 54	4145
Rover 414, 416 & 420 Petrol & Diesel (May 95 - 98) M to R	3453
Rover 45 / MG ZS Petrol & Diesel (99 - 05) V to 55	4384
Rover 618, 620 & 623 Petrol (93 - 97) K to P	3257
Rover 75 / MG ZT Petrol & Diesel (99 - 06) S to 06	4292
Rover 820, 825 & 827 Petrol (86 - 95) D to N	1380
Rover 3500 (76 - 87) up to E *	0365
Rover Metro, 111 & 114 Petrol (May 90 - 98) G to S	1711
SAAB 95 & 96 (66 - 76) up to R *	0198
Saab 90, 99 & 900 (79 - Oct 93) up to L	0765
Saab 900 (Oct 93 - 98) L to R	3512
Saab 9000 (4-cyl) (85 - 98) C to S	1686
Saab 9-3 Petrol & Diesel (98 - May 02) R to 02	4614
Saab 9-5 4-cyl Petrol (97 - 04) R to 54	4156
SEAT Ibiza & Cordoba Petrol & Diesel (Oct 93 - Oct 99) L to V	3571
Seat Ibiza & Malaga Petrol (85 - 92) B to K	1609
SKODA Estelle (77 - 89) up to G	0604
Skoda Fabia Petrol & Diesel (00 - 06) W to 06	4376
Skoda Favorit (89 - 96) F to N	1801
Skoda Felicia Petrol & Diesel (95 - 01) M to X	3505
Skoda Octavia Petrol & Diesel (98 - Apr 04) R to 04	4285
SUBARU 1600 & 1800 (Nov 79 - 90) up to H *	0995
SUNBEAM Alpine, Rapier & H120 (67 - 74) up to N *	0051
SUZUKI Supercarry & Bedford/Vauxhall Rascal (86 - Oct 94) C to M	3015
Suzuki SJ Series, Samurai & Vitara (4-cyl) Petrol (82 - 97) up to P	1942
TALBOT Alpine, Solara, Minx & Rapier (75 - 86) up to D	0337
Talbot Horizon Petrol (78 - 86) up to D	0473
Talbot Samba (82 - 86) up to D	0823
TOYOTA Avensis Petrol (98 - Jan 03) R to 52	4264
Toyota Carina E Petrol (May 92 - 97) J to P	3256

Title	Book No.
Toyota Corolla (80 - 85) up to C	0683
Toyota Corolla (Sept 83 - Sept 87) A to E	1024
Toyota Corolla (Sept 87 - Aug 92) E to K	1683
Toyota Corolla Petrol (Aug 92 - 97) K to P	3259
Toyota Corolla Petrol (July 97 - Feb 02) P to 51	4286
Toyota Hi-Ace & Hi-Lux Petrol (69 - Oct 83) up to A	0304
Toyota Yaris Petrol (99 - 05) T to 05	4265
TRIUMPH GT6 & Vitesse (62 - 74) up to N *	0112
Triumph Herald (59 - 71) up to K *	0010
Triumph Spitfire (62 - 81) up to X	0113
Triumph Stag (70 - 78) up to T *	0441
Triumph TR2, TR3, TR3A, TR4 & TR4A (52 - 67) up to F *	0028
Triumph TR5 & 6 (67 - 75) up to P *	0031
Triumph TR7 (75 - 82) up to Y *	0322
VAUXHALL Astra Petrol (80 - Oct 84) up to B	0635
Vauxhall Astra & Belmont Petrol (Oct 84 - Oct 91) B to J	1136
Vauxhall Astra Petrol (Oct 91 - Feb 98) J to R	1832
Vauxhall/Opel Astra & Zafira Petrol (Feb 98 - Apr 04) R to 04	3758
Vauxhall/Opel Astra & Zafira Diesel (Feb 98 - Apr 04) R to 04	3797
Vauxhall/Opel Calibra (90 - 98) G to S	3502
Vauxhall Carlton Petrol (Oct 78 - Oct 86) up to D	0480
Vauxhall Carlton & Senator Petrol (Nov 86 - 94) D to L	1469
Vauxhall Cavalier Petrol (81 - Oct 88) up to F	0812
Vauxhall Cavalier Petrol (Oct 88 - 95) F to N	1570
Vauxhall Chevette (75 - 84) up to B	0285
Vauxhall/Opel Corsa Diesel (Mar 93 - Oct 00) K to X	4087
Vauxhall Corsa Petrol (Mar 93 - 97) K to R	1985
Vauxhall/Opel Corsa Petrol (Apr 97 - Oct 00) P to X	3921
Vauxhall/Opel Corsa Petrol & Diesel (Oct 00 - Sept 03) X to 53	4079
Vauxhall/Opel Frontera Petrol & Diesel (91 - Sept 98) J to S	3454
Vauxhall Nova Petrol (83 - 93) up to K	0909
Vauxhall/Opel Omega Petrol (94 - 99) L to T	3510
Vauxhall/Opel Vectra Petrol & Diesel (95 - Feb 99) N to S	3396
Vauxhall/Opel Vectra Petrol & Diesel (Mar 99 - May 02) T to 02	3930
Vauxhall/Opel 1.5, 1.6 & 1.7 litre Diesel Engine (82 - 96) up to N	1222
VOLKSWAGEN 411 & 412 (68 - 75) up to P *	0091
Volkswagen Beetle 1200 (54 - 77) up to S	0036
Volkswagen Beetle 1300 & 1500 (65 - 75) up to P	0039
Volkswagen Beetle 1302 & 1302S (70 - 72) up to L *	0110
Volkswagen Beetle 1303, 1303S & GT (72 - 75) up to P	0159
Volkswagen Beetle Petrol & Diesel (Apr 99 - 01) T to 51	3798
Volkswagen Golf & Jetta Mk 1 Petrol 1.1 & 1.3 (74 - 84) up to A	0716
Volkswagen Golf, Jetta & Scirocco Mk 1 Petrol 1.5, 1.6 & 1.8 (74 - 84) up to A	0726
Volkswagen Golf & Jetta Mk 1 Diesel (78 - 84) up to A	0451
Volkswagen Golf & Jetta Mk 2 Petrol (Mar 84 - Feb 92) A to J	1081
Volkswagen Golf & Vento Petrol & Diesel (Feb 92 - Mar 98) J to R	3097
Volkswagen Golf & Bora Petrol & Diesel (April 98 - 00) R to X	3727

Title	Book No.
Volkswagen Golf & Bora 4-cyl Petrol & Diesel (01 - 03) X to 53	4169
Volkswagen LT Petrol Vans & Light Trucks (76 - 87) up to E	0637
Volkswagen Passat & Santana Petrol (Sept 81 - May 88) up to E	0814
Volkswagen Passat 4-cyl Petrol & Diesel (May 88 - 96) E to P	3498
Volkswagen Passat 4-cyl Petrol & Diesel (Dec 96 - Nov 00) P to X	3917
Volkswagen Passat Petrol & Diesel (Dec 00 - May 05) X to 05	4279
Volkswagen Polo & Derby (76 - Jan 82) up to X	0335
Volkswagen Polo (82 - Oct 90) up to H	0813
Volkswagen Polo Petrol (Nov 90 - Aug 94) H to L	3245
Volkswagen Polo Hatchback Petrol & Diesel (94 - 99) M to S	3500
Volkswagen Polo Hatchback Petrol (00 - Jan 02) V to 51	4150
Volkswagen Polo Petrol & Diesel (Feb 02 - June 05) 51 to 05	4608
Volkswagen Scirocco (82 - 90) up to H *	1224
Volkswagen Transporter 1600 (68 - 79) up to V	0082
Volkswagen Transporter 1700, 1800 & 2000 (72 - 79) up to V *	0226
Volkswagen Transporter (air-cooled) Petrol (79 - 82) up to Y *	0638
Volkswagen Transporter (water-cooled) Petrol (82 - 90) up to H	3452
Volkswagen Type 3 (63 - 73) up to M *	0084
VOLVO 120 & 130 Series (& P1800) (61 - 73) up to M *	0203
Volvo 142, 144 & 145 (66 - 74) up to N *	0129
Volvo 240 Series Petrol (74 - 93) up to K	0270
Volvo 262, 264 & 260/265 (75 - 85) up to C *	0400
Volvo 340, 343, 345 & 360 (76 - 91) up to J	0715
Volvo 440, 460 & 480 Petrol (87 - 97) D to P	1691
Volvo 740 & 760 Petrol (82 - 91) up to J	1258
Volvo 850 Petrol (92 - 96) J to P	3260
Volvo 940 Petrol (90 - 96) H to N	3249
Volvo S40 & V40 Petrol (96 - Mar 04) N to 04	3569
Volvo S70, V70 & C70 Petrol (96 - 99) P to V	3573
Volvo V70 / S80 Petrol & Diesel (98 - 05) S to 55	4263

AUTOMOTIVE TECHBOOKS

Title	Book No.
Automotive Air Conditioning Systems	3740
Automotive Electrical and Electronic Systems Manual	3049
Automotive Gearbox Overhaul Manual	3473
Automotive Service Summaries Manual	3475
Automotive Timing Belts Manual – Austin/Rover	3549
Automotive Timing Belts Manual – Ford	3474
Automotive Timing Belts Manual – Peugeot/Citroën	3568
Automotive Timing Belts Manual – Vauxhall/Opel	3577

DIY MANUAL SERIES

Title	Book No.
The Haynes Air Conditioning Manual	4192
The Haynes Manual on Bodywork	4198
The Haynes Manual on Brakes	4178
The Haynes Manual on Carburettors	4177
The Haynes Car Electrical Systems Manual	4251
The Haynes Manual on Diesel Engines	4174
The Haynes Manual on Engine Management	4199
The Haynes Manual on Fault Codes	4175
The Haynes Manual on Practical Electrical Systems	4267
The Haynes Manual on Small Engines	4250
The Haynes Manual on Welding	4176

* Classic reprint

All the products featured on this page are available through most motor accessory shops, cycle shops and book stores. Our policy of continuous updating and development means that titles are being constantly added to the range. For up-to-date information on our complete list of titles, please telephone: (UK) +44 1963 442030 • (USA) +1 805 498 6703 • (France) +33 1 47 17 66 29 • (Sweden) +46 18 124016 • (Australia) +61 3 9763 8100

CL21.9/06

Preserving Our Motoring Heritage

< The Model J Duesenberg Derham Tourster. Only eight of these magnificent cars were ever built – this is the only example to be found outside the United States of America

Almost every car you've ever loved, loathed or desired is gathered under one roof at the Haynes Motor Museum. Over 300 immaculately presented cars and motorbikes represent every aspect of our motoring heritage, from elegant reminders of bygone days, such as the superb Model J Duesenberg to curiosities like the bug-eyed BMW Isetta. There are also many old friends and flames. Perhaps you remember the 1959 Ford Popular that you did your courting in? The magnificent 'Red Collection' is a spectacle of classic sports cars including AC, Alfa Romeo, Austin Healey, Ferrari, Lamborghini, Maserati, MG, Riley, Porsche and Triumph.

A Perfect Day Out

Each and every vehicle at the Haynes Motor Museum has played its part in the history and culture of Motoring. Today, they make a wonderful spectacle and a great day out for all the family. Bring the kids, bring Mum and Dad, but above all bring your camera to capture those golden memories for ever. You will also find an impressive array of motoring memorabilia, a comfortable 70 seat video cinema and one of the most extensive transport book shops in Britain. The Pit Stop Cafe serves everything from a cup of tea to wholesome, home-made meals or, if you prefer, you can enjoy the large picnic area nestled in the beautiful rural surroundings of Somerset.

> John Haynes O.B.E., Founder and Chairman of the museum at the wheel of a Haynes Light 12.

< Graham Hill's Lola Cosworth Formula 1 car next to a 1934 Riley Sports.

The Museum is situated on the A359 Yeovil to Frome road at Sparkford, just off the A303 in Somerset. It is about 40 miles south of Bristol, and 25 minutes drive from the M5 intersection at Taunton.
Open 9.30am - 5.30pm (10.00am - 4.00pm Winter) 7 days a week, *except Christmas Day, Boxing Day and New Years Day*
Special rates available for schools, coach parties and outings Charitable Trust No. 292048